Heroes of the Metal Underground:
The Definitive Guide to 1980s
American Independent Metal Bands

ISBN: 9781627311403

Feral House
1240 W Sims Way #124
Port Townsend WA 98358
www.feralhouse.com
info@feralhouse.com

Designed by Ron Kretsch

Heroes of the METAL Underground

The Definitive Guide to 1980s American Independent Metal Bands

by Alexandros Anesiadis with contributions by Yannis Skarpelos

fh

To Nikoletta, Amaryllis, Ian Glasper, and the 1926 Family.
La Lucha 4 Sigue

CONTENTS

FOREWORD

HEAVY METAL IS NOT FOR THE FAINT OF HEART.

SOMETIME IN THE EIGHTIES ... IT WAS AROUND 2 IN THE MORNING, AND THE band was in full flight, roaring away. There were still several hours of metal ahead to enjoy, but I had other plans for the remainder of this particular evening. I walked out of Cheers in North Babylon, Long Island, with a wonderful girl from Connecticut who I'd just met, crossed the street to the parking lot to find my Camaro, opened the passenger door for my lady friend, closed her door, and was just getting into my seat when I heard, "There's the other son of a bitch! Let's get him!"

With a laserbeam glance, I quickly understood what was happening. Two guys had just jumped my friend and drummer, and apparently I was next. As they started coming toward me, I realized exactly who these two irate characters were. One was a martial arts guy who had previously been the boyfriend of my drummer's then-girlfriend, and the other was the ex-boyfriend of a girl I was occasionally dating. (Maybe he didn't know he was an ex!) They didn't like longhairs—or metal—and couldn't handle the fact that their ladies desired someone else.

To make a short story shorter: I figured, *Well, it's two—and possibly three—against one, and if they get me, what happens to this girl???* I slammed my door and revved the engine, hell-bent to drive over to my drummer to drag him into my car, but he'd already taken full advantage of their distraction, started his vehicle, and sped off. These guys were attacking like piranhas, meanwhile, pummeling my windows and fenders, so I fishtailed and shook them off, but one guy miraculously got up and lunged at the car again. So I spun the tires, knocked him over with the rear end of my Camaro, and roared off into the night...

They gave chase, but I eluded them on the wilds of the Southern State Parkway. When all was finally calm, cool, and collected once again, the lovely girl from Connecticut turned to me and said, "Wow, that was great! Really exciting, just like one of your songs!" And I said, "Ah, rock 'n' roll, it's a way of life!"

The very next night—or I should say early morning?—my drummer friend and I were in an after-hours club drinking vodka tonics with the two girls we'd almost been put in the hospital over, when bullets shattered the windows and everybody took refuge under the tables. The lesson I learned that day was that success, being famous, or drawing attention to oneself in any way is always a risky business.

These were the halcyon days when you could go out to a metal club any night of the week and there would be five hundred to a thousand people in the room ... even on a Tuesday night! The bands were always killer, and the audiences were always outrageously enthusiastic. These were also the days when you could go out with two dollars in your pocket and come home with fifty!

For at least ten wildly maniacal years, I spent every single night in one of those metal clubs between Long Island and NYC.

Back then, the groups did covers of songs by artists they were passionate about, while some of the more established groups did their own songs as well. Bands like Zebra were writing their own songs, which the audience was loving as much as their Led Zeppelin covers. Twisted Sister was also writing and performing their own songs, and they began releasing records soon after. Speaking of Twisted Sister, for a while there, I was dating a girl whose cousin was Mark "The Animal" Mendoza's girlfriend at the time, and I would occasionally run into him. It was inspiring to see those two groups charting their own paths and beginning to find success not only on Long Island and in NYC, but across the rest of the country and in Europe as well. The newly born underground press was telling the tales of what was happening in the metal world in various parts of the country—and especially what was percolating in the European scene.

Being keen students of night life and all things metal, we observed all that was going on in our particular sphere here on Long Island and decided that we were *not* going to do any covers. We would only play our own music. I think we may have been the first band on that scene that didn't do any covers whatsoever. As we started getting more and more press, other bands noticed and began adding more and more original music into their sets. I think we were influential in that regard.

Mind you, we were definitely on the rocket-fueled fast track—hungry, determined, and passionate about what we were doing. We'd only been together for about three weeks by the time we'd put together an album's worth of material.

With supreme confidence, we went into a small eight-track studio and began laying down these blazing songs we'd written. The recording sessions were quick and furious, and for under $1,000 in less than a week, we had recorded and mixed what became the first album.

Those early works of Virgin Steele's are really raw and wild, but they do capture the spark of a band completely in love with performing true, unbridled metal—the energy is focused, infectious, and radiant!

Initially, we made cassette copies of the album and sent them to all the various metal/rock magazines and fanzines. Interest began to build. One review of our first album in *Kerrang!* magazine said something like:

"It begins with the rumble of dramatic Bach-esque keyboards and guitar, but just as you settle down for some sensitive choral concept, there comes the stampede of rhythm, the wailing angst of effects-oriented axemanship, and the yelping, whelping of a true-tonsil stretching vocal warrior"!

I said to myself, "We may have arrived!"

Fan mail started pouring in, and Shrapnel Records president Mike Varney called to inform us of his intention to include one of our songs on his *U.S. Metal, Volume II* compilation album. The featured track was "Children of the Storm."

The train had left the station, and the momentum was building to a fever pitch. There was so much excitement and energy rising, the next step was inevitable: We needed to have the album out, truly and officially, on vinyl!

Over the years, people have asked me, "Why did you release that album on your own? How did you have the balls to do that at that time?" My reply has always been: Well, because we were alive and untamed, and we all firmly believed in what we were doing. I certainly knew that I wanted to document this unique moment in life as well as this particular era of my existence, and I knew that if we went for it, there was really no telling what this initial act of bravery might lead to.

The album was already recorded—the rest needed to be done. We found a talented artist to do the album cover, and if you notice on the rocket ship, he put the letters *N.W.A.H.M.*, which stands for "new wave of American heavy metal." We were staking our claim in the firmament.

I found a mastering lab to make the lacquer and a company to handle the actual manufacturing and pressing. We were off and running!

The initial pressing of 5,000 copies sold out in weeks, many from the trunk of my Camaro. I drove boxes of Virgin Steele records to distributors all over the East Coast of the States and shipped boxes to European distributors. (This was a truly great way to learn how the music business actually functions!) When the first pressing sold out, we pressed up another 5,000 copies, and before that second pressing sold out, we had several interesting label offers sitting on the table, staring up at us. The future looked grand and glorious. Our concerts were going well, we were sparking interest in record companies, and our fan mail was becoming quite compelling. There were two letters that clearly stood out: one was from a young band in the Seattle area that went by the name Queensrÿche, and the other letter came from a California group known as Metallica.

We eventually signed with a record company called Mongol Horde in the United States, and for Europe, we signed to a company in London called Music For Nations. Our first album was in fact their very first release! The catalog number was MFN 1 (Music For Nations 1). After signing us they signed Manowar, Ratt, Mercyful Fate, W.A.S.P., and Metallica, among others. It was an incredibly exciting time, the new waves of both American and British heavy metal, and magazines like *Kerrang!* and *Metal Forces* in England were very supportive, giving us great reviews and feature write-ups. In the United States, in addition to headlining our own shows, we began supporting many great bands like Motörhead, Krokus, The Rods, and the aforementioned Manowar, with whom we did a very enjoyable and successful European tour.

Everything you do in this business is a stepping stone. That debut album was the first arrow, catapult, or sword strike in our assault on the industry, and it enabled us to record the next album, which led to the next development, and so on. And speaking of sword strikes: Once we had started our journey, I commissioned a mad genius named Tom the Lawnmower Man to fashion me a massive Sword of Steele, which I still possess today. This glorious instrument can be seen on the cover of the *Wait for the Night* twelve-inch EP, as well as in numerous photos and videos since then, and it can be heard "singing" on the track "Fight Tooth and Nail" from our *Noble Savage* album! It stands as my testament to perseverance—to my dedication and commitment to this music.

People can listen to the albums, watch the videos, and hear the stories, but being there and living it every day—and even more importantly *every night*—was really something else. There was no internet then; it was all writing letters, being there at the gigs, and also tape trading, which one had to handle in real time. No downloading, no reaching a massive amount of people with one click. Yet the impact of everything you did felt immediate and rewarding, and probably more so. I think the value placed on each release was higher then because it was not as readily available. One had to work hard to seek and find what was out there. I think there is a certain take-it-for-granted aspect to the scene today, in comparison. We didn't always love every band we went to see in those days, or every single album, but we were always supportive and appreciative of what bands were trying to do, and certainly respectful of the fact that, because they were there doing their thing, they were helping the scene to grow and to continue.

One had to be very strong in those days! As my old soundman Mike Filosa (rest in peace, brother!) used to say, the gear was all "*Arrrgggghhhh, big, bulky, and useless.*" He hated moving the extra-large PA bins and the 480-pound Hammond BC organ around ... especially at the end of the night! We had a 3,000-watt PA, an enormous bass rig, three Marshall stacks, and all the drums miked in a tiny basement for rehearsals. All that had to be packed up and carried to each gig, and then reassembled for the next rehearsal! Our gigs and our rehearsals were incredibly loud. Kids would hear us and congregate outside our rehearsal space and listen all night. There was no social media, but it was an unbelievably social scene. You wanted to be a part of it—you didn't want to miss one minute. I would sometimes go to two or three different clubs in one night, since they were open until 4 a.m. (or later, if you got in tight with the owners), so it was easy to check out each different scene. You had Cheers, Hammerheads, Sundance, the Stage Door, all within a few miles of each other, plus so many other great venues within striking distance, like L'Amour in Bay Ridge and the Limelight in the Flatiron ... the list goes on. Radio helped, but I think the print magazines, newspapers, and fanzines fueled the scene even more. There weren't really any distractions. If you loved this metal music, you had to buy the records and go out to see the bands. If your favorite band wasn't in town playing at Madison Square Garden or the Nassau Coliseum, you could still always go to Cheers or any of the other wonderful venues, meet new people, have a great time, and hear a great band. I suppose nowadays, it would be like going to a rock festival like Wacken Open Air in Germany or Gods of Metal in Italy or something. Only this was every night! *And* all for only $3, might I add!

There is no denying the power that this music has for those who are deeply passionate about it. This is the combustible material we run on! This is the soundtrack to our lives, and for me, this has always been more of a way of life than a career. It has been and is still my inspiration, my magic, my refuge, and my reason for being. Those who have ears to hear will know what I'm talking about, and I'm sure that those who have picked up this book *definitely* know what I am talking about. Rage on!

David DeFeis
Frontman of Virgin Steele
April 26, 2021

INTRODUCTION

"WAIT, WHAT? A HARDCORE PUNK/THRASHER WRITING A BOOK ON THE independent metal bands of the 1980s? He's false!" some dedicated metalheads would scream just at the sight of my name. But hey, calm down! Take it as an attempt to glorify all those metal bands that released vinyl records on their own during the era (1980–1989, with some exceptions). I'm just trying to help all the shining diamonds of heavy metal get their deserved exposure to the world.

I had the idea for this book while I was finishing my first book, *Crossover the Edge*. Through many of the interviews I conducted for the first book, I identified that in the U.S., there was some common ground with the underground metal scene of the 1980s, whether this was in scene terms, in gig flyers, or even with shared musicians.

First of all, only U.S. bands are included in this book, within the time frame of 1980–1989, just in the interest of limiting its length. If the time frame was expanded, as well as the region reference (e.g., if Canada were added), I would have to write two books, not one! Other conditions for inclusion are that a) the bands have to have at least one vinyl appearance in the 1980s, with the record being self-financed, not financed by a record label (even indie labels don't count), and b) they had to musically belong somewhere in the range among hard rock, melodic metal, classic metal, power metal, and thrash metal.

However, to every rule, there is an exception, so I decided that bands that released a full-length record (not a demo) on cassette could be included, as well as bands with a more AOR or more extreme sound. But the core basis is undeniably classic American metal, the kind that "true metal fans" adore worldwide.

For this book, my comrade and co-writer will be Professor Yannis Skarpelos. Yannis, a dedicated metalhead, was fascinated when he heard about this book, and therefore the vast majority of the record reviews are authored by him. I didn't want to confuse metalheads with my opinions, so I thought that it would be best to offer them the perspective of a person whose opinion matters.

As you can imagine, the amount of work that's gone into this book was enormous. More than 130 bands were interviewed, and more than 600 bands were included. Lots of never-seen-the-light-of-day photos were borrowed directly from the bands. It was a project that took about 14 months and seemingly endless hours of research, interviews, reviews, and of course, writing. I'm more than happy that Richard Anderson and Cherry Red were the first folks to express interest in this book, since our first collaboration in *Crossover the Edge* was very successful.

So, what was it like to write the book that you have in your hands right now?

I have to admit that actually I was thrilled with the responses of the bands/musicians, as well as the fact that they all seemed to be down to earth and willing to offer their help wholeheartedly. Just like hardcore/punk musicians, independent metal artists are level-headed, kind, very supportive people, and throughout the process of writing this book I managed to create friendships that are definitely going to last. And that's not to mention some unbelievable surprise gifts that were sent to me, or the phone calls, personal confessions, and unpredicted emails/messages that expressed great love and honesty. Moreover, I came across bands and music that I wouldn't expect to like, but truth be told, there's a major punk influence in this kind of independent U.S. heavy metal, especially in the time frame examined. And no, I'm not talking just about Deuce!

And what could you say about the best intentions of American teenagers in the 1980s? It was those intentions—the purity of fandom—that led them to create the simplest but most original form of art, all based on their personal resources, and to deliver them through channels reminiscent of what the punk movement did earlier in the 1970s: producing their music, using their own (or friends') artwork, pressing their own records, and playing in backyards or home basements. Of course, the political stance of punk was absent, but on the other hand, recording, producing and releasing your own music, outside of the terms of the music industry—and in a time when it was unbelievably easy for a heavy metal band to sign a contract, but I'll discuss this one later—is a political act by itself.

I hope all of you enjoy it. And I hope that metalheads will shrug off the "Ah, that hardcore/punk crossover guy" impression of me and believe my true and honest intentions to offer this scene the research and exposure that it should've had. If not, hate mails are always welcome!

A NOTE ON THE HISTORY OF INDEPENDENT/PRIVATE AMERICAN METAL

IN THE 1980S, HEAVY METAL IN THE UNITED STATES FOLLOWED THE ROUTE of classic hard rock and heavy metal bands, as well as taking inspiration from the NWOBHM invasion from the UK. Even in the 1970s, there were bands like Alkana, Legend (*Fröm the Fjörds*), L.A. Rocks ("Cocaine"), Kammerzell, Axxe ("Rock Away the City"), Tracer, Wizard (1979 LP), Pratt (1979 LP), J. Paul Hancock, Armageddon ("Vampire State"), Scrooge ("A Waste of My Time"), Mizzouri Foxx, Rapscallion, Left End (*Ridin' Again*), Detroit (1979 LP), Centaurus (1978 LP), August featuring John Piette and Friends (1978 LP), Olimpus ("Death to Disco"), Zed (1979 LP), Skater ("Bad Boys"), Basstar Amber, Smokehouse ("For You"), Granmax (*Kiss Heaven Goodbye*), Blitz (Texas, 1978 twelve-inch EP), Sorcery ("Sinister Soldier"), Architect (1978 LP), Dartanyun ("Hot to Trot"), Taz ("Hot Mean Lovin"), Angus ("Want You to Take Me Out Tonight"), Roxstar ("She Takes Me Higher"), Flight ("Luvin Huggin & More"), Hot Flash (*First Attack*), Gorgon Medusa ("Sweet Child"), Imagination ("Fat Man"), Antigoni ("Rock and Roll War," 1979), Genghis Khan and the Mongol Horde ("Asian Invasion"/"My True Love," 1979), Totty (1977 LP), Liberty Bros (*No Time Lasts Forever*), Feathers ("You're a Labor"), Ramm ("Keep On Fallin'"), Badaxe ("Cry for Me"), Zane ("Step Aside"), Poobah ("Through These Eyes"), Jumbalayah ("Feel High"), Cosmic Eye ("Soft Love"), Wrath ("Warlord"), Cain (*A Pound of Flesh*), Luxus ("Brown Matter"), Locust (*I Must Be in Love*), Doc Rockit, Trixx (1979 LP), Blackhorse (1979 LP), Impeccable (*Live on the Rox*), Asia (1979 LP), Survivor (*All Your Pretty Moves*), Resistance (1979 LP), Squadran ("Fly Away"), Revolver (*A Piece of the Action!*), Tyranny ("Rock It"), Alexander ("Just Keep Holding On") Axes ("Can You See It Again"), as well as more famous ones like Manilla Road, Dokken, Sir Lord Baltimore, Kelakos (pre-The Rods) or Quiet Riot.

However, the common denominator of the 1970s metal bands that released a private LP/seven-inch is that, in terms of music, the sound could be described as "confused." In all those proto-private metal bands, you can find influences ranging from punk, garage rock, progressive rock, AOR, folk, heavy psychedelia, or music that bridges a gap between hard rock and heavy metal—too heavyweight to be regarded as hard rock, too lightweight to be regarded as pure heavy metal. There is a definite proto-metal edge among them, but few of them would appeal to true metalheads of today.

But what is "true metal"? Sure, you might have heard the term before. Weinstein (1991, p. 46) offers the definition of its polar opposite, "false metal," wherein metal fans used epithets like "poseurs, false ones, nerf metal, poodle bands, glam and commercial metal," in order to describe bands whose imagery was reminiscent of heavy metal, albeit their sound was usually lighter, but who "lacked the authenticity" of real heavy metal. These bands had a sound that was commercially driven, glossier, lightweight with glam fashion thrown in. Sweeter and more melodic. The term "false metal" was used to describe bands like Def Leppard, Mötley Crüe, and Poison.

THE TERM "FALSE METAL" WAS CHAMPIONED BY MANOWAR ON THEIR 1983 LP *Into Glory Ride*, where they declared "Death to False Metal" on the back sleeve. Manowar had all the components that fans of "true metal" love—the imagery, the epic heavy sound, the logos, the lyrics—so they're regarded by some as the truest heavy metal band. However, there are bands that are more lightweight than Manowar, more melodic, or less metallic (e.g., the early period of Cirith Ungol or even the 1970s period of Rush) that are still regarded as "true metal" bands.

To confuse things even more, Slayer's *Show No Mercy* era is regarded as true metal, whereas *Reign in Blood* is considered false, because even though the music was faster and harder, Slayer allowed too many hardcore/punk influences into their sound! Even more confusing, Metallica's *Black Album* era might be heavier and less melodic than, say, Warlord, but Metallica are considered false metal, since they went on to commercialize their sound, whereas Warlord kept the 1970s hard rock/heavy metal tradition combined with classical music influences. Meanwhile, Pantera's 1980s glam and power metal offerings are considered truer metal than their 1990s modern metal records, while bands like Machine Head are regarded hands down as poseurs by the same supposedly true metalheads.

Andreas Andreou, the mastermind behind the heavy metal record label No Remorse, says, "In my forties, terms like 'true metal' sound really old-school, even if we lived them and it's not something from the Jurassic period of metal music. While on the back cover of Manowar's second album (*Into Glory Ride*, 1983), you can read the infamous 'Death to False Metal,' we first read extensively about 'true metal' in the nineties and probably thanks to a band that 'true-metallers' don't really accept: HammerFall. While Manowar's definition of false metal is probably just a bold and egocentric statement (a cliché nowadays!), I can give you an example of real heavy metal. A passionate metalhead raising a fist in the air, five closed fingers, one for each band: Black Sabbath, Judas Priest, Iron Maiden, Accept, Saxon. Anything that strays from these bands' sound isn't real heavy metal. It might be metal, or heavy, or post-something, or some other metal subgenre, but these five have the classic, real heavy metal sound.

"However, a genre like heavy metal is not only about the music. It's something more, and only 'neighboring' music styles (for example, punk) can claim to be similar. The never-surrender attitude, the passion, the revolution, the knowledge and open mind regarding life and society, the eagerness to evolve but sometimes with a regressive taste, and the unending support for underground metal and the scene that surrounds it. You also need to fight for what you believe in and stand up for your rights. For life. Because Rome wasn't built in a day, and if metal is just a phase, or just an escape for someone, then it's not true metal they love. If one person ever personified true metal, it had to be Mark Shelton of Manilla Road."

George Tassis, a record collector and a major fan of the true metal sound, defines true metal as "the struggle to wed a conservative state of mind on the principles of heavy metal with a liberal way of conduct. The antithesis of musical elitism that aims at preserving an art form in defiance of sex, race, or ethnicity. Inherently flawed romanticism that succeeds in ways unseen. A bunch of peasants on the road of kings, offering another perspective of it, the one that pinpoints its philosophy rather than a strict musical definition."

Although we have the definition of false metal, the definition of true metal is confusing; the heavy metal philosopher Iron Skullet writes, "despite the elitism that is sometimes present in the term, 'true heavy metal' is a useful descriptor for separating bands that play near the center of the subgenre from bands with a hybrid or evolved sound. This is often relevant even within a single band's discography. For example, Black Sabbath's 1981 album *Mob Rules* is a true heavy metal album, while their 2013 album *13* is a blend of heavy doom."[1] The definition therefore of true metal is subjective, since one "true" metalhead could regard that all of Armored Saint's back catalog is true metal, whereas another could describe them as a true metal band initially that sadly later modernized their sound in the 1990s and 2000s. Crazy and confusing, the term "true metal" applies to many private American metal releases of the 1980s, since they comply with the strict general rules of true metal. They have the pure metal sound, the fantasy/heroic lyrics and imagery, the noncommercial vibe, and the obscurity. There are bands like Child Saint that released only a twelve-inch of two songs that are glorified by true metalheads. (In their own words, "These true songs erase discographies of much more famous commercial metal bands.")

Chris Papadakis, editor-in-chief of *Forgotten Scroll* zine/webzine (as well as singer of Afterimage and Ominous Sky, and radio producer of Mercury Radio), writes, "'True metal' was just a term used by bands, labels, and promoters as the main feature to develop a marketing plan. It does not represent any special value to me. I definitely have aesthetic criteria to sort different kinds of music and musical mixtures in my mind and decide what to keep for my ears and my record collection, but this is a complex and personal process/situation, not just for me but for everybody. Dividing bands into true or false categories is a nonsensical scenario for me, especially when you are doing it to sell more records, T-shirts, and concert tickets, 'cause in my opinion, this is what the 'true metal' thing is about. To make a long story short, music to me matters the most, and such terms like true metal are useless. To be true—as a band or a listener—in the matters of ethics, beliefs, and faith to your music and your aesthetic is a complex and personal story. It has nothing to do with any monikers or marketing plans."

The mystique that surrounds all those crazy rare private metal records offers points of authenticity among true metalheads, and it's followed by all the essential ingredients of heavy metal: the classic musical formula, the riffs, the visuals, the dedication to a specific status that doesn't stray. Even though this musical form is rather conservative and very claustrophobic, closed in its microcosm, it retains a special sincerity that someone must admit, regardless of whether they like the music or not. I mean, how many copies would you expect for a band like Heathen's Rage to sell? Bands like them attract metalheads who are dedicated and not going bananas for the flashy, overproduced metal bands that are destined to sell millions of records, distributed through major channels and advertised heavily. So, the sentiment created through the sounds and images of those independent metal bands plays a major role. This is why fans

1 ironskullet.com/2017/10/30/the-history-of-heavy-metal-part-i-the-difference-between-metal-and-heavy-metal/

would spend insane amounts of money on records, such as Street Child's 1989 self-titled twelve-inch; the combination of heroic cover artwork with the music and the low number of copies pressed (500) makes people spend over $1,000 for it.

But what is the connection between the independent/self-funded private American metal releases with true metal?

True metal bands are not by definition independent, and vice versa. However, independent bands that fall into the category of true metal are glorified like gods among the metalheads who gather around at festivals like Keep It True and Up The Hammers. Bands like Majestic Ryte (which only had one cassette EP of five songs in 1988) get not only a belated recognition from playing in such festivals, they gain even more of a cult status among fans of true metal. To reinforce this argument, when a band either a) is from the 1980s, b) has a stellar vinyl/cassette release from that period, and/or c) has a specific American metal sound that respects the classic metal tradition, that band automatically gains more respect from true metal fans than better-known bands that went on to change/modernize their sound or add nonmetal elements to their sound. Funny as it may seem, there's a good population of metalheads in Greece, Italy, Spain, Germany, Sweden, Japan, and of course the United States, who were disgusted with the modernization of the classic heavy metal sound and are searching deep in the underground to find bands that will quench their thirst for pure and honest metal.

Accordingly, one must mention that not all the private American metal releases of the 1980s were "pure" metal; in many cases, there were bands that would either border on melodic metal/AOR (Winterkat), punk/hardcore (Kratos, Black Task), hard rock (Beowulf), glam (Hendrickson, Lixx Array), progressive metal (Spectral Incursion), or even head for a heavier/faster metal sound, like Prowler's thrash offering. Again, the taste toward those bands is totally subjective; arguments arise over which is "true metal" and which is "nonmetal" or "false." And once again, quality, integrity, and authenticity also play a major role.

So, what could be described as true metal? A definition could be that true metal is attributed either to a specific subgenre of heavy metal or a phrase that defines a band/record with high levels of authenticity, integrity, and dedication to the real heavy metal as a whole (music, lyrics, imagery) as well as the band's approach (high-pitched vocals, old-school recording, flashy solos, and riffs that emanate from the classic heavy metal tradition). True metalheads believe that the definitions of true metal were born in the U.S. scene in the 1980s, with bands like Manowar, Omen, early Armored Saint, early Liege Lord, Jag Panzer, Manilla Road, Virgin Steele, and Warlord being among the foundations of this genre. What is common among those bands is that their sound generally rejects the older hard rock style, going out for an all-out-metal approach, and their heavy metal is played at the maximum level, not allowing external influences to creep in. While they sound more extreme than, say, Iron Maiden, Black Sabbath, or other NWOBHM bands, they don't sound as extreme as the thrash metal bands of that period (whose influences ranged from hardcore punk to NWOBHM).

Accordingly, those private releases often fetch big bucks. But what would be a starting point for getting into this endless hunt for private metal records? Is it just for collecting reasons, or is it the quest for pure, true metal? Record collector Elias Chatzialexis owns one of the world's biggest private metal collections and says, "To make a long answer short, I started collecting

American private metal because of Manowar. Starting around 1984, Manowar became my favorite band, and since I loved their epic style in music and lyrics, I tried to find similar bands. Of course, I bought every freakin' release by American metal labels of that era—Metal Blade, Azra, New Renaissance, MFN. But that was not enough (obviously). So, I started trying to find more unknown bands—the more obscure, the better. But even if I was considering myself a completist of American metal, I must say that the music was the key factor and not the rarity of the private metal releases.

"And there was an additional bonus: Boy, did the eighties have great fantasy picture sleeves!!! Okay, I understand, we're not collecting stamps, but if a private record has great epic music AND a fantasy cover, it becomes an American metal collector's wet dream. And all of the above also describe a lot of seventies hard rock private releases (today, most would call them proto-metal). So, you understand, it was a whole new world to explore, but the starting point was actually Manowar."

The DIY culture of independent American metal was a result of the cultural appropriation that NWOBHM initially did with punk. Punk was the one genre that embodied and championed the whole DIY philosophy in terms of "recording, manufacturing albums and merchandise, booking their own tours, and creating opportunities for smaller bands to get wider recognition and gain cult status through repetitive low-cost DIY touring" (Triggs Teal, 2006). In the punk world, the DIY culture wasn't just spread in recording/releasing music; it was also expanded to the production of fanzines and gig flyers/posters in the late 1970s. So, NWOBHM was the first metal movement that embodied the DIY attitude of punk and created a scene that could be regarded, as Alan O'Connor mentioned in his book *Punk Record Labels and the Struggle for Autonomy: The Emergence of DIY*, as "a field, a relatively autonomous space in society where a specialized activity takes place."

IT'S TRUE THAT THE EMERGENCE OF DIY IN PUNK MADE THINGS EASIER FOR the major record labels; no longer did they have to worry about signing the second-wave punk (or first-wave hardcore punk) bands and risk getting into trouble over their extreme sound or their explicit lyrics and artwork. So, they kept focusing on the markets of arena rock and pop, or even some of the "safer" heavy metal acts, since it's way easier to sign, promote, and advertise Robert Palmer than Discharge. Major labels were interested in the emerging NWOBHM as they saw potential sales: this is why Saxon signed to Carrere (their rock-oriented heavy metal had an impact on herbert punks, rockers, and bikers as well as younger heavy metal fans, which of course meant a bigger marketing pool), and why Iron Maiden signed to EMI (initially they had herberts, metalheads, casuals, and some punks following, plus a visual approach akin to the traditional comic art). There were many good bands, such as Jaguar, Witchfinder General, or Tredegar, that only gained minor exposure via signing to small metal labels, which were new at the time. The creation of these small metal labels filled in the gap between the DIY and major labels, and they focused on a niche marketing approach: for metalheads, by metalheads. Linking the cultural appropriation of metal from punk, small UK labels like Teesbeat, Rondelet, Trial, Ellie Jay Records, Direct Records, SRT, Brickyard Records, and Guardian Records N' Tapes went on to release records by both punk and NWOBHM bands in the early 1980s.

As mentioned, the early eighties was a very hard era for a true metal band to sign to a major label, especially in the U.S. The music market was very commercially driven, with acts like Styx, REO Speedwagon, and Pat Benatar being considered "extreme," while the rule was that artists like ABBA, Lionel Richie, and Stevie Wonder dominated the charts. However, in the American underground, there was a huge hardcore punk scene, a brilliant garage revival scene, an excellent power pop scene, the NYC avant-garde and noise scene, and of course the underground metal scene. The underground in the U.S. was boiling. But the penetration of major labels was pretty minor, if not nonexistent. Who would be so insane as to sign Black Flag in 1980, Teenage Jesus and the Jerks in 1979, The Barracudas in 1981, or Manilla Road in 1982? No major label would make money off these bands—and they could even lose money from legal issues, e.g., the PMRC going after Black Flag.

The first small independent metal labels appeared in the U.S. around 1982, with the most famous ones being Megaforce and Metal Blade; however, both of them went on to become "small majors." Heavy metal exploded in the U.S. by 1984 (in marketing terms); it gained even more airplay on commercial MTV shows, reaching "20 percent in 1984 from 8 percent the previous year" (Garofalo, 1997; p. 401) and having a peak in 1989 when "40 percent of all the albums sold in the U.S. were exclusively heavy metal" (Walser, 1993; p. 3). Right in between the increased sales, there was also the commercialization of heavy metal, either in the championing of glam/lite metal or in the perfection of the sonic element of heavy/thrash metal bands—for example, there is literally no comparison between Megadeth's sound on *Killing Is My Business...* with their *Rust in Peace* LP—in an attempt to gain more radio/video airplay as well as transforming it into a form of music that you could actually listen to at clubs. Through all those radical changes in the heavy metal market, there were bands that remained true to the core of heavy metal, refusing to commercialize their sound or follow trends like glam metal, thrash metal, progressive metal, and so on.

But this wasn't the sole case where bands remained in the underground, releasing their own self-funded records; bands that were not lucky enough to sign a contract with a small label, bands whose sound was considered passé, bands that simply wanted to remain in the underground, bands that didn't have the image or the music to upgrade to the big league, bands that due to internal conflicts couldn't go on. The world of DIY American independent metal is by no means an ideal world, which is to say that not all bands are great, even to the most dedicated metalhead.

This book is an attempt to chronicle the independent/private American metal scene of the 1980s, from both a research and academic point of view as well as from a fan point of view, thanks to Professor Yannis Skarpelos. Within the interviews, you will find not just academic stuff but also lots of great information about how and why this scene came to be, various musicians' personal beliefs about the underground metal scene today, and sentiments and stories that for the first time are seeing the light of day. I approached this book with respect and in a subjective manner, and I hope it will entertain you, offer you knowledge, and inspire you to seek out new-to-you bands. Enjoy!

heroes of the METAL underground

EAST COAST

M.C. BLADE

M.C. BLADE WAS A MAPLEWOOD, NEW JERSEY, BAND FORMED IN 1987, IN AN attempt to play their own brand of American metal that was rooted in the hard rock tradition of the seventies. Guitarist Pat Langone offers, "I think the best way of explaining would be to say the story is going to sound like a lot of other bands. The bass player, Tommy Bonassisa, was a childhood friend who lived one block over from me. I actually gave him bass lessons when we were still in high school. Tommy has an extremely good voice and to this day plays bass in multiple cover bands. Our drummer, Gary Blindt, was a few years older than us, and I met him when I was 16. He and another bass player were looking for a guitar player for a band, and even though they were over 21, they took a chance on me at age 16 because I could play and sing. Our keyboard player, Gerry De Santis, was younger than us; he was playing in a cover band with Tommy for a few years before M.C. Blade. Our second guitar player, Curt Knoth, was also a childhood friend we went to school with and who played in high school bands that we were all friendly with. He also played with Tommy and Jerry in the cover band. Mark, a.k.a. "M.C.," which stands for Mark Carolan, was of course the singer, even though he could play a little guitar and a little piano. He also went to the same high school; however, he was a few years older than us. So, we never actually worked with him in any of our high school bands.

"At one point in the early 1980s, I had the occasion through a mutual friend to start hanging around and working with Mark Carolan in a music store in a mall. We would always talk about our favorite groups and our musical accomplishments. At the same time, Mark was working as a VJ in a prominent New York City club called Danceteria. We would go and hang out and do all the things that you're not supposed to do in life right there in the DJ booth. Well, Mark was a bit of a songwriter and always carried a spiral notebook around, where he would write down lyrics and song ideas. He had some chords for a bunch of his songs, but he really had no idea how to put them together. That's where I came in. I started helping him organize his tunes and put guitar parts and arrangements together for him. To my surprise, some of the material was really good, and I felt that it needed to be put down on tape before it got lost.

"So, I called all the guys together and said, 'Hey I have a little bit of a project for this singer. Could you help me out?' They agreed, so we set about learning the tunes. Well, after a couple of rehearsals, things started sounding pretty good. So, we decided to ask a friend who had just opened a small four-track studio in the basement of his mother's video store if we could come down and put down some demos. And so, our first ten songs with M.C. Blade were born." M.C. Blade picked their best four songs, and the result was their self-released (on their own label, X-Calubur Records) *Step Into The Light* twelve-inch EP, that showcased a number of different influences.

"If I told you all the influences that we had over the years," Pat laughs, "I don't think you could fit it in your book. Let's just say we had many influences at many different times—all rock and roll, of course. The inspiration, however, for the kind of music we were making with M.C. Blade was basically a sign of the music for the times. Some of the influences you'll hear in that music is from the 1980s metal era, everything from the luscious vocals and melodies of Queen to the heavy guitars of bands like Judas Priest. At the time the band was putting this music together, I had just started going on the road with White Lion, and we toured extensively with bands all over the world. I was influenced a little by [White Lion singer] Vito Bratta, which is weird because he was influenced a little by me. Accordingly, there are so many albums and productions that have thrilled us all over the years, I couldn't even pick one. But if I was forced to, I would have to say any Beatles record, any Queen record, any Led Zeppelin record, and before this sounds like I'm a nut for English groups, you have to put in Van Halen, of course."

Step Into The Light contains four songs that to my (Yannis Skarpelos') ears sound totally in the tradition of 1970s American metal/hard rock, in the same genre as Kiss, Aerosmith, and Van Halen, with some UK 1970s hard rock (Queen) and a flashy production reminiscent of Judas Priest's early 1980s stuff—in between *Point of Entry* and *Screaming for Vengeance*, even though this comparison might seem odd! A bit blurry and roughly recorded, the production of *Step Into The Light* only adds to the authentic youth nature of the record, whereas in terms of songwriting, M.C. Blade offers powerful songs such as the title track. That would be worth the price of admission just by itself! M.C. Blade surely had potential, but sadly, this was their first and last offering.

"The scene was more or less what you would think in a small-town setting, with a bunch of kids running around in rock bands trying to compete in a friendly way," Pat adds. "But at the time M.C. Blade came around, I had already finished college at Berklee in Boston, and I had started working as a musician and a sound engineer. When we started M.C. Blade, I was actually working at a club/concert venue called L'Amour, which was considered the rock capital of Brooklyn. I had the opportunity to work with many headlining bands, including Cheap Trick, UFO, Paul Di'Anno, Judas Priest, Zebra, TT Quick, Celtic Frost, Voivod, King Diamond, White Lion, Iron Maiden, Frehley's Comet, of course, and many more that you can probably guess...

CUT TO THE CHASE:

M.C. Blade's *Step Into The Light* will satisfy fans of a kind of hard rock/metal mix, especially fans of the American metal bands. By no means a masterpiece, *Step Into The Light* is still a pretty rare record. The title song is the main reason to purchase a copy of *Step Into The Light.*

"As far as how we were treated, we weren't really what I would call an immediately popular group. Individually, everybody in the group was well known in the area for playing in other bands, but M.C. Blade didn't originally start out as a real band—just a recording project. As time went on, we decided to take the band on the road and do some shows to see what kind of traction we would get. But as fate would have it, Mark thought he was a rock star ahead of his time and started acting as such, so the rest of us decided just to dump it," Pat says with a bitter smile.

"To this day, though, you can mention my name anywhere in Maplewood, New Jersey, or South Orange, New Jersey, or even anywhere down the Jersey Shore, and there's a good chance I have plenty of fans and people know who I am. At the same time, I had the experience of working with Ace Frehley's Comet. You'll find Ace Frehley saying my name in the talking part of the song 'The Acorn.' Special side note to this story: I happened to be standing next to the drum riser of Jamie Oldaker when Paul Stanley and Gene Simmons got together with Ace for the first time in ten years. It was at one of his concerts at the Limelight in Manhattan, during the encore. It was one of the biggest times of my life to stand on stage with Kiss. There is so much more to this story, but maybe I should just write a book!"

M.C. Blade quietly disbanded in the late 1980s (Pat says that this might have been in 1988), and Pat continues to perform with his rock 'n' roll band, Swingin' Johnsons, and Tom Bonassisa with the New Jersey Party Band. Pat very kindly provided me (Alex Anesiadis) with a CD of 11 songs—all the songs that M.C. Blade released (plus a cover of David Bowie's "Ziggy Stardust")—that follow the same formula that Yannis Skarpelos mentioned before: the 1980s American hard rock/metal combo. Maybe an independent metal label would be willing to take a chance and release this as an M.C. Blade anthology someday?

STREET CHILD

HANDS DOWN ONE OF THE MOST WANTED HOLY GRAILS BY METAL collectors worldwide is Street Child's eponymous 1989 twelve-inch EP—something that is totally justifiable since we're talking about one of the highest-quality private metal releases overall. The initial pressing of 500 copies is nearly impossible to get hold of.

The story of Street Child starts in the mid-1980s in New York City. Bassist Rob Origlio recounts, "I was born and raised on the island of Manhattan. When I was 13 years old, two huge apartment buildings went up a block away from where I lived. That's when I met Jesse Odom. He was a year younger than me but already played guitar, and his brother, Doug, was a drummer. I always had a passion for music, but I wasn't playing bass yet. Jesse and I would hang around all the time and listen to music. We both loved Kiss. He introduced me to bands like Thin Lizzy, Ted Nugent, and such. I was a huge Led Zeppelin fan already.

"As time went on, I began playing in a band with some mutual friends of ours. Our drummer was Mackie Jason, who went on to be the drummer in Cro-Mags. When our guitar player left, we asked Jesse to step in, and he already had some songs written. We did a Sunday night at the famous CBGB. That band lasted for a little while, but we broke up. Around that time, Jesse got some recording equipment, and he began writing furiously. Almost a new song every week or two. It was me, him, and a drum machine. We were listening to bands like Iron Maiden, Judas Priest, and Black Sabbath. Our brand of metal was never big in Manhattan. The heavy stuff was either punk or hardcore. We would put ads in music papers looking for drummers and singers. We found a few good drummers. But the type of singer we were looking for was hard to come by. We wanted Rob Halford and Bruce Dickinson, but we were getting people that could hardly sing a note. Jesse was singing out of necessity. We found a drummer from Russia named Ted—we played with him for almost two years, and he wrote some great music, but he and Jesse just clashed after a while. We actually had Frank Ferrer of Guns N' Roses for a while. He went on to bigger things.

"Meanwhile, Jesse's writing was really maturing. He eventually met Nelson Wakefield, who was playing guitar in another band in the suburbs. Jesse asked him if he would play lead on our Street Child demo and if he knew a drummer who could cut it on the songs. He was playing with Ralph Arone and suggested he play on the demo. When those two guys heard the music, they were blown away and wanted in. We all felt very comfortable with each other and that's how the final lineup was born. We recorded at Sty in the Sky studios, which was owned by Josh Silver of Type O Negative fame. We all knew each other for a long time, since Jesse's brother played drums in a band with Josh years earlier. Our first gig was at the Limelight in New York. We opened for Waysted, and it was an amazing show. The rest is history!"

As Rob mentioned, it might seem weird, but with the exception of very few bands (Twisted Sister, The Rods, Anthrax, Frigid Bich, Virgin Steele, Dio, et cetera), the city of New York didn't enjoy a solid and big heavy metal scene. For a city as big as New York, with around 200 metal bands appearing from 1980 to 1989, it could be said that heavy metal wasn't as big as in other parts of America. New York, though, had already a huge tradition around punk, hardcore, garage, alternative, and experimental rock music, so this might justify the lack of a strong metal scene.

"The scene in Manhattan was never metal-friendly," Rob adds. "We had clubs that had rock nights or metal nights. You really had to go to Brooklyn or Queens or Long Island and Westchester. But some of the clubs were cool. We played New York and Westchester mostly, as far as locals. In Manhattan, we were the locals. But whenever we played out of the city, we always got a great response."

Playing metal, though, was the case for Street Child (even if they had connections with members of the New York hardcore scene), and Rob mentions, "Our motivation to form the band was probably the fact that we loved playing and we were very confident that we didn't sound like anyone else. Jesse and Nelson were two very different guitar players. Jesse played from the heart and was a great riff writer as well as a great lyricist. Nelson was schooled in music, so he understood odd time signatures and harmony. Some of the later Street Child music showcases that combination. Also, Jesse's voice was quite different from most of the singers of that type of metal. He had a baritone voice.

Street Child band photo courtesy Rob Origlio

"We wanted to share our music with other like-minded people ... the four of us liked a lot of the 1970s hard rock. I loved Kiss, Aerosmith, and Black Sabbath, of course. But Led Zeppelin really did it for me. I have an older sister, and she brought home *Physical Graffiti*. I was hooked. I grew up ten blocks from Madison Square Garden, and she took me to see Zeppelin! I was 13. As the years went on, Jesse would turn me on to a lot of new music. I remember he had *The Number of the Beast* by Iron Maiden. I heard Steve Harris, and I knew that was the bassist I wanted to be. Maiden was a big influence on all of us."

Street Child went straight on into Brooklyn's Sty in the Sky studio, under the direction of Josh Silver and the mononymous Sven, to record their rager 1989 *Street Child* twelve-inch EP. Rob says, "Jesse and I decided we wanted something that was more than just a generic demo tape. We wanted to impress someone at the labels who might get their hands on it. We wanted a vinyl album with album art. This was before the internet, so we would look in the backs of music magazines and music papers for small record plants that would produce a small number of albums and package them for not a lot of money. We found a place in Pennsylvania, I believe, that did the pressing and the packaging. The artwork was done by a friend of ours named Steve Chang. It was an actual painting he did just for us. Jesse gave him the basic concept of the track 'Street Child' and let him interpret it through the painting. We took the painting to a photo store, where they took a picture of it and shrank it down to album size. We printed only 500 copies. We sent some to the major labels, had some out at shows, and kept a few for ourselves. We had no idea that it would become a collector's item."

Rob adds, "I'm not sure of any other bands that had independent releases. We knew bands like Wench and Cro-Mags, but we weren't really paying attention to what other bands were doing. As far as we were concerned, we were the only Manhattan-based band that sounded like we did. As I as stated earlier, Manhattan bands were either punk, hardcore, or pop-oriented. We were a metal band."

Sporting an amazing heroic art cover (artist Steve Chang was also the bassist for the 1990s indie rockers Jupiter Sun), *Street Child* was released by the band's own Hell's Kitchen Records label in 1989 and to this day remains a definite classic, not only for underground metal but for classic American metal in general. With four songs that are fueled by the quality and power that only American metal bands could pull off in that time, Street Child stormed up their own brand of heavy/power metal—like a cross between Iron Maiden and early Fates Warning, with the vocals of Gargoyle. Highly melodic and anthemic, Street Child offer mid-tempo bangers such as "Erotic Insomnia," sing-along anthems like "Temple of Set" and the up-tempo apotheosis of pure Maiden-esque steel, "Building a Wall." Words cannot describe the perfection of the eternal eponymous anthem: "Street Child" is as classic as "Children of the Damned" by Iron Maiden. If you are not yet persuaded, I say that all metalheads will get goosebumps within the first few seconds!

CUT TO THE CHASE:

There aren't many words left to say about Street Child and their only release; fans of melodic yet powerful American metal, fans of Iron Maiden (especially the 1980–1988 era), fans of early Fates Warning, and fans of early Queensrÿche should try to somehow get their hands on *Street Child*.

"Our favorite moment," Rob says, "was without a doubt the first show we ever played as Street Child. It was September 1989. The Limelight was a converted church and had a really cool vibe. The stage was big, and the sound system was massive. They had rock and metal acts every Sunday night. Somehow, we got a show opening for Waysted, which was Pete Way of UFO. We were together for only six or seven months, but we rehearsed constantly. We were ready. We drew 200 people just for our band, which was pretty good for the first show of an unknown band. But we all had jobs and families, and it was our turf. Coworkers, friends, families all showed up to support us. It was an amazing show. You can see clips of it on YouTube."

Life's commitments were the reason that Street Child ceased to exist after a while. However, dedicated metalheads worldwide never forgot the name of Street Child, and by 2010, it was time for their sole record to get a proper reissue—by Buried by Time and Dust Records, with three bonus tracks. Of course, you can imagine the high quality of these three tracks, which leave us wondering how far Street Child could have eventually gone.

"I wasn't aware of a resurgence of interest in independent releases for metal bands," Rob says. "It reminds me of the 1980s, when Jesse and I would go to some independently owned record stores and find new bands. Sometimes you would buy an album just based on the way the cover looked. I remember when Jesse came home with Iron Maiden's *The Number of the Beast*. I heard Steve Harris, and my life changed. He totally influenced the way I played bass. Another memory I have is when Jesse bought Metallica's first album. I never heard anything like that before; I was immediately hooked. Sometimes I think about the *Street Child* release and I still can't believe it. It's very flattering, and it feels good to know that we did something that people still enjoy 30 years later. The reissue is a testament to how much the fans love the music. The fact that Nick from Buried by Time and Dust records took an interest in reissuing the album with extra tracks and a killer booklet says a lot."

Rob adds that in terms of the underground scene today, "there is definitely some kind of an underground scene somewhere. Look at bands like Rival Sons and Greta Van Fleet.

They are out there getting interest. But I don't know where the next big scene is going to be. In the 1980s, it was mostly the L.A. bands. The 1990s was Seattle's time to shine. It's all different now, since it's easy to download music. Record companies are different now. Different business models and such. Young bands not only have to tour constantly to make a name for themselves but also need to have a command of social media. It's hard out there for everyone. But when you're young and have no kids or mortgage, most likely you're going to live in a van and tour and do whatever you have to, because it's your passion."

I wonder if there will be an offer by European promoters that Street Child can't refuse (like the Keep It True festival or Up The Hammers festivals), so that metalheads could at least enjoy this band live. Additionally, a new reissue should be done, since the Buried by Time and Dust re-release has since sold out many years back!

HEATHEN'S RAGE

One of the mightiest American metal bands, and a band that still drives true metallers crazy just with their logo, Heathen's Rage from Yardsville, New Jersey, formed in 1983 and stormed the world with their majestic, ultra-powerful power metal.

"Heathen's Rage were already formed," bassist Mike LePond says. "They contacted me and set up an audition. I remember one of the songs I auditioned with was 'Deathrider' by Anthrax. I passed the audition, and I joined the band in December of 1985."

Initially, Heathen's Rage released two demos (the 1983 demo and *Fight 'til the End* in 1985), where all the harsh production only adds to the nostalgia. The shining diamond of Heathen's Rage is their bright, high-pitched vocals by Bob Pizzauro, and the Iron Maiden/Judas Priest formula errs on the side of Iron Maiden, with added influences of the American metal scene.

"We were very influenced by Anthrax, Virgin Steele, Riot, and Rainbow," Mike admits. "The record that inspired me most at that time was probably *Master of Puppets* by Metallica."

CUT TO THE CHASE:

The *Heathen's Rage* EP is a mandatory ultra-classic for fans who love their metal mean, hard, melodic, and traditional. The original copy on Rock Dream Records, though, is very hard to find. Totally recommended are all their re-releases and compilations, so for starters, the *Fight Till the End: The Lost Sessions* LP would be a great introduction to this awesome band.

The metal scene in my home state of New Jersey in the 1980s was amazing," adds Mike. "You could go out every night of the week and see kick-ass bands. Our scene was just as good as Los Angeles!" What's so rad in the case of Heathen's Rage is that they were an absolutely 100 percent pure metal band, yet they appeared on very diverse bills in the 1980s, alongside bands like Danzig or even the mighty Ramones! Christopher Wesley (lifelong friend and fan of Heathen's Rage, as well as the co-author of *Rage Days: The Illustrated History of Heathen's Rage*) mentions, "Their late singer, Gene Geary, played bass in an early version of Wayne/Jayne County's band back in 1974, and Marky [Ramone] was the drummer. Gene and Marky remain friends, and he tapped into that friendship to get Heathen's Rage on the bill for four Ramones shows in 1988."

In 1986, the time had come for Heathen's Rage to release their first vinyl album, the *Heathen's Rage* twelve-inch EP, also known as *Knights of Steel*. Mike says, "Our manager worked at a local metal store called Rock Dream Records. The owner of Rock Dreams had a record label, so we decided to release it on that label. We recorded the *Knights of Steel* EP for them, and the rest is history." That said, even though *Heathen's Rage* isn't strictly a private, self-released record, the fact that Rock Dream Records was a tiny label, which released only this record and the Tantrum LP that will be presented later, along with the whole family-type relationship that the band had with the owner of Rock Dreams, could stretch the nature of this release enough to be included here.

...And how could you not include a stellar release like this? What we have here is top-notch, first-class 1980s American metal that'll send shivers down the spines of all those who are nuts about this kind of stuff. Underproduced and raw, the three songs of the *Heathen's Rage* EP sound like a mix of NWOBHM alongside heavy metal bands like Metal Church and early speed metal like Anthrax—catchy as hell. "Knights of Steel" is an eternal metal anthem that reaches the highest peaks in heavy metal history, whereas the speed metal thrashing of "City of Hell" is simply menacing. "Dark Storm," which closes the EP, is a mid-tempo heavyweight, where the vocalist, Bob Pizzauro, sounds simply out of control.

Some shows followed, mostly in the New Jersey area, and Mike says, "My favorite show we played was with Megadeth at City Gardens in Trenton, New Jersey. I believe it was 1987." Of course, Mike also remembers the aforementioned Tantrum, as "they were from Trenton like us."The trend of excellent Heathen's Rage releases continued in 1988 with a new four-song demo, before the band called it quits later in 1990. Back in 2014, Heathen's Rage reunited and played festivals in Europe, and a number of compilations followed—the best one being the *Heathen's Rage Wooden Box Set*, a definitive anthology released by the Greek

HEATHEN'S RAGE PHOTOS COURTESY MIKE LEPOND

label No Remorse Records in 2015. "I see a huge interest for private metal in Europe and South America. I don't see it in the U.S., unfortunately. It's incredible that we became a cult band after just recording three songs. I think we could have been a huge band if we could have stayed together." Mike adds, "In many parts of the world, underground metal is alive and well. So many great bands are out there now. Unfortunately, it has come at a bad time. Most younger fans think music is free, and bands are getting killed by low album sales. Also, studios and record labels are going out of business all the time. In this atmosphere, I fear that no bands will be able to replace the great ones like Priest, Maiden, and Sabbath."

Heathen's Rage are definitely an ultimate fantasy for all hardcore fans of American metal, and the fact that they are active and featured on the 2019 *Knights at Switlik* album are hints that they're here to stay this time!

TANTRUM

ALONGSIDE HEATHEN'S RAGE, TANTRUM WERE ALSO FROM THE TRENTON, New Jersey, area—Groveville, specifically—and they formed in 1984 with the vision of playing pure metal, hard and loud. "Tantrum formed in 1984 with myself and Brian Mangini after years of writing songs with various other New Jersey metal musicians," John Riccio says. "This partnership was the beginning of a great new collaboration, adding drummer Nick Frascella and madman singer Chuck Bird ... we were all into Sabbath, Maiden, and Priest, with thrash directing us in a new approach." Tantrum quickly released their first demo in 1984, *Rock the World,* that contained four menacing metal songs, not unlike the traditional mix of Judas Priest with Iron Maiden, with a little bit of Accept and even a touch of NWOBHM bands like Angel Witch. "I was inspired by Tony Iommi, K.K. Downing, Brian May, and Ronnie Montrose," John adds. "Sabbath's *Sabotage* album impressed me and influenced my playing and writing. Moreover, the metal scene around the South Jersey area was very strong, with bands like Megadeth, Overkill, Slayer, and Metallica playing locally with their first albums just being released.

"Our motivation was to become a touring band and play the music we all put so much time into and loved to perform live. We always were well received at our shows," John says.

Rock Dream Records didn't miss the chance and released Tantrum's first twelve-inch, *Trenton City Murders,* in 1986. "We got albums from the record company with a promo album sleeve, no description on the jacket—when we disbanded, we stopped selling and distributing the remaining albums which had no stickers. We had to put the sticker on to label it; it was the first Black Album!" John laughs. "Metallica later did it. Theory at the time was they ripped us off—they were staying in our hometown of Old Bridge, and they were turned on to our music and record. Two years later, their *Black Album* was released, and 'Nothing Else Matters' sounded similar to Tantrum's 'Knights of Fire.'" Even though *Trenton City Murders* is not the end-all-be-all, it's still a very good effort from a band that took an approach to metal that's reminiscent of Sanctuary's *Refuge Denied* some years later. Sporting a very raw production, songs like "Call of the Beast" with its pummeling rhythm, its infectious chorus, and even some hardcore riffage is an ultimate classic. "Knights of Fire" is a haunting, dark, mid-tempo song with some crazy guitar leads. "Shot for Shot" reminds one of the style that bands like Steel Assassin proposed: explosive metal with very heavy riffs. And even though the title song, "Trenton City Murders," is the least memorable on the EP, it sure has its magic.

CUT TO THE CHASE:

Tantrum's *Trenton City Murders* EP would appeal to all metalheads who love their metal raw, speedy, and filthy, and also to fans of early Vicious Rumors, Destructor, and early Sanctuary. The original EP on Rock Dream Records can be a bit pricey; however, the reissue on Cult Metal Classics is way less expensive.

"Our best and most memorable show was opening for Megadeth in Trenton," says John. "TT Quick was a great band that also released private recordings, I believe ... but then again, there were so many unknown bands from that 1980s New Jersey era that are finally being recognized. It's an honor for Tantrum."

After disbanding sometime in the late 1980s, fast-forward to 2016, when the Greek record label Cult Metal Classics released the *Trenton City Murders* LP/CD compilation, which contained the classic 1986 EP in its entirety. It also included the tracks from the *Rock the World* demo and some other live and demo tracks, making it a very attractive package to satisfy all metalheads who couldn't find the original EP.

"There's great music out there still to be heard; our passion for metal was portrayed and withstood the test of time. Now I am going to rip up some guitar riffs! Yes, 63 years old and still a heavy metal warrior!" John laughs.

I can think of some people who would love to see Tantrum reuniting, recording, and performing, so there's always hope, thanks to the ever-young heart of John Riccio!

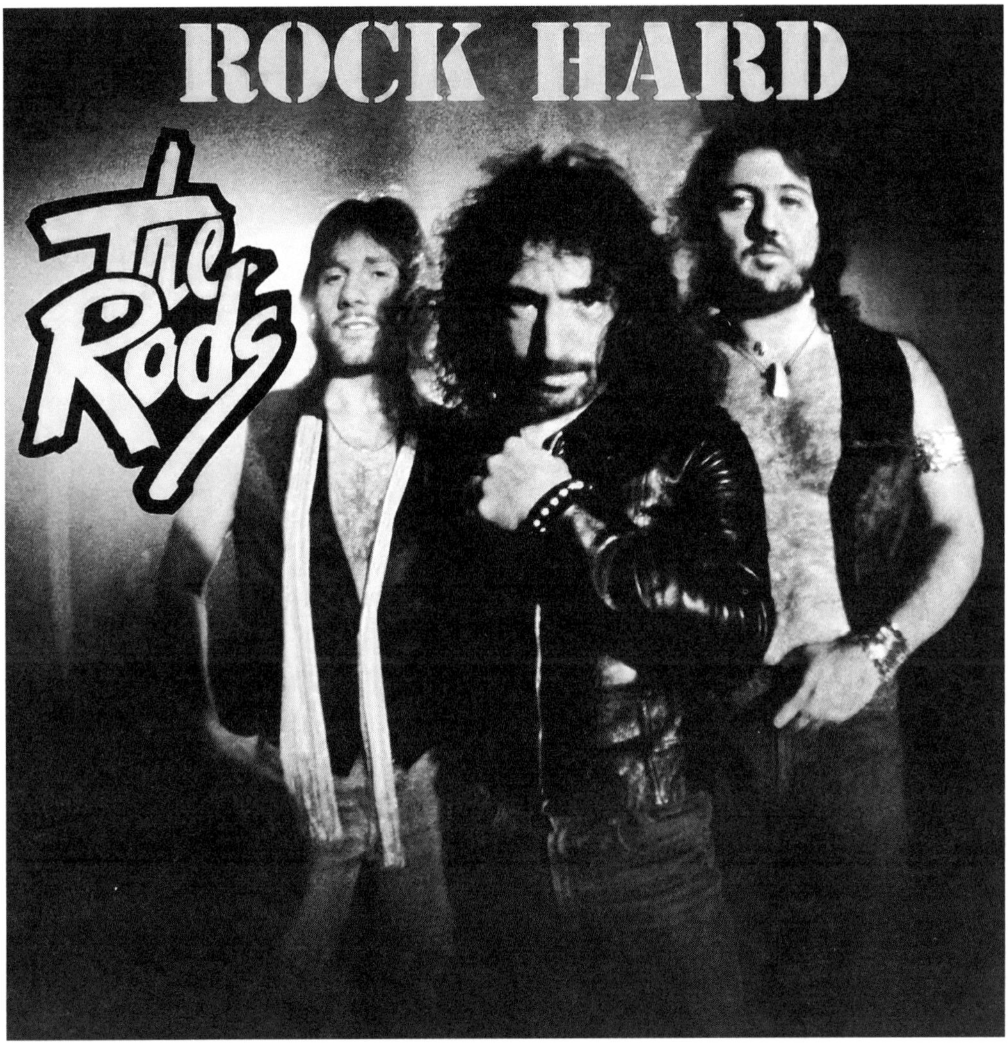

THE RODS

MOSTLY AS A REMINDER, THE RODS WERE CHOSEN TO BE INCLUDED HERE to refresh all metalheads' memory of what a great, long-standing band they are! Formed in Cortland, New York, in 1979, by David "Rock" Feinstein (guitar/vocals), Steven Starmer (bass/vocals), and Carl Canedy (drums/vocals). After the first album, Starmer was replaced by Garry Bordonaro. Feinstein started out playing guitar in the rock band Elf with his cousin, the infamous Ronnie James Dio.

"The Rods were influenced by so many great artists: Deep Purple, Hendrix, Jeff Beck, Cactus ... too many to mention," Carl, who was previously playing in the hard rock/heavy Kelakos, says. "We were laughed at when we first started playing originals. People thought we sucked, and we could clear a club in ten minutes. Little by little, we gained an audience, until we were packing the clubs. Local musicians thought I was wasting my time playing with The Rods."

THE RODS PROMO PHOTO COURTESY CARL CANEDY

Their first album was originally released independently as *Rock Hard* in 1980, on their own Primal Record Company, as was the *Crank It Up* seven-inch single (also in 1980), and Carl talks about their decision of initially releasing everything themselves: "We had no options to do anything but put it out on our own. We had it pressed in Texas at A&R ... we needed to get our name out there in order to get signed by a big—or bigger—label." Even though *Rock Hard* is an almost-great record, it still doesn't hold a candle to The Rods' subsequent releases, such as *Wild Dogs* LP and *Let Them Eat Metal*. The Rods' sound on *Rock Hard* is mostly based on the hard rock of the 1970s, like a blend of Kiss, AC/DC, Ted Nugent, and Deep Purple, with a slightly more metallic Judas Priest influence. However, still there are great tunes like "Power Lover" or "Get Ready to Rock N' Roll" and the title song "Rock Hard," which is maybe the heaviest and most metal on the album.

"It was our first show with Blue Öyster Cult at Broome County Arena in Binghamton, New York. It was my first arena show ever, and it was amazing!" Carl recalls. Carl was also the producer of many of The Rods' records, and he went on to pursue a career in production, with some of the greatest metal LPs ever produced under his belt. A few include Exciter's *Violence and Force*, Anthrax's *Fistful of Metal* and *Spreading the Disease*, Overkill's *Feel the Fire*, Helstar's *Burning Star*, and Possessed's *Beyond the Gates*, among cult classics like TT Quick's *TT Quick*, E-X-E's *Stricken By Might*, Rhett Forrester's *Gone With The Wind*, Attila's *Rolling Thunder*, and Centaur's *There's A Storm Coming*, among many others.

"Yep, it is true," Carl agrees humbly. "I produced a few bands with local releases." The first phase of The Rods lasted seven years, until 1987, and they released a good number of classic American metal records, such as their best ones, the 1984 *Let Them Eat Metal* LP and *Heavier Than Thou*. But sadly they disbanded, as their sound was too hard for the glam/metal fans of

CUT TO THE CHASE:

Bet most of you are already familiar with The Rods; if not, get at least three of their eighties records ASAP, with *Wild Dogs*, *Let Them Eat Metal*, and *Heavier Than Thou* being their absolute hits. Their self-released 1980 *Rock Hard* LP and the "Crank it Up" seven-inch are definitely great as well. Additionally, check out Killen and their superb 1988 *Killen* LP (on their own Victoria Records), which sounds like a weird cross between epic heavy/power metal and rough punk. Misfits, Manimals, or even Kryst the Conqueror come to mind. Terrific stuff!

the era, too traditional for the upcoming heavy/power metal fans, and not fast or rough enough for thrashers. Post-The Rods, all members played in innumerable other bands, among them Killen, Thrasher, and Lone Rager.

"We never thought our first album would become a collector's item," Carl says. "Now that it has, it's nice to see that fans are willing to pay for a collectible The Rods album. I wish we had more to sell!"

The Rods are back since 2010, with the two core members Carl Canedy and David "Rock" Feinstein accompanied by Michael San Ciro and Freddy Villano, having released three full-length LPs, always in the tradition of eighties-era The Rods: pure, classic American metal. "I believe that today, the metal scene is wide open," Carl concludes. "The only problem with the underground scene is that it's tough to get your music out to people. To make them aware of your new product. I love that music is accessible to fans. It's tough to make money for artists who do not tour and sell merchandise."

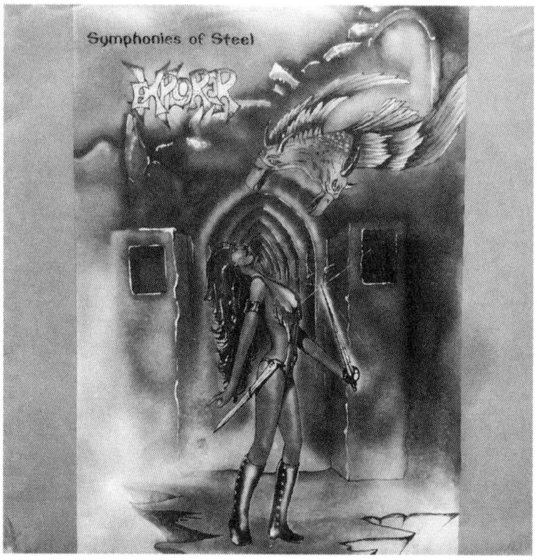

EXXPLORER

FORMED IN 1981 IN KEANSBURG, NEW JERSEY, AS EXPLORER, THIS LONG-RUNNING power metal band is definitely one of the most beloved in this book, and understandably, considering their recorded output through the years. "Explorer started as a cover band in 1981," guitarist Kevin Kennedy narrates. "The second 'X' was added when I suggested it after a second band also called themselves Explorer. We almost changed the name, but decided to just add a second 'X.' The initial lineup included me on guitar, Ed LaVolpe on second guitar, Charlie Shaver on vocals (later replaced by Lennie Rizzo), Jimmy Gardner on bass, and Mike Moyer on drums. Our biggest influences, in my opinion, were Judas Priest, Iron Maiden, Black Sabbath, and some Rush and Manowar. Judas Priest's *Sad Wings of Destiny* was a major influence for me!"

"The scene in Keansburg was custom-made for us ... clubs like the Old Tymer, Memories, and Faces were a few that we played on a regular basis, and they helped shape and mold the band into what we became," Kevin continues. "It really helped that our original vocalist, Charlie Shaver, was a key player in the Keansburg scene ... Charlie sadly passed away in 2018 (R.I.P.)."

Exxplorer were determined to gain more exposure, hoping to be approached by a record label, so they decided to use their own funds to put out their first record, the 1984 classic *Symphonies of Steel*, on their own Hot Hard Heavy Records. "We decided to release the *Symphonies of Steel* LP on our own after failed attempts to get a record deal ... after our limited release of 1,000 copies, Ed had mailed a lot of them around the world. This gained us an offer from the French label Black Dragon Records."

Symphonies of Steel is real ear candy for any fan of true American heavy/power metal; there's a definite Iron Maiden influence here, but Exxplorer retain a unique style of their own, mixing Queensrÿche with Rush, with shades of early Fates Warning. Lenny Rizzo's emotional, high-pitched vocals offer a very strong character to Exxplorer, but the best part is that their songwriting skills are tremendous. Listen to the opening track, "City Streets," which kicks off

CUT TO THE CHASE:

Symphony of Steel **is a quintessential American heavy metal LP that contains everything to make a fan of this sound wet his pants! A (not so) forgotten jewel in the crown of American metal history, *Symphony of Steel* is wholeheartedly recommended if you are into bands like early Queensrÿche, early Heir Apparent, and early Fates Warning.**

with a heavy Sabbathian riff and becomes a real powerhouse. The crushing "Run for Tomorrow" is anthemic and powerful as hell, while "Metal Detectors" is just top-shelf American metal.

Black Dragon Records offered Exxplorer a contract for a re-release of *Symphonies of Steel* later in 1985 (with a different cover and the band name as 'Exxplorer'), and Restless/Metal Blade offered them a U.S. re-release in 1986, again with a different cover! "I am not sure, but I think that our good fellows Liege Lord also released one record on their own, before they also signed with Black Dragon Records," Kevin adds.

Exxplorer remained active throughout all these years, offering shows in the U.S. and Europe ("The best memory for me was the original Exxplorer lineup playing together in Germany in 2015"). The band also released one (great) demo in 1985, and three LPs (up until 2011), offering pure American heavy metal, with the best being 1992's *Recipe for Power*, just for "Riding The Storm" and "Beg, Borrow and Steel."

"I love the fact that so many people still have interest in Exxplorer and so many other underground bands that arose from the 1980s," Kevin continues. "I don't see many old-school true original bands on the scene today, and it's sad what has happened to people actually purchasing the real product today ... the real underground scene exists today. But it is even harder than ever for them to succeed."

Members of Exxplorer also appeared with Dark Sky Choir (heavy/hard rock), Drifter (heavy metal), Skullshifter (death/thrash), Ashes to Ashes (heavy metal), S.A. Slayer, Narita, and Juggernaut.

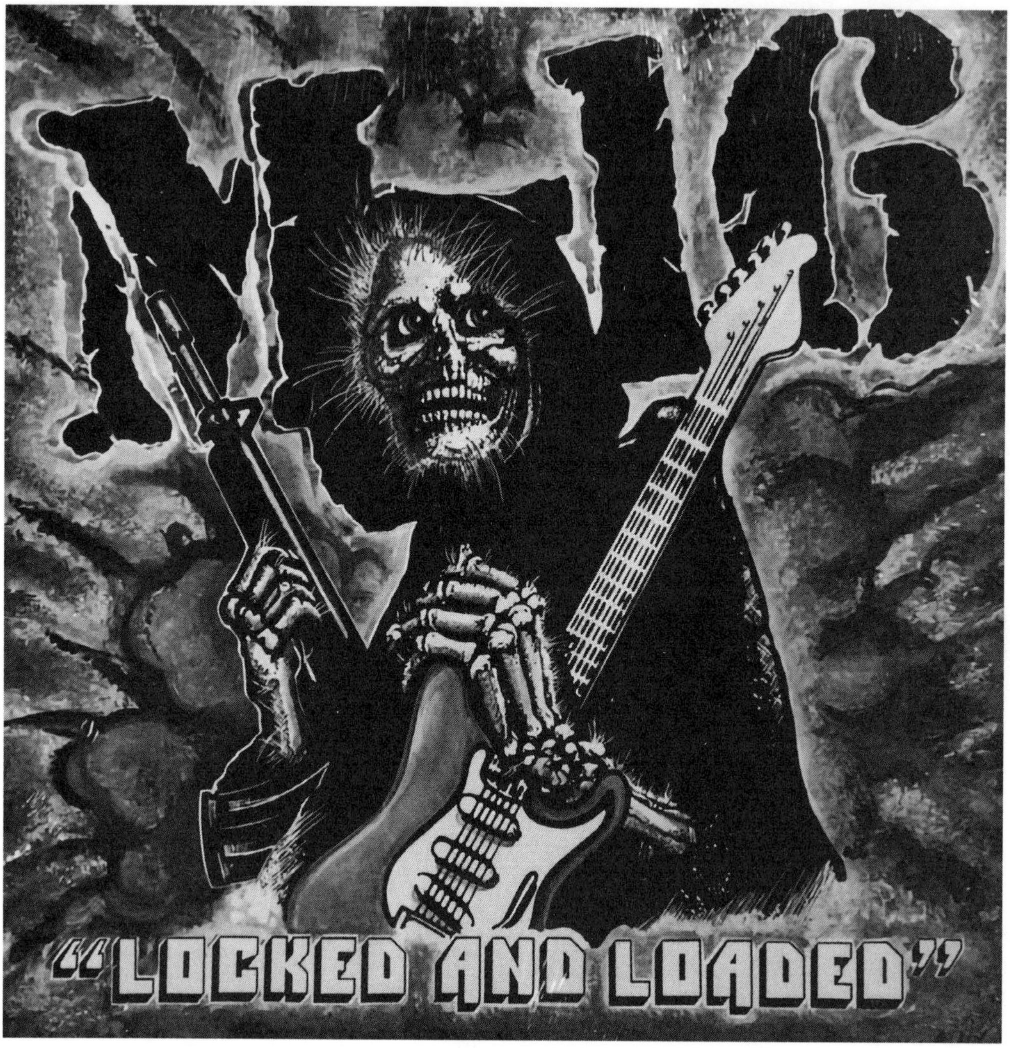

M-16

FROM UPSTATE NEW YORK, SCHENECTADY'S M-16 ARE DEFINITELY ONE OF the area's highest-quality bands, even though they released only one full LP, the 1988 *Locked and Loaded*. Lead vocalist Lenny Thomas narrates: "We formed in 1983 with the lineup being Greg Simmons on lead vocals, Glen Oliver on lead guitar, Gary Ranze on rhythm guitar, Steve 'Mote' VanDyke on bass guitar, and Tom Verrigni on drums. After numerous personnel changes over the next two years, they finally had all of the pieces fall into place with the 1985 lineup of me on lead vocals, Glen Oliver on lead guitar, Kevin Egnor on rhythm guitar, Steve 'Mote' VanDyke on bass guitar, and Pete Sivaslian on drums. We rehearsed in a little garage in Central Bridge, New York, and began writing our own songs while learning the latest songs of the eighties metal scene, practicing four nights a week most of the time when we weren't gigging. We opened for many national acts locally throughout the years, and in 1986 we took the opening spot for Poison when singer Bret Michaels became ill, and opened a show for Ratt at the RPI Field House in front of 7,500 screaming rock fans. We played all the local clubs in the Schenectady/Albany Capital District area and did a two-year Northeast club tour beginning in 1987, and promoting our self-released LP *Locked and Loaded* in 1988.

"From 1985 to 1990, we continuously packed the local nightclubs, from the smallest of clubs to the area's largest venues, with music lovers from all walks of life. When many bands were churning out the softer side of the synth-pop rock of the eighties, M-16 was known for their set list chock-full of the heavier side of eighties metal cover rock—with hits by Accept, Def Leppard, Iron Maiden, Judas Priest, Scorpions, and a fistful of originals as well. We were also known for our lineup of some of the most talented musicians the area had to offer, not to mention our high-energy concert-style shows, packed with rows of flashing lights, thumping speakers, and—yes, kids—Spandex and loads of hairspray!"

When asked about the initial intentions of M-16, Lenny responds, "You know the old cliché, 'sex, drugs, and rock 'n' roll.' We wanted to get signed with a major label, and in fact, we had interest from Atlantic Records, but our attorney advised us against the deal. At the time when I joined the band, I had just heard of Judas Priest and only knew the radio hit 'Another Thing Coming.' The band told me to listen to *Unleashed in the East* and learn the songs 'Green Manalishi' and 'Victim of Changes' ... Wow, I was blown away—to this day, it's the greatest album ever."

He adds, "M-16 were in general influenced by bands like Aerosmith, AC/DC, Black Sabbath, Iron Maiden, Judas Priest, Metallica, Ozzy, and Scorpions."

M-16 followed the route of hard work in the studio for years before perfecting their sound. "We started out just recording a two-song demo, which turned into a six-song EP, and after a few local recording studios screwed us, we decided to go with another local who put out other local bands' stuff, MCE Records. That's the studio and label we released *Locked and Loaded* on. It was re-released on CD a few years ago on Heaven and Hell Records, titled *Locked and Reloaded*, with some bonus tracks. Only 500 copies and they sold out. Apparently, he is putting out another run—I haven't heard anything yet.

"Anyway, after a few recording mishaps with demos at other studios and losing thousands of our own dollars that we saved from gigging, my mother and stepfather fronted the money to cover the cost of the entire process, from studio time, album artwork, printing, and distribution, which I believe at the time was around $5,000. We recorded it over a three-month period, and the tech accidentally recorded over it with his band. Needless to say, he was fired. We then re-recorded the entire album with the owner of the studio, Mark Ernst, in a two-week period and were rushed through the final mix process. Unfortunately, the studio closed and our master two-inch that we'd bought disappeared as well. We heard it was also recorded over. First run was 5,000 copies—sold out. Second run was another 5,000 copies—sold out. Nearly 4,000–5,000 sold overseas in Europe. We even received fan mail from Germany!"

Locked and Loaded can be considered a private metal release, since it was like the case of Heathen's Rage: a small recording studio put its stamp on the release, but the whole procedure was taken care of by the band itself. Don't let the record's cover carry you away, since *Locked and Loaded* contains nothing more than fine, professionally executed heavy metal in the American style. In fact, there are no hints of European heavy metal influences found here, other than the obvious, more American side of Judas Priest. It sounds absolutely like a product of the USA. The production of *Locked and Loaded* is flawless, giving the illusion that it was recorded with the backing of a major label. In musical terms, it stands somewhere in between hard rock and heavy metal, with the emphasis on heavy metal. Melodic, powerful, lyrical, *Locked and Loaded* will appeal to all the fans of bands like Dokken at their heaviest or Shok Paris at their most melodic. Even though the lyrics leave me cold—I never liked the cheesiness of metal romance and partying—songs like the headbanging "Tonite (It's You)" and "Why" are so inspired.

CUT TO THE CHASE:

Locked and Loaded **would absolutely appeal to all those into *Screaming for Vengeance*'s more American metal-styled songs (e.g., "Take These Chains"), and I wouldn't recommend it to the hard-line, epic power metalheads, as it would sound pretty soft to them. People who are into the more melodic side of heavy metal, though, would appreciate and love it. I can't really stand the whole drama of love songs, but can admit that in terms of execution and performance, *Locked and Loaded* is utterly professional. Re-releases of it on CD are also available on Heaven and Hell and Dyamond Roxx Series records.**

Lenny recalls, "One Saturday morning in 1986, I got a call from a local radio station, PYX 106—they had a Friday-night metal show and played our song 'Wasted Love' regularly—saying that Poison's lead singer had a diabetic attack and couldn't open the Ratt show at RPI Field House, and if M-16 could open the show. We needed 35 minutes of original music—no covers! At that time, we had just about that much. We accepted and played to the largest crowd ever for us—over 7,500. Obviously, we had quite a few fans booing, upset about Poison canceling, but it was general admission, so a lot of our fans were at the stage screaming in support. I did have to dodge some thrown quarters from some asshole haters, but we played on like professionals, and most people after the show said we kicked Ratt's ass. Definitely bucket list."

Lenny goes on to add, "I can remember China White, Visitor, Maxx Thrust, Triffid, and Divine Right from the wider New York area having private releases of some kind during that time, and those bands were definitely good." M-16 never released anything other than *Locked and Loaded* but remain active to this day, playing local shows and practicing in the studio from time to time. "I find it hard to believe that people are spending big bucks for our LP, but I think it's pretty cool at the same time—especially when I think back to all the time and hard work we put into it." Lenny smiles. "I think most loyal fans would rather purchase an album or CD, but unfortunately, with today's technology, we can never stop downloading."

HADES

FORMED WAY BACK IN JANUARY 1978, WHEN DAN LORENZO PICKED THE NAME from a mythology book in ninth grade, Hades, from Paramus, New Jersey, are still active to this day. They're for sure one of the most historic and underrated American metal bands ever.

"I started calling myself 'Dan from Hades' way back in 1978, the day I picked up a guitar," Dan Lorenzo, guitarist and founding member, narrates. "Initially, we were a cover band, playing live shows in the Paramus area, covering Cheap Trick, Aerosmith, Kiss, The Knack, and Ted Nugent. I will attempt to give you a short history of Hades, mentioning that our first record was a self-released 45 in 1982 with the songs 'Girls Will Be Girls' and 'Social Disease.' Paul Smith was our original singer. Riding Easy Records are actually putting those two songs on a compilation soon. In 1987 we released our first full-length, *Resisting Success*. We released *If At First You Don't Succeed* about 18 months later. We toured Europe in May and June of 1989 and then broke up. In 1999, we signed with Metal Blade and did three new CDs in three years.

"I loved Kiss and wanted to play guitar. Then I wanted to play my original music. I guess Kiss' *Rock and Roll Over*, AC/DC's *Highway to Hell*, and Aerosmith's *Rocks* were fundamental to my musical upbringing, heh!" Dan laughs. "The New Jersey scene was amazing until they raised the drinking age from 18 to 21 in 1982—but then again, it was still good for Hades from 1986 through 1989. We were pretty big in New Jersey, and particularly in northern New Jersey we were the scene."

> ## *CUT TO THE CHASE:*
>
> **If you are a fan of early American metal or a speed/heavy metal fan and you're not familiar with Hades, you have no excuse; you should check out their first two full LPs (*Resisting Success* and *If At First You Don't Succeed*) because both are incredibly mature, not only in musical terms but also lyrics-wise. Wish there were more bands like them in the 1980s.**

After lineup changes, Hades found a steady lineup in 1982 (for at least one recording), with the likes of Paul Smith on vocals, Dan Lorenzo on guitar, Joe Casilli also on guitar, Anthony Vitti on bass, and Tom "Agh" Coombs on drums. After four years of existence, Hades decided that it was time to release their first piece of vinyl, 1982's *Deliver Us From Evil* seven-inch (on their own Clown Records). "We had to put it out on our own because nobody would sign us, and we wanted to build a buzz," Dan adds.

The *Deliver Us From Evil* seven-inch differs much in terms of musical direction from later Hades releases; the brilliant "Girls Will Be Girls" sounds almost like a punk song with metal licks, whereas the flip side of "Social Disease" has a weird blues-rock style, mixed with hard rock. It's still good. Not recommended for hard-line metalheads, but this kind of stuff could also appeal to fans of KBD punk and metalheads equally! The then-newborn Megaforce Records offered Hades a slot on the compilation LP *Born to Metalize* in 1984, among bands like The Beast, Tortured Dog, and Sneak Attack. Their two tracks on the LP, "Rogue March" and "Gloomy Sunday," are both in the same style as *Deliver Us From Evil*, only more on the metal side of things this time. It's good, classic American heavy metal in the same vein of bands like Armored Saint and early Lizzy Borden.

The new lineup of Hades included Dan Lorenzo, Tom Coombes, high-pitched vocalist Alan Tecchio, guitarist Scott LePage, and bassist Jimmy Schulman, and they went on to release another record on their own, the 1985 *The Cross/Widow's Mite* seven-inch. On this single, Hades found the direction that they would keep up for many records to come: speed/heavy metal with a progressive edge, technical and bombastic. Both songs are huge classics of American metal, with "The Cross" having a more traditional approach and "Widow's Mite" affecting a weirder edge. Classic and mandatory stuff for everyone into early 1980s metal!

Actually, it was *The Cross/Widow's Mite* seven-inch that attracted small metal labels, with Torrid Records offering a contract for two releases (their classics, 1987's *Resisting Success* and 1988's *If At First You Don't Succeed* LPs); those records are pure gold for every fan of bands ranging from Fates Warning to Toxic and from Powermad to (Alan Tecchio's) Watchtower! It was time for Hades to reach for the sky, playing shows mainly on the East Coast. Dan says, "Playing Boston on December 30th, 1988, when we opened for Manowar and Nuclear Assault, was

maybe my favorite gig of the era. The crowd was loving us and we were fast and tight." But sadly, due to poor sales, Hades disbanded the following year.

"Yes, I can recall that Twisted Sister also had their first two 45s released on their own," Dan remembers. "It was such a fascinating time to be a heavy metal musician—there were so many different influences that were blending in the classic metal sound, and there was a massive number of big bands to follow!"

Following the 1989 breakup of Hades (or, as Dan puts it, "We never broke up, just took some time off...") Dan soon formed a new group, Non-Fiction, which issued its debut EP *Green* in 1989. After a stint with the group Watchtower, Tecchio returned to New Jersey and joined Non-Fiction as well, and each year, Hades played a reunion show at Newark's Studio One (1991's show yielded the *Live on Location* CD). When Non-Fiction dissolved upon completing their album *It's a Wonderful Life*, Lorenzo and Tecchio reformed Hades with Fuhrman, LePage (now on bass), and drummer Dave Lecsinsky. Hades released four more records: *Exist to Resist* in 1995 on Brainstorm Division, and then *$avior $elf* in 1998, *The Downside* in 2000 and *DamNation* in 2001 on Metal Blade Records. What a pity that Metal Blade didn't offer them a contract in the 1980s, because they could have gotten so much exposure. Torrid Records sadly couldn't handle things with such professionalism, even though bands like Exodus, Tension, Gothic Slam, and Mucky Pup were releasing classic LPs on the label.

"Phew, well, it's really flattering that people are actually still interested in Hades, and even paying some big money on our early two seven-inches," Dan says. "Sadly, everything is so different today, both in the mainstream music business as well as in the underground. I'm not fond of downloading at all. I really prefer the old-school way: buying records and CDs!"

Hades are still active to this day (2021), and they play shows from time to time!

MURDER SUITE

FROM CONNECTICUT, MURDER SUITE ONLY LEFT US A SEVEN-INCH OF TWO songs—but what a classic it was! Guitarist and vocalist Lenny Spickle narrates the story of Murder Suite: "We formed in the winter of 1984 in the small town of Milford, Connecticut. I had just finished high school and wanted to start or join a rock band. I looked in the local paper for musicians and found an ad for a band looking for a guitar player, so I called. That is when I first met Michael D. We talked on the phone for a bit, shared mutual interests in music and life. I was working at a gas station on the freeway, and we decided that Mike would bring me a cassette of songs we wanted to start out with. It included some Dio, Sabbath, Judas Priest, Iron Maiden, Accept, Whitesnake, and a few others. This was very exciting for me, as I really wanted to rock out and play in a band, and these were some of my favorite artists. Some of the songs I already knew, and the rest I learned right away. We set up a rehearsal at Mike's house—

he had a little studio in his attic. This is where I first met Fred Bemis. To this day, he's one of the best bass players I have ever met. At this point, it was just the three of us, Mike on drums (an amazing drummer), Fred on bass, and myself on guitar. From the moment we started, it was magical. We blew the roof off the house! We knew we had something special.

"Now all we needed was a lead singer and a second guitar player. I was at work one day and this long-haired guy in a leather jacket walked in and asked if he could use the phone. He looked like a rocker, so on chance, I just asked him if he played guitar. He looked back at me and said, 'Yes, I do.' This was the first time I met Mike Moleski. (Funny side note: I told him he could not use the phone at the gas station!) So I told him about the band we were forming, he was very interested and said he knew a really good singer. When he told me the singer's name, Carl Gent, I was floored. Carl was the local rock star hero! Here I was thinking, 'Holy shit, I'm going to meet Carl and he might sing in our band!' So, we exchanged info and set up a rehearsal. Mike and Carl showed up, we rocked, and that was the birth of Murder Suite.

"Some might wonder how we got our name. Carl owned a small hotel. Don't remember too much about it, but I think you could rent the rooms by the hour! There was a small banquet room that we turned into our rehearsal studio, and that became our hub and home. We now needed a band name. One day, over what I'm sure was many beers, Carl told us a story about what was probably a hooker that was killed in one of the rooms. So of course, instantly, we all wanted to see the room! Carl took us to room #17, The Murder Suite! I'm about 99 percent sure it was at that moment that was the band name. So, if you look at the cover of our record, there is a hotel key for room #17."

Lenny, when asked what motivated him to form Murder Suite, replies: "My motivation is the fact that I am first a music fan. I love music. It's that simple. I knew at a very young age that I wanted to play guitar. My first guitar was given to me by my Uncle Joe. He was a truck driver, and one day, he just came over and said he wanted me to have it. That is how it all started. I was around seven years old. I really didn't learn to play it; I just stood in front of the mirror with it, pretending to play along with all my favorite rock bands. It wasn't until I was 13 years old that I got my first electric guitar. It cost 35 dollars, and I made payments to the local music shop (Fladd Music) with my paper route money. The day I picked it up, it was pouring rain, and I had to wrap it in plastic to carry it home. I was the proudest kid on the planet! So basically, the motivation to start this band was the love of music, love of playing my guitar, and rocking with some of the most talented, coolest guys I had met."

Murder Suite didn't waste time, and they quickly went on to record and release their first and only seven-inch EP *Laugh Now, Cry Later*, which was out on their own Murder Suite Productions. "Not to toot my own horn, but it was my idea," Lenny adds. "I mean, what is the coolest thing a musician can do? Make a record! All I ever wanted was to have my name on vinyl. Here I was, playing in this amazing band, we started writing our own music, now we needed to record it. I saw an ad in a local paper for a local recording studio (Trod Nossel), and for 500 dollars, they included use of the recording studio, two songs, the engineer, and like 100 copies of the record. I thought, 'Holy shit, we are doing this.'

"So, I took it to the band, and of course, they were all in! What was the procedure behind its production and release? It was recorded and produced by the band and one engineer. We were just kids, had no idea what we were doing, so we brought our gear to the studio, set up, and played. To this day, one of the most memorable musical memories I have. First time ever in a recording studio, and first time ever recording. We all felt like rock stars. The songs were mixed, mastered, and pressed. They handed us a box of records, and off we went."

CUT TO THE CHASE:

I don't believe that anyone into the pure American metal sound won't at least enjoy the raw take of Murder Suite. Fans of Iron Maiden (1982–1985) will specifically love it, and it'll do the job for all those into Judas Priest and Accept's mid-tempo moments as well. A total banger!

Murder Suite's *Laugh Now, Cry Later* seven-inch contains two remarkable, ultra-classic diamonds of American heavy metal. The title song starts off with an epic intro, only to evolve into a raging metal hymn, like a much rawer, gutsier Iron Maiden. Murder Suite sound like they breathe metal in this one, and everything is perfect, from the vocals and the challenging guitar solo to the galloping rhythm. On the flip side, "Bad Guys Finish Last" is a hard 'n' heavy mid-tempo crowd-pleaser, more in the Judas Priest vein but still very good.

"We were all metalheads," Lenny admits. "Dio, Ozzy, Motörhead, Priest, Maiden, Mötley Crüe—anything that was on the radio in the early and mid-eighties, we played it. I had all the seventies K-Tel records—man, that stuff was good. But as far as rock or metal, it was Led Zep, and Black Sabbath, Ozzy. *Neon Nights* blew me away, and then when Dio came out with the *Holy Diver* and *Last in Line* albums, I knew I wanted to be a part of that music."

Murder Suite kept on rockin' until sometime in the late 1980s, playing local shows; meanwhile, Lenny joined Eden (post-August Redmoon) in 1986 and then again from 2004 to 2013, and he played in Animal in 1989. As of 2019, he played in Snew.

"It is absolutely awesome that people today seem to be interested in all the unknown metal bands of the 1980s," Lenny says. "Keeping metal alive, and hearing bands that didn't get the recognition they deserve. I am so honored that I hear from people all over the world that know who Murder Suite is, and want a copy of our little 45. We were a great band, and those songs kick ass! I hope to do another metal record and re-record those songs. Never in my wildest dreams could I imagine, this many years later, that record is sought-after. It's very heartwarming."

He goes on, "There is so much shit music being forced down our throats, we have to go underground for what's real, what's good. It's the times we live in. Sure, money is nice to have, but for me, it's not the money. It's the love of music and making music. If my music touches people the way music has influenced my life, take it, enjoy it! Rock till the end, my friends!"

BLACKSMITH

FORMED IN ALBANY, NEW YORK, IN 1983, BLACKSMITH QUICKLY BECAME ONE of the premier heavy metal acts in their area. Vocalist Heidi Black narrates, "Blacksmith was started by guitarist Dave Smith and myself. We'd had previous bands together, and once we had Tommy Roy and Michael Marino on drums and bass respectively, then we knew we had something great. So, we named the band Blacksmith, since I'm Heidi Black and Dave's last name is Smith ... and voilà! Forgers of metal, Blacksmith, was born. Around 1983, I think! Our personal influences were Led Zeppelin, Black Sabbath, the Runaways, Plasmatics, Ramones, early Metallica and Iron Maiden, and also classical music. *Led Zeppelin III*, which was recorded live in the studio, was definitely a huge inspiration for me. Still is. Years after I left the band and was working in radio, I got to meet Jimmy Page and Robert Plant, and holy fucker doodles, was that amazing. I was speechless. Just amazing. Now I have a dragon leg sleeve tattooed on my entire left leg, like Jimmy Page's dragon pants. I just love them."

When asked about Albany, Heidi says, "The scene there was amazing, someone was always playing locally and everyone went to the shows to support local music and share the experiences of all of the legendary bands and performers who played in the Albany area. Local people were, in general, really positive and supportive, not just of our band but of all the local bands and musicians. We really were one big rock 'n' roll family!"

After the 1985 demo, Blacksmith released a self-titled EP in 1986 that helped transform the band into one of New York's rising stars. Of course, it was a privately released record, aptly named *Blacksmith*, in a twelve-inch mini-album format. Heidi tells the story behind this release, adding: "We wanted to get our music out there, beyond the capital region of New York. And so, thanks to mainly our bass player Mike Marino's family, we secured financing, and the family of our drummer at the time, George Snyder, also helped us to secure a producer. We loved the studios where we recorded, Cathedral Studios. The production was contentious at times due to certain idiosyncrasies, which all creative people have. But we were really excited to be recording, and the release of the EP was received extremely well. We appeared in *Kerrang!* and other metal magazines a few times, which was such an honor! And also received lots of airplay on local radio and the various places we played in the Northeast. So, a happy experience for the most part."

CUT TO THE CHASE:

Blacksmith's first mini-LP release from 1986 is a very enjoyable and unique release that will please the hearts of everybody who's into weird metal that's challenging and structurally bizarre. It's definitely recommended. However, those into the dynamite metal of U.S. power/speed acts should also get their hands on *Fire From Within*. A sinfully underrated record!

The *Blacksmith* twelve-inch contains five songs of thunderous American heavy/power metal that reminds one of a beefier Bitch: stompy and heavy, a sound that bands like Savage Master attempt to recreate nowadays. Very challenging stuff here, with no-commercial/glam tendencies, and where Blacksmith suffer in catchy songwriting, they gain in power and authenticity! However, songs like the frenetic "Rock Hard" or "Louder than Hell" will please all fans of true, honest, and pure heavy metal! "I really can't remember any other local bands releasing an album privately at that time. It's all kind of a blur, haha!" Heidi laughs. "I know many of us recorded for compilation albums, which were released independently and got a lot of radio play. *Metal Luna Syndrome* I think was the title of one of them. There were so many great musicians and bands in this area back then. Thankfully, there still are! But it's a different vibe now."

Not long after the release of *Blacksmith*, original singer Heidi Black would depart and vocalist Malcolm Mania would step in. "Chris Caglione and I were in an all-original band called Sinistar," Malcolm adds. "We answered an ad in a local fanzine called *Metroland* for a singer and a drummer. We had two cassettes available as Sinistar, so David Smith had a good idea of what our sound was like already ... My main ambition is just creating music. I still to this day record all kinds of ideas, and sometimes, they become complete songs, and other times, they are like an old car that just needs the right water pump to make it perfect."

With the new lineup, Blacksmith released in 1989 the *Fire From Within* LP (on the small indie label named Tropical Records that also released records by Leatherwolf and Strut),

a real masterpiece of classic American metal that blends heavy metal with power/speed, in an intriguing and explosive manner! Songs like "The Beast" or "Hell to Pay" are simply incredible, and the full-length *Fire from Within* is a departure from the band's earlier sound. Here, Blacksmith sounds like Attacker, Liege Lord, or Agent Steel—that means razor-sharp, crazy American power/speed metal.

Blacksmith kept it up until 1991, breaking up and briefly getting back together for some shows in 2005. They are now back together for good, since 2011, releasing one compilation CD (*Strike While the Iron's Hot*, 2011) and then a 2012 version of the *Black Attack* (with Heidi Black) '86 single, as well as a new record, the awesome *Time Out of Mind* album from 2012, which time-travels you to the late eighties with its supersonic power metal sound (plus it includes a crazy cover of Ramones' "Blitzkrieg Bop"!).

As for their favorite shows from back in the 1980s? Heidi replies, "So funny—it has to be one of our early road trips to New Hampshire, when we played this place called the Zoo. Oh, my God, that was a rough place. Bullet holes in the walls, as one local guy put it, 'from the last band that played here.' Sheesh! We were about two songs into our first set when a beer bottle landed on the floor in front of me. 'Holy shit,' I thought, 'what to do, what to do...' So I picked it up and screamed really hard and smashed that bottle on the floor. Then we played 'The Zoo' by Scorpions like seven times in a row and all the locals loved us from then on. But it was meaningful for me because I learned how to turn a situation around pretty quickly! And that bar was in the hometown of the then-unknown GG Allin!"

Malcolm adds, "I don't want to glorify the 1980s, because the local scene in Upstate New York has always sucked. There was one club, so we played there more than anywhere else. It was called Saratoga Winners. We at least warmed up for a few good acts there, such as Wrathchild America, Nitro, Skid Row, The Great Kat. So many, I can't remember them all. But other than that, just a few dives, and believe me, we played them all. No shame in our game. Then again, I would have to say the most memorable show would have to be Headbangers Open Air Fest 2012."

As aforementioned, Blacksmith are still active today, in 2022, with plans to perform in Europe and the U.S., as well as some thoughts on releasing new material. "A real underground scene is definitely alive today, especially in countries other than the U.S. It'd be nice to see it more nationally accepted here, but still it lives nonetheless. I think everyone should pay something for the music they enjoy and support the music they love," Heidi adds. Malcolm agrees: "Being able to get music online for free for the most part has killed the industry for most people like us. Eighties metal is not exactly in high demand around here. I would love to live in Germany, where people yell out your name. That's all I really want—the same thing everybody wants—just to be loved."

DISCIPLE

STRAIGHT OUTTA BROOKLYN, DISCIPLE WAS ONE OF THE FEW NYC BANDS of the early 1980s that played in a strict heavy metal style (even though specific members had already a hardcore/punk background).

Bassist Charlie Ferrendi says, "Disciple went through a couple of formations; I was part of the second one in mid-1984. We met and got together in a Brooklyn studio named Slunky Sound Studio. I was playing with another band, and the members of Disciple were listening to us play and came in after we were done and asked if I would stay and jam with them. I said yes. This was 1984. The band was already locally known. And we jelled very quickly, and they asked that night if I wanted to join in. Little did I know that it was the drummer, C.C., playing with Dave Gonzales on guitar and Don Lord on vocals. Also, the band I played in before was a well-known band called The Fast. I was bouncing around playing with a few bands. Dave Gonzalez was

DISCIPLE PROMO FLYER, 1986

an excellent young guitar player with a lot of heart, and we played well together. C.C. and I are both Italian and made for a heavy rhythm section called the Italian Battalion. Don Lord was about 6'4" and had a strong metal voice. L'Amour, the rock capital of Brooklyn, was our home base, and Alex Kayne, the DJ, was a good friend. Disciple had a few good songs from the old lineup that we played, but we quickly put together our own songs, mostly by Dave Gonzalez laying down a riff and C.C. and I putting a solid rhythm behind it. It was kinda easy; we worked well together.

"Before I joined Disciple, they were involved in a battle of the bands at L'Amour with another local band. That band was Carnivore, our friends. Out of 20 bands, it was down to those two, but Carnivore won. Didn't really know of Disciple until I met them that night. Knew Keith very well, Big Pete [Peter Steele from Type O Negative] also. Good friends with Johnny Kelly of Type O. He actually was the drum tech for Disciple a few times. And I see, Alex, that you are in a picture with Vinnie from Agnostic Front! I played with him once in the A7 in NYC. I was playing with the guys in Ultra-Violence. And I played with Dave Manzullo and Charlie, the drummer!" Charlie recalls with joy, adding, "I guess I missed that boat, but I was there. I played in The Fast, which was a power pop band that came up with the Ramones and Blondie. See, I am 58 now, and I was part of the 1970s punk scene. Played Max's Kansas City and CBGB a few times. I even remember when the Sex Pistols came to the States, and it was very exciting!

"Thin Lizzy, Motörhead, Judas Priest, Ozzy, and Kiss were the bands that inspired us," Charlie explains. "The metal scene that was focusing around L'Amour was awesome, and everyone played there. A lot of big acts. Don Lord's brother, Matt Birkbeck, was our management guy, and he got the money together to do the EP after we were turned down by Island, Epic, and Megaforce."

Charlie mentions that it was unbelievably hard for a metal band in the 1980s to gain a contract with a (big or small) label; labels could afford to be picky because of the flood of high-quality bands of the era. So, after one cassette demo, Disciple went on to release on their own: 1986's *Disciple* EP on their own BSR Records. "We didn't press a lot, maybe 1,000 copies of it. We got some radio play on the local radio stations on Saturday night when they did their midnight metal show. We put a video out in 1986, which was a cut from the album named 'Neck Breaking Woman,' that was filmed at the Cat Club in NYC."

The *Disciple* EP contained five American metal songs, but it was a mixed bag; the hard rock/metal song "Neck Breaking Woman" is kind of weak, whereas when the band takes on a full-on metal approach like in "Beloved of the Butcher," the result is exciting. Lyric-wise, it's all party and women, something I can't connect to, but strictly in musical terms, *Disciple* contains real powerhouses, such as "Here and Now." This metal's 100 percent American—the only European influences of Disciple come from Judas Priest's more Americanized era, and I can hear some 1980s Riot in them, as well as Dio.

> ## *CUT TO THE CHASE:*
>
> **I recommend the *Disciple* EP wholeheartedly to all those into the classic American metal sound—not power/speed stuff, just plain, straight-up American metal. I'd love to see a compilation that included their demo and EP combined, so hey, reissue labels, go ahead!**

"My favorite show was at the Sundance on Long Island to a packed house opening up for Manowar," Charlie remembers. "People were three feet away from our faces, didn't really know who we were, but when we started playing, the house went absolutely nuts! Alongside that, we opened up for a lot of good bands both at L'Amour and the Sundance. Overkill, White Lion, Cinderella, Raven, and Keel were some of them."

Disciple dissolved later in late 1980s, leaving behind the heritage of their sole EP. "As far as the underground, I feel that I always was a part of it," Charlie sighs, "even though later life has thrown me a few curveballs. My wife and I are cancer survivors, and we have a special-needs son who we love. So, I've not been in tune with the current underground scene."

SIREN

DEFINITELY ONE OF THE UNSUNG HEROES OF THE AMERICAN METAL SCENE, Siren has been around since 1980, when they formed in Brandon, Florida, outside of Tampa. "As the 1980s progressed and the fires of heavy metal grew around the world, Brandon (and central Florida), for some reason, became a real ground zero for some great metal," drummer Ed Aborn tells me. "We were like one big, semi-competitive family. By the early to mid-eighties, bands like Siren, Nasty Savage, Savatage, Death, Obituary, Vengeance Inc., and many, many others called the Tampa area home. Studios like Morrisound Recording in Tampa became the go-to place to make your mark, when finances permitted. It was truly an amazing time with incredible energy and talent.

"Siren was originally formed in 1980. It was Rob Phillips on guitar, Hal Dunn also on guitar, Mike Martinez on bass, and Andy Flowers on drums, who I quickly replaced after one practice when he didn't show up.

"We were all huge fans of heavy metal bands like Judas Priest, Iron Maiden, Accept, UFO, Scorpions, and others," Ed explains. "When Siren first formed, we mostly played covers from these bands as well as lesser-known groups such as Angelwitch and other NWOBHM outfits. Like countless others, our motivation behind forming a band was to join the pantheon of heavy metal stars and achieve fame and fortune. With that as a distant goal, we actually enjoyed the camaraderie of the band life and performing around the local area. It was just fun to jam, play the songs of our heroes, and build up a following. We played A LOT of metal covers before starting to work on any real originals. Performers such as Wolf Hoffmann, Michael Schenker, and Steve Harris were revered as gods in the band's house. Posters covered the walls, and the music was played like a hymn in church. It's hard to pinpoint specific records, but some contenders would definitely be *Restless and Wild*, *Killers*, *Stained Class*, *Strangers in the Night*, and *Blizzard of Ozz*, to name a few. There was so much incredible music put out at that time. It's no wonder that heavy metal exploded in the early 1980s.

"We were very fortunate to live in an area where metal was the law! Brandon, Florida, really took hold as a metal hotspot in the early and mid-1980s," Ed continues. "Bands like Obituary, Nasty Savage, and Siren were able to break out and start to reach fans across the globe. In fact, before they changed their name from Xecutioner to Obituary, the Tardy brothers lived two houses down from where Siren would rehearse, at our singer Doug's house. That was one heavy street! There were several other local metal bands, and the scene as a whole was incredibly strong. In the greater Tampa Bay area were also bands such as Savatage, which really led the way for us as peers. Plus, there was a fantastic recording studio named Morrisound Recording that became legendary for heavy metal records and production. So, this whole region was a fantastic place to be back in the day."

By June of 1983, Ed had just graduated from high school and was preparing to leave for college at Florida State University in Tallahassee, which was about a five-hour drive from Brandon. In other words, he wasn't going to be home much. He was still friends with all of the guys and was excited to begin the next chapter of his own life. So Siren took a small break.

"So, it's now the end of 1983, and I'm home on Christmas break from college. Siren at that point was a non-entity. Hal Dunn, Mike Martinez, and Mike Furney had remained in touch and would eventually form the heavy metal glam band Atomic Opera over the next year with guitar virtuoso Todd Grubbs," Ed says.

"While on that break, I was hanging out with Doug Lee and remarked that we should get Rob and record a two-song, seven-inch single over the summer. My inspiration actually came from seeing how well my friends in another band, Nasty Savage, were doing with their music," Ed adds regarding their first seven-inch, 1984's *Metro-Mercenary*.

"Doug agreed that the idea of creating and promoting a Siren single sounded cool. So we set our sights to record during the summer of 1984 and we would see where things went after that. We discussed the project with Rob Phillips, and he was also on board. We recruited Ben Parrish, a friend of Rob's, to play bass on the two songs. We selected the songs 'Metro-Mercenary' and 'Terrible Swift Sword' to be the debut release. We felt that they were solid entries that reflected the main direction of the band musically," Ed says. "Upon my return to Brandon, the four of us set up in the living room of my house and started to work on

CUT TO THE CHASE:

I guess that time has come (at last!) that Siren can find themselves ranked higher in the metal world, and this is because they are one of the sincerest and highest-quality underground bands of the 1980s with a huge background history. I recommend all their records. And the release that concerns this book, the 1984 *Metro-Mercenary* seven-inch, is definitely one of the greatest independent American metal records of the 1980s.

the two songs for the single. Needless to say, it was rough, but it was raw and true. It was also very exciting to think that, at the end of the summer, we would have a Siren record in our hands and a list of contacts around the globe with which to share our music and seek our fortune.

"For some reason, we opted not to have a regular paper sleeve printed for the packaging," Ed goes on to say. "Instead, we had a folded insert printed locally and we placed those inside a clear plastic sheath along with each record in a paper sleeve. The package design was pretty simple. This was during a time where we had to have all of the text created on a typesetting machine. We were still half a decade away from the desktop publishing revolution. The front of the single was the Siren logo, which was designed by the brother of Nasty Savage drummer Curtis Beeson. In fact, if you look closely, you might notice that the Siren and Nasty Savage logos are similar stylistically. And now you know why! The records arrived in early August, and I remember sitting in Doug's living room as we set up an assembly line to put together and sign some of those 1,000 singles. I would be heading back up to school in a few weeks, and I had already met with Nasty Ronnie and received his list of fanzines, magazines, and some sage advice. It would be up to me to set the promotional gears in motion from the rental house I would be sharing with some school friends from the previous year. So, by the end of August, I was driving back up to Tallahassee with several hundred brand-new records, some semi-embarrassing promo shots, a list of media outlets from around the globe, and limitless young hope and enthusiasm."

Metro-Mercenary is a real treat for fans of hard-edged American power metal! Epic, raging, powerful *Metro-Mercenary* sounds very far away from their later delicate power/progressive metal, and it contains two tracks that will drive fans of this early power metal style crazy. Imagine a mix of early Savatage with Judas Priest, and guitarwise, a touch of Iron Maiden. Both songs rule, but I have a very slight preference for the more straightforward "Terrible Swift Sword." Haunting and exceptional. Classic stuff.

Initially, Siren kept it up until 1990, releasing brilliant demos like 1985's *Iron Coffins*, and headed for a cleaner sound on their classic 1986 *No Place Like Home* LP. This one sadly remains under the radar of most metalheads who love bands with a similar approach, like Savatage, early Queensrÿche, and Crimson Glory. I guess that the awful record cover of *No Place Like Home* didn't really help them either, but it's what's inside that counts, right? Their final LP during Siren's first era was the slightly tech-thrashy *Financial Suicide* (1989), which was very weird and challenging but still hot! Again, no one took notice. What a shame...

After Siren broke up, Doug Lee went on to perform and release records for German thrash metal band Mekong Delta—no wonder, since Siren's *Financial Suicide* was released on bass player Ralph Hubert's Aaarrg label. (Plus, did you know that Mekong Delta's Jörg Michael was the drummer in Siren's last gasp in 1990?)

"Most local bands from the Tampa Bay area were also putting out their own demos during the early and mid-1980s," Ed mentions. "These were mostly on cassettes. Some of the local metal bands that were releasing their own music were Nasty Savage (eventually signed to Metal Blade), Vengeance Inc., Atomic Opera, Oblivion, BRAT, Purgatory (Iced Earth), Obituary, and several others."

Of course, Ed (and Siren) hold very fond memories of their shows of that era, but they're not limited to the eighties: "Some of our favorite shows back in the day were ones where we would share the stage with other local bands like Savatage and Nasty Savage. One of the most memorable shows we played was actually at a small teen club where Xecutioner (later Obituary) opened for us. We used some flash pots and a concussion mortar during one song, and the guy who was handling that went WAY overboard. We ended up literally blowing the ceiling off of the place as well as most of our gear. Our most memorable show, however, was when we played the Keep It True Festival in Germany in April of 2018. After 30 years, they asked if we would get back together to perform again for a special show. It was amazing to play our songs again and watch thousands of people singing along."

And then, bingo! Siren reformed in 2016, with a new lineup—Ed Alborn, Hal Dunn, Doug Lee, Gregg Culbertson, and Todd Grubbs—and released two compilations (the *Lost Tracks from the Dead + 1* ten-inch and *Up from the Depths: Early Anthology and More*), plus a new LP, *Back from the Dead*, in 2018. And what a glorious return it was! Siren sound more excited than ever! "We are really amazed that people are still interested in Siren after all of these years," Ed says. "Any labels or organizations who support the metal scene and bands like ours have our respect and appreciation. Along with playing the show at Keep It True, one of the coolest things that has happened to us is the release of our early recordings in the *Up from the Depths* CD and LP packages. We put together an amazing two-CD set with a 24-page booklet in conjunction with Stormspell Records, along with an incredible three-LP vinyl set with replica seven-inch single on Underground Power Records. To have all of our early material plus bonus items and three new recordings be made available all these years later is truly an honor and something that we still can't believe. There is also a full documentary film coming out about our whole experience of being pulled back together for the show in Germany. We had such a great time preparing for the festival that we decided to record one more full album when we returned. We're just wrapping up production on that right now, to coincide with the release of the documentary. So, it's a busy time!"

Ed concludes, "We do believe that the family of heavy metal has never died—especially outside of the United States. We've seen that with other friends who are in active bands and got to experience it first-hand at Keep It True. There are millions of metal fans around the globe and, no matter where you live, we are all bound by that same love. There is certainly a hardcore group of metal fans that might be considered 'underground,' but most wear their love for the music on their sleeve these days. Be proud of your metal roots! As for the availability of music online these days, it's just the way that technology has gone. There are good aspects of the new order, such as the fact that bands can potentially gain exposure to a wider potential audience, but there are also thousands of other new bands struggling for that same attention. It's also no secret that there isn't really a lot of money to be made in music sales for bands that are not megastars. But that's really no different than how it was back in the day. Putting out an album back in the 1980s was no guarantee of success or money. In fact, even bands that went on to become huge often had some pretty bad deals from the labels. Personally, I enjoy the fact that I can very easily discover more bands that I enjoy via the internet. I support the bands that I like by seeing them perform live and buying their merchandise. Speaking for Siren, it is definitely a labor of love to make new music. We have no expectation of money or fame in the least. It's just fun to still work together after all of these years, and hopefully, some people will enjoy the fruits of our metal labor."

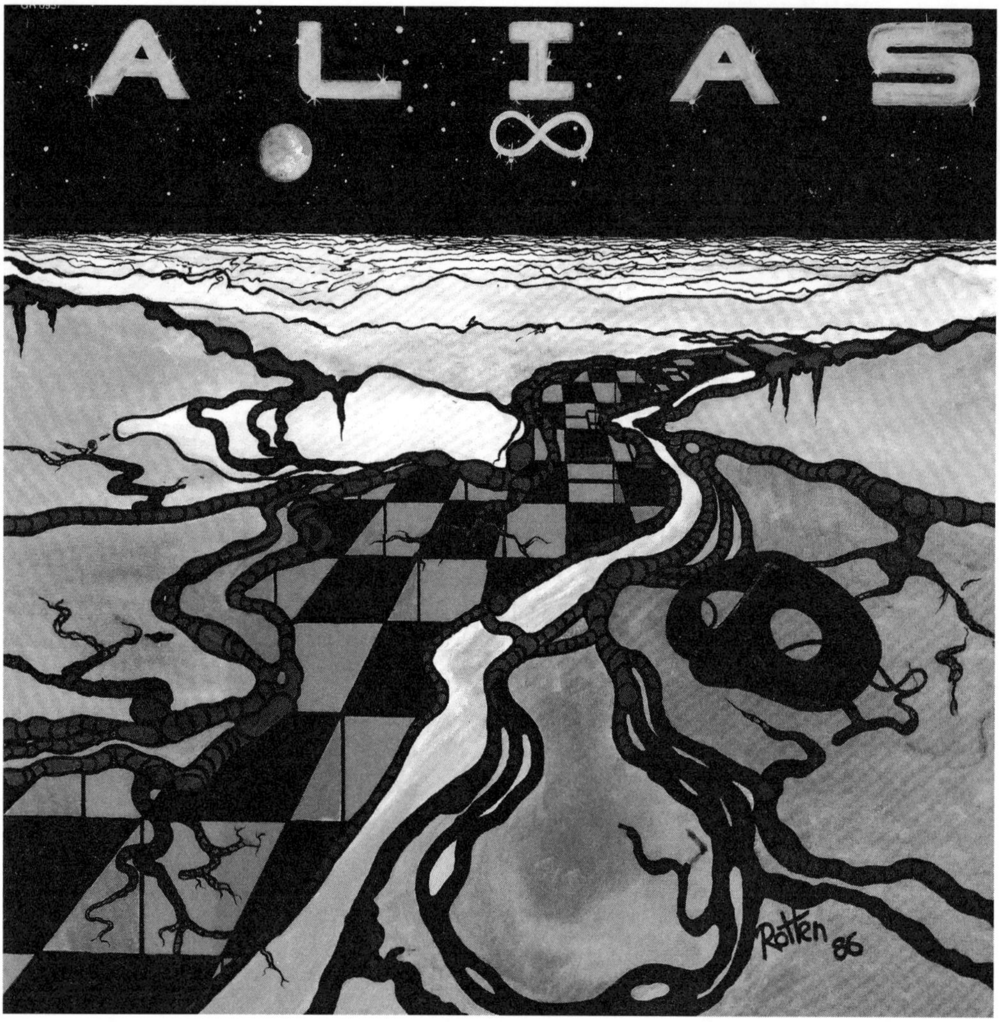

ALIAS

ALIAS WAS FORMED IN 1984 IN SARASOTA, FLORIDA, BY GUITARIST MARK Severns (later of Tyger Tyger and The Jeff Austin Project), drummer Phil Arnt, singer Tony Wise (ex-Crimson Glory and Tyger Tyger), and bassist Dirk Van Tilborg (ex-Attakk, ex-Crimson Glory, and later in Kamelot). The musicians joined forces from local bands Crimson Glory and Livewire. What is very extraordinary in their case is that Alias released their first record on a small indie label, while they went on to self-release their second LP. Phil Arnt tells their story:

"Me and Dirk were in a college band when we met in 1982—we played in local cover bands and talked about forming a new cover band. Dirk met Mark Severns at work and we formed a cover band with Tony Wise, frontman of the band later known, I believe, as Uncle Sally. Tony also fronted Foghat at some point. This early version of Alias was under another name, which may have been Tooth and Nail, but it escapes me exactly. Before Alias, our band name was Blitz, which is when we developed the first album, *Alias*. We had a number of frontmen over those first couple

CUT TO THE CHASE:

Alias from Sarasota, Florida (formed initially as Blitz), released the *Alias* LP in 1987 on the small indie Grudge Records, and the band took a different route than most, releasing their second LP, *Metal to Infinity*, in 1989 on their own label, Flame Records. This is actually the better of the pair, and while *Alias* is a good American power metal LP, *Metal to Infinity* is a whole level up. It's majestic American metal, reminiscent of bands like Ruffians and Steel Vengeance, and songs like "The Mirror" and "Ultraviolence" are massive bangers.

of years, and we played a lot of local clubs but couldn't attract an agent, probably due to our metal interests, who would book us live often enough to succeed playing covers. Eventually during the writing of the *Alias* album, we decided to name the band Alias.

"I had trained to be a musician since I was ten years old, so it only seemed natural to continue in the music business and at least give it a try," adds Phil. "All of us were very serious about our music and making a great product. I was personally shocked when *Operation: Mindcrime* was released. I thought we should just give up because it was such a great album, but later, I just used it as inspiration to be better. If you listen to my work on *Metal to Infinity*, you could hear the Queensrÿche influence during 'First Born.'"

In 1986, Len Jarrell (Surgeon, Unleashed Power) joined as vocalist and the band contributed "Authority" to the *Iron Tyrants Waging War* LP (a majorly rare compilation with obscure acts like Jewel Fetish, The Jaxx, Adonis, Fastuca, and Axist). Alias spent the rest of 1986 recording more music and performing throughout the South. That year also saw the band appear in mainstream metal publications such as *Kerrang!*, *Metal Forces*, *Metal Hammer*, and *Aardshock America*.

In early 1987, Alias signed with U.S.-based Grudge Records and recorded their self-titled debut album. With guest vocals on three tracks by Powersurge singer James "Jimbo" Marra, the album was released on August 14, 1987. To celebrate the release of the album, Alias headlined a concert sponsored by 24-hour music video channel V-32.

The *Alias* debut LP is a good start but by no means a classic, although there are some great songs like "You Can't Take Away My Youth," "Knight of the Realm," and the excellent "Take the Light." I have read/heard people dissing this LP because of the production, but I really like the harsh, weird sound that this kind of production offers—much better than any of the plastic crap in the modern metal productions. However, the band's greatest recording was about to be the next one.

"Alias' early experience playing covers didn't generate much of a fan base locally, and to be honest, we didn't have the looks or stage presence to succeed in the arena, which led us into writing our own material," Phil admits. "We produced both our LPs and then shopped them to Grudge Records (for *Alias*) and through our own private label, Flame Records (for *Metal to Infinity*). I remember having a conversation with Dirk and he was bemoaning about how hard it was without a management company, and I said make up a manager name—an 'Alias.' And he did, and it worked."

In 1989, Alias returned to Telstar Studios with new vocalist Carl Hayden to record their highly anticipated follow-up, *Metal to Infinity*. During 1989, the band also toured and produced several music videos, which received airplay on MTV, College Satellite Network, and MuchMusic in Canada. *Metal to Infinity* was released on October 1, 1989 in the U.S. and Europe, through Alias' own Flame Records. The band continued until 1990, when the members went their separate ways to pursue other musical interests.

Metal to Infinity is an outstanding U.S. heavy/power LP. A huge leap forward from *Alias*, the band sounded more mature and confident than ever, and songs like "Stormy Eyes" have a distinct touch of bands like Lethal or Queensrÿche, whereas pounding numbers like "Alpha-Omega" and "The Mirror" simply shred! Balancing between the sheer power of bands like Vicious Rumors and Shok Paris and the melodic lyricism of Queensrÿche and Fates Warning, *Metal to Infinity* is an unknown classic of this sound.

"Frehley's Comet with White Lion, that was by far our favorite show," Phil replies when asked. "This was around the time in Sarasota when there were absolutely crushing bands like Crimson Glory, Atheist, Belching Penguins and Neurotica. I think it's great that the interest in metal of our age is back," he continues, "but I haven't seen any money from either album, ever. I personally have many original Alias albums still wrapped in plastic ... These, I believe, are first releases from the master. And cassettes, which were duped early on before vinyl releases. There will always be an underground scene for music, it's how new bands launch their careers. The digital download has hurt me personally, but there is nothing I can do about it personally. Imagine seeing your hard work online for sale by hundreds of vendors and you have never received a penny from your work, ever. It is disgusting, and if I think about it, I get sick. Realize how much blood and sweat went into those two albums..."

STRYKER

STRYKER FROM FORT MYERS, FLORIDA, WERE A VERY ENJOYABLE, FEMALE-fronted American heavy/power metal band, formed in 1983. Rhythm guitarist Larry Farmer tells their story: "Steve Maitland and I were co-guitarists in a cover band called Marauder in the early 1980s. When the lead singer quit the band, we saw an ad that Sarah (who would become the vocalist for Stryker) ran in the local paper that said: 'Female lead singer looking for a hard rock band.' After she joined, we changed the band name and direction. We started adding originals to our sets. When we had enough songs, we started putting on shows and recorded an album. Jerry Young was added (on bass), and alongside came Lynn Baker (on drums).

"I would love to say that it was to express ourselves artistically and creatively, but I think in the beginning, it was about playing our guitars as loud as possible, haha!" Larry laughs. "All that creative stuff came later. As for our influences, these were Judas Priest, Kiss, and AC/DC.

"A bit of a lonely time to be a metal band in Fort Myers," Larry adds. "It was mostly Top 40 music being played in the early 1980s club scene, but there was a growing underground heavy metal movement that we were happy to be a part of ... I'm sure that there were other bands that released their records on their own, but I don't know of any releases. There was no social media to track those things back then—only word of mouth and local music magazines."

Stryker went on to take the big step of releasing their own record in 1985: the *Stryker* LP, on their Fastblood Records. Larry mentions, "There were no record labels interested in us at the time, so we thought that if we could record, produce, and sell enough copies, we could get their attention. Basic rhythm tracks (drums, bass, and rhythm guitar) were recorded at Link Brothers Studio in Fort Myers. All vocals, lead guitars, mixing, and mastering were done at Morrisound Studio in Tampa."

CUT TO THE CHASE:

This is one of the few cases in which a record can appeal equally to those ones who love melodic metal, as well as fans of true heavy metal. *Stryker* has at least six great songs, and it is a definite winner. If you can't find the original LP, be sure to get the Heaven and Hell Records re-release!

Stryker's only release is stunning. Melodic—but totally heavy—metal, with an atmosphere reminiscent of Barnabas (at their heaviest/weirdest possible), this LP contains just pure metal hymns like the opening "Plastic Man," the haunting "Nightmares," and the crushing "Vengeance Will Be Mine." What I also love about this LP is that it has the same approach production-wise as Heir Apparent's *Graceful Inheritance,* meaning that the emphasis is placed on the vocal and guitar melodies, with a thin but delicate sound. I wish more metal bands produced their material that way, rather than the modern ultra-bass heavy sound. Plus, I'm a sucker for female vocals, so what else can I say? *Stryker* is a minor classic!

Sadly, Stryker didn't have the chance to pursue a career in heavy metal—a pity, since they had the potential—and just managed to continue playing shows like at the National Guard Armory in Fort Myers. They called it quits later in 1987. Heaven and Hell Records re-released *Stryker* on CD in 2018—the first 100 copies came with a Stryker album art magnet—giving new generations of metalheads the chance to check out this awesome record. "I just think it's extremely cool that people still care about the bands from the early days of metal," Larry says. "There has always been an underground music scene, and it's not surprising that there still is one. Downloading has definitely changed the way bands get paid for their music, but people will always adapt to a changing market."

DEAD SERIOS

THE CRAZY WORLD OF DEAD SERIOS WAS BORN IN SATELLITE BEACH, FLORIDA, in 1985, and is still active up until today (2022). Dead Serios is a band that won't appeal to 100 percent of die-hard metalheads, but their schizophrenic case has to be reported here, because they were/are one of the most unique and diverse-sounding bands of the era of self-released American heavy metal. "Summer of 1985: New wave was winding down, hair bands were revving up, and the time was right for a real rock revolution," as vocalist Dead Lee Serios (known today as Christopher Long) tells it. "As an aspiring young musician influenced by an eclectic mix of Van Halen, the Ramones, Frank Zappa, Cheap Trick, Alice Cooper, John Denver, Motörhead, and Kiss, I was searching desperately for my own artistic identity during the mid-1980s. In the beginning, Dead Serios, like many of my early projects, also sucked. We had a few original tunes, but we were far from unique. Plus, I can't sing—a big problem for a lead singer. Initially, I also was ungraceful as a frontman. Ultimately, I became more comfortable (and graceful) onstage. As for the misspelling of 'Serios,' we weren't trying intentionally to come up with some type of cool eighties-style, Def Leppard-like moniker. 'Serios' is misspelled simply because the guy who designed our first logo smoked a lot of pot. When he laid out the original design, he ran out of space on the paper and reasoned that the letter U wasn't terribly significant. True story!"

CUT TO THE CHASE:

You like your metal crazy, weird, and fun? Do you love the schizophrenic tunes of Last Crack blended with the fierce rock 'n' roll sounds of Detroit and Motörhead, as well as the rough 1970s Kiss style? Yep, Dead Serios is for you, so pick up the 1987 *Who's Your Buddy?* LP as a starter!

Dead Serios' initial lineup included the aforementioned Dead Lee Serios on vocals, Rob Craig on guitar, Paul Dorland on drums, Jim Witherell on guitar, and Bryan Dumas on bass. This lineup released the 1985 *Dead In The U.S.A.* cassette, a crude attempt at classic heavy metal, theatrical and rough. "We spent the next two years writing, rehearsing, and playing everywhere we could. *Master of Puppets* and *Spreading the Disease* soon replaced *Metal Health* and *Pyromania* as my favorite LPs of the day," Christopher says. "Although I faced considerable resistance from early band members who lacked my vision, this newfound energy and attitude was being reflected in our music quickly. As a result, our sound and lineup soon 'evolved.' Then, I saw Alice Cooper in concert for the first time—another HUGE game-changer. I thought that if Dead Serios could merge our developing punk-meets-metal sound with an outrageous stage show and streetwise lyrical content, we just might be on to something—like a hardcore version of Saturday-morning TV."

Just like their first cassette, nearly all Dead Serios records were released via their own label, Long Song Records, starting with their first two seven-inches, *Dead Under The Tree & Heavy Metal Christmas* and *Screams In The Night*, both released in 1986. Both albums are full of good, entertaining stuff that verges between heavy metal and Alice Cooper, with a slight touch of 1970s NYC punk. Meanwhile, "Children of the Night" is actually a great tune!

"Before Dead Serios, there was NO original music scene in Central Florida—particularly in the area of Brevard County, known as the 'Space Coast,'" Christopher states. "Dead Serios deserves most if not all the credit for creating the scene. Bands all were standing around with their collective dicks in their hands, waiting for a leader. Dead Serios was that leader. WE called the shots. The local rivalry and backstabbing didn't ensue until after WE created the scene.

"Even in our creative infancy, Dead Serios was a very savage-sounding band. And we were having difficulty appealing to labels," Christopher admits when asked about his choice to self-release. "I wasn't going to stand around and wait for some label bigwig to give me permission to produce my music. So, I launched my own label, Long Song Records. We recorded in a popular hometown studio. Then I sent the master tapes along with handmade album cover designs to a pressing plant—usually in Tennessee. A month later, boxfuls of record product arrived at my apartment doorstep. I soon established a relationship with a large distribution operation out of New York—I shipped the Dead Serios product to them directly, and they in turn got us into stores across the U.S. Locally, I set up my own independent distribution operation, personally stocking numerous retail outlets throughout Central Florida.

"Alice Cooper, Zappa, Motörhead, and Kiss were our major influences, whereas *Billion Dollar Babies* by Cooper had a tremendous impact on Dead Serios," says Christopher when asked which bands influenced them most. "We've opened for an array of marquee metal/punk/hard rock acts over the years, including Ace Frehley, Marilyn Manson, Faith No More, Pat Travers, Anthrax, Cinderella, Slaughter, The Dead Milkmen, Circle Jerks, Great White, Faster Pussycat, Enuff Z'Nuff, Nuclear Assault, and many others. With those experiences come a myriad of additional engaging stories."

Dead Serios went on to release their first full-length LP in 1987, the great *Who's Your Buddy?*, which exposed the band in full force! Crazy, angular, weird, but lots of fun heavy metal, this album is unique and atypical of other bands of the era, with influences ranging from the Detroit scene (MC5) and Kiss to 1970s Motörhead and a little early Iron Maiden. *Who's Your Buddy?* is a record worth tracking down! After all, songs like "I'm on Fire," "Harbor City," and "On the Prowl" are sheer fun!

Of course, on stage, Dead Serios were frenetic, as evidenced by reviews from that era. "There have been SO many memorable/favorite shows. Our first national level gig opening for Anthrax in 1986 was a big one for us—it was 400 people jammed into a nightclub in Cocoa Beach, Florida. Anthrax was cool to us. Their tour manager was kind of a prick, but we learned A LOT that night," Christopher laughs. "I nearly got myself killed when I jumped into the pit during our opening set with GWAR in 1990—it's a long story. But my favorite show probably was a steamy outdoor local festival we headlined in July 1989. Temperatures were sweltering—and as our set ensued, people literally were worked into a frenzy. Cops took the stage, pulling people from the crowd, placing some into ambulances and others into squad cars. That might have been the gig when a gal in the crowd up front lifted her shirt in front of me, exposing her breasts as well as her new tattoo: a cartoon caricature of MY FACE tattooed between her boobs. Surreal, indeed."

Dead Serios' numerous lineup changes led to radical musical shifts, with the 1988 *Blow Chunks* cassette and the 1989 *Possessed By Polka* cassette album being mostly done in a crazy hardcore/crossover style reminiscent of bands like The Dehumanizers (that is, absolutely mental). Kudos to Christopher for keeping the band alive through hard times in the 1990s until today. "Major record labels clearly didn't embrace Dead Serios like the fans and press. An Interscope Records A&R rep once went so far as to tell me flat-out that our music 'sucked.' 'You ought to quit now and stop embarrassing yourself,' she recommended, with considerable arrogance and disdain ... Despite our lack of major label interest, we knew we were on the verge of becoming the next big thing in the early 1990s, when actually our days were numbered. The Seattle grunge movement was revving up and about to consume the entire rock world. And there would be little room in that world for a band like ours. The once-tight Dead Serios unit began to splinter, and before long, one by one, my bandmates all moved on to pursue other projects. Although I stuck it out for a couple of more years with various lineup changes, our window of opportunity had been slammed shut permanently by the end of 1992. I spent the next couple of years as frontman for the hillbilly/glam band, Glitterhick—an outrageous project in which I first worked with drummer Scooter Greenbud. In the early 2000s (along with Scooter on drums), Joe Del Corvo, Doug Gibson, and I began staging well-attended annual reunion concerts. But by 2011, I was pursuing Christian ministry, and despite continued fan interest, the Dead Serios story finally had come to a conclusion. Almost."

As aforementioned, Dead Serios are keeping it up till today, while Christopher is a successful writer with many books under his belt (check out *Superstar* and *A Shot of Poison*, absolutely amazing stuff). "Now at age 57, I'm uncertain regarding the long-term future of Dead Serios—rock and roll is a young man's sport, ya know. Our current lineup consists of me, Joe Del Corvo, Scooter Greenbud, and newly recruited guitarist Leonard Geezer. Although we've released numerous records over the years, we don't feel like we've truly 'nailed it' properly yet. Hence, we're expecting to hit the studio soon and have a definitive Dead Serios record released soon!"

RHED ASPHALT

"ABSOLUTELY CRAZY" WOULD HAVE BEEN THE BEST WAY TO DESCRIBE RHED Asphalt's musical style. While the band belongs in the American metal genre, what Rhed Asphalt did was far crazier even than Watchtower or Last Crack.

Rhed Asphalt formed in 1987 in Melbourne, Florida, and guitarist/vocalist John Feula mentions that "the band was formed by Jon Helpingstine and myself in junior high, just playing Motörhead and songs off *Kill 'Em All.* Jon was into ZZ Top and Billy Squier and played saxophone in the school band. I played him 'Don't Break the Oath,' and he was hooked for life. We then got together with Chase Solovicos. We were all 14 to 15. Jon came up with the name from our drivers education film—I just put the H in. Maiden, Priest, Rush, Accept, Sabbath, and Motörhead were our influences. Also the first albums by Mercyful Fate, Metal Church, Trouble, Jag Panzer, Celtic Frost and many others. Then a lot of prog, jazz, and fusion got in the mix.

"Most bands in Florida were kids practicing in public storage sheds," John adds. "We had our metal posters, drum riser, and a few stage lights. There was a party or two. Haha! When the cops came, you were done with practice. Eventually, we moved into a house we practiced in. It was infested with rats. I remember coming home one day, and they'd chewed the vinyl off my amp! We became good at self-promotion, getting lots of international press in the tape trading days, as well as in Florida magazines like *Jam*. Gigs were hard to come by, though. We played a festival that had Death on the bill once. Never got as far as touring. We'd play hard, no matter if it was a dead Monday night. I'd say, 'Goodnight,' and walk off after a show. Chase would stay up there for another five minutes bashing out a solo. Funny. He was always bleeding and destroying cymbals. I believe he still is!"

CUT TO THE CHASE:

Not "true metal" by any means, Rhed Asphalt's *The Obsession* twelve-inch is a gold nugget for everyone who's into bands that range from Nomeansno to Watchtower, from Toxic to Victims Family, or any prog/metal with balls and no pretense. I hope to see all their demos as well as this twelve-inch getting a proper re-release soon, since this kind of stuff should see the light of day somehow.

In 1988, the time had come for Rhed Asphalt to release their first, privately released twelve-inch record, *The Obsession:* "We recorded a single of *The Obsession* and our friend, Dan Meneely, made us a cool cover," John says. "We originally had a singer who quit before we drove out of town to record the song. I don't remember how the bass player, Ned Meloni, came to sing on it. Maybe he looked cool and worked at the local record store? Nice guy. We just recorded an instrumental, 'Creatures,' for the B-side to make it easier with no singer. Just some kids messing around."

Messing around? You must be crazy. What we have here is an absolute gem of some of the most crazily technical American metal of the 1980s. The title song sounds like ... well, like hard rock, heavy metal, and thrash combined, all under an improvisation jazz approach that would make Watchtower blush (since this band is more catchy than them by far). The flip side, "Creatures," is a mental instrumental, with shades of classic rock and progressive technical proficiency.

"The next demo, I began singing," John mentions. "It got us in one of those slick *Metal Maniacs* magazines you could buy at the 7-Eleven. That was a huge deal! Fun time. Later, we made the *Are They A Threat?* tape, which had songs like 'Pirates Life' and 'Blacklight,' and people liked it. Next, we made the more jazz-fusion-like *Admit One*, which didn't go over so well. The last tracks we did were the songs 'My Damascus,' which I put on my solo tape, *Thank You, Goodnight!* and a song called 'Blank Point,' which I think was kind of Coroner-like. Fast, jazzy, with a lot of parts. Maybe a little *Killing Is My Business*..."

The *Are They A Threat?* 1988 cassette was, again, self-funded by the band. You've been warned, though—we are talking about massively angular, challenging stuff here. By no means a typical prog/progressive metal band, Rhed Asphalt were a genuinely mental metal band, with influences ranging from free-form jazz to heavy and thrash metal, and they manage to keep the balance between paranoia and writing a catchy tune, but hey, still everything sounds like they're absolutely out of their minds! Through its seven songs, *Are They A Threat?* seems like it's from outer space. Check out "Maelstra," which exposes the absolute genius of Rhed Asphalt to its fullest.

"Locally, before us, there was Attika," John remembers. "They were power metal, and we really liked them. Also, Dead Serios, who put on an Alice Cooper-like show in our little town of Melbourne. Unbelievable! Prodigy, later renamed Oracle, were great. Technical thrash with a really good Geoff Tate-like singer. I love metal—I'll always go see Maiden, UDO, King Diamond, Voivod, Fates Warning, Raven when they are in Arizona (which is where I live now). Don't care for modern metal, but I always play Candlemass, Oz, and Manowar when at the gym. It's in my DNA!"

Rhed Asphalt continued on until 1995, when they parted ways. "I don't pay much attention to the interest in Rhed Asphalt. It's kind of like looking at your high school yearbook photo," John adds. "Jon and Chase were my best friends. We grew up together, lived together. We will always be like brothers, though we live very far apart now. I record with my band, Instant Hobo, and as a solo artist now. I think any artist is mostly interested in what he is currently doing. Overall, we were three nice kids who could get in a bit of trouble and who grew into skilled musicians. Rhed Asphalt was a good first step. Rough around the edges, but that's probably what made it interesting. There were opportunities that we just didn't have the guidance or experience to take advantage of. It was a big part of my young life in a time before the internet and cell phones, when I would run out to the mailbox and get letters and tapes from people all around the world. Amazing for some kids from Central Florida!"

ODYSSEY

UTICA, NEW YORK, ISN'T THE PLACE THAT YOU THINK OF FIRST WHEN THE phrase *American metal* is dropped on the table, but nevertheless, Odyssey were maybe the only metal band of the 1980s from this medium-sized East Coast town. Kyle "Ciola" Giglio, its vocalist, tells the story of Odyssey:

"We formed in the early 1980s as a bunch of 17- and 18-year-old high school guys looking to play some talent shows playing cover music. Mark Lace (guitarist) was jamming with Frank Amerotta (drummer), they met up with myself and Mike Mozzetti (bass), and the four of us formed a band called Vengeance. We then added Scott Kernahan (keyboards) and changed the name to Odyssey to get more availability to play—Vengeance seemed to be too hard of a name to get some jobs for a cover band. I chose the name from a Kiss song off the *(Music From) The Elder* album. I was a huge Kiss fan; other influences Odyssey had were Ozzy Osbourne, Dio, Judas Priest, Mötley Crüe, and then Bon Jovi, who was already becoming huge by the time."

CUT TO THE CHASE:

Odyssey's *Breakaway* twelve-inch will appeal to fans of melodic metal, but I think true metalheads won't appreciate it (since it would be too slick and soft for them).

Kyle adds, "At the time, the local music scene was great—a lot of venues and bars, as far as festivals also for us to play. We were well received and got radio airplay. We also did a lot down in Western Pennsylvania, as well as on college and university radio stations. Our most memorable show was for 11,000 people in Erie, Pennsylvania—it was an outdoor festival. The crowd was awesome. We actually went back to our hotel and I had to have security help us because there were so many people waiting to meet us and get autographs and pictures at our hotel after our show."

Odyssey recorded their first twelve-inch EP locally, at UCA Recordings Studios in Utica, and it was released in 1987 through their own label (Oddimobile Unlimited). The *Breakaway* twelve-inch included four hard rock/metal party anthems, with the title song being a definite high point for the band. Melodic and slick, with excellent vocals and keyboards as a driving force, *Breakaway* had everything a hard rock/metal fan would adore. The AOR influence is evident, of course, but still, the songs have a certain hard rock/metal edge. All four songs are, well, love songs, destined to hit the airwaves, and one can't say that everything sounds extremely professional. Obviously, fans of AOR mixed with hard rock/metal will definitely dig it. It's like a cross between Survivor's and Judas Priest's most melodic moments.

Kyle says, "We did the record because our manager at the time (who also ran our production), was our music teacher and said that we had the talent and look. It was becoming very popular in the MTV hair band era, and because we were young, it was a chance for us to try for something that other bands were achieving, except we were trying to do it in New York State rather than in L.A. So, we wrote our own material for a four-song EP, recorded it locally in Utica, and decided to shop it around and play and support the EP, as well as our other cover songs.

"I can recall that there were a couple bands from our wider area locally that did private releases, such as Mere Mortals and Matakopas," remembers Kyle. "I am very happy about the resurgence of metal bands today. I also feel very honored that the album has become a collector's item, as this was my first attempt as a 16- or 17-year-old in writing and recording music. An experience that I am so glad others are willing to enjoy."

Odyssey didn't make it in the music business—at a time when the competition between commercial metal bands was huge, it wasn't easy—and disbanded in late 1980s. "I do think that there's sort of an underground scene today. I am acquainted with the band from my area called Wicked, and they are doing it the same way that we did it back in the day: recording private albums, playing shows, big production. Very impressive. I do believe that the availability of downloading music for free does hinder artists who are starting out; there is no more revenue generated for the artists. So now, all that they create, it's more about generating revenue off of the performance and selling tickets. That's why tickets cost so much for live performances. It's the only way for the artist to recoup the revenue by performing their art, rather than selling it."

ARAGON

ODDLY ENOUGH, ARAGON REMAINS UNKNOWN TO THE FANS OF THRASH metal, even though they didn't lack any of the talent of their contemporaries. Formed in 1984 by four high school kids from Levittown on Long Island, New York, Michael Pope (guitars) narrates that "we started out playing covers from bands like Mötley Crüe and Ozzy, but we started to notice that bands like Metallica and Anthrax were starting to get more popular. We started writing our own material and broke away from mainstream metal and crossed over to thrash. We were young, very young; Vinny Ciminera and Rob Anderson were 15, Gerry Holz and I were 17. We would play the local Battle of the Bands and were probably the only young band in our area that was playing thrash metal. Most people hadn't even heard of Metallica yet."

Finding themselves already supporting touring bands such as DRI, Nuclear Assault, COC, and Flotsam and Jetsam, Aragon created a buzz for their sheer intensity. "I guess our biggest influence was Metallica—they opened up the door for us to start listening to the bands they

CUT TO THE CHASE:

I can't think of any dedicated thrashers not loving the straightforward approach of Aragon. I bet that fans of Nuclear Assault, Acrophet, and Powermad will especially dig them. And hey, why not—some of you folks who are into NYHC crossover will like them too.

were influenced by, and it came through in the original music we started writing," Michael explains. "For me, Metallica's *Ride the Lightning* album was a game changer. The ripping guitar sound at the time was just so different than what I was listening to. It forced me to work on speed picking on the guitar, totally different than how I learned to play ... when we started playing shows locally on Long Island, there weren't many venues that catered to our sound. There was one club, Sundance in Bayshore, that touring thrash and hardcore bands would play. Since there weren't many bands that caught on to that style yet, we would get put on the bill with them. The crowds seemed to like our sound; I think most people were taken back at how young we were. We rehearsed five days a week and were really tight live—I think it showed in our live performances."

After four years of hard work, they headed to Network Sound Studio (where Disciple and Toximia also recorded their material), and the process of working on their first LP started. "At that time, there weren't many bands from our area that had independent releases," Michael mentions. "Crumbsuckers, Ludichrist, and Hittman were a few Long Island bands that were releasing material and doing well... So the story begins with our managers at the time, the Mackay brothers, who had been releasing 45s with two local bands per disc on Arctic Records. We went in the studio and recorded one song, 'Dreams of Hell,' which they were gonna use for a 45, but it never was released. Instead, they thought we should record more songs and release our own album.

"We recorded at Network Sound in Brooklyn in the summer of 1986 and compiled enough songs for a long EP—or short album," Michael continues. "Our managers wanted us to record a cover song on the record: 'Stepping Stone' by The Monkees. We were totally against it, but we did, and it got a lot of attention. They set up Brokin' Records, and the album was released in 1988. By the time the album was available, Rob Anderson had left the band. We struggled to find a replacement vocalist, and the band disbanded."

Aragon's first release was a bombastic thrash metal rager, with influences ranging from the Bay Area scene (obviously Slayer's and Metallica's first two records), to the crossover of the NYHC scene. However, it cannot be filed under crossover thrash, since the metal element is prevalent, and it's just the whole vibe that's reminiscent of hardcore thrash. Released on their own label, Brokin' Records, songs like "Fallout" sound like a mix of Nuclear Assault and Powermad, totally powerful thrash metal, whereas "Killing the Innocent" sounds like a cross between Slayer and power metal! Filled with youthful energy, *Aragon* is from start to finish an excellent thrash metal LP and leaves you wanting more after only 21 minutes and six songs.

"I still recall when we opened for DRI at Sundance," Michael says. "It was great, it was packed, and we opened with 'Fallout,' the first track from the album. It was crazy—people were stage diving, running all around us. I think I was 17, and moshing and stage diving was something I hadn't experienced, so it was really intense."

Sadly, the departure of Rob Anderson in 1989 signaled the split for Aragon, and what a shame it was, since they had such potential. But wait! Aragon got back together in 2017 and are still active, and they have some new material in the works. Hooray!

"Back in the 1980s, if you told me in 2020, people will still be interested in our record, I would have thought you were nuts!" Michael laughs. "I think it was an interesting time in music, there was a shift in the sound, happens from time to time, but I don't think there is a way to predict it. Just the other day, I had a young kid from El Paso, Texas, send me a pic of his denim jacket with a patch of our album cover on it. That is a great feeling—makes all the hard work we put in seem worth it. I'm sure the other bands with private releases feel the same way. I think there is still a movement of underground music today—it's just easier to get a hold of via the internet. Young musicians are pulling influences from past eras, just like we did in the 1980s. The record industry has changed dramatically, but there will always be musicians pushing the envelope and creating. It's a natural cycle!"

FANTOM WARIOR

SADLY OVERLOOKED, FANTOM WARIOR FROM UNION, NEW JERSEY, FORMED in 1984 as Phantom Lord and are still active (as of 2020). "I had an older group of friends who lived in my neighborhood who had formed a band called Sabotage, and they asked me to join them," bassist John Chernack says. "I had another group of school friends who were the same age as me who I was already playing music with as well. Since both bands contained my friends and we were all playing the same type of cover tunes (AC/DC, Scorpions, Twisted Sister, Van Halen), I thought it would be a great idea to join forces and create one band with all of my friends. This is how Phantom Lord began! The motivation was to have fun playing music together, and the ultimate goal was to begin creating original music and playing out live in front of people. Our biggest influences musically were the big heavy metal bands of the 1970s and early 1980s, which we would cover. As a bass player, my biggest influence was Steve Harris from Iron Maiden and Geezer Butler from Black Sabbath! The first two Iron Maiden albums really left an impression on me and were what I cut my teeth on in order to improve my skills. As we grew as a band, in addition to albums like AC/DC's *Highway To Hell* and Black Sabbath's *Paranoid* and Scorpions' *Animal Magnetism* just to name a few, the early thrash metal releases like Metallica's *Kill 'Em All*, Slayer's *Show No Mercy*, and Overkill's *Power in Black* spoke to us. And we gradually became heavier, harder, and faster with the cover tunes we chose to play and with the music that we wrote."

FANTOM WARIOR FLYER WITH INSANIAC AT ST. THOMAS CHURCH, BLOOMFIELD, NJ, 1988.

With the lineup settling down to James Jensen (drums), Steve Schley (guitar), John Chernack (bass and vocals), and Keith Pires (vocals and guitar), Phantom Lord changed their name to Fantom Warior, and in 1985, the thrash metal wave that was spreading all over the American metal scene didn't leave them in the cold. On the contrary, they were absolutely fascinated with very early thrash metal bands, like Metallica and Slayer, and one can say that Fantom Warior is one of the hidden gems of first-wave thrash metal.

"We had a great scene at the time. Our first gig at the local recreation department had a great turnout, and our band and another local band that contained Mike Lepond were heavily supported by heavy metal fans in the area," John recalls. "We were very fortunate because every gig we did had a great turnout. It was the perfect time for thrash metal, and Jon Zazula's Rock'n Roll Heaven, which was in our area, was the epicenter on the East Coast for all thrash bands at the time. In addition to the local scene, we sent our demos out to fanzines around the world, which also gave us support from everywhere on earth."

Entering the studio in 1986, Fantom Warior released one of the best thrash metal demos of the 1980s. The *Morbid Invasion* cassette was an absolute rager that sounded like a cross between early Exodus and Slayer (plus some Destruction and Kreator thrown in): crazy, chaotic and rough thrash metal with a very slight hardcore edge (pretty obvious in the mental track, "P.T.M.")—this is the style of thrash metal that all people who are into this sound love, whether they prefer American or the German school of thrash! Production-wise, it was perfect too. A menacing but audible sound.

In 2015, *Morbid Invasion* was released on vinyl by Electric Assault Records. In 1987, among the frenzy of labels endlessly signing thrash metal bands, Fantom Warior put out their first

CUT TO THE CHASE:

I bet that thrashers worldwide will go apeshit for everything Fantom Warior recorded, since you really can't get much better than this when it comes to thrash metal! These raging, frantic thrashers will please the souls of everybody who's into Slayer, eighties-era Destruction, or even Sacrilege B.C. and Crumbsuckers.

LP on Token Records, *Fantasy or Reality*. John narrates the story behind it:

"Our guitarist's cousin, John, was studying to be in the music industry at the time, so he was a natural choice to handle the label side of things. We didn't feel we needed to sign with an outside label because John was creating his own label called Token Records. He was a family member of Keith's, and we wanted to help him out, just like he wanted to help us out. At the time, doing everything ourselves seemed best because we loved what we were doing and we could maintain creative control at all levels this way."

Don't be fooled by the bad cover art; kicking off with the absolutely frantic "Chosen Fate," *Fantasy or Reality* is not just a raw thrash metal LP—it's also inspiring, and every song will stick in your head. *Fantasy or Reality* sounds like a mix of the hardcore edge that Sacrilege B.C. had with Dark Angel and some of Slayer's faster songs. There is a huge hardcore punk influence as well (as in "Don't Criticize" and "Backstabber"), and overall, this is such a sweet and memorable thrash metal record. Not "true metal," of course, but still, I believe that metalheads who are into this sound will enjoy it.

"I have a few favorite shows that I reminisce fondly upon, but the one I would choose as one of my favorites was the show that almost didn't happen. The show was in Dover, New Jersey, at the Showplace," John recalls. "It was winter and I had just picked up my girlfriend at the time from work. I had three other friends in the car at the time as well. The defroster on my Chevy Impala was barely working, and as I cranked the window handle to open the driver's side window while coasting at about 10 miles per hour, we slammed into the concrete base of a parking lot utility pole, putting my vehicle out of commission. As John—a friend who was in the passenger seat—wiped the blood off of his head from the impact, and the rest of my friends—who were protected from injury by the massive Fender bass cabinet with two 15-inch speakers that sat on their lap—all agreed, the show must go on.

"We had to find a way to get there, even though it was 45 minutes away, and no one else in the vehicle drove. With no cell phones at the time, since it was the eighties, we went into the store where my girlfriend worked and asked to use their phone to call a friend who was already at the Showplace, waiting for us. He sped down and picked us up, and because of him, we made it to the Showplace just in time! We had a great crowd that night, and we killed it!"

Fantom Warior sadly called it quits in 1988, only to come back in 2012, releasing a single, "Retribution," a typical high-class thrash metal attack of yore, like nothing had changed for about 25 years. "Retribution" can be found on their 2014 self-released compilation CD *The Archive*, along with everything Fantom Warior ever recorded.

"I remember just about every band in the area at the time was creating their own independent releases," John says. "Rat Bones of Overkill was one of the leading forces involved in it at the time, and labels like Megaforce and Roadrunner were the labels that were very instrumental in signing some of the early thrash metal bands. I think the resurgence we've seen and experienced has been a wonderful thing. It gave us an opportunity to reunite and play together as a band live again, as well as to see old friends and meet new ones.

"When I discovered that our items were being sold for so much money by collectors, I had mixed feelings about it. I grew up not being able to afford expensive albums, so I don't want other thrash metal fans who want to buy our music to suffer the same fate. I have given freebies out for that reason. As for collectors selling our stuff at a higher price, that's a different issue. People who have deep pockets often don't mind and, in some cases, prefer to invest a higher amount for a unique item because it makes them feel good. The people selling the rare items have bills to pay, and often, that is why they are letting the items go. There are people who will always download music for free for one reason or another, but there are just as many people who are ethically opposed to doing that who will pay bands for their music. Of course, there are the collectors who set their own prices, for better and/or for worse. I am happy to see that there's a huge amount of fans both old and new who still love thrash metal music, continue to support it at all levels, and contribute to keeping the spirit alive. With all of this interest still alive 40 years later, I think we can all agree that thrash metal at all levels will never die—and that's a great thing!"

ALIAS MANGLER

FROM NORTH CAROLINA, ALIAS MANGLER WAS FORMED IN 1984 AFTER THE breakup of a band called Deffen. Scott Board, the singer, returned to Cerebus, his old band, while Jimmy Hinson (guitars), Terry Baker (drummer), and Brian Teale (bass) went on to form a new band. Jimmy Hinson explains, "We recruited Danny as our singer, and the four of us began writing songs together. I had been to a couple of Battle of the Bands shows in Raleigh at Dorton Arena. I said, 'We can go down there and win the next one.' We wrote songs and played some gigs, and I knew we had the potential to win. Well, our bass player decides only a few months before the contest that he doesn't want to play. So, we recruited Kelly Rowsey, and we hit it off right from the start. We continued to write songs and play until the day of the contest. We came, we saw, we conquered. Out of 32 bands, we prevailed and got the right to record an LP. It was a glorious day. We recorded the *Bite the Metal* album over a period of four or five days because that's all the time we had. We wanted to be one of the next big bands, like everyone else did. For the next three years, we played in clubs and festivals all over North Carolina. In 1988, we played our last show in our hometown, and we faded away."

CUT TO THE CHASE:

A solid LP, *Bite the Metal* will please fans of The Rods, Lizzy Borden's more melodic stuff, and Accept's 1979–1983 period. Definitely not a classic, but it's still an enjoyable LP, and you can find it for $100 to $140. There is a cassette version of it out there too (also with a run of 500 copies), plus Heaven and Hell Records re-released it on CD in 2018 with unbelievably bad cover artwork...

Alias Mangler were one of the many American metal bands that mixed the sounds of hard rock with heavy metal, but even though they surely had an American glam metal influence, oddly enough they didn't sound like one. "Our influences were Mötley Crüe, Accept, Ratt, Loudness, AC/DC, tons of bands from that era," Jimmy adds. "The biggest and the best and bands like us, trying to make it, all influenced one another. Early Crüe and Accept records were some of the most influential ... The scene in our area was great, lots of bands, but mostly, Alias Mangler and Cerebus were the top two. People who appreciated original music and stage presence were very supportive, and the cool thing was that they turned their young kids on to us. We were treated like rock stars in our hometown because people knew us and knew we were serious. They were genuinely sad when we called it quits. Thirty years later, the band Alias Mangler is still talked about in our area."

After winning the first prize in the Battle of the Bands at Dorton Arena in Raleigh, Alias Mangler got studio time at CMC Studios in Zebulon and pressed 500 copies of their forthcoming record. "Winning the contest put us in a position to record the LP—we would not have had the bucks to do so without the support of an independent label," Jimmy adds. "Steve Bass, the man who put on the contest, believed in us once we won. But the budget was very small to record and release the LP. Only 500 LPs exist! It was almost a demo album to generate more interest, you might say. It was done over a four- or five-day period, with mostly one or two takes on the songs. Plus, it was our first time in the studio. It took time to try to get some of the sounds we wanted, plus the studio we were in was still under construction. I look back, and I think we did the best job we could, considering our time and a lot of other factors."

Alias Mangler's first and only LP, 1986's *Bite the Metal,* was a super melodic, mid-tempo example of hard/heavy metal, focusing on the party side of things—lyrics about love and their dedication to heavy metal—and even though they had limited time in the studio, it is evident that they were very proficient musicians. The title song is an ode to metal, reminiscent of The Rods, whereas "Body Aches" is hands-down their heaviest song—ballsy metal with great guitar riffs, which also describes "Death on Foot" and the excellent "Take a Chance." *Bite the Metal* has a weird, nostalgic aesthetic, and even though it's not true metal, I can imagine some hardcore metalheads enjoying this album.

"We really also had some fun at our live shows, after the release of our LP," Jimmy recalls. "It's hard to name the most memorable show, because we had a lot of great shows opening for other bands and headlining. We gave it 110 percent at every show. Sweat reigned supreme! Probably the most memorable show was a multi-band outdoor show at Ernie Shore Field in Winston-Salem, North Carolina. It was 100 frigging degrees and women *and* men barely had anything on, due to the heat, and as you looked out on a sea of people, they almost all appeared to be naked. And we rocked them all."

Sadly, Alias Mangler didn't release anything else—they only had a session that was never released—and while they kept on playing in North Carolina after the album was released, they faded away in 1991. "I like the fact that people are interested in this stuff. A lot of hours of work and time went into the whole process of this music even existing," Jimmy mentions. "The quality of some of this music may be lacking, but the intent was there. Each band like us was trying to find themselves and working to get better. You had to start somewhere, and it was a good beginning. As far as it being a collectible, I get a kick out of that, and as a collector of many things, I understand it. Only 500 LPs exist. Power to the Mangler. I'm sure an underground scene exists today, but I'm just out of the loop. Downloading is good if music is just a hobby, but if it's your profession, you need to be compensated somehow for it, because it's time-consuming and hard work. The music business is hard!"

Among the bands that members of Alias Mangler went on to play in, Jimmy Hinson's hard-rocking Fair Warning are the best known. Terry Baker's 2017 death will probably keep Alias Mangler laid to rest, and maybe forever.

ROCKKIT

FROM BROCKTON, MASSACHUSETTS, ROCKKIT FORMED IN 1983, AT A TIME when the Boston scene was mostly hardcore punk and new wave-oriented. "I met David Fillingin in 1976 in junior high school," drummer Daniel Nottage says. "David played guitar, and I played the drums. I had started playing drums at the age of five years old. In 1980, we met Jim Spellman, an amazing young bass player. We formed a band called Firing Line as a three-piece, with Dave and I singing, and played a few local school dances. I joined a band called Crisis in 1982, where I met Mark 'Waste' Horne. One night, I went to see David and Jim, who had started a band called Rockkit with another drummer as a three-piece band. I was really impressed with the songs and the show. Mark and I decided to join David and Jim and started to work on some original music. That was in 1983."

Daniel continues, "I started to listen to music at an early age. My brother, Mike, was into all types of music. The Beatles and all the British Invasion artists. One day, he brought home an album called *Are You Experienced* by the Jimi Hendrix Experience. He sat me on the couch and gave me the album cover, and there was Jimi. He put the needle down on the record and 'Purple Haze' came blasting out of the speakers. My life was never the same after that. I wanted to play music! I got a Banana Splits drum set. I started to play along to all the music of the time. I started to take lessons and joined the school band in seventh grade. The next step was to join a band and play some rock music...

"In Rockkit, we were all into Aerosmith, Kiss, Montrose, Rush, The Joe Perry Project, and all the rock bands of the 1970s and early 1980s. David loved Joe Perry, which I heard a lot in his playing. Jim was into David Hull from The Buddy Miles Express and The Joe Perry Project. Mark was into Alice Cooper. My favorite drummers were Mitch Mitchell, Ian Paice, Peter Criss, and Neil Peart. The album that left me with the greatest impression and inspiration would have to be The Jimi Hendrix Experience's *Axis: Bold As Love*. I got that album when I was five years old, and it was the reason I wanted to become a musician. I have to also say that the album *Destroyer* by Kiss was the reason I wanted to really pursue a career in music."

As mentioned, in Boston in the early eighties, the music scene was more punk rock and new wave. The biggest radio station, WBCN, was playing that type of music, but Rockkit had already a four-song demo out that needed airplay. "There was a radio station named WAAF that played more rock and metal—and still does," Daniel adds. "They had a show called *Bay State Rock* that aired on Sunday night and played local bands. Our song 'Never Say Never' was number one for 21 weeks in a row. Russ Mottla, who was the station director at WAAF, really liked Rockkit and helped us get a lot of shows."

Rockkit chose "Never Say Never" and "Dark Horse" off their demo and decided to put them on a record, which they would release on their own.

"The main reason we put our record out on a private label was because we didn't want to wait for a major label to sign us, as we all knew how hard it was to get signed by one," Daniel admits. "Also, it was better to send them a record than a cassette, to show them you were willing to go a step above the usual promo kit with a picture and a demo tape. We started to look for a local label. We met Joe 'Count' Viglione, who had a label called Varulven International Records. He became our manager. We recorded at a studio in Boston called Downtown Recorders. Engineered by Joe Cuneo. We ended up sending it out to all the major record companies. We also sold them at our shows and local record stores."

The *Never Say Never/Dark Horse* seven-inch might not have been a 100 percent privately released record, but since Rockkit paid for its release, it can be considered as a privately released work that falls under the umbrella of a small label. That said, I can't think of anybody who's into raw American metal who wouldn't love "Dark Horse," a bombastic track with an explosion of metallic riffs, like Deep Purple played at 78 RPM with a damn raw sound! "Never Say Never" is mid-tempo, but still it's burning hot American hard rock/metal, like if Kiss had gone heavyweight and pumped up with adrenaline. "There were a few bands who released records on an independent label," Daniel adds. "We rehearsed at a place in Brockton, Massachusetts, called the South Shore Music Studios. The two bands that we did shows with, Split Image and Steel Assassin, also recorded an album there."

> ## *CUT TO THE CHASE:*
>
> **Anybody into the "hard-rock-gone-raw-metal" perspective, e.g., W.A.S.P. or Mötley Crüe at their wildest, would appreciate the *Never Say Never/ Dark Horse* seven-inch.**

Rockkit played a lot of shows in clubs like the Channel, Paradise, Narcissus, Bunratty Tavern, the Rat, Jimbo's, and Ranch House. Daniel adds, "The most memorable show would have to be opening for Sammy Hagar at the Worcester Centrum on October 30, 1984. A 12,000-seat concert arena. After playing clubs for all my life, playing a show like this was amazing. Playing for that many people was incredible. I will always remember the sound of my drums, like cannons blasting into the arena. We took the place of the band Krokus, who could not open for Sammy that night. The fans of that band were disappointed and started throwing quarters and ice at us, but after a few songs, they got into the show and started cheering. I'm proud to say we won the crowd over that night."

Rockkit split up later in the mid-1980s. Daniel mentions, "We always talked about a Rockkit reunion and got together a few years ago for a jam which was a lot of fun. Unfortunately, Mark 'Waste' Horne passed away on March 18, 2018. Mark was a friend to the very end and is really missed by a lot of people. Without Mark, we could never do it now ... However, I think it is great that there is a resurgence of interest toward private metal records and bands. It's a wonderful thing, knowing that people are still interested in Rockkit. I remember seeing our record on eBay and other websites and being amazed at the prices it was going for. Who would have known that after all these years, it would become a collector's item! The song 'Never Say Never' was also on a compilation album called *Massachusetts Metal* with other local rock and metal bands, which is rare too."

On a final note, Daniel offers his perspective on the current situation in the music industry: "I think it's sad that people are just downloading one or two songs from an album. Just imagine if a concept record like The Beatles' *Sgt. Pepper* or The Who's *Tommy* came out today—people would miss out on the whole experience of listening to it from front to back. Album art used to be a big part of an album also. Getting posters and other stuff included was another thing with a record. You don't get that with a download. I still buy a physical copy of albums and listen to them from front to back and always will. Thank God for bands like Dream Theater and Tool, who make albums for people who like to listen to the whole record and who even play them all the way through live in concert ... I think that it is easier for bands now to get their music out to the public through YouTube and the internet. But I still miss going to record stores and hanging out with people, talking about the new releases and waiting to pick up a new record. I am glad I lived when that was the thing to do!"

ASYLUM

RHODE ISLAND IS THE LAST PLACE YOU THINK OF WHEN YOU HEAR THE phrase "1980s heavy metal," and the small town of Westerly is even less likely to come to mind. However, not one but two pure heavy metal bands, Asylum and Matthias Steele, emerged from this place in the eighties, with the former releasing a record on their own label. "Asylum was originally formed in 1978 when myself, Tom the guitar player, and Jim the drummer were all in high school together," vocalist Donn Collings says. "After school, we split up for a bit and then got the band back together in 1985, wrote and recorded the *Nowhere Fast* EP, and played live shows ... When you're a skinny high school kid, getting girls is the motivation, but then after that, it was just so much fun! We were influenced by Aerosmith, Deep Purple, Thin Lizzy—that era of bands had the most influence on our sound. The album *Toys in the Attic* by Aerosmith was a game changer for all of us."

In 1987, Asylum released the twelve-inch EP *Nowhere Fast*, which contained four songs. "The EP was recorded and released to get more attention from possible record companies and agents," Donn explains. "We picked four strong original tunes and hit the studio, pressed it in New York, gave it away to every radio station, and sold it locally." John Piccolo of the famous New York power pop/new wave band The Shirts played the keyboards, and the result was a very raw and rough hard rock/metal record. "Night After Night" was the heaviest number, reminding one perhaps of early Twisted Sister gone power metal, and this song itself justifies you getting *Nowhere Fast*! The song "Nowhere Fast" is in the tradition of The Rods, gutsy hard-rockin' metal, and so is "Can't Keep Her Satisfied." Overall, it's a good—but by no means totally essential—EP.

CUT TO THE CHASE:

Asylum's *Nowhere Fast* is a decent EP that most completists of this sound will enjoy, especially for the song "Night After Night." Yes, it's not THE definitive metal classic, but there are still some enjoyable rockin' metal tracks along the lines of The Rods and early Riot.

"If I can recall, the band Run 21 put out some stuff, and a band named Cryer and a progressive band named Alpha all put stuff out," Donn mentions, referring to bands from the same area that also released records on their own. "The best gig was probably an opening show we played for the band Extreme at a concert club in Providence, Rhode Island, called the Living Room: packed house, we killed it, and after the show, we hung out with Lemmy and Philthy from Motörhead. Unforgettable for sure!"

Asylum was laid to rest by the end of the 1980s, and no members went on to join or form another band. "I think though it is great that metal music is strong and there are new bands bringing it to a new place—the new technology in recording and publishing is helping that," Donn offers. "I'm not so sure my stuff is a 'highly paid collector's item,' but if the music we created is out there, being listened to, that is awesome. As long as there are a few kids in a garage somewhere cranking out tunes, there will be an underground scene. I'm too old now to really know if it's happening or not ... I think the ease of getting music out today is great. Wish we could have had that to put stuff out!"

LEATHER NUNN

ONE OF THE MOST BELOVED AND SOUGHT-AFTER AMERICAN PRIVATE-release metal records was by a group of kids from Jacksonville, Florida, Leather Nunn. Jim Mehm, the band's bassist, says, "Leather Nunn was formed in 1983. Wade Williams (vocalist) and I met in a music store on Jacksonville's Westside and joined Jerry Brewer (guitar), John Gouchnour (guitar) and Jimmy Evans (drums). We were all guys living where Lynyrd Skynyrd was formed, and even though they were an influence, we all wanted to play a harder-edged rock and roll ... Every one of us loved bands like AC/DC, Judas Priest, Iron Maiden, Black Sabbath, Dio, and Kiss. The Kiss album *Alive II* probably had the biggest impact on most of us."

Leather Nunn started offering live shows in the Jacksonville area—not the most tolerant place for a heavy metal band. "We had a big band room next to a bar on a main street in Jacksonville, and we would have shows every weekend and have bands come from all over to open up for us," Jim says excitedly. "The locals hardly ever gave us trouble. The most trouble was when we played in some of the very strict redneck clubs in Jacksonville."

Yep, it was the 1980s, and rednecks all over the U.S. considered metalheads and punks to be the ultimate enemy! However, Jim recalls, "By far, our favorite show was when we played an outdoor show in Jacksonville Beach and there were people packed from the stage all the way to the ocean. It was an amazing spectacle that always brings me so many great memories."

CUT TO THE CHASE:

A milestone in privately released American metal history, *Take the Night* is an absolute gem for anybody into true metal sound—you can't get more true metal than this! Only 500 copies of the original pressing were released, and *Take the Night* fetches ridiculous prices. However, it has been re-released since, so you don't have to rob a bank to get the original!

Working on their own material endlessly, jamming like crazy, Leather Nunn perfected their sonic dimension and decided to release an album on their own. In 1986, they headed to Jacksonville's Key Studios, and Jim says, "We made a decision that we had gotten as big as we could in Jacksonville. It was time to make a record. We recorded at a Christian recording studio (Key Studios), so we had to be on our best behavior. The entire record was recorded in less than a week. Many of the songs were basically one-take live recordings." The result was the *Take the Night* LP, a crown jewel of the history of American metal! Hard, raw, and heavy, *Take the Night* is a record that combines all those classics of 1970s UK metal and NWOBHM but retains a definite, strong, and pure American metal character. Actually, records like *Take the Night* are the quintessence of American metal. The title song is an eternal anthem, "Taken Ground" is a hellish inferno, and "Mental Asylum" is a heavy roller coaster. Overall, Leather Nunn sound like a cross between Chastain and Ripper, heavy but dark at the same time. There's no room left to party for Leather Nunn—they are absolutely serious about playing their metal mean (as speed metal band Demonax requested).

"I can recall some bands from Jacksonville that released some stuff on their own too, though not 100 percent heavy metal ones," Jim adds. "The hardcore punk Stevie Stiletto and the Switchblades, Lethyl, and Jerry Mehm's Fate Awaits are some that I can remember."

Sadly, Leather Nunn was short-lived. After the end of their first tour to promote *Take the Night*, they got in an automobile accident, which meant the end of the band. This was 1987. But the quest for real American metal in Europe created a myth around Leather Nunn and their crazy-rare LP. "We didn't realize that it was getting popular in the underground scene. Wade and I moved to L.A. in 1989 and then sometime in the late 1990s, we started getting all these emails asking for albums," Jim recalls. "Before long, I noticed that an original LP was going for well over $1,000. And to this day, we still don't know how this underground movement began. We don't even know how people outside of Jacksonville found out about us because the LP was put out in 1986, before the internet. We used to give them away to friends and when trying to meet girls, never thinking the album would get as big as it did!"

Wade Williams contributed the track "The Albatross" to the *Labour of Love: Ricky Parent Cancer Benefit Project* album in 2006, which raised money to help cover the Enuff Z'Nuff drummer's

LEATHER NUNN PHOTO COURTESY JIM MEHM

medical bills. Today, Leather Nunn has a Bandcamp profile where you can find their re-released classic metal LP in various forms. "I know there is still an underground scene, but there are two types: the true music lovers and the ones looking at it for monetary reasons," Jim adds. "I have mixed feelings [about] downloading. In one aspect, if the internet was around in 1985, Leather Nunn might have become a worldwide-recognized band and still be together today. In 1985, there was really no way for a metal band from Jacksonville to become known. On the other hand, I feel for the musicians who spend a lot of time and money recording their music and get very little income for their work."

Post-Leather Nunn, drummer Jimmy Evans later played in Retribution in the nineties, releasing the classic metal CD *No Peace On Earth* with the band in 1994.

SLAMMER

FORMING IN 1984, SLAMMER FROM ALTOONA, PENNSYLVANIA, WAS A BAND that kept it up for quite a few years under different lineups. Todd Giornesto, its vocalist, says, "Slammer was already formed, and I was in a band called Black Angel. They wanted to change to a harder rock format. At the time, some of the former members didn't want to do that. So, they asked me to join, and I did. It was Rob Kruis, Matt Socoski, Ed Andrews, Bob Weidman, and me. And we proceeded as Slammer. We wrote music, did covers, played clubs and shows in Pennsylvania, Ohio, West Virginia, et cetera. The love of hard rock and heavy metal was our driving force behind Slammer, and we loved Black Sabbath, AC/DC, Judas Priest, Iron Maiden, and then Metallica, Slayer, Motörhead, along with all NWOBHM."

Quickly enough, in 1985, Slammer released their *Lethal Metal* demo (I couldn't find this one anywhere in order to review it, sadly). When asked about the Altoona scene, Todd replies, "It was very small ... we were the scene. At the time, there was a radio station called WFBG in

CUT TO THE CHASE:

A very mediocre record, *M.I.A.* is probably only for completists of American private metal releases. I'm sorry for the bad review I've given Slammer (because I couldn't find their other stuff anywhere, and believe me, I tried hard!), so this one applies only to their *M.I.A.* seven-inch.

Altoona that had a show on Saturday nights called *All Night Album Rock*. They played a lot of the new rock and metal from bands all around the world, and this really was our life connection to this music in our area at the time. At that time in the eighties, there was no internet. The DJs of that show were Jay Randall and Jim Price, and actually, we were very well received by them!"

Todd left the band in 1986, Denny Litman joined, and they released the *M.I.A.* seven-inch the same year. "Slammer wanted to get their name known in the metal world, so that's why they went on to release *M.I.A.* on their own," Todd adds. *M.I.A.* included two mid-tempo American metal songs, rough but forgettable. Not a classic at all, the record's songs both seem uninspired, while Denny Litman's vocals are a bit annoying. Oh, well.

Matt Socoski kept the band alive, and Slammer released the *Breakout* EP in 1988 and the *Locked Up* demo in 1993, neither of which seem to be available anywhere today. After his departure from Slammer, Todd Giornesto played in bands that I enjoy much more, such as the very good Beyond Reason, Chilling Vision, Giornesto, and the hardcore/metal band I Against I. When asked about the underground scene today, Todd says, "Underground still exists ... however, it got harder and harder to succeed in it. Some places are better than others, though. I think that the accessibility of music is great ... but it really destroyed the music scene. Lars Ulrich tried to tell 'em a long time ago. But no one listened. When I want an album, I go out and physically buy it. It supports the band more, and I like to have the physical copy of it. It is such a fucking joke, these sites like Spotify and some other music sources, which only pay the bands like half a cent for the published, recorded music."

Slammer were laid to rest in the 1990s, and Matt Socoski is still playing with a band based in Clearfield, Pennsylvania, as of 2008. Many years later, former Slammer drummer Jim Bagrosky, who took over for Bobby Weidman, went on to join Stept-On with Matt Day on vocals, and is currently with Bad Daze.

RUFFKUT

RUFFKUT FROM LONG ISLAND WAS FORMED OUT OF CHILDHOOD RIVAL friendships in 1984. Johnny Roggio was attending a Long Island high school, while Eugene Henriksen and his brother Tommy Henriksen went to another school. They all played in rival bands, and along this path, they went out with different girls from each other's schools, eventually becoming friends along the way. "Ruffkut was built out of necessity," vocalist and guitarist Johnny Roggio says. "Tommy and Eugene Henriksen approached me because my hair looked good, heh! I started out as the rhythm guitarist next to James Quinn, thus replacing and becoming the only guitarist in the band, after taking the lead by the helm and stepping out front. Mötley Crüe was our biggest influence as kids. Mötley Crüe's first LP was the model the band built itself on. We were also inspired by bands such as Van Halen, Judas Priest, Dokken, and many of the Los Angeles bands of the eighties."

While discussing the local scene, Johnny says, "The Long Island music scene was off the charts—it was thriving back then. It not only sustained the growth and development of new talent it provided, but also a needed group of bands, venues, and distribution for music outlets.

CUT TO THE CHASE:

Ruffkut's *Fight for the Right* EP will definitely please all those into early 1980s Judas Priest as well as bands like Hellion or Leatherwolf, or even Mötley Crüe (at their hardest).

Twisted Sister, Zebra, and so many more came from that same music scene. Locals both formed their own bands and helped them become pro and semi-pro bands that went on from there."There were so many bands of that era that had released their own records that it's hard to count, so kudos to you, Alex, for doing it!" Johnny laughs. "From our area, I can recall Zebra, Twisted Sister, Swift Kick, Cintron, and Kaiser, just to name a few."

Ruffkut went on to release its first and only twelve-inch EP, *Fight for the Right*, in 1984 on its own label, Ruffkut Records. When asked about the procedure behind it, Johnny replies, "We put *Fight for the Right* out because we couldn't find a label that would sign us. We did many a showcase to try to get a record deal, but we never seemed to fit the cookie-cutter stereotype they were looking for at the time. Our audience and fan base wanted a record, and we fulfilled that need. We did very well in terms of sales of that album, and it's still out there in the underground somewhere in the world."

Fight for the Right balanced between the classic heavy metal of Judas Priest, the party/glam metal of Mötley Crüe, and the melodic metal of Dokken. Even though this isn't my favorite style, I have to admit that it is actually a very good record—totally professional in terms of recording and musical execution, and it definitely has the mainstream metal flavor that was so prevalent in those days. But it still manages to keep its balance, and its five songs are pure gold for the fans of this style. "Run for Your Life" is a perfect Judas Priest-based anthem, melancholic and nostalgic at the same time, whereas the galloping "To the Top" is pretty perfect too. I'll pass on "Rich Bitch Lady" thanks to the lyrics, but again, in musical terms, it's great.

Of course, Ruffkut's fame went on to spread locally, and this got them slots on more shows. "One of the most memorable shows we did was opening up for Zebra at Stony Brook; that was our first enormous-sized audience we got to play for," Johnny remembers. "After that, we did go on to do many shows, especially at L'Amour in Brooklyn, opening for many national artists."

Ruffkut kept it up until 1987, and after the band's demise, Tommy Henriksen went on to play in Warlock, Alice Cooper, Hollywood Vampires, Doro, Rondinelli, Boink!, DiSViciOuS, Parade of Losers, and War & Peace, among many others, whereas Johnny now plays with the Beginnings, a Chicago tribute band.

On a final note, Johnny adds, "I think it's amazing that people still celebrate great music from the past. It keeps it alive—of the music that did stay alive. Some of us actually play in tremendously successful tribute bands that pay homage to bands we actually grew up with. The fact that our EP could even be called collectible is so humbling and warming to know. It is an honor to have people still listening to those tracks from our childhoods."

In regards to underground music, he says, "I truly believe in an underground for music. Some musicians are afraid of what they love to play, or there doesn't seem to be an audience to receive the music they want to play, and there is where underground is born. As far as downloading, well, none of us got rich from the music we produced back then, but to know it's still circulating and being listened to is a reward in itself!"

DEUCE

WRITING ABOUT DEUCE WAS SOMETHING I LOOKED SO MUCH FORWARD TO, since they were one of the first 1980s private metal bands, plus I loved their approach in terms of music! Deuce was formed in Maryland in 1979, and guitarist and vocalist Tom Gattis explains: "In 1978, my family moved to Maryland, and I immediately started a band. My mother built, by hand, a separate barn with a stage in it. So, I had a three-piece: me on guitar, drummer Chris Tinto, and bassist Steve Leter. My idols were this punk band from Wyoming called the Dirty Dogs (formed by Eric Ambel from Joan Jett and the Blackhearts), which is where I lived in 1977. They were a really bad (good) influence, so I was hell-bent on forming a punk band with a high priority on sleaze and smut of the most fun kind. Dead Boys, Ramones, Sex Pistols, Clash, Damned, et cetera were my influences. I absolutely hated heavy metal at that time.

Then one day, I bought this album with a corpse's head on it (inspired by a photo from the Vietnam war) and bam, I was hooked on Iron Maiden. It was like punk with better playing. So, I used to get bussed to the high school from the junior high school for math class, which is where I met Marty Friedman. I went to his parents' house to jam, and he played every Ace Frehley perfectly, and even better, he loved punk rock as well. He was hesitant at first to play in ANY band at all, and he would switch from punk to metal, depending on what week you caught him. I kept pestering the hell out of him to get out of his bedroom and do something with his talent, so I finally got him to join the band, and that made Deuce, in early 1979. At about the same time we got a singer, Eddie Day, who was with us about a year."

Tom describes why he decided to play music in the first place: "I completely fell in love with hard, fast music. It was the guitar sound, the squared wave to be exact. I was trained on classical flute, which of course produces a standard sine wave. But the moment I heard the squared wave, I was hooked. Interestingly, before I was tall enough to see over my dad's record player, he said I used to perk up to only two Beatles songs: 'Revolution' and 'Helter Skelter,' both songs with squared waves. So, I guess it's natural. Second thing was that I was a natural-born performer. I always felt like I was at my best in front of an audience."

Deuce's sound was totally unique, and don't forget, we are talking about the late 1970s, when even NWOBHM was in its formative years, and in the U.S., there wasn't a specific heavy metal scene yet. "The best band, by far, was Bad Brains. They blew everyone else away!" Tom declares. "And Kiss, Cheap Trick, Ramones, Dead Boys, early Scorpions, Riot, and Yesterday and Today (Y&T) were our basic influences," he adds, "whereas Marty also liked Sabbath. Literally, it was when metal and punk merged. The record that left the biggest impression for me didn't come out until the band was already together for a year or so, which is Iron Maiden's first record. That record exposed just how far you could take punk. You just needed touches of (dare I say it?) prog rock, strategically placed, then BAM! You have songs like 'Sanctuary' or 'Runnin' Free' (with a VERY punk beat). Everything changed after that.

"At first, the scene completely sucked," Tom sighs. "It was dominated by soft rock and Top 40, and if there were any hard bands, they sounded like Led Zeppelin or Southern rock, which was definitely NOT us. Marty and I had this saying, 'If you aren't feeble, if you don't suck, you can't be popular.' But then the myth of the barn started, and people started showing up. First just a few, but then it got so big, it was out of control. People were setting up small booths selling stuff, most of it illegal, haha! But our little practice barn had then become a nightly concert, so ALL of our practices were literally in front of an audience of some sort from day one. The stories that came from the barn years are so many in number that it would take a whole book, but they were great stories. People would pass out on Marty's pedals, or puke on the sound board. Once, Billy Giddings brought this brand-new white sash to hang over his drums, but the rest of us HATED elitism of any kind, so our bass player, Mike Davis, took Bill's sash off the front of the drums and wiped his butt with it and re-hung it, now with a brown line. Billy was mad. He threw away his shit-sash."

When asked about his proudest Deuce show, Tom replies, "About Deuce, let me say that THE thing I am proudest of is growing a band from the foundation up. I have had my share of opportunities to join other bands, but there is NOTHING like starting one from nothing and watching it grow and become internationally known. So that is by far the number one … but there were a lot of memorable shows with Deuce. There was one where we played this backyard party, like our second show, and we had to miss Priest on their *British Steel* tour. Then there was our first show, at a pizza place, where my mom had to come because I was 15—three years under the drinking age. Then there was this show where we played at a college for the deaf in D.C. It was the first show where we could turn up as loud as we wanted and no one would care. Then there was another show where we played at a summer camp for mentally disabled kids, and they all hit the dance floor. Believe it or not, we had the balls to play 'Cretin Hop' by the Ramones, and Marty sang it. One of the kids was lurching back and forth and hopping around to our music and then drooled on our singer, and he freaked out."

CUT TO THE CHASE:

Deuce's *I'm Saved* will please all you American-metal-loving metalheads, who like it rough, melodic, and catchy. Oddly enough, even though this is a mix of different things (such as American punk), it is still 100 percent metal. You actually can't get more true and pure metal than this! Just 1,000 copies were released, and many of them were destroyed or lost, so now it's a monster of a collector's item. For a much better price, you can get the collection that O.P.M. Records released in 1997, titled *Deuce*. Metalheads, pick up anything Tom was involved with, starting with Tension's *Breaking Point* LP. Ridiculously crucial and good stuff!

Tom goes on: "Then there was one show where I was singing and the house lights kept going on and off, so during a break, I asked why the lights were being turned on and off, and turns out they weren't; I was being electrocuted over and over. Of course, there were those shows where you have really stinky gas, and you know how band members move all over the stage? Well, whoever had gas would casually walk over to another member, then lay an egg, then split, leaving them to soak in the stench, so the victim would quickly move around the stage more. So that's when we started 'visiting' the drummer, because he couldn't run! I broke my leg on stage once, but I finished the song! Hurt like HELL!"

But there's more! "Once we were opening for Kix, another Maryland band, and my girlfriend at the time was really drunk and thought I was trying to pick up another girl backstage, so she punched me in the nose. I got it to stop bleeding before we went on, but then in the middle of a song, it started to gush blood everywhere and I couldn't stop it. It was really cool! We played in New York early on, and Marty had left his white Stratocaster in the truck, and it got so hot that the blue velvet inner lining of the guitar case actually melted on to the guitar—a white Stratocaster with fuzzy blue fur on it! Once, a guy in the audience tried to suck my dick, so I booted him in the face—hard. Not that I have anything against gays at all, you understand, but come on! If I am on stage, please don't try to suck my dick, especially if you're a dude. After all, I'm busy!

"Probably my favorite show was the first time we played Germany with Bruce Dickinson in Wardog," Tom concludes. "But the *best* show we played was in Baltimore with Overkill and Nuclear Assault. The crowd was fucking insane. Bobby Blitz was watching us play, and while he was standing with Billy Giddings, he said, 'I like that title of your song 'Wrecking Crew,' and I'm going to steal it.' Haha! Funny how that works. Great guy, that Bobby! Very cool."

In 1981, Deuce released one of the records most sought-after by metal collectors worldwide, the *I'm Saved* seven-inch, on their own Manta Records. "Marty's dad got reassigned to Hawaii, so he had to leave," Tom says. "In came Timmy Meadows, brother of Punky, with TONS of touring experience from being on the road with Angel and Kiss and Priest and the like. Since the very beginning, we had been writing our own music, so we wanted to put something out. So, my mom went to my dad, to the bank, everywhere she could to beg for money for us to put out something. We finally got enough together to buy studio time at the legendary Tracks Recorders in D.C. (Hendrix, Root Boy, Ramones) and literally our first experience in the studio was with an engineer and the great Neve 8038, with 16 Studor two-inches and Neumann mics. We had a day to record it and a day to mix it. Out came 'Bad Boys' and 'I'm Saved,' the single. My uncle, a professional artist, designed the center of the platter, and it was released about the same time that Iron Maiden's *Killers* acetate advances were pressed. We got one of those advances and it blew our minds. It was a lot like the reaction the Beach Boys had at the *Pet Sounds* release party, when someone brought in an advance copy of *St. Pepper's*. But we liked it, and we loved our little 45. Little did we know when we were throwing them around the barn and smashing them that they would be worth up to 300 dollars each in the future. It was just one of those things."

"I'm Saved" is an excellent metal/punk rocker, not far from Iron Maiden's early stuff, rough and very powerful, and at the same time unbelievably catchy—classic! On the flip side, "Bad Boys" is another excellent gem, along the same line of NWOBHM/U.S. punk mix. Plus, it has to be mentioned that Deuce sound totally wild for their era (this album is from 1981). I can't recall many early eighties metal bands in the U.S. with this sound.

Deuce went on to release another two demos in 1983 and 1984. Their awesome American metal-meets-NWOBHM-and-punk can be heard on many tracks—such as the perfect "Barn Burner," which sounds like a cross between The Stepmothers and The Crowd, or "Love's Massive Suicide"—as well as in early versions of songs that were re-recorded with the band that most of the members of Deuce formed after the band's demise in 1985. Tension was the continuation of Deuce, and in 1986, the band released the ultra-mega-classic *Breaking Point* LP on Torrid Records: an attempt at an apotheosis of heavy/speed metal.

"It feels great that more and more people today are interested in unknown heavy metal of the past," Tom says. "That genre and that specific process is key to keeping hard music alive. Always has been. If I ever record anything again, I want it small, on vinyl. The price that the Deuce single brings is shocking to me, but that's how enthusiastic true metal people are—they will pay for rare gems. It's the way music should be, actually. Here in the U.S., music in general is looked down on, even if you are famous. Doctors, lawyers, engineers, and nurses, all have higher status, and musicians—EVEN classical musicians to some degree—are looked on as scum. It's so ridiculous because it's one of the hardest things anyone can do. We have fucked-up priorities here in the U.S. In Europe, it IS different in that people tend to value the arts more in general. I can say that musicians are some of both the dumbest and smartest people I have ever met. Dumb musicians are REALLY dumb, but smart musicians are geniuses."

Tom Gattis' endless love for metal led him to form Wardog and Ballistic in the 1990s, whereas everybody knows Marty Friedman's route to Vixen to Aloha and then to Megadeth, among the countless other bands that Deuce members played in. Billy still plays with the power/progressive metal Alloy 20, whereas Tension and Ballistic are still on hold as of today (2020, that is).

"I don't know if a 'scene' exists, but I know I see a lot of retro-metal shirts on young people today, so it's not like it's dead," Tom responds when asked about the modern underground scene. "Having said that, I doubt if it will ever be like it was in the 1980s again. People in general went out more, interacted socially, face to face, and that is becoming a lost art. So, it's not just metal, but just going out and seeing anything is getting more and more rare. In a smaller way, I can't blame them. Going out, you get hassled a lot, from cops to the doorman at the club to ... whatever. So, why not fuck all that and stay home? Back in my day, there was a LOT less hassle, a lot less people fucking with us, and it was less dangerous. Nowadays, here in America, you don't know if you'll come home alive in some places.

"As far as downloading music, on the face of it, it is, of course, bad," Tom says. "But then again, for decades, record companies have had a stranglehold on music, making the decisions on who gets published and who doesn't, and a LOT of great bands have never happened to woo a record company executive to the point where they get signed. So, now you don't need them, don't HAVE to be on a record company, and this is a good thing. More people can be heard, and this is a really good thing. But also, some real crap is out there. In addition, small bands could not compete with big bands because the millions of dollars' worth of equipment wasn't available to them. But digital changed all that. Now you can record a record on your laptop. So, I guess I am torn!"

INTRÜDER

INTRÜDER FROM FLORIDA RELEASED SOME OF THE MOST VICIOUS AND raging true metal, and guitarist Ron Hanisco says, "I was in a 1980s band from Philadelphia named Teeze, and later changed to Roughhouse. I loved playing in clubs. With Teeze, we had a performance contract with Media Five from Allentown, Pennsylvania. They had us playing clubs six nights a week. They wanted Teeze to be a commercial music band. But I was metal to the core. So, I formed the kind of band I wanted and started my own thing…

"When I parted ways with them," he continued, "I had an old group of musicians that I jammed with. I got them back together, added a singer I met while in Teeze, and started the band with the connections with club owners I had made. Within months, we were playing clubs steadily. The lineup of Intrüder included me on guitar, Dan Cleveland on bass (later, Phil Martelli filled his position), Jack Robbins on drums, and Krazy Löu Hilaire on vocals.

"Our immediate inspiration was Judas Priest, especially the *Unleashed in the East* LP," Ron admits. "I was guitar-influenced, mainly Jimmy Page, but I loved the 1970s and 1980s metal players. As far as what influenced the band as a whole, it should be Accept's *Balls to the Wall* and *Metal Heart* and Judas Priest's *British Steel* and *Screaming for Vengeance*—they were top on the list."

CUT TO THE CHASE:

Are you into Kratos, Exciter, Knightmare, and American bands with a punk edge and a dirty raw sound in general? Intrüder's *Krush, Kill, Destroy* twelve-inch will absolutely do the job! Don't get turned off by the punk tag; this is 100 percent metal. It can be a bit pricey to obtain, since it ranges between 120 and 160 dollars, but it's worthwhile.

Intrüder went on to release their first and only twelve-inch, 1986's *Krush, Kill, Destroy* (on their own label, Inch Ruder Music), and Ron tells the story behind it: "I was sick of doing cover songs and wanted to motivate the band to move on to bigger things. I set the whole thing up. Saved all the money from our gigs in a bank account, and when I thought we were ready, I said, 'Okay, let's do this.' I wrote the songs, set up the recording, the mixing, the mastering, the artwork, the pressing, and packaging. I think it was a good move. Having an actual record out brought us some attention from local radio and offers to play better clubs."

Krush, Kill, Destroy only had two songs on it, but both of them rate as some of the most raging heavy metal ever to be released independently in the U.S. The title song is a mid-tempo burner, with a full-on passionate execution, reminiscent of early Attacker, whereas "Give Me Metal" is a total rager, with this punked-up Motörhead style that Exciter had—fast and venomous! Not for the faint-hearted white-collar metalheads, *Krush, Kill, Destroy* is as metal as you can get.

"While we played in the New Jersey area, it was great," Ron recalls. "We were treated like rock stars at every club. It was nice. When we made the move to Florida, not so much. It was like a time warp. They never saw bands that wore leather and Spandex!" laughs Ron. "Actually, my favorite shows came after Intrüder. I had formed a hardcore/metal band called Meatlocker. That's when things took off. We opened for Megadeth, Pantera, Biohazard, Agnostic Front, Overkill, the Exploited. All great bands. As far as Intrüder shows? Nothing could ever measure up to that."

Intrüder kept it up until 1987, and following their breakup, Ron formed Meatlocker in 1990 (hardcore/thrash) while Dan formed Raped Ape (thrash metal). "Meatlocker went on to be signed by Maze Records, Biohazard's first label," Ron adds. "They went bankrupt before we recorded, but I hold no hard feelings for the label. I really do think they were sincere, but just ran out of money. We later signed with Progress Records out of Denmark and put out one CD, *Triangle of Pain*, in 1994.

"The big band around the way, which released a private record in the 1990s, was Raped Ape," Ron recalls. "Accordingly, the Roidz were a big punk band at the time. In general, I think metal actually never left. If there is a resurgence, that's awesome. Bands have the means to put out their own stuff now without the huge price tag of pressing records or CDs. I love seeing indie bands actually have more access to the public now."

TITANIC

HEAVIER THAN THOU, TITANIC FROM NEW HAVEN, CONNECTICUT, ARE among the bands that were included in the classic series of *Metal Massacre* compilations released by Metal Blade Records (specifically, they're on the *Metal Massacre VII* LP with their song "Awakening"). But the band sadly never got a chance to extend their career further than just a private release.

"Titanic was formed in 1984 with Bob Torres on vocals, his brother Frank Torres on guitar, Robert Cretella on bass, and Freddy Mousinelli on drums," Alessio Zazzarino says. "Freddy and Frank quit the band, and then Bob Torres replaced them with me and Jim Donini one year later. Bob put an ad in the *New Haven Advocate* newspaper looking for a drummer, so I went to the audition—where there were 20 other drummers. At the end of the night, they chose me, and we started putting together songs for *Then There Was Rock* album. For about three months, we went into the TNA Studios in Wallingford, Connecticut, and recorded all the songs live with engineer Doug Snyder. We all had our families and friends there as we recorded, plus some wine. It was a lot of fun. Plus, we did about six months gigging around Connecticut. We wrote about 30 songs, and we also played covers of Scorpions, Dio, and Led Zeppelin, which we all loved. However, we had bad management and we, as a band, started to become frustrated. I wanted to do a European tour, but the rest of the band didn't want to; also, Metal Blade Records wanted all our songs, but the other members didn't want to give them the songs, so they offered only one song on *Metal Massacre VII*."

CUT TO THE CHASE:

Titanic's barbaric heavy/power metal sound will please all fans of this raw and unpolished style, especially those ones into the adrenaline-infused NWOBHM bands like Savage, Sledgehammer, or even Raven. The hard rock elements are there too, and while *Then There Was Rock* doesn't include the more delicate elements of the American metal sound, it surely has its audience.

Alessio continues, "Then, one of the members in Titanic started saying he wanted to play more pop, but I said no, because metal was getting more progressive and I wanted to get heavier and/or stay the same. After many arguments, I left the band and joined another band called WitchHammer from New Haven. I tried later to get Titanic back together as a band, but they all basically quit music, as far as I know. I've put a new band together now, which sounds a lot like Titanic, and I'm hoping to get a demo out soon.

"My motivation as a drummer and songwriter was that I wanted to follow the style of my favorite drummers and be like them," Alessio adds. "Vinnie Appice, Carmine Appice, bands like King Kobra and Dio. I wanted to be like them, with the same style, music and image. In Titanic we had a very good light show and sound system, alongside a smoke machine. All the shows were very good; we were always on the radio and people always came to see us. As far as inspirations for Titanic, these were Cactus, Dio, Black Sabbath, King Kobra, and we also liked Warlord, Mercyful Fate, King Diamond, Scorpions, Led Zeppelin, and Y&T."

Alessio also discusses the then-flourishing Connecticut scene (which, by the way, is one of my favorite scenes in both punk and metal). "It was very full of great bands in my area—you had Fates Warning, Legend, Obsession, ESP, Black Wÿtche, Anvil (not to be confused with the Canadian band), Dresden, and many other bands you would see just pop out of nowhere. It was so awesome; we all wore the leather jackets, had long hair, were ready to play shows all the time. It was a great feeling, and I still feel like that, even today. Many people and fans remember all the shows we played back then."

When asked about the current metal scene, Alessio says, "Today, musicians are indoors too much and it's hard to find them. And the new metal today, I think, is tuned down too much. I prefer guitar players with standard tuning. It sounds more like real metal to me."Titanic went on to record and release their first and only LP, 1985's *Then There Was Rock*, on their own White Lightning Records label. Alessio tells the story: "We decided to put out a private record because we wanted to build a following in the area and sell the records at Cutler's Record

Shop in New Haven. Alongside, we sold them in Rhymes Records to get on the radio, all of this leading up to finding a record deal. Well, we got Metal Blade interested in all our material, but the band would only let one song go. I thought it was a mistake, but there was nothing I could do. I would have given them all of the songs if I had a choice."

You can definitely hear the echoes of Robert Plant and Ian Gillan in Robert Torres' vocals (well, his are a bit crazier), and overall, Titanic sound like they had the time of their life while recording *Then There Was Rock*! Alessio's drumming is menacing and brutal, while the band sounds on some tracks (e.g., "The Otherside" and "Still of the Night") to be totally out of control. But what they lose in terms of inspiration, they gain back in terms of power. *Then There Was Rock* sounds more British than American, and actually like it came out of NWOBHM, like a pumped-up version of Savage. Even though it's not mind-blowing, I can't think of metalheads who are into this raw sound not loving "Precious Time" and its galloping rhythm, or the heavyweight "The Awakening," which ended up on the aforementioned *Metal Massacre VII* LP.

"Our favorite show was in West Haven, at the Masonic Temple," says Alessio. "We had put on a big party with four bands—all local bands. The place was packed, and the sound was great. We signed autographs at the end and many people drank a lot of beer and had a lot of fun there. I still see that show in my head even today ... it was unforgettable." Alessio adds, "A favorite band of mine was the local band Legend. Their album is called *Fröm the Fjörds*, and for me, their drummer, Raymond Frigon, is one of the best I've heard. They played locally and had one great album, and then their guitar player died young and they reformed the band into another name called Mercenary, which did a lot of good songs and shows too. Black Wÿtche was also another good band, with Mike Zweers on guitar."

After the release of the *Metal Massacre VIII* compilation in 1986, Titanic parted ways, and the band never revived. I believe they had potential to keep it up and to somehow, through stabilizing their sound and approach, pursue a career, but all these are just what-ifs. "I know that a lot of people like our album and I am happy about that, because we all put our heart into this band, and we played as well as we could and wanted very much to make a good album," Alessio adds. "It's the dedication that you put into something that makes it good. You have to completely love music and always keep your dreams first. I'm happy that I accomplished what I did; I still am very proud and wish I could go back to those days, and this is evident from the fact that today, I'm trying to recreate another metal-style band like Titanic and that classic sound of the 1980s metal.

"All music today is underground, because the radio stations refuse to support heavy metal. There is a rap agenda and demoralization process going on in Hollywood," Alessio concludes. "I think downloading has destroyed everything in music, all businesses. But if the radio stations played more metal on the radio, we wouldn't need to download it on the computer ... we could listen to it on the radio and go buy the actual record in the stores."

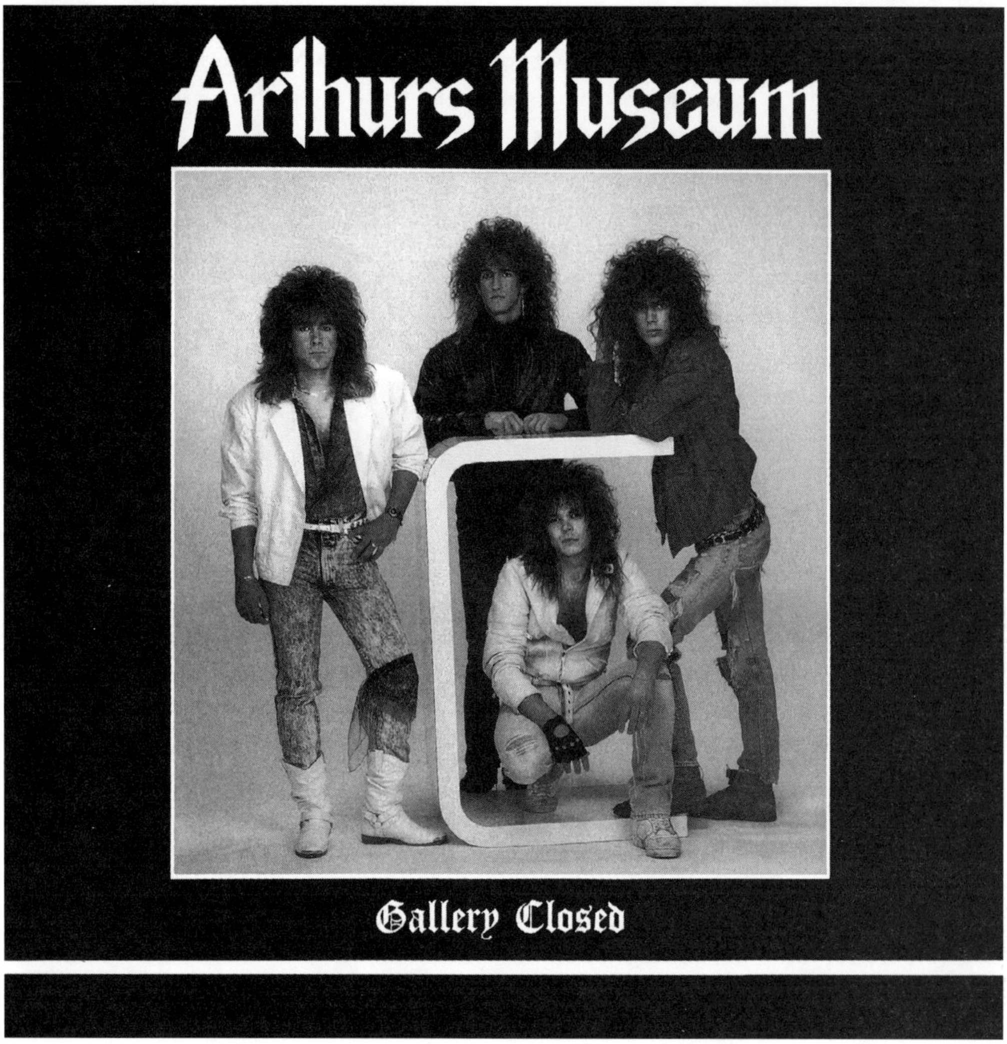

ARTHURS MUSEUM

MANY FAMOUS MUSICIANS EMERGED FROM THE INDEPENDENT METAL/HARD rock scene, and this is the case with Arthurs Museum. It was guitarist Richie Kotzen's first band, and he entered the rock 'n' roll world at the tender age of 15! "Arthurs Museum was already formed when I first saw them. My friend Buzz Saylor was the drummer," vocalist and keyboardist Brian Varhelyi says. "I remember talking with him during a set break, saying I need to find a band like his. They were really fucking good. He said, 'Why don't you join Arthurs?' I stated the obvious: 'You already have Richie.' (I think he was about 15 at the time.) Buzz said, 'No, I mean on keyboards.' I was primarily a guitarist when Buzz asked me to join. That's why I was surprised when he asked me."

Brian goes on: "Richie was already at the level of the rest of us 'older' guys, although he was shy and green. So, the band bought me a synth, and I was in the band. At that time, it was

Buzz Saylor (drums/lead vocals), Alisa Anderson (lead vocals), Danny Thompson (bass/lead vocals), Richie (guitar), and me (keyboards/lead vocals). Once we got serious about our own music and started recording and touring, there were some changes to the lineup; it was me, Danny, Richie, and new drummer Scott Lloyd, who was a friend of mine—we played in bands together previously. That's the lineup we had for the record. We played the East Coast club scene, opened for major acts, showcased, et cetera. Here's where you get different versions of the story, depending on who you talk to from the band. Bottom line was that Richie signed to Shrapnel, and the remaining three of us continued to record, but since our manager at the time was Richie's dad, we lost all support and eventually went our separate ways. Danny, Scott and I still play together from time to time and just last year recorded a single for our original vocalist, Alisa Anderson, who passed away from cancer. It's as yet unreleased, until we decide if an album will follow or if it's just the one song."

Formed in Reading, Pennsylvania, in 1985, Arthurs Museum was a guitar-driven AOR/ melodic metal band that followed the huge AOR wave in the U.S. Mind you, we're talking about the early to mid-1980s, and the underground was seething. There were youth subcultures everywhere in the U.S., and everything was reaching its peak.

When asked about the motivation behind Arthurs, Brian says, "I think it's the same for all of us: love for the music. That includes recording, and my favorite thing to do, which is to perform live in front of an audience. You need to feed the ego somehow, right? So, it wasn't about partying, although we did a little of that. It wasn't about the girls, although we did a little of that too. That's not why we started and why kept on to this day, though. Love of the music! Simple as that. As for our biggest influences? I'm sure this is probably different for all of us. Early on, it was Motown and classic rock. Zeppelin, Aerosmith, Yes. By the time the 1980s came around, it was Van Halen, Guns N' Roses, Journey. What people listening to our record today don't realize is that Arthurs was a progressive rock band in the beginning. It wasn't until the final lineup that things really got rockin'. But we never lost the progressive musical aspect of things. I think we had more depth to our music, instead of simply the hard-hitting party rock of the day, like Poison. We weren't big fans, so it was a bit surprising to find out Richie had joined them. The price we pay for fame and fortune, heh. In the end, turns out, it wasn't Richie's bag either. His music now is SO much better.

"The music scene in Reading, Pennsylvania, was jamming," Brian continues. "Lots of talented musicians and great bands, and this remains true today. Reading, Lancaster, Harrisburg. Our territory stretched to Philly and South New Jersey as well. So, besides Arthurs, there were bands like Poison, Heaven's Edge, and Cinderella, to name a few. We played a mix of covers and originals. Not sure why, but some of the bands in the local cover scene didn't like us. Perhaps they thought our manager (Richie's dad) was giving us a free ride, but he wasn't—we paid for everything, from production and crew, studio fees, et cetera. Paid for, not owned. Big difference there, as when we were 'legally divorced,' Danny, Scott, and I had nothing, including copies of the record, which, by the way, Richie was selling on his website for 300 bucks. All water under the bridge.

"Arthurs was inducted into the Berks County Rock & Roll Hall of Fame in 2016," Brian says. "We were invited for the ceremony and to perform. Danny and I were there, although unfortunately, Scott couldn't make it, and I didn't expect to see Richie. Rich, Sr. was there—hadn't seen him in a long time. It was nice seeing him again. After all this time there's no bad feelings. Until he went to claim the award while Danny and I were onstage performing. After our performance, we went in to see the award and pick it up, but we were told Richie's dad already got it. When I walked outside, I saw him standing there trying to hide it! Needless to say, I'm done with him, and never again will I give him the benefit of the doubt. I contacted the head of the Berks County Rock & Roll Hall of Fame and explained the situation, and he agreed to have additional awards made for the band members."

CUT TO THE CHASE:

Arthurs Museum's only album, *Gallery Closed*, will surely appeal to metalheads who dig the softer sounds of melodic metal, like Journey or even Styx and REO Speedwagon. I am not a fan of this style, but can surely appreciate a good effort. So, don't expect a barbaric and roaring sound—it's just delicate, smooth-like-silk stuff here.

Things were different in 1988, though, and all of Arthurs Museum's members were good friends too, so what could have been better than releasing their own LP? "We wanted to pursue a music 'career' and knew that we needed to write and record our own songs," Brian explains. "The best way to get noticed at that time was to have a record with sales to back it up. Record companies of the day wanted a finished product they could slap their label on and sell right away. So, we booked some studio time and began the recording process. We went way over budget and could have done the record for a lot less. But since we came from that progressive background, we wanted it as polished as possible. In hindsight, a rawer recording would've done just as well and saved us a lot of bucks. We did the basic rhythm tracks live. Richie overdubbed solos and additional guitar parts, and Danny and I did all the backing vocals. We'd both sing a part in unison, then again and again. Then we'd do the same with the next harmony part and so on. The vocals were huge! Lastly were the keyboards. Producer David Ivory and I spent a lot of evenings layering in keyboard parts, creating new sounds, mixing, et cetera. We used MOTU Digital Performer, so we had a lot of freedom with parts and arrangements. At the time, CDs were just coming into mainstream public use (our track backups were done on VHS tape!), but we decided on vinyl."

Brian adds, "We had a strong following. We played as much as possible, whenever and wherever. I think at the time, we sold around 10,000 copies, just locally. We had interest from a few labels, but in the end, Richie signed with Shrapnel. So, while he was off recording his first solo album, the rest of us were recording at his home studio and producing about another six songs or so. Richie wanted his second album to have vocals, and he asked if I would front his new project, so I did. We wrote some songs and recorded demos, which I still have."

Arthurs Museum's first and only twelve-inch EP was released in 1988, on their own label, KGS Records. Polyphonic, super-slick, and very professional, with influences ranging from Journey to Toto and eighties-era Rainbow as well as the then-emerging glam metal scene, *Gallery Closed* is a real treat for fans of this sound. I'm not an expert on AOR at all, but I say that "Life" and the heavyweight "No Turning Back" are more than good!

"We played a lot of cool shows as an opening act," Brian replies when asked about his favorite performance. "A cool one was with the Fabulous Thunderbirds. Jimmie Vaughan watched our entire set, came to the dressing room afterward, and told us how much he enjoyed what we were doing. A funny one (well, I think it's funny!), we were playing at Hammerjacks in Baltimore. Our opening act was a group of little boys called Menudo. Later, I realized it was Little Ricky Martin! But probably the most fun was a venue in Reading called the Silo. It was a two-tier club, with a lower floor and a balcony. We always packed the place with a lot of familiar faces."

Richie Kotzen left the band initially to pursue a solo career, and Arthurs Museum never replaced him, so everything ended in 1988. But their record still remains on the wish lists of metal/melodic metal collectors worldwide. "It's amazing and intriguing that people still search for *Gallery Closed*," Brian smiles. "I get calls, for example, from record shops in Germany asking how to get more copies. A new record probably would have new interest; perhaps we should re-release *Gallery Closed*. I'm not really sure I would even classify Arthurs as metal, but I guess people are? So, who's getting the money now, anyway? It's not me, heh!

"Underground scenes will always exist—it's the nature of the beast," Brian concludes. "It's great that there's still record shops overseas, where you can go check out some music and come home with an album, enjoy the cover art, and so on. We don't really have that anymore in the States. It's iTunes, Spotify, or Amazon. The downside to downloading music is that our collection becomes a shuffle play, a song from this artist or that one. There's no conceptualization anymore. Do we even know who we're listening to or what's even in our downloads? I think it's really sad, what the music business has done to music. They've killed it, and that's why there will always be an underground scene ... for those of us who still love music!"

VIKRON

IT'S ALWAYS VERY ENJOYABLE WHEN YOU RESEARCH BANDS THAT NO ONE has ever heard of whose members are still active today, even if they're minor bands. It's proof that rock 'n' roll has been running through their veins after all these years, no matter the level of fame and fortune.

Vikron formed in 1987 as a result of a band called Blessed Fury that Vick LeCar started back in 1985. "I was the primary writer and bandleader," Vick says. "The other band members felt that my writing was 'too commercial.' I have always believed that a song should be memorable, and in all honesty, let's just say that the other band members had 'problems' that clearly showed that music wasn't their first priority. So, I decided to start fresh with a new band. The band name is a play on this idea I had of a Viking and an avenging angel character. I know, you would think it's a play on my name, but it's not. One day, I was giving my friend Enzo a ride and I told him about it. I had gone through a few different ways of writing it and pronouncing it, but he told me that in order to pronounce Vikron, I had to get rid of the C after the I, and that's how the name was born.

When asked about Vikron's origins, he replies, "The formation of the band started when I ran into George Rodriguez, who aside from great drumming had an excellent way of organizing things. He was a huge help in that primary period of forming the band. Next, we auditioned bass players and found Joe D'Anduno, who was perfect for the vision. Next was the painful part: the lead singer. If auditioning every bass player in the Tri-State area seemed tough, the singer auditions were, let's say, a 'nut-cracking' experience. So, after countless auditions, this dude walks in, hyper as a squirrel on crack. He looked like a very young David Lee Roth and had a great personality to match. Brian 'Bri' G. Reskow. It was obvious that he was as nervous as a hooker in front of God, yet he was smooth in his delivery and pulled it off. I said to myself, 'This is the guy, we found him.' And that's how Vikron was born.

"Personally, I still love all the 'mother bands,'" Vick says about his influences. "Led Zeppelin, Deep Purple, Queen, and Black Sabbath. At the time, Mötley Crüe, Judas Priest, and the whole heavy metal scene were in full throttle, so we were collectively heavily influenced by them as well. The record that most influenced me, I have to say, was Deep Purple's *Machine Head*. Aside from the obvious magnitude of the album, the songs, the sounds, and the amazing mix of styles, from blues to classical to pop, into a heavy rock style that was so unique. You have solos that were delivered with such skill and feel. They really spoke to me. When I was a child, all I listened to was pop and classical music. Rock music was the first thing that made me feel untamed, ever. It's something that was in me, and rock music spoke to that. Now, take the guitar solo on 'Lazy,' for example—it starts with this mellow tone, yet it's aggressive at the same time. Then it explodes into this wild screaming solo. It really took me somewhere else. It made me become a better player, in that it pushed me to become obsessed with my playing."

As he's talking about the New Jersey scene in the eighties, Vick recalls, "Rock was king at the time. It was everywhere. Everyone played and looked the part. We always had a blast and had our own following. The locals always treated us great—they would even help us promote the band. Once, we did an interview at WDHA radio and fans showed up in the parking lot with homemade banners and jackets with the band's logo and were having a tailgating party. That's when I knew we were up to something. I believe if you give people great music and treat them well, you will have die-hard fans for life. To this day, I still get fans contacting me just to tell me how much Vikron meant to them.

"We regularly played a club called the Showplace in Dover, New Jersey," Vick adds. "It was awesome. So many great memories. The most memorable time that comes to mind right now is at this one show where Bri disappeared from the stage in the middle of a song. Oh, man! He felt into a hole that was in the middle of the stage covered by a very thin piece of plywood and a rug! But he kept on singing! Now that was a great show! And here's some rock 'n' roll trivia: that hole was originally made by Leslie West of Mountain. The club just never patched it up correctly!"

Vikron's story is reminiscent of other New Jersey bands (Heathen's Rage, Adrian Dodz, and Tantrum) that released their own records via a small record label (Rock Dream Records). Vikron, though, released it through Broccoli Rabe Records, a super-small label that also released other indie hard rock/metal bands like Sting, Broken Promises, and The Tans. "Without getting into too much detail, because it is unbelievable what goes into a DIY outfit, I have always been the kind of person to take matters into my own hands," Vick adds in regards to the release of their first and only seven-inch. "I didn't know anything about the business. We are talking nothing at all. All I knew was that professional bands write songs, record albums, and sell them, so I put together the songs I wanted for the 45 and we hit the studio hard. The production of the record began with song selection. We used to cover 'Long Cool Woman in a Black Dress' by The Hollies live and would receive a great response from the audience every time. That made it an easy choice for the record. Funny enough, we got more airplay with 'King of the City.' After song selection came the decision of where to record, of course. Luckily, in the same building as the rehearsal studio was Broccoli Rabe Studios. It was brand new, and everything was state-of-the-art. Beautiful place! Obviously, it was the right choice.

"But there was one problem," he goes on. "We began recording, and while getting the drum sounds, I noticed the in-house engineer had a know-it-all attitude. Quite arrogant. So, I had to hire an outsider who was familiar with rock music and works more than he talks. Enter Bill Berends. Sonically, for the gearheads out there, we chose Ampex two-inch tape after trying many different tapes. I used a Marshall JCM900 4100 and a Kramer Barretta guitar. Candy-apple red really makes a difference. This is pre-white Les Paul. Hard to imagine life without my Les Paul...

"The release was interesting, in the self-promotion aspect," Vick continues. "Major labels ran the show, as we all know. The footwork is unlike anything we do digitally today. Almost everything was done in person, face to face. We called every radio station in the Tri-State area. We went down to every record store we could find, and they would accept the record on consignment only. Doing everything yourself teaches you a lot, which I think is great. That's today's standard, and I think it allows artists like myself to release things unfiltered."

So, Vikron released in 1986 their only seven-inch, *King of the City/Long Cool Woman in a Black Dress*, which contained the aforementioned Hollies cover plus their own original song. Mixing Judas Priest with Mötley Crüe, 1980s melodic American metal is written all over them both. It's not something crucial to a collection, but it's definitely enjoyable: "King of the City" is memorable and presents a band that had potential to progress further.

"There may have been some bands in our area that released their own records, but I was not aware," Vick admits. "It was unheard of at the time, because what East Coast bands were shooting for were demos to impress record executives, in order to get signed to a major label. Which is completely understandable. What you have to understand is that at the time, there was a mold for artistry. A 'mother band' would set the standards, and record companies were only interested in cashing in on the trend and not developing a new artist and the musical vision. The art of being an original band has always been very simple in my eyes. Be yourself, genuine. Follow your vision. Never compromise. And that's it! There is such excitement when you are creating your own music and then to see and hear your musical vision come alive."

Vikron kept playing shows locally until 1989, and then faded away. Vick LeCar went on to play with the (much better) Platinum, releasing one pretty good heavy/power metal LP on Rising Sun (*Iceman* in 1990), as well as pursuing a solo musical career and releasing several of his own CDs.

CUT TO THE CHASE:

Vikron's only effort is a good but not too memorable release; I will rate it as a must for completists, but other than that, it's simply okay, melodic heavy metal. However, *King of the City/ Long Cool Woman in a Black Dress* is very pricey, so good luck. And fans of heavy/power metal will definitely enjoy Platinum's *Iceman* LP.

"The resurgence of classic heavy metal is great," says Vick. "I think it's great to see that our hard work was not in vain. What is really interesting is that these bands and records were not signed to majors nor heavily promoted by labels. Which goes to prove that even if it's indie, it will rise up if it's great music. Who knew that our seven-inch would be today a collector's item? Ha! I could use a new Corvette. All joking aside, it feels great, and I am very appreciative of the fans. Especially knowing how hard it is to find this 45, seeing people going to great lengths is unbelievable."

On the subject of the current metal scene, Vick responds: "There are pockets of people all around the world who love rock and metal. There are also many musicians and artists, both old and new, continuing the tradition. Just look at the rock and metal festivals across the globe! When I go on tour, I always hear bands complaining about charts and what's happening in the mainstream. It's an epidemic! Focusing on the wrong aspects. Range. Technical ability. Gear. Style. Yes, that's all important. But if there is one piece of advice that I pass on to all the artists I meet, it is to focus on the songwriting. The song. You can be amazing in any other aspect, but the vehicle that brings that to the people is THE SONG. Without that, you really have nothing at all. With that said, it really angers me that not just my own but ALL of our efforts—hours of work, years of developing craft, and dedication to music—gets stolen by online pickpockets. Luckily, we have artists in the community like Steven Tyler working on projects such as the Music Modernization Act (MMA). We need more people getting involved in that aspect. What we are asking for is fairness in our business."

He adds, "On the other hand, streaming is a great way to share music with fans around the globe. But when it comes to paying for music, it seems no one wants to take out their credit card. Try that with anything else! It comes down to understanding that is our work and how we make our living. If record companies can find a model that works for both the record company and artist, things would be very different. But nowadays, they are practically useless. They take no risks on anything new. And I'll say it again: Fair. So, it has come full circle. Releasing your own music and managing your own business was and always will be the way in my eyes. Cheers and long live rock 'n' roll!"

BLACK DIAMOND (NY)

THE HISTORY OF PRIVATELY RELEASED AMERICAN METAL CONTAINS MANY stories about bands formed by childhood friends; this is also the case with Black Diamond, named after the Kiss song, who hailed from Long Island. Guitarist and vocalist Bobby Huber tells their story:

"I was friends with Patrick Hull since we were kids. We grew up in Farmingdale, New York. He began playing the drums and I began playing the electric guitar. I was 13 at the time. It was 1976. I didn't even know how to tune it when I first started out! I was mesmerized by the sounds I was able to create, and I was instantly hooked. At the time, we were both huge Beatles fans ... I would try emulating their moves and style. That guitar was absolutely horrible to play. Many of my classmates had started playing at that time as well. We used to trade off ideas and learn from each other. I used to spend hours just sitting in my room learning every inch of the fretboard. Never took a lesson, just loved to play. I eventually saved up enough of my paper route money to buy my first real guitar, a Gibson S-1. We hooked up with a bass player named Jimmy. I remember borrowing Kiss' *Alive II* from Pat, who kept telling me how great they were. When I put that album on and started gazing at the pictures in the album, I was instantly hooked on them. My musical interests took a whole new direction. We played our first gig when I was 15. It was a Sweet 16 party in a backyard. We played our butts off, doing everything from Zeppelin to Skynyrd. I remember walking out of there with my amp in a wagon. There was a large crowd out front in the street. We walked out and someone yelled, 'Where's the rest of the band?' What a great feeling that was for me.

"We named the band Black Diamond and gained a local following," Bobby continues. "There were lots of other local bands that were formed by people I'd played around with early on. I found myself writing a lot of my own material that we worked into our playlists. After a while, we only did my originals. I didn't want to be a cover band when I had the ability to write. People seemed to love the music we were making, so I kept at it. It seemed like second nature to grab a guitar and come up with a cool riff. The lyrics seemed to come to me out of nowhere. The band matured, and our musical influences did as well. I started scouring the local record store for albums and bands that piqued my interest, which included UFO, Judas Priest, Scorpions, and a few other obscure bands. I think UFO's *Strangers in the Night* really moved me the most. We also loved the heavyweights at that time, like Black Sabbath, Led Zeppelin, and—believe it or not—a couple of Southern rock bands. Southern rock was huge in my high school in the late 1970s and early 1980s."

Black Diamond's lineup comprised the aforementioned Bobby Huber on vocals/guitars, Pat Hull on drums/vocals, and Vinny Torretta on bass (Joey D. Uttarro, later of the band Uttarro, was a member for some time as well), and as a trio, they released their one and only *Black Diamond* LP in 1982, on their own label, Diamond Records. "That record was the number-one requested album on some metal station in the Midwest for months!" Bobby laughs. "A few local New York bands had released private-label stuff as well, but I don't think they really took off."

To this day, *Black Diamond* remains a stone-cold classic of the early era of American metal; it's actually very intriguing when you listen to it and find out it's a full-on 1970s metal and NWOBHM band, right on the verge of the American metal explosion, playing the purest form of pre-true metal. Don't expect crazy rhythms, galloping drums, or high-pitched vocals—this is just heavy metal reminiscent of early Manilla Road, Black Sabbath (fans of their seventies albums will especially enjoy this), Kiss, Deep Purple, and seventies-era Rainbow. Songs like "Now and Forever" stand out as solid rockers, with a total NWOBHM approach that kind of reminds me of the same atmosphere Trespass had on *One of These Days*. Meanwhile, "Mezmerizor" is like a mix of Judas Priest and Black Sabbath, a charming tune with simple but very effective riffs. The album's closing number, "Last Dream," is really its highlight: heavy metal filled with passion that starts out slow, vast, and murky and progresses into a total epic powerhouse, with a marching drum beat. Absolutely spectacular!

Sadly, Black Diamond didn't quit their day jobs—but they kept releasing some quality metal music until disbanding in the 1980s. Bobby admits: "I am thrilled with the resurgence of interest in bands and music like ours. I think people have become inundated with the stuff that's out there. Those days brought forth some of the best talent around. We don't really have music or musicians like that anymore. Music no longer comes from the heart. Today, musicians (if you want to call them that) are just looking to write Top 40 hits. They want money—understandably, of course—but the real grit that makes great music is long gone. I believe the masses are craving something different. Unfortunately, there is not much being created today that feeds that hunger. That is what is driving people to the past. To go back to the music that actually had meaning and substance. So, yes, I do believe this underground scene exists. People are thumbing through albums again. Looking for an interesting record or band to explore, just like I did back in the day. Rather than listen to what Disney says we should listen to.

CUT TO THE CHASE:

You simply can't ignore Black Diamond's only LP if you're a fan of pre-1983 American true metal. Very heavy, very atmospheric, and with that weird edge that will give you goosebumps, *Black Diamond* is wholeheartedly recommended to everyone into the true metal sound. It's definitely above par, to say the least, with some moments that are actually breathtaking!

"Another issue," he adds, "is that downloading music is both good and bad. Unfortunately for musicians, who depend on making a living with it, they're losing out. The only way to make money now is by gigging. There are too many cover bands and tribute bands out there. The artistry in writing is slim to none. The plus side of downloads is the ease of acquiring songs that you may have otherwise never heard."

Already in their mid-sixties, the Black Diamond members still remain friends, and guess what—they are somehow back! "We are still at it. Just recorded a new album. We have since changed the name to Storm Beneath. We are beginning to play the local circuit again, which, by the way, seems to be thriving! Speaking of downloads, our album *Out From Under* is available on iTunes. Believe it or not, there are a couple of songs on there from our original album, *Black Diamond*."

DARKSTARR

ONE OF THE MOST BELOVED HOLY GRAILS OF HEAVY METAL COLLECTORS worldwide is DarkStarr's twelve-inch EP. DarkStarr was formed by guitarist Dave Sestito in 1980. Dave had previously been in a band called Reostat in Fairport, New York, with bassist Phil Newton. Shortly after Reostat broke up, Dave recruited his old bass player, Phil, and then found local drum legend John Schalaci. The trio jammed on mostly original songs and a few cover songs—hard rock with a touch of Pink Floyd sprinkled in—and played significant free-form jams in many of the songs. Later that year, Sestito heard John Meyers playing folk guitar and singing at a friend's party and was extremely impressed, thinking that John was the missing component that could complete the band. He approached John that evening, but John said he wasn't interested in joining a band. Finally, after several weeks of Sestito's prodding, John agreed to jam with the trio and joined the band shortly afterward. Through multiple jam sessions, the band began to click and developed a unique sound, style, direction, and chemistry—and DarkStarr was formed.

"I wanted to play music for a living from a very young age," Dave says. "The guitar I picked up at eight years old was actually my brother's guitar. He didn't play it much, and I seemed to be a natural at it. I started taking lessons by nine years old, but I was too impatient to read music. I remember asking the music teacher to just show me some chords so I could get started. I eventually dropped lessons and learned to play by ear, plus I learned from jamming with other local musicians who played better than me. Later on, I began to write my own songs. I believed in original music and wanted to blend the sounds of the times along with my own styles, plus express my feelings and tell my stories and observations using music."

Dave says, "As for DarkStarr, we took the most influence from Rush, UFO, and Pink Floyd. Guitarists' sounds like Alex Lifeson, Michael Schenker, and David Gilmour were a huge influence and can be heard throughout DarkStarr's music, blended with my own playing and the band's overall style. No particular record made an impression over another per se. All music back then was interesting and dynamic in one way or another, and the band was open to many styles."

DarkStarr started playing shows since the very start, mostly in the Northeast. "Back then, there was a thriving live music scene that welcomed both cover songs and originals," Dave adds. "In the beginning, people used to enjoy DarkStarr playing cover songs like Rush, Judas Priest, Pink Floyd, Joe Walsh, and others. However, after the DarkStarr record was released and played on WCMF 96 radio, fans came out in great numbers to hear our originals. DarkStarr was treated like celebrities and highly regarded, especially in our home area of Upstate New York. Fans would buy drinks for the band, lined up on stage, and ask us to autograph posters and records! It was a wonderful time."

DarkStarr's first music appearance on a record was their track "On the Road Again" which was included along with several other local bands' songs on a compilation album called *WCMF 96: Homegrown 2* in 1981. Dave explains how they then decided to release a record on their own:

"Once we had enough original music to record our own full record, John Meyers' brother became a money backer in New York City and funded the recording of the first DarkStarr record. It was recorded and produced at PCI Recording in Rochester, New York. The record was sold locally and in the United States by several sales reps and agents associated with the band. The record eventually found its way into Europe, where it gained a following, but by the time Europe was ready for the band to tour, the band had broken up. We would have preferred to enlist a record company versus private press, but releasing it directly had advantages that left the band in control of the sales, distribution, and profits from the records. In hindsight, engaging a record company would have expanded sales and the band's following much faster."

This precious little diamond, the 1982 *DarkStarr* twelve-inch EP, was released on the band's label, Galaxy Records, and is a prototype of hard-to-heavy metal crossover. While overall it's not flawless, it has at least three songs that every metalhead into this kind of stuff should listen to. What's very exciting in this case is that they manage to combine the European heavy sound of NWOBHM and Black Sabbath with the more melodic American hard rock sound, and they do it in a very stylish and posh way. The album's opening "My Deepest Regrets" is a pounding heavy metal number, and maybe the best they ever wrote. Amazing stuff. "Finding My Way"

CUT TO THE CHASE:

I don't think anyone into the heavy/hard rock sound won't at least love some of the tunes off DarkStarr's only release! It's a minor classic of the American private metal genre, but it can be really pricey to get the original—so why not get the Cult Metal Classics reissue? It's the music that counts, and in the case of *DarkStarr*, it is absolutely exciting. Fans of NWOBHM, you'll love it.

kicks off like a ballad before growing into a heavy rocker monster, whereas the amazing "Hard Rocker" kind of reminds me of Thin Lizzy's more metallic material. Actually, the only mediocre song on this twelve-inch is "Stand Aside."

Pelican Productions, the band's management company, saw the band's large fan base and club draws. They began booking the band heavily at three to five nights a week. Unfortunately, Pelican took the commission proceeds and invested them into pop band Duke Jupiter. Pelican was looking for a pop chart payoff instead of promoting DarkStarr in a longer-term effort in the rock world. In early 1983, Dave Sestito was laid off from his full-time job and began managing the band. By this time, the band was getting tired and had little time to write new songs. It had been three solid years of heavy playing and travel, with no help or focus from Pelican Productions to propel the band forward. Dave recognized that playing in the Northeast and the poor performance from their current agent were not doing the band justice. He tried to move the band to California, where the music scene was flourishing and there were good rock agents available, but unfortunately, he was too late. John Meyers had had enough and wanted out, and the rest of the band members were tired and wanted a break. The band officially played their last show in 1983.

"Our largest, most memorable show was opening for The Rods," Dave recalls with a huge smile on his face. "They pulled up in a limousine and we were all really impressed, but also a little depressed, seeing as all we had was an old van that we all had to cram into. The stage was much larger than we were used to and it took a song or two to get the mix and blend right. However, the audience loved DarkStarr, and we made quite an impression at that show!

"I can recall quite a few bands that also released their records on their own," Dave adds. "A band called Cheater from Rochester was another local band that put out original music. The guitarist for Cheater was named Don Mancuso, and he would go on to play for a band called Black Sheep, which had a record and label. The Black Sheep singer was Rochester native Lou Gramm. They broke up after their equipment truck broke down on the way to a major gig and everything unraveled. Eventually Lou Gramm auditioned for the band Foreigner and got the part, which obviously became a huge success. I still go out to hear Don Mancuso play in local venues now and then and we talk about the old days."

Approximately five years after their breakup, a record executive in California heard the DarkStarr record and was very interested in DarkStarr reuniting to make a new record. By that time, they had disbanded and some members had moved out of state. Timing and fate just missed aligning to relight the DarkStarr ... but at least Greek label Cult Metal Classics reissued their *DarkStarr* twelve-inch in 2020!

"It is good to see resurgence toward some very good writing and musicianship from decades ago," Dave says. "Back then, you recorded live on tape with little edits and overdubs. There was no pitch correction, no lining up any timing that's off, and no correction of instrument sounds. What was recorded is what was heard: a raw but true sound. It's an honor that DarkStarr is included in a wave of collectors who treasure and appreciate original music from the 1980s era."

When asked his opinions on the current state of underground music, Dave replies, "There is a huge underground music scene that has expanded over the years. This is a wonderful thing, to preserve music of the past and appreciate the musicianship that went into it. I do think the internet makes it easier to be heard and discovered today. Back in the 1980s, during the DarkStarr era, you had to promote yourself by playing live and through newspapers, posters, radio, and word of mouth. It was very difficult and took more time to gain notoriety and grow a following. On the other hand, I don't appreciate free music downloading at all. This is the sweat and hard work of artists who are already undercompensated for the many years of hardship and expense it takes to hone their arts and skills. It should not be exploited for free. Even now, my company DLS Effects (www.dlseffects.com) designs and produces guitar effects for some very big artists like Alex Lifeson, Frank Hannon of Tesla, Styx, Rascal Flatts, Daughtry, and many others. I still purchase their CDs even when they offer them for free. This is to help support their art—and the hardships they endured along the way!"

STRANGE FLESH

I WAS TORN ON WHETHER TO INCLUDE STRANGE FLESH FROM PROVIDENCE, Rhode Island, in this book or in my last book *Crossover The Edge*. My decision to include them in *Heroes of the Underground* was based on the fact that Strange Flesh were mostly a metal rather than a hardcore/punk band, even though they included such elements, and even though they seemed to be mainstays of the hardcore/punk scene—as well as their whole aesthetic. It was very metal in lyrics and imagery. Strange Flesh formed in 1983, and their second vocalist, Graham Batting, has more than a few words to say about their story:

"I first heard of Strange Flesh in 1984 when I was a student at University of Bridgeport in Connecticut. I had been active in punk and hardcore since the late 1970s, and even though I had moved on from hardcore and was getting more into metal, I still went to see shows at underground clubs. A friend at school suggested we go to the Anthrax club in Stamford,

Connecticut, to see a show—one of the opening bands was called Strange Flesh, and we had a good laugh at that name. We got to the show, and the live Strange Flesh show was pretty funny to us. They were a three-piece punk band with two girls on guitar and bass and a very uptight-looking guy on drums. My friend Karen and I got the impression that it was a lesbian act who'd quite possibly enslaved a man to fill out the rhythm section, as the songs were a bit harsh, excessively confrontational, and generally displeased with the state of things in general. Both girls were hurling insults at anybody who'd walked in or out of the club during their set, saying things like 'Sorry we're not young boys with hooded sweatshirts and high-top sneakers!' They seemed pretty bitter, and the music wasn't that great. Nevertheless, I couldn't turn away; it was a glorious disaster.

"Fast-forward three years, or maybe two and a half. I'd been kicked out of University of Bridgeport after just the one year and had moved back to Providence, Rhode Island. I was a dishwasher by day and a barfly by night, where I met a kid named Mark Mathieu who was dating my friend Kelly, who played bass for my friends' band Coat of Arms. I soon learned he was playing guitar for Strange Flesh, which gave me a good laugh. 'Are they still lesbians?' I asked, to which he said that the drummer and bass player were actually Steve and Julie Parker, husband and wife, and it was they who had started the band many years before. My assumption was way off-base! He had replaced a guy named Paul Feta who'd replaced the girl I saw playing guitar at the Anthrax. We soon found out we both shared a love of the new crossover metal born out of hardcore, and he petitioned the band to give me an audition on vocals as I'd sang for Rhode Island's first hardcore band, the Idle Rich, from 1981 to 1986 (with a two-year gap in the middle). The audition went well, and in the spring of 1987, I was the new lead vocalist of the band I'd laughed at three years prior!"

The final lineup of Strange Flesh included Julie Parker (bass), Steve Parker (drums), Don Sanders (guitars), Mark Mathieu (guitars), and Graham Batting (vocals), and Graham says: "My first show with Strange Flesh was in late May of 1987, opening for Dirty Rotten Imbeciles at the Living Room in Providence, which was somewhat poetic, as I had done the illustration for D.R.I.'s three-song *Violent Pacification* seven-inch four years before. My drawing was supposed to be the cover art, but the postal service was slow in delivering my illustration in time for the EP to go to press, so they made it the lyric sheet graphic as well as printing up T-shirts of it. Now I was going to be in the local opening act for D.R.I., which had since grown in stature. That first show was insane with well over 800 in attendance. I remember looking out at the crowd halfway through our set, a seething throng of punks and metalheads churning en masse and screaming for more, and feeling like I was home at last."

Graham continues: "After a few shows, I got the idea that my friend Don Sanders, who'd been guitarist for the Idle Rich, might be the perfect addition to the group, as he was insanely good on guitar both rhythmically as well as on solos. I knew he might find our format a tad sophomoric, but he was always up for a laugh and at that point not doing anything musically, so we arranged an audition for him after Mark and I taught him a few of the songs. I remember the feeling that night at our warehouse rehearsal space after Don plugged in and ripped into the songs; we had something potentially big, and it was all coming together. You could see the difference in the next few shows we played. The kids went from mental to ballistic, and

CUT TO THE CHASE:

Yep, I know, the hammer will fall on me for adding Strange Flesh to this book. However, you should get their 1987 EP if you love bands like Knightmare (Manchester, New Hampshire), early Exciter, Warfare, Iron Gypsy, and of course, Motörhead. There are still copies of the *Strange Flesh* seven-inch floating around out there.

they were actually screaming for encores. Musically, I didn't think we had anything special to offer, but we all performed with sincerity and an intense desire to make our shows, more than anything, fun.

"The band with that lineup would not make it to 1988," Graham sighs. "In early November of '87, we went on a ten-day tour with dates in West Virginia, Tennessee, Nebraska, Missouri, and Pennsylvania, and the shows were well attended and well received. We sold a lot of records and T-shirts, but by the third night, Steve and Julie were booking Mark, Don, and myself into one motel and then taking off to find one for themselves without telling us where. Julie was not a fan of the drunken antics of the two guitar players and myself. I don't really blame her. The apogee of her frustration peaked after our Nashville gig at the motel after the show. I had passed out on a folding cot, only to be awakened by Steve screaming at Mark and Don while holding one of my ankles in the air and pointing at my crotch.

"'What the hell is going on?' I mumbled.

"'LOOK AT WHAT THEY DID TO YOU!!!' Steve screamed, still pointing at my crotch. This was when I realized I had no pants on, Julie wasn't currently in the room, and the room's door was open to the parking lot. I sat up to see what Steve was pointing at, my one leg still elevated by him, and discovered that Don and Mark had used indelible ink markers to redecorate my testicles: one red, one black.

"'DO YOU THINK THAT'S FUNNY??!' Steve screamed at me.

"'Well ... yes?' I replied.

"'WELL, I DON'T!!!' he bellowed, slamming my foot back down to the cot. 'AND IT'S INCREDIBLY DISRESPECTFUL TO JULIE!' he continued, then went on ranting for a few minutes before leaving with Julie for a new motel. The three of us giggled like naughty kids who had just been yelled at by their dad. After the tour, I knew we were never going to play together again. Everyone knew it. It's a shame because we were on our way to something, and there's no one to blame; it was just bad chemistry."

In 1987, Strange Flesh released a record on their own label, Death Head Records, and Graham discusses the process behind this seven-inch release:

"The idea to put out the record was Steve's; he had done all the research and cost analysis. I have no idea how he found out about Frank Gardner's basement studio, as I was often drunk back in those days, so information of any real value was fleeting at best, if Steve ever even told me. We would've loved to put out a full-length LP, but it just wasn't in our budget range. We figured we could do a full-length record later on and maybe find a label to assist, and in the meantime, our little record would aid in that venture. We recorded our three-song seven-inch EP in August of 1987, having debated which songs should be on the release for a few weeks prior during rehearsals. Our practice space was in an old mill building in the Olneyville section of Providence, where you could almost throw a saddle on the rats, and the rents in the neighborhood were as cheap as the prostitutes hanging around the dollar store. There were no acoustics in our space, and I screamed the vocals through a small practice amp, engulfed by the tornado of sound produced by a twin-guitar attack, bass, and drums."

Graham continues, "It never occurred to any of us that we hadn't clearly heard what we sounded like, that is until we got into the studio. I think we were all a little surprised at how good we sounded. Not great, but good enough. Steve's drumming was full and robust, whereas when we played live or at practice, we'd only heard the extreme highs and lows. Julie's bass playing was way more complex than previously suspected—she was all over those scales at just the right time and her sound was punchy and fat. The perfect thunder for the guitars' lightning. Mark's rhythm guitar work provided the blistering fuzz, while Don's searing leads were the bionics. We needed to build ourselves better, faster, stronger. It was a shock that took a few takes to get over, but we smashed through the basic tracks in one day.

"The vocals were, for me anyway, a bit of a trick," Graham adds. "This was the first time I, or anybody else in the band, had heard the vocals clearly. For the most part prior to recording, I'd been screaming to be heard, whether at rehearsals or live shows, but now everything was as clear as crystal ... and a bit disorienting. It was also the first time the other band members had heard my lyrics, and I took a good bit of ribbing for it too; at one point, while listening to the playbacks, Steve turned to Mark, saying, 'How can you sit back and mentally relax knowing what you were before?' making fun of my lyrics on the song 'Something's Wrong.'

"'Gates of Hell' was written by Steve years before I'd joined the band," Graham says. "They had recorded it previously for a demo tape with Steve singing from behind the drums, but now we had the opportunity to really get ridiculous and decided to add 'secret messages' and a goofy faux-Latin prayer to Satan at the end. The song was a fan favorite that we always ended our live sets with, so we felt honor-bound to give the kids some next-level nonsense as thanks for their support. During the intro breakdown, if you listen carefully, you can hear Steve, Mark, and Don ominously chanting the pre-chorus: 'Do you fear him? Are you scared? Get down on your knees, boy, it's about to begin!' Then just before the vocals come in, you can hear Don 'screaming' as his soul falls into Hell. Really scary stuff! For the ending, Mark scribbled out some Latin phrases he remembered from his days at Catholic school and handed me the paper, saying, 'Grammatically, it's not correct, but it'll do.' After telling the engineer what we wanted to do, he threw on some vocal effects and we added the 'satanic chant' during the cacophonous outro. I personally loved the effect because it sounded like the demons from *The Evil Dead*, which was one of my favorite movies. Don, Mark, and Steve also threw in some chants of 'Satan... Satan... Satan...' that you can barely hear as the song dies out. Julie opted not to take part in any of this tomfoolery, which was a portent of things to come. When we listened to the final playback, we were rolling on the ground giggling like four-year-olds who'd just heard the word *doody*."

Graham was already a pretty notorious artist in the underground punk, hardcore, and metal scene, having created many flyers among other works, so he was the one who created the visual art for Strange Flesh. "While the record was being pressed, Steve and I coordinated the sleeve design, logo, and lyric sheet. I had done illustrations for D.R.I., Verbal Assault, a bunch of flyer art for bands like Bad Religion and the Adolescents, so here was my opportunity to craft the look of a band I was actually in. It was a lot of pressure. For the band's logo, I wanted it to look unique. Aggressive without being too over-the-top or corny. A lot of the new metal bands were trying a bit too hard with some of the logo design back then; it was the dawn of the viney, spikey logos you could barely read, so I wanted something high-impact yet low on cheese factor. Furthermore, everyone in the band came from a punk rock background, so we weren't inherently metal to begin with. I'd been a huge horror fanatic my whole life, so I decided to emulate the fonts that were popular on the horror novel covers of the day. I added a few fangy-looking spikes, just to make it a little extra dangerous for the viewer's eyeballs.

"For the cover illustration, I copied myself," Graham adds. "I had designed an evil screaming face for a friend's fanzine three years prior that never came out, so I had this unused artwork lying around. I redrew it, but this time, I added some horns ... because, you know ... evil. For the back cover, I used one of my bats that I'd been doodling in sketchbooks for years—these guys would show up randomly on the corners of pages or in the margins of notebooks, and now I had a chance to use one on our release. With all that taken care of, we just had to wait for the vinyl ... but there was a problem when it finally showed up. We put the record on the turntable, and while it sounded like the master tape, it was awfully quiet. I mean, sure, you could turn the volume up to hear it loud, but you'd have to remember to turn the stereo down before you put another record on—otherwise, you'll blow out your speakers. This was a huge disappointment, and we didn't have the time or the resources to figure out why this happened or to fix it. It was one of those like-it-or-lump-it moments that you just roll with, but for our genre, it was a particularly unfortunate faux pas. It became glaringly obvious when DJs would play it on local college radio stations back in those analog days; it's kind of hard to convey you're a scary crossover hardcore/metal band when R.E.M. comes on afterward and blows you out of the water. We lamented to ourselves that all of this would be fixed when we record our full-length album ... but that would never happen."

The *Strange Flesh* 1987 seven-inch is quite a fascinating release—at least if you like your metal raw and dirty. Do you remember Canadian bands like Iron Head or Iron Gypsy? If you do, you get the clue. There's a huge dose of Motörhead in Strange Flesh's sound, but you can also hear the echoes of early Iron Maiden as well as touches of the crossover era of Agnostic Front (*Cause for Alarm*) and Crumbsuckers. I know that die-hard metalheads are not fond at all of all this stuff, but the whole feeling here is 100 percent metal: the aesthetics, the 'evil' sound—everything here oozes metal. I'm very fond of the crossover stuff, and actually, alongside the early hardcore and the indie/punk crossover genre, the crossover between hardcore and metal is my all-time favorite genre. The opening "Decline" is a total Motörhead-based anthem, whereas "Gates of Hell" sounds like Cro-Mags going evil metal, and the closing "Something Wrong" sounds like a more metallic (and much tamer) Crumbsuckers.

"The apogee of our absurdity came on the day of our three-song seven-inch single release party," Graham laughs. "We had recorded the songs in August of 1987 in the basement home studio of Frank Gardner, and on September 27th, we headlined a matinee show at the Rocket in downtown Providence. We had spent the previous night as well as that morning stuffing records into sleeves while drinking beer and watching professional wrestling on TV. One wrestler, 'The Million Dollar Man' Ted DiBiase, captured our attention in particular because he would pull audience members into the ring to humiliate them for money. We thought that was great! So, when Don broke a string during our fourth song, we decided to incorporate some of that debasement into our set. Steve pulled out a five-dollar bill from his pocket, and I defied the audience to produce a sniveling pathetic worm to lick the sweat off my bare foot in front of the entire assembly. We didn't have to wait long: A young blonde girl cut a swath through the crowd, from the back of the room to the front, hurling herself onto the stage, and we had ourselves the loser we'd hoped for.

"As I mentioned previously, I was a dishwasher by day, and it being the summer, my feet were particularly ripe," Graham says. "Nevertheless, all she had to do was lick the bottom of my foot a few times and the fiver was hers. Once my sock and sneaker were removed, I offered my foot to the kneeling lass while holding onto Mark and Steve, who stood aside me for support. Suddenly, my foot disappeared into the young woman's throat ... she was into it. I was unprepared for this development and started to panic a bit, but the room was going bananas. People started throwing beer all over the place and the roar was deafening. I tried to shake my foot loose, but the young lady would not relent, and she kept sucking on my foot as if it was a popsicle. Finally, she let me go and snatched the five bucks, along with my sock, and disappeared into the cheering horde.

"After our set," Graham says, "I was at the bar with my girlfriend and the foot-sucker appeared, asking me to autograph my own sock, which I did. After she left, a nearby patron suggested that signing the sock might've been done in error, as the girl was heavy into Satanism and black magic and the chances my sock would end its day on an altar were strong. Who cares, though—we all had a blast that afternoon! By the fall, we had built up a pretty strong fan base and our shows were consistently well-attended affairs. We found similar crowds in some nearby out-of-state venues, particularly in Burlington, Vermont, where we had a strong following. Musically, we shamelessly copped riffs from bands like the Cro-Mags and the Mentors, though lyrically, the songs swung between sincere soul-searching, like in 'Something's Wrong,' to the absurd, such as our fan favorite, 'Gates of Hell'—which we'd intentionally served up as the satanic fare that organizations such as the PMRC (Parents Music Resource Center) were so terrified of corrupting our nation's youth."

The crazy days of Strange Flesh were over, and Graham concludes: "Following the break of that lineup, we all went our separate ways. Don, Mark, and I toyed with the idea of starting a new band with a different bassist and drummer called Bloodweiser, but it fizzled out after a couple of drunken rehearsals. Don went on to start Medicine Ball with the old bass player from the Idle Rich days. Mark never found another band to join. I joined a local metal band called R.O.T. but suggested we change the name to Mechanikill, which we did, but after a year of practicing and only playing out a couple of times, that collapsed. Steve and Julie continued on as Strange Flesh, but it was never the same, at least from my perspective.

"By 1991," he says, "I quit music altogether, not really enjoying the direction 'underground' was taking. It was all a sham at that point. Sure, you could still find some amazing musicians or bands that had an original sound or style, but there was overexposure from media outlets, little to no interest from younger fans in the roots/organics/influences of underground music, and just too many bands. Everyone was in a band. Folks always talked about the scene, how it's so important to support the scene. In my day, you didn't even think about a 'scene.' If you loved music, you sought it out; nothing or no one could stop you from finding it. Your parents could smash your records, concerned politicians could campaign about the evil and sin hidden in the new music that was perverting the youth, but none of this could stop you. You found the music and you loved it. By the early nineties, everything had become commodified, everything had turned into a pantomime of those it genuinely inspired, it was all style/little substance. A kid could go to the mall and buy whatever costume they desired, join whatever tribe they fancied, and find validation on music television channels that transmitted the uniform, protocol, and locations for these pantomimes. The joy of discovery was domesticated. Joe Strummer called it: they'd turned rebellion into money. It went from music creating a scene to the scene creating neutered music. People were throwing bands together just so they could play out, with no attention to developing a sound. They all sounded the same; they all looked the same."

As for their only release, Graham adds, "From time to time, I'll get a text or email from a friend who found our record in a used record store or a yard sale; it's weirdly comforting to see it pop up so many years later, never knowing where or when that will be. I also (rarely) get contacted through social media from someone who discovered the EP and wants to know if I'm 'the guy from Strange Flesh.' You realize that was the point of the whole thing: you and your bandmates were trying to make somebody's day a little ... different. Not necessarily better or worse, but something that made them take notice. The idea that our record is a collector's item defies sanity. When I hear this, all I can think about is Mark, Don, and I stranded at the Admiral Benbow Inn in Memphis, Tennessee, taking photos of trophy-class bowel movements and using 12-ounce cans of Budweiser for scale, or firing bottle rockets at the gas station across the parking lot while innocent travelers tried to fuel up their vehicles. It's funny what you think is funny when you're young, drunk, and don't own anything.

"Strange Flesh has become part of my identity, even though it has been 32 years since putting mouth to microphone with them," Graham responds when asked about his best shows. "Some of my fondest memories are with the band. There was the time we opened up for the Mentors, and backstage, Il Duce let us tap his big fat belly. So many friends of the band were concerned the Mentors would sexually assault Julie, but they were nothing but gentlemen to her. Or the time we opened for the Exploited during the height of the AIDS crisis: the show promoter was handing out prophylactics at the door and gave us a whole box to 'distribute' from the stage. We threw hundreds of packets of rubbers into the audience, thinking we'd done our part, but minutes later, the condoms returned to the stage, inflated and bobbing and bouncing around like some perverted episode of *The Lawrence Welk Show* while we ripped through our set. There was the show in Lincoln, Nebraska, in the basement of the local community center, which was a basketball court: no stage, no barrier. We set up under one of the backboards. When we started our set, there was a polite separation between fan and band, but the kids kept inching closer and closer. By the end of our set, we were swarmed—surrounded by the punks and metalheads, all going berserk right alongside the band. I've never experienced anything like it before or since: a crowd comprising a small portion of performers and the majority fans, all equal. A massive throng pounding it out, no stage, no division. Kids who I would never see again, but for that one night, and we surged like old friends who hadn't seen each other for decades. It was a shared love of intensity and music, we'd all been looking for it for years and were finally finding each other: monster music for lonely kids.

"Upstairs and outside that little Lincoln, Nebraska, community center, cornfields stretched in every direction into the darkness. Later that night, after the show, some kids came back to the motel with us to drink beer and hang out. One of the kids' mothers had sent him to the show with a care package of food, figuring we would need it ... which we did! Among the food items was a package of American cheese; we melted a slice on a lightbulb on one of the lamps in the room. The lightbulb exploded and the room was plunged into darkness!"

BLACK VIRGIN

BLACK VIRGIN WAS A BAND THAT I WAS RELUCTANT TO INCLUDE IN MY FIRST book, *Crossover The Edge*, and I can safely say that they fall right in between that book and *Heroes of the Underground*. However, I chose to include them here because they are much more metal than punk, plus they released a self-financed seven-inch! Formed around March 20th, 1982 (memorably right after the death of Randy Rhoads), Black Virgin were a New York City band that kept it together for quite a while. Cathy Burke (drums) was in a punk band called The Reactors that released *The Seduction Center* seven-inch in 1979 and just happened to take an ad out to jam in a three-piece unit. That's when Kenny Lienhardt (vocals, guitars) and Jimmy Strain (on bass, and now in the still-active power thrashers Forsakken) auditioned her. Kenny and Jimmy had a band named Voltage in the early days before Black Virgin, but they'd had trouble keeping a drummer after their first drummer went off to the Navy. When Cathy was hired, the name changed to Black Virgin.

Joe Cerna, the second bassist for Black Virgin, explains, "Life on the streets of the Bronx was hard, all of us just surviving and being rebellious, and having to defend ourselves. Our lyrics reflected rebellious anthems at everyday injustices in life, on the streets, and in our city of five boroughs, New York City. Kenny was good at journalism through college, so he had a unique charm and savvy for lyrics, not to mention we were all metal and punk fans. I joined in 1984."

BLACK VIRGIN FLYER "JUSTICE FOR GERMANY" 1991 TOUR

As for Black Virgin's influences, Joe adds, "It would have been groups like the Dead Boys, Girlschool, Motörhead, Ramones. These were our initial influences as well as some early thrash/hardcore à la Suicidal Tendencies, Cro-Mags, and hard rock like AC/DC. There are too many to mention. It's amazing, how much inspiration you can get from many artists and many songs of any given genre to inspire creativity. Cathy loved good drummers such as Buddy Rich and John Bonham, Kenny had a raw guttery-sounding guitar with an old-school twang. I had more of a Steve Harris or John Entwistle playing ability, so you can imagine their tastes in good music. It's diverse."

Black Virgin's 1982 demo included two venomous, raw, and underproduced anthems, kind of reminiscent of New Hampshire's Knightmare, and this goes for the punk approach too (even though Black Virgin have a definite metal edge). "The locals treated us with respect if they liked their teeth, haha," Joe laughs. "Besides, we never cared; we wrote and blasted our music our way, not giving in to what the 'fans want.' Just makes a band a bunch of pussies, in my opinion. Speaking of the locals and the scene, the club/bar scene was much better back in the early 1980s, before New York City raised their rents and forced almost everyone out by the mid-nineties. There were plenty of clubs then, and in the city, everyone loved music. We'd did it all, from posting flyers on every telephone pole to actually mailing letters to fans, the old-school way. Most of the places had specified metal/punk/rock or dance nights, so people would show up accordingly."

Black Virgin put out a record as quickly as possible, and the only way to do it was by releasing it on their own. "It was actually the best decision we ever taken," Joe admits. "We got decent success on the local scene with the single, and the band was getting a following in Europe through advertising and mail order sales of the single. Through that correspondence, we managed to get picked up by a local record company (Metal Enterprises) and we flew to Germany and toured for two weeks with a subsequent recording deal to follow, so we jumped at that chance. It was just a one-time thing to get some decent exposure and develop a good following in Europe, which we did. It brought us back to Germany four more times to play or to open for other acts."

CUT TO THE CHASE:

Even though I love it, I would not recommend the *.44 Killer* seven-inch to fans of strict or true heavy metal. Its weird punk edge is awesome, but I know that metalheads won't digest it. Either way, it's great, and metalheads will definitely be into Black Virgin's first LP, *Most Likely to Exceed*, which is a real crushing metallic assault.

Black Virgin's 1983 *.44 Killer* seven-inch is such a weird—but good!—release. Reminding one of the Super Heroines gone metal, with a sloppy yet charming sound, it's dark, raw, vicious. This is by no means your ordinary metal, and it borders even on the gothier punk, yet it retains a metallic approach. Both songs are so eerie, and even though they aren't catchy, the chaos in this release offers a certain allure. "Feel the Steel" progresses in an agonizing way, and Cathy's vocals have to be heard to be believed! Highly original and unique heavy metal, all the way.

Kenny Lienhardt took the vocals on their next release in 1986, the awesome *Most Likely to Exceed* on Metal Enterprises, and the band went for a full-on metal approach. Actually, it's demonic American power metal like Iron Cross (Florida), very heavy, with NWOBHM influences (from Venom to Cloven Hoof), and fantastic songs like "Blood Brothers" or "First to the Worst."

"Believe it or not, one of the best gigs was an 'Audition Nite' at L'Amour in Brooklyn. And a few gigs in Germany in little clubs, abandoned factories, and outdoor festivals were a blast!" Joe adds. "We also played regularly in New York City in a little dive called the Underground; it's long gone now. Gone are those good days of seedy clubs in New York..."

Black Virgin kept on releasing demos up until their demise in 1996, in the same sonic-assault style of raging, fearsome American power metal. They were last active in 2018, and many compilations and re-releases have emerged, like the splendid *Most Likely to Exceed* reissue on the New York-based WYLN label.

"The underground scene today exists more than ever," Joe says. "There are just so many bands, I can't keep up with them all. Also seeing more 'seclusive'-type bands that write in a more cultish sense. There are so many genres now, more than back in the day of just punk, rock, and disco! There are thousands of talented musicians who will never get a chance to be heard, and with all these smaller companies, it's a good way to exploit and get your material out to as much people as you can, without having to deal too much with the big business of the music industry. An artist is freer to be an artist with smaller companies representing him. As for the whole downloading issue, it happens, it isn't cool, but that is our human abuse of technology, and if people are gonna do it, they will. Though now, songs are so cheap and you can just buy what you like. It's a small amount of chump change, but it's something. When people snatch your music, it means that more people are becoming hip to your art ... so either way, somebody is listening to your music. However, it's incredibly hard to make any sort of money in the music biz now."

DAGGER

THE METAL SCENE IN BALTIMORE IN THE EIGHTIES WASN'T HUGE, BUT IT WAS definitely high-quality! The city was home to some absolutely fantastic bands like Have Mercy, Wrathchild America, and Rancid Decay, among other bands that are still to this day huge faves of true metalheads worldwide, like Lofton and especially Apollo Ra and Assailant. Dagger was somewhat unrecognized in the Baltimore metal scene, and they still remain active (as of 2021), after starting up in 1987!

"The band was formed around 1987 with guitarist Paul Leopardi and bassist Phil Mahoney; both searched for a quality drummer and an additional guitar player to start a cover band," vocalist Rob Olds says. "Luckily, a guitarist named John Lejnar lived in a house with Paul, and finally me and Barry Moss (from Chicago) were added to the final lineup. We rehearsed for a good six months before playing shows, and Dagger started out at Paragon in College Park, Maryland. Our influences were the many metal bands coming out in the

CUT TO THE CHASE:

Dagger is a band not to be missed by anyone into the melodic metal sound of Q5, Fifth Angel (especially their second LP), or even Pretty Maids and Dokken. The *Enchanting Me* seven-inch is a bit rare to find, but be sure to get the *Dagger: The Deep Cuts '89 –'99* compilation!

1980s, mainly mainstream hair metal bands. I think *Pyromania* and *Led Zeppelin I* were my favorite albums. In the beginning, people commented on my voice sounding like Geoff Tate of Queensrÿche, and so their *Operation: Mindcrime* became and still is my favorite CD.

"The Baltimore scene was pretty bad back then," Rob confesses. "People were not that loyal; they'd say they would come but never show up at your gig. We finally started getting a following especially in Baltimore at the Rage and at Jaxx in Virginia. Both club owners appreciated us as good musicians. We opened up for some big names—bands that really helped us. But still, there weren't that many clubs that supported the metal bands, and most people were brainwashed by the songs played in radio."

In 1989, Dagger released their *Dream Stealer* cassette, containing six songs of good, melodic (not hair/glam!) metal. Actually, Dagger struck a balance between the melodic metal of Q5 and the more hard-rockish metal approach of late-eighties Queensrÿche, creating a highly enjoyable result. But they wanted to spread their name even more after this release, so they decided to release a seven-inch, which included two songs from the demo cassette ("Enchanting Me" and "Take Me"). Rob tells the story:

"Well, we didn't have the money for studio time, and we sort of floated around until a guy named Tim Hammer believed in us and used his own funds to record the first demo and then the seven-inch. Things were going great—we were drawing a crowd and placed our originals in our sets, and they received good support. Then we were scheduled to go to New York and remix a song in some high-dollar big-time studio (I forgot the name). Well, we got up there, and producer started talking about costs, which had already been discussed before we went up. Tim got cold feet and called the whole thing off and basically abandoned us. We were heartbroken ... but still, we had our releases on our hands."

Dagger's 1989 *Enchanting Me* seven-inch is a high-quality, very professional recording of pretty melodic metal—the flip-over track "Take Me" is especially tuneful, and yes, Rob Olds sometimes sounds like Geoff Tate here, particularly in the lower register! A decent release for anyone who's into this sound.

Dagger initially kept it up until 1998, took a 20-year break, and are back at it as of 2019, playing shows again (mostly locally). Rob recalls, "We did play at Hammerjacks and that was pretty cool. Maybe my favorite show of ours. As for Maryland bands, of course Kix and then Child's Play were getting a lot of things going on, thus we really respect them."

When asked about the resurgence of interest in Dagger, Rob replies, "It feels awesome, and I'm very proud that we are finally noticed for our originals. Our music was different—everyone else wanted to sound like Kix. I think we were one of the few bands who didn't sell out. But I don't think A&R reps didn't know what to do with us. We were so diverse. Today, I feel honored that out of the thousands of bands, that Heaven and Hell Records heard something they liked and called me out of the blue," referring to the label's 2019 *Dagger: The Deep Cuts, '89–'99* compilation. "Never heard of them, and don't know how they got a hold of one of our songs. So, our first seven-inch is a collector's item? I don't know about that, but does look like there is a resurgence, and that's cool. It's good music! A lot of talent around back then."

Rob adds, "Our CD is coming out real soon, and I'm hoping for the best. I'm very excited, and we're reforming Dagger to do some shows. First show we hope to do is a CD release party with other bands locally that played with us back then, or with some of the Heaven and Hell bands that are in the Tri-State area."

KNIGHTMARE

I HAD SOME DOUBTS ABOUT ADDING KNIGHTMARE FROM MANCHESTER, NEW Hampshire, because in my ears, they are one of the wildest metal/punk crossover bands, like a mash-up between Dead Boys, Motörhead, and Judas Priest. However, I stepped back and decided to include them in this book and not in *Crossover The Edge*, because of their huge amount of self-released records. Formed in 1979 by Al Mead (vocals, bass), Tim Koukos (guitar, vocals), and Bill Connell, who was replaced in 1984 by Steve Piaseczny (drums), Knightmare still remain one of the greatest unsung heroes of their genre. A shame, 'cause their sonic output was exceptional.

"Knightmare was formed on a cold snowy night in Manchester, New Hampshire, on the notorious East Side, with an unrelenting unrealistic style sound and power that spurred the trash metal sound and opposed the glam movement of the late 1980s, fighting the PMRC and the restrictions forced on the music industry," drummer Steve Piaseczny says. Vocalist and bassist Al adds, "We were a high school cover band for a long time, started playing local bars in Manchester. We mixed in some originals over several years. When we finally decided to record, we had around 20 songs, and we recorded them all. Ten were put on the *Mindless Mayhem* LP. We tried for a while to shop for labels, but we ended up doing it on our own ... the other ten songs were put out on our second record, *Evil Dreams*, two years later on another label, which didn't do much for us. Sadly, very few copies exist. We had a few 45s as well, here and there."

When asked about their influences, Steve responds, "Drum-wise, we were influenced by Don Brewer of Grand Funk Railroad and Bill Ward of Sabbath. Guitar-wise, it was Alvin Lee and Ten Years After, whereas our bass influence was of course Lemmy." Al Mead also chimes in: "There were really so many different influences! We actually started in 1979 and played all the stuff we loved. Sabbath, Scorpions, Rainbow, Deep Purple, Rush. There were many punk rock bands that we also liked, and then metal came out. Motörhead, the Plasmatics, Fear, Dead Kennedys, et cetera. Meanwhile, I also played with GG Allin and the Scumfucs as well. But I would say that Motörhead's *Ace of Spades*, and *Coup d'Etat* by the Plasmatics were huge influences."

"Our music was a little unaccepted in our area, being too fast, loud, and heavy. All our gigs came out of Boston, Massachusetts, which had a surge in the thrash metal scene. There was slam dancing, skinheads and punks, and we had a fan who died in the pit at the Channel," Steve recalls. "Manchester was okay," Al adds. "We set out to play Boston and other towns as much as we could too, but mind you, we got kind of mixed reactions as we evolved."

Knightmare's first release was the 1983 *Still Insane After All This Treatment* seven-inch on their own label, Beaner City Records, which also released punk band Fly's On Shit's 1986 cassette *Nerve Damage*. Raw, pissed-off, and venomous heavy metal is the best description for its two songs. It's punk-fused metal, but not crossover/thrash—mostly a mix of seventies punk with the same era of metal. You already know that I love that stuff, so I'll just add that this sounds like a four-way train crash between Dead Boys, The Stooges, Motörhead, and Judas Priest!

"Putting out a slab of vinyl was most musicians' dream at the time, I think," Al declares, while Steve adds, "We wrote recorded, produced, and arranged all our tunes in our own studio in Manchester, only 'cause we were told it could not be done and also sound good. We used TASCAM equipment—we had a basement studio and rented four-track recorders to do the records. Later, we got an eight-track reel-to-reel for our *Great Day to be Dead* release. That one never made it to vinyl, though!"

Knightmare were massively prolific, recording about five demos in 1986 before making another one on vinyl. Meanwhile, they played constantly on the East Coast, especially in Boston and Connecticut. "I guess my favorite gig would be when we played in Boston opening for Motörhead and hanging with Lemmy. We also had the privilege of opening for Megadeth twice in their heyday," Steve recalls. Al mentions, "We had so many great shows! Played with Motörhead, Megadeth twice, Flotsam and Jetsam, Blue Öyster Cult, Molly Hatchet, Circle Jerks, Gang Green, Testament."

Knightmare's next release was the 1987 *Mindless Mayhem* LP, again on their own label Beaner City Records. Their brand of punkish metal reaches the top on this one, with anthems like "Complete Control," "Technology," and the psychedelic instrumental "Never Be." Moreover,

CUT TO THE CHASE:

Yes, it is true that Knightmare will be of little interest to fans of pure metal. However, if you are a fan of Overkill L.A., early eighties Motörhead, or Jeff Dahl's Powertrip, Knightmare is a mandatory band. As you can imagine, I really love their sound! Knightmare's *Still Insane After All This Treatment* seven-inch and *Mindless Mayhem* LP both are highly recommended for everyone into the dirty, raw stuff!

there's a great Dead Boys cover, "Sonic Reducer." What else could you ask for? *Mindless Mayhem* is rough and awkward but has a great charm, especially if you love your metal atypical.

"GG Allin was from New Hampshire and had many releases out on his own," both Al and Steve confirm. Both of them were huge fans of GG's. "We used to hang with him at a crazy-ass bar named the Zoo. GG was just hilarious," Steve says.

Two more demos followed in 1987 and 1988, titled *Great Day to Be Dead* and *Louder than Words* respectively, and then Knightmare's grand finale took form over two releases—this time on a small indie label, Antithesis Records in South Carolina. Initially, it was the 1989 LP *Evil Dreams*, and as crazy as it might sound, Knightmare were rougher than ever here! *Evil Dreams* is maybe my favorite record from this band: outstanding lo-fi punk metal, the songwriting reaches its peak this time with great songs like "Better Off Dead," the title anthem, or "Domination"—all tracks that remind me of Overkill L.A. and their 1985 *Triumph of the Will* LP. Finally, later in 1989, they released the *Begin Again* seven-inch, which included two LP tracks for promotional reasons. By 1990, Knightmare were laid to rest, although they held a reunion show on June 16, 2001, playing a six-song set at Chantilly's Speedway Lounge in Concord, New Hampshire.

"It's amazing that people are still after Knightmare records!" Al exclaims. "Several years ago, the phenomenon started, and lots of collectors wanted copies. I sold most of what I had. I think Tim still has a bunch." Steve says, "I think the resurgence in interest in old vinyl is great. I still have mine and a great turntable that is computer-friendly. As far as value, we never took any money from our gigs; all our money was paid to the soundmen, and merch sales went to recording and production costs."

Finally, Al closes, "I think the modern world of music is great; you can record on your own and put it out yourself much easier. I think a lot of bands still try to put out full-length CDs, which is a waste, I believe. One song at a time with a great video for YouTube should be the goal in today's environment. With all the download outlets, it is easier, faster, and cheaper than ever before to get your stuff out there." As well as in Knightmare, Tim Koukos played in Red Right Hand (thrash metal) and Fly's On Shit (punk), and Al Mead played in Tearabyte (thrash), Al Lee Slime (thrash), Decrepit Mind (thrash), Prime Evil (death metal), Storm of Hate (thrash), Mutants (punk), Sycoman (thrash), Fly's on Shit, and of course with GG Allin and the Scumfucs.

KRYST THE CONQUEROR

MISFITS (1977–1983) ARE ONE OF MY ALL-TIME FAVORITE BANDS—ABSOLUTELY in my top 20 bands ever. Each and every release of the early Misfits is pure gold in my book, regardless of whether you're a punk, rockabilly, or metalhead, and even if true metalheads massively disagree, everyone should at least own two Misfits records.

The case of Kryst the Conqueror (also from Lodi, New Jersey) is a whole different issue though: following the first breakup of Misfits, bassist Jerry Only—then known as Mo the Great—and his brother, guitarist Doyle Wolfgang von Frankenstein, decided to form a band in 1987 that had a whole different approach than Misfits. Where Misfits was a total punk band (well, that headed into hardcore on *Earth A.D.*) with satanic imagery and lyrics, Kryst the Conqueror was classic heavy metal, with Christian lyrics and imagery! David Calabrese (a.k.a. Dr. Chud), the band's second drummer, explains, "It was a band that Jerry Only and Doyle (the Caiafa brothers) tried putting together after the Misfits, 1987–1995.

They released a four-song EP, and it was a straight-up Christian metal band with Conan the Barbarian imagery. I started playing with them around 1993–1994, because their regular drummer The Murp (who later played in Sardonica) would miss a lot of rehearsals. So, I would sit in and practice with them. Before the band got off the ground, they retained the rights to use the name Misfits, so they put Kryst the Conqueror aside, and that's how I got to write and play drums for the Misfits.

"I don't know where the drive comes from to wanna do this your whole life," David adds, "but it's all I ever want to do in life, to be in a band. I can give two fucks about marriage or kids or a nine-to-five job or conforming to society's rules. I did my own thing my whole life and don't regret anything!" When he was in Kryst the Conqueror, in terms of influences, David says, "Mine were Led Zeppelin, Queen, Aerosmith, Rush, and Wings, while the Caiafa brothers loved Iron Maiden. My inspiration came directly from records like Led Zep's *Song Remains the Same*, *Wings Over America*, Rush's *Hemispheres*, and Queen's *News of the World*."

Doyle then started the Doyle Fan Club, sending the message to the old Misfits fans on things about to come—and not just this project. Danzig's post-Misfits bands Samhain and Danzig were considered by Doyle to be "way too satanic and evil," thus he wanted via Kryst the Conqueror to send a different message—actually the polar opposite of Christian metal!

"The scene in New Jersey/New York was amazing," David says. "I played out three nights a week to mostly full houses. It was a fun time. It's not anything like that anymore, so I'm grateful my youth was spent being creative and performing. I'm never treated badly by fans; other musicians probably give out more drama than fans."

Kryst the Conqueror hired Jeff Scott Soto (then of Yngwie Malmsteen's Rising Force) to do the vocals for their first and only album, 1989's *Deliver Us From Evil*; one of the book's exceptions, *Deliver Us From Evil* was never released officially on LP, but it was released as a limited-edition Christmas package for the Doyle Fan Club, containing a CD and a cassette (in the same release), a Kryst the Conqueror flashlight, three stickers, a hat, and a copy of Doyle's (as Mo The Great) info letter!

In musical and lyrical terms, those who read my first book, *Crossover The Edge*, already know that I gave it a pretty bad review. But this is only for the lyrics; I could never understand how a rock 'n' roll band could have pro-Christian lyrics, and in the case of Kryst the Conqueror, this is even more shocking, considering the members' past career in Misfits! Never mind the cheesiness of the whole "for our Lord we will die" lyrics—this is actually a very enjoyable release, and dare I say a minor classic of American underground metal! *Deliver Us From Evil* had surely a strong Iron Maiden influence (Dickinson era, 1982–1988)—all beefed up, though, falling in between the American power metal of Omen, the classic Dio/Rainbow sound, and Iron Maiden's *Powerslave*. The album was released privately on the band's label, Cyclopean Music (a label that also released albums by Slaughtered Grace and The Empire Hideous); fans of this style will flip over tunes like "In God We Trust" and "March of the Mega-Mites," whereas "Spellbound" even incorporates some more punkish elements of their past. Another weird thing, though, is that *Deliver Us From Evil* was never released properly as a full long-play release, and only five songs were included on the aforementioned first pressing, even though the band had recorded a full LP of songs (for a total of 13).

Also, throughout their existence, Kryst the Conqueror never performed live! They survived as a non-active band until 1995, when Jerry and Doyle reached an out-of-court settlement with Glenn Danzig, granting them the rights to perform as The Misfits. The last lineup of Kryst the Conqueror (including Dave Calabrese a.k.a. Dr. Chud) transformed into the second coming of The Misfits, releasing brand-new records, and (surprise!) some old Kryst the Conqueror songs such as "Dr. Phibes Rises Again" got a new, punked-up treatment.

CUT TO THE CHASE:

With the whole Misfits-related collecting mania worldwide, sadly, you have little to no chance of finding the original release of Kryst the Conqueror's *Deliver Us From Evil*. But you can get the 2019 *Soldiers of Light: The Complete Recordings* CD for a pretty decent price.

"Playing in Osaka, Japan, with The Misfits was pretty rad! The crowd would sing louder than we played, and people would be diving off the balcony," Dave says. "Besides KTQ/The Misfits, there were/are many great bands from the area. Lodi was an extremely musical little town, and a band named Sardonica would be a good start."

Kryst the Conqueror were laid to rest, and Misfits are keeping it up to this day (as of 2021) in various forms—the last one being with the original lineup.

"Music just doesn't seem as special as it once was. The ritual of album art, reading the lyrics, checking out the credits, getting those seeds out of your weed with the gatefold sleeve days are gone. Checkin' out bands live is gone because most of the venues are gone. The ever-creeping death of the digital age is upon us. No one seems to care, and downloading just cheapened the sound," Dave sighs. "I hear the difference, and it blows! I've still never bought an MP3 and it's 2021. Seriously, every band needs to turn Spotify and Pandora into commercial sites for their music; it's a concept I came up with a few years ago. I'm doing it now, I get paid for putting a commercial up on Spotify—if ya like the song, then buy it, but you aren't getting the full song there. Go to Spotify and search for Dr. Chud's 'We're the Garbage Pail Kids' and listen to the whole track, and you will all see what I'm talking about!"

OBLIVION

ANOTHER EXCEPTION TO THE RULE IS THE CASE OF OBLIVION FROM LANSDALE, Pennsylvania. They were added to this book for specific reasons, even though they didn't manage to release an LP, just a 1989 cassette with a run of 100 copies which were sold exclusively at their shows. Surely, there were thousands of bands from that era that released at least one demo; however, Oblivion's sole release was chosen to represent bands that released their full-length record on cassette. Drummer Paul Kendikian tells the Oblivion story:

"In early 1988, I was desiring to start an original heavy metal band. I contacted Chris Hafler. He was an amazing guitarist, even though he was just 15 years old. He introduced me to Bill Majoros. Bill was an equally amazing guitarist. He was 17, as was I. We rehearsed twice, and with their guitar playing and my bass playing, I thought we were the next Iron Maiden—oh, well! Then Chris bowed out. He wanted the whole spotlight, to be the solitary guitarist in a band. I quickly had a friend of mine audition. Shawn Gilmartin was not our ideal singer, but he impressed us enough with his range that Bill and I decided to keep the 23-year-old (not sure) at least temporarily. The next six to nine months consisted of us consuming a lot of beer and drummers. It was very difficult to find a drummer that could keep up with our speed and understand our complexity. One drummer who was pretty good lived an hour away. I spent four hours per practice driving him back and forth, and then he quit. He said it was too much work. Another drummer we loved also said our songs were too physically demanding.

"We rehearsed several times per week, as we wrote our songs," Paul continues. "Most of the writing was Bill's. He was incredible. He would bring in a mostly completed new song on a very consistent basis. He opened my eyes to the craft and turned me into a prolific songwriter. Shawn started contributing lyrics. He and Bill were working well together. Bill's lust for ridiculous speed, and his and Shawn's influences pushed our music into the death metal realm more than I had wanted. We called it death metal. It might be labeled speed metal now. I have no idea! However, I was loving the material, and I was not writing fast enough to shape things differently. I contributed a song, and parts of a couple of others. We had the material, and we were desperate for a drummer. Chris Hafler introduced us to his future brother-in-law, A.J. Galluppi, who immediately became our drummer."

When asked about the songwriting process, Paul says, "I had outgrown the various cover bands that I had performed in. I wanted to write songs. I wanted to be a rock star! I never did play covers again. I have also never found the right band members to promote my songs. I have currently (as of 2021) a band named Score. I wrote, performed, recorded, and mixed my latest album, *Across the Rock*, almost all by myself."

Oblivion formed right in the heyday of American power metal as well as thrash metal, and inevitably, their sound was influenced by both subgenres. "Bill and I are big Beatles fans. He liked King Diamond too, and Yes is one of my favorites. Iron Maiden was my biggest influence for my bass playing. Shawn liked a lot of the underground punk and metal bands of that era. Stormtroopers of Death and GWAR, among others. There is no question that the record that set the bar for all of us in that genre of music was *Master of Puppets* by Metallica. One of the very few covers we performed was 'Master of Puppets.' Also, don't forget that we were a young band from Philadelphia suburbs. Shawn and I lived in a town full of drugs and criminals. Bill and A.J. lived in a quieter Mennonite/Quaker area. There were some original rock/metal bands playing the club circuit, and our debut produced surprisingly positive energy from the crowds. The audiences grew at a shocking rate. The reaction was amazingly positive both in numbers and enthusiasm!"

CUT TO THE CHASE:

Good luck finding Oblivion's only release. All copies of *Oblivion* are majorly rare and have never ever appeared for sale or on auction in the digital world!

Oblivion decided quickly to put out their first official release on a limited run of 100 copies, which was the 1989 *Oblivion* cassette. "We simply wanted a recording. Record companies were scouting us, but we still wanted our own recording," Paul says. "We used Bill's four-track TASCAM cassette recorder. We started with the drums—we recorded them in the factory where we rehearsed. We used a few very cheap microphones. I then recorded all the bass lines at my house. We did not know how to punch in. Everything was recorded from the start of the song to the end. We recorded all the vocals at our factory as well. Bill added the guitars at his house, and Bill mixed it. I doubt that I helped at all. We did not have the resources to distribute it much back then—we just sold it at shows."

Oblivion is a release that falls exactly in its time and place. Reminiscent of Powermad, Lääz Rockit, and Cold Steel, it has its fair share of melody and power, with a combination of power and thrash. Even though the recording's quality is mediocre, there are songs that can be regarded as massive, such as the opening "Paralyzed" (which has a slight NYHC touch), "Cold Steel," the punk-fueled "Get a Life," and the epic "Final Day," which sounds like Flotsam and Jetsam!

Oblivion's name spread fast in the Philly area, and Paul says, "After our first shows, the momentum of the crowds was building enormously. Every show we played set the attendance record for the club we played at. That would probably make our last show the best, although I don't remember it, and we had no idea that it would be the last show. The one show that I am proud of is caught on video. We played the Telford Inn in Mantua, New Jersey, and we set the attendance record on a beautiful Labor Day weekend. Labor Day is a holiday at the end of the summer, and in Philadelphia, hundreds of thousands flood the New Jersey beaches. There is no nightlife in our area. The bars are empty. In one of the videos, Shawn points out to the crowd the packed club—damn, memories!"

Friction in Oblivion regarding musical direction led the band to disband in late 1989—a pity, just one year together. Galluppi and Majoros later played both in Steelwynd (power/progressive metal), Crystal Fate (power metal), and Elvenfire (instrumental power metal), whereas Kendikian nowadays performs with Score.

"The local underground scene consists of a generation of, in my opinion, very misguided artists. They think that there is a level of respect due to them if they record live. They want their recordings on vinyl. As a recording artist and engineer, I think they should graduate from that junior high school mindset and rehearse more. We left the static, muddy frequencies of vinyl in our basements 30 years ago for a reason. If they want to be retro, they can put down the prescription medications and learn to play their guitars. Accordingly, easy downloading is a cancer to songwriting. If I cannot control the distribution and revenue of my songs, I am a lot less motivated to write them. If you can download my songs for free, there is less motivation for you to see me perform live. Music, like socialization among people, is almost becoming virtual rather than social."

KILL VAN KULL

FROM NYC, KILL VAN KULL FORMED IN 1983 AND ARE STILL ACTIVE TO THIS day (as of 2021), with some intervals in between. Vocalist Rick Cabrera narrates their story:

"The long version is that I met Danny Mills (guitar) when I started working at a New York City brokerage firm. He found out I was a singer, and I let him hear some of my originals. He loved what he heard, and we started jamming with two musicians he knew. In a strange twist of fate, the drummer was beginning to miss practices, and on my commute home one night, I ran into a friend of Vinnie Raschella's (drums). I had played with him a few years earlier and knew he was a good guy and solid drummer. It turns out that he was injured in a violent unprovoked attack, which severely injured his eye. I wanted to pick up his spirits and reached out to see if he wanted to jam with my current band, The Rock Exchange. He came down with his eyepatch and rocked that night. Immediately, we asked him to join the band. Soon afterward, we had to replace the bass player, and Vinnie knew an amazing bass player he had played with before.

KILL VAN KULL BAND PHOTO COURTESY RICK CABRERA

Enter Billy Pritchard Cardinale. Adding his playing and songwriting skills, the band took shape. One day the four of us were driving together and were thinking of potential band names when Vinnie and Danny were mentioning all the kills (rivers) that are all over Staten Island. They simultaneously said 'Kill Van Kull,' and we just knew—it was the perfect name that really suited us. After some exciting shows in the Staten Island, New York, music scene, we finally impressed and recruited a remarkable lead guitarist, Scott Pedersen, to complete KVK.

"Forming Kill Van Kull was a way of being creative and having it heard and seen. We wanted to be a working, successful band. But even with that said, we enjoyed all the fun and camaraderie," Rick adds. "The Beatles, Aerosmith, Black Sabbath, and Van Halen were our biggest influences, specifically Aerosmith *Rocks*, Black Sabbath's *Black Sabbath*, Kiss' *Alive*, The Beatles' *Sgt. Pepper's*, and Van Halen's *Van Halen*.

"In the early and mid-eighties, the music scene throughout New York was outstanding. All the venues had great crowds that enjoyed live music. The locals were tremendous with their energy and support," Rick recalls. "The shows at L'Amour in Brooklyn were always the standouts. The crowds, the energy, our performances, the intensity were all amazing."

Kill Van Kull were already active for four years when they released a record. After having no luck finding a proper label in the very strict music industry of the 1980s, they formed their own label, Kullco, and released the 1987 *Eye of the Storm* twelve-inch EP. Rick says, "The music industry, as always, made it difficult to make a name for yourself and be heard by the executives. The 'who you know' sometimes was as important as the 'what you do.' By doing a private press, we attempted to open a different door to get noticed. *Eye of the Storm* was mostly a live recording done in one day and mixed the following day. The studio was a two-hour road trip away, where we enjoyed the recording experience but also the ridiculous and lifelong memories from that weekend."

Eye of the Storm contains four tracks of classic heavy metal with a huge Iron Maiden influence! However, there's also some melodic metal elements, which impart a diverse sound. I'd say that they sound like a cross between Iron Maiden and Diamond Head on at least three tracks. The title song is a brilliant instrumental, whereas "A Piece of Love" is maybe the best song on this EP—a manifesto of technical orgasmic metal! "Yesterday's Love" is the only mediocre song here, whereas the opening "Burn it Up" balances between party metal and classic metal. Good stuff.

CUT TO THE CHASE:

***Eye of the Storm* could have been a tremendous classic of self-released American metal if all four songs were on the same level of greatness as "Eye of the Storm" and "A Piece of Love." But sadly, they're not, and overall this is a mixed record.**

Kill Van Kull released a demo in 1989, in the same style, and then split up. The band got back together for two years in the nineties and have been back on since 2004. In 2006, KVK released the *Edge of Sunrise* CD, again on their own label.

When asked what he thinks about people searching for the Kill Van Kull stuff even today, Rick replies, "I think we were stunned in disbelief at first, but certainly proud and excited for the attention."To be honest, we are not so sure if a metal underground scene exists or not today. The only way to be sure is to see the crowd back out in full force and supporting the rock scene. I myself have also been performing with another local original band, Scottish Widows, but the clubs don't always have large crowds. The acts are usually top-notch performers, but the crowds aren't consistently there. And we think that the easy access via downloading hurts the artists as well as the venues. They also rob the fan of discovering those 'hidden gems' that may be on albums that won't be found if only the hits are downloaded and get airplay!"

DAMIEN (NEW YORK CITY)

NEW YORK CITY'S DAMIEN FORMED IN 1982 AND HAD MANY DIFFERENT members throughout their run. Starting out as a cover band, this changed in late 1983 when the new lineup focused on writing their own material.

"There were two prior guitar players before I joined," bassist Pat Lano says. "Their names were Christian Paladino and Jimmy DeVito. When I joined, it was Bobby Blake, who's on the *Face the Danger* album. I did not desire to play cover music at that time. I wanted to do my own songs, so did Troy Bova, the vocalist throughout all the Damien incarnations. I decided to write songs, and we spent roughly ten months writing the material for the *Face the Danger* album, rehearsing as much as five to six times a week to get the songs where they needed to be to record them on tape."

The new Damien lineup included Troy Bova (vocals), Pat Lano (bass), Frank Reilly (guitar), and Nicky Cioppa (drums), and the decision was made: they were destined to play like their idols! "*Alive!* by Kiss was probably one of my biggest inspirations, but I also loved Rush, Aerosmith, the Rolling Stones, and of course, you can't leave out Led Zeppelin and Black Sabbath," Pat explains.

"The eighties were a great time for hard rock and heavy metal music. There were many clubs that welcomed you with open arms, whether you were original or a cover band, and you actually got paid. I could name a few for you: the Rising Sun in Yonkers, New York, was the first place everybody started, including Twisted Sister, Metallica, and Raven. Long Island and New Jersey also had many clubs, like Hammerheads in Long Island—that was a very big club. In New Jersey, there was the Soap Factory, and Manhattan had the Great Gildersleeves. Also, the Cat Club, Limelight, Traxx, and of course CBGB."

Damien went on to release their first LP, 1985's *Face the Danger*, on their own label, Danger Records. Pat describes how this happened:

"It was very hard to get signed to a record label in that time, so I must've been sending off our material to the major record labels. If they contacted you, you got a showcase where you could perform for them, but this didn't necessarily mean you were going to get a record deal. So, we tried this road, and it did not work for us. We decided to play gigs, save that money, and produce our own album from start to finish. It was a very costly endeavor at that time! It was not like today—we spent quite a bit of money to get the *Face the Danger* album out to the public. We put it in local record stores around the Tri-State area and got some local radio stations to play it, and we received a great response!"

Face the Danger is an uneven yet still good LP. There are some great moments, such as "Tables Will Turn," which kind of remind me of Diamond Head, along with the title song "Face the Danger," and "Between the Sheets," their heaviest number. Still, though, it is not a classic, and songs like "Hang on to Your Head" or "Angel for the Night" are just mediocre.

Damien split about 1989, then got back together initially in 2006 and again in 2010. Although at the moment they are inactive, in 2006 they released their *Say Your Prayers* EP as a CD-R, which included songs that were written and produced between 1986 and 1988. A huge leap forward from *Face the Danger*, *Say Your Prayers* sadly didn't get a proper release. Top-notch

American metal with enormous driving power here, and each and every song is bombastic. From the opening "Say Your Prayers" and the heavyweight "Queen of Pain" to the awesome "Judgement," this album is just pure metal perfection!

CUT TO THE CHASE:

Although the *Face the Danger* LP is decent, it's for completists of private American metal. On the other hand, the *Say Your Prayers* EP is real gold, and you should get it at any cost! A real forgotten jewel of classic metal, hopefully it will see the light of day someday as a proper release. Not to be missed!

"The only other band that was indie that comes to mind was BlackLace. We were in the same rehearsal studio as Anthrax, and we watched them get signed," Pat recalls. "I'm not so sure about being highly collectible, but myself and all the members of Damien appreciate that people love the music that we created 30-something years later. It's nice that people can go back and find artists and music from that time."

Pat ends by offering his view on music downloading today: "I don't know if I would call it underground, and as for the downloading part of it and getting a hold of the music without paying the artist, it is a little unfair to us. The sales of CDs and vinyl albums and, of course, T-shirts give the bands the revenue to continue and record new music, and to support their families. Without this, you're not going to see a lot of people releasing material, especially in that genre."

Damien members played in a number of bands after the band split up. Pat says, "In the past eight years, I have done four different projects and had the honor of recording six songs with Neal Smith from The Alice Cooper Band! With my new band, we just did a four-song EP called *So Rude*. The band is called Crude-N-Rude, and we have two releases out!"

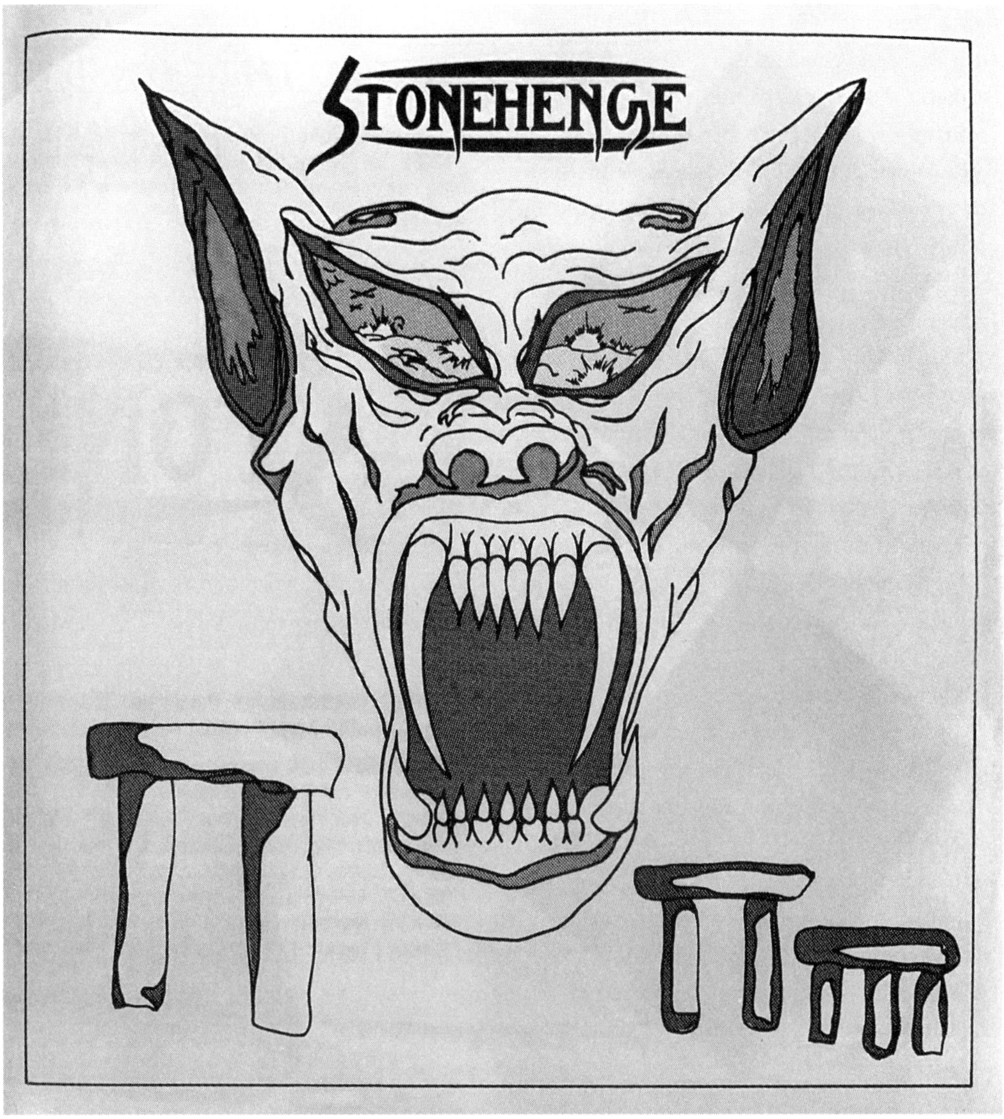

STONEHENGE

SO STRANGE! ALBANY, NEW YORK, MUST HAVE BEEN THE PLACE WITH the highest proportion of unsigned metal bands that self-released records in the eighties, such as Blind Legion, Blacksmith, China White, and of course, Stonehenge. Formed in 1983, drummer Mike Normandin narrates their story:

"Stonehenge was a band founded by myself and my brother, guitarist Chris Normandin. We were young (I was 17 and my brother was 14) and our mother was the band manager! Later on, bassist Jim 'Wildman' Duke, vocalist Andy Libertucci, and second guitarist Pat Ginnelly were added. Our intention was to write and play our own originals as well as perform popular rock/metal cover songs. We all really had dreams of making it big someday. In the early days, our influences definitely included Iron Maiden, Queensrÿche, Dio, and Black Sabbath. For me personally, it's tough to mention my favorite records, because there were so many! *All the World's a Stage* by Rush, *The Song Remains the Same* by Led Zeppelin, along with early Iron Maiden, Black Sabbath, and Dio albums and *Unleashed in the East* by Judas Priest come to mind.

"The Albany scene," Mike adds, "was very vibrant—lots of bars and clubs to play. We often would pair up with other bands or shoot for warm-up gigs for national acts. We were always treated with respect and had a great following and reputation in our scene."

CUT TO THE CHASE:

I know that there are more than a few people out there who are suckers for the early Iron Maiden sound—so, Stonehenge is for you! The band definitely has its own character, but fans of Iron Maiden's first LP will flip over the *Cats Eyez* seven-inch. Wish I could find a copy of their demo, *The Warriors*, someday too. I'm very curious about its sound.

Stonehenge wasn't just a cover band—they also wrote their own material, and they were ambitious enough to release it by themselves! Mike tells the story behind their 1985 *Cats Eyez* seven-inch:

"We wanted to share our original music and to be discovered, and we were hoping it would be a way to get signed to a major label. We figured that that's what Queensrÿche did with their EP, so that's what we were hoping would happen for us. We recorded it at a popular local studio, Arabellum Studios, and had it sent out to be duplicated. It was a big deal for us as the time, and something we took a tremendous amount of pride in—both the songs as well as the artwork."

Containing only two songs, *Cats Eyez* is a real keeper for everyone into the early Iron Maiden-meets-American metal sound. The title song is an amazing, powerful tune, kicking off with a drum beat reminiscent of (later-to-be-released) *Painkiller*, and bordering on American power metal. The flip side, "Heavy Metal Woman," continues in the same vein, sounding almost like something off of *Iron Maiden* or *Killers*! Rough 'n' ready heavy metal, totally quality stuff.

"We had many fun shows, but probably our first one—that was the one I remember the most. We had a sound company, lights, fog machine ... it was a big deal! But we weren't the only Albany metal band with a self-released record. China White, Legion, and Blacksmith come to mind. Great bands, and they also had a strong passion and desire to succeed."

In 1986 lineup changes took place, and Doug Montanye was the new vocalist, as well as John Nania (formerly of China White) as the new bassist. The new Stonehenge released only one demo, 1986's *The Warriors,* which I sadly couldn't find in order to review. But zines refer to it as a huge step toward the epic metal sound. Wow!

Stonehenge folded in 1987, and Chris Normandin performs now with the death/grind (!) band Axe to Grind. Mike discusses the current interest in pure heavy metal: "I think it's great! It keeps the legacy alive, and it's nice to be still considered relevant, especially after all these years! It's very flattering to think something we did so long ago still means so much to the fans and metal collectors in the world. What a great compliment to receive, particularly from fans who really know their music. Very humbling to say the least..."

About the scene today, he says, "The underground metal scene today is very strong, and the internet has made that scene more visible than ever before. As for downloading, my opinion is that it's sort of the nature of the beast in today's high-tech world. As a recording artist, I don't necessarily agree with free downloading, but I also think from a musician/income standpoint, ticket sales and merch sales are where it's at now, not really music sales. The music has almost become secondary, not in all cases, but in many. Bottom line is that it's easier than ever to share music today, which ultimately is great for the music industry, especially new songwriters and bands."

X-CALIBER

JUST A TINY TOWN ON THE OUTSKIRTS OF WESTMORELAND COUNTY, Irwin, Pennsylvania, can boast that one of the most terrific American metal LPs was created there! X-Caliber was a short-lived but brilliant epic metal band that recorded just one release. Bassist Bruce Fleckenstein narrates their fantastic story:

"I was recruited to play bass by guitarist Jim Yedlick. He contacted me. He was either informed by word of mouth or saw me play. I was playing with a band called Alpha Centauri around that time. We played in the North Huntingdon, Pennsylvania, area. Jim was local to this area. At first it was just Jim and me. He had big plans. He mentioned the past of X-Caliber and stated that they were a bar band. He was determined to get away from that and wanted to go big and concentrate on original material, including a record contract. His plan included Kevin Donegan as lead vocalist. Kevin was a member of X-Caliber but at the time was living in West Palm Beach, Florida. Jim was assured he was in and would relocate when the time was right.

"So, Jim came to me with a demo tape recorded at Micro Mix Studios in Latrobe," Bruce continues. "It had the songs 'Runaway,' 'The Sword,' 'Rocks Alive,' and 'Some Day.' I figure Kevin and Jim were probably the main writers here. I know the past lineups of X-Caliber included different members—I know most of the names and still hear about and see some of them at times. A few still have bands that perform. I live in the area where it all started now, Irwin. At the time, I ended up being the only one from Elizabeth Township; whereas everyone else was close to each other, I wasn't that far. I began working on these songs from the demo. Soon after, Jim and I started rehearsing together. This included freshly written material. Some ended up on the LP. We were in pursuit of a drummer, and Donnie Poland was the next member added to the lineup. We then started to rehearse as a three-piece.

"While this was all going down, there were some good times to be had. Jim was a guitar teacher at the local music store, and he had a lot of talented students. I know and have been in contact with a few of them recently. A couple have been very active guitar players to this date. This brings me to the next added member, Jerry Conrad. He was a student of Jim's. Jim brought him to us one day and said, 'Here's our new guitar player.' Donnie and I were like 'Okay,' so the four of us started working together. Not only did we concentrate on the material for the LP, we had some heavier, more collaborative stuff for another LP. We rehearsed a lot! Had high expectations. Was anticipating the meeting with Kevin. We booked studio time at Air Craft Communications in Dormont, Pennsylvania, and Kevin came up from Florida around Christmas. We were concerned that he had a cold when laying tracks down in the studio, but it seemed to turn out pretty good. Kevin ended up returning to Florida until a later date. He ended up moving back to his hometown.

"I was musical from a young age," Bruce adds. "Listening to Mom's LPs, eight-tracks, classic rock mostly. I started playing trumpet in school when I was nine or ten. Learned how to sight-read soon after. Started getting involved with guitar with a neighbor, maybe around 12. Met up with some others and wanted to get more involved. Bass seemed to suit me better. My 13th birthday brought me a bass. I listened to a lot of LPs, learned songs from my favorite bands. I performed live at this age. What really got me going was some friends and the first serious group, Alpha Centauri ... I found out fast that I liked the excitement and attention. Also, all the fun times with the band and meeting new people. Can't begin to say how much music has been a part of my life!"

As for X-Caliber's influences, Bruce offers a huge list of them: "Well, we all had many of course ... Iron Maiden came out with *Powerslave* at the time. You can hear this on the material that was written for the second LP. Jim could play Eddie Van Halen solos note for note. All of them! I can hear a lot of his style in Jim's writings. Those two stick out the most right now. Jerry was into some stuff coming about, and we were pretty much with him: heavier stuff, Metal Church, Slayer, et cetera. But again, there were so many influences. Tons of classic rock, metal like Dokken, Queensrÿche, Stryper, Twisted Sister, Rush, The Who, Boston. Even Anthrax, S.O.D., Metallica—you get the picture. We used to cover stuff at rehearsals.

"The scene back then was great!" Bruce smiles. "The locals loved us, and it spread to my hometown. Jerry and I were still in high school at the time. We were local celebrities. The scene? We created our own with a couple of big full-production shows. We weren't a bar band.

We had a house for a while that was a scene in itself! Our scene was also a lot of work and dedication from us and those around us. Support from family and friends was huge. Financial backing was necessary."

After two years of existence, X-Caliber went on to create X-Caliber Records, and released their only record, *Warriors Of The Night*, in 1986. "How did we do that? Well, it was Jim's hard work and never-quit attitude," Bruce says. "Forming a corporation with private investors. Jim was the man. He was overwhelmed and needed help. He would share ideas with me. I understood most of what was involved. He had to create a publishing company that was named Exor Music. Also, he created a record company, X-Caliber Records, Inc. The goal was to land a record deal with a major label. Not like he didn't try, but we could not generate enough interest there."

CUT TO THE CHASE:

Yep, *Warriors Of The Night* is a wet-dream release for everyone with a slight interest in the real American metal sound. Everything here is nearly perfect, from the music to the artwork, so you know what to do. The original pressing, though, is pricey, and even though No Remorse re-released it in 2017, all 300 copies have disappeared! Anyway, get it at any cost!

Warriors Of The Night is a tremendous LP. It includes all the qualities and elements that make American metal so great. Epic and dark, mystical yet melodic, songs like "Runaway," "The Sword," and the title track are sheer epic metal anthems, whereas tunes like "Tell Me Why" and "Told You Not to Run" are more in the classic American metal genre, with a resemblance to Judas Priest. X-Caliber sound like a cross between Medieval Steel (well, on their best tracks) with early Exxplorer. So, *Warriors Of The Night* is a mandatory purchase for everyone who's into this stuff.

The future for X-Caliber was shining bright, and this was evident too in their shows: "Definitely the Dynasty show was my favorite," Bruce says. "It was a club with a lot of history in the White Oak/North Huntingdon area. There was a blizzard that dumped a lot of snow that evening, and so we were concerned about the turnout that night. Our friends, family, and fans weren't gonna miss this debut! The count, probably just paying customers, was 850. This was a full production show, sound, lights, a castle wall, a 250-foot backdrop, a live three-knight battle on stage! Video production, et cetera."

When asked about fellow indie metal bands of the era, Bruce says, "Yeah, I knew what was going on at the time—there were many private metal releases. I'm sure you probably heard of Valhalla. Private release? I think. We were buddies with Genghis Khan. Hung out with them during the recording of the second album. Later, I played in a band with a couple of them for a while. Iron Cross' *Warhead*: was it a private release? There were probably more, but those are the ones that I'm recalling now."

Sadly, X-Caliber disbanded in 1987, leaving the second LP on the shelves, unreleased. Hopefully, it will get a proper release someday, as I'd love to hear their evolution from *Warriors Of The Night*. Following X-Caliber's breakup, members didn't perform with other bands—or at least haven't joined so-called "proper" bands, releasing demos and records, et cetera.

When asked about the renewed interest in X-Caliber, Bruce responds, "I think it's great! I wish some of this interest was around back then. It may have helped with us becoming more successful." *Warriors Of The Night* has been re-released by both Heaven and Hell Records and No Remorse Records in 2016 and 2017 respectively. "It makes me happy that we did something that turned out to have such demand. Seems the whole package is what makes it so desired. Music, concept, artwork, limited release on vinyl, era, self-release, following, et cetera. We put our all and our hearts into it. Makes me feel good that others enjoy it. I like the messages that I've received!"

As for the state of the underground, Bruce says, "Real underground? I'm not quite aware of what all goes on these days. I believe there's an underground scene. I'll bet other countries and the U.S. both. There are local acts here. I really hate to see people not get paid for their product. Some people realize the value and try to back local acts, but still, downloading a record by a small band is something I'm against. Paid, this may be great. The ability to have media available worldwide is tremendous! I know that a download doesn't generate much revenue. I prefer vinyl nowadays, which is a costly process."

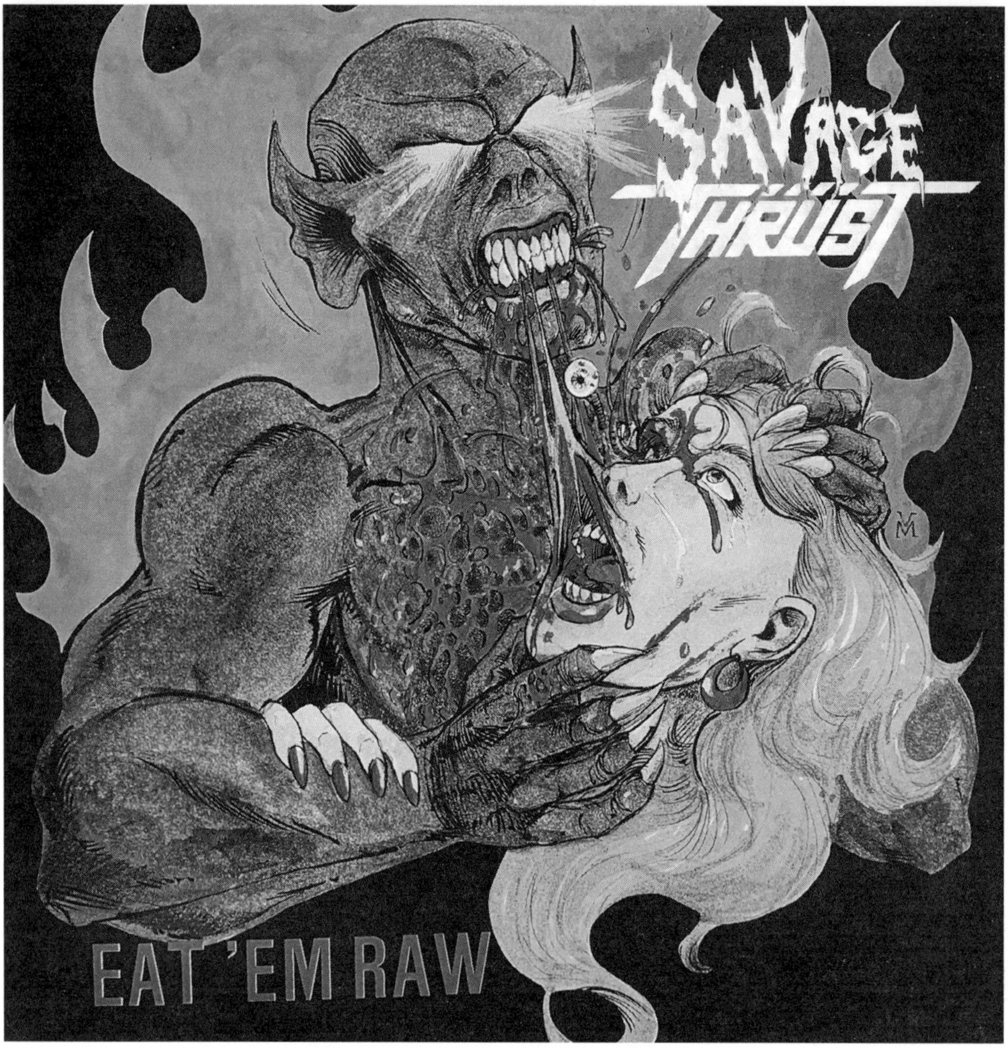

SAVAGE THRUST

FROM NEW YORK CITY, SAVAGE THRUST SADLY REMAIN SOME OF THE MOST unsung heroes of American metal—a shame, since their musical output will cause everyone who's into speed/thrash to flip! Formed in 1984, founding member and guitarist Pat Donofrio tells their story:

"Initially, it was me, Ed Varuolo on guitars (R.I.P. 2018), Mike Smith (vocals), Bob Boch (drums), and Jim Gellentien (bass). We went through a few bass players until Mike Puch, of the hardcore band Sworn Enemy, joined and fit the band until the end. We all came from the same neighborhood in Staten Island, New York. At first, we were a cover band, playing Judas Priest, W.A.S.P., Iron Maiden. Then after about three months, we started writing original stuff. The first song we ever wrote was 'Crown of Thorns' and it was chosen for the compilation album *Speed Metal Hell II*. We just wanted to be an honest power speed metal band and hoped to

CUT TO THE CHASE:

Any speed metal fans out there? Do you remember bands like Evil Dead, Toxic, Powermad, Destructor, or even Helstar or Liege Lord in their faster songs? Well, then, Savage Thrust will absolutely be highly enjoyable for you. But *Soon Revenge/Agony & Extacy* is surely a good record (yet not a classic), and *Eat 'Em Raw* is their best effort.

play at the legendary metal club L'Amour. In a very short time, L'Amour called us to play our first show playing with Fates Warning. It was big stuff for us! Then we played with many of the greatest names in metal like Manowar, Overkill, Armored Saint, Anthrax, Exodus, and also with M.O.D., Ramones, and Nuclear Assault. The local scene on Staten Island was just starting to accept bands playing the faster, harder thrash metal. We basically were the first band in our area to be playing that type of metal. We were turned down by basically every metal record company, for one reason or another. One label offered us a deal but wanted our firstborn child to be signed away ... so we turned it down. We happened to do a short tour in Mexico, and we had no choice but to have the album put out independently.

"My favorite show was playing with either Manowar or Exodus. Both nights were packed full, and the crowds were crazy! We were building a nice following," Pat recalls about his favorite shows of Savage Thrust's. "We felt we were better than 80 percent of the bands that were signed to the metal labels. So, at some point, when the grunge scene started to take form, I saw the metal scene dying before my eyes. And no record deal—something that left me dead inside."In 1986, Savage Thrust went on to create their own zine named *Thrüstazine*, after they released their first demo in 1985, the crazy speed/thrash *Demo of Doom*. Their later *Live Pain* demo came out in 1987, once they'd already made their a pretty hot name for themselves in the underground metal scene, thanks to the inclusion of their excellent track "Crown of Thorns" on the 1986 New Renaissance compilation *Speed Metal Hell II*.

On their own label, Polydisc Records, Savage Thrust released the *But Soon Revenge/Agony & Extacy* seven-inch in 1987 as well. Heavy and hard-hitting speed/thrash metal, with the high-pitched vocals of Michael Smith, the demo reminds one of early Flotsam and Jetsam, Heathen, and Overkill on "But Soon Revenge." They head for a more power metal approach on "Agony and Extacy," which is also a real winner.

The next three years were rough for Savage Thrust, since they couldn't get a decent deal with a label, and the change of trends both in the metal scene—death metal was starting to replace thrash, glam metal was reaching its peak in 1987 and 1988—along with the upcoming rise of the grunge era left Pat disillusioned. "It was late 1989 when I decided to leave the band, and I was replaced by Rob Antilla, who is a good friend of mine. Actually, I just spent the last six days at Rob Antilla's house in the mountains, writing new music. And from a songwriting standpoint, it's gonna blow people away. We've had close to 20 years to reflect. The new music might finally put us on the map as true contenders of the thrash/speed/power metal scene!"

Savage Thrust finally managed to release their first LP in 1990, *Eat 'Em Raw*, on the Mexican label Avanzada Metalica: Mexico's first independent metal label, formed in the late eighties by journalists Georgui Lazarov and Carlos Hernandez. This is definitely the band's best moment: weird, angular, punishing speed/thrash with a huge dose of brutality. Check out "Speed or Bleed" or "The Vice." Overall, *Eat 'Em Raw* might bring to mind Helstar (*Distant Thunder*), Toxic (*World Circus*), Overkill, or Powermad. It's a certain quality of speed/thrash that only American bands could pull off at the time.

Two more demos followed in 1991, *Demo '91* and *New Demo*, still in the same style, and then Savage Thrust were laid to rest—for a while! The band's first renaissance took place over two reunion shows at L'Amour in Brooklyn in 2001. Today, Savage Thrust is back together, having last reunited in 2018.

"Ed Varuolo passed away in August of 2018 and we held a memorial show," Pat says. "It was meant to be our last performance. However, we've since decided to keep going due to the fact that ... we still got it! And we're currently writing some new material and hope to play some of the bigger events, like festivals. At this point, we can choose where and when.

"Today, the Savage Thrust lineup includes Rob Antilla too, a good friend. Mike Smith no longer sings; Rob handles vocals as well. Bob Boch is on drums. And we have a new bass guitar player, Tommy Walters, from the old neighborhood."

On the current online interest in Savage Thrust albums, Pat says, "As far as our records being collector's items, that blows my mind. I had to buy a copy of *Eat 'Em Raw* off eBay because I gave all my copies away. The first pressing sold out very quickly, so the guy who reissued it gave me a bunch of copies on CD. So, I'm good! As for today's scene, it is totally different than the scene I know. It's so hard for a young band. But with the internet, it's a lot easier than back in our time. So, we will test the water, and see what's next for Savage Thrust!"

VOYEUR

I BET THERE AREN'T MANY OF YOU WHO'VE HEARD THE NAME OF VOYEUR, and if not, you missed one of the most obscure yet exciting privately released seven-inches of the eighties! Yep, some grandiose talk here, but let's begin the story of Voyeur, who formed in 1985 in Mansfield, Connecticut, with drummer Tim Yasui:

"In 1985, I was attending the University of Connecticut Graduate School of Business, working on my master's degree in business administration while playing drums in various hard rock/metal rock bands all over New England to help pay my tuition. The dual lifestyle ingrained me into the New England rock community, which was significantly more active at the time than my hometown of Williamsport, Pennsylvania, where I'd learned to play drums at age of nine. Because the drinking age was only 18 in Connecticut back then, the nightlife and music scene was really hopping! Hartford, Connecticut, is right smack halfway in between

Boston, Massachusetts, and New York City, so there were tons of major acts barnstorming through the area, and the college radio scene was amazing as well. Working also as a broadcast DJ on weekends at the University's radio station while attending graduate school also enabled me to play music over the airwaves of WHUS 91.7 FM, which I loved. It was not uncommon for me to invite local Connecticut and Massachusetts metal bands into the studio to play their original songs—it was a lot of power for a young kid who was addicted to metal music!

"Hence, how I met my partner in crime, before we evolved into the original band, Voyeur: a long-haired guitar virtuoso named John Donovan, a.k.a. 'Justin Tyme,'" Tim continues. "We clicked immediately over love of the same music like Michael Schenker and UFO, Yngwie Malmsteen, Loudness, Ratt, Judas Priest, et al. John was already writing some cool original music and we rehearsed as a duo at his family's home in beautiful Avon, Connecticut. Soon, we had enough original songs for our first EP. For bass guitar, I recruited John Cianfaglione, whom I had played with in my previous New England band, Destiny. For lead vocals, I recruited (and actually had to pay out of my pocket) a frontman named John Code, who hailed from the local top-drawing metal band Cryer. We recorded four songs (only three made it to the EP) in one day."

Tim's story goes way back to the seventies: "I had already been playing in bands for over ten years back in my home state of Pennsylvania, prior to moving to Connecticut to attend undergraduate school at nearby Trinity College. My first band at age 13 was called BESO, Spanish for 'kiss,' and so we played all Kiss covers, followed by my stint at UConn. The motivation to form Voyeur was simply to play music that John and I both loved! It was my first band to play all original music, which was a big step and challenge, coming out of mainly cover bands back in Pennsylvania and cover bands as an undergrad. After our Voyeur EP release in 1986, Justin and I moved out to Hollywood, California, together in the hopes of making Voyeur 'famous.' Less than one year after he and I moved to Hollywood, I joined London—former members included Nikki Sixx, Blackie Lawless, Izzy, Slash, Fred Coury, and Steven Adler from Guns N' Roses) and signed a record deal with Noise Records. Justin joined Dave King's band, Flogging Molly, and I believe he played on one of their albums.

"Justin was a Michael Schenker/UFO/MSG freak, and he shared with me a ton of that stuff," Tim says when asked about the band's musical influences. "But we both also loved Loudness, Judas Priest, Yngwie Malmsteen—back then, it was known as 'melodic metal.' My drumming inspiration personally came from John Bonham from Led Zeppelin, but I would be lying if I didn't include some of the flashier drummers like Tommy Aldridge and Tommy Lee. *Physical Graffiti* to this day is my all-time favorite rock album, and I remember at age 15 memorizing the drum parts on that entire double album."

When asked about the scene that Voyeur hailed from, Tim replies with nostalgia: "Eighties-era New England was amazing for music back then. Before I eventually got to live up there to go to college, Boston had been widely considered the rock 'n' roll capital (before Hollywood took its place). That area was the home of Aerosmith, The Cars, Boston, The J. Geils Band, Jon Butcher Axis, James Taylor, and so many other legends!"

Voyeur went on to release in 1986 their only record, *First Glance*, in a seven-inch EP format through their own label, Yasui Records, and Tim relates the story behind this release:

CUT TO THE CHASE:

Voyeur's *First Glance* seven-inch is a magnificent piece of heavy metal. It will definitely appeal to different camps of metalheads, since the ones into melodic metal will enjoy the passion and the style, and those into true metal will love the total metal approach. Are ya into (early) Dokken, Judas Priest (*Screaming for Vengeance*), early eighties Riot, or early Yngwie Malmsteen? You should get *First Glance* in your collection by any means!

"While working on my MBA, I had the opportunity to get academic credits for forming my own indie record label and releasing an audio album. The result was a three-song mini-EP called *First Glance* that I recorded in East Hartford, Connecticut, at the same recording studio where the first Fates Warning album was recorded. I pressed it at an Ohio vinyl pressing plant (now since closed) and had to make a class presentation with the finished product. Great learning experience for me, as it was the first time I had to file a sound recording copyright, obtain the appropriate logos, schedule photo shoots, and market and sell the seven-inch. I had to take out a college student loan of 5,000 dollars to pay for it all!"

Tim continues: "To my surprise, ten years later, in 1995–1996, I was contacted by a vinyl distributor who told me that my Voyeur seven-inch was a widely sought-after record in the collector's market and could I please send him several hundred copies. Right when I thought they were all sold out, I remember seeing that, on eBay in Australia, my seven-inch was selling for 100 dollars—totally blew my mind! Eventually, I sold some there, and in Greece, even—the strangest places for a mid-eighties melodic metal band, especially in the late nineties. I do have one or two small boxes left, so if anyone is reading this interview and would like to purchase a very rare seven-inch, please email me at timyasui@sbcglobal.net!"

Let me be clear, and I am by no means exaggerating: Voyeur's *First Glance* is one of the greatest seven-inch EPs to ever be released by an American metal band. This is it, simple as that. Everything here is utter perfection, including the songwriting—"Stand or Fall" could have easy been a major hit for a big band, while "Hot Touch" would be an obvious crowd-pleaser. Serious, professional, over-the-top heavy metal, and Voyeur remain one of the biggest what-ifs of the American metal underground. I can't even imagine what the future would bring for them. *First Glance* has a definite early 1980s-era Judas Priest approach, with the crazy guitar shredding of Malmsteen and/or Blackmore. However, they reveal something that very few bands have: their own character.

"I recall only a handful bands from New England having released their own stuff," Tim admits. "Run 21 was one of the top New England bands back then, featuring drummer Stet Howland, who went on to drum for W.A.S.P. and so many other huge names. Joined Forces featured Jimmy Bell on guitar, who went on to play guitar in House of Lords, and they were able to do that as well. At that time in New England, it was not as common for bands to press and release their own titles. But some of the aforementioned bands with regional interest were able to successfully release their music on their own small indie labels."

Voyeur throughout their short-lived existence played just one show (!) and Tim has a few things to say about it: "The ONLY live show that Voyeur ever played was in the University of Connecticut grand ballroom in 1986. As the metal music director of WHUS 91.7 FM, I organized a fundraiser to raise money for the non-commercial radio station, which I called The Northeastern Hard Rock Showcase. I booked all the cool local metal/hard rock acts including Run 21, Joined Forces, Band (from Boston), and Sweet Pain (from New York City). We packed the place, broadcast live over the airwaves and on local television, all while raising a few thousand bucks for our radio station! We recruited the same session players for this show that had recorded the three tracks with Justin and me: John Code, who at the time was singing for the Connecticut band Cryer, and bassist John Cianfaglione, whom I had played with previously in the cover bands Destiny and later Adonis."

After Voyeur, Tim Yasui pursued a great career in Forty Thieves, Spiders & Snakes, and London, as well as one on the executive side of the heavy metal music industry. "After moving to Hollywood in 1987, I made myself a pretty decent career working full-time for indie metal labels like Metal Blade Records, Massacre Records, Century Media Records, and now at Cleopatra Records. One thing I learned from those experiences is that the metal genre will never die; it just keeps morphing, but its global reach is undeniable. I was blown away by the reaction to Voyeur decades later, especially after seeing our album on eBay for 100 bucks. But alas, in the digital age, I've since made the EP available on iTunes.

"There will always be underground metal in its various genres," Tim concludes. "The difference now is that young indie bands can easily record albums digitally at a fraction of the cost in the eighties and nineties and can post their music up on the internet at a snap of their fingers. In a way, it's a good thing, since it evens out the playing field for unsigned bands to get their music out there to the masses—even without the help of a record label. Now even my nine-year-old daughter is able to make a digital presence online. I hope to co-write songs with her and one day record an album with her—and release them online too! She's already familiar with Michael Schenker Group!"

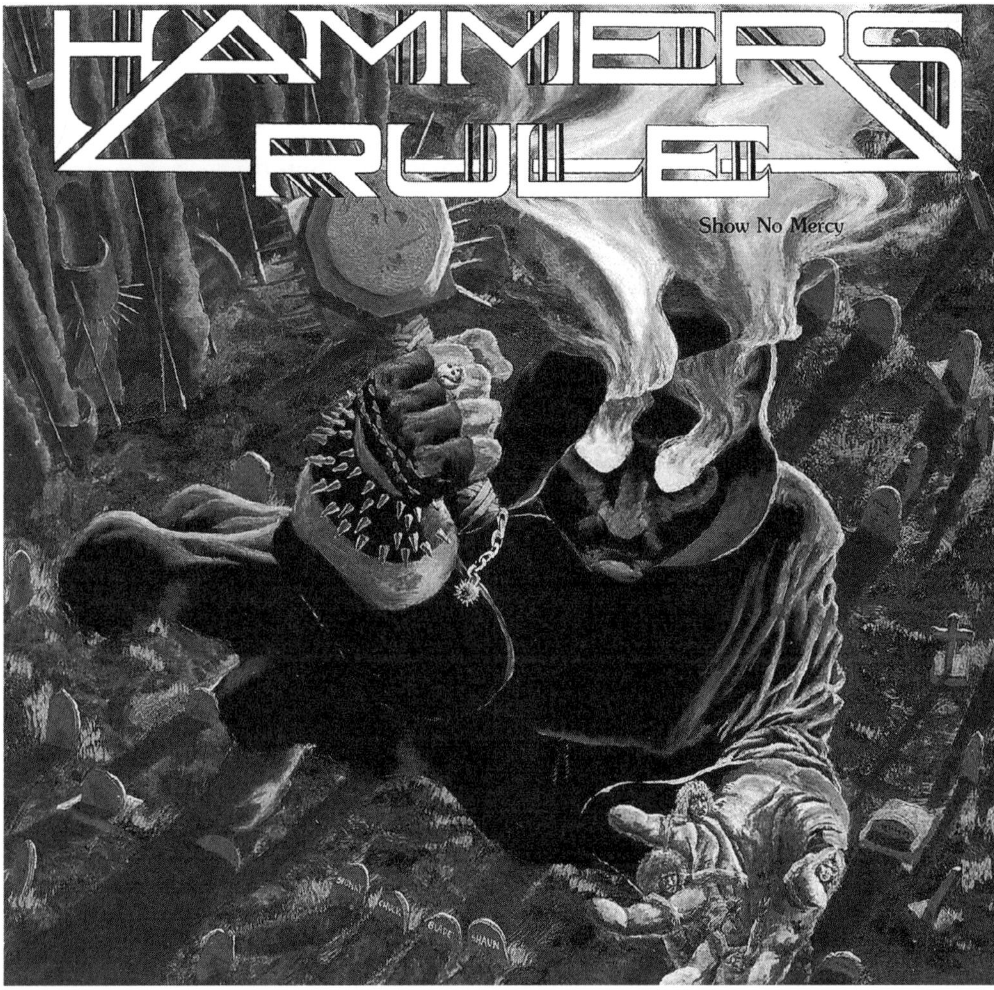

HAMMERS RULE

BACK TO THE METAL SCENE IN BALTIMORE, MARYLAND, INTRODUCED IN the Dagger section, it must be mentioned that Hammers Rule was one of the best bands to ever come out of this small but strong scene. Vocalist Frank Duncan tells their story with such enthusiasm!

"We started out in 1978–79 out in a small working-class suburb of Baltimore, Maryland, called Dundalk. A few of us guys who were in the same commercial art class in high school got together, smoked a lot of weed, and listened to cool records ... and after a while, we soon discovered that we all shared the same interest in music (hard rock and heavy metal). Somehow, we rented and practiced in a room at the Dundalk YMCA, jamming out on our favorite cover tunes and smoking lots of pot. After graduating from high school, we decided to become an actual rock band, calling ourselves Fate and consisting of Bill Wiscott playing lead guitar, Todd Ferguson on rhythm guitar, Dave Zidek on bass guitar, Keith Crass on drums, and myself on lead vocals (a.k.a. Cory Silvertin). The name of the band changed from Fate to Dream, and later to lots of other names, but in 1980, we eventually settled on the name Hammers Rule."

About that band name and how they picked it up, Frank shares, "It was actually taken directly from the 'special thanks' credits on Iron Maiden's self-titled first LP. I believe it stated something like 'Special Thanks to all the Headbangers, Hellraisers, Hellcats, Hammers Rule OK'... at that time, we had no idea that Hammers Rule referenced their favorite soccer team. Anyway, during the early eighties, we played anywhere we could. Mostly school dances, bars, and plenty of festival events in the local Baltimore and Washington area, getting quite popular for our high-energy show and unique choice of cover music at the time. Instead of gravitating to the dance and pop scene, we played medleys of Alice Cooper, Led Zep, Bad Company, Judas Priest, Bowie, Iron Maiden, and ended our last set of the night performing the entire first side of Rush's *2112*. It was a great time for music."

Frank continues their historical narrative: "About that time, we acquired a super talented lead guitarist from our neighborhood named Ronnie Mechlinski, eventually known as Spunki, and an amazing young bass player named Shawn 'Hollywood' Henley. Both had awesome playing ability and incredible stage presence as well. Needless to say, we all became really great friends and bandmates, but Ronnie got an opportunity to move to the Midwest and decided to relocate out to the Denver area in Colorado (Pueblo), where he began playing in another band called Justin Sane. So, Hammers Rule (lineup number two) in Baltimore just sort of dissolved. I became the norm: met a cool girlfriend and found a good job at a big grocery store, while still keeping in touch and remaining close friends with Ronnie. It wasn't very long before I became really bored sick of my normal working life in Maryland and took Ronnie's advice: I sold everything I owned, hopped on a Greyhound bus out to Colorado, and gave this dream a shot. Moved in together with Ronnie, began writing nonstop original heavy metal music and planning our future as (hopefully) the next great heavy rock 'n' roll band on the planet. Calling ourselves Destiny, because ... we are the FUTURE!!! At least we believed that."

During the early eighties, it was a great time to be alive and making our own music. No limits, just gotta be as creative and interesting as possible. Like we were treading new grounds musically. New wave, punk, metal, techno—so many diverse audio sounds and visual styles were out there to inspire us with fresh ideas and give an artist some creative motivation. Also, MTV was very young and just beginning to influence the youth of the world's mindset and fashion sense. But personally, the only damn thing we wanted to do at that time was simple: write, play, perform, and record our own music. And the only way to learn that, and the industry, was hands-on: just do it, and live and learn as you go. Which is exactly what we did. There was no such thing as the internet then, so we were completely on our own. Any songs that I needed to reference ideas or facts on was done in an actual brick library building. (Do you remember those? Haha!)"

And what about their motivation for forming and being so dedicated to Hammers Rule? Frank says, "I think James Hetfield of Metallica said it best: 'We were fans first. If we weren't up on that stage, we'd be out there in that audience, rocking out with them.' So true. If we weren't listing to our favorite albums, we were hanging at the local record store buying the most recent metal band's album for our own collection. We attended every rock concert or local metal gig

CUT TO THE CHASE:

I really loved the Hammers Rule story as well as Frank Duncan's narrations—I have pages and pages of our interview left in my files! And yes, if you like good, straightforward American metal, get the *Show No Mercy* LP—its original first pressing on Tangents Records, which is the white-colored record, can be obtained fairly easily.

available. So, as you can see, forming a band of our own and playing music was really just the natural next step for us. Playing music in a band was more like this incredible yearning passion deep down inside that became our whole reason for living. And very seldom did we ever make any money doing it—it literally was just a labor of love. It was that inner passion that drove us to constantly create and produce our own version of what our favorite bands were already doing. Like they say, imitation is the best form of flattery, and we had plenty of great influences to inspire us, for sure."

And as for the bands and records that were Hammers Rule's main inspiration, Frank rattles off quite a few. "In our early years, it was bands like Deep Purple, Bad Company, Alice Cooper, Led Zep, Aerosmith, Frampton, Queen, Bowie, AC/DC, Van Halen, and Kiss. Basically, all the really great commercial hard rock acts from the seventies. I could go on and on and on ... Blue Öyster Cult, Pink Floyd, Triumph, Black Sabbath. I think I saw Terrible Ted [Nugent] in concert about seven times back then. I'm sure there were many other great bands that I'm forgetting to list here, but you get the picture. By imitating these bands during this era and playing this cover music, I believe this is what gave Hammers Rule our hard rock and heavy metal music foundation. Once this music became easier for us to imitate and perform, I think we began leaning toward more technical and musically challenging artists, such as Judas Priest, Yes, UFO, Scorpions, Rush, and Iron Maiden. It was at this time that we went from playing in the bar band approach into an almost concert act, while still playing the rock clubs. The recordings that followed were absolutely some of the top LPs to affect our sound: Deep Purple's *Machine Head*, Kiss' *Alive!* and *Destroyer*, AC/DC's *If You Want Blood, You Got It* and *Highway to Hell*, Judas Priest's *Sad Wings of Destiny* and *Unleashed in the East*, Rush's *2112* and *Hemispheres*, Alice Cooper's *Billion Dollar Babies* and *Greatest Hits*, Pink Floyd's *Dark Side of the Moon* and *Wish You Were Here*, Black Sabbath's *Black Sabbath* and *Heaven and Hell*, Iron Maiden's *Iron Maiden*, *Killers*, and *Number of the Beast*, all early Led Zeppelin music, and so many more. But I guarantee you these particular albums listed here definitely gave each member of Hammers Rule creative motivation."

Regarding Baltimore in the 1980s, Frank offers us a very extensive and detailed description: "The music scene in Baltimore during my younger days was exciting and fun. Perfect for any teenager looking to get laid, hear loud music, and catch a good buzz. Just about any night of the week, you could find a club with a local rock act playing somewhere. I remember the Seagull Inn at that time was a very popular, small venue that always showcased upcoming rock bands like us. They attracted musicians and rockers from all around, booking semi-pro acts from nearby states as well. So, we spent a lot of time hanging out there. This was way before

Hammerjacks, but as I said, there were still plenty of great rock bars in the area featuring new bands, so on any given night, me and my buddies would travel within a 30-mile region to party at these nightclubs. We'd socialize and promote ourselves, maybe find a new connect or possible gig along the way. Some bands were super talented, some were just okay, but almost all the bands were doing the same cover music/original music formula at their gigs. They would play three 45-minute sets for each gig and slip in their original material whenever they could. It's a little hard to recall their names, but a few of the better Baltimore-area local bands I remember were Mannekin, DC Star, Wrathchild America, Mystic Force, Madam X, Bootcamp, Jesse Bolt, The Ravyns, Dead End Kids, and Kix. On a side note, Bootcamp had a low-budget music video that was being played on MTV, very seldomly, but it was cool that local boys were seen on TV. This was the year MTV actually started establishing itself, so all this was new and fresh to us. The Ravyns also had a hit song on the radio, and that tune was even featured in the eighties teen film *Fast Times at Ridgemont High*. It was called 'Raised on the Radio.' Not metal music, but they were talented musicians. New wave and punk were alive and well in mainstream music at that moment, and metal acts (like ours) were becoming harder to find locally ... but they were still there, if you knew where to look.

"I also remember a local commercial metal group called Face Dancer that became very popular then. The word was that they got signed, recorded a great album on Capitol Records, but got brushed aside by the record company who decided to push their other commercial rock prospect, The Knack, instead. Shame, since they were really damned good. One really super talented band in our area was called Crack the Sky. Never made it big, but they were absolutely fantastic. I think the only band that I do remember, which was playing the Balto/Washington area club circuit, and which I feel really Made It, was a high-energy act called Kix (originally called Shooze). They started out doing the 50/50 formula at places like the Seagull Inn and later Hammerjacks, playing mostly upbeat AC/DC songs and tossing in punky brash original tunes here and there. Great band live. The frontman was one-of-a-kind fabulous. I believe they went on to get national—possibly international—fame. 'Don't Close Your Eyes' was a pretty big hit here on the charts, and the video played quite often on MTV. Back then, I think, as a band, you felt that any artist who got played on the radio or MTV were absolutely on their way to stardom. Shows how naïve we truly were."

Hammers Rule moved to Colorado, playing the local metal clubs. "Some of the Colorado bands that I remember were Child's Play, Justin Sane, The Willies, Satan's Host, Castle Rock, Mau Mau 55, and Jag Panzer from Colorado Springs," says Frank. The band's first attempt on vinyl, 1984's *Show No Mercy* LP, was recorded and released there on their own label, Tangents Records. Frank explains, "This is when Hammers Rule decided to scrounge up some cash and go into a professional 36-track recording studio and record the *Show No Mercy* album in 1984. So, Ronnie Mechlinski, our guitarist, somehow got us into American Studios and soon began recording our first record, *Show No Mercy*. People treat you differently when you have a professional-sounding album out. Soon after the record was released, we noticed that we suddenly had the validity we needed. The record had established us as real musicians striving to be professional recording artists. I recall that, even when we finally had returned back to our old stomping grounds, the local people of Baltimore had a newfound respect toward us and treated the band better. More like we were their homeboys, on our way to super stardom. It was cool."

Show No Mercy, with its fantastic cover/logo artwork, grabs you instantly. It's straightforward, no-frills American heavy metal that sounds very basic in terms of sound, but at the same time is damn catchy and sincere! It has its flaws, but I won't refer to them; songs like the excellent "Pool of Piranhas," or "Hammers Rule" and "After the Bomb" are simply intriguing and genuine, whereas "Castle Walls" is maybe their most exceptional track! Too bad, though, that the other 50 percent of the LP is generic party/metal, since Hammers Rule could really have become a great, true heavy metal band.

After releasing *Show No Mercy*, Hammers Rule released an EP in 1985 called *After the Bomb* on Web Records, the label that also released Satan's Host's first LP, whereas Germany's Metal Enterprises Records re-released it in the same year, including the complete *After the Bomb* twelve-inch plus five extra songs from *Show No Mercy*. However, constant touring, substance abuse problems, and many personal and financial issues caused detrimental changes in personnel. "In 1985, Shawn 'Hollywood' Henley was married and was replaced by Blitzkrieg bassist Miles Marlin," Frank mentions. "Soon after, drummer Chuck Hohn left the band to pursue other musical interests, so to continue touring, he was replaced by drummer Mike Venus. The band traveled and toured across the USA, ending up back in our hometown Baltimore/Washington region."

The band's grand finale was 1987's *Spontaneous Human Combustion* LP on Metal Enterprises, which was a really decent effort with good songs, such as the title track, "Madman on the Loose," and "White Widow," but things were already starting to fall apart, so by 1988, Hammers Rule disbanded. Post-Hammers Rule, Frank Duncan made a guest appearance in the Baltimore band Manifest, on their *Find a New Place* CD, and also formed a heavy metal band called Pool of Piranhas.

"Just to offer some final words," Frank—who's literally unstoppable—adds, "So, to recap: We started out in Baltimore as big fans of metal, played tons of gigs, got a huge fan base, MTV and new wave music took over, and we slowly faded away. Then, we moved to Colorado, rebuilt the band, recorded an album, got cred, traveled all around the USA supporting our album and playing gigs, and eventually worked our way back to Maryland, where suddenly we were considered upcoming stars. Funny how life comes full circle sometimes, huh?

"When Hammers Rule moved back to Baltimore again, we were working on great new material and video concepts for the second album, scoping out professional music production and management, with a big plan to hook up as an opening act for a larger established band that was already on tour, like Maiden or Saxon or similar. This way we could play to larger audiences, continue promoting our album and EP, and hopefully move to the next level with the second LP. But sometimes life throws a monkey wrench into your engine, and that plan never came to light. Oh, well ... shit happens. But wow, man, what a ride we had!"

SPECTRAL INCURSION

FROM HAVERHILL, MASSACHUSETTS, SPECTRAL INCURSION ORIGINALLY formed in late 1985 as Trinity, and the band played their first live show before changing names to Graven Image in 1986. With the recruitment of singer Rob Tadiello in 1987, they changed their name again, this time to Spectral Incursion. Bassist/vocalist Art Melonas says, "I started playing with Steve Lytle (guitar/vocals) and Jay Frasca (drums) in 1983. Steve and Jay were three years younger than me, but even though they were very young too (I was 15 years old and they were 12), they were both great players, so we started jamming and learning some Sabbath tunes. Then I started getting some riffs together, so we started doing original songs. I had a bunch of riffs to get the band going, which gave Steve Lytle a kick to get him going on writing riffs. The more I sat down with my classical guitar and a nice big joint, the more riffs I came out with. When you're young the mind is full of so many ideas, they just keep pouring out. At the time, we were very big into Sabbath, Rush, ELP, progressive rock-type stuff, so our early riffs were a reflection of the music we listened to—we wanted to create a band with lots of cool riffs!"

Art says, "Steve Lytle and I were big into Rush, Sabbath, Iron Maiden, and early Scorpions stuff, but we were discovering new and old music at the same time. We would go down to the record store and find new music, so we would have a Slayer album and also find older music like Jethro Tull. And Jay Frasca, the drummer, was big into John Bonham from Led Zeppelin; he could already play the full 'Moby Dick' drum solo at age 12. But the most influential record to me was *A Farewell to Kings* by Rush!"

At the time, in the mid- to late eighties, thrash was the big underground thing, and we liked thrash," Art mentions. "We listened to it, but we didn't want to be just another thrash band. We never set out to be a metal band; we just played what we played, and when we played at clubs, we would always be grouped in with metal bands, thrash bands, et cetera. None of the metal bands we played with liked what we were doing because we weren't following the scene, but we didn't want to follow the scene. Moreover, I've heard that in places like San Francisco, all the thrash bands were friends, but it wasn't like that in Massachusetts; it seemed like every band hated each other. But we did make some friends while playing out."

In 1988, Spectral Incursion went on to release the excellent *Nowhere Fast* demo, from which four tracks were later included on the band's first vinyl offering, which was also released through their own label in 1989, the *Spectral Incursion* twelve-inch. Art tells the story behind it:

"We had a first recording prior to them, which was recorded at a country studio—the engineer never recorded a rock band before—so the original Graven Image/Spectral Incursion demo tape was recorded very poorly. The *Nowhere Fast* demo tape was recorded in our hometown, Haverhill, Massachusetts, at Double Edge Music. We went in with a new singer and friend of ours, Rob Tadiello, we recorded a bunch of tunes and played more gigs, but the fans/friends couldn't get used to the band having a new singer, so we decided to go back to a trio. The engineer at the studio, Dave Spaulding, knew of a place in New Jersey that could press a record for us. So, I re-recorded the vocal parts, and the engineer had the four songs pressed onto an EP. I can't remember, but I think that the 500 copies pressed cost us about 500 dollars. The father of a friend of ours had a printing shop, so we had him print out the cheap sleeves that came with the EP."

Spectral Incursion is a stellar release and definitely one of the most challenging the American metal underground ever put out. Imagine Voivod and Watchtower blended with Slauter Xstroyes, with a melancholic edge ("Beneath Your Lives") and an element of thrash ("The Other Side"), with "Last of the Torment" being the best song on the classic twelve-inch EP. While searching for more info on Spectral Incursion, I also came across obscure bands of the same era like Myramainz, Sedition, Savage Choir, Silo, Brothers Grimm, and Suiciety, and it's a damn shame that bands of this quality never managed to put out a record in their heyday—just demos.

What is pretty fascinating is how the *Spectral Incursion* twelve-inch went on to be heard in some European countries. Steve Lytle was also the guitarist for the excellent Methuen, Massachusetts, punk band The Broken Toys, and Art adds, "I didn't know people were back into the underground scene and records. The only reason our EP got around the world was because Steve Lytle brought a bunch of our EPs to Europe when he did a small tour with The

Broken Toys, and he spread our EP around those places (mostly in Germany)."

After another demo in 1991—the (also excellent) *Middle of Nowhere*—Spectral Incursion disbanded later that year, with Steve and Art both later playing in Doctor Smith alongside drummer Jim Mazarakis. However, in 2010, in preparation for the release of the Spectral Incursion two-disc compilation *Anthology* by Stormspell Records, the band reunited with Rob on vocals under their previous name Graven Image and recorded totally new versions of old songs from the Graven Image demo. And they've been active since then!

"I don't recall any really memorable shows," Art admits. "A lot of times, we would play metal on Tuesday nights in Boston, so the clubs were pretty bare on a Tuesday night. We did back up Hallow's Eve in Boston at the Channel nightclub, we played all around Massachusetts and a few places in New Hampshire, we played a show with Satan's Warriors (later to be renamed Anal Cunt) and Afterbirth, which included Terry from the band Grief. That was a fun show!"

Art closes our interview: "I feel bad for any of the bands coming out today. The music scene is just flooded with bands, and no one will ever get their music heard with so much music on the internet. What we tried to do in Spectral Incursion was to create original sounding music—and a lot of that is lost today. Everything has been done."

CUT TO THE CHASE:

Into some of the weirdest metal ever? Are you a fan of Voivod's most progressive moments, Watchtower, Slauter Xstroyes, or even Sacred Blade, Militia, Toxic (*Think This*), or Blind Illusion? You need the *Spectral Incursion* twelve-inch, simple as that. Crazy, bizarre, and at the same time 100 percent metal to the bone, this is an EP that will appeal both to progsters and true metalheads alike. I think 80 to 120 dollars is a pretty good deal for this EP (considering its past sales history), but let's also wait for some special deluxe re-release of all their stuff! Anyway, this one's mandatory at least.

RESLESS

RESLESS STARTED OUT AS A HIGH SCHOOL METAL BAND TOWARD THE END of 1983 in River Vale, New Jersey, when Kurt E. Stahl (guitar/vocals) got together with Jim Cardinale (guitar), who lived five or six houses down the street from him. Jim said he knew of a drummer who he'd heard was pretty good, Kevin McCarthy. It didn't take long for the three to put some songs together. Kurt says, "This is exactly the Resless story; we started out as a high school band when I asked 16-year-old drummer Kevin McCarthy to join my buddy and neighbor, Jim Cardinale, to jam with us. We instantly hit it off and starting writing tunes. The first two were the two that ultimately ended up on the Resless 45, 'Don't Understand' and 'The Power.'

"To play very loud and heavy music and to meet girls—that was our focus!" Kurt laughs. "It was all influenced by Kiss, Cheap Trick, Thin Lizzy, UFO, and Judas Priest. Specifically, Kiss' *Dressed to Kill* and Cheap Trick's *Heaven Tonight* blew my mind when I was a teenager.

"We were a bit of a locally famous group," Kurt adds. "We were filling clubs with a following that would bring banners and signs with songs on them. That was pretty damn cool! The locals were very welcoming."

About their decision to put out a record on their own, Kurt responds, "We were teenagers and didn't have any kind of connection with record labels but knew we wanted to be heard. The procedure was pretty simple, honestly. We took the nine songs we had written, went into a local studio, and belted them out. I didn't even have a great amp at the time. I actually used my boom box as my amp. The sound you hear of my guitar is fed through that. Pretty damn good sound, I must say! Although *Kerrang!* thought it sounded like trash cans banging together. I was totally okay with that. Only 500 copies were produced. We sent promos to fanzines around the world and garnered five-star reviews in each of them. We sold copies at local record shops and at shows. Fan mail started to pour in, and much of it was pretty interesting, to say the least. Not bad for kids in their mid- to late teens!"

CUT TO THE CHASE:

Resless are one of the early-eighties American bands that based their sound mostly on the incoming (in America) NWOBHM style, with Judas Priest and early Iron Maiden influences. The 1984 *Restless Metal* seven-inch is a real beauty, but a great rarity too!

In 1984, Resless released their *Restless Metal* seven-inch on their own Flying Dog Productions, which includes two fantastic, pure heavy metal anthems—with the emphasis on heavy. Both "Don't Understand" and "The Power" are done in the tradition of Judas Priest of the late seventies and early eighties and NWOBHM. Catchy, rocking, overall great American metal that still has a connection with the UK sound of the era, rather than with the then-emerging American metal sound.

"Of course, there were many metal bands that put out their records on their own too," Kurt adds. "My friend Dan Lorenzo's band, Hades. They put a 45 out, and we did it right after they did. Dan was awesome for helping us through the process."

Resless went on to recruit a new bass player. "We needed a bass player, and a friend of ours knew one who mopped floors at a local record store. We paid him a visit, and as soon as we walked in, he knocked the mop bucket over, and we knew right then he was our guy: Dave Messinger," Kurt says. And then they were back in the studio in late 1984 to record six more songs; however, these songs ended up as demos only.

Resless kept it up, though, and performed locally for a couple of more years. "Probably a gig we did with King Kobra is my favorite. Those guys were very cool, and kick-ass musicians. I'll have to say the most memorable was when our bass player, Dave, accidentally knocked down a set of Marshall stacks belonging to the band Tangier. We got into a fistfight with them and then ended up partying with them after the gig, because we blew them off the stage!"

Resless then took a long break, only to become again active in 2018. "Getting all of this great metal out to people even after many years is really cool, man," Kurt says. "Lots of great music that needs to be heard by bands that never had the chance. It's pretty wild that our output has become a highly paid collector's item. You put yourself out there, good things happen. I'll continue doing it as long as I can.

"I'm not sure if an underground metal scene exists today. I certainly hope so. As for the whole downloading issue, on one hand, I'm cool with it because music is made to be shared, and on the other, I think we should be paid. In the end, people will do what they do."

At the close of our interview, Kurt says: "In 2019, we put out those nine songs, remixed and mastered, and called it *Unearthed*. Nine killer songs. I'm in the middle of remixing and mastering songs from 1985–1989 that will be under the Resless name, but they were done during other iterations of Resless when we were called Dirty Blonde and then A Thousand Times. I just feel these songs need to be heard. We're also going to be part of a book about the New Jersey metal scene in the eighties. Written by Alan Tecchio of the bands Watchtower and Non-Fiction as well as the legendary photographer Frank White. In November of 2021, RidingEasy Records will be releasing a compilation called *Scrap Metal: Volume 1* that will include our song 'The Power.' Psyched about that!"

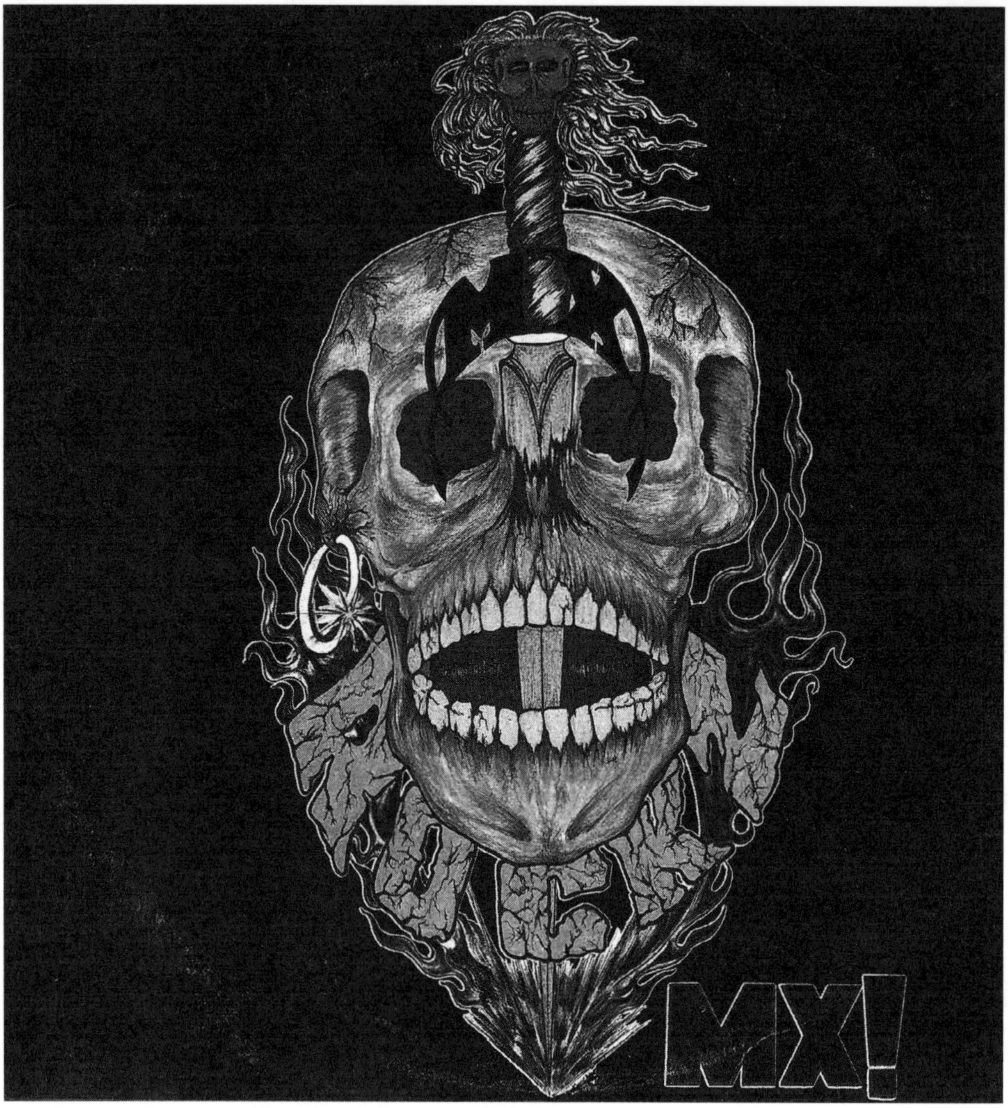

MX

FORMED INITIALLY IN 1982 IN MACON, GEORGIA, AND THEN RELOCATED TO Atlanta, MX—since renamed MX the American—have a huge history in the underground metal scene of the East Coast. They're still active as of 2022, after a hiatus between 2006 and 2018, partly due to the death of "Rad Ray" Terrell's son. "We started in Macon, Georgia, in July of 1982 with me on bass and backing vocals, Alan Carden on the guitar, David Stamper on lead vocals, and Wade Bradley on drums," says bassist, vocalist, and founding member "Rad Ray" Terrell. "Shortly after doing a demo at the Otis Redding Foundation and mixing at its Capricorn Records, we hired Michael S. to become the lead singer in 1985. After making the decision to find bigger audiences, Michael S. and I moved to Atlanta and hired Kris Madsen on lead guitar, Sam Couch on guitar, and Chris Cook on drums and percussion. The band was complete then to record the infamous

CUT TO THE CHASE:

If you're into the classic American metal style that's based more on heavy rock (with a metallic production) rather than in the American power metal vein, you need to get the *Rockz* LP as well as the *Out of Control/ If You Really Love Me* seven-inch. Also recommended is O.P.M.'s *MX* compilation LP. I'm guessing, however, that hardcore metalheads will have limited interest in those releases.

Rockz album. My motivation to start MX was to be able to express my musical outlook and expression my way. Our musical influences are/were Jimi Hendrix, Motörhead, Ozzy, Judas Priest, Iron Maiden, Scorpions, and Anthrax.

"Atlanta had a really great metal/thrash scene," Ray adds, "with clubs like the Metro Plex, 688 Club, the Masquerade, but the locals were a really tight-knit group of militant skinheads and hair farmers, especially in the downtown and Little Five Points areas of Atlanta. However, through our existence, we played lots of great shows here, like opening for Slayer, then Megadeth ... I can't really put my finger on an exact specific show, since we did a lot of shows with a lot of great bands! Hell, we've opened for Red Hot Chili Peppers, Overkill, Quiet Riot, Butthole Surfers, Sister Hazel, Fates Warning, Paul Diano's Battlezone, Mercyful Fate, and King Diamond!"

MX have a very interesting distinction as a band: all their records, with the exception of their latest, 2021's *Appalachia Voodoo Factory*, have been self-released on their own label, Radical Recordz (and its variants). Accordingly, their first LP, 1986's *Rockz*, was also self-released, and Ray explains, "After shopping our demo around here and there, I finally said, 'To hell with it ... let's do our own album, our way, and not worry about what other companies and bands thought about it,' and I hooked up with Hugh Harrer with Transmedia Sounds Studios on the outskirts of Atlanta, in Lithia Springs, Georgia. We made a decision on doing eight songs and set to work on it, finished it in 1986, then went to print. A lot more gigs came our way then, along with some really good response and some mixed responses. A lot of people were saying stuff like 'You can't put out your own record!' Well, we did it, and did it our way. Best thing we could have ever done!"

Rockz is a verging-on-excellent American metal LP that blends heavy rock with the rising-at-the-time classic American metal and NWOBHM. With awesome songs like the thunderous "Electrocuted Madness" which is reason enough alone to buy this record, the opening headbanger of "Hyway to the Top," which sounds like a cross between Twisted Sister and W.A.S.P., or the melodic "Straight Line," *Rockz* is wholeheartedly recommended for everyone into the classic American metal sound of its day.

MX released another record of pure heavy metal in 1988, the *Out of Control/If You Really Love Me* seven-inch (wild stuff here too!) before heading into the nineties in first a more alternative rock and later modern metal direction, releasing six full-length CDs. In 1988, John Haupt from O.P.M. Records released the excellent *MX* LP, which compiled the band's old eighties demos, obviously from their heavy metal days.

"There were also other bands with private releases, such as Panda, Wrongful Death, Masada ... I remember a lot of them," Ray says. "Most had demos. I'm really glad that early metal bands are having a resurgence; it's nice to know people respected and at least listened to what we did. You do a lot as a musician just to get a pat on the back, and then if your album actually becomes a collector's item, like the MX album *Rockz,* it's just awesome to have been a part of it all!"

Still active, and still releasing records in a modern metal style, MX continue to perform mostly in Georgia. "I still believe that there's an underground scene," Ray asserts. "Some places, it's off the chain, but back in the 1980s and early 1990s, it rocked! As far as download sites, I'm a fan; I just wish all of them promoted the bands on their site more. But overall, now a band can be heard worldwide at the click of a button. Back in the day, we had to search for places to send them to, and then hope it actually got there. We just somehow stumbled on the right person that could do something to help the band."

CARNAGE (SOUTH CAROLINA)

FANS OF ROUGH, BLUE-COLLAR AMERICAN METAL, TAKE NOTICE. FORMED by kids at Spring Valley High School in Northeast Columbia, South Carolina, in the mid-1970s, Carnage holds their own place in the history of underground American metal.

"Initially it was Albert 'Chip' Anseman, Bruce McLeod (guitar), Nick Pagan (drums), Keith Woodward, and a host of other musicians came until Andrew went. They played covers. I was living at a drug halfway house and met the guys when attending Spring Valley High," vocalist Stuart Johnson (a.k.a. Jack Hammer) narrates. "After school, Carnage drifted apart. Pagan, McLeod, and Woodward made their marks in the local new wave and punk scene, but Anseman moved to Florida. He lived in a motel and worked as a maintenance man. Around 1982, I was working at a local punk club when I ran into McLeod and Dave Alewine (bass). They were looking for a singer, so we worked on forming a band. We recorded some songs, but it just wasn't jelling. Alewine told me about jamming with a guitarist and drummer who had recently returned to town. He thought

I'd be a good fit and I got together with them. The drummer (I don't remember his name) didn't care for my vocal style. But Anseman and I connected instantly. We worked with the original songs Anseman wrote and put lyrics to poems that I had written for the purpose of using them for songs. In the notebook was the beginning of a short story I was writing for a local contest. Anseman found the notebook one night and set the short story to music. It appeared on the album as 'Killer.'

"After that," Stuart continues, "we had weekly meetings where we fleshed out song ideas, then brought those to the rest of the band ... we rarely played gigs, but instead focused on working toward the goal of recording the album. Just before the recording of the album began, the drummer left suddenly. He is remembered as 'Skip Towne' in the notes on the back of the original LP jacket. So, we recruited Rick Griffith, a drummer in the local scene, to do the drums on the album."

CUT TO THE CHASE:

As you already know, I can't get enough of this kind of venomous, awkward, raw American metal, in the vein of Knightmare or Brocas Helm. Actually, Carnage seems to combine the punkiness of the former with the epicness of the latter! The 1986 *Carnage* LP is a tremendous classic (there, I said it!), and you can get the original pressing along with both the Heaven and Hell and Lost Realm CD/ LP re-releases, titled *Massacre*, which include their massive 1985 demo too!

"I wasn't scheduled and didn't play with Carnage, but we were friends," drummer Rick Griffith says. "I played drums in a rockabilly band and before that a punk band, so they knew I could play. The drummer they had had some kind of an addiction problem and wasn't able to play, and they asked me. We practiced twice, and I recorded the songs on a cassette player, and when I was in my car, I listened to them, and then when we went into the studio, I did all the songs in one take except two. Funny, in one song, I knocked a cymbal stand over, and on the other song the studio engineer noticed I was growling while I played and he asked me to stop doing that. I did a couple of live shows with them—it was fun. Now there are only three of us left, since the guitarist died of a drug overdose..."

In 1986, Carnage released the eponymous *Carnage* LP on their own label, Pyle M. High Productions; those who admire the much rawer stuff (like, ahem, me) will definitely fall in love with Carnage's ultra-barbaric, brutal, and menacing approach. The punk aesthetic is all over this album, and how could it not be, since several members had a background in the punk scene? However, this is still total, raging American metal that reminds me of Cirith Ungol and Knightmare (New Hampshire)—just like a blend of Motörhead with early Iron Maiden and the gloomy sound of Dead Boys, and the epic elements of Manilla Road, and the street attitude of NWOBHM (e.g., Sledgehammer). Songs like "Killer" and "Omega Man" have to be heard to be believed, whereas "The Astral Inn" is an epic metal masterpiece. Here, Carnage had gone on to become even more brutal than their 1985 *Bring on the Victims* demo cassette, which was already very raw, and this LP represents the band's peak.

In 1989, Carnage released two songs off their LP on a seven-inch titled *This Is the End*, on Amethyst Records, the South Carolina label that also released stuff by Commandment—and this was the end of a brilliant band. Rick Griffith adds, "I like the fact that there is a renewed interest in the underground scene of metal's heyday. Classic rock radio has already missed the opportunity to expose the deep cuts and more obscure bands. For example, among music lovers like myself, Crack the Sky is the best band from the late 1970s that most people never heard. Big Star inspired decades of new wave and indie-rock jangly guitar sounds, yet at best, they had a cult following. The same with metal. Signed bands like Savatage, At War, Wargasm, and Diamond Head (to name a few) never got the audience they deserved. Heaven and Hell Records had a large stable of independent metal bands from that era, and the mastermind behind that label is doing a great service to the true devoted music lovers who (like me) think their favorite music is stuff they haven't heard yet. I am very happy that they chose to re-release the Carnage record. There most likely won't ever be a reunion—I can't envision Carnage without Spike Marshall. But it is a great memorial to my brother that his music is still reaching people's ears."

"I really didn't know about the Carnage album being a collector's item until the early years of this century," Stuart says, "when I was doing sound at a venue in my hometown. I had Hellacopters play my stage and I wore a Carnage T-shirt I made while studying commercial graphics. They recognized the logo from the album cover and conversation ensued. I was stunned to find out that people actually collected the record. I also found the listing of us in the Encyclopaedia Metallum. I have to say that I was very pleasantly surprised!"

Finally, Stuart mentions, "The internet changed the landscape of how music is made, promoted, and distributed. Some of it good, but in many ways, it has made it harder to establish a foothold in the business. But I think that, throughout history, there's always been a dilution of the soul of art in general when it becomes a product for sale. But then again, marketing music is how it gets into more ears. So, it's a necessary evil. Is there an underground scene? Maybe. But mostly regional and local scenes. In the digital age, YouTube, SoundCloud, and Bandcamp have replaced underground networks like the one that I got my copy of Metallica's *Metal Up Your Ass* through."

This Carnage piece is dedicated to the late Spike Marshall. You can check out some more stuff by the band by searching for "Carnage Columbia SC Metal Band" on Facebook.

SINISTER ANGEL

ATLANTA'S SINISTER ANGEL HAVE NOT ONLY LEFT THEIR FOOTPRINT ON the history of American metal, the band also remains active today! Emerging from the ashes of the seventies metal band Warrior[3] (Rick Norris on drums and Greg Bolton on guitar), Sinister Angel set the bar pretty high from day one. "Many different factors fall into effect for me, then and now," Greg replies when asked about his motivation to start a band. "I think you want to combine all of your biggest influences into your own monster. Being a youngster, well, of course, you wanted the girls and stardom ... plus I never ever wanted to get a real job!"

Jim Staggers was also added on bass, as well as vocalist Billy May. Sinister Angel members all met each other while enrolled at the Music Business Institute at the Art Institute of Atlanta, studying sound engineering and copyright law, and their goal was to record and release their own brand of American heavy metal. Boy, have they succeeded! "Back on the first album, our

3 Another band also emerged from the ashes of Warrior: Hallow's Eve, with Stacy Andersen and Tommy Stewart.

CUT TO THE CHASE:

Into true American metal? The original *Sinister Angel* twelve-inch will make you cry, and it's not gonna leave your turntable for months! You'll probably spend between 90–120 bucks to get it, and my advice is to also get the *Enter the Gates of Hell* LP. The 1984 twelve-inch will appeal equally to fans of early Fates Warning as well as to fans of the most complex Iron Maiden stuff. And why not—people who are into Liege Lord or even Slauter Xstroyes would admire it too!

overall coolest influence was Alice Cooper!" Greg says. "Ace Frehley was my idol on guitar, along with Tony Iommi and Ted Nugent. I think Rick's influences were Neil Peart and Neil Peart, haha! Jim Staggers is simple—Steve Harris, throw in some Geezer Butler, and let's start jamming, boys!

"In 1984, it was becoming almost a trend to release an EP with four to six songs to get signed. We recorded six tracks, I think, in four days. And it sounded like shit, but it was what it was," Greg sighs. But in my humble opinion, he is wrong. Their *Sinister Angel* twelve-inch contained some absolutely amazing, powerful, unique-sounding American metal that bordered on both epic and power metal, with hints of progressive metal! Its four songs are absolutely challenging, thundering, and inspired, and the raw production offers so much power to the band. Unexpected pace changes, weird structures, and passion for hot metal are all found in *Sinister Angel*, and I dare you to compare "The Last Alternative" with any classic eighties American metal song. Of course, Iron Maiden and Rush influences are heard here, but what you get is a menacing dose of great, original stuff.

Following the release of Sinister Angel, the band decided to move to Los Angeles. "Rick and I grew up in Atlanta, and Bill grew up in Mississippi," Greg mentions. "We were usually well accepted in Atlanta ... then when we moved to Hollywood, oh, my God! We were early-twenties kids; hell, Bill was still in his teens! Jim and I moved out first to get a gig and slept in the car by the ocean on Highway 101 and wherever we could for a while. To summarize, life for us in L.A. and the scene was just dog eat dog. We always had a noose hanging around our necks. From going onstage and the cord from my amp head being unplugged (awkward!) and blowing the circuit breakers to assholes dropping rows of fireworks down on your face and heads! Priceless."

In 1985 in Los Angeles, Sinister Angel released a four-track demo before fading away. "We got the chance to meet many bands that were like us up to then; there were a few in L.A., but in Atlanta, not so much," Greg says. "We did have past and present bandmates from Hallow's Eve, Necropolis, and Bloody Gyres."

Fast-forward to early 2001, when Sinister Angel reformed with three of the original members—Rick Norris, Billy May, and Greg Bolton—and released a new album in late 2012 titled *13 Skulls*. Again, the album was recorded and released on their own, this time with a more modern production and style. This album kind of reminds one of Ozzy's post-*Osmosis* stuff as well as nineties-era W.A.S.P., but it still has the melodies and the hooks. However, the band's first twelve-inch was re-released with bonus tracks in 2018 by the Greek label Cult

Metal Classics, titled *Enter the Gates of Hell*. As you can imagine, the bonus stuff is as legendary as one might think: American metal that fans of this style will just go apeshit over. “Avenge the Innocent” will bring you to your knees!

“I think the uplift of independent labels are the future of the music industry,” Greg says. “It’s extremely easy to record your own tunes in your own home these days, to cut out the big labels fucking you over a barrel and then telling you to make them a sandwich and clean the gutters on your way out the door. There’s always been an underground scene with a pulse of its own! If you can’t find it, you’re not trying hard enough! It’s not at fucking Starbucks, is it? My opinion of music being available to download at the drop of a hat is: It’s awesome if the artist isn’t getting dicked on royalties! Which is nothing new and may never change...”

As of this writing in 2020, Sinister Angel are still active, so let’s cross our fingers for a new release soon!

BLACK TASK

ONE OF THE HARDEST-SOUNDING AMERICAN METAL BANDS, BLACK TASK, even though they can't be filed under the 'true metal' umbrella, were definitely a wild bunch, delivering their totally aggressive metal with a passion. Formed in Philadelphia, Pennsylvania, in 1984, Steve Kristiansen (guitar) tells me, "The first name of the band was Maidenhead and consisted of Warren Ay on vocals/guitar, Eric Az on lead guitar, Gus Santiago on bass guitar, and Jim Trub on drums. Warren was dating my sister, Karen Kristiansen, and expressed a concern about getting an additional guitar player to relieve him of his dual duties. I eventually joined the band, sharing lead guitar duties with Eric. This band was doing mainly cover music, i.e., Priest, Motörhead, Deep Purple, et cetera.

"In 1986, we decided to write original music with a heavier/hardcore edge," Steve continues. "Eric Az did not care for that direction, so he left the band, leaving me as sole lead guitar player. After his departure, we decided to rename the band. We used the first letter of the four members' last names: T (Trub), A (Ay), S (Santiago), and K (Kristiansen), and the color Black seemed to be the appropriate word to place in front of Task."

Black Task released initially a four-song demo titled *Spikes to the Wall*, and it was as raw and brutal as you might imagine. All four songs clocked in under three minutes, whereas the title track and "Harbinger of Death" have to be heard to be believed. Totally out-of-control stuff. Black Task had a definite metal sound, though, that was fueled by the ferocity of hardcore, even though the end result was 100 percent metal.

"Some of our biggest influences were Motörhead, Metallica, Slayer, and Venom, along with older bands like UFO, Deep Purple, and Riot," Steve acknowledges. "I was influenced by some hardcore/punk too, but it was prominently stuff from Venom, Slayer, a lot of black metal-type music. While it may not seem to be the style of the music Black Task was playing, I would say Pink Floyd's *The Wall* was the record that left me the greatest impression and inspiration.

"Fortunately, the original music scene in Philadelphia was thriving," Steve adds, "but as far as heavy/thrash metal, we were the only band doing it. It took some time, but we were able to turn over a substantial fan base in the area. We had many memorable shows at the Empire Rock Club in Philadelphia, but I would have to say my favorite was our show at the Penny Arcade in Rochester, New York. We initially were supposed to support Metal Church there, but because of a problem in their organization, they pulled out and we played the show solo. The entire event was a great experience, with a local radio show the night before, and the fans were great at the show the following day."

Black Task went on to release their first twelve-inch EP, *Black Task*, in 1985, on their own label, Damnation Records. "It was self-produced, as you can tell by the quality, in a local recording studio," Steve adds. "We initially pressed 1,000 copies under the name Damnation Records and sold them at shows and through the mail. Back then, there was a huge underground scene throughout the world for this type of music. This helped us get our record contract with a label from France named Axe Killer Records."

Black Task is a brutal masterpiece of speed/thrash metal, with the hardcore/punk influences floating all over (especially in songs such as "Firestorm," which has a very Discharge approach) or "Smash Your Face." In fact, all the four songs on this EP are crushing, relentless pieces of metal noise. The power of the band didn't leave record labels cold, and as mentioned Black Task was offered a one-album contract by Axe Killer.

The result was the *Long After Midnight* LP in 1986, which could be regarded as the most American metal of Black Task's catalog. Almost gone were the hardcore influences (with the exception of "Burning the Sky"), and *Long After Midnight* sported a definite metal edge. They're a heavy/speed-styled band (with the emphasis on heavy) that put out some excellent tracks, such as "The Terminal Frost" and "The Road Burns."

"Anvil Bitch, great local band that would open for us at the Empire back in the day, and shared a same approach with us," Steve recalls when asked about other local bands who put out indie albums. "They were the only other band doing this type of music. I believe they have recently reformed and are doing some shows in the area!"

CUT TO THE CHASE:

Black Task are not a band you can call true metal by any means, since their hardcore-fused sound makes their heavy/speed metal edge pretty extreme. Fans of Razor, early Exciter, Destructor, and Venom, as well as those who fancy the crazy early NYHC sound of Urban Waste, The Mob, or The Abused will enjoy the *Black Task* twelve-inch, whereas more traditional metalheads will definitely enjoy the *Long After Midnight* LP.

Black Task called it quits sometime in the late 1980s, with some of their music getting re-released in the aughts. Bestial Burst Records re-released their two demo songs in 2006 on a split seven-inch with Incriminated, and the "Polaris" digital single was released in 2010. Also in 2010, Radio Raheem Records, a hardcore/punk label out of New York City, released the compilation LP *Black Task/Spikes to the Wall*, which included their first twelve-inch and the *Spikes to the Wall* demo.

Following the dissolution of Black Task, Warren Ay went on to form a progressive metal (!) instrumental band, recording under his real name, Warren Appleby, and releasing a huge number of albums upon which he plays everything.

"I think this resurgence of interest from old metal is incredible," Steve adds, "and I would say we have today's communication technology to thank for that. I believe it helps nourish real underground scenes. Downloading was a great evolution for the music industry. It helps talented artists get their music out there with ease but, in the end, still requires hard work and passion for the music."

heroes of the METAL underground

WEST COAST

RUFFIANS

RUFFIANS ARE ONE OF THE BEST-KNOWN BANDS IN THIS BOOK, NOT ONLY thanks to their high-quality sound and material, but also due to the fact that some of its members went on to other popular bands afterward. Formed in Berkeley, California, in 1983, Ruffians was made up of a group of like-minded friends who listened to much of the same music. Craig Behrhorst (guitar), Luke Bowman (drums), and Chris Atchison (guitar) started the band. "We rounded it off with Dan Moura on bass, who I'd been friends with since grade school," Craig adds. "Everyone in the band was from Berkeley except for our singer, Rob Bonstin. Rob was the first singer for Ruffians before Carl Albert and later Rich Wilde. This was 1983, a time when friends from the neighborhood could form a band. We all grew up together and then matured as musicians and songwriters throughout the years that we played together. Ruffians' first show was at the Mabuhay Gardens in San Francisco in December of '83. Our friend Paul Baloff from Exodus was there and gave us a big thumbs-up—Paul knew his rock and metal!

"We've been influenced by the bands from our youth, such as Deep Purple, Judas Priest, Thin Lizzy, Scorpions, Rainbow, and UFO. NWOBHM bands like Iron Maiden, Tygers of Pan Tang, and Saxon made a big impact on us as well," Craig offers. "There are so many records that I've been inspired by! The albums that I learned to play guitar to were *Led Zeppelin II* and the first Montrose LP. I loved live LPs, so UFO's *Strangers in the Night*, Thin Lizzy's *Live and Dangerous*, Judas Priest's *Unleashed in the East*, and Scorpions' *Tokyo Tapes* were a big influence. AC/DC *Powerage* and Aerosmith *Rocks* were huge for me as well."

Ruffians kicked things off with their 1984 four-song demo. If you expect the typical underproduced, lo-fi recordings of the era, you'll be shocked: This is a totally professional recording, bringing great power, all of which ended up on their seminal 1985 self-released EP *Ruffians*. Craig, when asked to describe the release of *Ruffians*, explains: "We wanted to get our music out to the world and didn't want to wait for anyone. My sister Lorrie Behrhorst, who was managing the band at the time, was instrumental in making Ruffians' first release possible. She pitched the idea to the band and made it happen. We got some private funding and went into Studio D in Sausalito, California, in January of '85. We recorded and mixed those six songs in about 24 hours! It went really fast. I sure wish we'd had another 24 hours to hone in the overall sound and re-take a few tracks, but it breathes with youth and excitement. The EP was released to the masses on May 1st, 1985. This was a hands-on lesson on how a record was produced and released, start to finish. Lorrie created Victory Records along with our own publishing company, Victory One Music. We registered our songs with BMI to have total control of our product, publishing, royalties et cetera. This was also a crash course in the business of promoting a record. We sent the record to every college radio station in the county that had a metal program, along with many radio stations in Europe with metal programs. We started getting heavy rotation, along with letters from European and American magazines, asking us for interviews and photos. Lorrie then licensed the EP to SPV Records in Europe and FEMS Records in Japan with a lucrative return. while retaining the rights to our music. This helped to establish Ruffians on a global level."

Ruffians is hands-down a moment of glory in the history of American private-release metal; shining like a diamond throughout its six songs, the album reveals a nature and class that very few bands of the era had. From the opener, "Fight for Your Life," it's obvious that Ruffians have a character all their own. "Wasteland" is great too, with its mid-tempo rhythm and infectious chorus, and the only mediocre moment comes with "Bad Boys Cut Loose," which takes a more glam metal approach. "Run for Cover" is top-notch stuff, and so is "Eyes of Fire." Ruffians closes with the ballad "You're All I Need," and the initial pressing, 1,000 copies, on the band's own Victory Records label quickly vanished.

"The Bay Area music scene was great! We were teenagers hitting our twenties, we felt alive, and anything seemed possible," Craig says. "All the Bay Area bands in the eighties were lucky to have professional clubs to play in. Venues such as Old Waldorf, the Keystone, and Wolfgang's were great clubs where many national acts and local bands played. The Mabuhay Gardens and Ruthie's Inn were great too, not as pro, but reckless and a shit-ton of fun. These places were our clubhouses, where the bands, fans, and friends hung out. All the bands and locals treated each other with mutual respect and seemed genuinely interested in one another. Around this time, metal and punk converged at the clubs. Punk and metal bands and fans began to hang out together at some of these clubs, and everyone got on well. We were all there for the love of music, to get drunk, get laid, and have a good time!"

RUFFIANS FLYER WITH LIZZY BORDEN AT RUTHIE'S (CLUB)

Vocalist Carl Albert left Ruffians later in 1986 to join Vicious Rumors and was replaced by Rich Wilde. Overstatement or not, Rich managed to fill Carl's shoes successfully, and the result was the 1987 four-song demo. No surprises here: It was still top-class American metal, with the terrific "Do or Die" and "Through Your Eyes." Sounding like an American heavy/power metal version of Dio, the 1987 demo proved that Ruffians could continue ... but they chose not to and disbanded in late 1988.

When I asked Craig about his all-time favorite shows, he answers: "We played the Stone in Berkeley, California, with Slayer and Lääz Rockit on January 27, '84. That was our first 'hometown' show, and the crowd was wild and really supporting us. I'm pretty sure this was Slayer's first Bay Area show. They overdid it on the eye makeup, and some of the Bay Area fans let them know it wasn't cool. I don't think they wore the eye makeup again! The Kabuki Theater shows in San Francisco in '84 and '85, supporting bands like Y&T and Loudness, were all great shows. The most memorable show may be when we played the warm-up show for the Bang Your Head!!! festival in Germany in 2004. The band had just reunited and our European fans had been waiting a long time to see us at this point. It was packed to the rafters. The crowd was singing the words to all our songs from the first EP ... it felt really special."

After Ruffians disbanded for the first time in 1988, Craig played with Two-Bit Thief (a band with members of Attitude Adjustment), along with Control, Vain, Dusty Skull. "Back in the eighties, there were a few bands that put out seven-inches such as Anvil Chorus, Violation, and Head-On, who were all Bay Area bands. A rock band named Wizard from Hayward, California, put out their own album, and a rock band named Roadrunner from Marin County put out their own EP," Craig recalls. "I think it's natural for music lovers to try to find all the hidden gems. One band's album might have a time period or geographic connection that leads you to another album. When you get into certain bands, you want to hear the bands that inspired them—for instance, Steve Harris from Iron Maiden cited Uriah Heep and Wishbone Ash as major influences. So you say to yourself, 'I better go listen to them.' The same goes for AC/DC and Chuck Berry. 'Better find me some Chuck Berry!' I'm honored that someone would pay good money for an original

CUT TO THE CHASE:

You might have noticed that during the whole of this Ruffians piece, I didn't write a word in regards to the band's influences. This wasn't on purpose, but it reveals the strong character of the band. No imitation, only absorption of the band's many influences. Ruffians sound like no one else, setting the bar very high with their first twelve-inch EP. I think that metalheads into bands like Gargoyle or early Queensrÿche (minus the very high vocal crescendos) will especially enjoy it, since it is meat-and-potatoes basic and damn catchy. You can get the original version on Victory Records, as it has been re-released many times, with bonus tracks too. If you like it, also get the CD compilation *There & Back*, which contains their 1984 and 1987 demos, as well as the *Desert of Tears* LP.

pressing of Ruffians' first album. With music streaming in full swing, prices are coming down, along with the fact that our first album has been re-released quite a few times."

Ruffians reunited in 2004, with re-releases and a new LP in 2006, titled *Desert of Tears* and released on German label Metal Heaven Records (among others). Even though in general I'm not a fan of the post-eighties metal bands/records, first and foremost due to the production values—I can't stand ultra-clean, pop-ish, radio-friendly productions—this is not the case for *Desert of Tears*. It retains the eighties production spirit, and moreover, it hasn't strayed from the tradition of the band. Heavy and a bit blurry, which imparts a great nostalgic approach, *Desert of Tears* is a little more hard rock-oriented in comparison to the Ruffians' past, but you get the excellent "I Believe," "I Will Fly," and the bombastic "Live by the Sword." Certainly not as classic as *Ruffians*, but still a good album that sadly sailed under the radar of most metalheads.

"There will always be an underground scene in every part of the world all the time; we just don't know of them all," Craig replies when asked for his thoughts on the underground scene today. "In music, the underground seems to be made up of a younger crowd. There's a scene here in the Bay Area now; there seems to be a lot of Doom/Sabbath-type bands at the moment, along with some cool old-school metal bands like Hellfire. I think it's great that music is so easily accessible and can be shared with the masses. It opens a lot of doors for bands who can expose themselves on a worldwide level without having to be signed to a record label. With that said, the market is a bit oversaturated, but if you're honest and the band is good, people will pick up on it. That's what takes you to the next level. The negative side of downloading is that people don't have such a strong connection to the album. Albums were made with a specific running order in mind, even down to the seconds that were placed in between songs. This was the way the band wanted it presented to the listener. The running order was etched in your brain, you knew the artwork, the producers, the engineers, the catalog. The platforms that music is presented to us on now is in jukebox form, which is cool, but if you dig the band, you should listen to their album track by track."

The history of Ruffians is connected to so many classic and diverse bands, since Ruffians members appeared also in Villain, Proudflesh (featuring members of the punk band Crucifix), Now, and Vicious Rumors, among many others.

CIRITH UNGOL

THE SPIRIT OF AUTHENTIC, TRUE, GENUINE, SERIOUS-MINDED HEAVY METAL is embodied in bands like Cirith Ungol. Never following any musical trend, Cirith Ungol—their name was taken from J.R.R. Tolkien's *The Lord of the Rings* and means "Pass of the Spider" in the fictional Sindrian language—formed in 1972 in Ventura, California, and their musical and historical route is simply fascinating. "Rob Garven (drums) and I first met in English class in seventh grade in 1969, and had common interests in Ferraris and *The Lord of The Rings*," bassist/guitarist Greg Lindstrom says. "After a brief stint in the band Titanic, formed in 1971 with Pat Galligan (later a member of the punk band Angry Samoans), then Jerry Fogle, Rob, and I broke away to realize our dream of playing heavier music, forming Cirith Ungol. Almost immediately, we started writing original songs, along with our versions of songs by Sabbath, Budgie, Thin Lizzy, et cetera. Mountain was also a really big early influence on all of us, in the way they would do extended jams. It wasn't until 1975 that Neil Beattie (a.k.a. Terry Dactyl) became our lead singer. He was more glam-inspired than the rest of us, but he put on a really wild live show, with black widow spider fingertip extensions for 'Shelob's Lair.' Even though he was a great performer, Neil's voice didn't quite fit in with the direction we were headed, and we parted ways after about a year. We spent the next couple of years writing a lot of songs and playing all the L.A. clubs as an instrumental power trio, playing alongside bands like Quiet Riot (with Randy Rhoads), Y&T, and Van Halen and going over amazingly well. We tried out a number of singers, but nobody clicked until 1979, when Tim Baker, who was our head roadie at the time, tried singing lead on 'Hype Performance.' That version is the first song on *Servants of Chaos*. The rest is history!"

The initial 1972 lineup of the band included Greg Lindstrom (as a bass player then), Robert Garven (drums), Jerry Fogle (guitar), as of 1975 Neal Beattie (vocals), only to be replaced in 1976 by Cirith Ungol's classic mainstay vocalist, Tim Baker. As for Greg's motivation for forming Cirith Ungol, he says, "I wanted to do something worthwhile with all those guitar lessons my mom made me take in fifth and sixth grade! It really is amazing how much quicker your skill level increases when playing with other people. We were only 14 and 15 years old, and through constant jamming, we got better pretty quickly, developing our own style. And it's a pretty cool feeling when you can write a song and play it with your friends.

"Very early on, it would have to be Cream, especially the live stuff on *Wheels of Fire* and *Live Cream*," Greg answered when asked about Cirith Ungol's favorite bands. "We used to jam on 'Crossroads,' 'N.S.U.,' and 'Spoonful.' A little later on, Black Sabbath emerged, and of course, they were a huge influence to anyone who plays heavy rock. It is hard for me to pick a single record, but for me personally, most of my favorite albums were created in the golden age of heavy rock, the early seventies: Captain Beyond's first album, Trapeze's *Medusa*, Scorpions' *In Trance*, BÖC's *Tyranny and Mutation*, Stray Dog's first album, Night Sun's *Mournin'*, and Thin Lizzy's *Vagabonds of the Western World*. As for greatest impression, although not necessarily an album, but seeing Iggy and the Stooges play at the Whisky during their *Raw Power* tour was the most intense concert I've ever seen. Witnessing the power that Iggy had over the audience, and the way he fed off their energy, was incredible."

Ventura wasn't exactly famous for its heavy/rock scene—actually, the only Ventura artist I can recall from the seventies was the jazz/fusion composer JoAnne Brackeen—which meant it wasn't all roses for Cirith Ungol. "We tried to make a scene, but locally, this is more of a laid-back surfing and country/western community. But always, there are a handful of rockers in every community," Greg mentions. "We had silver-and-black bumper stickers that read 'Cirith Ungol Heavy Metal.' Without an internet, it wasn't so easy to be a metal fan back then!"

After releasing two near-perfect demos (*The Orange Album* in 1978 and the *Cirith Ungol* demo in 1979), Cirith Ungol took their fate into their own hands, as their sound was very challenging for the then-emerging hard rock/heavy metal scene. It was the late seventies, when NWOBHM was just starting in the UK, and the American metal explosion hadn't even started. So, Liquid Flames Records was born in 1980, a label started by the band itself. On Liquid Flames, they went on to release their first LP, the 1981 *Frost and Fire* with the addition of Michael 'Flint' Vujejia on bass. Rob Garven explains, "After years of trying to get the attention of the Los

Angeles record industry, we decided to create the mother of all demos, which turned out to be *Frost and Fire*. It had to be an offering as polished as any released by major labels, and I think we succeeded. In order to get radio airplay, which was essential at the time, we put on that album what we considered were our most commercially accessible songs. It was recorded at Goldmine Recording Studios in Ventura, California, on a TEAC 80-8 eight-track machine. To cut the album, we went to one of the best mastering labs in the L.A. area, Allen Zentz, and the record was pressed on German Teldec vinyl by an audiophile-quality pressing plant, KM Records. We used Michael Whelan's masterpiece, *Stormbringer*, for the cover art, and I did the layout of the cover, and it was printed by the company that was printing all the major label covers, Ivy Hill Communications. We were lucky to have a dear friend, Randy Jackson, who helped us finance this project, whom we promptly paid back shortly after its first pressing. After we manufactured the original batch, we tried to get major label interest, but when that did not succeed, we went to find record stores to carry it. We were friends with Brian Slagel, who at the time worked at a record store near Los Angeles called Oz Records and was starting to form his own record label, Metal Blade Records. He connected us with an import export media company, Greenworld Distribution. We eventually signed a deal with them to distribute the album worldwide."

CUT TO THE CHASE:

I guess (and hope) that everybody who got this book is already familiar with Cirith Ungol, so their chapter serves as a reminder of what a brilliant band they are! If you haven't heard of them, well, what we have here is one of the most sincere and honest metal bands ever, regardless of genre. As for *Frost and Fire*, I strongly recommend this LP not only to true metalheads but also to fans of progressive rock, to those weirdo psychedelic rockers who want to gather each and every record that has even the slightest influence of psychedelia, as well as to fans of 1960s/1970s punk. Yes, *Frost and Fire* is complex, but not complicated! Get it, and then get their whole discography!

Frost and Fire is a terrific record, and I won't hear any objection to this! Well, I know that many people prefer Cirith Ungol's later (also excellent) output, due to the fact that they sound heavier, more epic, more angular, and more metallic, but still, you can't go wrong with *Frost and Fire*. Highly innovative and unique heavy metal here, with influences ranging from progressive rock (early Rush), sixties psychedelic rock (as in the perfect "What Does It Take"), the hard rock of Scorpions and Deep Purple, Blue Cheer as well as the proto-punk of Iggy and the Stooges (especially "A Little Fire"), Thin Lizzy mixed with seventies punk ("Better Off Dead"), progressive rock mixed with Ramones ("Edge of a Knife") ... and still keeping its 100 percent heavy metal character. *Frost and Fire* is a mandatory listen if you want to get deep down into the nature of Cirith Ungol, and it is sadly underrated when compared to their other records.

"I can't say we were the first band to ever do this, but we were certainly the first band in the L.A. area during this era to put out an album of this caliber, without major label support," Rob adds.

After the release of *Frost and Fire*, Cirith Ungol started performing more frequently, and when asked about his favorite shows from that early era, Rob replies: "A memorable early show was put on with Brian and Metal Blade Records at Wolf & Rissmiller's County Club in Reseda, California, with Pandemonium and Bitch, who along with us were on Metal Blade Records' first compilation album *Metal Massacre I*. All the bands were emerging metal bands in the L.A. area, and even though we were all competitive, it was a fantastic show. That was an amazing venue, and we played there several times over the years. Several of the early videos of the band are from that club!"

Cirith Ungol later signed to labels (Enigma, Metal Blade, and Restless), and the band released three perfect metal records this way (*King of the Dead* in 1984, *One Foot in Hell* in 1986, and *Paradise Lost* in 1991. The best of the three is *One Foot in Hell*, in my humble opinion. However, *Paradise Lost* includes the best song they ever wrote, "Chaos Rising." Cirith Ungol went on to disband in 1992, tired and disappointed by the state of the heavy metal scene—sadly, during the eighties, it was all either big bands (Iron Maiden, Judas Priest, et cetera), thrash, or glam metal, so bands like Cirith Ungol found it pretty hard in terms of commercial success. It doesn't matter, though, since artistically, Cirith Ungol were successful.

After their split-up, Greg Lindstrom made two albums with Falcon, but the other members either gave up music or their whereabouts were unknown. However, fast-forward to 2015, when Jarvis Leatherby organized a rehearsal with guitarist Jim Barraza and drummer Robert Garven, where he played bass. Tim Baker attended but did not sing. Having received offers from various festivals, like Keep It True and Up The Hammers, Cirith Ungol decided to reform! Not only did they reform, but they also went on to re-release their old stuff, as well as releasing new fantastic records, like nothing had changed since the eighties: the *Witch's Game* twelve-inch, the *Forever Black* LP, the *Brutish Manchild* flexi seven-inch, the *Half Past Human* twelve-inch, and the *I'm Alive* double live LP.

Finally, Tim Baker shares his thoughts on the modern renaissance of Cirith Ungol: "The resurgence of interest in anything that has to do with rock music and, of course, hard rock and metal in particular is always a good thing. Having a bit more interest can only help the scene as a whole, whether that means more record sales, concerts, merchandising, and media attention—it's always welcome. The vast majority of metal bands are always in a constant struggle for survival, ours included, and more interest and support for the entire realm of metal helps lift us all. As far as some of our stuff becoming what you refer to as collector's items, that happened because the band was inactive for such a long period of time. Metal Blade has always done a good job of trying to keep things in print over the years, but some of our catalog has been subjected to long stretches of unavailability due to various issues. This, of course, led to tons of bootlegs: records, CDs, T-shirts, and other things, some of which are actually pretty good! Haha! Our drummer, Rob, the Master of Disaster, actually has a battle vest covered entirely with bootleg Cirith Ungol patches from all over the world!

"You can count me as a believer!" Tim laughs. "Being able to finally play in many festivals around our planet for the last few years, and seeing such an incredibly vibrant scene and support for heavy metal out there, is truly amazing! Getting to be a small part of all that, and getting a chance to share the stage with some legends of the underground—and of course, to be able to meet so many of our long-suffering fans and friends—really makes all the lost years seem like they were meant to be. And of course, we all hope that soon, things will get back to some sort of normal, and we can all once again live the dream together. The internet has made the world so much smaller, and everything is right at your fingertips, including music. This is quite the double-edged sword for bands trying to stay afloat in the music industry. Of course, ease of access makes it so much simpler to find new music, bands, anything else you can think of. It helps that you can get yourself out there instantly, instead of like in the old days, when we were completely relying on print media, radio stations, and word of mouth. But it also makes it so much easier for people to just upload the latest thing without doing anything to support the bands they love, like buying officially licensed products from the bands or the labels they're on. I do know that a lot of people who are into the metal scene actually make the effort to try to support the music and the bands they love, and this is truly appreciated by everyone involved in the painstaking process of making that music. I will speak here for every musician I know and say a huge thank-you!"

BROCAS HELM

A SERIOUS HIGHLIGHT OF THIS BOOK, BROCAS HELM REMAINS TO THIS DAY one of the best bands that the American independent metal scene ever offered. You actually can't get much truer than Brocas Helm, which always brings to mind bands like Cirith Ungol and Manilla Road—it's some of the most respectable stuff ever to come out of heavy metal.

Brocas Helm formed in 1982 in San Francisco from the ashes of the band Prisoner, featuring guitarist/vocalist Bob Wright, Jim Schumacher (bass), and Jack Hays (drums) as the core members. A second guitarist, John Grey, was added until 1984. Jim Schumacher narrates:

"Ah, well, back in the way-back times, I moved up to San Francisco from Southern California. Of course, I immediately started looking for a band. After a few auditions, I ran into Bob's band, Prisoner, and they needed bass. So, we played a bit, but it wasn't really metal ... it was good rock, but Bob and I wanted to go hard. So, we disbanded Prisoner, and the two of us started looking for musicians. We picked up John Grey and Jack Hays. Bob and I started writing songs, whipped them into shape, and even played a few shows. One day down at the Record Vault, the guys there asked for a demo tape. We didn't have a damn demo tape. Didn't even know we were supposed to. So, we whipped up the *Into Battle* demo and sold it at the store there. Eventually, we recorded the entire *Into Battle* album and started looking for record companies. Most of them had very bad deals. After some negotiation, we put out the first LP on First Strike Records. There were a few hard feelings on that, two big issues being: they changed the cover a few days before printing without notifying us. Second, they changed the mix of the album. And that probably explains another of your questions: why we later put out our own label..."

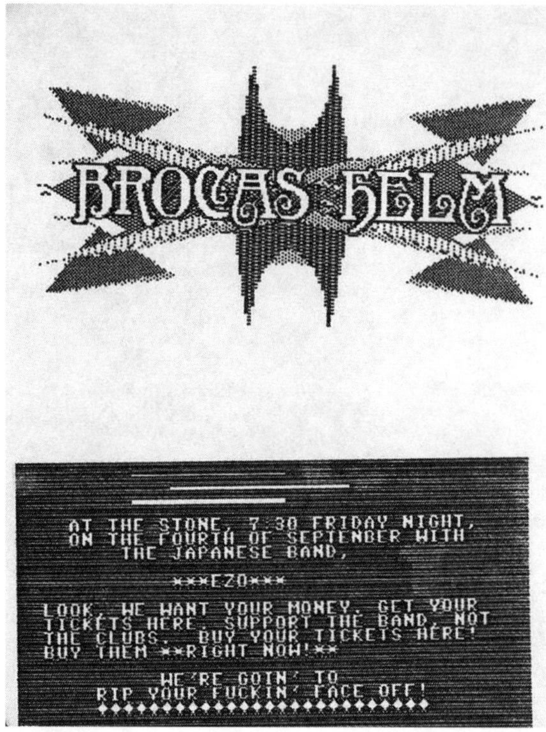

BROCAS HELM AND EZO FLYER

When asked about his influences, Jim responds: "Bands, hm, I used to listen to Deep Purple, Uriah Heep, that sort of thing. Grand Funk Railroad, who are a lot better than you probably think. Deep Purple's *Machine Head* was probably my first monster album. Then there was UFO, Scorpions, that sort of stuff.

"[The San Francisco scene] wasn't really as big as people think ... there were a few clubs to play metal in, but mostly they were pay-to-play situations, where you had to buy tickets and sell them yourselves. A lot of the bands lived in the same neighborhoods and knew each other, but although we knew the other people and hung out, it wasn't like we partied with them every weekend or anything. Most of the bands were okay guys, but once some shitheads pulled some political crap and managed to bump us down from the headline to a lower spot. There's a vid of that night—pretty sure at the end, I shouted, 'That's all the metal for tonight, next up, The Wimptones.'"

Brocas Helm released *Demo 1* in 1983 and the 1984 *Into Battle* LP (the U.S. release by First Strike Records and the Euro release by Steamhammer). If you blend early Iron Maiden, 1970s Motörhead, Thin Lizzy, NWOBHM and Black Sabbath, and filter them down to the raw American rock of Dust and Blue Cheer, what you get is genius, authentic, angular but catchy, highly original, and overall brilliant heavy metal. Songs like "Into Battle" sound unbelievably epic, yet they're having so much fun, whereas "Warriors of the Dark" or "Dark Rider" have to be heard to be believed—totally bizarre, yet so damn catchy! The recording mix left the band disappointed, though, as it didn't offer the punch and the chaotic edge that Brocas Helm had.

CUT TO THE CHASE:

Brocas Helm are the true epic metalhead's wet dream since their first demo in 1983. Their 1984 *Into Battle* LP came out through a small indie American label (First Strike Records), while it was also released in Europe by Steamhammer. However, their second LP, 1988's *Black Death*, was released on their own label, Gargoyle Records, and remains to this day a moment of glory for epic metal. Tremendous stuff here, barbaric and awkward metal, so unique that no one else could ever reproduce it. Brocas Helm still keep it up strictly in the underground, releasing excellent records (and many of them on their own) from time to time, and they are still active as of 2021. All their records are mandatory listening if you have even a slight taste for epic heavy metal!

The band decided to take their fate into their own hands, and after the 1987 *Black Death* demo, they went on to release the *Black Death* LP in 1988 on their own label, Gargoyle Records. "*Black Death* was recorded entirely at Bob's house, in our rehearsal area. At that point, we decided to take control of all aspects of the records, so no one could fuck with anything, and it would come out the way we intended it to," Jim adds. "More work, but more control."

Tom "T-Bone" Behney was recruited as a second guitarist, and the result is one of the most tremendous records that epic metal has ever offered. A whole level up from *Into Battle*, *Black Death* is a sheer attack on the senses. I know that Jim Schumacher might argue with me about that, but I say this record sounds like a punk band gone heavy metal and played to the extreme. (Actually, this also happened in the UK with the band English Dogs!) Unbelievably crazy, chaotic, inspired, and insanely executed metal to the max, with hymns like "Black Death," "Prepare for Battle," and "Fall of the Curtain," while "Fly High" will always be an eternal anthem. Production-wise, this is also totally mental—almost sounding like an organized chaotic car crash. This is actually a pinnacle, not just for American epic metal but for heavy metal as a whole.

Contrary to what most believe, Brocas Helm never disbanded—they just took it easy later, still releasing demos (like 1989's *Helm's Deep*) or EPs like *Ghost Story* (1997) and *Skullfucker* (1999). And of course, they continued performing from time to time. "The most memorable show ... all the European stuff is great. This is what I wanted when I started playing music. Long before you were born," Jim laughs. "But probably the most awesome show was our first show in Athens. It was our first show out of the country, and we didn't really know what to expect, but the Greeks were awesome. They took care of us from the time we hit the airport until we left. So much shit was happening, and the crowds were so excited. American crowds are jaded, and a lot calmer than Europe—it's kind of sad. Some of the metal festivals, like in Chicago, are picking up, but the Europeans still rule."

In the early aughts, Brocas Helm became a power trio and were way more active, releasing initially the great live LP *Black Death in Athens* (recorded at their 2001 show at An Club, Athens, Greece) and then the excellent *Defender of the Crown* LP (2004), where they progressed the sound of *Black Death* in an even crazier direction. Again, I know that Jim will strongly disagree with this opinion, but I surely hear a punk edge, even though it's 100 percent metal. A split live seven-inch with the mighty Manilla Road followed in 2007, and since then Brocas Helm have re-released their old stuff such as their demos on the 2012 *Demonstration of Might* double LP.

"Am I happy that *Black Death* is a collector's item?" Jim responds to my question. "Sure. It's nice to feel appreciated. At the same time, we license reissues, so anyone can get a hold of the music. I've never been one of those guys who would sue fans for downloading music either. (I'm sure you know who I'm talking about.) The music is for everyone, so if you can't afford it, I don't really care if you download it. But, if you're making money from selling our shit and not paying, that's a different story."

As for a metal scene today, Jim says, "There's always an underground scene, there's so much stuff available that people don't even know about. The internet has made a lot of new stuff available (not all of it's good—you gotta wade through it). But the most awesome song is waiting around the corner somewhere ... some guy in a basement wrote it and needs to record and publish. There's been a lot of bands that just faded away, waiting for something to happen. You need to do it yourself. Write the song, record the song, and put it somewhere. If you can't get a contract, put the damn thing on YouTube, get some exposure. And what's the place, Bandcamp? You can go there these days (says the guy who's never tried it, haha).

"The music scene now is kind of like the anime scene in the past," Jim concludes. "We would order VHS tapes from Japan, someone would translate and subtitle them, and then we'd pass around tapes (like demo tapes) until the generations became too bad to see. At the time, there was a very small amount of stuff available. Now, there's way more anime available in America than you have time to watch. Music is similar to that now—you have to have a reliable source or friend recommend stuff to you, or you just wade through everything looking for the gold nuggets."

GOTHAM

GOTHAM WERE A LAST-MINUTE INCLUSION IN THIS BOOK, AS I WAS TRYING TO contact them for about a year. Formed in 1982 in the Bay Area as Vienna and then renamed in 1986, Gotham's story is told by Dan Lewerenz (drummer) and Steve Rice (guitars):

"Gotham was formed after Vienna guitarist Ricky Torres left the band suddenly," Dan begins, "while Steve Rice came on board to complete the new band and name Gotham."

Steve picks up: "I came into the band when they were still called Vienna. The singer, Matt, and I went to school together and he stopped by my place one day and asked if I'd like to try out for the band, since their guitarist quit. So, since I was pulling my pud anyway looking for bands, I gave it a shot, and it worked out."

"I had wanted to play the drums since I was nine years old—my two brothers played guitar. So, I played in bands with them a lot growing up," Dan says, while Steve adds, "If you play well enough to get on a stage, it's kinda the motivation you need to grow as a musician. Now guys can just sit in their bedrooms all day masturbating over prerecorded tracks and drum loops, but playing with real people is more fun. Just like sex!"

Being from the Bay Area, Gotham was exposed both to the top-quality heavy metal of their birthplace as well as the touring bands—after all, the Bay Area scene was thriving in those times. "We were all on Judas Priest, Iron Maiden, UFO, Michael Schenker, et cetera," Dan explains. "The music scene in the San Francisco Bay Area was unbelievable then, shows almost every night. We came out the same time Metallica did. The locals and our fans were rockin', great people."

"I will agree with Dan," Steve laughs. "UFO, Rainbow, Priest, Maiden, Scorpions, Sabbath, and on and on for me. For the other guys, I think it was the Bay City Rollers and the Monkees! Haha! Even though the Bay Area was thriving, it was fairly good if you played thrash and smoked dope with Testament or sniffed crank with Exodus, but if you didn't know those cats, it was rough. In San Jose, there was more of a hair bear cokehead crowd and the bands all wanted to be Ratt or the Crüe. So, since we played shit that had a Queensrÿche/Crimson Glory-type thing going on, it was a tough sell to the posers."

Gotham went on to release their 1989 *(12 O'Clock and) All Is Well* seven-inch on their own Crazy 8 Records, and both Dan and Steve have a few words to share: "We decided to record a few tracks at Prairie Sub Studios in Cotati, California," Dan begins. "Did two songs in one weekend. We had the 45s pressed ourselves and then ran an ad in San Francisco's *BAM* Magazine to give them away for free to promote the band. We shipped them all over the world!" Steve says, "Well, no one was going to sign us without a proper demo or production. Our first single was killer because we spent the cash, but the second demo production was a mess because the band got to be a mess, with drugs and bullshit."

Gotham's *(12 O'Clock And) All Is Well* seven-inch is a shocking release! Unbelievably heavy, ultra-powerful American metal, with an killer sound and two fantastic songs. Gotham reminds me of a mix between Metal Church, Vicious Rumors (Albert era), and Crimson Glory. The musicianship is just top-notch, whereas the production offers even more power to the material. This is seriously one of the best seven-inches that the American metal genre ever offered, and it sadly remained unknown for many years. Check out "The Witness Stand" and you just won't believe this magnificent piece of plastic.

Gotham recorded three more songs in 1989 in Sunnyvale, California ("Starshine," "For the Wicked," and "She Will Sleep for Years") that were added along with the two Vienna tracks ("Shall We Ride Tonight" and "Scream the Night Away," recorded on May 30th, 1986) to the *Gotham* compilation LP in 2003. "We had so much fun when Gotham was around," Dan recalls with a huge smile. "We played a show with Simon Wright's band, the drummer from AC/DC. Three days after the show, a box showed up at my shop. His roadie had accidentally picked up my drum case and took it in their van to the next show. Simon was kind enough to ship it back to me. I thought that was a cool move."

"C'mon, at that time, it was Metallica, Forbidden, Testament, Lääz Rockit—great bands all around," Steve remembers. "Some of the bands local to us in the Bay Area that might have released an independent record were Sleaze, Mad Anthony, or Tramp."

Gotham dissolved in 1990, and Steve Rice pursued a great career in metal, initially with Imagika (power/thrash metal) and later with Kill Ritual (thrash metal).

CUT TO THE CHASE:

Gotham's 1989 *(12 O'Clock And) All Is Well* is a real treat for all fans of American heavy/power metal! It's got two songs of highly inspired American metal, with "The Witness Stand" being my favorite—a true classic! The price is between 40 to 60 bucks. Be sure to also get the *Gotham* LP compilation on Doomed Planet Records.

Dan and Steve add a bit more about their *Gotham* seven-inch release nowadays being sought after by metal fans worldwide as well as the underground scene today. "I think it's great that fans are still rocking to our stuff and the youth are showing more interest in heavy metal music," Dan says. "I've seen the prices on our disc that came out in the late 1980s. It's insane but flattering at the same time. I'm not sure there is much of an underground music scene at this time, but things change, people's music listening interests evolve. I hope it comes back strong. Music downloading these days is great in some ways and bad in others. It gets new music out there to the masses. but the artist is really getting screwed by the services garnering most of the monies and profit that's owed to the artists of the world."

Steve concludes: "We aren't getting a red cent (from the seven-inch), so I guess I really wouldn't know. It's cool that people still enjoy the tunes, considering however small a fan base that really is. I'm sure there's plenty of bands going around as usual, because there's always some pimple-faced punk kid looking to make noise and get people to listen to it. But obviously, the punk better not ever think about making any money off it—99 percent never do, especially when your music is disposable, like it is today."

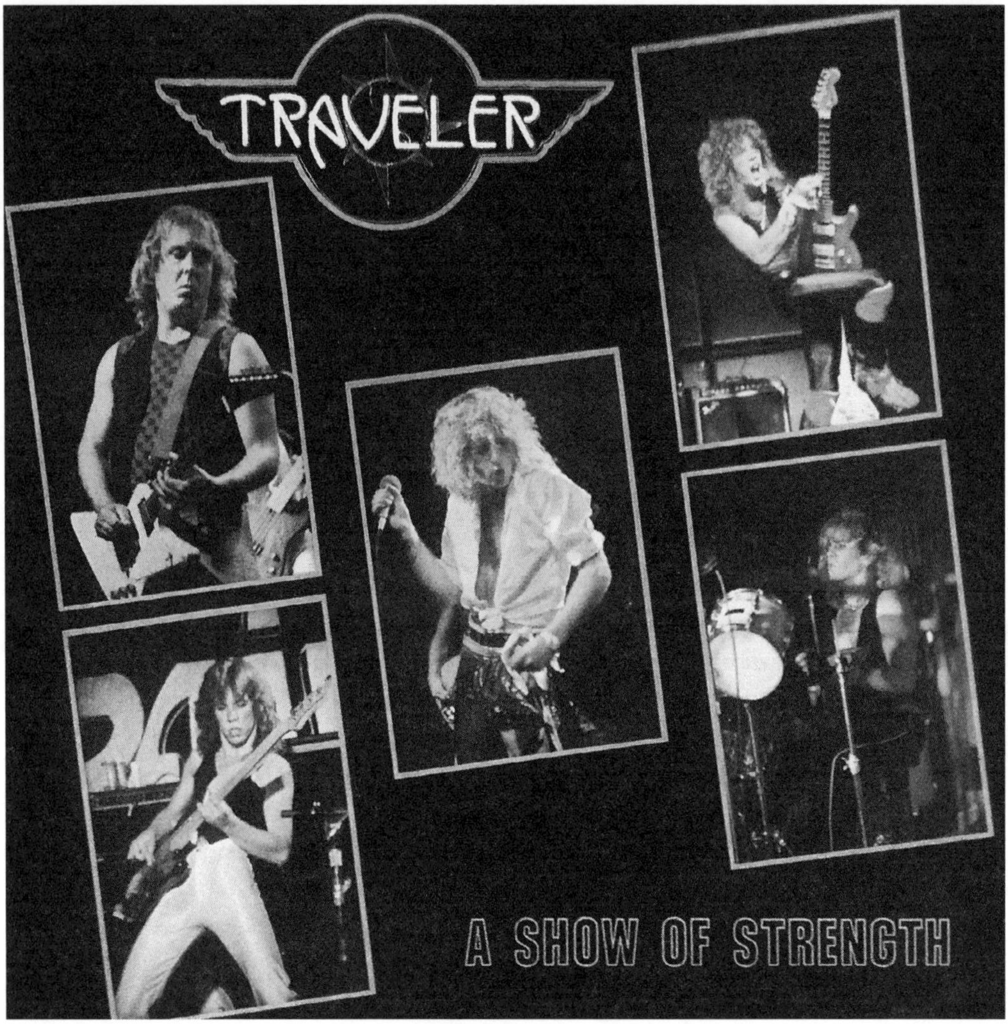

TRAVELER

THE CITY OF SANTA CRUZ, CALIFORNIA, IS NOT FAMOUS FOR HAVING AN exceptional (in terms of numbers) metal scene in the 1980s. I can recall only Wrekking Machine and Rude Awakening, which was Luke Pabich of Good Riddance's first band. But Santa Cruz's Traveler was definitely a great hard 'n' heavy combo. Vocalist Stevie Satain, formerly of Allies, tells the story:

"Traveler was formed in 1983 after I had been in a couple of different bands. There was a huge network of bands and people at Bobby Allen Studios in East Palo Alto. I think this is how we grabbed Eddie Yrure and Brad Beldner." The first lineup of Traveler included Carey Washburn (guitar), Brad Beldner (guitar), Rob Strom (bass), Eddie Yrure (drums) and Steve "Satain" Smith on vocals. "Our motivation for forming Traveler was simply the love of music and the love of that lifestyle. For me, it was the competition and the camaraderie as well. We were all so very diverse. We loved hard rock, but we grew up on everything from soul and

CUT TO THE CHASE:

If you are into early NWOBHM or Y&T and Diamond Head's hard rock songs, look no further, 'cause Traveler will suit your tastes perfectly. I wish they'd have kept it up and headed for a sound that riffed on the metallic approach in "Lost in the Darkness," but this is the magic of "What if?"

funk to Southern rock. From Aerosmith's *Rocks*, Derringer's *Live*, and Kiss' *Live* to local favorites like Yesterday and Today, Ratt, Mötley Crüe, Missing Persons—all were favorites at one time or another. The Whitesnake *Saints & Sinners* album was a wake-up call and inspired us because of the new sound it produced."

I'd also like to add Diamond Head as an influence that I hear in Traveler's great sound. It's maybe the Whitesnake element that both they and the British band filtered through their sound, but you can understand how this is translated in music terms: gutsy, melodic, hard 'n' heavy rock, equally balanced with the new metal sound.

"Our local scene was incredible and so much fun. We did consider our scene to belong in the Bay Area or L.A.," Steve adds. "There were also two bands from Santa Cruz that, like us, went on to release their records on their own: Redvette and Head-On."

Traveler then released their first seven-inch *Wishful Thinking/Bay Area Lady* on their own label Relevart Records in 1983; both melodic and rockin', tending more toward the hard rock side of things, these two tracks are definitely winners. I can even discern the NWOBHM influences here. "Wishful Thinking" has a more lightweight Tygers of Pan Tang effect!

Traveler's name was not to be ignored, and Steve adds, "We were determined to keep up with the competition here in the Bay Area." Crazy as it might sound, Traveler played in fairly exotic places such as Guam, and they also toured Japan! "These are our three standouts: Keystone Palo Alto, opening for Joe Perry of Aerosmith, any show in Guam, and our last show in Nagoya, Japan. The Japanese fans loved melodic metal and hard rock, and we had the time of our lives there!"

Traveler didn't get a record deal and decided to record and release their next and final twelve-inch EP, *A Show of Strength*. This 1984 release kicks off with the "Rock n' Dance" metallic rocker—explosive stuff! "Out of Control" sounds like a mix of AC/DC and Accept with some Diamond Head worked in; Steve sounds so much like Sean Harris here. This is the case in "I Need You" too. The EP's closer, "Lost in the Darkness," on the other hand, is a galloping metal monster—epic, thunderous, amazing! "*A Show of Strength* was just that: a product of very hard work," Steve says. "Something got lost, though, in the mastering, and it sounded weaker than I would had liked. Nevertheless, I was very proud, and we worked our asses off to get this done.

"I really love the fact that there are still people out there who dig our sound," Steve adds. "Sadly, I really don't know much about the underground scene of today ... However, music is for everyone, and I don't care how they get it. If you record it, then it's there for people to get a hold of to hear."

Traveler faded away sometime in the mid-eighties, never to be reunited, and I found no other projects or bands that their members were later involved in. But their legacy lives on through these forgotten-in-time jewels!

CHILD SAINT

RESPONSIBLE FOR ONE OF THE MOST SOUGHT-AFTER PRIVATE METAL RECORDS lately, Child Saint was formed in 1983 by guitarists Brian Scott and John Specter in Orange County, California. They added manager Rick Rayl for some direction, along with vocalist Greg Thompson, who was later replaced by Bob McCormack. The lineup was stabilized with the addition of Steve Hardin on bass and Gary Schultze on drums. Gary explains, "John and Brian wanted to create metal music. Rick suggested that if they wanted to take it to the next level, they needed to get out of the garage and get a true rehearsal space. They also needed a killer rhythm section and vocalist. Bassist Steve Harden joined in 1984, and I joined in early 1985. After we went through a couple of vocalists and did some shows in Orange County and Hollywood, Bob McCormack joined in 1986."

CUT TO THE CHASE:

To fans of true metal, Child Saint's 1988 twelve-inch is considered golden. I'm not going bananas over it, but I still consider it a decent piece of American metal. Fans of early Trouble will definitely like it. It used to be very rare, until a box of sealed LPs by the band was recently discovered!

In 1985, Child Saint released a three-song demo with Greg Thompson on vocals that oozed pure metal all over. Although it has an amateurish rough production quality and a totally obvious Iron Maiden resemblance ("To Die in the Sun" is absolute Maiden worship), this is true heavy metal played to its logical extreme, especially on "Made of Metal."

"Biggest inspiration for sure was Judas Priest and Iron Maiden," Gary says. "Our sound and look were very similar. Probably for me, *Number of the Beast* and *Screaming for Vengeance* were heavy influences. We were based in Orange County but did a lot of shows on the Sunset Strip in West Hollywood. Troubadour, Gazzarri's, the Whisky, et cetera," Gary adds. "We had a decent following. We were well received. However, we were not hair metal, so getting a record deal proved to be difficult."

With the addition of Bob McCormack on vocals, Child Saint went on to record and release the 1988 *Child Saint* twelve-inch EP on their own. "We were not getting any financial help or record deals, so we decided to do an independent release. Rick helped to bankroll the process, and we picked a couple of songs and recorded in Garden Grove, California," Gary narrates. The result was a two-song minor classic of American metal, with "I Am Future" being a heavy grower, almost doom-metal-like—kind of a more heavy metal-styled early Trouble. The re-recorded "Child Saint" was a heavyweight too, like Black Sabbath gone seventies-era Judas Priest.

There are so many rumors swirling around the song "Child Saint" in reference to Dave Mustaine, but I will let you find out for yourselves. (Just read the comments on YouTube videos and forums in regards to this song.) There is nothing out there to confirm it officially, so it would be a risk if I stated it as a fact, but ... do your own research.

Oddly enough, Child Saint never split up but were on hold from 1991 until 2006, when they independently released the *Live in Los Angeles* CD, recorded live at the Dancing Waters club in San Pedro, California, on May 21st, 1988. "Our biggest moment for me is when we opened up for Saxon at Jezebel's in Anaheim, California," Gary replies when asked about his favorite Child Saint show.

"Another independent cassette that was released in our area was a band called MadelFang. I went to high school with a couple of those guys. Katon from Hirax was another guy I went to school with," Gary adds. "It seems like the renewed interest in old independent heavy metal recordings is happening more in Europe, not so much in the States. I really have no idea about an underground scene today. If the internet had been around in the eighties, we would have sold a lot of music."

As of 2019, Child Saint are still active.

TRAITOR

NOT MANY BANDS RELEASED A SEVEN-INCH FLEXI DISC ON THEIR OWN, SO Traitor from Orange County, California, are the outliers here! Formed in 1984, Traitor's heavy/power metal sound will definitely give fans of this style some goosebumps. "Traitor was a band that was looking for a singer in the mid-1980s," vocalist Tim Karr narrates. "I had just moved to Hollywood from Montreal, and they had an ad out for a singer. I auditioned and joined the band. It was the first American band I ever joined. A lot of fun!"

Traitor comprised Danny Byrne (guitar), Brian James (guitar), John Gonzales (drums), Truman James (bass), and Tim Karr, and with this lineup, they followed their dream of becoming another great American metal band. Their formation happened right in between the rise of both glam metal and thrash, but this was beefy heavy/power metal, underproduced but gutsy as hell.

CUT TO THE CHASE:

Good luck finding the *Feel the Steel* seven-inch; it's not that pricey, but it is damned rare. *Shot Down*, on the other hand, is both rare and pricey. Obviously, both are recommended for people into the early-eighties American metal sound. No extreme stuff or epic overtures here, just simple, honest American metal!

"I've been in bands since I was 16," Tim says. "At first, it was mainly to meet girls, but as my songwriting developed, it became a positive outlet for creativity. Kept me off the streets and out of jail! I think all Traitor were really into the Scorpions and Judas Priest at the time, maybe Ratt. Personally, the record that had the greatest impression on me was *The Rise and Fall of Ziggy Stardust*. It spoke to me. It was so dirty and dramatic. 'Rock 'n' Roll Suicide' is one of my all-time favorite songs."

Traitor didn't want to miss the train on the American metal wave, so in 1984 they released the *Feel the Steel* seven-inch flexi, which contained only the title song. The label that released *Feel the Steel* was actually a studio, Hot Fudge[2], where Traitor used to practice. "We used to rehearse in a city called Bellflower in California where the band had a lot of friends," Tim says. "The scene was pretty cool, and everyone was very supportive. I lived in Hollywood, which was a 45-minute drive away, so I didn't hang out very much there. A lot of time spent sitting in traffic on the freeway in my girlfriend's car."

"Feel the Steel" is an amazing, ultra-exciting, melodic heavy metal track, both rough and catchy. It kinda mixes NWOBHM with American metal, having the weird anti-commercial edge of the UK bands as well as the magic of the American bands, like a rougher Armored Saint or a more heavyweight early Savage Grace. Bellflower's Erika Records, a minor independent label back then, later gave Traitor a chance to release a twelve-inch EP, *Shot Down* (1985).

"We were signed by a label called Erika Records. Small indie label. The funny thing was, they got the record deal after I had left the band. So, they asked me to come in and do the vocals. Other than coming in and doing my parts, I wasn't really involved otherwise," Tim says. "The rehearsal space was pretty big, and we would have parties with a ton of people who would listen to a set to get feedback on new songs. Those were crazy days!"

Shot Down included "Feel the Steel," but you should purchase it if only for the heavy/power dynamite "The Way It Used to Feel." The power and hooks on this song are simply incredible—American metal lovers, you will explode! The mid-tempo "Have You Ever" is excellent too; even though by today's standards the production sounds a little bit stale, it's actually offering a character, a sheer nostalgia. There IS a definite glam metal influence (e.g., "Traitor"), but the passion for raw metal is here ("Shot Down"), and even though *Shot Down* isn't a first-class American metal LP, it has its great moments.

Traitor kept it up until 1988, then fell apart, and some members went on to have musical careers: Tim Karr played in Cincinnati's China White (releasing two demos) as well as a solo

2 Hot Fudge Productions released another seven-inch, the hip-hop record *Rappin' with Ronnie*, but it still remains a mystery whether it was a joke or not. Fact is, Traitor self-released and produced their first album.

career, and he's active today, whereas Truman James Cruickshank still plays in small bands. "I think good music is good music, regardless of when it came out," Tim adds. "It's great that people still appreciate it after all these years. I've noticed a lot of kids are getting into music from the old days, when people played an instrument and actually sang songs. No synthesizers, no loops. Brian James [Cruickshank], who played guitar in Traitor, passed away a few years ago. I wish he was still around to see how much people appreciated his music..."

About the underground scene, he says, "Personally, I think the underground scene has become mainstream. Since you don't need a record company anymore, you can pretty much record an album and release it yourself. Which is awesome! The gatekeepers have fallen. The artists have taken over. Although I think getting easy access to music via the internet is amazing, the piracy of music is a real problem. I've just finished recording my new record, *Lost in the Ether*, which took two years to complete. A lot of time, creativity, and money goes into making it. No one thinks they're going to get rich on record sales anymore, but seeing songs available for download for free just adds insult to injury. So, if you hear music that speaks to you, that helps get you through the night, you might want to consider supporting the artists who created it. They need you as much as you need them!"

TAIST OF IRON

FROM TACOMA, WASHINGTON, TAIST OF IRON IS ONE OF THE MOST UNIQUE-sounding bands of its time when it comes to heavy metal. Formed in 1982, vocalist Lorraine Gill says, "Mark Glabe (bass) and I were playing in a band called Ruz Skullen at the time we met Bill Pearson (guitar), who was the founder of Taist of Iron. We were playing some concerts at a local grange called Midland Hall. Bill saw some of our performances and approached me about singing for this new band he wanted to form. He originally was going to be the singer, but then he saw me and decided to hire me and teach himself lead guitar instead. However, when he asked me, I said no. I was dating Mark Glabe at the time and didn't want to leave Ruz Skullen. Then he approached Mark, and Mark agreed. Mark then talked me into joining with him. I finally agreed. And Bill Pearson was the driving force behind forming the band. He had a very clear vision of what it would all look like and stand for! He was a powerful driving force, and I will always feel grateful for his vision and tenacity. It's because of him that we were known around the world!"

Jeff Massey was added as a drummer, and the first lineup of Taist of Iron was complete. As for their influences, Lorraine says, "Black Sabbath was by far one of the strongest influences for the band itself, as was Randy Rhoads and Iron Maiden! My personal influences for writing were not from the metal realm, however. I was very much into progressive rock, and I was also very much into theater and acting. The foundations of my lyrics stemmed more from progressive rock and some of my spiritual values of the time. I also loved the very theatrical aspects of Taist of Iron: I was lowered from the ceiling in a coffin for one concert, shackled to the drum set for another, et cetera."

CUT TO THE CHASE:

Taist of Iron's *Resurrection* is an American metal classic, but there's a lot more to it than that. This is one of the few records that could appeal to massively different camps out there. True metalheads will love it because it's pure and unique; however, its sound could also appeal to fans of occult rock too, or even psychedelic rock fans. After all, songs like "Feeling You" or "Cross of Fire" have a weird edge, straight out of the psychedelic sixties.

The metal scene in the Pacific Northwest—Seattle, Olympia, and Portland—was already starting to take off, and Lorraine remembers, "There were some amazing local bands playing metal, Queensrÿche and Culprit to name two. (Geoff Tate went to the same local high school in Tacoma that my son later went to.) The scene was so much fun in the early days! Everything was brand-new. I loved being a girl playing metal back then, and I still love it. We had a pretty good local following, although I couldn't tell you how good—I was a bit behind-the-scenes back then."

Just like Queensrÿche, Taist of Iron decided to put out their first record on their own. "Ultimately, it was Bill's decision to create the label for the record," Lorraine adds. "There was an amazing local record studio, T.J. Landon Recording Studio, that helped us to make it all possible! The guys traded physical labor on building T.J.'s new studio for recording time. That was a great help."

In 1984, Taist of Iron released their now-classic *Resurrection* LP on their own label, Iron Records—some of the most eclectic, angular metal of the 1980s! Sometimes ethereal ("Feeling You," which is sheer magnificence, as well as "Evil"), sometimes more straightforward ("The Gates," "We Give Life"), and with Lorraine's fantastic vocals, Taist of Iron sound like no other band. If I were to mention some bands with similar approach, I'd say Sacred Blade, or Tyrant but weirder. There's a definite 1970s Black Sabbath aesthetic here too, but overall, *Resurrection* is highly original and unique, with characteristics that very few bands of their era had.

Unfortunately, Taist of Iron split up in 1986, but they reunited in 2012 and have been active since then, releasing the *Taist of Iron* CD in 2017. The album sounds like a follow-up to *Resurrection*—great, original, underground stuff!

"I have to mention my four most memorable concerts!" Lorraine laughs. "First one, playing the Troubadour in West Hollywood. Second one, playing at the Dancing Waters in San Pedro,

California, two weeks after Blue Öyster Cult played there. Another very favorite one was the local concert we played out of our practice space, when I walked over to an ungrounded light bar and got the shock of my life! I actually blacked out! And finally, the night we played at the Bicentennial Pavilion here in Tacoma, Washington, with Culprit. We had a very elaborate stage set-up with a ten-foot crypt with a door acting as our drum riser. In front of this and alongside are tombstones, and at the very front of the stage, an eight-foot metal fence that spans the whole front of the stage. I crawl out of the crypt in the fog, so the audience just gets a peek at me, then out behind me comes Uver, our mascot, a seven-foot guy in a long black cape with a hood. As he is stepping over me, he loses his balance and grabs hold of the fence. The whole thing comes crashing down onto a live mic! Oh, there is one more most memorable concert: the Keep It True festival in Germany last year (2019). My absolute most favorite time on stage ever.

"I love that there has been and is now new interest in the older, more obscure bands of the eighties," Lorraine joyfully adds. "All of these bands were the front-runners in the current metal scene, and I am glad that I was and still am a part of it. I am so proud to be part of a project that still is a collector's item even now! I feel the underground metal scene absolutely exists and saw the evidence of it at the Keep It True festival last year. Underground metal is alive and well!"

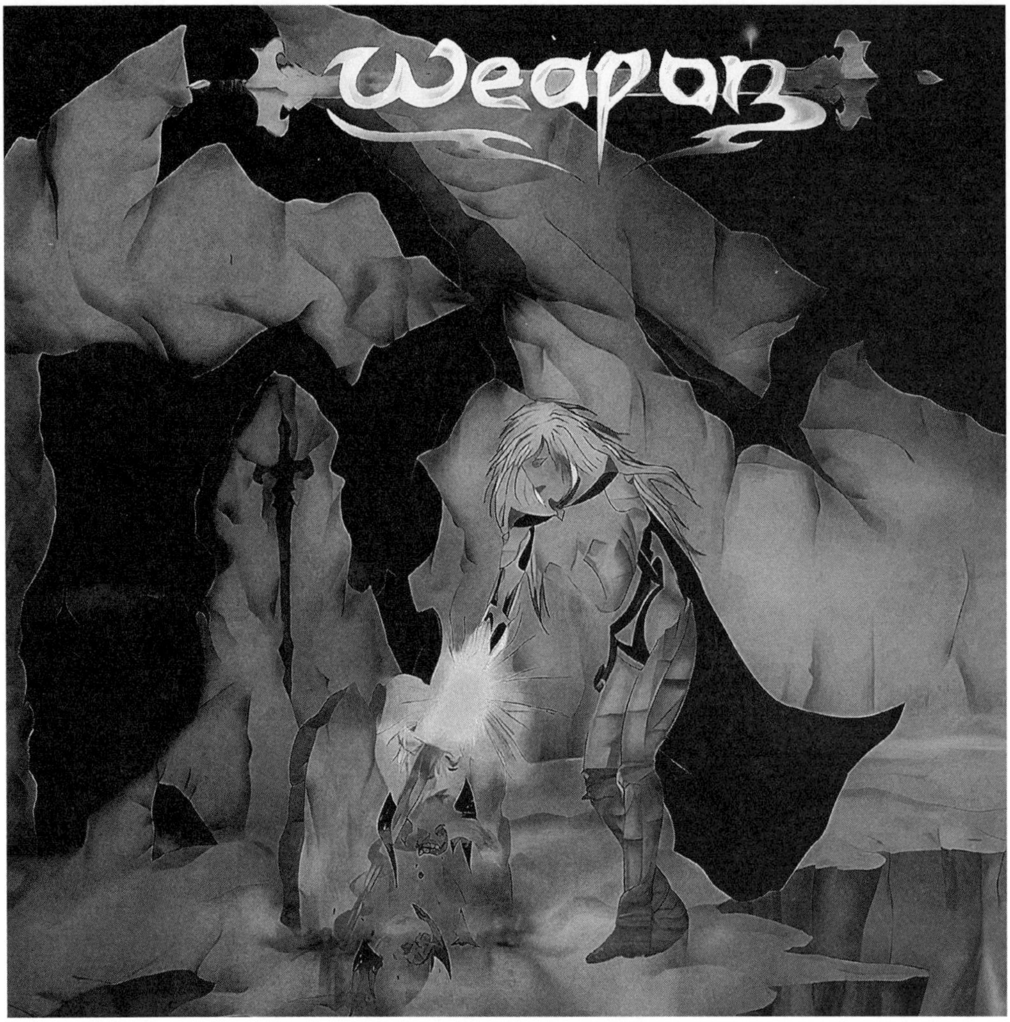

WEAPON

FOUNDED BY GUITARIST/LEAD VOCALIST JOHN ANDRADE IN 1985, WITH BRAD McAfee on bass and Duane Waider on drums joining in 1987, Weapon from Los Angeles were a short-lived band that took their cues both from the glam metal uprising (mostly in terms of image) as well as the growing popularity of classic heavy metal in the UK. "The scene was extremely competitive in Hollywood back then, record labels were everywhere looking for the next big thing, and the local bands were at the front of the pack fighting for a record deal," drummer Duane Waider narrates. "We were influenced by many bands, but the ones that come to mind are W.A.S.P., Mötley Crüe, and Led Zeppelin."

Actually, Weapon sounded like a cross between W.A.S.P., Mötley Crüe, and eighties Judas Priest, while McAfee's bass lines had that Steve Harris pounding style. And even though their looks were more akin to the glam metal style, their music was much wilder and rawer in general. So, they decided to put out their first and only LP in 1988, titled *Weapon*.

CUT TO THE CHASE:

I bet fans of raw, classic American metal will love the *Weapon* LP. Don't be misguided by the band's stylistic choices; what we have here is raw and wild American metal that would please all warmongers of this sound. As mentioned, it's not a definite classic of the genre, but it still sounds fresh even today!

"John Andrade had found backing, so it just made sense to do it ourselves instead of waiting to get discovered, so to speak," Duane adds. "We recorded it in Hollywood at Sage and Sound and mixed it at the Music Lab in Silver Lake, here in Los Angeles ... I also re-released it on CD in 2015 on Snailworx Records, which is a label I am signed to and do A&R for."

Weapon is no classic by any means, but still, it's a very good, enjoyable heavy metal record. Its beautiful fantasy cover might prepare you for an epic metal attack, but *Weapon* is a heavy metal LP done the American way: powerful and pure. Tracks like the opener, "Come and Get Loose," along with the frantic "Ultimate One" and "Smokin Axes" are 100 percent heavy metal, sounding like early W.A.S.P., albeit much rawer, mixed with UK metal and NWOBHM. John Andrade's vocals might be a turn-off for some, but he is definitely passionate, and his performance is totally energetic, whereas Weapon in general sound very technically proficient. Especially the heavyweight closer, "Speedy Leeds," with its punishing riff and build-up on the exceptional rhythm section. Crushing stuff.

"I still have very fond memories of our appearance at the Whisky a Go Go in Hollywood for our record release party in 1988 ... it was a killer time to be on the Sunset Strip back then. Lots of energy."

Weapon called it quits in the early 1990s, but their legacy remains in the American independent metal scene thanks to their sole release. "I think it's absolutely awesome that the old private metal labels/bands are being rediscovered. I'm thrilled to see that people still have that ingredient to wanna get heavy and utilize an open mind," Duane adds. "As for our album becoming a highly paid collector's item, I think that is very flattering and humbling, and I'm kinda speechless. I do feel there's an underground scene as strong as ever—however, I think it has gotten misconstrued as a mainstream vibe, due to the internet being so transparent. Downloading music for free I think sucks majorly. It has completely raped the music business blind and has taken away any chance of there ever being a new rock star developed as we know it. Those days are gone."

SOLDIER (SAN FRANCISCO)

THE CHRISTIAN METAL SUB-SCENE WAS BLOOMING IN THE 1980S, AND WHILE I have a major opposition toward Christian (or any religion) rock, history has been written, and it can't be undone. Soldier's case is another exception to the "records only" rule for this book, because it would be an absolute shame not to have any reference to a band that released one of the most exceptional cassettes of American metal, 1988's *Babylon*. "Marco Allen (bass) and I had just quit a secular band we were in and decided to go looking for a drummer and guitarist," vocalist Jimmy Arceneaux says. "Rick Hunter (guitarist) came into a record store we both worked at, we got to talking, and the rest is history. I think Adam from Golgatha told Rick what we were looking for, if I remember correctly ... the initial lineup included Al Whalen from Golgatha on drums, later to be replaced by Jason Souza."

CUT TO THE CHASE:

Soldier's *Babylon* is a real hidden gem in the history of underground American metal. Yep, it's a cassette, but this one needed some exposure in this book! I think that fans of different styles of metal will definitely enjoy it. Plus, it's more proof of the level of quality of eighties American metal—a band as magnificent as Soldier didn't get a record deal, for God's (pun intended) sake!

Formed in San Francisco in 1985, Soldier was right in between the rise of American thrash in the city and the outburst of glam metal in Los Angeles. However, they chose to play vicious, ultra-heavy power metal in its finest form. "We just wanted to do something we felt was missing in Christian music, being a more commercially driven heavy metal (but still powerful) outfit, ya know? Of course, there was the ministry aspect, but we wanted to be more into classic metal music than most of the thrash stuff that was coming out at the time," Jimmy explains. "Speaking for myself, I was into Lizzy, Alice Cooper, Sabbath, Zeppelin—you know, legendary 1970s bands. Oddly, Marco was way more into rockabilly, Springsteen, a lotta punk rock. He was our wild card. Oddly enough, he helped write a lot of the music and the lyrics with me. It helped to have his vibe in the writing, which is what made us a bit unique, in my opinion."

San Francisco being a leading force for the heavyweight metal bands of the West Coast, Soldier might have had a hard time with their more delicate metal sound, but Jimmy says, "I booked one of the biggest metal clubs at the time. Most of the bands (Death Angel, Exodus, Vicious Rumors) were very cool to us. Of course, we had a few folks who really hated what we were about—and we were not surprised by it at all. We did our thing and had fun, no matter what people thought of us."

Soldier was included in the *California Metal Volume II* LP compilation in 1988, alongside Vision, Emerald, Recon, Judea, Mastedon, and Ransom, with two brilliant tracks of melodic, Judas Priest-like metal. "Borderline" is actually a top-notch example of this style! But the best was just around the corner, with the release of the *Babylon* cassette album the same year.

"We just knew we wanted to do it ourselves to have more control over it," Jimmy says. "We knew a song like 'Angel' may have a harder time being put out by a Christian label, as it was about a person and relationships. Back then, it seemed every song had to have the name Jesus in it to be taken seriously by that community. So, we gathered our funds, went into a full-blown studio, and did it with help from friends."

Explosive, fun, totally metal, and over-the-top professional are just some ways to describe *Babylon*; from the opening "Louder Than Hell," a real power metal anthem (reminiscent of Vicious Rumors), to heavyweights like "One of a Kind" or "King of the City," this is heavy/power metal with a slight glam edge that's absolutely memorable and inspired. Meanwhile, songs like "First Time" and "Deadly Weapons" reach Q5 levels of greatness! An absolute shame that no label back then was interested in releasing such a brilliant recording.

"There were so many bands that did the same thing as we did," Jimmy says. "You know, Golgatha, Believer, Crossforce ... it was a fantastic era for heavy metal. I cannot remember the name of the event, but my favorite was held at the Olympic Velodrome in L.A. somewhere. All of the heavyweights were on the show, Bloodgood, Barren Cross—the other (Holy) Soldier band. Ironically, the day had been mostly under cloud cover, and when we played, the sun came out, to which *CCM* Magazine said was a 'sign.' They were kinda joking, but it was cool and funny!"

In 1989, Soldier released the *Louder Than Hell* demo that included two new songs, one re-recording of "Angel" and four live takes, but the band called it quits in early 1990. After Soldier, Rick Hunter played in Regime (hard 'n' heavy) and Discern (death/thrash), while Jason Souza played in the notorious hard 'n' heavy Christian metal band Guardian.

While Roxx Records re-released a deluxe LP discography of Soldier in 2018, *Babylon & Beyond - 30th Anniversary,* Jimmy adds, "Honestly, I am shocked people still care about our older releases. Not saying we are not proud of them! It's just very humbling to see a cassette we sold over 30 years ago on eBay for ridiculous amounts of money. Staggering, really."

Jimmy also offers his point of view on the current metal scene: "I have been a talent buyer (booker) for years—back in the old days, you would make a cassette copy of an album and turn your friends on to it. The only difference then was, most folks would then go out and buy the same album, 'cause you wanted the cover and the liner notes and whatnot. These days, most music feels like it's treated like background music ... but it is getting better, and people are starting to go old-school, much like the 1970s, and getting back into music again. Which is great, in my opinion!"

VALOR

One of the hidden treasures of American private metal belongs to a Christian metal band from San Francisco named Valor. Formed after the demise of Golgatha, which released the *Prisoner* demo in 1985, bass player Adam Alvarez teamed up with Jim Maxwell (drums), Chris Price (guitars), and Michael Brueck (vocals), and created one of the best ever releases of American metal, which remains under the radar of metalheads worldwide. They were actually an early pioneer of the Christian power/speed metal genre following the proliferation of hard rock and glam rock Christian acts of the eighties, and they played the popular clubs in San Francisco and Los Angeles as well as a variety of additional venues and some charity performances.

Drummer Jim Maxwell says, "Valor was formed by bassist Adam Alvarez in 1986 after the breakup of his previous band, Golgatha, a hard rock-styled Christian band. Alvarez retained vocalist Michael Brueck and me, the former drummer from Saint, and together we searched for a guitarist after Todd Price left. Chris Price was called in for an audition and was subsequently hired. Price brought with him the speed metal genre that Valor became known for. The combination of the hard-driving, fast-paced music combined with Brueck's classic rock vocals differentiated us from other acts of their time. Vic Sardon was hired as the second guitarist, and we recorded our demo tape, *Masquerade*. Because Golgatha had gained some fame, we were able to hit the ground running with an existing fan base."

In 1988, due to their rising popularity, Valor was invited to perform live on television to promote their upcoming *Fight for Your Life* album. This television appearance included a live performance of five completed songs and an interview of the band members (that I couldn't find, unfortunately). However, things seemed to be on the correct path for Valor, and Jim talks about the process behind their only release, the fantastic 1988 *Fight for Your Life* LP. "By the time, our musical influence included a diverse set of metal and progressive rock styles presented by bands such as Judas Priest, Metallica, Slayer, Iron Maiden, and Rush, and we were desperate to have a release out soon, so we decided to do it on our own White Stone Records. We were so excited to finally hold our first album; it was such an achievement for us."

Fight for Your Life is a tremendous piece of power/speed metal: clever, unique, and 100 percent metal to the max! You can hear all the motifs of like-minded bands such as (early) Helstar, Jag Panzer, and a touch of the ferocity that Savage Grace or Liege Lord had. There's not a weak moment on *Fight for Your Life*, but if I had to pick the three best songs, these would be the thundering pounder "Fight for Your Life," the absolutely mental speed metal track "Accept Him" that reminds one of Agent Steel and clocks just over one minute (!), and "Valor," a huge headbanger that sounds like a cross between Helstar and Attacker. Great stuff!

Jim offers a few words on *Fight for Your Life* and its later re-release: "I have seen original vinyl copies of *Fight for Your Life* sell for as much as 300 dollars. Both nationally and internationally. The band's continuous popularity and various requests from fans for Valor to come back had enticed me to urge Price to join me in the remixing and remastering of the *Fight for Your Life* album as a 30-year anniversary re-release. We contacted Alvarez and Brueck and all agreed to contribute to the project. It was determined that the rhythm guitar and bass parts needed to be redone, so Price retracked the rhythm guitar parts in my tracking studio (CFZ Studios). Adam Alvarez was unavailable and gave permission to allow another bassist to assist with the retracking. The world-renowned Uriah Duffy (Whitesnake, Christina Aguilera, Sly and the Family Stone) was brought in to retrack the bass parts on the album. In December of 2018, me and Price went to 513 Studios in Arizona to oversee the remixing of the new and existing tracks. Owner of 513 Studios Catherine Vericolli, Piper Payne of Neato Mastering, and Grammy winner and Iron Maiden's own mixing engineer Jared Kvitka were hired to complete the task. The album was remastered at Neato Mastering by Payne. The scheduled re-release date took place in the second quarter of 2019, and the vinyl pressing was completed by Second Line Vinyl in Oakland. A limited number of vinyl pressings of the original 1988 recording was available in the first quarter of 2019. Me, Price, Brueck, and Sardon are currently (as of 2021) working on fresh material for a new album to be named *Resurrection*."

CUT TO THE CHASE:

I rate Valor's *Fight For Your Life* LP very highly; it is definitely one of the best Christian metal albums ever made, and it's also one of the greatest records to be released by an American metal band of the eighties, period. Heavy, fast, and metal to the bone, this album is a must-have if you have any love for the early, unpolished power/speed stuff.

Valor disbanded during their heyday in the 1980s. "Vic Sardon left the band and was never successfully replaced," Jim adds. "In 1989, Adam Alvarez left Valor and was replaced with jazz-rock bassist Tom Gage. We continued to play shows and perform new material until our breakup in late 1989." Jim recalls some of Valor's highlights: "Most memorable show: there were several, probably with Bloodgood, White Cross, Deliverance, News Boys, and Vengeance, just to name a few. I videotaped everything in those days. My bigger shows, though, were with Saint in the early eighties, originally called the Gentiles, formed by Russ Koch, John Mahan, and myself."

Valor got their *Fight For Your Life* LP finally re-released in 2019, both in its original version and its remastered version, offering the chance for today's metalheads to enjoy this masterpiece. "There is always an underground music movement, but it has changed a lot, 'cause basically, anyone can do it now from home," Jim believes. "Lots of competition, and much of it is not very good. I think downloading entire albums is not good, as the musicians can't survive on music alone as it is. I am old-school (and old) and don't like the 'cell phone era.' Although one good thing of the Facebook era is that I have been able to reconnect with musicians from the past!"

HAMMER HEAD

From Bellingham, Washington State, Hammer Head (or HammerHead) wrote their own chapter in the history of American metal. "We formed in the winter of 1984 with Greg Martin on lead guitar, Dave Fender on drums, Don Cooper on bass, and Tom Cooper on guitar," Don Cooper says. "Dave and Greg met me at a bar in Bellingham called the Underground and asked me if I would play bass for them. I said yes, and at our first practice, our first song was Black Sabbath's 'Paranoid.' We rocked it and knew that we had something going. My brother Tom then joined the group. We put out an ad in a paper called *The Rocket* in Seattle for a lead singer. Our first choice was Jeff LaRue from Culprit, but we never got him to actually sing for the band; that's when Pete Mainzer came to Bellingham and joined the group. I was working at a local fish plant at the time and submitted a list of band names to the group. Hammer Head was on that list, and that's what we chose for the band."

In 1984 Hammer Head released their first demo named *Speed Metal* (on cassette), which included five songs. The demo appealed to the underground metal scene, and "Masters of

CUT TO THE CHASE:

Hammer Head's *Rock Forever* LP would please most fans of the American metal sound, mostly those ones in angular-styled groups such as Culprit or Glacier—mid-tempo stuff with power and creativity. You can find *Rock Forever* fairly easily, and I am so honored and happy that Don Cooper sent me a free copy of it as a gift!

Frustration" appeared on New Renaissance Records' compilation *Satan's Revenge* LP in 1985 (with the band's name spelled 'Hammerhead'), creating a buzz around the band. *Speed Metal* included ragers such as the aforementioned "Masters of Frustration" and "Money," but the other songs had more of a hard rock/metal edge. It's a nearly perfect demo in terms of professionalism, with that classic American heavy metal sound—melodic but at the same time hard, and with exceptional guitar playing.

A fan club cassette was also released in 1985, containing six songs, but I couldn't find it anywhere to review it!

"We then moved to Tacoma, Washington, and all got a big house together where we practiced in the basement," Don says. "The neighbors hated us. That's when Pete wrote the song 'Neighbors,' which is on the *Rock Forever* album. We then went to Triad Studios in Redmond, Washington, where Queensrÿche had been recording. Also, Steve Miller was in there recording at the same time. During the day, we were using Steve Miller's equipment, and at night we recorded our album, as they didn't want to move any of their gear.

"Robin Trower, Jimi Hendrix, Frank Zappa, and Carlos Santana are my influences," Don says when prompted. "At this place, we were almost signed by David Geffen and Geffen Records but couldn't close the deal. Wendy Dio was also interested in us," Don sighs, adding, "In 1987, there were already huge bands in our area. Culprit was huge, as so was Metal Church."

Hammer Head then went on to record and release their first LP at their own expense in 1987, *Rock Forever*. Again, what's so evident in Hammer Head from the start also appeals here: totally professional approach, both in terms of production as well as excellent musicianship. *Rock Forever* has some (well, many!) excellent moments of brilliant American metal, such as the opening "Arakian Nightmares" (one of the best songs the band ever wrote, hands down), "Rock Forever," a brutal cover of Queen's "Stone Cold Crazy," the re-recording of "Master of Frustration" and "Holocaust." I think this was the style that most fitted the band: hard-hitting heavy metal, rather than the hard rock/metal mix of some songs.

Sadly, the release of *Rock Forever* brought major changes to Hammer Head: "My brother Tom was the first to leave the band after about a year in Tacoma," Don says. "My girlfriend was killed in a car accident in 1989, and I soon left the band and moved back to Bellingham. The band continued on with Brett Habel on bass. We've had a couple of reunions with Dave Fender, the original drummer, but Hammer Head has continued on with other musicians with Pete Mainzer as the lead singer."

Hammer Head remain active today (as of 2020), and Greg Martin put a group together called Stories Under Stone. Don Cooper is playing in a band in Wyoming called Coupe DeVille.

"I was kind of shocked to find that our album *Rock Forever* is selling for 250 bucks on eBay!" Don exclaims. "I think metal is just as popular today as it ever was. A lot of bands are great (and some are not so great), but I like lots of different music as long as it has a screaming guitar!"

SNOW

SNOW FROM NEWPORT BEACH, CALIFORNIA, WHO LATER RELOCATED TO Los Angeles, are one of the bands whose members went on to appear in or form much bigger bands. In their case, Carlos Cavazo played with Quiet Riot and Ratt, Tony Cavazo with Hurricane and Dangerface, and Stephen Quadros with 7th Sun and Showtime Networks (in addition to becoming a famous broadcaster of martial arts!). Formed in 1978, Snow's story is narrated by bassist Tony Cavazo:

"Snow started long before the inception of the band. My brother Carlos Cavazo (Snow, Quiet Riot, Ratt, Rough Riot) and I shared a room when we were young growing up, and we were both into music. We practiced and learned together. We had a friend, Perri Strong, who played drums, so we formed a band called Speed of Light. We started learning heavy metal songs by bands like Black Sabbath, Montrose, and Boston, to name a few. Then we began

CUT TO THE CHASE:

Snow's eponymous ten-inch is recommended to both casual and die-hard fans of the hard 'n' heavy sound. Fans of early Quiet Riot or Krokus will love it.

playing backyard keg parties and tried playing school dances, but they thought we were too hard-rock; they wanted more dance music. So, we stuck with backyard parties where people wanted us to play and promoted our own concerts, all the while still living with our parents."

Tony continues: "When we left our parents' house and moved to Newport Beach, California, our drummer, Perri Strong, left the band to pursue a different career. It was then that we changed the name of the band to Snow. During this period, we acquired a band manager, Stewart White, who helped us book gigs and was the driving force behind eventually moving to L.A. After searching for a different drummer, we came across Roger Singer, who lived in Newport Beach. And we also came across a singer named Fred Dehut (R.I.P.). After several rehearsals and recordings, we started playing small clubs like the Cuckoo's Nest, playing covers and originals. After several gigs, we parted ways with Fred Dehut and found Doug Ellison through a newspaper ad. We invited him over and, after working with him, felt he was the right guy. We started writing songs, playing small clubs, adding more of our original music to each performance.

"After about a year," Tony says, "we decided that if the band was going to go any further, we would need to move to L.A. So, Doug, Carlos and myself moved to Arcadia, a city just outside of L.A., into a small house and set up a little recording studio. After moving to Arcadia, our drummer, Roger Singer, left the band. We immediately started searching for a drummer in the paper ads and found Stephen Quadros, who was already playing the L.A. scene and knew a lot of people. We went to Hollywood, where he lived, met with him, and invited him to our studio. When he came to the studio, we jammed, and we all quickly realized that everyone there brought a powerful amount of energy to the table. We started recording original material and began playing at the Whisky, Starwood, the Troubadour, and the Woodsound, just to name a few. At that point, Snow was officially formed.

"It wasn't really a motivation as much as it was inspiration from the current heavy metal bands like Black Sabbath, Bad Company, and many others," Tony admits. "Watching them on TV and seeing them live inspired us to want to be performers as well ... so, Snow's biggest influences were Black Sabbath, Montrose, Boston, and Bad Company. The record that left the greatest impression and inspiration was Black Sabbath's *Paranoid.*"

About their move to Los Angeles, Tony adds: "In Newport Beach, there really wasn't much of a scene. That's why we decided we needed to move to the L.A. area. The scene in L.A. was much more happening and powerful. Newport Beach locals seemed like they didn't care about heavy metal music at the time. In L.A., the locals loved us."

Snow, active since 1978, found a hard time getting signed by a label, since it was 1980 and heavy metal wasn't the next big thing—the NWOBHM invasion had started in the UK, but in the U.S. other musical styles were prevalent. "Due to the rise of new wave and punk rock, we were unable to get a record deal, so we decided to put out a record on a private press," Tony recalls. "The procedure was no different than any other recording session: lay the basic tracks and do vocals and guitar overdubs. We had to release it ourselves. We sold them at gigs and to our friends."

The result was the *Snow* ten-inch EP, an unusual format, that was released in 1980 on their own label, Dynamic Records & Tapes. The album included five songs of pure and wild hard rock/heavy metal crossover! From the almost-power-metal powerhouse of "Bad Generation" to "Crack the Whip" and the melodic "No Way to Treat a Lady," *Snow* is definitely a product of its time, and even though you might find its approach nostalgic today, this is where its magic actually is! It takes you back to a different era, when things were much more carefree and easygoing. All the band members are exceptional players, so it's totally understandable why they later pursued much bigger careers.

Snow appeared with their song "Crack the Whip" on the *K-WEST L.A.'s Hottest* compilation LP in 1981 and disbanded after a while, only to reunite in 2011 (!). They're still active today, with original members Carlos Cavazo, Tony Cavazo, and Stephen Quadros, along with Andrew Freeman (The Offspring, Lynch Mob). A double-CD anthology was released on 2017 on Escape Music as well, which included all their studio material plus a live appearance at the Starwood in Hollywood from May 2, 1981. Tony adds, "Some of the Starwood shows were the most memorable. We were in a monthly rotation at the Starwood!"

As for other local metal bands that were recording privately at the time, Tony says, "There were some other indie metal bands that I can remember. The underground was so strong back then, and I can remember Smile and A La Carte from our area. I do believe there is a scene today, just not as powerful as it was back then. It's much smaller because the fan base is smaller, but it is growing. The kids from the eighties are slowly catching on to the metal music of the seventies and eighties. It's good that it's easily accessible, but there needs to be a better system in place for artists to get paid for all the downloads. These days, releasing an album is like giving someone a business card. In other words, the artist doesn't necessarily get paid when their songs are downloaded. In my opinion, the internet killed the music industry. There is something magical about purchasing an album and having to wait until you get home to play it. Nowadays, everyone wants instant gratification. Most young people today will never get the experience of purchasing an album the way we did."

Snow continue to perform from time to time in L.A., and Tony concludes: "Releasing a record on our own back then was important because at the time, there wasn't much of an industry for metal and hard rock bands. Snow is bigger than me, and for it to be considered a highly collectible EP makes me feel honored. It's nice that people want to collect a piece of L.A. metal history. Bands like Snow paved the way for other bands that went on to great stardom."

CHILDZ PLAY

BOISE, IDAHO, CERTAINLY HAS A MUSIC SCENE, COUNTING SEPTIC DEATH, Paul Revere & the Raiders, Built to Spill, and Treepeople among its local bands, but when it comes to heavy metal, Childz Play might have been the only band that this city produced in the entire decade of the eighties!

"Childz Play was formed in 1980 by myself and bassist Ray Van Cour," guitarist Mitch Hoitt says. "We were in a band called Ace. I asked Ray to show up early for practice to see what my originals sounded like with bass behind them. Ray grew very interested in the originals, and when Ace broke up, Ray decided to stay with me, hence the beginning of Childz Play. Ray and I met another drummer who we practiced with for a while, and he introduced us to a great younger guitar player, Jeff Fultz. All that was left to find was a singer, so we had Curt Caldwell come audition. I had known him from a band I was in prior to Childz Play. Todd, the drummer at the time, handed Curt some lyrics to sing—they were way off from what we wanted—and then Curt and Todd had an argument. Curt left with Ray. Jeffery Fultz (guitar) and I left together. Curt and I knew Troy Nickell from the previous band we were in, so we met Troy in a parking lot, played the tape of originals for him, and he was in. For three years we kept our nose to the grindstone and practiced only, having an occasional party to test the songs in front of people. Word of mouth got around way before we ever played live.

"The motivation behind forming the band was I had these tunes in my head and I couldn't get them out!" Mitch smiles. "I kept hearing the whole tune like a record—I could hear all the parts, and I'm multi-instrumental, so I could play all the parts; I would show the guys the basic parts that I was hearing and then they would take those parts, polish them, add their own mojo, and create some great tunes. At first, I used the KISS theory ('keep it simple, stupid,' that is) which worked well for bands like AC/DC. We all figured if the music was simple but had drive, people would easily relate—which they did very successfully. There were always a few quotes in our heads, such as Van Halen: 'When you have four or five people who want it that bad, it's going to happen.' And the Scorpions: 'No matter when you play, there is always someone watching for the very first time, so put the show on for THEM.'"

The scene in Boise wasn't something too spectacular at the time, and Mitch adds, "It was happening, but I found it mundane. Kind of different bands trying to see how well they could copy someone else's tunes. We were on a mission for originals, and after a few other musicians came to one or two of our parties, it kind of caught fire here and exploded with bands writing their own tunes. Childz Play became huge once we decided to go live; all the other bands were still trying to write, and we already had about two hours of tunes ready for shows. We found the guy with the biggest sound system and the guys that had the most lights, and once we did our first couple shows, they wanted to stay with us. As bands got their list together, we would have some open for us. It was a win-win situation, since we needed them for a longer show, and they needed us for good exposure. Those were great days and times for all involved, kind of looked back on as golden times to a lot of the population in Boise.

"We had so many Spinal Tap moments throughout our career," Mitch laughs. "I guess my favorite gig was in Sandpoint, Idaho, where we played there because it was a small town surrounded by a few cities, so we could get a lot of people. We were so loud, the plaster from the ceiling in the old theater was falling on people. A bunch of funnies happened too, like with Ray's wife learning on the curtain ropes until she figured it out, so we had one note (from the learning session) that went for like four minutes! By the time the curtain opened, there was so much fog, no one saw the band till almost the end of the song!"

Childz Play were definitely enjoying their small rock 'n' roll dream, but it was about time to release something on vinyl, and their *First Toy* LP on their own label, Playmates Records & Tapes, was released in 1986. Mitch adds, "It was the result of a whole lot of people believing in us as a band, believing how good we were, believing we would put Boise on the map, parents believing in their kids, et cetera ... We decided to put the album out when we met a friend of Ray named Kevin Mitchell. Kevin owned a tire store in Seattle and loved good rock 'n' roll. He started kicking the idea of recording around with us after a show and went back to Seattle. He called us later for us to arrange to come out to Seattle and be recorded, with us being paranoid about

CUT TO THE CHASE:

Childz Play's *First Toy* LP will definitely make two camps of metalheads happy: the ones who love the classic American metal sound, and the ones that are into party/glam metal. It has something for everyone!

sounding good. We hit the practice place hard when we recorded at the Music Source in Seattle; our engineer had done recordings for Aretha Franklin, Mötley Crüe, Metal Church, and a slew of top-notch acts."

He continues: "In the studio we had practiced the songs so much, we did them all on the first take. The engineer told us that was something unheard of. But we were just happy saving money, since the Source was 175 dollars per hour and we were recording in a three-million-dollar studio! Dave Raynor, the engineer, did us proud with the final mix and buttoned up the masters to go off to the presser. The demo presser came a few weeks later (I've still got the one and only), we released it at a huge show after the albums arrived, and we went on a mini tour because, at that time, the record stores wanted our album—and we were happy to oblige."

First Toy LP has a definite hard/glam edge; however, it manages to retain its strong heavy metal character with great results. There is an obvious Mötley Crüe influence here, but their sound is strongly rooted in bands like Judas Priest (up until *Screaming for Vengeance*), Scorpions, and Accept. Overall, this is a highly enjoyable record, with crowning moments such as the heavyweight "RIP," the mix of party glam metal and Judas Priest found in "Thinking of You," and the galloping "Feel It," which reminds me of early Saxon gone American!

"After the original scene blew up, that was the next big thing. Quite a few bands came out with their own tunes—some great, some not so great, but everyone was proud of their accomplishments," Mitch says. Childz Play moved to Los Angeles for one year, from 1988 to 1989, and then to Seattle until 1993, when they split up.

"Today, there are some killer bands out there, and they are too many to list. Our album becoming collectible? I've seen a couple being sold on eBay. One went for 400 bucks, one for 900 bucks, and it made me feel great, but I was happier when I found out there's an underground radio station in Japan still playing the album. Imagine that!"

Post-Childz Play, guitarist Jeff Fultz played in Bloodwitch (heavy metal), Seemless (stoner metal), Cult 45, Dead of Night, Gozu, Birch Hill Dam (stoner metal), and Mellow Bravo (rock 'n' roll). Troy Nickell played in the blues-rock Revolution Blue. Childz Play continued on in the 2010s, reuniting from time to time to offer local shows.

Sadly, Mitch Hoitt passed away while this book was in the works, in 2020. It's a pity that such a kind, enthusiastic, and lovable person has left this world. So, the Childz Play chapter is dedicated to the memory of Mitch Hoitt.

"A real underground most definitely exists today, even more than it did back in our day. There's a digital studio in every musician's house (including mine), and there are a million tunes out there to listen to, to find that one that turns your wheels. It is a whole different animal. As far as downloading? That's what happened when CDs killed vinyl. Analog went away, and so did the feeling of the analog sound, but the good thing that happened because of downloading was that you get to see your favorite band live in concert, because once again, it's back to the show."

SUSPICION

DOKKEN, QUIET RIOT, TWISTED SISTER, AND RATT (ALONGSIDE THE UK'S Def Leppard) had a fair share of influence in the early eighties American metal scene, especially on the bands that were more into the party rock sound than the heavier and powerful style of classic American metal. Suspicion, which formed in 1981 in San Diego, California, started off as a heavy metal band that later went in a more glam metal direction. Guitarist Mick Moore explains, "I had previously been in a band that I formed called Frantic. Since none of us had a real job, it was up to me to beg and borrow to get us to shows, put gas in the van, et cetera. When I tried to reimburse myself for gas money, one of the guys in the band accused me of skimming money, so I quit and formed the first version of Suspicion. Ironically, we ended up opening for Frantic and blew them off the stage. It was the perfect payback for their accusations. Frantic went on to disband and fall apart soon after. So, the first phase of

CUT TO THE CHASE:

Suspicion's *Hollywood Nites* twelve-inch EP isn't a classic for sure, but will make fans of eighties melodic/party metal happy, with a huge dose of nostalgia to boot. Good, well performed, and catchy, this one's for fans of early Dokken, Ratt, or even Q5.

Suspicion was heavily influenced by old Scorpions, Accept, Riot, and Iron Maiden. *Virgin Killers* by the Scorpions and *Restless and Wild* by Accept were the main albums influencing the band at the time.

"Growing up in San Diego, we were lucky and had a thriving metal scene," Mick recalls about the local scene of the 1980s. "Bands like Ratt, Asphalt Ballet, Stone Temple Pilots, and Rough Cutt came out of San Diego, along with Eddie Vedder, Jewel, and of course, Iron Butterfly. We quickly proved ourselves both musically and when performing live, so we had a strong following and pretty much sold out every venue we played. We wrote solid, groovin' songs with a heavy sound that attracted both men and women, so Suspicion soon rose to the top of the leading acts. We opened for many famous bands that passed through the area, like Riot, Poison, L.A. Guns, and many others. Our fans were loyal, and we soon discovered that if we wrote for the girls, the guys would all show up as well.

"Opening for Riot featuring Rhett Forrester, for sure," Mick replies when asked about their favorite show. "We loved Riot and especially the *Restless Breed* album lineup with Rhett Forrester. To be able to open a couple of shows for them in that lineup was a dream come true. We kidnapped Rhett after the last show and just buried him in a ton of blow. The poor guy got so fucked up, he missed his bus heading to the next show in Arizona. The same happened to Phil Lewis and Tracii Guns after one of the shows we played with L.A. Guns. We partied so hard at my house, the band left without him, and he had to catch a ride back to L.A."

After the release of two demo tapes (*The Garage Tapes* and *Liar 4 Love*, both in 1985), Suspicion went on to release their first twelve-inch EP *Hollywood Nites* in 1987, which the band members financed themselves. "We had interest from several labels, but with all labels, they wanted to control the writing, the song composition and layout. We didn't want someone telling us what to write, or how to sound, so we ditched our contract and released the album *Hollywood Nites* ourselves," Mick adds. "We hired a guy who had a small studio and was a professional writer for local commercials and jingles. He was all we could afford at the time, so we had him engineer the recording, and I did most of the producing by the seat of my pants. We learned a lot about layering and multitrack guitars and vocals."

Hollywood Nites is a good piece of melodic metal with a touch of glam. Throughout its six songs, it is pretty obvious that Suspicion were having a ton of fun, and the musicianship and production values are ace. There is a definite Mötley Crüe touch (the vocals, basically), but the guitars sound much more like the classic metal of early Ratt, eighties Scorpions, and early Dokken. The whole party attitude is all over the record, making it a fun listen with catchy tunes like "Here We Go Again," the excellent "Bringin' on the Heat," as well as the title track.

"There were lots of bands that put out their own stuff those days," Mick recalls. "Rough Cut, Asphalt Ballet, Aircraft, Victim, Kaos, et cetera. Most were barely acceptable garage quality but with great hooks and lyrics. We all traded each other's albums and for the most part helped each other out whenever possible. There was a lot of support among the bands in San Diego, and most were good friends as well as friendly rivals! I think the writing of bands from the eighties had great hooks, great guitar tone, and decent production values, even if it was produced in a low-budget studio. The songs and the chops were memorable, and that got many bands past the shitty mix or production. Our music was solid and kind of crossed that gap of metal, with glam, so we created a strong, heavy 'Driving Heavy Melodic Rock' kind of sound. Girls liked the hooks, and guys liked the heavy guitar and drums. Overall, it made a good, fat-sounding selection of songs, without getting too bubblegum-sounding."

Suspicion later released one live album, *Live at the Troubadour in 1989*, as well as the *Wasted* EP in 1990, which was their final release before disbanding ... only to release a *Greatest Tracks* CD in 2003. They never reformed, nor have they released anything else since.

"Music today is so scattered," Mick concludes. "Most of it is a rehashing of bits and pieces of other songs taped together, and the quality of the writing has gone more rap-sounding, so I think the quality of many of these musicians, if I can even call them that, has suffered. That's not to say that there aren't many great guitar players and solo artists out there. The writing to me just isn't what it used to be, and the melodies lack imagination and creativity, unfortunately. Everything sounds so prepackaged and overproduced. Rap is huge, and until it burns out and opens the door for something fresh, we will still get hundreds of Run-D.M.C. wannabes and crappy rap sampling from Queen, Van Halen, and AC/DC. Not that some aren't clever. I really like Eminem. That's some quality shit."

EMERALD

FORMED BY GUITARIST DAVE ENOS IN FONTANA, CALIFORNIA, IN 1977, Emerald's initial lineup included friends of Dave's from high school, but soon changed. Throughout their career, in fact, the band didn't have many stable lineups—on the contrary, people were coming in and out of Emerald consistently. Dave's brother-in-law, Larry Philips, joined after Dave heard Larry performing "Victim of Changes" by Judas Priest and was astounded.

"Black Sabbath's *Master of Reality* is probably the album that made the biggest impact on me," Dave admits. "The scene in the eighties, the L.A. music scene was pretty saturated with bands from all over the country. It was really hard to break through with the extraordinary amount of bands in L.A."

It took nine years after their formation (and many personnel changes) for Emerald to secure a steady lineup and get around to releasing their music. It was Dave Enos (guitar), Larry Philips (vocals), Joe Palma (bass), and Kyle Morrett (drums and synthesizer) who went on to record and release their own album in 1986, the *Armed for Battle* mini-LP, on their own label, Metal

Gem Records. "We decided that if a record company wasn't going to offer us a chance, we would take matters into our own hands," Dave says. "The album cost us 13,000 dollars to make. We pretty much produced it ourselves. We used a few different studios. The problem was that we didn't have any money left over for any marketing or distribution. If it weren't for a chance meeting with our (now-) friend Jürgen Hegewald with Hellion Records, we might never have been distributed throughout Europe and Asia."

Armed for Battle has this magical American metal quality, as Emerald blend Judas Priest, UFO, and Scorpions into their sound, creating a mystical, uplifting masterwork. Songs like "Look to the Stars" and "Teenage Suicide" have that element that only bands from the eighties American underground metal scene could pull off. Emerald is not crazy-fast power metal but pure, traditional American metal, with emphasis on sentiment and atmosphere. The mini-LP's closer, "Judgment Day," is maybe my favorite, with a heavy and pounding rhythm galloping through the strong melody. Excellent stuff. And even though people tend to classify Emerald as a Christian metal band, the truth is that certain members were Christians, but the band didn't fall under the umbrella of Christian metal. And how could they, since their formation predated this sub-scene? "I can't recall any other band from our town to record and release a LP on their own," Dave mentions. "Sammy Hagar is from our hometown, but I don't think that he ever released anything independent.

CUT TO THE CHASE:

If you are into the classic American metal sounds of Saint or Philadelphia, albeit with a more magical touch and an epic atmosphere, you will love Emerald. It's this type of totally seventies-influenced American metal that always strikes a chord for people into calmer, more melodic stuff, rather than frenetic power metal. *The Armed for Battle* EP is very rare, though, and on the wish lists of many collectors in the world, but there is always the option of the *No Remorse* re-release, as well as the split CD compilation with Oracle (released in 2001 on Magdalene Records).

"Probably our album release concert in 1987 is my all-time favorite show of Emerald's!" Dave says. "We had a chance to meet our fans one on one after the show. We hung out with them and signed merch. It was amazing."

Emerald's inclusion on the 1988 *California Metal II* compilation, with two excellent tracks ("Traitor" and "Born to Die"), regrettably didn't bring them a contract with a metal label, and they disbanded shortly after. Dave Enos and Larry Philips later formed Seventh Sign (and Enos formed Last Daze as well), Kyle Morrett played in Sacred Faith, and Roger Martin—who played bass for the band from 1984 to 1986, and again starting in 2019—was the most prolific of all, appearing in Once Dead, Die Happy, Holy Right, and Vengeance Rising, among many other bands.

The resurgence of interest in pure heavy metal, combined with the re-release of *Armed for Battle* by No Remorse Records in 2018, brought Emerald together in 2019, with a new LP in the works! "I'm both amazed and humbled that people actually show interest in getting the original

Emerald LP, as well as the re-release," Dave adds. "It has also motivated me to get back into the studio and make more music. I'm currently working on a project that should be completed by the end of the year. Plus, today, there is definitely an underground scene again. I'm not sure how much here in the States, but in Europe—and especially Scandinavia—it's pretty substantial."

On a final note, Dave adds, "Downloading for bands like us is probably both a blessing and a curse. Without it, we probably wouldn't have been as widely known, but with it, the opportunity for pirating is much more probable."

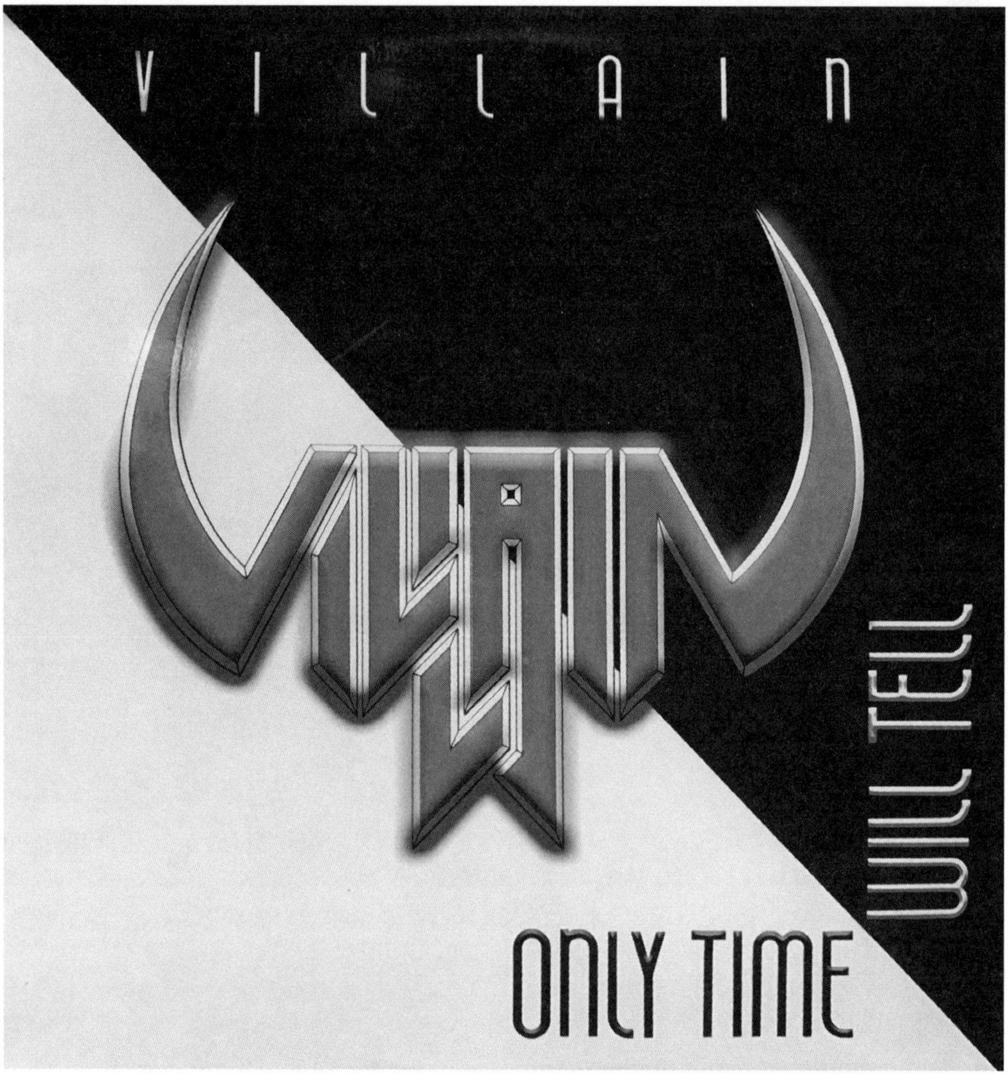

VILLAIN

VILLAIN FROM MODESTO, CALIFORNIA, WERE AMONGST THE BRIGHTEST starts of American metal in general, and not only because Carl Albert and Tommy Sisco went on to play in Vicious Rumors. In fact, Villain was managed by Vicious Rumors' Geoff Thorpe, and their quality as a band was evident from the very beginning.

Formed in 1984, bassist Tommy Sisco says, "Villain was already on its way to becoming a band before I was invited to join. The band was in a town about 30 miles away from where I lived. I had met their original singer, Kenny Lea, a few times at local shows and parties in the town of Stockton, California, where we both grew up. He called me one day and asked if I would be interested in coming out to audition for this band he was in called Villain. At that time in my life, I was so hungry for success that I instantly said yes, even though I was already putting a band together with another guitar player. Not long after that, Kenny and I drove out to Modesto, where Villain had a practice room, and I had my shot at becoming their bass player. That was the first night I met Leon B. Smith (guitar), Greg Noll (guitar), and Rob Quillen (drums). I was pretty excited, so it's all a blur and I don't remember a lot of details. I must have rocked hard enough, because they asked me to join the band before I went home that night.

"Villain was the brainchild of Leon B. Smith," Tommy continues. "From the beginning, he had a complete vision of what he wanted it to be. It would be something our music scene had never experienced before. Hopefully something the world had never seen. Once he connected with Greg Noll and they started writing music together, Villain's sound came together quickly. Leon once told me that the band's logo came to him in a dream and the moment he woke up, he sketched what he had seen. After I joined the band, we refined the logo through an artist friend who I grew up with. Our singer, Kenny, was a great guy and sure had the right look, but his vocal style just wasn't what we wanted. He was older than us and took things at a much slower pace. We were ready to take on the world, but he was more cautious. Had to think about things too much. Wanted to go left when we wanted to go right. It got to a point where it just wasn't going to work for us anymore, but the thought of finding a new singer in our area was not something we were looking forward to. We didn't hear a voice in any of the other local bands that screamed, 'I'm the one.'

"One day, Greg Noll said, 'I grew up with this guy Carl in Sonora,'" Tommy adds. "That Carl would be the late, great Carl Spencer 'Ace' Albert. The only problem was, he had moved to the San Francisco Bay Area and was singing for the band Ruffians. They'd recently released their first record and were doing pretty good. Certainly not the best scenario for us to ask him to come join our little outfit back in Modesto. Ruffians were doing a show at the Old Waldorf in San Francisco, so the four of us decided to drive to the City and ask Greg and Rob's old friend if he would consider leaving Ruffians to join Villain. It sounds crazy, even writing it here! But we thought, 'What the hell, you never know until you ask.' We were young, brave, and desperate! As our luck would have it, he wasn't happy as the singer for Ruffians. He told us that he liked his bandmates, but they were just too different than he was. For Carl, friendship and companionship was always the most important part of being in a band. He, Greg, and Rob had a history. He loved Leon's vision and fire. For me, Carl and I just got along. It was a brother thing. I'm pretty mellow, and I think he felt I was a good balance to some of the craziness that the music scene could bring. It was the eighties, after all!"

Tommy continues, "Once Carl was in the picture, we started focusing on writing original music right away. The talent in that band was way too large to be contained. What a travesty and a waste it would have been to continue playing cover songs. Once Carl joined, the creative energy in that band exploded! Leon, Greg, and Carl were unstoppable as a creative force. This is clearly evident on *Only Time Will Tell*. That record was recorded in two phases—that kind of money was not easy to come by back then—but completed within the first year after Carl joined. Some of the songs were already written but were refined by the five of us together, while some of them were written just before the recording session.

"We all had incredibly diverse musical likes though. We were open to pretty much all styles," adds Tommy. "I'm truly thankful that the stars aligned and brought us together. My exposure

CUT TO THE CHASE:

Only Time Will Tell **is a bright star in the history of American metal, and it is totally recommended to everybody into the classy sound of white-collar American metal. Meanwhile, Villain certainly has its own character, and maybe this is the most crucial factor in their case.**

to NWOBHM was pretty limited. I was a Kiss, Aerosmith, Ted Nugent, Kansas kinda guy and was just getting into UFO and Thin Lizzy when I was asked to audition for Villain. A few of the songs I remember learning for the audition were 'Desert Plains' by Judas Priest, 'Emerald' by Thin Lizzy, 'Die with Your Boots On' by Iron Maiden, 'I've Got the Fire' by Montrose/Maiden. This opened up a whole new world of music to me that I hadn't been exposed to before that. And from then and on, it was basically NWOBHM. There were too many LPs that we loved for me to name just one or a few, and I'm sure it would be a different list for each of us. A lot changed for the band when Carl Albert joined forces with us. All of a sudden, the walls of our creative limits came crashing down. There was nothing Carl either couldn't sing or wouldn't try to sing. For me personally, hearing Kiss' *Destroyer* for the first time is what inspired me to play bass. After that, all bets were off. I thought Rob Grange from early Ted Nugent records was an awesome bassist. Rush's *2112* was a holy-shit moment for me. Another dimension altogether!

"Our motivation was to be rock stars!" Tommy laughs. "To share this magic with as many people as we could. To follow in the footsteps of the bands and musicians that inspired us to pick up our instruments in the first place. To really think about it, we didn't have a choice. Once the music stirred within us, forming a band was what we had to do. It was a knowing in our bones. This would be our path no matter what we wanted. I'm sure most musicians will say something similar—we just didn't have a choice. Music was our flame, and we were there to hold that torch high for everyone to see. However, our music scene was pretty small. San Francisco was booming with music in the mid-eighties, but we lived about 100 miles away. Towns around us were small and we didn't have very many places to play. But the places we did play ... we rocked them like nothing they've ever seen or heard before! Our fan base grew pretty fast once we started playing shows in our area. We started getting recognized when we went places. It felt good. It felt right. What we were doing at that time was unlike anything any other band was doing. There weren't any bands around us that could compete. Especially with a voice like Carl's."

In 1986, Villain recorded and released the *Only Time Will Tell* EP. Another case of a private metal LP released through their own label, Relentless Records (which also released Aggression's Secretary Strut seven-inch in the same year), *Only Time Will Tell* stands until today as a crown jewel of American metal. From the opening frenzy of "Kamikaze" and the brilliance of "Kids of Crime" to the heavyweight powerhouse effect of the title song, *Only Time Will Tell* has the words *bona fide classic* written throughout. True American metal of the highest order, technocratic (metalheads like to call that stuff 'white-collar metal'), virtuosic, professional, melodic, but most of all inspired, *Only Time Will Tell* has only one weak spot: the Queen cover, "Tie Your Mother Down." This is not in terms of execution, only that I bet a faster song would suit them much more. But yes, Villain sound like they are on fire.

Regarding the making of *Only Time Will Tell*, Tommy says, "Not long after Carl joined the band, a friend, Roger Maxwell, invested some money into us and we went to a 16-track studio in Sacramento, California, to record a three-song demo. We tracked 'Kamikaze,' 'Only Time Will Tell,' and 'Kids of Crime.' When Carl lived in the Bay Area, he met and became friends with Tambre Bryant, who was a partner at L&L Productions. At some point along the way, we started working closer with Tambre, and she ultimately became our manager. Tambre and her partner, Michael Oliver, helped us get organized enough to go back in and record more songs, with the plan to shop us to some record labels. We even had a meeting with Mike Varney of Shrapnel Records, who offered us a deal, but we ultimately turned it down, thinking the terms weren't fair. He told us that he wanted to choose the songs that were to be put on the next few records, and Leon was absolutely against that. He wanted an album full of guitar burners like 'Kamikaze.' We weren't a one-trick pony—we weren't only one style, and we didn't want to get trapped into Shrapnel's stylistic hole.

"In hindsight," Tommy says, "that might have been our worst decision, because a few years later, after Carl left Villain and joined Vicious Rumors, they were offered that same deal ... and we all know how much of an impact their career has been on the scene! After several rejections, we all decided that Villain's music was too good not to get out there! Tambre took it upon herself to do all she could to make it happen. Without her, *Only Time Will Tell* would have never seen the light of day. She was and is a brilliant driving force within the American metal scene. Once it was all in motion, I asked my childhood friend Rick Rummel to help design the front cover artwork, and Tambre created the back-cover graphics at home on her first-generation Mac computer!"

Tommy adds, "There were a few shows already that we loved, but when we supported UFO at the Fox Theatre in Stockton, California, which is my hometown, in 1986, it was our first sold-out theater show and has to be at the top of the most memorable of shows for us. At one time, there was a video of that entire show, but sadly, it has since been lost. We also supported Racer X at the Stone in San Francisco. It was one of our earliest shows in San Francisco, and to play a sold-out show at the iconic Stone was amazing! We became friends with the owner of a restaurant in Modesto called the Pizza Machine. He told us he wanted to start having live music at his venue, and if we built the stage, we could play there whenever we wanted. Some of our most rockin' local shows were at this venue. The live tracks on the 2003 re-release on Hellion Records were recorded on a boom box at this venue. They're pretty rough recordings but are the last unheard recordings of us from that time."

Tommy Sisco and Carl Albert went to Vicious Rumors right afterward, and Villain disbanded, only to reunite in 1995 with a new lineup, wherein Leon B. Smith and Greg E. Noll were the only original members. This resulted in the Japan-only CD release of the full-length *Chequered Past*; it's damn sad that Villain went on to incorporate the (trendy at the time) groove-metal sound of Pantera. Gerry De Leon's voice is amazing, but the groove-metal style doesn't do Villain any justice as a whole, and even though there are some really inspiring songs (such as "Time 4 a Fight" or "Shackles"), overall it would not appeal to the so-called true metalheads.

"I remember being in Germany several years ago while on tour with Vicious Rumors when I wandered into a record shop," Tommy recalls. "I come across this glass wall display showcasing an original copy of our *Only Time Will Tell* vinyl album. It was priced at 1700 euros!! I couldn't believe what I was looking at. Not only was there an actual original copy of the album, but they were asking 1700 euros for it! After so many years of looking back at Villain's musical history, to see fans truly appreciating what we did is difficult to describe. We're honored, we're humbled, we're proud, and sometimes we feel a little melancholy. Each of us has wondered over the years what our lives would have been like had we done something a little differently. Said no when we should have said yes. Made the choice to sign with Shrapnel. Caught the attention of Megaforce Records with our demo. Been asked to sign on to a tour. Who knows? It was a different musical landscape back then.

"Now that we're in the digital age," he says, "music fans of all ages have direct access to music from all over the world. I salute those heading up the labels that keep the machine moving forward. With folks like Tambre Bryant at Relentless Records, Brian Slagel at Metal Blade, Chris Poland at Eclipse, Alfie Falckenbach at Mausoleum Records, and so many others, we're sure to have access to a bounty of quality classic as well as new music for many years to come. It's really too bad that all this music sharing doesn't generate any income for us old rockers, but in the end, it's about having that moment in our lives available for anyone who wants to take that trip. It represents our legacy that will outlive us all, and I'm good with that."

After the release of *Chequered Past*, Villain called it quits, but in the later years. The label Cult Metal classics re-released *Only Time Will Tell* in 2002 (with two bonus live tracks!), and Hellion Records went on to release the double-LP compilation *Time Machine*, which included *Only Time Will Tell* plus demo and live songs, in 2004.

"It's my belief that music—not just metal but all rock 'n' roll—will endure and survive," Tommy states. "There will always be a group of friends getting together in a garage or basement because they just got a new guitar or bass and an amp, maybe some drums. Making a whole lot of noise that annoys their parents and neighbors and really not giving a shit! They just keep banging away until one day they realize that what was once noise is now a kick-ass song and a unique sound. That feeling, which is unlike any other on this planet, will always sustain the underground scene. Why? Because there will always be that kid somewhere, and it only takes one of them, to infect that feeling, that desire into their friend or the kid they met the other day. Next thing you know, there's that new band we've been waiting for, the one that blows your mind, playing in a way we never thought possible, reminding us that that feeling is still possible. It's perpetual. It's inevitable. I, for one, don't believe it will ever die."

RAZORMAID

ONE OF THE GREAT MYSTERIES OF THIS BOOK WAS WHEN I FOUND BANDS that were 100 percent metal but which were not included even in the most extensive metal databases. This was the case with Razormaid, whose record I came across at a record fair in the UK, with a "private metal" sticker grabbing my attention instantly.

Guitarist John Kirk explains, "Razormaid was formed in El Cajon, California, in 1985 by me. In 1986, while I was playing in a local band, I met our future drummer, Dean Clarkson. I had wanted to form a band with Dean, so I left the band I was playing in to do so ... I wanted to form a band that was based on my vision of songwriting style, with big choruses and hooks, performance with two guitarists, soloing in harmony, and trading off back and forth. So, Thin Lizzy, Scorpions, and King Kobra were big influences. Thin Lizzy and King Kobra for their dual lead guitars in harmony, and Scorpions for the vocal and songwriting style as well as their

Razormaid band photo Tony Cable

performance. Dean and I moved to Northern California in the winter of 1986, where I had a place in the woods to write and arrange music, along with a local bassist. With the help of Bruce Turgon (formerly of Warrior, Lou Gramm, and Foreigner), we recorded a three-song demo. Bruce produced it and sang on it, as we had no vocalist. Summer of 1985, we moved to Reno, Nevada, to link up with vocalist Jamie Lee, guitarist Curt Mitchell, and bassist Dave Wix. In Reno, we soon became the most popular metal band, and are loved and played on the radio there to this day."

The three-song demo created a buzz around Razormaid's name, and they managed to get slots on touring bands' shows. "The most memorable shows were with Y&T at Lawlor Event Center in Reno, and Molly Hatchet at a club in Reno," John adds. "Molly Hatchet treated us very well. Danny Joe Brown personally brought us beer on ice, and the guys in the band were standing side-stage, waiting to compliment us as we walked off stage. The worst was opening for Joan Jett. Her band and crew were very rude to us, yelling 'Razormaid sucks!' at our crew and fans during load-out."

Being in Reno didn't actually help Razormaid gain exposure to the world of metal music, so they opted to put out their first record on their own. "I had met an investor, Rob Wood, and we decided to record and produce our own album. It was the step we needed to take to get local airplay and create a groundswell of fans, as well as to have product to use to garner attention from labels outside the area," John says. "We recorded and mixed it at Starsound Audio in Reno. With the help of Dave Hogle, in 1987, we pressed 1,000 vinyl records and 1,000 cassettes. We later remixed it at Granny's House in Reno and released it on CD."

The result was their first and only full LP, 1987's *First Cutt*. I'll attempt to describe this LP the best way I can, since I'm not an authority on the melodic metal, but ... *First Cutt* is simply amazing! From the first notes of "Sooner or Later," it's evident that this is a perfectly professional metal band that has worked its ass off to produce something so high-level. The

CUT TO THE CHASE:

Dude! I have to be completely honest, as always. The whole musical style of bands like Razormaid leaves me cold (don't forget, I'm a punk rocker!), but in their case I have to admit that *First Cutt* is a perfect melodic metal LP that will remind you other acts of that period, such as Letchen Grey or Agentz, although Razormaid are more guitar-driven. Absolutely essential to all people into the melodic metal sound. The piece on Razormaid is dedicated to the loving memory of Dave Wicks, the band's bassist.

production is crystal-clear, and even though some metal fans regard *First Cutt* as an AOR LP, the truth is that it's a gutsy melodic metal LP, reminding me of New York City's Hittman (their second LP). There's no element of pop or glam metal here—it is absolutely metal, but it's delicate and powerful at the same time. You can't argue with the definite metal character in songs like "Fight for Your Love" or "Livin' on the Run," and class is the word that's written throughout the album.

"No other bands, while we were in Reno, had private releases that I know of," John mentions. "When I went to Los Angeles in 1989 and formed Bangalore Choir with David Reece (formerly of Accept), I brought guitarist Curt Mitchell into the band. Razormaid began getting mentioned in articles about Bangalore Choir as press wanted to know where we had come from and about our past projects."

Razormaid called it quits in 1988. "It was amazing that the internet has been instrumental in bringing awareness to Razormaid, and many indie bands from the 1980s and 1990s," John says. "When the internet began, we remixed Razormaid's *First Cutt* and released it on CD. We began selling the CD in Japan, Greece, Norway, Germany, et cetera, by just linking with people online. When YouTube was created, people began posting it. Then when Yahoo and eBay were created, people began selling their used albums, which brought attention to the fact that they existed. But since we only originally pressed 1,000 albums, they soon became an item that collectors wanted, being so rare, which drove their worth up exponentially. It's really amazing that a whole new fan base has become aware of our music. In 2016, *Loudwire* Online Magazine listed Razormaid's *First Cutt* at number 25 in their top 30 hair metal bands! The internet has created a real movement for previously unknown artists and music, creating a platform for artists to be heard and build a following on their own terms, without the greedy hands of the music industry. On the downside, few artists are getting paid for their work as everybody is freely downloading it. In Razormaid's case, most of the CDs for sale on the internet are bootlegs, and we don't receive a cent."

GRINDING MACHINE

AS CRAZY AS IT MIGHT SOUND, FOR A SHORT TIME, GRINDING MACHINE from Los Angeles included the notorious David Marks, who played guitar with the Beach Boys, The Moon, and David Marks & The Marksmen! Guitarist and vocalist Vince Lauria describes Grinding Machine's beginnings: "It was basically between 1983 and 1985. Me and drummer/keyboard player John Cosgrove used to write a lot of instrumental guitar pieces together. I would play them, and John would record the sessions with a small reel-to-reel tape recorder. It was a lot of fun, and we started the formation of 'Blood of the Beast' and other basic songs that would later be released on our album. It was a personal statement for us: We wanted to create something that we wanted to do, and our own vision with it. At that time, we were damn serious about it, and we rehearsed six or seven hours a night!"

Grinding Machine's musical influences varied, and as Vince tells it: "I was teaching guitar in Los Angeles, so I was constantly exposed to different bands of the time; Ozzy, of course, and

CUT TO THE CHASE:

Definitely weird, Grinding Machine's *Cosmic Illusion* LP has its moments, but I'll recommend it primarily to completists. Even though it's not catchy, nor 100 percent professional, it still has a specific charm.

Black Sabbath … Iron Maiden, Mötley Crüe. We loved those metal bands, and my job was to figure out the guitar solos for students, so I was pretty familiar with how the heavy metal songs were created. So, I don't know if there's one record that was the most influential to all of us! I think that everything Jimi Hendrix did was huge, for everyone in the band, but regarding to pure, real metal, it has to be the *Number of The Beast* LP by Iron Maiden."

Dan Ferguson was also added as a keyboard player, and both Brandy Haile and Dee Dee Andros handled the background vocals. However, Grinding Machine always remained the vision of Vince and John. "As for the story of David Marks, well, he was 15–16 years older than us, but he really had a great energy! That's how we managed to play Gazzarri's, which was a very notorious club on the Sunset Strip. When we played, the locals were pretty responsive to us; they treated us nice, and we liked it."

When asked how they put out their first and only LP on their own, Vince admits, "It was Rafael Garcia's thought. I still work to this day with Rafael. He put up the financing; we did something like a crowdfunding, gathering money from friends in order to fuel things up! Then, we hired Dan Ferguson, who was a top studio engineer and guitarist—he played on the theme song for a then-popular TV series, *The Rockford Files*. He had a great private studio, and we started recording there. My ex-girlfriend, Brandy, also sung on it. We just used so many friends of ours! I remember that time that Jim Keltner (who worked with George Harrison, John Lennon and Ringo Starr) helped us, 'cause he liked what we were doing! There was a bit of a buzz with the band then!"

In 1986, Grinding Machine released their *Cosmic Illusion* LP, a record that bordered on melodic metal and shred at the same time; however, it was also totally weird, something that adds to the charm of this record. The opening "Born to Rock" is a galloping heavy metal ripper, and the instrumental "Grinding Machine Theme" is just superb, while "Blood of the Beast" has a mental aesthetic, like Alice Cooper on meth. *Cosmic Illusion* definitely has its moments.

"My favorite gig with Grinding Machine?" Vince asks. "The Gazzarri's show, definitely a great show. I don't recall, though, bands from our area with a private release at the time.

"I'm so busy nowadays with my online school, teaching guitar, that I don't really know whether people are interested in Grinding Machine, or in general, anything that has to do with the underground metal scene," Vince says. "Hey, I love metal, still and always do, and I have a clear vision of what's happening in the current metal scene, but I feel that a lot of the new stuff isn't played anymore … so much is done with loops, effects and those kinds of things. I'm old-fashioned, I like to listen to a band with musicians who can make some mistakes, as long as everything is executed with a passion. Music has more soul when it is actually played."

Grinding Machine faded away in the late 1980s, and as of 2022 Vince is still a music teacher. As for his opinion on downloading music, he believes that "Napster, Soulseek, those kinds of things devalued music to a degree; a musician can only make money nowadays performing live. On the other hand, though, some rare or classic records are getting re-released, thanks to the exposure that they got via downloading."

AIR RAID

LIVERMORE'S AIR RAID MIGHT HAVE PUT OUT ONLY ONE SEVEN-INCH (and remain relatively unknown even to the most loyal heavy metal fans), but the band had a huge history in the Bay Area metal scene, starting in the late 1970s.

"I joined a band that was already formed, and then it took on new directions," guitarist Tommy Merry says. "It went through several variations, starting with Manny Daluz (an incredible drummer) and Bob Starkweather (bass), who are both deceased, and Eric Johnson (guitar). When I joined the band in 1981, we got a bit heavier right away and started incorporating double leads, like Iron Maiden and Thin Lizzy. A few years later, we incorporated a new dedicated frontman, Johnny O'Dea, on vocals. The band was getting a LOT heavier at the time we broke up. By the time we got seriously heavy, it was Kiss, Iron Maiden, Thin Lizzy, Judas Priest, and Rising Force, whereas my personal favorites then were Iron Maiden's *Killers*, Judas Priest's

CUT TO THE CHASE:

The *Rock Force* seven-inch is simply a prototype of excellent American metal of the highest quality that will please everybody into the sound of NWOBHM mixed with early American metal. Fast but not thrash, heavy but not doom, *Rock Force* succeeds where many of the newer bands miss. Through its authenticity and honesty, as well as its non-negotiable inspiration, it manages to create the atmosphere for the perfect, total American metal.

Unleashed in the East, and Rush's *Hemispheres* (that was on my turntable 24/7)."

Tommy adds that things in the local heavy metal scene weren't always nice and easy. "When we first started, it was the 1980s, so of course, the scene was very competitive. All of the bands seem to hate each other. They'd go to your show and stand in the back row with their arms folded, haha! However, there were tons of bands! In the area of Livermore, there were all kinds of band styles: thrash, college rock, new age. It was a small town but easily had over 50 bands that were trying real hard to push through the roof. We'd head out to Palo Alto or San Francisco to play the bigger venues. A few of us bands regularly opened for bigger acts like Lita Ford, Metallica, Tony MacAlpine, Armored Saint, and Michael Schenker."

With their sonic approach expanding from hard rock to a more heavy metal sound, in 1983 Air Raid released their first offering, the *Rock Force* seven-inch, on their own Mapa Records. "We recorded at the highest-quality studio we could afford, which was with recording engineer Tom Size," Tommy says. "We then mastered it at Audio Arts in San Francisco, subsequently releasing it as a 45-sized 33 ⅓ RPM, so that it would have higher fidelity."

The *Rock Force* seven-inch includes two fantastic songs of pure American metal that would surely please fans of true metal too. I would call "69 in a 55" an absolute heavy metal hymn—a mix of NWOBHM with American metal (like early 1980s Riot), fast and anthemic, with crazy Maiden-esque guitar licks—while the flipside track, "Anytime," is a heavy rager.

"Our drummer Manny Dauz (and his longtime girlfriend, Sherry Rapp) were the driving force when it came to promotions and pushing the band forward," Tommy says. "After our first single was released, we had band dues, in which we all put in approximately 200 dollars a month, until we saved enough to record a full album. We continued to put in dues. We had a giant custom-built drum riser with fog lights and pyrotechnics built into it. We took our stage performance as seriously as our music. Next, we went on to record at one of the Bay Area's biggest studios, Fantasy in Berkeley. But the album was never released. And most of the tracks were lost. At the same time we were there, Sammy Hagar was also there recording *VOA*, and Starship was recording *Knee Deep in the Hoopla*. From those sessions, I still have one track that I'm working on remixing, which is called 'Road to Ruin,' and which was one of our heaviest tracks we ever wrote as a band! At that time, our bass player was John Souza, brother of Zetro [a.k.a. Steve Souza] from Exodus, between 1986 and 1994. Around that time, it wasn't uncommon for the guys in Dublin Death Patrol and Chuck Billy to drop by our studio, because Air Raid was getting heavier, and they were excited about the direction we were heading in.

AIR RAID BAND PHOTO COURTESY TOMMY MERRY

"We played with early Lita Ford and Ratt, but probably the most memorable was playing with Metallica at Keystone Berkeley," Tommy remembers with a huge smile. "It was about five months after *Kill 'Em All* came out, and they were young and raw. They almost had a *punk* quality to their music in the early days. Mosh pits were still in their infancy, and it was more like slam dancing to metal."

Air Raid disbanded in 1986 without releasing their (lost) LP. Johnny O'Dea went on to play with Snyper (and release two great demos of pure metal), whereas Tommy Merry plays still with his current band, Gamma. "I am one of the few that are left from my generation of underground metalheads. Many have died, and many look like (and are) insurance salesmen. I've been blessed to have kept my edge by pushing myself daily to continue to master the guitar, and to create and be more passionate with my songwriting. I have a new album coming out with some varied styles on it. Some instrumental shred, some fusion, some dark pop. Since traditional record labels have all but died, there are NO RULES. Just go for what you know. I tell anyone who will listen: Release your album, put it out there, with no attachment to outcome. It may go viral, or it may only impact the life of 100 people. But isn't that what it's all about?"

Tommy goes on, seemingly unstoppable. "Music has always owned me. I can't stop playing. I tried once for a few years, before Gamma featuring Davey Pattison reached out to me to be part of the reformed version of Gamma (formed by Davey and Ronnie Montrose back in 1979). Our original singer, believe it or not, is in his seventies and his voice is still incredible—he just keeps getting better with time. Once I finally embraced the idea of playing music just for the fun of it, more success came my way. I could whine about the digital download thing like some old rockers do, but I think it's cool. I mean, our society is totally immersed in music now because of digital downloads. However, it has made it nearly impossible to make a living at it. My buddies, who are in some pretty notable metal bands, still work a day job when they're not on tour. They tour all over Europe, do metal cruises, then a lot of them come home nearly broke and head back to their day jobs. So yes, that part sucks. However, they are livin' the life. And THAT'S what it's all about!"

Rock Force is a collector's item today, and Tommy grins, "I had hundreds of these records at one point, and over the last 30 years, I slowly started getting rid of them, So, I could kick myself in the ass for that! That being said, I am truly grateful that people still find a treasure in the heart of our metal. I mean, if I had only known that this metal thing would hang in there this long ... Those who are new to the scene are in for a wild ride, and us originals are very humbled by the continued life our music has had. I do believe a new wave of strong underground metal and that hard rock is building once again. I offer free guitar lessons at my website, TommyMerry.com. It's my way of giving back for the gifts I was blessed with, and helping those young and upcoming shredders get some free insight from my 40+ years of playing professionally."

WOMBAT

FORMED IN LATE 1983 IN HOLLYWOOD, CALIFORNIA, WOMBAT'S STORY IS narrated by drummer Scott Beasley: "I joined the band in early 1984. Tom Clowry had finished schooling at the Musicians Institute of Technology in Hollywood, Jim Davis had recently moved to L.A. from San Jose, and Tom Cronin was a friend of Tom Clowry's and was the vocalist. I grew up in Agoura Hills, California, and felt that I had outgrown the local music scene there, plus I knew Hollywood was the place to be if you're going to make it. So, I answered a classified ad in the *Music Connection* and auditioned for the band. Apparently, they had tried out quite a few drummers and were not very satisfied with what they had seen, because on the original phone call, Tom sounded a little discouraged, stating that they were looking for a Neil Peart-type drummer, and my response was 'I am Neil Peart, Jr., and I have exactly the same kit!'

"I kind of think Tom didn't believe me," Scott continues, "but when I showed up with the kit, I seemed to understand exactly where they were musically, judging from the fact that the jam went really well. And when I walked in the door of my house after the audition, the phone was ringing, and I was in. Two weeks later, we were playing at Gazzarri's on the Sunset Strip. About six months later, we sadly informed Tom Cronin that we wanted to look at other vocalists, and I must say he took it very well, considering the disappointment. and remained the best of friends with the band from then on. After a short search, we found Bruce Martin from Oak View, California, and we must admit that he was pretty dedicated, because he was driving 84 miles each way for practice two to three days a week. And that is pretty much, from my point of view, the formation of the band.

"It's always hard to describe your sound to someone," Scott says, "but I always told people we were like a cross between Rush and Iron Maiden. I believe that those bands definitely had an influence on our sound, although Tom Clowry and I each had a bit of a background in the jazz fusion greats as well. Tom's favorite player was Jaco Pastorius, and like me, he was a huge Neil Peart fan. That particular era in Hollywood was so hair-makeup-and-Spandex-oriented, where the joke was 'If you're prettier than your girlfriend, you'll probably get a record deal.' But believe it or not, it was pretty true, if you look at bands like Ratt and Warrant and Poison. But we were much more musically and instrumentally detailed. Many of our songs had bass leads as well as guitar solos. I'm a much more syncopated and accent-heavy type of drummer. Our songs, in my opinion, were much more than just your average simple groove-heavy metal for 13-year-old girls that was so common in Hollywood at the time."

Scott adds, "As far as I could tell, this was the absolute peak of the Hollywood days. There were thousands of bands out there at the time. It was amazing to go out there on a Friday or Saturday night with the bumper-to-bumper traffic cruising up and down the Strip and thousands of people walking the sidewalks in their coolest heavy metal clothing, trying to pick up on women and promote their band. It was standard procedure to go out there during the week and put your posters over other bands' posters, and it was ridiculous! It was hard to put a poster on a telephone pole because they were solid staples and nails! We finally started spray-gluing our posters up, and eventually, we got a ticket in the mail for littering! It was so competitive that sabotaging another band's equipment during their show was not unheard of. My favorite time of the show was actually sound check, because all of the bands had to be there and it was always apparent by the end of sound check who was going to blow whom away. And not to sound immodest, but in my opinion, we always walked out of sound check feeling pretty good. Now, of course, that does not translate into a record deal! We were not prettier than our girlfriends and we never got a record deal!"

So, Wombat had to find a way to release their music and offer it to their fans, and what was the best way, other than doing it themselves? Scott describes the process behind their first and only twelve-inch EP, *Wombat*, released in 1987 on their own label, Wombat Records. "With the only interest having come from a few small independent labels, and even then, nothing was really materializing, we started looking into the possibility of borrowing some money. We ended up doing that when a friend of Bruce's agreed to loan us some money. We had a payment schedule, and I'm proud to say that we paid him back in full with interest.

"We took that money and spent about 90 percent of it on recording at Skip Saylor's two-inch 24-track analog facility in the Larchmont District," he says. "I think that Skip was pretty well versed in exploiting the dreams of the young and inexperienced. He insisted that we sign over three percent of any future monetary gains and declared himself our producer. He didn't spend a lot of time maximizing the quality of the raw sound that was hitting the tape—in other words, preproduction sound check. And during the mixdown process, he would send us upstairs to watch TV while he and his engineer supposedly came up with five different mixes for us to choose from, which in my opinion was just a tactic at padding the hourly cost, because we would come back and maybe he would have turned the treble up or the bass up a little, like you were doing it on your car stereo. In other words, there wasn't very much difference in the mixes. But we didn't really know any better, so we took what we got. I think the record actually sounds halfway decent, but the bass is a complete mudfest, and the vocals could have used a little more work."

CUT TO THE CHASE:

Wombat's self-titled twelve-inch EP will definitely appeal to all the eighties American metal lovers, especially those who like their metal party-style. But be warned: in musical terms, Wombat is certainly not a glam metal band. It's heavy and technical, and I wish they had dropped the party attitude, because if they had, they could've released some pretty magical stuff!

The *Wombat* twelve-inch EP sounds totally professional, clearly coming from a band that worked in the studio a lot. Tight musicianship with a strong and heavy sound, this party metal album will definitely strike a chord with all fans of this style. The four songs are enjoyable, but the best one, the opener "Radio," is a total anthem taken from of the Iron Maiden book of songwriting—even though it has still the party attitude. But yes, "Radio" has a tremendous metallic riff and style that makes the purchase of this twelve-inch mandatory! And the Rush-gone-Iron Maiden flavor of "Got to Do Something Now" makes it another gem. The rhythm section on this one is out of this world, exposing the real technical proficiency of Wombat.

"One very memorable event was when we were playing with Hollywood Rose, which eventually combined with L.A. Guns to become, well, you know who," Scott laughs. "Anyway, during the bass solo, all of a sudden, everything went quiet for about 20 seconds—which, of course, nothing looks worse than technical difficulties. Anyway, some of the band or crew from Hollywood Rose had pulled the power from Tom's bass amp, and if I remember correctly, they got a nice little beatdown afterward, haha!

"But believe it or not," he adds, "I think our favorite shows occurred at private parties. We used to pay for our advertising in *BAM* Magazine by playing private parties, many of which were at my house in Agoura Hills, which was by far the largest contingent of our fan base, which was generated by our acquaintanceship with the people. Which is all you got when you're just starting in Hollywood and have not yet created a buzz. The private parties are usually absolute chaos, with hundreds of people stuffed into a house and the surrounding yards, and we would wait until everybody was in and paid their five bucks and the beer was gone before we started playing, because usually during the third or fourth song, the cops would close it down. I had a Ventures cover band that I'd been playing with for years, and there was also The 502s and Harum Scarum. I would have to say that was my favorite of our private shows. We also did a Battle of the Bands that was put on by the band Armored Saint, which translates to: it was a showcase for Armored Saint. It was called L.A.'s Top 25 Showdown. It felt like quite an honor to be included and it sure was an elaborate affair—they had a world-class festival-type stage and backstage set-up!"

Wombat wrote their name in metal history and were laid to rest in the late eighties, leaving behind their twelve-inch EP and some great memories.

"In regard to the resurgent interest in the American metal scene of the mid- to late 1980s, I think it's great. I have had friends look us up on the internet and find stuff all over the world," Scott says. "It always blows my mind. I mean, we sold our records individually for seven bucks or less, so it blows my mind to hear that people are willing to pay significant money for them! I'm not really aware of much of an underground scene; I live in Northern California now, and although there is a very good music scene in Chico, California, and I was involved in a very well-regarded funk band called Sofa King, I still feel that I am in musical exile up here. The thing about Hollywood in the 1980s was that you had to get a record deal to get any kind of large-scale exposure, and people came from all over the world to do it. So, joining or attempting to join a band was as easy as getting a local classified newspaper, and there would be hundreds of ads, looking for players of all types for all kinds of music. I still think of it as a large stroke of luck, but Wombat was the first band I auditioned for, and I'm very happy for that because they are great people and players.

"When Wombat eventually stagnated and died," Scott says, "we decided that we wanted a recording studio. I have a background in building houses, so I built us—on a limited budget—a wonderful set-up with a great main room, a small isolation booth, and a control room. Jim Davis really fell in love with twisting knobs and is a well-regarded producer to this day. He is also a monster guitar player, but he really doesn't play anymore. Even when working with people like Steve Vai, he gets more satisfaction out of recording them than when he plays the guitar himself. A couple of years ago, I literally had to beg him to pull his guitar out—he still has the same guitar in the case for years—so now I believe he at least keeps it a little more available. Like I said, Tom is still actively playing all the time. Bruce, I believe, ended up owning a stage, sound, and lights company that provided the equipment for outdoor shows. I have a seven-year-old son, and I continue to work in the construction field, but I will never stop playing the drums!"

SHADOW (KENNEWICK, WASHINGTON)

PHEW, TALK ABOUT OBSCURE AND CRAZY UNKNOWN BANDS! SHADOW FROM Kennewick, Washington, is maybe one of the oldest bands included in this book. "We started off in 1970 in the town of Kennewick, Washington, when a trombone player, Kris Knutson, in our high school stage band was asked to put together a bunch of players to play at a party," guitarist Cliff White says. "He asked the drummer, Art Bennett, and me from stage band to play, as well as another guitar player, Ray Leonard, and a singer, Dave Kesterson, who he knew. When we got to the party, we found out that it was being held at a church, and the pastor refused to let us play. So, we all went to the singer's house to jam.

"That night, we decided to start a band," Cliff explains. "At practice the next week, we decided that we didn't need a trombone player and we didn't need a second guitar player, so Ray Leonard volunteered to play bass, and we said goodbye to the trombone player. We named the band Ozone, and we were on our way. After months of rehearsals, we needed a way to break into the business. We met a keyboard player who had previously played in a band that had a booking agent and had just moved into town from Spokane. We started rehearsing at his house, and his old booking agency started tossing us gigs that other bands didn't want. His mom came up with the name Shadow. We all liked the name, so we adopted it. Several months later, we dropped the keyboard player because he refused to travel more than 60 miles away to play any show. Then we started rehearsing at the drummer's house. We tried out a few other guitarists, but none of them meshed with us. So, we decided to go for it with what we had.

"At this time, in 1972, we had a pretty good local following and were playing in the local clubs, even though we were all underage," Cliff continues. "We were able to play the clubs as long as we didn't stray from the stage, and if we needed to use the restroom, we had to get a cocktail server to escort us there and back. In 1974, we submitted a demo tape recorded on a TASCAM four-track to The Good Music Agency, a booking agency in Missoula, Montana. A few weeks later, they contacted us and said they wanted to see the band play live, and they booked us for a Friday and a Saturday at a club in Missoula. After seeing the band, they asked us to sign a booking contract, which gave them exclusive rights to book the band. We signed the contract, and the next month, we headed out on the road."

Cliff adds that, basically, they were the ones who started the local heavy metal scene. "We grew up in a small town in Washington state where the only clubs were country/western venues. That is ... all but one, which was called My Place Tavern, and that's where we really got our start. They usually booked rock bands out of Spokane, but thankfully, they decided to give us a weekend show because we were willing to play for half the normal pay that they were giving to bands booked from out of town. Our first night there, we were approached by someone from the local musicians' union, who told us we would no longer be able to play there or anyplace else in town unless we joined the union. So, we went to the next musicians' union meeting, paid our dues, and joined the union. The union members were made up entirely of county/western players, and right off the bat, you could tell that we were unwelcome and that

CUT TO THE CHASE:

Shadow are one of those bands that only left two or three songs behind, but all of them are pure gold! Shadow's style will please different kinds of audiences, from the true metalheads and hard rockers to the retro-lovers and those who love the evil sounds of bands like Mercyful Fate. Absolutely classic stuff.

they didn't want to have anything to do with us. All they really wanted was the money from our dues. They were down-home country/western players, and we're the long-haired, no-good, hippie teenagers. But it all turned out okay. The president of the union told us we didn't have to attend union meetings anymore ... but to make sure we didn't forget to send in our dues! Other than that, we had tremendous support from the locals, even though we weren't really that good. Still, I believe we had a fantastic following, as we were the only rock band in town at that time.

"We all lived in a small town in southwestern Washington state where there wasn't much to do," Cliff adds. "I don't think there was really a conscious decision on anyone's part to start a band. When we got together to jam the first time, I think somebody said, 'Hey, we don't sound that bad. Maybe we should start a band,' and we all just said 'Okay, let's do it.' The album *Smokin'* by Humble Pie was the album and band that left the greatest impression on us. I don't think it had too much influence on our musical direction, but we analyzed every song on that album forward, backward, and upside down. We used to listen to a few seconds of each song and then would pause it and talk about what had we just heard. It still remains one of my favorite albums of all time! Some of the other major influences were Kansas, ZZ Top, early Scorpions, and later on Van Halen."

In 1980, Shadow was offered a slot on the soundtrack of the movie *New Year's Evil*, and this led to the release of the title track seven-inch on the very small indie Cannon Records—but in fact, Cannon only handled the distribution. As Cliff describes:

"We were playing at a club in Reseda, California, and someone came up and talked to our bassist about the possibility of performing in a movie. They were really searching for a punk band but liked our original music and thought it would fit in the movie. After a few weeks, we met with the president of Cannon Records, as they wanted to sign us to a movie deal, but also they were planning on releasing an album of the movie soundtrack. We had been touring the U.S. for six years nonstop, and this was the first time anyone had offered us anything. So, we jumped on it and signed a movie and recording contract with them. The procedure was quite simple. They wanted a live sound, as the band was going to be playing at a live event in the movie. We set up our equipment in the studio. They set up all the microphones, and then they just started recording as we were playing. There was no overdubbing or heavy use of effects. Basically, they just wanted a raw sound. If someone made a mistake, we started recording the song over from scratch. And we continued just like that for each song that they wanted to include in the movie. They promised us that when we were ready to work on the album, we would re-record everything and do it right. But right now, they just wanted a raw live performance. The release of the 45 was a complete surprise to us. We were not informed that they were going to release it to radio stations all over the country. When our booking agency told us about the release, we were pissed off beyond belief. They had promised that we would be able to re-record everything with proper production values, not the soundtrack version. Later on, we were glad they released the 45, as Cannon Records soon went out of business and we would have ended up with nothing."

SHADOW (KENNEWICK, WA) FLYER AT SKYWAY (CLUB)

The reason that Shadow was included in this book, even though their release wasn't independently released, is because *New Year's Evil* is such an obscure and difficult-to-define release. It was a record that was sent to radio stations throughout the U.S. without the band having any knowledge of this, and then Cannon went bankrupt, and only a few copies ended up with the band! In musical terms, Shadow is one of the most exciting bands to be included in this book. This seven-inch is just pure gold, even though it lasts six minutes in total. The track "New Year's Evil" is a hard/heavy metal steamroller, reminiscent of seventies Scorpions mixed with Uriah Heep, whereas the flip side of "Simon Bar Sinister" is an unbelievable, pure metal crusher: upbeat, dark, and evil sound that predates Mercyful Fate!

"As far as I know, we were the only band from our area to have a private release. I think we were the only band from our area that was able to move beyond the confines of our hometown, in fact," Cliff adds.

"There were two shows that were far more memorable than all the rest," Cliff says. "But if I had to pick one, it would be the show that we played in Denver in 1980. We were playing at a club in town when we got an offer to play at a three-night Battle of the Bands contest being put on for Colorado bands at the Rainbow Music Hall by KAZY Radio. Even though we weren't really considered a Colorado band at the time, we had been playing there quite a bit and had one of our biggest followings there. The best bands were being offered a track on the KAZY compilation album, *Thunder on the Mountain*. The owner of a club called Mr. Lucky's was kind enough to let us skip playing his club for the first two hours of our show there, so that we could play the Battle of the Bands, as long as we finished out the night at his club. It was a magical night. The Rainbow Music Hall was packed to capacity, and there was standing room only. The crowd was extremely receptive and that helped us put on one of the best performances of our careers. And best of all, we got one of our best songs included on the KAZY album!" Cliff laughs while recollecting.

Shadow split up later in the 1980s, leaving behind a fantastic piece of music heritage. "Honestly, I didn't know there was a resurgence of interest toward private metal records and bands," Cliff admits. "In 1989, I gave up on trying to make a career out of music when I realized that I was not making enough money to properly support my growing family. When I moved from Los Angeles to Phoenix, I put away my professional music ambitions and started working for a national banking company. My interest in music eventually faded to the point that I no longer kept up with anything going on in the music industry. But since I retired from my banking job, I've made a return to the world of music! However, I'm only interested in writing my own music for my own enjoyment and rarely ever listen to anyone else's music."

SHADOW

THE HISTORY OF EIGHTIES AMERICAN PRIVATELY RELEASED METAL IS FULL OF fascinating stories, and the story of Shadow is one of them. Shadow formed in 1986 initially as Brain Damage, and amazingly, the band came to life during the Cold War by soldiers in the United States Army, in the German town of Schweinfurt. Drummer Kirk Streiter explains:

"I came along in late July 1986. When I came to Schweinfurt, my first roommate was a guy named Jason Penner—he was the singer for a band called Brain Damage (the original formation of Shadow). It was either my first or second night and Jason mentioned he had band practice, so I told him I played drums and I asked if I could tag along. They had a guy named Jimmy playing drums, and my initial thought was that he was a great drummer, maybe a little arrogant, but I thought I was just as good as he was. I remember Jason complaining about Jimmy's consistent tardiness and lack of dedication when it came to practice. So, I came up with this plan. I would go to the rec center and sign up for the drum room about half an hour or so before Brain Damage was supposed to practice. That way, I would already be there playing when they showed up. It paid off immediately. Jimmy was usually late, so I would get to jam a tune or two with the guys, and it eventually led to Tony asking me if I wanted the gig after a couple of hefeweizens at Maggie's. I was in!"

Living in the small city of Schweinfurt was by no means a drawback for Shadow to fulfill their dream of creating a unique heavy metal band. "I thought we were treated fairly well by the locals! We had quite a few fans," Kirk adds. "Of course, 'Ich spreche nicht sehr gut Deutsch,' but I don't think they were ever talking bad about us, haha! I remember the other musicians being supportive. We rented a room at Herr Geyer's place down by Sennfeld Lake, just outside of Schweinfurt, and there were a couple other bands that rented there. I remember the dudes from Vendetta and Horny Arbiter hanging out. There were a few other bands as well—the names escape me right now, but they were good people! There weren't a lot of places to play, especially during the winter. We played mostly fests and smaller clubs."

When asked about the band's influences, Kirk replies, "I'm not trying to be a smart-ass or anything, but I think you could listen to the album and figure it out. I mean, 'Fate of Evil' sounds like something Iron Maiden would have written, LOL. I would say the biggest influences for the band would be Iron Maiden (obviously), Black Sabbath, Ozzy, Dio, and Led Zeppelin. Album that left the greatest impression is definitely *Led Zeppelin IV*. John Bonham didn't just play the drums; he expressed himself THROUGH his drums, and not just on that album. That's just the album that introduced me to the band. John Henry Bonham is the greatest drummer to ever live! My biggest inspiration was definitely anything by AC/DC. Phil Rudd, he drives the songs. You don't just listen to AC/DC—you take a ride. Phil always plays a simple beat that is PERFECT for the song (much like Ringo always did), and I discovered that I could play those simple, driving beats early on, and that was a HUGE inspiration to me."

Shadow went on to release the first and only record, the *Iron Umbrella* LP, in 1989. It's not a 100 percent private pressing, as the German music publisher Knock Out Music Service helped them out with that. Kirk tells the story behind it:

"In my mind, it was to get a good copy of the music I helped to create. We had recorded ourselves with a little boom box tape recorder several times, either Tony or Monte bought a little four-track recorder that we used a few times, and we even went to a small studio somewhere in Schweinfurt and made a four-song demo. The quality of recording was good with that one, but personally, I wasn't happy with my performance. I think we just decided that the only way we were going to get noticed was if we put something out ourselves. One of my biggest regrets was that I didn't immediately return to Germany upon my release from the Army to try to promote the album. Woodhouse Studios and Herr Tomas Schnabel (a.k.a. Sam D. Jones) helped us with *Iron Umbrella*, and what a blast it was! This would actually be best answered by Tony. Tony and Ingrid (Sawyer, Tony's girlfriend/band manager of sorts at the time) got the money and hooked up with Tomas at Woodhouse Studios. Tomas also happened to be the guitarist for the Jan Kaveh Band and knew the process well from his experience releasing his own album. I think we just gave him free rein, and he did what he did. The entire process was a blast! Me and Scott actually stayed a few nights at the studio and had a great time hanging out with Sam D. Jones, drinking hefes, doing shots of Jaeger, eating 'Bambi meat' (LOL, a little inside joke), and watching him mix the album.

Next to the births of my children, it's probably the most memorable time of my life."

Iron Umbrella is a shining example of an American metal record from start to finish, with the influences of Judas Priest, Accept, and Twisted Sister being evident. Brilliant songs here, like "Numbered Man," the emotional "Fate of Evil," and the menacing "Nerves." Its rough production offers huge power to the material, making it an archetype for anyone who wants to play good melodic metal with a mean sound. The album's closer, "Iron Umbrella," has a fantastic intro riff, which progresses into a real metal hymn. *Iron Umbrella* will surely please all fans of real metal.

CUT TO THE CHASE:

***Iron Umbrella* is an amazing record, full stop. I really love its weird edge, as well as the underproduced sound that offers such character and originality to the recording. It's totally recommended for every fan of classic American heavy metal of the eighties. Sadly, it hasn't been yet re-released, and so only a few copies float around.**

Throughout their existence, Shadow played some shows that Kirk recalls vividly. "My favorite show would be the 'wig gig,' as we've come to name it. It was during the Brain Damage days. Jason and I went out and bought a couple of wigs and wore them onstage. Looking back at some of the pictures, I looked pretty silly, but we didn't care—we just wanted to be rock stars! My most memorable show would definitely be our first gig after releasing the album. We opened for the Jan Kaveh Band. Jan Kaveh was more of a pop/rock band, and we were metal, so to say that we felt out of place playing to their crowd is an understatement! We finished our first song and it was dead silent. I'm pretty sure we played our entire album plus a few tunes we had written but didn't record without so much as a peep from the crowd. They just sat on their hands and stared at us like we had dicks growing out of our foreheads. It... was... BAD!"

Kirk also offers some memories on bands from their area (which he considers to be Germany) that released records on their own. "I've mentioned Jan Kaveh Band numerous times—they had a private release but they weren't a metal band. Vendetta was local, but I'm pretty sure they were signed. They were really cool guys. Horny Arbiter was another Schweinfurt band at the time, don't recall whether or not they had an album. I think they did, but I'm not certain."

Shadow split up in 1989 but got back together in 2003 to record an acoustic set of the original LP, as well as several unreleased Shadow/Brain Damage songs. Then they broke up again.

"I'm not only a member of the band Shadow," Kirk admits, "but I'm also a fan. I LOVE our music. I still listen to it on a regular basis, and I'm very proud of what we created. The band never officially split up in my mind. We just separated and went about our own lives. I consider Monte, Tony, and Scott my brothers, I still have regular contact with the guys, and if I ever had the opportunity to reunite and play a few shows with them, I would move heaven and earth to make it happen. It's great to see that there are people out there that appreciate not only our music but the music of every independent metal band of the era.

"When I first found out about the whole underground eighties independent metal scene," Kirk continues, "I was astonished at how big it was. There were some amazing bands, and some amazing music. It's sad that none of us were really recognized at the time, but the music has stood the test of time. Over the years, I've received numerous emails from people all over the world (Brazil, Portugal, Spain, all over Europe—I'm talking everywhere!) either expressing appreciation for the music or asking where they could buy an album. It's a great feeling to know that music I helped to create moved someone to go through the painstaking process of hunting me down in search of their own copy. That's just plain wild!

"It blows my mind, to be perfectly honest. I only wish I knew where all my copies went; maybe I could make a few bucks!" Kirk smiles. "In all seriousness, I am extremely flattered. I think the desire of any musician who creates their own music is for their creation to be appreciated. It's a nice feeling, to know that there are people out there that appreciate my music."

On today's scene, he says, "There certainly is an underground scene for the record collectors. I know for a fact that I have people constantly contacting me asking about the album, if I have any I would sell, do I know where they can find one, et cetera. As far as live music, I think it would be awesome if there were some sort of live music scene for underground eighties metal. I've kept my chops up over the years, and I'm fairly confident I could pull off a tour. It would actually be a dream come true."

Finally, on the issue of downloading music for free, Kirk adds, "As a music fan, I think it's great! All kinds of free music! As a musician, it has its pros and cons. I think it could be a good thing for independent bands, the gigging, touring road bands. It gets their music to more ears, which leads to more fans and larger crowds. The internet has somewhat become what the independent/private releases of our day were. However, I also think that it could be a bad thing. Sites like Reverb, Soundcloud, and the sort have almost an oversaturation of music, and a lot of it is AMAZING music, but there's also a lot of complete and utter shit on those sites too. It's easy to get lost in the crowd. Back in our day, if we bought a vinyl album, we usually sat and listened to the entire thing, and even if we didn't really like it first time around, we would give it a second, third, and fourth shot at winning us over. These days, there's so much out there that I might listen to 15 or 20 seconds, then move on to the next band, unless it's something that really grabs me."

ASSASSIN (SAN DIEGO)

NOT TO BE CONFUSED WITH THE MANY OTHER BANDS NAMED ASSASSIN, THE Assassin from San Diego, California, formed in the summer of 1983, when Thom Beebe and Vincent Cavarra were working at a local guitar store in San Diego.

"We both had just left bands that don't really need to be remembered, and were currently not gigging and said, 'What the heck, let's get a group together,'" Vincent narrates. "We obviously decided it was going to be an original direction to pursue, as we both were tired of the cover groups out there banging away. Thom had been in a local band a few years back called Child and had some songs under his belt, so we started learning those tunes right away. So, we took our time in finding other members. At first, we actually had a female lead singer, but she rejected the band's name. So, as fantastic as she was as a singer, we had to move on. Our drummer was Leroy Vega. God, what an animal on the drums. Simply the loudest and most rock-solid drummer I've ever played with. A nice guy as well. Leroy then brought in a singer he had played with before in

CUT TO THE CHASE:

Assassin from San Diego are pure gold and will appeal both to fans of American pure metal, as well as those into that hard 'n' heavy mix. I can't think of a metalhead who likes Judas Priest's *Screaming for Vengeance* who would not like the Assassin seven-inch, whereas those who are deep in the American metal underground with draw comparisons to bands like Ruffians and their heavy, melodic metal.

other groups, Pete Papps. Pete has a very strong voice for such a little guy, kinda like Ronnie James Dio. So, he was on board. The first bass player we had was Neil Foote. Good player, but he had other interests at the time, so he departed rather quickly. Then I remembered a guy I met a few years back who was an absolute monster on the bass, John Osmon.

"I really don't remember much about the first times we played," Vincent says, "just that it was incredibly loud! It was just perfect. It wasn't too long after we made sure our songs were tight that we started booking engagements, and off we went. We opened for many of the national acts that came through San Diego at that time and were well regarded, which earned the band opening slots for national acts like Alcatrazz, Girlschool, Coney Hatch, Wendy O. Williams, King Kobra, Poison, Precious Metal, L.A. Guns, Raven, Blue Murder, Grim Reaper, Anthrax, Rough Cutt, and Slayer. We grew up with and were friends with many of the bands that started in San Diego, like Ratt, Rough Cutt, and guys like Jake E. Lee (and I should also mention guitarist Jennifer Batten, who toured with Michael Jackson several times). So, the environment and music scene in our sleepy city was an incredible seed of creativity, looking back.

"I was influenced early on by the pioneers of heavier rock, such as Jimmy Page, Van Halen, et cetera," Vincent continues. "Thom was influenced largely by Ritchie Blackmore as well as Clapton for sure. I also listened to lots of Rush in order to learn the odd time signature stuff! Other members' influences ran the gamut from Chicago blues artists, some well-known and some not, to even jazz! For me, if the music is good, no matter the genre, it should have an influence on you as a musician."

When asked about which records influenced him most, Vincent responds, "As far as a record that left me with the greatest impression, wow, that is a hard one being as all of it left an impression on me ... I'll throw *Houses of the Holy* in there, and surely Van Halen's debut album. For the other members, it was a wide spectrum, from jazz artists to blues. Funny that when I look back, most of us never really owned heavy metal records, because we were IN it ourselves, if that makes much sense!"

When discussing about the San Diego scene of the day, Vincent says, "I touched on it above a little, but when you are in it at the time, it seemed like things were not really that great. Part of the problem for many of the bands back then was that we were so close to Los Angeles that some people looked down on bands from San Diego. I guess that is a natural phenomenon. But now with the benefit of hindsight, it was a very vibrant music scene, especially compared to today. There seemed to be quite a few venues to play, and they really supported the original bands. The local turnout was really awesome, and all bands had wonderful, faithful fans. Of course, there were still many 'cover band venues,' but those mostly catered to the slightly older bar scene age groups, whereas the original venues were under 21."

Assassin's time to release a record arrived in 1984, and their youthful energy couldn't be stopped, which is why they decided to record and release one on their own label. "There were many bands that put out their product on their own back then ... Victim, Aircraft, Bible Black, I'm sure I'm missing some. In the early nineties, also I was in a band called BlackList (which included some of the Assassin members) and it was really quality stuff, holds up even today. Anyway, after we got quite a few shows under our belts, it was time to go into the studio, so I asked my parents to help us out, and they did! That first investment got us started, and through the help of some other generous friends, local DJs, and sports people who we knew, we had enough to complete a nine- to ten-song EP. This was our hope anyway, to shop the material to major labels, but it was a different time back then, no internet to self-promote music. So, even after getting a lot of interest generated, it just never happened as we would have liked. Yes, we had an agent/manager at the time, but it just never panned out. So, we decided to release a 45 (remember, this was in the eighties), and we used our song 'Treason' as the A-side and 'All Your Love' as the B-side. (Funny note: As it happened, there was a screwup in the printing of the labels, and both sides were stipulated as A-sides.) So, we pressed 1,000 copies of our single, and I guess they are in demand now, whatever that means."

Assassin's self-titled seven-inch came out on their own label, Assassin Music, and included two songs of bright and brilliant American metal. "Treason" is a heavyweight anthem, like a pumped-up Judas Priest gone proto-power metal, catchy as hell, with excellent musicianship and solos, while "All of Your Love" was somewhere in between Dio-era Black Sabbath and Whitesnake, but heavier and definitely American metal-flavored. Both songs are not only catchy and great but also boast perfect production. In general, Assassin remind me somehow of Ruffians and/or Shok Paris, which is definitely a compliment! Both songs were also included on several compilation LPs, including *Metal Madness: Volume One*, *No Substitute for Steel* (with "Treason"), and *California's Best Metal* (with "All of Your Love").

"We had so many fun shows, seriously, that this is hard to narrow down," Vincent says. "I think our show with Alcatrazz is up there for me. The rush of a young 20-something kid, playing in front of thousands of people, was thrilling for me. We also did a headlining show in Tijuana, Mexico, that was really insane. Crowds rushing the stage and the Federales (police) clubbing kids on the head was disturbing. We barely made it out of there and back into the States!"

Sadly, Assassin split up in 1986. Peter Papps formed Red Alert, Vincent Cavarra formed BlackList with John Osmon and Leroy Vega, and then formed BG Hunter with John again. In 1993, he moved to Coos Bay, Oregon, and played with Toyz. Thom Beebe formed Copperhead, which lasted until 1994, and in 2004, he formed a metal/blues band called Gun Metal Blues. As of 2012, he and his wife, PK, are in the band Steampunk Willie. John Osmon still lives in San Diego and currently plays with a Deep Purple tribute band (Deeper Purple, along with Dave 'Bundy' Imondi) and a Van Halen/Sammy Hagar tribute band (OU812). Leroy Vega joined Stress and played on their 1988 EP (available on the CD reissue of the Stress album *Killing Me Night and Day* on Deep Shag Records).

"I think the resurgence of small independent releases is due in part to the commercialization, in my opinion, of music in general," Vincent believes. "As such, I think today, the overall quality has suffered, and many are looking to grab something good—are longing for real music. There was a hunger you could almost feel in these recordings. It is palpable. Again, for many in that era who recorded their material with hopes of major labels picking them up, I think the bands were really trying to do their best stuff. Not all of course were great, or even good, but for the ones who kept at it, played a lot of shows and got tight, they put out some really good material. I know I still will sometimes put on one of our songs and say to myself, 'You know? Not bad, not bad at all.' And to be honest, as far as our stuff being considered collector's items, well, I'm VERY flattered. Like I said, I know we did some good things, and I'm very proud of that!"

Assassin came back from the dead in 2010 for an anniversary performance at the club 4th & B in San Diego, but prior to that, Deep Shag Records released a CD compilation in 2009 named *Assassin*, which included the seven-inch EP, six tracks from a previously unreleased 1985 album, plus five tracks from a live appearance at San Diego club Straita Head Sound in 1984. It's a collection that will appeal to all the fans of the band.

"Seeing that I'm almost 60 years old, I'm trying to stay away from the 'underground scene,' if you know what I mean," Vincent laughs. "But seriously, I now co-own a recording/video studio, and I see a lot of great music being recorded. It is relatively easy to put music onto the internet, but that is a double-edged sword, so to speak. You have a ton more music out there, but this also means you have a ton more crap out there too. And the major labels are kinda still around, of course, but they will not invest or take a chance on new talent, not like they used to do. Also, the downloading factor has surely created this ease to acquire music for the consumers, but this has also resulted in less revenue for the artists, and is a tough thing to 'regulate' and make fair for all involved."

ELYSIAN

ELYSIAN FROM SAN DIEGO WERE NOT JUST A FANTASTIC HARD/HEAVY METAL band, but they also played a huge part in the musical history of San Diego, even after their breakup. Prior to forming Elysian, guitarist Dan Colquitt and bassist/vocalist Jimi Lyons were in a band together called Matriarch. Drummer Joel Maitoza, who was previously in the band Metal Arsenal, auditioned for Matriarch but didn't get the gig. Shortly after, Matriarch disbanded. Dan and Jimi wanted to start writing original material and contacted Joel to join the band. So, in late 1983, Elysian came together, and Joel adds, "We were influenced mostly by European heavy metal. Primarily Scorpions, Judas Priest, Thin Lizzy, and UFO in addition to many others. Mainly guitar-oriented rock and metal. Probably *Go For What You Know* by Pat Travers, early Scorpions, and Michael Schenker would have been our most favorite records."

Initially, Elysian had a small but dedicated following in the area. "Locally, we did very well; however, there wasn't much of a rock/metal scene at the time in San Diego," Joel says. "New wave

CUT TO THE CHASE:

Blinded by Sound **is an utterly brilliant, hard 'n' heavy American metal record, and one of the few cases where a record of this kind will appeal to fans of hard rock, heavy metal, and true American metal equally. Don't get me wrong over my overexcitement about it—I'm a punk rocker, so I'm approaching everything here with an unprejudiced ear. This is simply ace.**

and ska were very popular, so we would end up playing at high schools and backyard parties mostly. We played this 'Locals Only' festival at this huge venue in Del Mar, California, with like 20 bands and only about 50 people showed up. We still played like it was a packed house. It was fun to be on a big stage!"

Even though they were very young, the members of Elysian were already accomplished musicians, and they decided to put out their first LP on their own label. "Honestly, we were all really green at the time, just starting out and didn't really know anyone in the music industry, so we never even shopped to labels," Joel says. "We decided to do everything ourselves and just hoped people would like it. We had about 13 or 14 songs written and decided which ones would be the best to record. We recorded the entire album live in one day and spent an additional three days tracking guitar leads/overdubs and vocals. I believe we mixed the entire album in two days and mastered it at EMI in Hollywood, California. I think everyone in the band agrees that there are a lot of things we would have done differently during the recording process, but you can really hear the excitement and energy in the tracks."

Elysian put out the *Blinded by Sound* LP in 1986, on their own L.C.M. Records, and if you are a fan of the hard rock/heavy metal mixed sounds, this is simply a precious gem! The funny thing is that Elysian don't sound American at all, since their major influences come from Europe, and when the band decide to step on the heavy metal side of things, it's pure magic. Songs like "Mystic Warrior," "Blinded by Sound," and "Hell Season" will make true metalheads cry out of happiness. *Blinded by Sound* is full of total quality, and all three members are fantastic players. This exciting and unique release sounds like nobody else—you can't even really distinguish the bands that influenced Elysian. Well, maybe some seventies Judas Priest and Rainbow with the heavier side of Thin Lizzy.

"There were only a few popular local metal acts that were pressing up their own vinyl, but most of them just had three-song demos on cassette," Joel recalls when asked about local bands that released their own stuff. "The more popular ones I remember were Bible Black, Assassin, and Ratt. And the resurgence of interest toward private metal records is awesome. It gives future generations a chance to research what we worked our entire lives to accomplish and to relive a little history. So many famous musicians had to start somewhere, and it's important to know where their roots came from. Sadly, it's extremely difficult to find any original pressings of our only album, *Blinded by Sound*. That being said, we haven't received any money from album sales, since I'm sure the album has been bootlegged numerous times."

Elysian disbanded about a year after the release of *Blinded by Sound*, and Joel Maltoza went on to play with Gangland (a power metal band featuring members of Sound Barrier and future members of Fishbone!), releasing one demo in 1988 and later relocating to New York to drum for the mighty alternative rock/funk/metal/hardcore 24-7 Spyz, exposing what a proficient and great drummer he is. He's also playing funk/hardcore/metal in Shockhead.

"There are so many great bands out there still putting out great material that nobody has ever heard of," Joel mentions, adding, "I'm torn on the issue of downloading. Although it gives people the opportunity to discover new music, it's hurting the musicians because they don't end up getting paid for all their hard work."

THE RH FACTOR

FOR DECADES, ETHNOMUSICOLOGISTS HAVE BEEN RESEARCHING THE variations of musical styles according to numerous elements, including age, gender, date, music and other factors. The case of American metal has its own specialties too: you had barbaric metal bands coming out of New York City, epic metal bands from rural America, and many melodic metal bands from places like Los Angeles.

This is the case of The RH Factor. Formed in Los Angeles in 1984, bassist Von Babasin says, "I was playing and recording with a rock group in the early 1980s called Uranus. I had produced and directed a music video, 'Lonely Streetfighter,' a track on our first album, *Maiden Voyage*, that was released in 1983 on ZYX Metal in Germany and throughout much of Europe. But by the time we had a pressed copy of the album in our hands, the band had broken up. So, we tried to put together a new Uranus to try to salvage the record deal. That was when I met guitarist Robb Howell. We did a few recordings as Uranus; however, the indie label we were with thought our sound was getting 'too heavy,' so they let us go. Robb was working on an album with another group at that time, named *One Step Closer to the Sun*, but he had no name for his group. I had shared a story with him about a song my father, jazz bassist Harry Babasin, had recorded with a vibraphonist named Robert Harrington, called 'The RH Factor,' and released on his *The Jazzpickers* album in 1956. I always felt it would be a great band name. So, Robb asked if I minded him using The RH Factor as his band name for the album release in 1985, and I said no problem. Shortly thereafter, I took out a loan from my credit union and booked ten straight days in Lake Tahoe at a studio named Cougar Run and started writing and recording under The RH Factor name—and for the next ten years.

"My personal motivation is that I am an artist and musician," Von Babasin adds. "To deny it would be to deny myself. It is as much a part of me as eating and breathing. Being brought up by a professional musician, I saw no other way of life. I was in my first working cover band at 17 and played and recorded for a decade before I started producing my own music. I have been playing now for more than 47 years, across three original bands, recorded nine albums, and released six of those and one feature film soundtrack. I am not with a group at this moment, focusing my time on producing my father's documentary, *Harry Babasin's Jazz in Hollywood*."

When asked about the band's influences, Von replies, "I would have to say that Frank Marino and Mahogany Rush were the largest influences on the overall sound of our The RH Factor. Robb was a protégé of Frank's, and our two drummers, Dave Goode and Jimmy Marcos, have both played and recorded with Frank. I believe the SG that Robb played at the time was once owned by Frank. My biggest influence was my father, who also became a great source of inspiration for the entire band and everyone I've ever played with. Dad was a visionary and innovator of the West Coast jazz movement of the 1940s and 1950s, who introduced pizzicato cello to jazz as well as recorded the first forms of the bossa nova. They don't come more inspirational.

"We were always well received by the public, but we never garnered any label interest," Von Babasin sighs. "They would label us (Uranus) as a 'hybrid band' by today's standards. After *Cries of the Night*, we played live locally and put together the music for a second album, *Jams*. We also went through personnel changes in the time we were together—we started with Johnny Thrasher as our vocalist on *COTN* in the eighties, moving to Eric Fling in the nineties on *Jams*, and I mentioned Dave and Jimmy on drums. We also had a keyboardist named Greg Nichols when we did the movie in 1992. We had recorded the basic tracks for a new album in 1995, but personal problems forced Robb to move to Idaho, and he took those tapes with him. They were never completed, to my knowledge."

In 1985, Von Babasin's first lineup released the *One Step Closer to the Sun* LP on MCF Records, with Robert Howell (guitar, keyboards, vocals), Greg Fisk (drums), and Bob Ridgway (bass). It's a good fusion of heavy metal, hard rock, and AOR, with at least two great songs: "One Step Closer to the Sun" and "The Calm." However, the lineup for the second The RH Factor LP changed to Johnny Thrasher (vocals), Jimmi Marcos (drums), Von Babasin (bass), and Robert Howell, and Von Babasin describes the release of the 1988 *Cries of the Night*:

"Curiously enough, I have no idea how you've ever heard of this record. We produced it with money from a private investor, and we never secured a distribution deal from anyone.

CUT TO THE CHASE:

The RH Factor is a band that will appeal to different camps; melodic metalheads into Q5 or Dokken will love them, and fans of hard rock/metal like TKO or Krokus will definitely appreciate them too.

As a result, we never knew of any release or impact it may have made anywhere. The same with *Jams*. It released on a CD, and we never had any distribution that I ever knew of. There may have been something I was never aware of, but I think *Jams* is even more rare than *Cries of the Night*."

Cries of the Night was released on their own label, Tem Records, and sticks with the same formula as *One Step Closer to the Sun*, only this time heading in a more metal direction and with much greater gusto and style! Fans of Q5 (their second LP), Heir Apparent's second LP, and M16 will be totally thrilled with this release, with killer songs like the title track, the great "A Chance to Run," and "Need You to Stay," which is maybe the best song they ever wrote. Mid-tempo melodic metal at its best!

The RH Factor played many shows at their peak, with Von Babasin recalling some of the best ones: "The coolest rock show we did was opening for Foghat and The Outlaws at Fender's Ballroom in Long Beach. Our band manager at the time, R.J. Cobb, was also the stage manager at Fender's, so he got us the opening slot for the concert. While that was an awesome experience, the best show I have ever played with any group was with a form of The RH Factor when we opened both days of the First Annual Long Beach Jazz Festival. R.J. got the stage manager gig for the festival, and he approached Al Williams, who was booking the talent for the show. Al was a jazz drummer who had played with my dad, and when he heard I was in the group, he booked us. Of course, we had to play jazz! So, Johnny sat this one out, which was probably a reason why he left soon after, and the core—Robb, Jimmy, and I—added Jim Yeager on keys and Elpidio Cobian on percussion. We were the only group to play both days, on the same bill as such artists as Hubert Laws, The Rippingtons, and Stanley Clarke. The biggest stage I'd ever been on, 80 feet by 58 feet, at the Rainbow Lagoon, outside of the Long Beach Arena, overlooking the *Queen Mary*. After the performance on Sunday, we were interviewed by the legendary Chuck Niles on KKGO Radio (now KKJZ), who had known and interviewed my father a number of times. It was one of the great honors of my life.

"I don't recall any other independent bands from my area with a private release," Von continues. "I remember always running into The Offspring at the rehearsal facilities we used to go to, but they were far from independent by 1992, hahaha!"

The RH Factor kept it up until 1995, until they disbanded. "Funny, I have also worked in film production all my life, mostly in special effects, and there is a resurgence of appreciation of the real, practical special effects we used to do over the CGI that dominates effects movies of today," Von Babasin mentions with excitement. "Music is much like that—we used to record on two-inch analog reel-to-reel masters and mix down to digital, preserving that warm sound you get from tape. There is a resurgence in vinyl too, over the sterility of digital. As far as our record being a collector's item, it's ironic, though, and even more so for my father. At least his albums are truly collector's items...

"I would say there has always been an underground scene for whatever your preference, more today than ever before. There's an audience out there for everything, so you just have to find your niche. Don't plan on paying the bills, though—if you can, more power to you, but plan on doing it for the love of doing it or don't waste your time. There is only one credible way to earn a living on your music in this market: licensing for film and television. Write all your own music, own all of your copyrights, own all of your publishing, and place your music everywhere you can get it into. And, for God's sake, be fair to your bandmates. Nobody gets a paycheck in the lean years, so if you do 'make it,' then everyone should benefit equally once you do."

Finally, Von adds, "Robb was in touch for many years but has disappeared. Haven't heard from Johnny or Jimmy in ages. I continued to play and record with Dave Goode in a new band we formed called ONOFFON. Dave and Eric are still my good friends!"

PROWLER (SAN DIEGO)

WITH THE EXCEPTION OF PSYCHOTIC WALTZ, WHICH FORMED IN 1987 BUT whose career took off in the 1990s, and Infamous Sinphony, San Diego is rarely referred to in the history of eighties heavy metal. But Prowler also calls the city its hometown. This band formed in February of 1982 when Doug Eidsmoe and Keith Larson met at the record store where Keith was working in Escondido, California, about 30 miles north of San Diego. They talked about forming a band, and Doug put an ad in the *San Diego Reader* for a singer and drummer. Recent Indiana transplants Paul Valentine (later of the hardcore band Social Spit) and Wally Thome answered the ad, and with the addition of Kurt Fonseca, a friend of Keith's, Prowler was born.

"I'll give you the chronicle of Prowler's lineups," Rob Palmer, the band's vocalist, says. "The first Prowler lineup from March to December 1982 was Wally Thome (vocals), Keith Larson (guitar), Kurt Fonseca (guitar), Doug Eidsmoe (bass), and Paul Valentine (drums). George

Cataulin replaced Kurt on guitar in January of 1983. Wally and Doug left in June 1984, and Ron DeBlanc replaced Doug. I joined in November of 1984, and the classic Prowler lineup was set. Keith and Ron left in October 1987 and were replaced by Hugh Muncie and Andy Jermstad. That lineup lasted from October 1987 to April 1988, when the band broke up. Quite a few changes in the history of Prowler, right?

"The metal scene was exploding everywhere, and we wanted to be right in the middle of it and creating our version of a killer metal band," Rob adds. "Accept, Iron Maiden, UFO, Motörhead, Judas Priest and Loudness were our idols, and the record that left a huge impact on us was Accept's *Breaker*. Such a classic!"

CUT TO THE CHASE:

Prowler's *I Love It* seven-inch is a brilliant record, and I strongly believe that fans of American heavy metal in its most basic and raw form (e.g., Omen's *Battle Cry* and early Shok Paris) will definitely appreciate it. A bit hard to come by even today, but why not get the 2015 *Prowler* compilation LP from Fils du Metal Records, which includes everything they recorded?

In 1984, Prowler released a six-song demo, and some hints of their greatness are already there, in anthems like "Nosferatu" or "Highway Robbery," which sound like Saxon, Accept, and Motörhead blended together. But the best was yet to come.

"There was a good scene in Southern California, and lots of places to play at first, but as time went on, it became difficult to get shows that underage kids could go to," Rob sighs. "We never achieved a huge fan base, but we were well known in the area."

In 1986, Prowler put out a record on their own. "We were tired of waiting for labels to offer us a contract, plus we desperately needed to have something out," Rob explains. "It was actually the best decision that we could take, instead of sitting on our asses and waiting to get signed. The problem was that we had fallen right in between two major trends in the heavy metal world: glam metal and thrash metal. So, it was practically very difficult for a pure heavy metal band like us to draw some attention."

On their own Scumdog Records (a label name that Paul Valentine used later for a demo cassette of Social Spit), Prowler released their 1986 seven-inch *I Love It*, which remains one of my favorite American metal releases! Two heavy metal crushers, mid-tempo and as heavy as possible, and every word, every note is oozing with power. Prowler took their cues from Accept, obviously, but what differentiates them from the Germans is the brilliant voice of Rob Palmer, who sounds like some of the rawest American metal singers of the era, like Omen's J.D. Kimball. Both songs rule, with "Temporary Insanity" being a real powerhouse. Prowler had both the talent and the hooks.

After the release of *I Love It*, Prowler did a West Coast tour, even playing some dates alongside the mighty Mentors! They kept it up until 1988 when, disappointed by not getting further attention from a record label, Prowler was laid to rest.

"These were absolutely good times," Rob smiles. "I never regret what we did with Prowler. We could have progressed it further, but that's life!"

HANS NAUGHTY

HANS NAUGHTY WAS ONE OF THE BANDS WHOSE RELEASE OF A SELF-FINANCED and self-promoted record led them to a contract with a label. Formed in Los Angeles in 1981, their story is narrated by vocalist Dan Sullivan:

"Terry Broadbent (guitarist) and Jim Flanigan (drummer) were living in the San Francisco Bay Area, and me and Mark Crowley (bassist) grew up in a small farming town called Marysville in Northern California. I moved to the Bay Area at 19 and played in a few bands as a drummer. I decided I wanted to front a band, as I was singing from behind the drum kit, so I answered an ad I found in *BAM* Magazine. I remember the audition; I actually showed up in freaking leopard-skin Spandex and fur boots, haha! I guess that worked, 'cause I got the gig. Terry and Jim had a different bass player at the time named Kevin, but he was more prog-influenced by the likes of Rush, Triumph, et cetera, and we wanted to go more arena rock. So, I called Mark and he moved down.

HANS NAUGHTY BAND PROMO IN METAL_ON_METAL ZINE NUMBER 06, 1988.

"Our first gig was at the Mabuhay Gardens, which was a notorious punk club on Broadway in San Francisco," Dan says. "The Mabuhay was known for punk with a capital P, featuring the likes of Pearl Harbor and the Explosions and the Dead Kennedys. So, they booked us on an off night. It was a Tuesday night and a torrential rainstorm, but we went in there and blew the doors off the place to about 15 people, LOL. Dirk Dirksen, who managed the place, was really impressed and continued to book this part metal/part rock band in his punk club until we were packing it on weekends. At this point, other clubs took notice. like Bill Graham's Old Waldorf and also the Stone across from the Mabuhay, and we started playing the bigger clubs."

While detailing his passion for music, Dan adds: "I was really into sports in high school, playing football, but I picked up the drums and really liked that. I realized I wasn't going to have a career in sports, so I said, 'Fuck it, I'll be in a band.' Me and Mark started a band called Atomic Warhead and we played the local high schools. We really loved it, it felt good on all levels, and all of a sudden, girls liked me, so that wasn't bad either. Anyway, after high school, I had a talk with my mom and told her I wanted to pursue music, and she encouraged me to move to the Bay Area because that was the only chance I'd have at success."

Hans Naughty had a definite melodic/commercial metal background. Dan says, "In general, I'd say these bands had a big influence on Hans Naughty: Van Halen, AC/DC, UFO, Ozzy, Judas Priest, Ted Nugent, and Lynyrd Skynyrd. Specific albums were Van Halen's *I*, *Highway to Hell* by AC/DC, *Screaming for Vengeance* by Priest, and *Strangers in the Night* by UFO."

Dan wants to pinpoint that there were two eras for Hans Naughty: "The first one was the San Francisco Bay Area scene, and the second one was the Los Angeles scene. The Bay Area scene took to us right away. A 'right place, right time' scenario. We rose up really quickly there—we went from a rainy night with 15 people at the Mabuhay Gardens to headlining Metal Mondays at Bill Graham's Old Waldorf in about a year. In hindsight, I think we should have stayed in the Bay Area, but me and Terry took an investigatory trip to L.A. and stayed with a band called Angeles. We crashed at Stephen Pearcy's pad for the weekend and fell in love with the scene, so within the next year we had relocated to L.A.

HANS NAUGHTY FLYER FOR JUNGLE PRODUCTIONS, 1988.

"L.A. loved us too," he goes on, "but we were not as big of a band there. Mötley Crüe had just got their big deal—they were a band that we played with in the Bay Area—and folks like Dokken and Great White and Ratt were beginning to break. One of our first gigs in L.A. was opening for Ratt at the Troubadour, where we were well accepted and got a positive response, soon headlining places like the Roxy and Gazzarri's (and the Troubadour!). I think, hands-down, it was a show at the Troubadour in West Hollywood that was my favorite show. It was the night before the US Festival in San Bernardino, and guys from Van Halen, Judas Priest, and Scorpions were in the crowd. I couldn't believe those guys were in the crowd while I was onstage—what a surreal moment to look out and see your rock heroes watching you! A close second would be playing Metal Mondays at the Old Waldorf—always packed, and always a great time. Or maybe playing with Mötley Crüe at the Old Waldorf, which was great as well. We played with Metallica at the Stone, but their audience sucked, and we almost got into a brawl with some of their fans after our set."

Hans Naughty were about to explode, but they really needed to put a record out soon. Dan describes the story behind their self-released 1985 seven-inch, *We're an American Band*, on their own Naughty Rock Productions. "Okay, this is where it starts to hurt, heh. We only released independently because we couldn't get a major label to sign us. We had big-time

CUT TO THE CHASE:

Okay, I'll just keep it short and sweet: If you by any chance happen to be a fan of the L.A. metal bands of the eighties, like Dokken and Ratt, Hans Naughty will be an ideal band for you. However, their sound is much more powerful than either of those bands, with a guitar that somehow reminds me of heavy/power metal bands at times, and this is actually the most enjoyable part.

management, but somehow, we just couldn't get over the hump with a major. Atlantic was grazing around us but never bit, and with the scene changing with bands like L.A. Guns and Guns N' Roses breaking into the scene (both of which we knew and hung out with), our window of opportunity was beginning to close. Iron Works Records wanted to release our music, so basically, we gave them the best-sounding demos we had and they mastered them and released them.

"And the sad part," Dan says, "is we had recorded five incredible songs with Don Dokken producing and Michael Wagner engineering! They were stellar-sounding and radio-ready, but our financial backer didn't pay the studio the final bill and we were never given the masters. This was before we had the big-time management. Our backer was a stripper with money. Oh, well!"

Hans Naughty's seven-inch, *We're an American Band,* includes the Grand Funk Railroad title song cover, but the B-side, their original "Where's All the Music," is a perfect representation of what they could deliver! Warning: This is by no means your typical lite-sounding glam/metal—it had a huge, powerful sound that bordered between heavy and power metal, with party metal elements added by the lyrics and the fun aesthetic. Hans Naughty even remind me of an American party-animal version of The Cult on this song, and this is maybe because of Dan's excellent vocals—but I don't want to be unfair to all the other members. This is just great.

Hans Naughty got the chance to release some records for Iron Works in subsequent years, but I really don't want to refer to this specific label, and will draw a line by mentioning that no matter how great a band was, none of them found a career via Iron Works. (It was other labels that helped bands like Overkill, Liege Lord, or Jag Panzer to achieve a career in music, not Iron Works.) That said, in 1987, Iron Works released the *Paint the Town Red* twelve-inch LP that every fan of glam metal should have in his collection—very powerful metal with the usual party edge—as well as the *Tears in the Night* 1987 seven-inch picture disc and the *Paint the Town Red* cassette. Hans Naughty also gained some fame due to their inclusion on the soundtrack of the movie *Beach Balls* (1988) with "Say Hey Hey," and kept it up until 1993.

"Well, first off, if someone's selling our stuff online, I want my cut," Dan laughs. "But yeah, I think it's great that some people are interested in Hans Naughty. Our scene was a very unique time in rock 'n' roll history, and I can see why folks would be interested. My daughter, who is in her early twenties, tells me she wishes she had been part of the 1980s!"

Members of Hans Naughty are also connected with other bands. Steve Stamato played with the thrashers Détente, Lover of the Bayou, and Naked Soul, Dan Sullivan with Honkystomp, and Mark Crowley with Black Bambi.

When asked about the state of the underground metal scene today, Dan replies, "The whole musical landscape and how music is being delivered has changed dramatically. Either we keep up or become obsolete. Knowing how to monetize music today is way different than when I was coming up. On some levels, it's better for the artist, as they have a direct connection with a potential mark through the internet, and on other levels, it's worse, as you have to give away music … it's a mixed bag that my daughter and I are trying to figure out as I am getting ready to release her music this year (2020)."

CHILDHOOD'S END

CHILDHOOD'S END FROM SANTA ROSA, CALIFORNIA, WAS A SHORT-LIVED project by Dino Alden (guitar, bass, sound engineer, and producer), Steve Russey (drums), and Jennifer Hall (vocals), and left their mark with just one brilliant twelve-inch, 1984's *Childhood's End*.

Dino Alden explains, "It was so long ago, so let me try to remember! This would have been around 1979 or 1980, so we were just kids around 16 or 17 years old. I met the original Childhood's End guitarist, Gary Miller, at a local music store where I was taking bass lessons. The drummer, Steve Russey, went to the same high school I attended, and we met through a mutual friend. The original singer was a guy named Brian O'Dwyer who was in his twenties, but he didn't join the band until around 1981 or '82. Jennifer Hall joined in later and we recorded our twelve-inch with her ... we all shared the love of creating music, having fun, and in the spirit of all the bands that we were fans of.

"Speaking of bands," Dino continues, "we were big fans of most of the popular rock bands that came out when we were kids: Queen, Rush, Yes, Rainbow, UFO, Kiss, Van Halen, Cheap Trick, Black Sabbath, Boston, Led Zeppelin. It was only natural that we would be influenced by their work. For me, albums like Queen's *News of the World*, Rush's *2112*, Yes' *Fragile*, Boston's and Van Halen's first records, Rainbow's *Long Live Rock N Roll*, and Black Sabbath's *Paranoid* were hugely influential to me. I still love those records!"

In Santa Rosa, says Dino, "There was no real scene where we lived at the time. Most of the bars that would allow rock bands were pay-to-play and had poor sound systems, if they had anything at all! Often, we would get Tuesday nights at country bars and, not surprisingly, the regulars would hate us! Plus, because all of us except Brian were underage, we either had to stay in the dressing room or go outside when we weren't playing. So, after a while, what we wound up doing was playing shows at house parties instead. Those were enormous fun because there would be loads of kids our age who were into much of the same stuff. So, we decided to put out our record on our own, 'cause it seemed like the thing to do to help us get better bookings, have something to sell to our fans, and to help us get noticed by the record labels."

Childhood's End went on to release their first and only twelve-inch, as Dino explains: "It is a terribly drawn-out story. First, we went to a small home studio on the west side of Santa Rosa. Those recordings came out worse than the recordings we were doing in my folks' garage. Then Brian suggested we go to Prairie Sun Recording, which is in Cotati, a small town south of Santa Rosa. So, we went there, met Mark 'Mooka' Rennick, and he recorded three of the four songs. But by the time we were working on the third song, 'Out on Your Own,' we had fired Brian, and Gary couldn't continue on, so it was just Steve and me. So, in addition to playing the bass, I wound up playing the rhythm guitars on all of the songs. Mooka suggested we hire Peter Marrino of Le Mans to sing the lead vocals of the songs. Pete also helped me write the lyrics to 'Out on Your Own.' Later, we got Greg Vorobiov to play lead guitar on three of the songs. But then Le Mans got signed to CBS, so Pete suggested we check out his girlfriend at the time, Jennifer Hall, who was also an amazing vocalist. We loved her voice too, so we redid all the lead vocals with her."

Dino continues, "At some point, we got Josh Ramos (Le Mans/The Storm) to play lead guitar on 'Out on Your Own.' Then I wrote 'You Better Run' and we recorded that at Beggar's Banquet in Santa Rosa. For that song, we got Dylana Nova Scott (VAIN) to play lead. Sadly, because it took so long and was so expensive for Steve and me to finance, our original goal of a full album was shelved. Also, even though we finished the recording in summer of 1984, we didn't have enough money to do the artwork, mastering, and record duplication until the beginning of 1985. To make matters worse, my father was diagnosed with brain cancer in June of 1985, so I was helping my mother running their business and taking care of my dad. Furthermore, at this point, Steve was getting a lot of pressure from his folks to pursue something more lucrative, so he was fading out of the picture. By the time I was contacting record stores and distributors, there was really just me left in the band. When my father passed at the end of 1985, I just didn't have much enthusiasm to continue promoting the EP, and that was that for Childhood's End."

Melodic hard rock/metal (with a slight AOR touch) is the style here on the Childhood's End twelve-inch, and they do it with gusto and style. Everything in the band sounds totally

CUT TO THE CHASE:

Into the melodic sounds of bands like White Lion, Shy, or even Hellion? Grab a copy of the *Childhood's End* twelve-inch—it definitely has both the quality and the songwriting chops.

professional, from the production to the execution of the songs, and there are some definitely some talented people here—everybody's an accomplished musician. Vocalist Jennifer Hall offers a huge kick, and there's no song that lacks for inspiration. For favorites, allow me to choose the excellent opening "You'd Better Run for Tomorrow" and the heavyweight "Out on Your Own," which sounds like Judas Priest playing AOR/hard rock.

"At the moment, I'm not recalling many," Dino replies when asked about other Santa Rosa bands that released their own records. "I'm sure I'll remember more later, but one that I remember was a band called The Electric Toys. They released a single called *Electric Energy*. They were a new wave band, sort of like The Knack. I really liked the song live, but I never heard the recording. I think Skitzo started putting out records around 1985 or 1986. Skitzo is a wonderful heavy metal band, stylistically like Black Sabbath, and is still playing around the Bay Area."

House parties, getting themselves slots on bigger events ... things were going good for Childhood's End for a while. "There was a house party on Pacific Avenue in Santa Rosa that we played, and that was a total blast!" Dino says. "In addition to our instrument amps, we also had a pretty large and powerful PA. The crowd was right in our faces, and the sound was so epic. We totally blew them away!"

Regarding the private metal releases of the day, Dino says, "A lot of people poured their hearts and souls and money into these recordings but never had a chance of getting that many people beyond their own small social circles to hear them. It's a wonderful thing that, now through the internet, this material can be enjoyed by many more people. Even though I find it hard to believe that people are paying big money for the *Childhood's End* twelve-inch! You know, very few copies were ever distributed worldwide because of the whole cancer issue with my dad. I think there might be only about 50 copies of the vinyl EP in Europe and maybe another 50 in the U.S. And that's it! We only had money for 100 copies in the first pressing. We had a second pressing of 300 copies, but they arrived right in the middle of when I was helping my mother care for my dad. Also, and I didn't learn this until after my father passed, but the second pressing had been shrink-wrapped too tightly, so virtually all of the second pressing was warped. I still have 200 to 250 copies of the second warped pressing in storage."

Childhood's End were laid to rest by 1985, never to reform. "I'm just surmising, but I think there is a vibrant underground scene today," Dino posits. "First, there are always fans and collectors out there looking for new (to them) bands and artists. Second, I know that labels such as Heaven and Hell, Eonian, and others are re-releasing private metal recordings from that era, so there is obviously some level of interest. However, downloading is a double-edged sword. On one hand, it allows people to hear stuff they would normally never have access to. On the other hand, the artists never see any financial reward for their labor. For example, I know that on one guy's YouTube channel, there has been over 100,000 views of 'You Better Run,' which to me is mind-blowing! I can only guess that people have stumbled across it because we took our name from the Arthur C. Clarke novel, or people know about the Pink Floyd song, or Marillion's, and then saw the album artwork and gave it a listen. But regardless of how people stumbled upon it, I won't see whatever paltry sum YouTube pays for all those views. So, there is the rub: vastly more people are aware of the material and are able to freely enjoy it, which is awesome, but the artist doesn't get rewarded. This is because of the internet laws that have given vast disproportionate deference to content delivery over the content itself. Hopefully, a more equitable balance will be struck in the future."

DIAMOND CLAW

DIAMOND CLAW FROM LONG BEACH, CALIFORNIA, FOLLOWED THE OPPOSITE route: they initially signed to a very tiny indie label to release their first record, and then went for a private release on their second one. Moreover, in a male-dominated scene, Diamond Claw were one of the very few metal bands with an all-female lineup.

"Diamond Claw formed in 1984," vocalist Debra Billingsley tells me. "Mary Jo Godges a.k.a. Mary the Maniac on bass, and myself, Debra Billingsley a.k.a. Debby Do. We hooked up with Jenny Thornburg a.k.a. Jenny T. Shred, on guitar, and Pamela Galloway a.k.a. Bam Bam Pam on drums. I knew Jenny and had played with Mary in another band. I introduced Mary to Jenny, and then Jenny introduced Mary and me to Pam. We all decided to play together to see how it sounded. It was magic. We all got along fantastic and became best friends. We rehearsed together five nights a week. We wrote all the songs for Diamond Claw. It was the best time of my life playing with that band! We were an all-female band motivated to be the best we could be. We worked very hard at it, and everyone in the band had different influences. My personal influence was Judas Priest."

The Southern California metal scene was at its peak in that era, and Debra recalls that the scene was amazing. "Everyone was out watching live bands. The clubs were packed. We headlined clubs from Hollywood to Orange County. We played the Roxy, Whisky a Go Go, Troubadour, Gazzarri's, Fender's Ballroom, Bogart's, the Dancing Waters, and Jezebel's. The locals loved us. Diamond Claw was a popular local band—but it was other bands that paved the way for us, The Runaways and, of course, Girlschool!"

Rehearsing endlessly led Diamond Claw to become a real tight-sounding combo, and the band developed a distinct sound, evident on their first 1987 twelve-inch EP, *No Hate in Paradise*. "We wanted so much to put out a record," Debra admits. "Mary the Maniac, our bass player, was a disc jockey at KNAC and found us a producer and a very small record label. Ron Goudie from Enigma Records produced us, and Blackjack Records signed us to their label. That EP was on 60 college radio stations. We were distributed in the U.S., Japan, and the Netherlands. We had local write-ups, a write-up in Germany, and a write-up in *Kerrang!* magazine by the time it was released!"

CUT TO THE CHASE:

Diamond Claw's *No Hate in Paradise* is still under the radar of most metal fans worldwide, and it's a shame; those who are into the melodic metal of Dokken or the classic American metal sound of the eighties (that is, without any rough NWOBHM influences) should get it, because it's a high-quality release. The guitar tone somehow reminds me of Heir Apparent's *Graceful Inheritance*, but this is where all similarities end, because Diamond Claw aren't an epic metal band—this is just a comparison to show how sweet and delicate they sound!

I consider *No Hate in Paradise* to be a semi-privately released record (whatever this might mean); Blackjack Records was the baby of Bill Overholtzer of the new wave band Q 16, and the label exclusively released that band's records. At the time, Diamond Claw's EP was the first on this label other than Q 16's releases; it was followed by an LP by a band called Hard As Nails/Cheap As Dirt, and Blackjack Records then folded forever. That said, *No Hate in Paradise* is a beautiful melodic metal record (not glam, not AOR—this is 100 percent melodic metal), and what makes an impression from the beginning of "Hail to the Queen" is the technical proficiency of Diamond Claw's members. All of them are accomplished players, but allow me to refer specifically to Debra's excellent voice and Jenny's absolutely crushing guitar style! Check out songs like "Shooting Star" or the closing "Danger Eyes," a real heavy metal rager. Great stuff.

Diamond Claw could have pursued a great career in metal, but strangely, no record contract came in from a bigger label, even though the band got regular slots on live shows. "I have no favorite show, but one of the most memorable was stepping over Wendy O. Williams at Fender's Ballroom in Long Beach," Debra remembers. "We had the privilege of playing the venue with her that night. She asked us to open for her at Bogart's after we played the Fender's Ballroom show. Of course, we said yes!"

Diamond Claw self-produced a one-song demo cassette titled *Sex Thing*, which was shopped around to labels in 1989. Unfortunately, no one snapped the band up, and Diamond Claw split up before the year's end, disappointed, only to appear again in the nineties to independently re-release their *Diamond Claw* CD in 1996, which keeps up with their eighties sound.

Debra Billingsley would later join the jazz/pop band Token Angel, releasing the 1996 album *Let It Go*. Mary Jo Godges later reappeared as a member of Phantom Blue, appearing on their 1998 *Full Blown* EP, whereas Jenny Thornburg worked as a technical engineer for bands like The She's and Gringa.

"I would like to add that Hellion was one of my favorite independent bands of the 1980s," says "I love Anne Boleyn's vocals. Another all-female band in the streets in the eighties was Leather Angel.

"And I love the resurgence of interest in metal records and bands. It is exciting for me to see the youth at metal concerts watching the old ones play and watch young metal bands form. Metal forever, I say. I wasn't aware that my output had become a collector's item, but I love to hear that. Haha! Live original shows aren't as popular in the U.S. as they were in the eighties, but I do think the metal bands march on, and there is a drive to keep it going. I am so glad you can hear bands on the internet that you wouldn't have not heard years ago. I am glad it's out of the hands of the big record labels and radio stations. There are some brilliant bands out there that you wouldn't have heard if it wouldn't have been for downloading..."

VICTIM

VICTIM WAS FORMED IN SAN DIEGO IN THE SPRING OF 1983 BY THE MEMBERS of two different cover bands: Brian Paul Thoryk from the band Desire, and Rocky Randolph, Mike Pfahler, and Junior Solis from the band Syndrome. The week they formed, all the members went together to attend the historic second day of the US Festival, a showcase known as Heavy Metal Day, and were compelled to begin writing original material.

"It was a decision that was instantly taken," Brian says. "I'm a songwriter at heart and have always written all material for the bands I've been in. I was in a punk rock band called the Skull Busters when I was 15 or 16 and also wrote all the music and lyrics. Even today, I currently produce fun songs and videos of all kinds and write all music and lyrics.

"Our influences?" he asks. "Oh, well! In general, all of the other members had their roots in heavy metal: Scorpions, Accept, Judas Priest, Rainbow, Van Halen, Rush. My roots are all

CUT TO THE CHASE:

If you are into early Exciter, Savage Grace, or even the faster Diamond Head tracks, you will love both *Power Hungry* and *By the Neck*. Sadly, Victim's only exclusively privately released LP, *Dirty Mean & Nasty*, is pretty mediocre. But get the other two!

hardcore punk," Brian laughs. "I saw all the early shows with Misfits, Minor Threat, X, The Cramps, Black Flag, et cetera. My all-time favorite band is the Sex Pistols and my favorite album is *Never Mind the Bollocks*.

"The San Diego locals liked us but were a little jealous because we had radio play on one of the *KGB Home Grown* albums put out by radio station KGB-FM, which was an advantage over the other bands. There were some other independent metal bands from our area that I liked, like Snakebyte, Assassin, Prowler, Bible Black, and Raven Mad," Brian recalls.

Victim's musical direction differed from the bands of their era and place. It wasn't glam metal, and it wasn't early thrash metal; it was a weird yet intriguing heavy/speed combo that took its cues from Judas Priest, like a more beefed-up *Screaming for Vengeance*. And this was initially evident on the *Home Grown '84* compilation LP that included their song "Victim," which also had a video clip. Their musical approach didn't help much, though, nor did their geographic location, and Victim couldn't get a contract to release a record.

"We personally financed all our albums," Brian sighs. "It was tough to get signed out of San Diego. Back then you really had to move to L.A." Contrary to what most people believe, Victim's first album, the *Power Hungry* LP, was released via a small indie label in 1984, and not by the band itself, even though it was financed by Victim. The small label Pop Records, which also released albums by the pop/new wave bands This Kids, The Origin, and X-Offenders, was behind the *Power Hungry* LP, and it's a very good record. At songs like "The Bridge" or "On the Street Tonight" it even reaches classic levels!

Victim's story includes a strange incident, though. After the release of *Power Hungry*, Victim immediately recorded a follow-up titled *By the Neck*. However, unexpected financial difficulties left the band unable to complete the release process, with the record being left at the studio, unfinished and abandoned! It only saw the light of day in 2014, thanks to Stormspell Records, and with the help of Mike Harris—their original recording engineer, who kept the master tapes—the metal world was graced with Victim's finest moment by far! *By the Neck* includes nine songs, five of which were unique to this LP, while one ("Hot-n-Frigid") appeared on their final self-financed album, *Dirty Mean & Nasty* in 1985.

Dirty Mean & Nasty is their weakest effort, unfortunately; it's not bad, but it doesn't hold up either to the power of *Power Hungry* or the inspiration of *By the Neck*. The songs here are tamer, more Dokken- and Mötley Crüe-oriented. Still, there are some good songs, like "Pedal to the Metal," but I'm not a big fan of this style.

"We were offered many shows," Brian adds. "But opening for Ron Keel at San Diego State University was the most awesome!"

Victim ended their short-lived career in 1986, with members Tom Hogue and Mark Arrington appearing later in bands like Malady and Hard Echo respectively.

"I think the metal resurgence is awesome because the music in the 1980s was raw," Brian concludes. "I am happy everyone thinks *Power Hungry* is a collectible, but I actually think *By the Neck*, the lost album, is our best work. But since it was only found and released a short time ago, people are just discovering it." On the subject of downloading and the underground scene, he says, "I don't like that downloading is almost free, as it drives smaller musicians into poverty. I know there is a serious underground scene in South America because we have a ton of fans there. Especially in Brazil!"

SACRED RITE

FORMED IN 1979 AS SABRE, SACRED RITE FROM HONOLULU, HAWAII, REMAIN one of the best hidden gems of the American metal scene of the eighties that are still active to this day (as of 2022). "Sacred Rite's formation started as far back as 1979 in Honolulu, Hawaii, with myself and drummer Kevin Lumm," guitarist Jimmy Caterine tells me. "We were very young, about 15 years old! It was hard finding players who were as ambitious as we were, so it took a couple years to find the right fit. Mark Kaleiwahea (vocalist and guitarist) came into the picture in 1980, and he had both the vocal and guitar skills that we were looking for. We went through a few bass players and finally found Peter Crane through one of Kevin's neighbors in 1981. We played a lot of parties and local events, mostly playing covers of our favorite metal bands. We did start writing almost right away ... we saved all our money for two years to record and independently release our first record in 1984. We actually brought in a rangier singer. So, we were a five-piece for about five months, but after much deliberation, we let him go, and Mark went in to retrack all the vocals. We stayed with that lineup until we split up the first time in 1990."

As for their musical preferences in the early Sacred Rite days, Jimmy says, "We loved music and mostly the metal that was coming out of Europe at the time. We loved it all. And we were musicians. So, it only seemed natural to put a band together. There were so many bands then that it's hard to choose. Kevin and I loved Judas Priest (the first five records especially), Iron Maiden, Saxon—just all the great European stuff. Mark liked all that as well but was a little more apt to like some of the straightforward stuff like Ozzy and Sabbath and some American stuff like Y&T and early Mötley Crüe. Peter Crane was very eclectic and was a huge fan of The Beatles, Pink Floyd, Yes, and King Crimson as well as the metal."

Honolulu wasn't known for its huge metal scene in the eighties. However, every band that came from Hawaii was special and brilliant in musical terms; from bands like Rat Attack, Aloha, and Liquid Mirror to the more notorious Hawaii, Vixen, and of course, Sacred Rite, it seemed that there was something very interesting going on. "When we started, there wasn't really a metal scene in Hawaii," Jimmy says. "Over the years, between 1980 and 1984, Sacred Rite was one of the three bands that helped build the metal scene, which flourished through the rest of the 1980s in Hawaii. The other two bands were Hawaii with Marty Friedman and Aaronsrod. It was a happening scene until we all left to pursue touring."

After recording a couple of demos (which were never released) in 1982 and 1983, Sacred Rite began the procedure of releasing their first record on their own label. However, the story here is quite interesting, since they went on to release it again, with a whole new cover, after later signing with a small indie label, Axe Killer, that re-released the album in 1985. Jimmy tells the story behind the *Sacred Rite* 1984 LP:

"We had recorded several demos between 1982 and 1983. We shopped to record labels and they all said the same thing: 'You are a great band with great players and songwriting skills, but it's not commercial enough. You have to simplify your music.' We just loved what we were doing and couldn't compromise. So, the obvious thing to do was to record it ourselves. We went into the studio and self-produced our first record along with Pierre Grill. Back then, it was way different than it is now. After you sent your stuff off to get mastered and pressed, you had to make tons of phone calls to find distributors, and most of them would only take 100 to 300 copies and see how they did with it before they would take a larger amount of records. I led this whole campaign, as I was a business major in college and had the best business acumen at the time. I pressed 1,000 records, as I didn't want to put us too far in debt. I managed to get three distributors, and the records were gone in a couple weeks. I pressed 3,500 more with a different cover, and those were gone in a month. Axe Killer Records picked up the album after that. So, there are three versions of the record. No Remorse Records did also a limited vinyl press of 500 before our show at Keep It True in Germany in April 2019. So, there will now be four vinyl versions of the record, along with the CD version released by Marquee Records in Brazil back in 2013."

Sacred Rite's first LP is a real shining diamond of American metal; it's especially fascinating that they sound fresh and genuine even today, nearly 40 years after its release. From the

CUT TO THE CHASE:

Sacred Rite is a band that you should by no means miss if you are into the classic American metal sound, although it's a bit speedier and more powerful. However, Sacred Rite don't fall into heavy/power or speed metal categories—they are first and foremost a classic American metal band, with some added punch. I'd guess that more than a few of you love early Iron Maiden as well as late 1970s/early 1980s Judas Priest, both of which are represented here, and so for those who do, Sacred Rite's first three records are simply mandatory! However, their self-released *Sacred Rite* 1984 LP is a classic independent metal release, and you can choose among its many pressings. Amazing record, anyway!

opening heavy/speed metal heaven of "Wings of Pegasus" to the crazy "Revelation" and the epic heavyweight "Executioner," this is simply a top-notch record of pure, mature, and technically proficient heavy metal. Sacred Rite is clearly influenced by Iron Maiden (Peter Crane's bass lines sound *so* Steve Harris) as well as Judas Priest. Finally, I shall mention that my favorite song off Sacred Rite is "The Blade"—just listen to it and you'll be shocked by the huge dose of talent and songwriting evidenced here.

Jimmy adds, "Our second release, *The Ritual*, was also an independent release—even though it was not released by ourselves. We had decided that we made more money when we were doing it ourselves than with Axe Killer, as they did not promote it the way I thought they would. But *The Ritual* got picked up right away by [Dutch label] Boudisque on their Megaton sublabel, which we stayed with for the third record, because they paid for everything and we didn't have to pay out of pocket for any of the album's production."

Sacred Rite continued their career through the 1980s, releasing two more LPs: the abovementioned (and equally good) *The Ritual* in 1985 and *Is Nothing Sacred* in 1986, and the future seemed bright for them and their unique brand of American metal. "It was a fantastic time back then," Jimmy remembers. "We played a lot of great shows for large crowds, 6,000+, and even more for smaller crowds (up to 1,000). But the most memorable was the very first large show for about 8,000 people, when we opened for Triumph in our hometown of Honolulu, just before our first record was released."

Their relocation to Tulsa, Oklahoma, in 1987 didn't help them much, sadly, and internal friction led Sacred Rite to break up after the departure of Kaleiwahea in 1989. Dee, Crane, and Dickerson carried on playing under the names Beauty Knows Pain and Tragic Nancy, changing styles and employing various other members and ultimately being reduced to a classic rock cover band. Dickerson quit Tragic Nancy in 1994. Dee and Crane worked together in a Las Vegas classic rock cover band called Time Machine until 1996.

Sacred Rite reformed in 2003, now back in Hawaii, and released the *SR-IV* CD in 2003 and the *Resurrection* CD in 2007 as well as some compilations. To this day, in 2022, they're still flying the flag high. "I love that bands are taking it upon themselves to get their personal voice heard," Jimmy adds. "Going with a label doesn't allow that. Labels are all about money, and they stifle creativity. The only drawback today is with the internet—it is much harder, in my opinion, to make enough money. It's the world of free music. And it does make it tough on the artist. We did well enough back in the day to be able to keep making music and putting it out, because at least most people were paying something for the product. In fact, I recently released a metal album with my band, HereAfter. I think it is awesome that Sacred Rite is still on the list of classic underground metal, and I am thrilled about it. It makes me feel like I did something timeless!

"Luckily, there is still a strong underground scene, and it is very large," Jimmy continues. "A lot of people love metal. It is great that bands can get their stuff out there, but the drawback is that there isn't a lot of money, which still makes it hard to produce things that are as good as you may want. I am lucky that, over the years, I have been able to build a formidable studio and can make records to my heart's content, but I have invested 50,000 dollars into it over the years. Most of the younger musicians have to record everything in the box. I don't think things sound great until you can blend digital and analog. That might be an old man's opinion, but that is what I think. It takes money to build it...

"What I would like to see is more appreciation for the artist," he concludes. "It is our heart and soul that we are putting out there, and it does deserve a little more in the way of connection, whether it be monetary or some sort of connection that lets the artists know that what they are doing isn't for nothing. I, of course, am satisfied. I never thought that Sacred Rite's legacy would have stood the test of time. I thought it was over in 1989. But it still keeps going. It's wonderful."

heroes of the METAL underground

CENTRAL / REST OF THE U.S.

MEDIEVAL STEEL

BANDS LIKE MEDIEVAL STEEL HAVE HELD A HIGH CULT STATUS AMONGST die-hard metalheads, and there was always a mystery surrounding this phenomenon. The truth is, even if Medieval Steel just wrote their eponymous track and disappeared, their name still would have been carved into the annals of relentless, total heavy metal.

Formed in 1982 in Memphis, Tennessee, vocalist Bobby Franklin says, "I was outside my apartment, working on my truck, and I was singing with the radio, and a guy who lived in an apartment a couple doors down heard me and wanted to record me. A couple days later, I went to his place and recorded a few songs, like Journey, Zeppelin, and Judas Priest. I didn't think nothing of it. And then he took the tape to a friend of his named Chuck Jones (later the guitarist of Medieval Steel, R.I.P 2014). That following weekend, Chuck was knocking on my door, saying, 'We need to form a band! You are a great singer!' About a week or so later, we had our first jam session, and it was magical! Mind you, I've always liked Elvis, but I started out singing in church. If I had to pick an album that may have influenced me, it would have been Judas Priest's *Stained Class*—that one is totally awesome!

"There were a few good bands like Cobra and Southern Creed, to name a few, but when we broke out, we took over the scene," Bobby states. "Cobra released their album with a private release too."

In 1984, through their own label, Sur Records, Medieval Steel recorded and released their first twelve-inch, simply titled *Medieval Steel*. Bobby mentions, "The reason we released it on our own was that we didn't want to be told what to put on the record, or when to release it—we wanted complete control. As far as process in those days, everything was analog, and we

CUT TO THE CHASE:

Surely most of you already know about Medieval Steel, one of the most notorious underground American metal bands to release a record on their own. There was a time in the nineties when people went apeshit over their first release, the *Medieval Steel* twelve-inch. So, if you are a fan of early Queensrÿche, early Manowar, Manilla Road, and early Liege Lord, you know the deal—get it as soon as possible. Get everything they released, actually, 'cause this is some of the most glorious epic metal you can find!

were able to get a deal with a studio where we could record our stuff on their downtime."

A major collector's wet dream for many years, *Medieval Steel* ranges from good ("Echoes," "Warlords") to great ("Medieval Steel," "Battle Beyond Stars"), and this is as pure and true metal as it gets, with a roaring sound akin to early Queensrÿche mixed with Manilla Road. Medieval Steel gained a huge cult following due to this record, and I can totally understand the enthusiasm over it, even if I don't find it flawless. Still, the brilliant two songs on this twelve-inch are unbelievable—much bigger bands never recorded a track as glorious as "Medieval Steel."

Oddly enough, after the release of the EP and with the same lineup, the band, while dealing with Megaforce Records, changed its name to Fire Choir and followed a totally different musical direction! Even if there were recording sessions, nothing was officially released, and Bobby Franklin left Fire Choir to reform Medieval Steel with Scott Jones on guitar in 1985. "It was a beautiful time to play metal music," Bobby says. "Our most memorable show was back then, and it's a tough one to choose! It would have to be the first time we played at the Memphis Fairgrounds, where there were over 5,000 people. We opened for Accept and Quiet Riot. There have been too many since then to name!"

The band sadly never signed to Megaforce, and this brought lineup changes. Steve Crocker became the new bassist and Chris Cook the new drummer. With this lineup, the band stayed together until 1992. However, they managed to release the 1989 demo, a fantastic piece of work that, to my ears, is even better than their EP (in musical terms). This is evidenced by awesome tracks like "Eyes of Fire" and "To Kill a King." The second coming of Medieval Steel arrived in 2003, when the band reunited for two years, re-releasing all their stuff on 2004's *The Dungeon Tapes* CD. After another breakup, the band got back together in 2011 and is active today, with another release under their belts: the excellent 2013 *Dark Castle* LP.

"I think it's wonderful that bands like Medieval Steel are finally getting their due. As far as collectibles, we are still bootlegged, so we won't get the money we are owed," Bobby says. "There is a real underground scene—we see it all the time when we tour, and it is wonderful. However, the internet can be good as far as getting your music out there, but then it can be bad as far as people bootlegging you."

ASSASSIN

WITH AN APPROACH HEADING FOR A HARD ROCK AND HEAVY METAL MIX, Assassin from West Mifflin (suburban Pittsburgh), Pennsylvania, formed in 1983. Keys player Lawrence Donovan explains, "Assassin was formed before I came along, actually, the core members being Billy Toth (guitar), Rick Darr (bass), and Mark Bailey (vocals), who were still involved when I joined. Their two-guitar attack had changed, and they were originally looking for a double-threat guitar/keyboard player. I guess the pickings were pretty slim, at least among the hard rock/metal musicians, in my area. I auditioned, but wasn't confident I was going to get the gig, because I play guitar one way: badly. I remember that when I did get the gig, Rick Darr wasn't sold on a one-guitar + keyboard lineup, and it was going to be a challenge to win him over. We were still mostly doing cover music, since that's what really sold in our area. Original music was a purview for 'artsy' bands (at least at first, as far as heavier bands were concerned), and we stuck to the tried and true.

"Assassin was formed in Pittsburgh, Pennsylvania, in a rather austere Rust Belt-riddled rock scene," Lawrence adds. "I'm not using that term Rust Belt specifically or pejoratively, but there was a certain stagnation of music in the scene here, except for punk and blues. Pittsburgh was a burgeoning market for punk/new wave acts. They even had a few bars in the Shadyside area dedicated to that crowd. There was nothing like that for metal in the area."

In 1983, using their own funds, Assassin released their first seven-inch EP, *Fools Don't Know/ Feels So Good*, mostly to promote their music as much as possible. Printed in 500 sleeveless copies, *Fools Don't Know/Feels So Good* attempted to attract interest in Assassin with its two melodic hard rock/metal songs. "Fools Don't Know" was indeed a great tune, mid-tempo and catchy, mixing Scorpions with Dio. "Most of the originals were already written by my arrival into the band, so I worked out the keyboard parts to highlight and accent the sound, in a live setting with some synths, a B3, and sound FX. I did some backing vocals live as well," Lawrence adds. "We started to incorporate more heavy bands that included keyboards into the repertoire (Uriah Heep, Deep Purple, Dio, Ozzy, Rainbow, Rush) and it seemed to go over well. We were touching new areas in the heavy metal/hard rock crowds, and we were getting some steady gigs. And let's not kid ourselves here: I played a lot of bass lines and sound FX at first, since we still played a lot of AC/DC, Accept, Black Sabbath, et cetera, and I didn't have a whole hell of a lot to do on stage. We started working originals in (mostly written by Toth/ Darr/Bailey), and we were, amazingly, getting great responses. It seemed the hard rock/heavy metal crowd was ready, after all, for some local, original music!"

Even though their first LP, *License to Kill*, was released by a small indie Pennsylvania label (Micro Mix records, which also released the pre-Holocross band Iron Cross' *Warhead* LP), metal collectors worldwide consider it similar to a private release. "We decided to record what we had and went with a private label, recording in an old church (ironic!) in Homer City, Pennsylvania. It was a great experience, and everything went pretty smoothly, from what I remember. It was mostly a matter of money, why we went the route we did with recording privately. Our new drummer's (Jeff Coffer) father put up a lot of the money for the recording, if I recall. We had a great time recording, even having a group of amazing fans come in to do the background vocals on 'Wild and Crazy,'" Lawrence recalls.

The result was the *License to Kill* LP, and even though it had its weaknesses, songs like the title track (an unbelievable pounding hymn), the Dio-like "The Assassin," the Saxon-meets-America "Made in the USA," and the beautiful atmospheric "In the Night" make it worth the price of admission. There's also melodic hard rock/metal stuff that fans of Dokken, Q5 (at their hard rock-est), or Dio would definitely appreciate.

"After the release of *License to Kill*," Lawrence adds, "we were starting to get bigger gigs, in larger venues, and garnering a lot of fans. We got some opening gigs, like Steppenwolf, in front of a large audience. This translated into us being considered one of 'the' bands around the area to see. We played a lot of biker shows, which were always a lot of fun. We ended up playing on a pavilion rooftop once, because we feared our equipment may have been damaged from all the rowdiness that ensued. It seemed the local scene was beginning to grow, with the advent of bands like Def Leppard making heavier stuff more poppy, for lack of a better word. Hard rock and metal bands were now drawing more women, that's for sure, and where the women go, the guys go, and the booze sells! This is a win-win for musicians and venue owners alike. We saw a larger upswing of women in our audiences, too, which was great to see. A form of music that tends to exclude half the population is kind of counterproductive, in my opinion.

"There were many bands that were up-and-coming rivals when we were playing, bands like 18 Names, who leaned hard but were much more traditional AOR rock than we were, and Streetheart, who did all covers and were more progressive rock. And 18 Names did release an album, which was pretty good. They featured a woman lead singer," Lawrence mentions when asked about the Pittsburgh metal scene of the era.

CUT TO THE CHASE:

Assassin was at least an honest band, with its own melodic style of hard rock/metal; even though today their songs might sound very nostalgic, there's definitely an edge to many of them. I would suggest both the two-song seven-inch and the *License to Kill* LP to all the weirdos seeking true and pure hard rock/metal in the American style.

Assassin broke up in 1986, and vocalist Mark Bailey went on to the heavy metal Triple X for a while. No reunions whatsoever after their demise, although Assassin offered their contribution to the American metal scene, and manic collectors will always search for their records. "We never made much money back on those albums, but that's okay," Lawrence says. "I can say I was part of a groundswell of great music back in the day. I know that it's a difficult thing, trying to regulate who has access to music these days, with downloading and streaming. I think that if there's any way to get the music you like, that's great, since radio, once the prime source of finding new music, is almost a dead art form. I am more than a little disappointed that the artists are not being compensated for their work, however. If it was easy, everybody would be writing, arranging, and recording. but it isn't. It's hard work, made to look easy. Artists should be compensated for all this hard work, in my opinion."

The resurgence of interest in American private metal recordings led to the re-release of *License to Kill* in 2016 on both CD and LP, by Heaven and Hell Records and Alone Records respectively. "I've seen a lot of genres come and go in Pittsburgh. Grunge came after the hair metal bands had sort of became parodies of themselves. The grunge scene didn't last very long in this area, as the blue-collar rock did then and still does dominate the scene. Eighties bands seem to be a recent phenomenon, and the resurgence of that scene has been pretty cool, since there was a lot to like about eighties music. I've also seen a resurgence of progressive rock/metal tributes; Rush and Queensrÿche tribute bands seem to do very well. I am particularly fond of progressive metal. Bands like Dream Theater and Symphony X, being full of keyboards, of course, are very common in my playlist. The fact that there are collectors of private metal record collectors out there has also been very good to see. I'm glad there are still those people out there who are interested in bands like Assassin."

HALLOWEEN

WHEN THE DISCUSSION GETS TO THE HORROR/THEATRICAL METAL OF THE eighties, the name-dropping includes big ones like Mercyful Fate and Lizzy Borden, Satan (UK) and Hell (UK), alongside Ripper (Houston, TX), Death SS (Italy), and obscure ones like Trop Feross or Dwarr. But one band set the bar unbelievably high, and it's had a cult following since 1983—even though it never made a huge breakthrough in the metal world. This band is Detroit's Halloween.

Formed in 1981 under the name Bitch, it included current vocalist Brian Thomas, hailing from a band called Alcatraz (not the Graham Bonnett/Malmsteen band), Rick Craig from the band Limousine, bassist Ed Reynolds, guitarist Mark Scott, and future Seduce drummer Chuck Burns.

HALLOWEEN BAND PHOTO COURTESY GEORGE NEAL

Reynolds did not play any shows with Bitch, as he was booted and replaced by George Neal. In 1983 on Halloween night, Bitch officially became Halloween when they played a show at the Falcon Lounge in Detroit. George Neal adds, "When we were called Bitch, the stage show started with a porcelain skull that was a candleholder and a bag of cobwebs, and that grew into what it is today. When we found out about another band called Bitch with singer Betsy Bitch, we decided we needed a new name. Halloween was chosen for many different reasons, the main reason being that we were already using Halloween stage props such as candelabras, cemetery gates, dry ice, spiderwebs and pyro when we were called Bitch. It has considerably expanded since!

"When we went on, it was simply just for the love of music," George admits. "At that time, Kiss had taken off their makeup and Alice Cooper was not doing much of his usual stage show, and all of us were (and still are) great fans of theatrical stage music. We wanted to give that to the people to keep it going. So, yes, it was Black Sabbath, Kiss, and Alice Cooper regarding our biggest influences, most significant being *Welcome to My Nightmare* by Alice Cooper. To me, that album was theater on vinyl."

The Detroit heavy metal scene in the 1980s has a rep for being pretty wild, and George confirms: "It was amazing. Before we were acknowledged worldwide, the Detroit fans were the motivation that pushed to keep us going. If it were not for our dedicated fans here, I don't think we would have the inspiration to press forward. We owe them everything that we are."

The first strike of Halloween took place in 1984, when they released their first seven-inch *Trick or Treat* LP on the label that would be their driving force for quite some years, Motor City Metal Records. Only 300 records of *Trick or Treat* were pressed; only approximately 200 are in circulation today, as the other 100 were never given away and are still in boxes that have since gone missing. The crazy and bombastic sound of Halloween is already evident here, in its most primal form. "Trick or Treat" is real dynamite, falling somewhere between the then-emerging American power metal sound and NWOBHM—like a cross between Grim Reaper and W.A.S.P. and Savage Grace. The B-side, "She's a Teazer," is a mid-tempo heavyweight track à la early Savatage with a Judas Priest touch. Absolutely catchy!

Halloween was literally on fire with their explosive shows in the Detroit area, and they didn't miss their chance, taking their fate into their own hands. In 1985, the band released their first full LP, the now-classic *Don't Metal with Evil* LP. "At the time, a DJ, Doug Podell,

CUT TO THE CHASE:

Everyone should at least have one Halloween record in their collection, and this should be *Don't Metal with Evil*. It's one of the most mind-blowing records that independent American metal ever offered, sheer heavy metal played to the max! Certainly a top-20 private metal release.

at a major radio station in Detroit, WLLZ, approached us about making a video ('Trick or Treat') in the studio," George says. "*Don't Metal with Evil* was done on a limited budget. We actually recorded that album twice. The first one was not good enough to release. We found a recording studio in Eastpointe, Michigan, called 'The Disc' that was within walking distance of where we were staying. We decided to go in just to see what a real studio would look like. They mainly recorded gospel music. We really didn't have the funds to record. We managed a deal with the studio for $2,000 for a 30-hour block straight. We recorded from the first note and through to the last song, plus mixing, all within 30 hours. Not a lot of time..."

Don't Metal with Evil is one of the American metal records of the 1980s (just in general, independent or otherwise) that every metalhead should have. It's heavy (and I mean HEAVY) metal of the highest order, reminiscent of a heavier and less commercial version of Twisted Sister, more like a much crazier Grim Reaper or a more street-metal version of early Mercyful Fate. Tracks like "What a Nice Place" and "Scared to Death" have to be heard to be believed, whereas anthems like "Tales from the Crypt," "To Fight the Beast," and "Don't Metal with Evil" are inspiring. As for the production, its roughness adds so much originality to the music—it's one of those cases where, if it were recorded any other way, it would pale in comparison with the original mix. That said, *Don't Metal with Evil* is a real breakout from a band that never got the attention it deserved. Too heavy for classic metalheads and too tame for thrashers? Who knows!

"Okay, I think there were/are many great moments in Halloween live performances," George smiles. "But the one I will never forget is when we did a live broadcast at Harpos in Detroit on the radio with WLLZ. It was the first time that I stepped on stage and saw a venue that size packed beyond standing room only. I could have walked on the crowd, shoulder to shoulder, to the front entrance. Another one is when we played with Queensrÿche for the first time during the *Warning* tour. To this day, Eddie Jackson and I still keep in touch."

Sadly, Halloween's problem was that they couldn't maintain a steady lineup. Following the release of *Don't Metal with Evil*, drummer Bill Whyte and founding guitarist Rick Craig both departed. Enter guitarist Billy Gray (later to join Invain, which changed their name to Fair Game) and drummer Tommy Stewart (who later joined Lillian Axe, Fuel, and Godsmack), known then as Tommy Scott. But this incarnation of Halloween didn't last long, even though they released an excellent 1990 demo. Shortly after the demo was released, Tommy Scott left and was replaced by Billy Adams. Gray stuck around for a short time afterward, ultimately leaving to play in Fair Game full time, although he returned in 1991. But this is just a small piece of Halloween's ever-shifting lineup issues, so let's stick to the 1990 demo, which was a real treat.

The 1991 lineup of Halloween included George Neal (bass), Donny Allen (guitars), Brian Thomas (vocals), Billy Adams (drums), and Tim Wright (guitars), and they released their second album, *No One Gets Out!*, once again on their own label, Motor City Metal Records, this time on cassette and CD.

Very classy and pretty thrashy, *No One Gets Out!* is an attempt to modernize their sound. Now bands like Overkill and even Metallica are added in the list of influences, and the album features great songs like "7 Years," "No One Gets Out!" and the superb "Kings," which sounds like Dio playing power metal. However, I think that Halloween lost their early edge and uniqueness with this release.

The band continued through the difficult times in the nineties and up until today, releasing quality metal. Their 1997 *Victims of the Night* LP is way above par, whereas their subsequent CDs—with their last offering being 2012's *Terrortory*—are still good stuff for anyone into the modern American metal sound. Halloween's name is still relevant with the metalheads of the underground, and George adds, "I think it is a great thing. It reflects that people are still passionate about old-school metal. It amazes me the broad range of ages of people, from very young and up, who have heard of us and our music. Sometimes, it is overwhelming in a good way ... don't forget, there were many Detroit metal bands like Weapons, Seduce, Scarlet, Wulfhook, Ezra, and others that released records on their own as well.

"It absolutely exists—it is as strong as it ever was," George concludes about today's underground metal scene. "Music, either underground or mainstream, will always exist. Downloading is a bittersweet situation. The positive about downloading is that it gives people easier access to music and makes it easier to discover underground metal as well as mainstream music. The negative is that it can be very easy to steal or [indulge in] illegal downloading and sharing. It makes it harder for bands like us to record another album without the funds to do so..."

GUNNER

THE STORY OF PRIVATE AMERICAN METAL IS FASCINATING, NOT JUST FOR bands that went on to become bigger, or for bands that were coming out from places with a challenging metal scene. It's also extremely interesting to discover bands from smaller scenes or metal-unfriendly places. This is the case of Gunner from Flint, Michigan. Formed in 1982, Gunner's story is narrated by Joey Bredow, on vocals and guitar:

"Well, it started with me and Keith Christian (vocals, drums). Both of us were in different bands playing cover music in and around the Detroit, Pontiac, and Flint areas in Michigan. We both were tired of playing other bands' music, and we were both songwriters. So, we got together down in his mom's basement, which was also our rehearsal room, and started bouncing ideas off one another of songs we had in mind. Keith had some great guitar riff ideas, and I added riffs and melody lines that I'd put together. The really cool thing about this is that most people didn't know that Keith was the drummer and I was the singer and guitar player for Gunner, but when we wrote most of the songs, Keith would be playing the guitar and I would be playing the drums. We both played many instruments! We would start to play a riff, and I would say, 'That sounds great. Now to G ... yeah, that sounds cool, now go up to B,' and so on, until the song was finished. We had about 15 songs we wrote at first. So, then, we had to record them. We borrowed a four-channel cassette recorder (remember, this is the eighties) and started the process of recording. We ran a 16-channel snake cable upstairs to the living room and into a 16-channel mixer and then into the cassette recorder. The only bad thing is that when the person being recorded needed to do another take, we had to run up and down the stairs. And, of course, bump the three tracks down to one, and so forth.

"Well, we finally got all the songs recorded," Joey continues, "but we still needed a lead guitar part inserted into all the songs. So, Keith used to play in a band with a guy named Dan Medawar (who also loaned us the recorder), and he played lead guitar on all the songs we wrote for that recording session. So, now we had a cassette recording of all the songs and had to put together a band to go play them. First, we went out looking for a bass player. I knew Ron Cousineau from his band playing the same clubs that I played and approached him about the possibility of playing in the new band we were forming. We gave him a copy of the tape, he listened to it, liked it, and said he was in. Next, we asked Dan, who played all the leads on the tape, but he said he couldn't do it. So, we looked around for a bit and found a guitar player up in Flint by the name of Joe 'Hot Wire' Arnold, and he said yes after listening to the tape and our vision of being an all-originals band. With that, Gunner was complete. We started playing only our originals around the same areas we were from, and we quickly built up a following.

"The metal and rock music scene was still energized," Joey adds. "The rock radio stations had the biggest listeners, and they were playing new music from new bands. They were going strong as ever. The fans loved us, we were playing to packed audiences in the clubs. We knew people who knew people who were famous, and they were going to tell them about us. We had a talent agent from RCA Records who said he was going to mention us to them and was sure they would like us. We just wanted to make it in the industry. Of course, we liked Alice Cooper, Mötley Crüe, Ozzy, Judas Priest, Def Leppard, and all of the great bands back then. But our main inspiration was getting that contract!"

In 1985, Gunner sought to release their own record, a non-sleeve seven-inch, *Love on the Roxx/Take It or Leave It*. Perfectly executed American metal with a slight hard rock edge, "Love on the Roxx" was a mid-tempo rager, melodic and powerful and as catchy as Twisted Sister, while "Take It or Leave It" was an absolute metal hymn, fast and menacing, like a mix of Judas Priest and Def Leppard, going on an all-out metal attack. I have also managed to listen to some of the songs Gunner recorded prior to the release of this record, and all I can say is that their demo songs were good, but they weren't as mature as those on the seven-inch.

Regarding how they released a seven-inch on their own, Joey explains, "Well, it was the next logical step to take. Cut a record, sell it to the fans, and show the big guys that you were serious. We also knew we would need a music video to back up the record—remember, MTV was going strong back then. So, before we even went to RCA, we'd already recorded and had our 45 pressed with our own money. We knew we were not going to get rich off that record.

But we had something for the fans—CDs were just coming out and were expensive, and a lot of people did not at that time own a CD player. I knew we could have just made our songs into cassette tapes, but records, they were better. So, we wanted to go to a recording studio and have some songs professionally recorded. I'm not really sure how, but we contacted a Flint recording studio to see if we could get in. The producer and owner of the studio was Bernard Terry. He was newly famous for recording and producing a Flint band called Ready for the World that just had a hit with one of their songs, 'Oh Sheila.' So, we booked a spot on an off-night at the studio and recorded five songs. We debated which two songs were going to be on the record and came up with the songs 'Take It or Leave It' and 'Love on the Roxx.' Bernard made me a copy of those two songs to be sent to a mastering and record pressing company that he'd suggested, which was named QCA. The record was never officially distributed. It was just sold to our fans.

"After the release of our seven-inch," Joey goes on, "there was a show at the 300 Bowl in Pontiac, Michigan. It was packed. That's when the AR guy from RCA came out. We went to New York and had a meeting with Wendy Goldstein, who said she liked it but wanted to hear more. So, we sent her more. Again, she liked it but wanted to hear more. Okay, we got the hint. We never got the RCA contract. But we did make our record!"

But that was the end for Gunner. Sadly, they disbanded, and they didn't leave anything else behind, even though the demo tracks are floating here and there around the internet. A small nugget of gold buried in the history of worldwide metal.

"I think it is great when guys (and gals) get together and actually play music," Joey replies when asked about the resurgence of interest in private eighties metal. "Musicians are getting hard to find nowadays. Everybody wants to be a rapper or pop singer, doing their thing with a recorded background track. I think the resurgence of private metal records has mainly been in the European countries and also is thanks to the new demand for vinyl records in those countries. I'm seeing all the big metal and rock acts doing huge tours over there. As for my record being a highly paid collector's item, that's news to me. But I am flattered by the compliment, that some 30-plus years later, people are still enjoying our music. Not many bands from back in the day can say that!"

As of 2020, Joey Bredow still writes and releases music as Joe Pops Bredow, this time more in the psych-pop territory. I'm a sucker for this kind of stuff, and songs like "Still 1969" are genius, but I don't think today's metalheads will appreciate them.

"I really can only speak of what's here in Michigan," he says about the metal scene today. "Yeah, the underground scene here is still alive in places like Harpos, the Token Lounge in Detroit, and the Machine Shop in Flint, and a lot more all over the state. It's still going strong and never really went away. Michigan is an industrial state. They work hard and play hard. Metal and hard rock music was made in Michigan. As for my opinion about music being so easy to get downloaded, I take it you might be hinting at pirated music? Hey, all the way back when they invented cassette recorders, people were copying music. They would wait until a song they liked came on the radio and record it. All the kids did it. The big difference is the radio stations paid a nice royalty to the artist per play. And sooner or later, the person would go buy the record just for the cover and the artwork. Now that being said, only the bands who had recording contracts where paid, and those who didn't have a contract were never heard of. And most bands who did owed the company a lot of money. So, bands like the Goo Goo Dolls and Thirty Seconds to Mars never saw any money from their hit songs.

"But here is what's good about having downloadable music," Joey concludes. "You don't need the radio stations to have your music heard. If you think your music is good enough, you can submit your songs to as many *internet* radio stations all over the world as you want. And most will play it, without you having to pay to play. Of course, they don't pay hardly anything in royalties, if any at all. But your music and you and your band are getting known all over the world. Downloading is an inconvenient consequence of having music that sounds good enough and wanting it so much that someone needs to get it without paying for it. So, I have to think about it in another way. Music is advertising. There was a time when you did a concert tour to help sell albums. Now you use your music to help get people to come see your concerts and sell merchandise (T-shirts, CDs, photos, and maybe even vinyl records). So, I guess my opinion of someone getting my music via downloading is this: Plain and simple, it's better to be known and have listeners hearing your music and losing your 99 cents per download than to not be known or heard at all."

CUT TO THE CHASE:

I don't think that anybody who appreciates the more rockin' side of American metal won't appreciate Gunner; actually, the two songs from the seven-inch would be a blast for those into this style. I'd love to see a Gunner discography, including demo recordings, be released by a metal label. Joey was super kind enough to send me four copies of the *Love on the Roxx/Take It or Leave It* seven-inch as a gift, which I distributed to friends (except for one, which I kept).

OUTRAGE

THE ONLY HEAVY METAL BAND TO COME OUT OF BATTLE CREEK, MICHIGAN, in the eighties, Outrage falls under the radar of most metalheads. Bass player Brent Everest narrates the band's story:

"It all started out with four people who were as green as grass, and only one of them had a clue as to what they could do with their axe. Best of friends who just wanted to shake some windows. Lifelong friends, truth be told. Then, a mutual friend introduced me to them. But I'm thinking this is way too far back, heh. Outrage started out with just a group of friends that progressed with time and became something we all were proud of. No matter our part. We went through many members, but each one had an influence. There was never a bad vibe between any of us. Throughout all the lineup changes, we were just friends. And I for one consider that the strangest shit ever, but that's the way it happened!"

Outrage's lineup took the form of Brent Everest (bass), Dale Hertel (drums), Scott Marshall (guitar), and Don Nelson (vocals), and the band "didn't have specific influences as a whole," Brent admits. "We were individually inspired by our own favorites. But personally speaking, at that time I was inspired by and still love Steve Harris and Gary Lee. Well, you probably know him as Geddy. His mother had a strong Polish accent, so 'Geddy' just stuck!" Outrage's guitar player, Scott Marshall, says, "At the time, my main influences were probably Eddie Van Halen, George Lynch, and Yngwie Malmsteen."

"I decided to form a band since I was watching my oldest brother pretend to be a rock star with his band in his bedroom in the seventies. I felt the calling back then!" Brent smiles. "I was the youngest of five. I had to endure all of my siblings' crushes and interests. Because of that, I love all music." However, it wasn't all wine and roses. "The locals were fantastic," Brent says. "It was the other local bands that made life shit. Outrage never threw anyone under the bus, but our so-called friends found it easy to do so. I still find that a sad reality. These were people that I grew up with. Who we partied with, we hung out with. Sad."

CUT TO THE CHASE:

Still hidden under the radar of even the most dedicated metalheads worldwide, *Outrage* is a record with at least three or four songs that would appeal to the passionate fans of heavy and razor-sharp American heavy/ power metal.

In 1989, Outrage released its first, and only, self-titled LP, and it's an all-out attack of vicious heavy metal, especially in tracks like "Lazerblade," "Angel in Black," and "Down Under." The results here are unbelievably exciting: razor-sharp, gates-storming heavy metal of the highest order. "Red Hot Sally" is a great rockin' American heavy/power anthem, and so is "Love on Ice." Heavy, hard-hitting sound, reminiscent of bands like early Attacker (albeit less power-metal) or Shok Paris, *Outrage* will at least quench the thirst for some good American metal. This record was the result of hard work, as well as of having Outrage play alongside bigger acts in their area. "We opened up for Autograph, we also opened up for Meat Loaf. Truth be told, we shouldn't have turned down the gig with BÖC. But that's just my opinion. Our Halloween parties rocked—these were by far my favorite shows of Outrage's!"

Outrage were one of the (literally) thousands of metal bands that formed in the eighties in the U.S., intrigued by both the NWOBHM explosion as well as the American metal of their time, but they were one of the few that left us with a self-released record.

"I don't recall any other local bands pressing any records," Brent says. "It wasn't as easy as today, where everyone has a recording unit that can burn CDs. It's nice to know that people are searching the past for some entertainment. It shows that they're kind of fed up with the mass-produced crap being shoved down their throats, you know, the bubblegum pop bullshit. Well, to be quite honest? I wish it was this lucrative back when we needed it most. That being said, we put our heart and soul into that music and gave our best at every gig, no matter how small. I'm just as proud of it now as I was then, and it's a great feeling, knowing it's still appreciated worldwide.

"I believe there is an underground scene for sure. There always has been and always will be," Brent states. "Underground scenes of any sort are like a private club that everyone wants to be a part of because of the like-minded individuals. But downloading? Toughest question ever and always. I feel it's like bootlegging if you don't use legit sites, but I don't blame anyone for seeking out the others because the 'industry' has put such high prices on everything. I do love the fact that you can discover a lot of different bands just by browsing your phone, though. It surely gets your name around worldwide quickly. To sum it up, it's a double-edged sword, and I'm just as guilty as the next person of running with it."

CENTURION

CENTURION FROM CLEVELAND HAD THE HONOR OF INCLUDING MUSICIANS who later played in famous bands (such as Integrity, Purgatory, and Mushroomhead), and their genre of heavy metal is totally unique and exciting. Formed in 1984, guitarist Dave Felton tells me, "Centurion was created by Rich Ronges and his schoolmate, drummer Mark Lee. I was recruited shortly after, followed by frontman Denny Giardina.

"Back then, it was pretty cool," Dave says. "We were still in high school, so we had tons of friends coming to the shows. We were totally influenced by Kiss, Ozzy, and Black Sabbath, but it was Ramones too—you know, all the classic stuff."

Centurion went on to play with many local bands, such as Mayhem (with Sacred Heart members), and after a few years of their existence, they released their first and only self-financed LP, *Cross and Black*, in 1987. "We wanted something with staying power," Dave admits.

"Cassettes were cool and more convenient but kind of disposable in a way. Vinyl records just had more clout and were a lot cooler to look at."

Cross and Black is definitely a great LP, and the fact that it has so many different influences makes it even more special. Centurion is not your ordinary heavy metal band, since they manage to combine a buzzsaw punk sound (reminiscent of the Stepmothers) with doom-laden Black Sabbath song structures and a weird atmosphere that's reminiscent of early Manilla Road. The whole thing sounds a lot like Knightmare from New Hampshire! "Rebels Freed" is a menacing galloping metallic beauty, "In the Night" is definitely the most punked-up number, and "The Power" sounds like Omen with layers of noise. Bone-crushing stuff!

CUT TO THE CHASE:

Don't turn your back on Centurion if you are a 100 percent metalhead! We are talking about an all-out metal band, so give them a chance, 'cause *Cross and Black* is simply excellent. Their doomy atmosphere will appeal to fans of the weirdest and most obscure metal, such as Druid, and I can think of some metalpunks who'd be into them too!

"I think it's cool from a nostalgic point of view, that people are still interested in Centurion," Dave tells me. "But then again, if *Cross and Black* is a highly paid collector's item, how come I'm not seeing any money? Ha!"

Centurion also had two songs included on compilations, and both are tracks that weren't released on *Cross and Black*. The first one was "Peacefully" on the *Northcoast Steel: Cleveland Heavy Metal* LP (1988), and the second one was "Be Warned" on the *Convicted to the Avant Garde* cassette (1989). Unfortunately, both are ridiculously rare now.

Centurion split up around late 1989, and its members went on to play in bands like (216) (hardcore), Integrity (hardcore), Mushroomhead (nu metal), and Hatrix (thrash metal), among many others.

"The downloading thing is just an evolution of the industry," Dave says. "We used to make copies of albums back in the day, which doesn't seem that different to me. The internet just makes it easier. To me, the real problem is oversaturation. No A&R people are out there looking for quality. Seems like a lot of new music with not much substance these days. Disappointing."

PURGATORY

CLEVELAND, OHIO, IN THE EIGHTIES WAS ONE OF THE MOST VIBRANT HEAVY metal cities in the United States. And when saying "heavy metal" in this context, one should add that there were countless bands that played raw metal in its purest form, from Shok Paris to Black Death, from Mystik to Sacred Few, from Breaker to Jagged Edge. And Purgatory is no exception, since they've been blasting their rough metal from 1984 to 2018. Vocalist Jeff Hatrix tells their story:

"Prior to Purgatory, Kenny Easterly and I were in a Cleveland band called NI4NI. An Eye For An Eye, when written out in the long form. I needed a change and moved down to Louisiana for about a year. Jammed with a band called White Heat—not the hair band—and did my first experience in studio tracking. Upon returning home to Cleveland, I set about forming the new band that Kenny was up to reforming, but the other guys were no longer an option. So, we put an ad in the local *Cleveland Scene* magazine and hoped for the best. A friend named Ralph Strimple knew of a guitarist/bassist team that he thought very highly of. This ended up being Greg Perry and Mark Alexander, and the rest is history."

Jeff also discusses his musical background, which led him to become a singer: "I found a copy of Grand Funk's *Survival* at 15 while walking down the road back home, and it changed my life. I grew up on The Beatles, The Rolling Stones, and others, but this band from nearby Flint, Michigan, sold out Shea Stadium in NYC faster than The Beatles, and did a much rawer take on 'Gimme Shelter.' Then there was Maiden and Priest and anything else I could get my hands on, really. Anything to sing along with worked for me. No country, of course, but otherwise, I was screaming it."

The Cleveland scene was thriving back then, Jeff adds: "Cleveland loved metal, and it was alive and well when Purgatory was happening. Breaker, Shok Paris, Destructor, Black Death, Wretch, and the Spudmonsters were happening in a huge way. Sadly, the death of a great friend, Dave 'Holocaust' Iannicca from Destructor, ended the scene momentum for quite a while. The scene now is still always active, though, as there are many bands and just as many venues. Cleveland truly rocks!"

Even from the beginning, Purgatory created quite a buzz, initially with their 1985 demo—their musical approach was clearly something to keep an eye on. They put out their first twelve-inch, *Purgatory*, on their own J.U.F. Records. Jeff Hatrix recalls, "There were a couple big fans, Bill and Ed, who believed in the band very much, and we decided to make a four-song EP and see what happened from there. It was at a studio, Britain Square Sound, that to my knowledge really hadn't done anything that heavy prior. All we had before that were boombox tapes, so it was nice to have a proper release. It wasn't long after that that Bill Peters came calling and we were a part of the Auburn family. Good times."

Purgatory is a metal-to-the-max release, and the band's sound is different from the classic American metal sound. A weird but intriguing mix of heavy, speed, and, thrash, Purgatory sounds like a pumped-up Iron Maiden meets Accept and Overkill on this release, with Jeff Hatrix's vocals landing somewhere between Udo and Halford. Purgatory is simply menacing, with excellent tracks such as "Valley of the Shadow of Death" and "Purgatory (Shattered Vision)." The only drawback is the really weak production, and even if I'm a sucker for raw and brutal sound, in this case, the low production quality literally steals power from the band.

"It was a Cleveland show called 'The Anti-Valentine's Day Massacre,'" Jeff adds, while mentioning his all-time favorite Purgatory show. "It was cool to play with the rest of the Cleveland metal royalty, if you will, at the time. Purgatory got a lot of love and it felt really good to be included, as a part of those big names."

Local label Auburn Records didn't miss the chance and signed Purgatory later in 1985. "I do know it was happening," Jeff replies, when asked about the prevalence of self-releasing metal albums in Cleveland at the time. "Until anyone got signed at whatever level, the common practice was coming up with your own cool-sounding label name. Ours prior to signing to Auburn was J.U.F. Records. I can't remember the meaning behind it, but I bet it was something cool..."

The band's 1986 Auburn release, *Tied to the Trax,* is definitely their brightest moment—it's sheer heavy metal mayhem, again with the same influences and much better production.

CUT TO THE CHASE:

***Purgatory* is a superb twelve-inch for those into bands like Abattoir, Savage Grace, early Overkill, or Tension. If it weren't for its terrible production, this album could have been a brilliant moment in the history of privately released American metal. Luckily, the *Tied to the Trax* LP is a different story, and it's a record that everybody who's into the heavy/speed sound should get.**

There's great songwriting here, such as the title anthem, the Savatage/Liege Lord-reminiscent "Fear of the Night," and the speedy bulldozer "Deep into the Red." Not to be missed if you are a fan of heavy/speed metal!

Things weren't as good later for Purgatory, however. In 1989, they released the decent (but not outstanding) *Dr. Pain* cassette (on their J.U.F. Records), and lineup changes led to the breakup of the band in 1990, with several reformations though in 1991, 2003, and 2018. Today, Purgatory remains inactive.

"I think a lot of people self-release, and that is admirable. I would like to see how my new band does on a label, because I feel a lot of my releases have been, for lack of a better word, self-sabotaged. It is nice to see bands having faith in their own product, though. More power to them," Jeff adds. "I take great pride in reading that people refer to Purgatory as 'eighties speed/thrash metal at its finest!' And that it's a shame we never had another release. There was one planned called *Dark Alley Surgery*, and we felt that this album really would have broken us ... I also appreciated having toured with Lamb of God later in life, to have heard from them that they grew up on my band Hatrix and asked why I stopped doing it."

When asked about the underground scene today, Jeff says, "A real underground scene exists today, for sure. But it does depend on where you are. There are strong, vibrant scenes all over the world, but at the same time, there are dead zones, I guess I would call them, at least at the bar level. Who knows—maybe there are bands rehearsing away, where people have yet to make their discovery. Music being available by download is still a work in progress. Labels themselves admit that the CD is a dodo. I believe downloading helps an unknown band rocket to the forefront, while it can, at the same time, cripple a high-level artist into becoming just a memory. As long as a band stays cutting-edge and always pushes the envelope as opposed to becoming too comfortable, they too can have a future. It is a double-edged sword. Do you want to be relevant, or are you happy with past accomplishments?"

Post-Purgatory, Jeff played in a huge number of bands, Hatrix and Mushroomhead among them, whereas founding members Mark Alexander, Kenny Easterly, and Greg Perry played in bands like Mystik, Chemikill, Attaxe, and Zyklone.

BREAKER

AMONG CLEVELAND'S BRAND OF ROUGH AND FIERCE METAL BANDS, Breaker is not just one of the most historic but also one of the greatest exponents of pure, high-class metal that Cleveland's still offering. Formed in 1982, Breaker is still active today (with a pause between 1991 to 1999), and bassist Ian Shipley reminisces on its early days: "As I recall, me and Jim Hamar (vocals) were previously in a band with drummer Matt Schindelar (who was later—and still is—in Destructor). Jim had a friend who was a guitar player, and he and his band needed some help finishing a recording, so he asked if Jim and I were interested in finishing their project. We had our own band, but we were just gonna help 'em out."

Ian continues, "Our music at the time was more Iron Maiden-ish—I even played bass with my fingers 'cause Steve Harris was my idol. The music, though, that the Breaker guys played was much more UFO-, Scorpions-, and Accept-influenced, and this was very interesting for both Jim and I to pursue. We helped them with their songs, but there was a friend of ours who asked

CUT TO THE CHASE:

You can't go wrong with bands like Breaker. The essence of American metal, in its most genuine, innocent, and authentic nature, is right there for everyone who needs a good dose of that music. I would definitely recommend all the stuff they recorded and created, and in terms of this book, you'll be very lucky if you can find the ultra-rare *Blood Money* seven-inch from 1983. However, pick up *Get Tough!* for starters—it's a real masterpiece of serious and mature American metal!

us (meaning Jim Hamar and our band) to play a party for them, as well as the Breaker guys too. So, we all got together, all played the party, and after that, we liked working with Breaker so much that we eventually joined in, even though it was too hard for us to leave what we have started with our band. I was 18 at the time, in 1982. We wanted to play heavy music, and I loved that I was playing with guys who were musically better than me (and a bit older!). Jim and I made the change, and this was a lot of fun.

"We definitely liked the European style of hard rock and heavy metal," Ian adds. "For me, though, it was all Scorpions and Accept at the time. And this is how Breaker got their name, off the eponymous song by Accept. I thought it was one of the coolest songs ever! The music scene in Cleveland was young, with hard/heavy bands coming before us with some level of notoriety, but there was a band that we felt very dear toward, Snake Rock ... they were the ones who helped us get our first shows. They got us started, and we started drawing people to shows! But it was time for us to put out our music, our record—that was the *Blood Money* seven-inch in 1983."

Breaker was a brilliant live band, and Ian explains how the seven-inch *Blood Money* was released via their own label, Breaker Music. "A lot of our success goes to our fellow Clevelander, Bill Peters, who still has a show on college radio every Friday night called *Metal and Metal*. He saw us at a show and offered us a place on his compilation LP that was released on his Clubside Records in 1983. Among the bands were Black Death, Sacred Few, Shok Paris, Sorcerer, Jagged Edge, Cerberus, and Mistreater, and we got the chance to release two songs of Breaker's. We had a long relationship with Bill—actually, we are still good friends—and he did so much for the Cleveland metal scene, since he later became the founder of Auburn Records! So, in conclusion, Bill Peters was the one that lit the fuse and made us wanna make our own record, the 1983 *Blood Money* seven-inch."

Breaker sounded tough as nails even in their early days. *Blood Money*'s two songs ("Blood Money" and "Afraid of the Dark") are just pure examples of American metal. While "Blood Money" is harsher and more straightforward, bordering on American proto-power metal, "Afraid of the Dark" has a certain melodic, mesmerizing quality, and you can hear the early Accept influence here. (I would add Scorpions and UFO to the mix too.) Terrific and diverse stuff! Breaker set the bar very high right from their first release.

"There were a lot of bands that we maybe helped or inspired to record their own stuff," Ian mentions. "We were pretty big in the Cleveland area, and when we started going, it was like showing to other bands that 'Hey! You can do it too.' I'm proud of that, and some of the bands in Cleveland are still our friends."

Breaker initially kept it up until 1991, releasing many demos as well as the (now-classic) 1987 *Get Tough!* LP, a record wholeheartedly recommended to any metalhead with a taste in good old American heavy/power metal. The band broke up in 1991 but reunited in 1999, releasing the excellent *Accept* EP along with many more demos, compilations, and live albums.

"I am always searching for something new to listen to," Ian admits. "I constantly try to find new blood, 'cause it's enjoyable and really fun to follow new bands—like Whores from Atlanta, Georgia, for instance. I can understand the whole frenzy around 1980s American metal, but I am more of a guy who always searches for new music, new bands. So, I'm honored that Breaker's 1980s stuff is a collector's item, and I managed to find this out in our 2017 gig for Bill Peters, when people flew from all over America to see us. It was extremely flattering, to say the least!"

Members of Breaker—there were way too many in the band's existence!—also appeared in many other bands too. Let's stick, though, with the initial lineup, starting with Ian Shipley, who played also with the hardcore/crossover The Spudmonsters, Wretch, the crossover band Civil Disobedience (covered extensively in my book *Crossover The Edge*), as well as Concussion and Lovesick. Don Depew played with Terminal Lovers and Destructor, and Jim Hamar played with Nightcrawler, Rotterdam, and Havoc (the band that released the excellent *The Grip*), whereas later members of Breaker appeared in bands like Brat, Nick Giannakos and Alchemy, Abdullah, and Breaking the Halo, just to name a few.

"I think there is an underground scene for sure ... bands that play in very small venues. I feel bad, though, for musicians today that try to make a living through music. People nowadays are addicted to everything that is free; in the old days, when we started, people checked out a band, bought their record or CDs, and listened to the whole thing. Today, people listen to songs, not albums. They just stick to one song they saw on YouTube. I like to do my research, and I usually end up finding many more other bands/records that are connected to the band that I originally liked, but not many fellows follow that 'musical tree.' For example, there's a band I found out about recently named Mutoid Band—attractive, musically challenging, tongue-in-cheek stuff. The drummer also plays in Converge, and I got into them too. A totally fantastic band! That said, nowadays is a different world ... bands have to find other ways to make money, so some of them are also [visual] artists, so some try to sell things with their band logo on them (e.g., coffee). They have to make money in ways other than their music. I wish things were different, and that their art was respected for what it is. I wish I could help those new bands in some way..."

WHITE BOY AND THE AVERAGE RAT BAND

A BAND THAT REMAINED A MYSTERY FOR MANY YEARS AFTER ITS disappearance, only to re-surface in 2011, White Boy and the Average Rat Band formed in 1979 in Toledo, Ohio, and founding member guitarist Mike Matney tells their story:

"In order to understand about the formation of White Boy and the Average Rat Band, you need to know a little about the history behind the name. I grew up in a small rural town in Southwest Virginia. My mom was the piano player in the local Baptist church, and I was always into music. I first had piano lessons in the first grade, then got my first guitar at eight. Grew up playing music in Mom's basement with my buds. In 1980, two weeks out of high school, my parents helped me move to Nashville. There, I took Ron Keel's place in a band called Taboo. For a time, I was the only white guy in the band, so band leader Kriss Famous designated me 'White Boy.' Flash forward six months to a year, and I'm back home for a while. A local gentleman, Eb Baldwin, had a record store with a little four-track studio in the back. Eb was an old World War II vet with a wooden leg. He always wanted to record an album, so we became friends and struck a deal. I did some work for Eb in return for recording time. I would go in the evenings with either Tim Gilbert or Jerry Hogeston, who were both drummers. We would just jam and lay down the drums and guitar. Then over the course of the next few days, I'd go back and fill in the bass, vocals, and lead guitar. Flash forward a few months and Eb passes away. I barely get the masters out of the studio after Eb's kin come to town. We save up some yard-mowing chore money and have it pressed.

"As far as what inspired the band or the music the most," Mike continues, "you have to remember I grew up in a small rural town. Rock and roll was in its heyday, all this great music coming out, and there were no venues in our town, so we did the homegrown thing. I can remember in the sixties, when my mom and dad got a stereo. I used to lay for hours with my head between the speakers, listening to her 45s of Elvis, the Everly Brothers, early Stones, and my most prized possession, the *Something New* album by the Beatles. Then, growing up in the seventies, I was always deep into the music that was coming out. One of my first concerts was Black Sabbath in 1976—coincidentally, that was the first time I ever got high on weed. Both left a huge impression. Always dug that three-piece sound. ZZ Top, Robin Trower, Frank Marino. All huge influences. And then there's Priest. Don't get me started on those guys. They're the best. I spent a lot of time listening to the live album from Priest and *Tres Hombres* by ZZ Top, come to think of it."

Relocating to the town of Richlands, Virginia, was the next move for Mike, where, he says, "The scene where I lived was nonexistent. There were no bars or nightclubs in this small coal-mining town in Southwest Virginia. Only churches, lots of churches. Snake-handling, long-sleeved dresses only, women never cutting their hair, et cetera. Rock and roll was of the devil, and heavy metal was the worst! So, I spent a lot of time when I was young walking that line. I still do. I think it comes through in my music too. That constant struggle between the spiritual and the secular world produces a conflict that inspires. How cool and fitting to be on the Heaven and Hell label. As far as how I was treated in my hometown, it was fine. Never a prophet in your hometown. Which is to say: I'm always just Mike here, not White Boy. Nobody here is gonna let me get the big head.

"Just a short story here," Mike adds. "A few years ago, our town council came to me and asked if I would play their 4th of July celebration, as they were trying to get one organized. They said there was no money, but if I played the following year, there'd be money and we would be the hometown band. We played, people came—it was a big success. Following year, same thing—they asked if I would play for $250 so they could afford to add fireworks, and I said yes. The following year, they went out and hired an out-of-town band for $10,000 and never called us or said anything. So, yeah, now there's hard feelings..."

On their own label, Tradewind Records, White Boy and the Average Rat Band went on to release their self-titled LP in 1980, which is regarded today as a forgotten classic of the American metal sound. Mike explains: "From time to time, I get asked about the label that the record came out on, and it makes me smile. Jerry Hogeston's dad had a small studio at

CUT TO THE CHASE:

Are ya into the crossover metal/rock sound of Riot, early Anvil, The Rods, or early Saxon? Get *White Boy and the Average Rat Band* at any cost, 'cause this is a wild record! Also get their later records from the 2010s—same style, same quality!

one time. He recorded country and gospel locally. That studio was gone long before I was around. But we would set up and jam in the old building where it used to be. There on the wall was a sign for the old label that Jerry's dad came up with. We just thought it would look cooler if it looked like we were on a label, so..."

The *White Boy and the Average Rat Band* LP is a perfect example of where hard rock was already starting to move on in the early 1980s in the U.S. Grounded in Kiss, UFO, and Motörhead but embracing a much heavier sound and approach, this LP serves today as a prototype for the hard rock/metal crossover genre. Very powerful and very metal (especially "Neon Warriors" and "The Prophet Song"), at times harsh ("Maybe I'm a Fool"), and most of all great fun to listen to ("Leaving Tonight on Vacation"), it could alienate younger generations of metalheads that are used into much slicker, clean-cut sounds. However, *White Boy and the Average Rat Band* is an excellent record that can appeal to fans of hard rock and true metalheads at the same time.

"There have been a few memorable shows from that era," Mike responds when asked about his favorite show. "Winning that very first Battle of the Bands with the original band and right out of the chute, so to speak, was awesome! We partied for days, and it really set the bar pretty high for upcoming shows. In recent years, after reforming the band, we played at Whisky a Go Go in Los Angeles, and that was awesome too. Made even more so by the fact they knew who we were. I had a friend, Ron Garmon, who was working with *L.A. Record* at the time, and he timed the release of the article about us with our appearance at the Whisky, and the whole experience got to be a little surreal."

A lack of interest from bigger labels (as well as changes in priorities in their everyday lives) caused White Boy and the Average Rat Band to disband in the mid-1980s, only to reform in the fall of 2011. As of this writing in 2021, they're still active and have released two more great records (*White Boy and the Average Rat Band II* and *Love My Ride*), in the same style, like nothing changed! "The current renewed interest in private pressings and vinyl in general is great, in my opinion," Mike adds. "A move back to more substantial artistic endeavors, or maybe just people of that age wanting to reclaim a little piece of their youth—for whatever reason, I've benefited for sure."

He goes on: "When I learned that the album was doing well, I was told by my childhood friends Glen and Gary's dad, Mr. Allinson, that it wasn't the fact that the album was all that great—it's just that it was rare. Mr. Allinson was not above keeping my ego in check. Mr. A was in the mining business and had come over from England. He was also a record collector. First blues, then metal. He ran with some big names. I'll never forget the time he brought Henry Vestine from Canned Heat to my mom's basement for band practice. I give him a lot of credit for getting the album out there on his list. Mr. A called me in the 1990s and asked if I had any more copies of the album. He said he would give me 50 dollars apiece for them. After

I gathered up a few and went to see him, I realized that he was getting $150 apiece at that time for them. At that time, he advised me never to release the album, as it would endanger the value of the original. The only thing I knew him to be wrong about (other than the fact that he was an atheist)."

When asked to say more about the album's scarcity, Mike replies, "I would be remiss if along about this point if I didn't say something about the bootleggers. My first encounter with them was Roach Records. The album looked just like the original, except there was an address for Roach Records on the back in the upper right-hand corner. Once, I decided to investigate, so I used Google Street View. The address was the Church of Scientology in Los Angeles. The album was bootlegged at least twice that I know of, by Roach and Rocket Scientist Records. I thought about trying to stop it at one time, but I had to ask myself if that might do more harm than good. I've always wondered how many copies those guys really sold ... Anyway, along comes Jeremy at Heaven and Hell Records in 2016, and 38 years later, the album gets its first official release and I'm touring. I love it. We're constantly having people bring their albums (bootlegs and all) and say they drove for miles to see us. We get this a lot, and also 'This is the one show I never thought I'd see.' The beauty of the Heaven and Hell release is this: People who could never before afford a copy of *White Boy and the Average Rat Band* can now have an official copy and not some half-ass MP3 burnt from a bootleg. Cheers!"

CHALICE

FROM MIDDLETOWN, OHIO, CHALICE FORMED IN LATE 1970S AND ONLY released one seven-inch, but they kept it going (on and off) for quite a while, playing local shows until the late 2000s. Guitarist Michael Wilmot explains the formation of Chalice:

"Chalice originally was three of us who grew up together and literally learned to play together. There was myself, Doug Martin who played bass, and Rick Manning, the drummer. Doug and I grew up on the same road. In fact, he showed me some of my first chords on guitar around age 14 or so. He started playing with the drummer, Rick, and Rick's brother, Roger, on bass. They soon invited me to join, and shortly thereafter, Roger left to pursue girls and cars. Doug started playing bass. We originally called ourselves Brimstone, but just after high school, we renamed the band Chalice ... We played in a lodge group, doing country for a while. But rock was where our hearts were at.

"I would say without a doubt that our biggest influences were Deep Purple, Grand Funk, Black Sabbath, Uriah Heep, Hendrix, and Zeppelin. Our favorite record back then was Deep Purple's *Made in Japan*, and then Grand Funk's *Live* was also a big influence, the band itself went through various members, with me and Rick always being the core of the band."

> ## *CUT TO THE CHASE:*
>
> **Chalice are the definition of the obscure heavy metal band. In just two songs, they managed to convey all their personal relationships, their experience of growing up together, releasing a record, and fading away—creating something innocent and pure that has the word honesty written all over. I can't imagine that there's one single person into the classic heavy metal sound of the early eighties who won't get goosebumps from the two songs on the *Take It Away/ Shoot for the Stars* seven-inch.**

Chalice went on to record and release their only seven-inch, *Take It Away/Shoot for the Stars*, in 1981, which was released without a record cover; pressed by QCA Records, it was produced by Floyd Jones and is his only known work. The obscurity and rarity of this single goes hand in hand with its quality, since it contains two absolute great hard 'n' heavy tracks (emphasis on heavy). Sounding more European than their contemporaries, Chalice displays their Rainbow and Ozzy influences on the galloping "Shoot for the Stars," and there's definite Dio and Blue Öyster Cult influences in David "Seaweed" Seacrest's vocals (R.I.P. 2010).

"Take It Away" is another catchy, classy number, and the NWOBHM influences are absolutely obvious here too—Chalice embraced the new metal sound that had just arrived from the UK and weren't following the strict American 1970s metal path.

As mentioned, Chalice were playing local shows on and off for many years, whereas bassist Charlie Grau also played in the melodic heavy metal nineties act Unbound.

ARCH RIVAL

FROM DAYTON, OHIO, ARCH RIVAL IS A LONG-RUNNING AMERICAN POWER metal band that still remains unknown to the vast majority of metalheads (even though guitarist Michael Harris later enjoyed a very successful solo career and other members went on to play in much more notorious bands, such as Darkology). "Arch Rival rose from the ashes of Tyrant in 1986, which featured myself, Greg Martin on drums, and Gary Rigmaiden in its final lineup," Michael Harris says. "Arch Rival had the intent of writing original music. After several lineup changes, we evolved into our classic lineup with Steve Snyder on vocals."

Early versions of Arch Rival included Aaron Wallace on vocals and Jeff Dennis on guitar, and Michael adds, "It's always been all about the music to me, and I think I can speak the same about my bandmates, so my very first bands were a vehicle for playing my favorite cover music, which eventually evolved into the welcomed challenge of composing, recording,

ARCH RIVAL BAND PHOTO COURTESY MICHAEL HARRIS

and performing original music ... Our four members have quite a diversity of influences. Personally, I'm into more progressive bands like Rush, Kansas, Yes, and some old-school metal like Sabbath or Priest. Steve is more into a Motown style, mostly because of those great vocalists, plus he's from the Detroit area. Greg likes more bluesy rock, such as ZZ Top or Aerosmith, and Gary likes CCR, Rush, and Led Zep. A good middle ground between all of us would be King's X. As far as which influences actually come out in our music, we'd rather our fans tell us!

"The Midwest has always had a strong rep for supporting music," Michael continues, "so we built a pretty insane following in the first lineup of Arch Rival. After all, it was the heyday of the 1980s. Later, when we got Steve and released *In the Face of Danger*, our fans really got behind us more as an original act. If you wanted a major deal, you had to prove that you had a sizable following, and the best way to build that following was to put out your own recording and prove to a label that your band would be a solid investment for them..."

Arch Rival's first release was the 1986 *God Bless America* seven-inch, on their own independent label. It's absolutely professional white-collar American power metal, with huge dynamics and catchy songwriting, as evident in tunes like "Ridin' High" and "Pedal to the Metal." If the recording were higher-quality, this would have been a flawless American metal release!

In 1989, Arch Rival released the demo *There Is No Escape*, following a similar pattern, and Michael adds: "Then our ex-soundman, Chris Armstrong, who worked at a studio in Nashville, also set us up with a producer, Mike Clute. So, we went down and recorded *In the Face of Danger* and released it on our own label, and David Chastain eventually helped us land deals in Europe and Japan."

The 1991 *In the Face of Danger* CD was released on the band's Windmill Records, and this time, Arch Rival took a much different musical route, abandoning American power metal for a more melodic approach, balancing between heavy metal, progressive, and modern hard rock. However, they did it with great gusto, and the result is jaw-dropping. Arch Rival sounds like a

CUT TO THE CHASE:

Arch Rival surely need more attention—especially from metalheads more into the melodic metal sounds of, say, Ten or even King's X. However, their *God Bless America* seven-inch will satisfy all those into early American power metal with its attitude and intensity.

world-class act with songs like "Me Against the World" or "Fortune Hunter."

Michael says, "Opening up for Bad Company at our local sports arena, Nutter Center, is one of my all-time favorite shows of that era. There were quite a few metal bands that released also their stuff on their own throughout the lifespan of Arch Rival. Prizoner, for one, was a really talented band from Cincinnati."

After one live CD, one demo cassette, and the 1993 *Wake Up Your Mind* CD, the band went on hiatus after their 1993 tour, as Michael opted to focus on his solo career. They got back together for one year in 1996, then again for three years in 2008, and since 2011, they've been on hold.

"People searching for indie metal releases—this is obviously really cool for those types of bands," Michael adds. "I think true music listeners have realized that there's a lot of fantastic music out there that hasn't reached the mainstream. And with the advent of independent/home recording studios, a quality mix can be achieved by the bands themselves without a large investment. It's a very good feeling for me too, regarding Arch Rival—writing music that lasts is what any serious original act should strive for."

When asked for his thoughts on the underground scene today, Michael says, "There is definitely a big underground scene nowadays—with the advent of the internet, it's easier than ever for lesser-known bands to be heard and to develop an underground following. It used to be fanatics trading cassettes, such as in the early days of Metallica, but now it's all at everyone's fingertips online. The negative is that the internet's almost oversaturated with bands, so only the strong and persistent will rise to the top ... Sadly, though, it has become pretty much impossible for artists to make a living exclusively off of the recordings that they've given such a large percentage of their lives to. So, if you really want to make a living off of music, you have to pound the pavement and tour. The CD or LP has now become either a piece of musical art or an advertisement to tour."

ROSIE

ROSIE ARE A HARD ROCK/METAL BAND FORMED BY EX-THE GODZ GUITARIST Mark Chatfield in Columbus, Ohio, in early 1980. The name Rosie was inspired, as Chatfield tells it, "by the old tale of Rosie Palmer and her five sisters." Guitarist Ed Means says, "Around 1979, Mark Chatfield left The Godz and wanted to start another band. That band eventually became Rosie. We went through several different members over the next couple of years. Around 1980–81 a group from Atlanta came to Columbus, Ohio, to play. That band was called Smokin'. Bob Boos, Carl Shelor, and Robert West all came from that group. Sometime in late 1981, I joined, and we began to record the album *Precious Metal*. Previous to that, Rosie won a national Battle of the Bands in Daytona Beach, Florida, which resulted in us recording an EP titled *Rosie*. That EP in its original 45 RPM format has become very rare and usually commands a steep price, when you can find one. That EP was later released in a 33 RPM format, which is also somewhat rare.

CUT TO THE CHASE:

Rosie is another great example of a band with a hard rock background that crossed over to the then-emerging heavy metal of the early eighties. Their approach, though, doesn't sound retro at all. The *Rosie* twelve-inch EP still sounds fresh, and it's recommended to everyone into bands like Kiss (especially its late 1970s era), early Dokken, Quiet Riot, or Stryper.

"Having fun and meeting women was my motivation to play music," Ed laughs. "I loved guitars and the feeling of playing in front of a live audience—when they are singing along to your songs, it's unbelievable! My personal favorites have to be the Beatles on Ed Sullivan. At the time, I wanted to play baseball as a career—it would've been an awful decision, since I sucked at it! When I saw the Beatles, I thought, 'Yeah, I would love to do that!' But again, in Rosie, we all got to grow up with the same type of influences."

Hard rock and heavy metal were starting to take off in the United States, and Ohio was no exception. "The scene in central Ohio was really great," Ed says. "There were many clubs that wanted both original music and cover bands. We were treated very well by the hard rock/metal fans. We worked very hard to do what we do, and it really paid off! We opened for many famous bands during that time. We all seemed to enjoy our shows most of the time. There are many traveling stories ... of course, it was the 1980s, so there was some drinking, and other stuff (ahem), but overall, we really enjoyed what we did."

Rosie debuted with a self-titled, self-released, four-song twelve-inch EP in early 1981 and contributed a further track, "Sorry (I Forgot Your Name)," to a radio station sampler LP album titled *Q-FM 96 Hometown Album Project, Volume 3*. A very interesting fact is that the *Rosie* EP was released as a twelve-inch *and* as a ten-inch in the same year, the latter being a format that was very rare in American metal. Actually, I can't recall any other ten-inch releases from any eighties American metal bands that released their own records.

The *Rosie* twelve-inch EP is a great example of hard-rock-to-heavy-metal crossover, with the emphasis on hard rock. It contains four exciting songs, with the best one being the opening "Under Control," a real dynamite track with a major Kiss influence! The more metallic period of the band, though, started when bassist Jay Chesbro was replaced by Ed Means, and is on full display on the full-length studio album *Precious Metal*, recorded and issued by Doubletree Records in 1982. *Precious Metal* has a sound that's more akin to Dokken, and it's way better than *Rosie*. However, Rosie's career was in turmoil, and Ed explains, "Our *Precious Metal* LP was done at a local studio ... but the final mix was done in Atlanta by Ed Seay. At the time we were locked in a contract with a manager. We had major label interest, but due to the aforementioned manager, we were involved in a legal battle with him for several years!"

After a tough start in 1984 due to management problems, Chatfield opted to join Bob Seger's Silver Bullet Band for a lengthy tour. This left vocalist Carl Shelor to take over guitar duties as well. Bassist Robert "Wild" West was then succeeded by a new member, Tom Courteney. With Chatfield returning from the Seger tour, Rosie went into Bison Studios and started working on what was to be their next album. With Shelor and Chatfield as the principal songwriters from the start, the music flowed, and they realized they were writing some of Rosie's best music. A pity, though, that that album never came to be, as Chatfield got another call from Seger, and Rosie was left to look for a replacement.

Fast-forward to 1988, when Mark Chatfield, who had opened his own guitar shop in Columbus, Cowtown Guitars, contacted Means and Shelor about a possible Rosie reunion. After some planning, it took place over two nights and was recorded as a thank-you to the band's loyal fans. Rosie's second and final album, the 1989 LP *Rosie Live!*, was recorded at the Alrosa Villa venue in Columbus on November 25th and 26th, 1988. (This venue later became infamous as the place where former Pantera guitarist "Dimebag" Darrell Abbott was gunned down onstage in 2004.)

"There were a couple of other bands around Columbus, Ohio, with independent releases. The fact that our albums have become collector's items is great ... for the band. But we don't get any money from that. We were never about the money anyway ... we loved what we did," Ed says.

Chatfield still performs with Bob Seger's Silver Bullet Band, with occasional reformations of The Godz, and also plays with Ohio band Luvhead. Rosie broke up in 1996, got back together in 2007, and plays the occasional live show every now and then, but the members have no plans to record again. However, they are still active as of 2021.

"The internet has been both good and bad for the artists, I suppose," Ed concludes. "When you had to do a major release, there was a bit of a filter regarding quality. There were a lot of good bands that were never heard by the masses. Today, you hear it all—and it's not always good! As far as the underground today, I set an example in Columbus. Just one club left, and they try to keep it going!"

PROPHECY (MONTANA)

METAL MADNESS WAS ALREADY SPREADING OVER THE U.S., AND EVEN IN towns and cities that didn't have a thriving rock 'n' roll scene, there were young metalheads forming their own bands. Such is the case of Prophecy from Missoula, Montana. "The band started in 1979 when four rockers dropped out of high school to play in the local bars," guitarist and lead vocalist Doug Koester says. "We soon started working with a local booking agency and became a top draw in the state. Prophecy had a few changes in the lineup early on, and the lineup on the *Prophecy* album was in place by 1980." This comprised Doug Koester, Brent Magstadt (guitar), Tracy Sprain (bass), and Gordy Robertson (drums). "We only wanted to play rock 'n' roll, the music of our age and time," Doug adds, "and we all favored the great 1970s hard rock and metal bands, such as Deep Purple and Black Sabbath."

We quickly became a local favorite and stayed busy touring Montana and the inland Northwest," says Doug. Throughout their existence, they played a pretty extensive list of live shows: about 1,200 shows in five years! "We played five to seven nights a week for four years. There are many memorable nights!"

With so many original songs in their list, Prophecy decided to put out their own record, founding Metal Arc Records in 1984. Doug says, "We recorded the album in Missoula through a mobile recording studio. It was recorded on two-inch tape and sent to press with the help of the booking agency. Of course, everything was on our own label."

CUT TO THE CHASE:

Prophecy's sole LP is a brilliant attempt of hard rockin' metal (or metallic hard rock—call it what you like). *Prophecy* could appeal both to fans of early Iron Maiden, Judas Priest, and Accept as well as fans of Whitesnake and Dokken.

The result was the 1984 *Prophecy* LP, and while described as a hard rock release, the truth is that there's a huge metal edge to *Prophecy*. This is evident in absolutely fantastic songs such as "Killer" (akin to early Iron Maiden and eighties Thin Lizzy), "Night of the Executioner," with its very Accept/Judas Priest style, and the wild melodic metal of "Key to Confusion." Surely, there are pure hard rock tunes too (such as "The Experience" or "Don't Tease Me Please"), but still, these are flavored with a slight metallic touch. This one's a release that will please fans of both camps!

"I can't recall any other hard rock bands from Missoula that put out original music and recorded albums," remembers Doug. I didn't come across any either, at least not from that period.

Prophecy disbanded in 1985 and never reformed, while Tracy Sprain played later in the Minneapolis melodic metal band Gemini (and released three records in the nineties), and Doug currently (as of 2021) plays in country-rock band County Line and rock 'n' roll band Wild Prairie Smoke. "There is and always will be an underground music scene," Doug concludes. "Access to music is easier than ever before, and the variety of music is enormous. It is much easier to produce and distribute original music than it was when Prophecy was around. Plus, I am damn happy that people are still interested in Prophecy today!"

XCURSION

NOT MANY PEOPLE ARE FAMILIAR WITH XCURSION FROM LAS VEGAS, NEVADA, even though all the members of the band were previously (or after) in pretty famous acts such as Ferrari, Kuni, Vinnie Vincent Invasion, Rhoads, Quiet Riot, and Slaughter. In fact, Xcursion was the first band that Mark Slaughter, who later achieved huge commercial success in his glam/hard rock band Slaughter, was ever in.

Bassist Kelly Garni says, "Xcursion was a band that already existed since 1981. They had dismissed their bass player, Dave Filozof, and were set to travel to San Francisco to record an album, which we did. The band was heavily influenced by two bands, Triumph and Raven, both three-piece bands. The album came out just great. There really wasn't any kind of musical scene back then in Las Vegas. So, we played wherever we could: backyard keggers and a few clubs. I only did about eight shows with them and we were very well received.

"My favorite show with them was at a club called Captain America's. It was the first show, and although they told me they used pyrotechnics, they didn't tell me when. A few went off and then I was standing too close to one that I didn't even know was there, and I got blown up on stage. Nevertheless, I finished the show!"

CUT TO THE CHASE:

Xcursion's records are prototypes of classic American metal, and you can place them between bands like The Rods, early eighties Riot, or Dio. The Xcursion twelve-inch is good, but not a mandatory purchase. On the other hand, the *Ready to Roll* LP is amazing and will please every fan of this sound!

Initially appearing on a set of Starstream Records compilations called *KOMP FM 92 ROCKS Las Vegas*, starting with their song "Stay with Me Tonight" on the first volume in 1981, Xcursion then released two records on their own label, Rampage Records, kicking it off with the *Xcursion* twelve-inch in 1983. I initially thought that this would be a hard rock/heavy record in line with Dokken or Ratt, but what a fool I was! This is fist-pumping, raging heavy metal, like a cross between Dio-era Sabbath and Judas Priest. There are at least two great songs: the vicious "Mouthful of Steel" and "Skull Queen." However, Xcursion suffers from terrible production.

"What few bands there were back then didn't last long and were not that memorable," Kelly adds. "I think the internet changed the way bands can sell music and promote themselves without the influence of having a 'boss,' like they do with a record label. I'm very thrilled that Xcursion's records have become a collector's item. I never made a dime off of them, but at least the records have prestige!"

Al Rumley (later of the heavy/power metal band Apocrypha) replaced Kelly Garni just prior to the release of Xcursion, and the lineup for the next and final record was Mark Slaughter, Al Rumley, and Anthony White. Their 1984 *Ready to Roll* LP is their finest moment—even though they mellowed their sound down, it's still great classic American metal, this time with good production and terrific songs like the title track and the steamroller "Over the Edge" (which might even be pre-power metal?). Actually, when Xcursion play fast, they thrive, as in "Tear It Down" and "Ridin High."

Xcursion's demise came in 1985, when Mark Slaughter went on to play with Vinnie Vincent Invasion—Mark didn't miss a chance in order to pursue a good career in rock 'n' roll.

As for today's scene, Kelly says, "I don't think there's much if any underground scene, as bands generally plaster themselves all over the internet to draw crowds. As far as music downloading, it's a trade-off: you get to promote yourself for free, but your music goes out for free."

DESTROYER

IT WOULD HAVE BEEN A DAMNED SHAME IF A BAND AS GREAT AS DESTROYER hadn't been included in this book. Largely unknown to even the most hardcore metalheads, Destroyer from Cincinnati, Ohio, recorded only a few songs, but many more famous metal bands never achieved their level of brilliance! Kenny Burck, Destroyer's drummer, narrates their story:

"We were all always childhood friends, living in the same small Cincinnati suburb, our families knew each other, et cetera. Around the time we met, two of us (Rick and Kenny) were in a band named Destiny, and Scott was in a band called Freeloader. In 1984, both Destiny and Freeloader split up on the same day after some shady things took place between their other bandmates. Without being able to remember all the exact details. Destiny called Scott from Freeloader shortly after the split, and Scott joined Kenny and Rick as their bass player, and Destroyer was formed. My personal motivation stems from the day that I opened Kiss' *Alive II* and saw Gene, Paul, Peter, and Ace. I listened to the album and knew from that moment that I wanted to be in a band. My family has a history of musical talent, so from a young age, I was taking piano lessons, strumming the guitar, and playing the drums. For myself, as the drummer in Destroyer, in order, my biggest influences were Kiss, Iron Maiden, Dio, W.A.S.P., Judas Priest, and pretty much all eighties metal bands. For impression/inspiration records: hands down, it's Kiss' *Alive II* and *Number of the Beast*."

> ## *CUT TO THE CHASE:*
>
> **Destroyer will make your blood boil in the best way possible if you are into the most sincere, decent, and bombastic American metal! As true as it can get, *Black Angels* is a terrific piece of art but a damn rarity today to obtain. Hopefully, a label will reissue all of Destroyer's stuff someday soon. On a side note, did you know that Kenny Burck is the brother of famed New York City street performer The Naked Cowboy?**

When discussing the local scene at the time, Kenny tells me, "The area we are from in Cincinnati is called Greenhills. It's a small suburb that was built after World War II, where everyone knew everyone and families were very friendly and gathered often. Being teenagers within this community, our neighborhood and families supported our music projects. We were the biggest thing in the area at the time! To put it simply, all the other bands were lame, and we tried to put on a show like no one else was doing in a small town or in our age group (16 and 17). During our shows, we had friends or younger brothers use aerosol cans with lighters to shoot flames behind us on the stage. We also had skulls with holes in them and would put smoke bombs inside of them. We went door to door and collected coffee cans to paint black and make our own custom lighting. Our vision was that of huge metal bands, but on a teenager's budget. We wanted to stimulate all senses when people were watching our shows, like Kiss and Maiden."

Rick adds, "Greenhills is well known for producing musicians, some of whom inspired us to play. Growing up and watching the local bands play on the steps of the community building made me want to form a band and play there. We ended up playing there quite a few times."

Composed of overexcited youngsters, filled with passion for heavy metal, Destroyer couldn't wait for a metal label to pick them up, so in 1984, they released their *Demo 1984*. The record contains two songs, "Taboo" and "Flag of Victory," and under the old-school, unpolished, rough production, you can hear a band that had the magic touch. Beautiful heavy metal songs, in the purest form, like a cross between Black Sabbath, Rainbow, and Iron Maiden—melodic, heavy, and unbelievably catchy! This is where the heavy-metal meter hits tilt—it can't go more metal than this. Epic, pounding, and totally inspired stuff, this demo will make all true metal fans cry.

Meanwhile, Destroyer had built themselves a small reputation, since they were performing live in the area. "Bogart's in Cincinnati—W.A.S.P. and bigger eighties bands were playing this venue and continue to today. Playing this venue was an awesome experience. A local place in Greenhills called John L. Sullivan's, where all our local friends, family, and neighbors could see us play and support us," Kenny adds. "Brandy's Waterwheel in Middletown, Ohio. We couldn't wait to play this show we were hired to do. When we arrived, the bar was closed that night, and no one was to be found anywhere. No one called to cancel our gig. Being young and relentless, we decided to take the letters off their advertising sign and arranged them to say, 'Destroyer says fuck you!'"

Destroyer went on to release their first seven-inch (named *Black Angels*, 1985) on their own: "At that time, we had tons of original songs, we were dreamers and wanted to be nothing more than rock stars!" Kenny smiles. "The three of us put all of our money together and decided we wanted to put out a record. If the funds would have been there, we could have put out several. We went to a studio in Kentucky (south of Ohio) called Group Efforts Studio and we printed it/had it pressed on vinyl at a place called Queen's City Records in Cincinnati. We sold the singles for two dollars each to our friends in high school, put some in local record stores that sold local bands' music."

Black Angels included just two songs, but boy, what a piece of art it is. Even better than the demo, Destroyer totally rips on this seven-inch. It would be hard to believe that still today, a metalhead with a passion for the pure American metal sound wouldn't fall to his knees and scream over this one! Absolutely excellent, utterly inspired, class-A American metal. To make comparisons, just imagine bands like early Metal Church at their very best, or the power/speed metal of early Fates Warning, but much rawer and to the point. "Black Angel" is a damn catchy headbanger, whereas "The Grave (Six Feet Under)" is a menacing pounding number that catches you by the throat.

"I can't recall any other bands from our suburb of Greenhills, but there were a few from Cincinnati. Prizoner, CJSS, Freeloader, and Thruster. Freeloader put out an album around the same time but it's totally different music," Kenny says.

Sadly, Destroyer split up a few months after their release of *Black Angels*. It took the band until November 2019 to reunite—for one show in Cincinnati, which was the first time they'd played together in almost 35 years!

Kenny points out, "I find it very odd, after all this time, that people are coming out of the woodwork and taking interest in Destroyer like they have been over the last five to ten years. Sometimes, I think if they would have been this interested 30 years ago, who knows where we could have made it. However, I can't say that I blame them, because all the music on the radio and modern artists all suck balls, and if we as musicians and those interested in music want to find new things to listen to, we have to go backwards in time! Commercial music is garbage for the last two decades!

"I truly don't think there is an underground scene currently," Kenny replies when asked about the state of indie music today. "Even in the mid-nineties, I think there were still some underground scenes in different areas of the U.S. Maybe it's my age, but I don't think there is anything that kids are doing with the underground music world like we were doing in the eighties. First, I hate downloading music, and never have! I want the artwork from the albums and CDs to collect and appreciate. I want to hold the music in my hand and truly collect the music. Second, if YouTube, MySpace, Pandora, et cetera would have been around 30 years ago, then I think Destroyer would have made it worldwide. These kids today are able to get their names out through so many avenues because of the internet. Musicians in general are able to watch tutorials and learn from others online, unlike us 30 years ago."

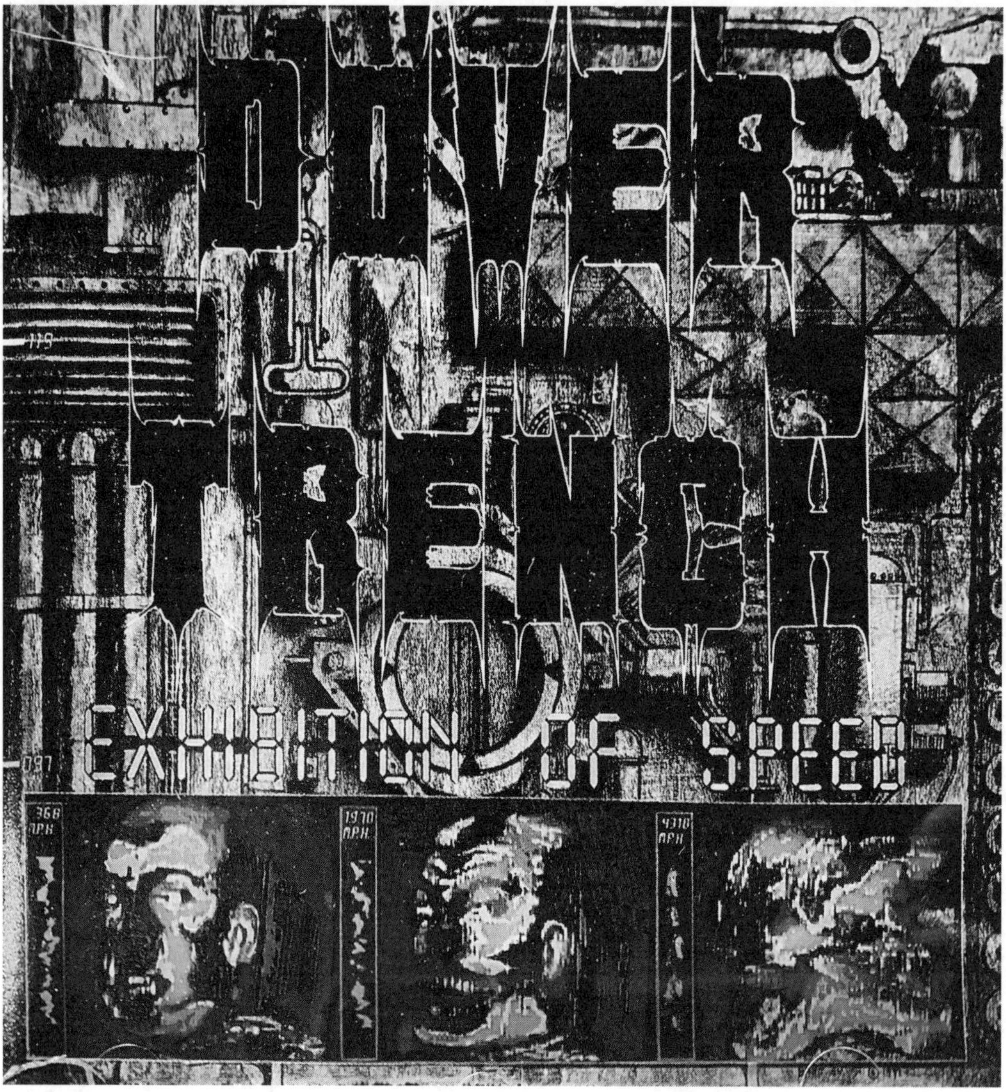

DOVER TRENCH

SOME METAL FANS WILL ASK, "WHAT'S DOVER TRENCH DOING HERE?" BUT I wanted to include them as a total exclusion to the rule, just to show the transition from vinyl to CD in the early nineties, and I was also motivated by the fact that their name rarely gets mentioned, even though their own brand of thrash metal was top-notch. Bassist David Chaney narrates their story:

"Eli Freeman started the band with various members in 1985 in the small town of Sierra Vista, Arizona. I joined the band in the winter of 1986, and Eli and I are the only original members from that time until my departure in 1992. I joined the band, had two nights of rehearsals, and my first show with the band was in Tucson and was filmed for a local TV broadcast. The full band members at that time were Eli on vocals, myself on bass, Joey Durham on guitar, Jim Mattingly on guitar, and Mike 'Smiles' Lawrence on drums. Other band members in the early Sierra Vista days were Doug Floyd on guitar and Blaine Askew on guitar. Matt Pimple on drums and Tom Biancino on guitar had joined the band before we made the move from Sierra Vista to Tucson.

"My motivation to join was lack of anything else to do musically in such a small town," David laughs. "And we all had a love of punk and metal music ... punk and metal music was Dover Trench's biggest influence in the beginning. And it also made us one of the earliest thrash bands. Bands like the Dead Kennedys, Black Flag, TSOL, Part Time Christians, Iron Maiden, Queensrÿche, and also crossover bands like early Red Hot Chili Peppers and Suicidal Tendencies were big influences. Dover Trench started out doing covers of some of these bands, and you can hear those influences in our original songs like 'God Bless Iran,' 'Mutilation,' 'Judge Dredd,' and 'Kill the Bitch' in the early years of Trench and then, in the later years, in songs like 'Tight as a Vice,' 'Married Murderer,' and 'Friction Burns.' The album that left the greatest impression in those early years was S.O.D.'s *Speak English or Die*."

But what about their place of origin, Sierra Vista, and the underground scene there? David replies, "We were lucky in the Sierra Vista days, since it was such a small town. We would play anywhere we could, backyard parties to our infamous Mosh in the Wash, out in the desert. We gained a lot of fans in those days who stuck with us even through the move to Tucson. Having that fan base in that move helped us a lot. We also had the appeal of punk fans and metal fans alike in Tucson, so with the move to a much bigger market, we grew quite rapidly. After the move to Tucson, we did nothing but practice, and that grew to a practice schedule of five nights a week, and the band got extremely tight. So, with that and the fact that we would play any show offered to us, our fan base really took off. Our Halloween parties were outlandishly huge. I also have to credit the mentality of the band back then. We loved being musicians, and we loved to practice. It's not like it is nowadays, in this age of distraction, where you can't even get a bandmate to return a text, let alone show up for rehearsals."

The raging thrash of Dover Trench appeared in their early recordings, the *Dover Trench Demo* 1987, and the 1989 *Hard... Fast... Loud* demo—crazy thrashers with a slight crossover edge (e.g., "God Bless Iran"). David describes those early days:

"We put out a three-song demo cassette on our own, mainly just to get the music to the fans. It had 'Judge Dredd,' 'God Bless Iran,' and one more song on this demo. This demo was recorded, mixed, produced, and mastered all in one night by the guy who owned a recording studio in Tucson. It was Eli, Blaine, Doug, Matt, and myself who recorded those three songs, and we called the demo *Hard... Fast... Loud*. Eli and I were driving home from a strip club one night, a couple days after that recording, and we got to talking about this guy who wanted to manage us and we agreed that no matter what, no one outside the band is going to want this more than us. So, Eli, my sister, and I took the master of those three songs and dubbed off our own cassettes, made our own labels and liner, and we mass-produced the tapes from my sister's apartment. We gave a lot away and sold them at shows and whatnot."

David continues, "Tom had replaced Doug in the band, and we went back into the studio and recorded *Mutilation* and added it to the tape. Before we could do up a well-printed liner for the cassette, Blaine was replaced by David Hembree, so Hembree's picture was included on the new *Hard... Fast... Loud* liner. This second run of the demo was sold in local record stores as well as shows. With David Hembree in the band, we started writing the material that would become the album *Exhibition of Speed*."

Sadly, it took Dover Trench a while to release their first CD, 1991's *Exhibition of Speed*, on their own label, Speedcore USA Records. By then, thrash metal took a step back, with death metal becoming the hottest name in extreme metal, while the grunge explosion left little room for metal bands to gain exposure. David gives the story behind the release of *Exhibition of Speed*:

CUT TO THE CHASE:

Dover Trench are a definite hidden gem for all thrashers to find out about. I just wonder why no label has yet come in contact with members of the band in order to re-release *Exhibition of Speed*. Absolutely crushing, this record/CD is a total must-have!

"This time, we recorded all the songs in one night, then mixed them another night, and then got the recordings set up for mastering on another night. This was all done with the same producer from the first demo. We had a local artist do the cover and new logo and take the pictures. We sent the master with all the designs for the liner off to manufacture, and in two weeks, we got the finished CDs and cassette tapes. Most of the money to produce our albums came from shows. Each band member did not take a percentage—it all went into the band as a whole. We held a huge record release show that was sponsored by the then-national radio station Z Rock, which helped get the word out about the band. What some fans don't know is we wrote a whole album of material that we recorded a pre-demo for, which was never released. Some of those songs, I believe two, we played live at the *Exhibition of Speed* release show. But only the band members have the recordings of those songs. There is also a song called 'Mr. Sinister' that we never released, but I think it's out there, if you just look for it."

Exhibition of Speed is one of the most glorious underground thrash records ever; it's a shame that a record of such creativity, inspiration, and professionalism still remains under the radar of even the most dedicated fans of thrash metal. Frantic, brutal, fresh, and genuine thrash that blends influences from Metallica, Slayer, Voivod, Sadus, Dark Angel, and Kreator, along with ultra-fast crossover such as Ludichrist or Lethal Aggression—all via excellent musicianship! Brutal blasts of songs like "Friction Burns" and "Married Murderer" are just utterly crazy, while "The Immortal Few" and "Acid Test" are simply unbelievable, crazy, technical thrashers. It's actually bizarre that Dover Trench manage to sound so chaotic yet homogenous at the same time.

When asked about other bands in the Tucson area that released indie albums, David responds, "The only band that self-released their record from our area was Malignus Youth. I'm sure there was a lot more, but Malignus Youth is the only one that comes to mind at the moment."

Exhibition of Speed shocked the underground, and Dover Trench had their moment in the local scene, supporting major bands that were coming to town. "Playing with Slayer was cool because it's Slayer," David says. "Pantera was cool because no one can really play a show with them again, so that is something the band will always hold close. But for me, on a personal level, when the band played with Testament, that was my favorite. The guys in the band were so personable and down-to-earth. During load-in, the guys in Testament would sit at a table with me and Tom and joke and hang out. Testament was like us hanging out with ourselves. They even treated our road crew great."

Lack of further exposure—as well as the radical change in the metal trends by 1992—led Dover Trench to disband, only to come back later in 2007 and 2015 for some shows. But this doesn't mean that members were inactive! David Chaney later played in Doomsday (thrash), Jarra (heavy/doom), Luminatus (symphonic metal), Malo de Dentro (metalcore), and Omniscient (black metal), while Matt Pimple also played in numerous bands, with Sleeping with the Witch (groove metal) being his latest. Eli Freeman and Blain Askew played in Scar Strangled Banger and Doug Floyd in The Four Pigs.

"With the advance in technology, it's so easy to get music for free," David says about the current climate in the music scene. "So, nowadays more and more bands and artists are going the private route. And with technology, it has become so easy to record digitally in these times. I come from an era of going into a studio, setting up my amp, and getting the best possible sound, and then trying to get the best recording of a song from start to finish with as little 'punching in' as I could. Compare to today's digital recording, where I go into the studio with just a bass, plug into a computer, and there's a hundred different amps I can pick from with thousands of different plug-ins for filters and EQs that can be used at a click of a mouse. I can play a few measures, and then it can be cut and pasted wherever it's needed. Even mis-fretting or mis-picking can be fixed without re-recording if your producer is good."

David continues, "And of course, a lot of bands are now recording themselves. So, it is natural that bands are producing, releasing, and promoting themselves, and technology has made all this easier. And bands these days have the ability to reach a greater number of fans through social media instead of printing out flyers and posters from back in the Dover Trench days. And bands can now run their own websites and sell their music and merch at a minimal cost to the band. As far as *Exhibition of Speed* being a collector's item, that really blows me away. It's amazing, and it humbles me. Every band wants their albums to do well, but for *Exhibition of Speed* to be such a collector's item after all these years is a great feeling and unbelievable at the same time.

"There will always be an underground scene, more so with the advancement in technology that this age has to offer. When it comes to downloading music, it's always been a tough thing being a musician, but really it all comes down to the fans. As long as a musician is pleasing themselves first, there will always be fans, no matter how the fans get the music. There has been music 'downloading' for many years, if you think about it. We had record albums, and when cassettes came out, we had the ability to take our records and record them onto cassettes. And then we could record from one cassette to another. CDs came out, and again we could burn from CD to CD, or record to CD, or transfer from cassette to CD. So, in reality, the idea of downloading has been around for many years before the personal computer was mass-produced. Technology has made downloading easier than ever; that is a fact. I do believe that, because of fans getting their music for free, it's made the ticket prices for bands' live performances and merch skyrocket."

SLAYER

NO, THIS IS NOT THE SLAYER, NOR IT IS SLAYER FROM SAN ANTONIO. THIS IS a short-lived band from Phoenix, Arizona, that was formed in 1982 by Dave Roberts (vocals), Darryl Ogawa (guitar), Eddie Hosmer (bass), and Johnny Ray (drums). "It started in the South Pacific on some tiny islands in Micronesia," Darryl tells me. "Eddie and I went to high school together back in the seventies and used to jam together, playing anything we could at the time. The music scene was essentially nonexistent out there, so trying to figure out what the driving force behind that was is pretty much a mystery. Both of us ended up in Phoenix, and the opportunity moved us to Tucson to see about getting Johnny Ray on board."

Eddie adds, "We'd heard of Johnny Ray, but we felt very fortunate to play and write with him.

"It certainly felt like forming the band was what needed to be done. That's just what you do. We were trying to find like spirits," Eddie says. "We all just brought our own personal

CUT TO THE CHASE:

Slayer's only release, 1982's *Dangerous Appetite* LP, remains both a major rarity as well as an item that only few hardcore metalheads are aware of. Musically, it is pretty good hard rock/metal. Not a classic, but always enjoyable.

influences, since Darryl and myself basically grew up musically together and we had many of the same influences. I would add Yes, Black Sabbath, UFO, Led Zeppelin, Doobie Brothers, and The Beatles." Darryl also mentions Rush, Queen, Thin Lizzy, Van Halen, and Aerosmith.

"Queen, the first album blew me away. The tones, dynamics, arrangements, and vocals were all inspirational," Darryl reminisces. Eddie says, "Rush's *2112* was just an eye-/heart-/mind-blowing experience for me. Words cannot express what that did to me..."

Originally, Slayer were not from Tucson, Arizona, which is where their only album was written and recorded. Darryl and Eddie were living two hours away in Phoenix and moved to Tucson specifically to get Johnny Ray in the band. "We were not familiar with the scene; we were on a mission. I remember the locals embracing us very nicely when we played," Darryl says.

Slayer decided to put out their record on their own. Darryl says, "It was the thing to do and, at the time, what we thought had to be done," and Eddie adds, "We felt doing a six-song EP on vinyl looked more professional and showed how serious we were about the craft and the business of music." Eddie also says, "From what we remember, we wrote the songs pretty quickly, spending all our time on only that one goal. We weren't working day jobs, so eating was not high on the list. We had some friends helping us out in that department. Recording on two-inch tape puts your playing front and center, and no one wants to waste studio time, so going in prepared was a must. I consider that all part of the production. We went in and recorded them, mixed them, got them mastered and then pressed."

Somewhere in between hard rock and the emerging heavy metal scene of its day, *Dangerous Appetite* is rough yet melodic, silky yet powerful, melodic yet fist-pumping. A metallic rocker with six songs that range from good ("Dreamer Blue," "Candy Cane") to very good ("Fighting Fire" and "Loyalty"), it's like a more basic Rush blended with UFO and seventies-era Riot. *Dangerous Appetite* will appeal to fans of all the aforementioned.

"We played quite a few shows following the release of *Dangerous Appetite*," Eddie remembers. "We played a club called the Night Train in Tucson. It was a big club with a great high stage. It felt so good to play the stuff live and have people enjoy it. It was one of those evenings where you felt good about the show. However, since we weren't originally from Tucson, we had no knowledge of the other local bands at the time. This was 1982, and we had our noses buried in our project."

Slayer disappeared later in the mid-1980s, but their *Dangerous Appetite* is still here to remind us what a great band they were. "I wasn't really aware that people were still interested in the underground metal like us," Darryl continues. "I was made aware of it in 2013 when I reconnected with Johnny Ray," Eddie agrees. "He had mentioned something about it and I found it hard to believe. I think it's great because there are some really good hidden gems out there."

"Is our record really a collector's item?" Darryl says in surprise. "I kinda feel like Darryl... If there are people out there enjoying our efforts from back then, I think it's great, and I thank them sincerely," Eddie says. "After all, there is still an underground scene, although I haven't been involved in it, but have heard it's there," Darryl concludes, with Eddie adding, "I think it's there, and I'm glad people are supporting drums, bass, guitars, and vocals."

"The internet changed everything in the way music is listened to and distributed. There's good and bad, but it's just the way it is these days," offers Darryl regarding the whole issue of downloading music. Eddie supports him: "There was something special about going and purchasing the album, unwrapping it, putting it on the turntable, hearing the needle hit the vinyl, and listening to that song begin to play. Reading the cover and inserts ... it was an experience."

ROC LOCHNER

MASTERS OF MELODIC HEAVY METAL ROC LOCHNER FROM TUCSON, ARIZONA, formed in 1980, when the band members were still in high school. Robby Lochner, guitarist, tells me, "We played at our high school, as well as house and desert parties, but under several different names. Riff Raff and Oakenshield were two of them. Me and Dan Felgar were the only two in the band from the early incarnations when it became Roc Lochner. People kept calling the band 'Rob Lochner's band,' which I didn't want. When my brother Charlie joined the band, the neighborhood friends started calling us Roc Lochner which ended up sticking.

"My biggest inspirations in the early days of the band were Van Halen records," Robby says about his musical influences. "They were the way of the future at that time. As for the band collectively, TNT's *Tell No Tales* and then *Intuition* were influences. Other than that, we were hearing some of what was going on the radio and MTV but were trying not to be influenced too much by what was going on. We were focused on getting our own identity."

"The music scene was amazing for us. We were the most popular band in Tucson for ten years," Robby adds. "Over the last five years, we became arguably the most popular band in the region. Thousands of people would come see us play. In 1984, when we played a new venue called the Roxy, just shy of 1,500 people were packed in like sardines in this 800-capacity venue. We were treated like rock stars, although we were not...

"The scene was vibrant back then," he continues. "If we played somewhere and only drew 500 people, we looked at it like a failure. No other band locally could bring in the people like we did; however, the smaller bands could draw 100 to 200 people a night. This was an amazing time that we'll never see again. The scene had an air of excitement, an electricity that can't be truly described, only to say that shows were an event that no one wanted to miss..."

When asked about his favorite show they played, Robby replies, "There are many memorable shows but one that stands above the rest. In June of 1982, we played on the banks of the Tanque Verde Wash [near Saguaro National Park in southeastern Arizona]. We built a street scene out of eight-by-tens and painted red bricks on them, with painted doorways and windows. We ran the amps and PA off a generator, ran a snake about 100 feet out into the wash, and buried it in the sand. We backed up a pickup truck out there and had the soundman run from the back of a pickup truck. We put flyers out to most of the high schools in town. The turnout was guesstimated by the police to be about 5,000 people. The police had a helicopter flying overhead for about an hour before they finally stopped the party. One cop said to me, 'What are you guys, the Rolling Stones?' There was designated parking along the dirt road leading up to the wash and a whole area by where we put our set-up. All that was packed. The police had set up perimeters on a road called Tanque Verde Loop. They had blocked each end, which was one mile apart. That whole mile had cars parked all the way down on both sides, and they turned away cars that were coming in. That was the biggest show I had ever played prior to playing with Rob Halford in 1994. People in four-wheel drives were coming up the river bed and parking outside of the crowd of people. The show was broken up before we finished our set. I still remember packing up and feeling incredibly high from the experience. I have never felt that high from a show before or since!"

The whole frenzy regarding Roc Lochner wasn't something that occurred overnight; the band had been working crazily hard both as a band as well as individuals, perfecting on their own their sound and technical abilities. But more than that, they could write great tunes! With the lineup being Rick Travis (on bass), Troy Richards (on drums), Robby Lochner (guitar), Ken Triphan (vocals and keyboards), and Charles Lochner (rhythm guitar), in 1985 Roc Lochner released their self-financed LP, *Roc Lochner*.

"We had decided to do our own release because we wanted to break through," Robby says. "How else would a band who knew no one in the industry get attention, other than to write and release vinyl? We had demo'ed material at a place called the Sound Factory and had done some basic four-track demos prior to doing the first release. We then did the recording; it was supposed to be released in 1984. It took until June of 1985 to get it released. We originally assisted in the mixes, which were pretty decent. They sounded somewhat aggressive, warm, fat, but every test pressing we received would not be able to play properly on a turntable. The needle would jump off the record. Probably too much low end. Our bass player's older brother had a former bandmate who was living in L.A. who then had a studio. We got him to test-mix a track, which

CUT TO THE CHASE:

The 1985 *Roc Lochner* LP will please those who are into melodic metal—albeit with a punch. Just imagine Fifth Angel's *Time Will Tell* LP for a similar style. But allow me to recommend to you the 1998 compilation LP on O.P.M. Records—this is the band's best moment!

sounded great. We paid him 2,000 dollars to mix the rest. The problem was the guy was a coke addict and he took the money and had an assistant do the rest of the mixes. They sounded horrible. We ended up going back to the engineer at the Sound Factory, and at this point, he wouldn't take any input. His mixes sucked, but that's what we were stuck with. We did sell all the vinyl. I only own one copy..."

Roc Lochner was an excellent LP of pure melodic heavy metal that sounded like it was on a major metal label—just so professional! What is very significant in their case was that everybody in the band was a proficient musician, and this resulted in six tracks of awesome American metal. "First Sight Love" is dynamite, whereas "Headlines" will please all those into hard-rockin' metal. Even though the atmosphere was very glam-oriented, *Roc Lochner* is still an American metal record. Roc Lochner kept it up until the late 1980s when they self-released the *Seventh House* cassette in 1989, a crazy rare item today that I couldn't find anywhere. Robby says, "Our second release, *Seventh House*, is something that I haven't seen anywhere and don't even own a copy! Sadly, we only released it on cassette.

"There was a metal band called Aftermath from our area that had a release right after us. I think they may have two vinyl releases," Robby recalls about other Tucson-area bands who recorded on their own labels. "Our bass player who joined up with us in 1984 had a release just prior to ours. He recorded in the Sound Factory as well, over the years 1982 and 1983, and released in 1984. There might have been releases by a band called Street Pajama before us and a band called The Next, though I'm not sure."

Roc Lochner faded away in the late 1980s, and Robby, an amazingly gifted player, found himself playing alongside Rob Halford in his nineties heavy metal band, Fight, and since then in Jack Russell's Great White. In 1998, O.P.M. Records released a compilation of Roc Lochner that, to me, still is their crowning moment: unbelievable, terrific, melodic American metal, this time with no glam influences, but all the songs coming from 1980s demos. It's the best stuff they ever recorded! Just check out "Hammer Me," "Moon Over Phoenicia," and "Body Heat"—bombastic, melodic American metal, like Lizzy Borden mixed with Fifth Angel!

"I had heard that a signed copy of our first release was displayed in Tucson at a record store, asking price of 100 dollars. This was probably around 2002," Robby says. "I went into that store when I was in Tucson shortly after that and it had been sold. I asked a girl working there about it and she started telling me about the band and how they were popular way back when. I eventually told her who I was."

Robby adds, "I do think it's cool that it is a collectible. I think that the situation, though, today with so much 'free music' is a double-edged sword being able to get music so easily. There are some cool things about it and some not so cool ... As for getting music, it's cool that, to actually own the physical copy, you still have to hunt for it. To hear it is probably not so tough, but actually holding vinyl or a cassette is a different thing."

ASHBURY

ASHBURY DIDN'T COME OUT OF NOWHERE; AN EARLY INCARNATION OF THE band formed in 1978 in Oklahoma. It began as Ashbury South, a cover band that disbanded in 1980, with brothers Rob and Randy Davis relocating to Tucson, Arizona. The two brothers performed as an acoustic/electric two-piece before adding drummer Dave Carpenter, guitarist Lee Smith, and bassist Noal Morris, and Ashbury was born.

"We grew up in a music-filled household," guitarist Rob Davis tells me. "Our dad loved music above all things, other than his family. He was in the military, and when we were very young, he was stationed in France for three years. During that time, we had no television, just a stereo, and music was played all the time. The artists included everyone from Johnny Cash to Buddy Holly, from Elvis to Fats Domino and Chuck Berry; from Herb Alpert and the Tijuana Brass to Faron Young, from Jerry Lee Lewis to Hank Snow. So, you can see that this was a wide exposure to different styles and genres, and we listened—we really listened!"

Rob continues, "Randy began playing drums at age nine and began piano lessons at 11. He showed talent right from the start and an understanding of music theory well beyond his years. By 12, he was playing bass guitar, and lead guitar by 15. At 18, just after graduating from high school, he began making his living as a musician, playing in house bands in large venues in Texas and Oklahoma. I began playing with him while he was in high school, but it would be a couple more years before we began working together. All told, we have been performing together off and on for over 40 years. After a few years playing in cover bands, forming our own band seemed an obvious choice. The main reason we formed Ashbury was to play original music that we were writing ourselves.

"Our biggest influences were the classic rock bands of the seventies," Rob adds. "Jethro Tull, Black Sabbath, Wishbone Ash, Rainbow, and many others. Our biggest single record influence was Tull's *Thick as a Brick*. Also needing mention would be Tull's *Aqualung* and Sabbath's *Paranoid* and *Sabbath Bloody Sabbath*."

Ashbury had already been together for three years when they put out their magical music on a record. "Randy and I never tried to be part of the musicians' clique," Rob admits. "We were (and still are) ignored by the local press, and the main reason is never having signed with a label. We are the ultimate independent band: never signing, only licensing labels to manufacture, distribute, and sell our albums. So, when we refused to sign with any label, the only reasonable course was to write, record, and produce our debut album ourselves. We distributed it through Tower Records in the U.S. upon its release. We rejected an offer from Polydor Records in September of 1983."

The result was the major classic LP *Endless Skies*, released in 1983 on their own label, Ashbury Music. It's simply incredible, melodic hard rock with a heavy metal feel, and above all, more epic than your average power metal band. Everything in this release is of the highest quality, from the terrific fantasy cover art to the songwriting. Songs like "Vengeance" or "The Warning" will just send chills down your spine, whereas "Mystery Man" or "Endless Skies" are eternal rock hymns that deserved a much bigger audience. *Endless Skies* is mostly an acoustic LP, but that doesn't strip away any of its epic, powerful feeling. Balancing among the classic hard rock of Wishbone Ash and Rainbow, the riffs of Black Sabbath, the pomp of Styx, as well as folk rock and even Southern rock, this is really one of the crowning moments in the history of metal that sadly never got the recognition it deserved.

However, their vision of recording and releasing their music totally on their own, as well as handling everything that had to do with the band, started falling apart just a few months after *Endless Skies* was released. By November of 1983, Ashbury weren't together.

Fast-forward to 2010, when Ashbury were only sort of back together just for occasional shows. But they also released two excellent records, *Something Funny Going On* in 2010 and the *Eye of the Stygian Witches* LP in 2018, as well as one cassette in 2013, titled *Out of the Blue*. They wanted to do it their way, so this time, they did it! "Since then, we had several great shows, but both Keep It True appearances, both Muskelrock shows, Psycho Las Vegas, Hammer of Doom, and both Ragnarokkr shows were among the best," Rob says.

"As for the days in the eighties, I recall a fellow Tucson band, Atrophy, that released two pretty memorable metal records—though not independent, but still great," Rob mentions.

"We are truly pleased about the *Endless Skies* original pressing being a highly sought-after collector's album. They are quite difficult to obtain these days. The original pressing was for 1,000 copies. I've heard they may go for as high as 400 euros or 500 dollars."

Regarding the current climate in the music industry, Rob adds, "The music scene is a constantly changing and evolving platform. We do believe there is a true underground music scene, but there are now so many people trying to promote and stage their own festivals that it is becoming convoluted. YouTube and downloading sites help to promote a band's music but ultimately take away from possible income. I wish people would listen more on digital sites like Spotify, Deezer, Google Play, et cetera, as there is at least some payment (although it is minuscule) to the artists and labels. The next time you want to promote a band's new release, do it via a Spotify link instead of YouTube—you will be supporting the band and label in a more productive way. Music is a very important part of our culture ... and the underground scene is vital to avoid the major labels from controlling everything that is released. Support your favorite bands, and keep the independent artist alive!"

CUT TO THE CHASE:

Ashbury's *Endless Skies* is a timeless classic of hard rock/heavy metal, and it's a mandatory release to have, whether you are a fan of hard rock, heavy metal, true metal, or just great music in general! I don't want to moan, but this time I'll do it, since I have seen many bands as great as Ashbury be overlooked in heavy metal databases—this is simply ridiculous. Ashbury might not have the heaviness of, say, Manowar, but they are 100 percent epic and majestic, plus they definitely have many metal elements in their sound! Get *Endless Skies*, then get everything else they released.

WYZDOM

WYZDOM FROM MINNEAPOLIS IS ANOTHER GREAT OVERLOOKED METAL band of its era. Formed as early as 1980, the band went through different musical phases throughout its existence. "The idea of Wyzdom came to me when I was in The Russ Erickson Band, so when the band ended, I formed Wyzdom," says Mark Nesser, the band's vocalist and keyboard player. "I wanted to create a band with a harder edge and a deeper mystical meaning. At the time, I was studying many occult philosophies and that really influenced me ... I would go through many member changes, with me and Dave Sanborn (guitar) being the longest-standing members. We lasted over ten years and had over 100 songs (including three unreleased albums). The members of Wyzdom were influenced by many bands from Deep Purple and Def Leppard to The Beatles. I was personally very inspired by Aerosmith and Led Zeppelin, but Rainbow's *Long Live Rock 'n' Roll* album really moved me and still does to this day. Ronnie James Dio and Robert Plant were my heroes."

Since Wyzdom wasn't from Los Angeles or Chicago, they found difficulties in getting signed by a big metal label. "Wyzdom was based in the Twin Cities (Minneapolis and Saint Paul, Minnesota), which did have a very good metal scene," Mark mentions. "The problem was, there were few metal bands being signed from our area. The locals were very unreliable, because sometimes we played for 200 people in an average club, and sometimes there would be only 25 people. When we went on tour with the Minnesota metal band Slave Raider, we got to perform for up to 5,000 people every night."

Mark and Dave recruited new members Tom Garvey (drums) and Max Luebeck (bass). Living all together in a band house called the Zoo really helped in dedicating a lot of time to practicing and writing a lot of songs! After working on their first full-length (unreleased) album, *Philosopher's Stone*, the band went into Blackberry Way Recording Studios at the same time Hüsker Dü was recording there. Wyzdom recorded several songs there, including "Not Afraid to Be Strange (newer version)," "Won't Be Too Long," "Wake Up the Night," "Bridges of Magick (newer version)," "Sad Eyes," and "Philosopher's Stone." After running out of funds to complete the project, the band created a demo, which they sent to Warner Records.

Being persistent, Wyzdom self-released 2,000 copies of their 1985 seven-inch EP, *Wake Up the Night*, containing two songs. Both tracks are classic melodic metal with keyboards, mostly heading for the Rainbow route rather than the AOR route. The title song is a nice hard 'n' heavy number, while the flip side, "Not Afraid to Be Strange," is slightly more melodic but still good.

"We put out our own seven-inch vinyl because we were trying to get signed by Warner Records at the time and we wanted to give them something that would impress them more than just a cassette demo," Mark says. "We put out our full album, *Through the Looking Glass*, later on a friend's independent label, because we had been turned down by several labels and really wanted to give something to our fans."

With the new drummer, Tom Garvey, the band focused on playing as many shows around town at clubs like the Payne Reliever Church and Ryan's Corner, both in St. Paul. They also embarked on their first tour, but after only a month, the bus they were using to tour had an unrepairable electrical fire, so the band returned to the Zoo. They were broke and disillusioned, and once again members quit, leaving only Dave and Mark again. Mark took a Wyzdom demo to the local concert on Deep Purple's *Perfect Strangers* tour, and after the show, with the help of a special friend, got backstage to give the demo tape to their keyboardist, Jon Lord. A later communication reported that Jon had liked the music, especially "Philosopher's Stone," and was going to pass it on to their label, Polydor Records. After several failed contacts, though, a deal was never made.

In 1988, the band decided to record a whole new album and found investors to finance it. *Through the Looking Glass* would originally feature 12 songs (later to be only ten) including new versions of "Bridges of Magick" and "Not Afraid to Be Strange." The cover of this Wyzdom album was an art collage created by Steve Janke. After the band finished mixing the album, things got weird again, because the investors and bass player Rick Kremer stole the Wyzdom master tapes. They were trying to negotiate to get part ownership of the songs. After Mark Nesser hired a music lawyer, which he paid for out of his own pocket, he got the master tapes back and finished the album, removing the two songs that Rick Kremer had any writing credits on, because Rick

CUT TO THE CHASE:

Wyzdom will definitely satisfy fans of the crossover territory between hard rock and heavy metal, albeit with a more melodic touch. Fans of Q5 or Nightshade will love it. The *Wake Up the Night* seven-inch is slightly rawer than their later stuff.

was fired from the band—and because of all the pain he had caused them. Steve Janke got credit on the inner sleeve as the bassist for this album. Tom Dades filled in as bassist for the band, so they could finish shows they were contractually obligated to play. At one of the multi-band shows they were playing in Stillwater, Minnesota, Mark's cousin Adrienne Nesser would introduce Mark to her boyfriend (now husband), Billie Joe Armstrong from Green Day.

Through the Looking Glass cassette is a mixed bag, in my opinion; when Wyzdom play pure metal, like on "Bridges of Magick," they totally shred, reminding one of all the classic melodic American metal acts like Heir Apparent. But when they head for a more commercial AOR-based approach, I think that it doesn't fit them, even though fans of AOR will surely like them because the quality is definitely there.

A new Wyzdom bassist, Mike Marshall, was finally hired and the band went on a tour to promote their album. They played all over the Midwest. Mark Nesser shopped the new album to many record labels and caught the interest of Twin/Tone Records, but a deal was never made. Once again, with the band broke and disillusioned, members of the band quit. This time, Mark Nesser decided to put Wyzdom on hiatus and join several local cover bands (Challenger and X-Rated) to pay some bills. Tired of the cover band scene, Mark joined the band Jeppeto's Fire as their new lead singer, where he met JP Bohn, a great drummer who would soon become the drummer when he reformed Wyzdom.

"All the opening shows that we did for Slave Raider were amazing," Mark smiles. "Their audience really connected with us, and we started building a large following from those shows ... Plus, I remember there were several other bands from our area that put out private releases, like Nasty Nasty, Regime, Riff Raff, and Gemini, but didn't get the same attention that we did from our release."

Mark joined Wild Child and got burned out in 1988 from playing five nights a week and touring for almost a year with them; with no record deal in sight, Wyzdom were laid to rest for good, and Heaven and Hell Records re-released *Through the Looking Glass* on CD in 2019. "There's a lot of lost metal/hard rock music from a lot of talented bands that needs to be brought to life. Also, I feel that a lot of the music of today is missing that energy, excitement, and mystery that Wyzdom had," Mark believes. "The music scene now is so oversaturated with amateur bands that it actually makes it very hard for someone to sift through all the trash to find the gems. If there's a real underground scene existing today, it's lost in the flotsam and jetsam. Another problem is that the record industry doesn't support most bands anymore, and because of digital downloading and rip-off services like Spotify, most of the signed bands are struggling to pay their bills. Most bands make all their money from performing live and have to tour almost nonstop to make money."

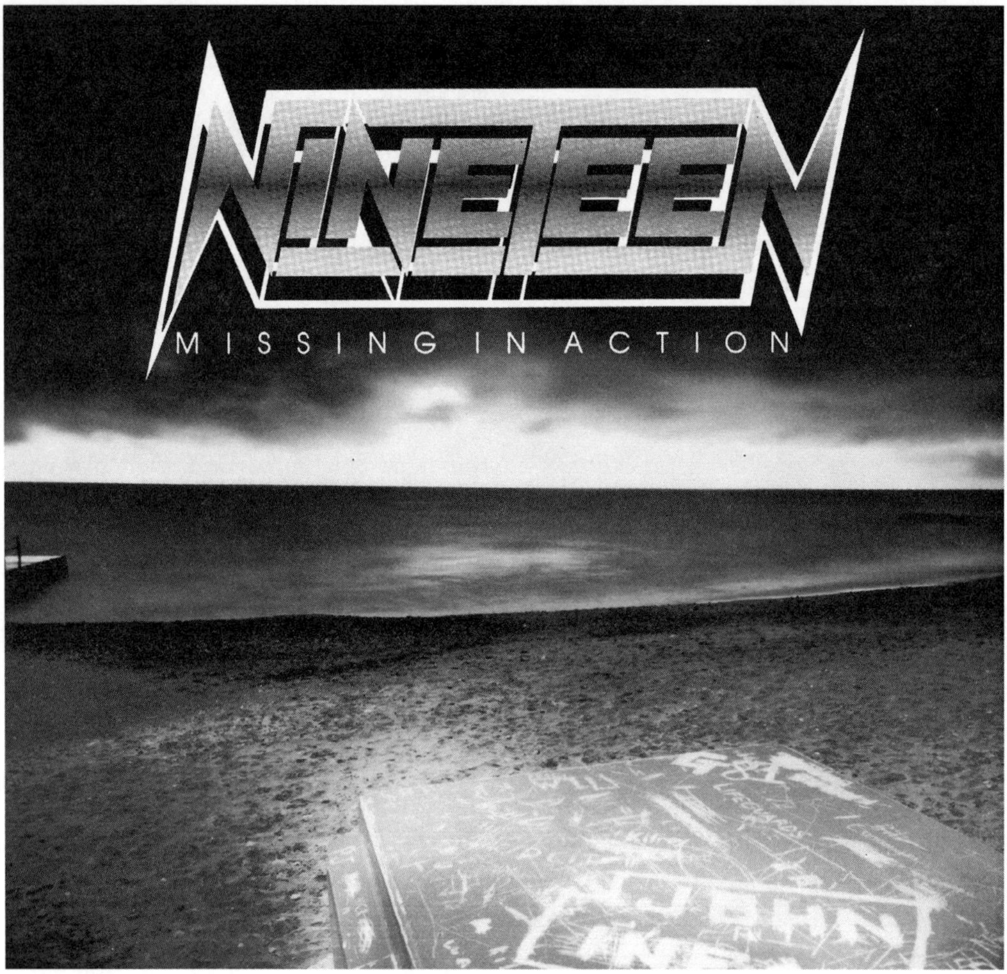

NINETEEN

JUST A FEW MINUTES AWAY FROM CHICAGO, THE LITTLE TOWN OF Bridgeview, Illinois, has its own submission in the American metal scene of the nineties—a small one, since the only known bands from Bridgeview were Tera (progressive metal) and Nineteen. The latter managed also to release a record on their own, and Linas Olsauskas (vocals and keys) tells their story:

"I had a music background, as did most of the other members through their grade-school band elective. I played piano and trumpet, Ron (Dieken) played sax, Jim Kerwin played percussion. The original four members went to the same high school. Our music interests morphed into electric guitar and so on. Long story short, no fun to play your guitar by yourself, so Ron, Randy (Adamski, guitar) and Jim formed a band. They needed a singer and asked me if I would be interested, although I had no experience. This all happened after graduation. At the time, the band was named Axis and played covers. The intent was to play graduation parties and fests..."

Recalling his favorite shows with the band, Linas says, "One of the most memorable shows, and for all the wrong reasons, was a Battle of the Bands we participated in at Condesa Del Mar banquet hall in Alsip, Illinois. Of six bands, I think we placed fifth and nearly got booed off the stage! After that we regrouped, we came to the conclusion that we'll never sound as good as the original bands we covered, and every band out there had their own clique of followers comparing how well each band played a cover of the same song. So, we decided to write our own music. We changed the name to Nineteen (we were all 19 years old at the time, and back then nobody had just a number for a band name), and I went and studied voice for a period of three years with Thomas Siliti from the Lyric Opera of Chicago, and the material for *Steel Trax* demo was written. The lineup now included also Paul Kamp (guitars) and Steve Dunne (drums)."

Linas continues, "Back in the late 1970s the exposure to any band was a different music experience: Rush with *2112* was spacey, Black Sabbath was dark, Rainbow was mystical, Kiss was makeup, the Runaways, all-girl and raunchy ... different identities. My first concert was the Kiss *Alive II* Tour. Favorite bands included Zepp, Van Halen, Scorpions, Def Lepp, AC/DC. Everybody in the band had their own favorites, with Pantera and Megadeth added later on..."

In 1985, Nineteen released their first cassette mini-LP named *Steel Trax*, and Linas describes the process: "This was the 1980s and MTV had just started. Metal had really started taking off. At the time, I was working at a record store chain named JR's Music Shop and was assigned the position of import buyer. Metallica, Anthrax, Slayer, Queensrÿche, and Pantera were still at this time on indie labels. We decided to go into the studio to cut a cheap eight-track demo to shop our music for larger shows, and maybe a record label. The idea was that if they can do it, we can do it. *Steel Trax* was recorded, and for a small investment of a couple hundred each, we packaged 500 copies on cassette with cover art and a lyric sheet to send out and test-market our product. About a year to the day, we opened a triple bill with Rock Corps, an Alice Cooper tribute band, and Tough Love, an all-girl rock band, all in front of 3,000 people at the same place, Condesa Del Mar. And killed it. We were supposed to play covers. We opened up with 'Hellion/Electric Eye' and played all of *Steel Trax* for the next half-hour. Sold out of all 500 cassettes the next few days. JR's was a big benefit. They let me sell Nineteen's merchandise. My presence there working and their willingness to carry indie product started a Southwest Chicago metal scene, a hangout for local musicians. JR's had 19 stores in the tri-state area. We packaged another 1,000 cassettes and sold out of those. That was another step in the decision to go back into the studio and record what is now *Missing in Action*. We had a bunch of great shows, but that one is probably most memorable—being the acceptance point and real turning point of the band."

The 1985 *Steel Trax* cassette contains seven songs of pure, melodic heavy metal, in the tradition of early Queensrÿche with a Judas Priest touch, and there are some absolutely inspired tracks here, such as "When the Hammer Falls" or "Forever and a Day," a real anthem! There is a good dose of melodic hard rock there too, but this is done with great gusto, such as in the excellent "Can't Please Every Body," when they combine AOR with powerful heavy metal!

"The music scene in Chicago, band-wise, was lame," Linas sighs. "Stagnant for the longest period. Not known for metal. The last bands to make it big from the region were Styx and

Cheap Trick. The Midwest had a real stigma. The West and East Coast were the hot spots. Anthrax was forming, Mötley Crüe was forming. Jumping a little forward here, but in an effort to secure potential national radio play, I had my girlfriend at the time mail a test pressing of *Missing in Action* from Florida when she was visiting her grandmother, to displace the band or disguise the fact we were from Chicago. EMI/Capitol Records was doing the mixdown and vinyl pressing. I sent out blank test pressings with no name of the band on it and included what looked like ransom notes, using clippings from magazines that said 'Hey, Z Rock, listen to this. Songs marked in yellow are potential nut-kickers from America's newest metal band.' Side A: 'The Soldier.' Side B: 'Street.' I had return shipping labels from Jem Imports (being the record store import buyer). Two days later, we made national radio play on two stations, dubbed 'The Mystery Band.' The radio station requested anybody with any info to call in. They got flooded with calls. We made heavy rotation for about a week. Created a mountain out of nothing. Had some major label interest, and then things got pulled when they found out we were not published yet with BMI or ASCAP. Technically they were not supposed to be playing it if no royalties were being paid out. Kind of like a union thing ... but oh well, we managed to get some airplay, at least!"

CUT TO THE CHASE:

If you can handle the whole aforementioned identity crisis, *Missing in Action* is a pretty decent LP, especially for fans of early eighties American metal (in the pre-power days). I wish that *Steel Trax* would get a reissue on vinyl someday, because this is their best—and most metal—moment!

In 1986, Nineteen proceeded to create their own label, Express Records, and released their sole LP, *Missing in Action*. Seemingly suffering from an identity crisis, this very enjoyable record has great metal songs ("Brazil (Room 101)," "Queen of Angels," and "Run for Cover"), AOR ("Nightlife," "Where's Your Love") and metallic hard rock ("Streets," "Two Hearts"). *Missing in Action* is inconsistent but still good.

"The only other band from our area that we were friends with that went same route self-producing vinyl was Slaughter Xstroyes," Linas recalls. "If I could offer advice on producing a record, it would be: Make sure everybody is on board. All members of the band must have an investment. Having no manager means that someone needs to take charge making the decisions. In a band where I was late to the party, after a while it became my party, at my own expense. Too easy for people to walk away at the slightest criticism from within or even outside of the band. You'll never sell out an album and grow the following if you can't tour the album. By that time, it's almost too late to assess people's commitment level ... If you saw the movie *The Dirt*, it would be the same example as Vince Neil listening to his girlfriend. Left me with a bit of bitterness toward the first lineup guys who appeared on the album. As a result, I own everything—the name, the rights, trademark, publication. Nobody else wanted to step up. Making an album on your own is expensive!"

Nineteen kept it up until 1989, releasing one more demo cassette in 1988, *The New Breed*, which I sadly couldn't find anywhere. Members of Nineteen didn't appear to play in any bands after the band's breakup, and Linas adds, "I have been removed from music for so long ... Today's problem is you don't know what's good. Everything feels disposable and sterile. Back 20 or 30 years ago, you got album jacket inserts, you could read who they thanked, who produced it, where it was recorded, who was credited, photos from shows, lyric sheets, et cetera ... Even album artwork gave a little peek into maybe a concept album or a band's identity. There is an abundance of music, so you can't rely on likes or numbers of downloads. And I don't talk to enough people to know or hear about what's good that's underground or not really discovered yet. That was our job at the record store. That said, I am astounded our *Missing in Action* album sells today for 30 dollars. I had a hard time getting rid of the ones I had 30 years ago for five bucks!"

WINTERHAWK

WINTERHAWK IS ONE OF THOSE BANDS THAT, IN THE PRE-INTERNET DAYS, enjoyed massive cult status and were one of the first to find their first, independently released record, *Revival*, get a reissue in the 1990s. Formed in 1977 in Chicago, Illinois, guitarist and founding member Jordan Macarus narrates:

"Every band has a story, and there are similarities and differences. Our story is very disconnected. I learned some guitar as a kid outside of Philadelphia—a little inspired by The Monkees and The Beatles, could play a few songs. We moved to Downers Grove, a Chicago suburb, when I was ten; then I bought drums from a friend for 60 dollars when I was 12 and started playing in a 'band' at 13. Then I moved over to guitar when our guitar player moved to Florida. And from age 15 to 17, I played some rock covers with a band named Rage that was me, Paul Filinovich, and Mike Powers. And then Winterhawk started when I was 17."

CUT TO THE CHASE:

Get *Revival* at any cost, whether you are a rocker, a fan of progressive rock, or a metal fanatic. This is one of the few occasions where the quality of a record reaches unimaginable heights and also has something for everyone.

Regarding their influences, Jordan mentions, "We dove right in for the short time we were really together. For Doug Brown, I think it was the James Gang and Joe Walsh. Steve Tsokatos, well, he could listen to everything! He managed Tempo Records in Downers Grove when I met him. As for me, early on, it was Deep Purple, Ted Nugent's *Tooth, Fang & Claw* and *Call of the Wild* from 1974 (before he lost his supposed Native American spirit). Yes' *Going for the One,* and catching a lot of bands working concerts. As a stagehand in 1980, I got to watch Frank Zappa rehearse, which was the greatest single music lesson of my life. I took guitar lessons from Nick Brown, Steve Brown's older brother, a fantastic rock and jazz guitarist who wound up as a session player and career musician in Los Angeles.

"The bar scene was good at first, from 1977 to 1979, when the drinking age was 19. Then it really tightened up for original bands," Jordan recalls. "We were sort of a phenomenon in our hometown, but not too much else. Although we did well opening for a few touring bands: Budgie, Jefferson Starship, Black Oak, Steppenwolf, and a few more..."

Jordan also sheds some light on the somewhat confusing Winterhawk story, describing the lead-up to the recording and release of their first LP, *Revival*, on their own Lambda Records in 1982: "After Doug and Steve Tsokatos quit together in 1980, Chris Mazur ('Maze') and I went to college. (Way more affordable back then.) And while there, we revisited the tapes, talked to Doug Brown about getting back together to make a record. He brought along Scott Benes, and Maze and I did some studio/producer research and found Dr. Caw, referred by Mike Rasfeld and Danny DiSilvestro, and launched the record project.

"Steve Brown did the album cover, and we did everything as efficiently as we could, with not much money," Jordan adds. "We rehearsed for seven weekends, then recorded for like a week—for 110 studio hours. We signed Doug and Scott to a deal so we could try to gig for a year, and then evaluate where we were. Doug and Scott quit about six months after the record release. The underlying problems with Doug and me were rooted in our first meeting in early 1977. Drummer Rich Mezger said he wanted to start a band with me, and we started banging out a few ideas. Then he told me that Doug Brown and guitarist Dan Searight wanted to audition, and that they were willing to split up if we didn't want them as a team. I was more interested in a keyboard player, like Deep Purple, than a second guitar, but they were both so good that we just got started. The problem was that we were doing the audition in my parents' basement, and I kind of ran the audition; but Rich had told Doug and Dan they were auditioning me..."

Jordan continues: "So, I think Doug always thought I was kind of arrogant or Machiavellian (and I'm sure I was some of that), and that stayed under his skin since I sort of took the reins and started writing a lot once I heard him sing. (Doug is still one of the greatest all around talents I've ever known.) But since Rich was the first guy to get kicked out or leave the band, neither Doug nor I knew about the 'manipulated' initial meeting. Doug 'always' thought I was auditioning for them, and I thought the reverse. About six months after making the record, Scott and Doug quit for the last time."

Revival is one of the most adventurous and fascinating records the American hard rock/ metal world of the 1980s ever offered. It actually crosses over different territories, balancing between the progressive rock of Rush and Yes, the melodic and lyrical hard rock of Scorpions, the fist-pumping hard rock of Thin Lizzy, as well as the early proto-metal elements of Deep Purple or even Southern rock. Charming, melodic, progressive, yet still catchy, songs like "Period of Change" or the amazing "Free to Live" are unbelievable—but then again, *Revival* as a whole is top-quality.

"I am happy that, with Winterhawk, I had the chance of playing so many excellent gigs," Jordan smiles. "In the old days were the big crowds with Jefferson Starship in 1980, the record release at NIU in Dekalb, Illinois, in 1982, and several great shows with the 1982 live band, including Doug Brown, Scott Benes, Rex Carroll, and Chris Mazur. But since our reformation in 2006, there are so many great ones: the shows we did with BOTD, Alehorn at Double Door with Slough Feg and Manilla Road and more ... Ragnarokkr in Chicago, Athens in 2013, the 2018 Keep It True in Germany, so many..."

After the band's first breakup, Jordan followed a solo career, releasing a good number of CDs, and the name Winterhawk reappeared in the 2000s with the release of the *There and Back Again* CD (live and unreleased material) album in 2002 and the *Wind from the Sun* CD in 2003, which includes early nineties recordings. Winterhawk got back together in 2006 as a gig band, finding fertile ground in the new generation of metalheads.

When asked about other indie bands from the Downers Grove area, Jordan says, "Just like us, there was a young band in the early 1980s named No Secrets, a rock band from the same hometown. After us, there were some heavier bands and some other good younger bands..." And as for the renewed online audience for Winterhawk's records and privately released metal in general, he replies, "Haven't really thought about the resurgence of interest in the 1980s metal. Sounds cool! Bands that are in a good position to tour can do all right, if they stay after it. I'm honored about *Revival*, and I'm glad it's making money for some folks out there. We benefited from some of that.

"It is what it is, and that's probably cool," Jordan concludes about the current situation in the music industry. "Like I implied in my long story above, the future of economics in my head is where we get paid to conserve resources, regenerate the soil, water, airs, bees, et cetera—and don't lose ourselves in an economic system that rewards a lot of greed and has lost touch with those fundamentals of life on Earth. I'd like to make enough for a dignified honest existence, and to kick some live music out once in a while. There's a lot of amazing music out there, and this access gives people opportunities to hear many diverse things."

IVORY TIGER

FORMED IN 1986 IN CHICAGO, IVORY TIGER WERE ONE OF THE MANY GREAT metal bands the Windy City offered. Formed by Kenneth Eichmann (bass) and Michael Salisbury (guitars), both ex-members of Orphan Allies, their intention was to release some good American heavy/power metal in line with the metal bands of their generation. "Soon enough, Timmy Petersen (of Vengeance) was added on drums, and we also got a fantastic vocalist whom we knew from the Chicago metal scene, Bob Hoffman, from a band named Axis," Kenneth says.

"It was all about making great metal music; we loved Queensrÿche, but at the same time, we had so many different influences. Heart was a band we all loved ... we also didn't want to be 'bar stars,' a.k.a. a cover band that would please the audience with covers that had already been played to death," he adds.

Ivory Tiger didn't lose any time; they were already stalwarts of the Chicago metal scene as members of Elixir since 1980, the band that evolved into Orphan Allies, and were very confident about their musical stance. First was the 1986 Demo (*Demo 86*) that they released on cassette, containing six pure metal songs with definite influences from Dio, Black Sabbath (Dio era), Judas Priest, and early Queensrÿche. There are some great moments of raw, unpolished heavy/power metal here, such as "Ride the Wind" and "Prisoner of the Mountains & the Sea" (with its heavy Dio style!), as well as the thundering "The Stand." But this demo was nowhere near the greatness the band later achieved!

CUT TO THE CHASE:

Ivory Tiger's *Metal Mountain* is a real pearl of eighties American metal. This is one of the most classic and flawless records of that era you can get, and I have to give the band extra points for not having an obvious Iron Maiden influence (unlike their many peers!). Classy, totally unique heavy/power metal. Also check out Orphan Allies and their 1986 *Running from the Law* LP—it's absolutely great as well!

"We were desperate," Kenneth recalls. "Michael was frustrated that we still couldn't get a record deal off a label—it was very hard getting signed—so we recorded our own four-song EP and had *Metal Mountain* printed on vinyl in 1986 on our Ambush Records label."

Metal Mountain is one of this book's most mandatory records to get, if you want to understand what privately released American metal is all about. This is a total rager, professional to the max and at the same time as heavy as the purest metal can be. The production was done at Solid Sound Recording in Hoffman Estates, partly by Michael Salisbury and by an unknown producer named Steve 'The Outlaw,' and it offered Ivory Tiger all the beef they needed for their sound. These are four glimmering tracks of incredible American heavy/power metal—among them the absolutely crushing "Stand Up (Watch Out)" and "Chandar," and the title hymn "Metal Mountain." Here, Ivory Tiger sounds way more unique than they did in their demo, as though they were finding their own style.

"I have very fond memories of Ivory Tiger times," Kenneth recalls. "Like the 1985 Alpenfest show that was packed and everybody went crazy. We were definitely one of the first metal bands in our area to release our record on our own, and we had a small—but dedicated—following in the area."

Even though they attempted many times, record labels didn't end up signing Ivory Tiger—they were unluckily too heavy for the glam/metal crowd and too slow and melodic for the fans of the thrashers who were dominating the metal charts in that era. So, in 1989, the band moved to Florida and changed its name to Amber Rose, taking on a more melodic metal approach. Amber Rose split up in 1992, which was also the end for Ivory Tiger.

The Greek label Cult Metal Classics heard the pleas of hardcore metalheads who were asking for this rarity to be re-released, and voilà, in 2017 *Metal Mountain* got a reissue as an LP containing all of Ivory Tiger's songs, both from the demo and the EP. "Of course, there is a strong and vital underground metal scene," Kenneth replies when prompted. "Even today, now and then, I get messages asking me if I was the bassist of Orphan Allies and Ivory Tiger! But then again, I still love music, I still love playing just for my personal pleasure, in a small band, no matter what the musical style is. This is my life!"

HAMMERON

CHICAGO WAS SURELY ONE OF THE PLACES IN THE U.S. THAT OFFERED loads of high-quality metal acts in the eighties, and Hammeron are a prime example. Formed in 1980, Hammeron is also included as an exception in this book, because they released their first LP on the tiny, now-classic Chicago indie label Silver Fin Records. I was torn between including them and Paradoxx, the other Silver Fin heavy metal band, but decided to write about Hammeron because their *Nothin' To Do But Rock* LP is a huge classic.

"Hammeron was originally formed by Peter Pagonis (drums), Mark Cutro (guitars), Carlos Basili (guitars), Scott Guigliardio (vocals), and Vito di Palma (bass) in 1980," guitarist Mick Vega says. "However, the lineup that released *Nothin' To Do But Rock* didn't even include one founding member! It was me on guitars, Danny Vega on bass, Brian Trǫch on vocals, Jack Lazor on guitars, and the late Jeff Ward on drums. We had so many influences, ranging from Queen to

Queensrÿche; however, we were always closer to Iron Maiden and Black Sabbath, in the Dio and Ozzy era. I guess, though, that it was *Killers* by Iron Maiden that was a tremendous shock for all of us, a record we could all identify with."

HAMMERON ON THE COVER OF THE JUNE, 1985 ISSUE OF *ILLINOIS ENTERTAINER*

Their regional popularity earned them a slot on the various artists compilation *Chicago Class of '85* (released by Silver Fin) with the track "Marching Off to War," a hard-hitting yet accessible metal song written by guitarist Jack Lazar, who writes most of Hammeron's original material with bassist Danny Vega. Rounding out the group are lead screamer Brian Troch and drummer Jeff Ward, formerly of Powerage. Ward replaced Pete Pagonis, who hit the skins on "Marching Off to War." At the time of this release, Mick Vega indicated that the group plans to record an eight-song demo of original tunes, then shop for an independent label deal.

Then in 1986, the Silver Fin label called on Hammeron once again for their track "The Only One" on the label's *Chicago Metal Works Battalion #2*, another massively exciting anthem of pure heavy metal. However, nothing could predict what would follow when the LP was released.

"Chicago was always treating us great, even though the local scene was highly competitive," Mick adds. "The scene back then was so vibrant, and there was so much enthusiasm from the fans ... we offered many memorable shows through our existence. However, there are two shows I recall most fondly. One was opening for Mötley Crüe at the Limelight, for MTV's Halloween Horror Special, during their *Theatre of Pain* tour. The other one was at the Thirsty Whale with Manowar ... actually, the show with Manowar was a turning point for us toward a heavier sound."

Ready to explode, Hammeron couldn't wait anymore, so they grabbed the chance Silver Fin offered them, and in 1986 they entered Tanglewood Studios in Brookfield, Illinois, to record their debut album *Nothin' To Do But Rock*. Mick discusses their choice to accept Silver Fin's offer:

"It all started in 1985, when our drummer Jeff Ward was working with the local booking agent Tony Labarbera, who was also the founder and owner of Silver Fin Records. Tony included us in the two aforementioned compilation LPs, creating a real buzz around our name, and it all came as a natural progression—we had to put out our record on Silver Fin! Back then, there were no CDs yet, so we did records and cassettes of our first LP. No Pro Tools obviously, and compared to today, it was a real challenge."

With the excellent production by engineer Frank Pappalardo, Hammeron on *Nothin' To Do But Rock* were hitting their apex; heavy, emotional and straightforward metal, with influences

CUT TO THE CHASE:

Hammeron's *Nothin' To Do But Rock* is just a great example of how great was the self-released metal in the 1980s. Professional, emotional, sincere and honest metal played by fans of this style, with great songwriting and a starting point of influences being Iron Maiden and Queensrÿche. Also get the 2014 *Wired for Sound* LP that collects their later demos, which might not be as good as the first LP, but still they are decent. You really need *Nothin' To Do But Rock*, though—this is U.S. private metal at its best!

ranging from Iron Maiden to Queensrÿche and Dio/Sabbath, *Nothin' To Do But Rock* is surely one of the highlights of this book. Songs like the opening bulldozer of "Silent Victim," the melodic masterpieces "Why Lie" and "So True" as well as the superb epic "Sands of Fyre" are tremendous offerings by a band that should have kept it up. Bands like Heir Apparent, early Crimson Glory, and of course their fellow Chicagoans. Paradoxx, Decoy Paris, Ironhawk and Ivory Tiger come to mind when one hears this record. Chicago had a very specific heavy metal sound that was melodic, yet not wimpy or commercial, and it's present here in spades.

"Many bands from Illinois self-released their stuff back then," Mick says. "War Cry, Paradoxx, Cuttlass, Vengeance, Felony, Zoetrope, Love Hunter, Demented Ted, and many more." In 1987, Hammeron released a demo for a second album, which remained unreleased up until 2014, when the Greek label No Remorse Records gathered their 1987 demo and the later *Sponges* demo and released them all on one LP, aptly named *Wired for Sound*.

By 1990, Hammeron were no longer together; however, all the members of the last lineup pursued great careers in rock and heavy metal. Jeff Ward played in Ministry, Lard, Low Pop Suicide, Nine Inch Nails, Pigface, and Revolting Cocks before committing suicide in 1993. Mick Vega played in Beyond, MadDog, Sindrome, Rising Up Angry, Damien Thorne, and The Plague. Jack Lazor was in Widows Rose and Aleph Null, while Pete Pagonis went to Damien Thorne (and released the great heavy metal LP *The Sign of the Jackal*). Brian Troch was very active, playing with Shooting Hemlock, Znöwhite, My Infected Soul, Cyclone Temple (appearing on their excellent power/thrash *I Hate Therefore I Am* LP), The Reign of Terror, Flywater, Rising Up Angry and Taz. Danny Vega also played in Widows Rose, Cosmic Fury, the excellent thrashers Aftermath, Lost Cause (a brilliant crossover combo), Aleph Null, Bunker Hill, Mind Bomb, and Roller.

"It seems to me so strange that *Nothin' To Do But Rock* has become a collector's item, with people paying big bucks to get it," Mick adds. "I mean, I like it, but I can't understand it! It's flattering though."

Hammeron broke up in 1990 and never reformed, with members playing later in the abovementioned bands. "I think that there will always be an underground metal scene, whether this is big or small; new people are always getting involved and bring their energy to the underground. And the fact that people today can acquire music easily is just perfect; the more music gets out, the better it is both for the fans and the bands. I don't get people who moan over downloading music..."

DECOY PARIS

ANOTHER GREAT BAND TO EMERGE FROM THE THRIVING 1980S METAL SCENE of Chicago, Decoy Paris formed from the ashes of Head First (a band that you can read more about in the last chapter) in 1985, featuring John Nomikos (bass), Wes Overall (guitar), and Lorenzo Joseph Martinez (vocals), and to be later accompanied by Vince Ochwat (drums).

John Nomikos says, "The formation of Decoy Paris came to be when Wes, Larry, and myself were in a five-piece band called Head First in the early 1980s. We played locally in some clubs and decided to record a 45 that was released in 1984. We only printed 1,000 copies, just as a promo. After some musical differences, we parted ways and became a four-piece band. The key to that was finding a superior drummer. Then came V.V. Machine (Vince Ochwat) on drums, and we became Decoy Paris in 1985. Played the local circuit for a while and decided it was time to record some originals. We went into the studio in 1986 and recorded the *Love on the Run*

CUT TO THE CHASE:

Decoy Paris is one of the classiest acts of this book. Their finesse and style are totally over the top on the *Love on the Run* EP. One strange thing is that they can appeal both to those who are into melodic metal as well as fans of true metal, but I guess that this has to do with how their sound uses only the best elements from the melodic metal style of the eighties. Plus they do have a pretty heavy sound! Get *Love on the Run* in its original form, but I would also check out the Shiva Records re-release because the box set of this release is unmatchable!

EP, and it was released in 1987. Again, we only printed 1,000 copies for the promo. In 1998, we released a CD with the old songs and added four new originals. That's our story!"

John describes how Decoy Paris developed their unique sound: "Wes and myself were raised in a musical family, which only enhanced our love for music. My grandfather and mother both played violin on the Greek island of Amorgos, where they were born. Wes' parents were musicians and singers here in the U.S. Larry and Vince just had it."

John continues, "The motivation for forming a band was the love for music. It was always my dream as a child, and it never left me. As far as the influences, all the great bands in our era! Led Zeppelin, Deep Purple, Black Sabbath, et cetera. But the most important one that did it for me was Grand Funk. Once I heard Mel's thunderous sound and playing, that's when I started playing the bass. I had a minibike, which I loved, and traded it for a bass guitar after hearing Mel. Started playing, and I never looked back."

The Chicago scene was very competitive at the time, John adds: "The scene where we lived wasn't like California, of course, but we still did well and were treated with respect." Decoy Paris released their first twelve-inch EP in 1987, *Love on the Run*, on their own label, Head Start, upon which they also released their earlier band Head First's seven-inch. "There were also other bands in Chicago that did private releases, like Paradoxx, and Ironhawk. We decided to put our records on private press because we felt we had a good product, and whether we were able to get a record deal or not, we wanted our music out there. We produced our recordings and had control of the releases."

Love on the Run is an excellent prototype amalgam of hard rock/metal that's a little more on the metal side, without the cheesiness of the American hard rock of the time. One could say that it's melodic metal, and this classification isn't far off from what Decoy Paris attempts. The result is superb: catchy and totally professional tracks that bear resemblance to Fifth Angel or a rockier Queensrÿche (as in the fantastic "Secrets of the Heart,") or the pounding "Love on the Run." This EP is surely a hidden pearl in the ocean of private metal releases.

The song "Take Me in the Night" was also included on the *Chicago's Class of '87* compilation, and Decoy Paris played shows locally, with John offering, "My favorite show was our record release party. It was a big success and had a great crowd ... we were blessed by having a great road crew, led by Mike Luczak. They made us feel like rock stars!"

Decoy Paris never signed with a "big" metal label, but they continued along their way in the underground, initially up to 1999, releasing the *Decoy Paris* CD compilation in 1998 (again, on their Head Start label), which included *Love on the Run* plus five new songs, again in the same musical style. After a big pause from 1999 to 2015, Decoy Paris are active as of 2021, and at last, their *Love on the Run* record got a great reissue treatment from the Greek label Shiva Records in 2014.

"I think the resurgence of interest is a wonderful thing," John adds. "As far as the EP's price as a collector's item, I'm happy for the collectors and honored to be a part of it. But I think it's more about how rare the records are and not as much about the music ... I do believe that an underground metal scene exists, due to the fact that today's music is nothing like the old days, in my opinion. But as far as the downloading of music goes, I'm not really a fan. Some of my best memories were when a new album was released: I couldn't wait to go to the record store, buy the album, and go home, play it, and look at the album cover while it played, wishing one day it would be me. The anticipation and excitement of the whole experience was awesome! But unfortunately, this has been lost now in the digital age."

SORCERY (CHICAGO)

ANOTHER EXCEPTION TO THE TIMETABLE RULE, BUT AN INEVITABLE ONE, since Sorcery was one of the most significant bands of their place and time in terms of privately released American metal. Formed in 1976 in Chicago, Sorcery's two self-released LPs remain to this day a metal collector's wet dream. Drummer Kieran Hoening tells me, "Sorcery was formed in the mid-1970s by Kirk Bryk (Brykowski) and Paul Koster. Guessing 1975 or 1976, Kirk was on lead guitar and vocals, Paul on rhythm guitar and vocals. Having gone through less dedicated musicians to fill their voids of drums and bass, they approached a few members of a local garage band called Spectrum to fill their needs. I was their light man at the time. John Mrozek was the drummer and a very good one, with above-average vocals! He tried out and easily won their approval! They also grabbed the bass player, Chuck Dorrington. He was eventually dismissed but did come back at a later date to run sound for a time. I was brought on shortly after to run lights and effects."

Kieran continues, "Kirk and Paul were extremely dedicated! Practices were Tuesday, Friday, Saturday, and Sunday and usually lasted at least three hours. That band was together for approximately two years. John, though an outstanding musician, had his problems with feeling ill or other excuses and missing practice. Kirk and Paul wouldn't have it, and that eventually became his demise. He did become a very prominent drummer in the area all the way until his death in 2011. He was still a great friend 'til the end. Being good friends with John since the fifth grade, I always messed around on his kit. He taught me a few things, and I had a small kit of my own. Kirk and Paul wanted me to sit in just to keep them in practice. I was a little torn because of friendships, and I thought there was no way I could keep up with those guys!! Well, I did fill in, all along thinking that I was doing just that? After a few months, they told me they wanted me to be their drummer. I was like 'No F-in' way!!!' They said that we would figure out a way to get me a new kit and they were happy with me showing up for practice and giving my best effort. Needless to say, in a short time, I was sitting behind a brand new Tama Imperial Star 12+1, a monster kit at the time, which I still have. Dave Maycroft was added playing bass, a coworker of Paul's. He wasn't very good, LOL. Don't get me wrong, haha, neither was I, but I worked hard to get better and did, and ... Dave didn't. To continue my thought, John also shared the lead vocals mainly with Paul, singing the higher parts. So, after he was let go, here was that void to fill. We tried out several candidates and ended up giving the lead vocals to Tim Barrett."

Sorcery was maybe one of the first American metal bands that displayed a Black Sabbath influence and went on to progress it the American way. "Our biggest influences for the band started with the almighty Black Sabbath!" Kieran smiles. "Paul was fanatical about them, and Kirk was a huge fan of Tony Iommi's. I loved them as well! The early days of the band contained cover music as well as originals. A lot of the covers were Sabbath! Haha! We did copy some lesser-known bands such as Captain Beyond and Hawkwind. We also dove into some of the mainstreamers at the time, including Kiss, Nugent, UFO, and Montrose, to name a few. But again, any of Sabbath's earlier albums would fit into the category of most impressionable for us, up to *Technical Ecstasy*. Kirk also was a big fan of Hendrix's.

"The local scene was just that," Kieran adds, regarding the Chicago rock and metal scene of the day. "Chicago, being a large market, had everybody and their brother in a bar band! There were plenty of bar venues in the area to go out to see local acts at, any day of the week. Haymakers, Beginnings, the Thirsty Whale, and the Edgewater were a few of the often frequented on the circuit. Sorcery was not a circuit band. Kirk was more content to rent larger halls and promote our own shows. That statement could have been eventually Sorcery's demise? The self-promoted shows cost a lot of money and happened too few and far between ... Between the shows was just the long practices four nights a week or, in the latter days, messing around with studio work. Which was also a big expense! Sorcery was kind of isolated because of that. We were definitely the loudest band, though, in the land. Plus playing an all-original slate, we were maybe viewed as nonconformists? We didn't care! We were still dedicated to our cause, and those that didn't like it could simply fuck off."

Sorcery went on to release their first (masterpiece) album, *Sinister Soldiers*, in 1978. and they were so confident about their work that they managed to do a whole double LP of 50 minutes of music—a very rare, if not the only, occasion in the privately released records of American

CUT TO THE CHASE:

The *Sinister Soldiers* double LP will appeal to a variety of different crowds. From epic metalheads to those into hard/heavy crossover, and even fans of psychedelic hard rock, this LP will strike them all hard—it is certainly one of the most classic releases ever in American metal. The *Till Death Do We Part* LP is still very good, but I find it to be less wild and adventurous than *Sinister Soldiers*, plus it sounds in places like Sorcery wanted to aim for a more commercial side. Again, though, this is another great hard 'n' heavy release. Both LPs go for ridiculous amounts of money among collectors nowadays, so always be sure that you're getting an original and not one of the bootlegs that appeared after 2000.

metal. "While John was still the drummer, the band had gone into a small studio in Evanston, Illinois, to do some demo tracks of our original music," Kieran mentions. "Likewise, after I became drummer, and new music was created when we went back in to that studio for more demo work. All the time thinking it was for promotional reasons. Tim was not there yet for the newest demos. He was brought in on a periodic basis to put his vocals on the tracks. Having had the taste of the studio work and becoming better at my drum skills, I started to lobby for Kirk to get back in to record a real album. Several months went by, a few gigs and of course practices. I forget—where were we? We were traveling in our van somewhere, a little drunk and disorderly. That's when I would usually lobby Kirk, and one day, all of a sudden, he hands me the first album! Shocked would be an understatement, but excited! Couldn't wait to get home and play it! I did so and was somewhat disappointed. Even though it was an album, it was sometimes overproduced and sometimes underproduced demo work. Not to mention that 'Fly the Sky' had John's drums on it and not mine...

"Paul immediately quit the band," Kieran says. "Being the founding member, not being included in the production, and the final product was too much for him to swallow. The shame of him leaving was that the band lost the creator of some of its dark lyrics! (e.g., 'Schizoid,' 'Arachnid,' 'Snowshit') Not only that, he coached, encouraged, and pushed me personally to get to where I was at, skill-wise."

I don't share Kieran's disappointment with Sorcery's first LP; *Sinister Soldiers* is a terrific piece of classic early American metal—not proto-metal or whatever, but actual pre-NWOBHM American metal, heavy and rough. The band put the album out in 1978 on their own label, Century Records, and the result was like a cross between Deep Purple and Black Sabbath. Sorcery managed to release a hands-down classic double LP, with killer songs like "Fly the Sky," the beautiful instrumental "Sugar Sweet Lady," and the menacing and pounding metal explosion of "Schizoid." If I could compare their style with other American bands of the day, these would have been Manilla Road and Survivor. (The *All Your Pretty Moves* band from Shreveport, Louisiana, not the pomp/AOR rockers of the same name.)

Sorcery also enjoyed playing gigs in the Chicago area, creating a small fan base. "The Woodstock Opera House was my first gig, and a really cool place to play," Kieran says. "I wasn't very good at the time but got through. Some of the others were the Rialto Square Theatre in Joliet, Illinois. A beautiful place, much too nice for the likes of us. Hemmens Cultural Center in Elgin, Illinois, was a perfect acoustical room, even with our volume! Once, we promoted a large party to include 50 kegs of beer and like five different bands. We had a professional stage and light system set up in the middle of a field. We had a great turnout."

In 1980, Sorcery put out their second (and last) self-released LP, *Till Death Do We Part,* on their label, Sentry Records. With a more rock 'n' roll influence that's evident mostly in keyboard-driven songs such as "Ogre" and "Borderline," this is an actually very good LP, though not as brilliant as *Sinister Soldiers*. This time the influence of Black Sabbath was reduced, and Sorcery headed for a more Deep Purple meets Rainbow meets Cream sound, but still songs like "Ruby Red" and "Right to Survive" hold the Birmingham style. Also check out the striking "Fly Away," with so many melodies reminding one of Ashbury or even Scorpions.

Regarding why they went with private releases, Kieran states, "The only person who would know the whole story is Kirk. My best guess is because Kirk was the money behind the band. He created Century Records, once again fitting in the mode of self-promotion. I'm not sure if there was some copyright infringement with the Century title? Once again, that is only a guess, seeing as though the label was changed to Sentry Records on the second album."

Sorcery disbanded quietly in late 1980, and vocalist Tim Barrett later performed with Aleister Crowley, Canterbury (releasing a private rock LP in 1981), and Sea of Monsters, among other bands. Sorcery never reformed, and their case remains one of the biggest what-ifs.

SALEM'S WYCH

ONE OF THE TRUE METALHEAD'S HOLY GRAILS WAS RELEASED BY Salem's Wych, a band that formed in 1983 in Bridgman, Michigan. Bassist Keith Jann narrates their story:

"Salem's Wych had already been through a few lineups before I joined the band in 1984. I was good friends with Bill Neff, and we happened upon each other one night, at which time he told me about how he had been jamming with Mark for a while. They were looking to record a vinyl EP to use in a promo pack to try to get signed by a label, and at that point, they had been having trouble finding the right guys for the band. They needed a bass, another guitar player, and a vocalist, and that was my beginning with Salem's Wych. After a few trials and tribulations, we finally settled in on Tom and Ron in late 1985 or early 1986. We recorded through the spring and into the summer of 1986, and then Mark was able to put it all together and get it pressed on vinyl. We figured out that a full album wasn't going to be much more expensive than an EP, so since we had enough songs for a full album, we went for it. We released the album on October 31, 1986, on Halloween. Mark worked at a local record shop and through their connections was able to get some distribution help for our album. It's been rather amazing to me how *Betrayer of Kings* has become such an underground metal vinyl classic over the years and am very proud to have been a part of such a classic! On a little side note: I was 18 years old when I joined the band and turned 21 a week after the album's release. I was the youngest, Bill and Tom were about a year older than I was, and Ron and Mark were the old guys, haha!"

With the lineup stabilizing as Keith Jann (bass), Bill Neff (drums), Tom Bronicki (guitar), Mark Gast (guitar), and Ron Johnson (vocals), Salem's Wych was influenced by many greats of heavy metal as well as other diverse influences. "For me, I grew up with a musical family, so I have a lot of different genres of influences, but I had an older sister with a pretty cool vinyl album collection full of sixties and seventies rock 'n' roll, and I loved to listen to her copies of Black Sabbath's *Master of Reality* and *Paranoid*. They were an early influence before I played the bass. About the same time that I started playing the bass, which was age 16, I was at a friend's house and told him I was playing the bass, and he asked me if I had heard any Iron Maiden, and I said no, so he put on *Number of the Beast* and it completely blew my mind to hear the bass played that aggressively! So yeah, Steve Harris and Iron Maiden and Geezer Butler and Black Sabbath, as far as metal goes, were definitely it for me. Salem's Wych was perfect for me because Bill, Mark, and I definitely thought alike. Of course, Bill and Mark also had their own personal influences as well. Later, when Ron and Tom joined, we had already written most of the material, so they had a little bit of input, Ron more than Tom."

Even though in northwest Michigan there were also bands like Medieval, things were rough for bands of southwestern Michigan. "Here in southwest lower Michigan, back in the early to mid-eighties, the music scene didn't favor bands that were playing original material," Keith adds. "Any music hotspot wanted cover bands. Also, at that time, if you weren't a 'metal' band with guys basically dressed up like girls ('posers' was what we liked to call them), the venue didn't want anything to do with your band. Radio stations, even the more underground stations, wouldn't play local original bands. It was very disappointing, believe me! Of course, with a name like Salem's Wych, we scared all the locals, LOL, we were being accused of being devil worshippers and sacrificing small animals. It was crazy! The only thing being sacrificed back then with us was a lot of Budweisers! And of course, the time we were sacrificing trying to achieve our lofty goals of rock 'n' roll stardom! At one point, we had a really nice lady who wanted to try to start a local regional magazine to try to support the local music scene. She was from northern Indiana and featured all genres. But local religious groups came after her because of her support of the metal scene and our band, around that same time that you had Congress debating whether to start rating albums due to their content. She even had threats of violence if she didn't stop her support of metal bands and our band in particular. Vinnie Vincent and Dana Elcar of the Vinnie Vincent Invasion were on tour in our area at the time and even came into town to try to help bring to

CUT TO THE CHASE:

Betrayer of Kings will definitely please everybody who's into the epic or true metal sound, since it includes some absolutely great songs—prototypes for this kind of music. Epic, mysterious, barbaric, but very catchy, _Betrayer of Kings_ has some moments of unbelievable greatness. Fans of Omen, early Liege Lord, look no further.

light that this lady was being threatened just because she was publishing a magazine that also supported metal. Sadly, it eventually resulted in her giving up on the idea..."

But Salem's Wych didn't give up, and went on to record and release their first LP in 1986, on their own label, Metal War Records. The album was titled *Betrayer of Kings*, and Keith tells how it came to be:

"I'll have to give Mark props on this one. When I ran into Bill that first day, that was the first time anyone I ever jammed with in our area had come to me with an idea of that nature. Like I said, this area of Michigan at that time was not big on booking original bands into the venues in this area. So, the idea was to produce an EP at first, get some band pics and a band biography together for promo packs to send to bigger labels, to try to get signed. Back in that day, we didn't have the internet, so you needed the backing of a big label because of the costs involved with production and pressing and getting distribution—quite a monster to conquer. Especially when we were working day jobs at the time as well. Mark knew that John Zilke had a professional eight-track recording studio at his house. We started by getting all the drum tracks down, then I laid down the bass tracks, then Mark laid down all the guitar tracks except a couple lead fills by Tom. Then vocals came last, and then Mark did the final mixes and produced a master tape. Then he and Randy Locatis were able to find someone to do the pressing and cover production. Mark had a local artist, whose name escapes me right now, volunteer to do the artwork for the album with Mark's visual concepts.

"Once we had the finished product," Keith says, "just to add some hype and creepiness to the whole Salem's Wych album release, we released it on Halloween. We also released the album as a cassette tape. On the production part, Mark wrote the guitar parts, did the arranging, wrote the lyrics. Bill and I wrote all our own parts and helped in writing the musical aspects of the songs. So, Bill and I had major input and say as to our instruments and the tracks laid down for the album. So, while Mark definitely did most of the legwork, the musical aspects were more of a collaboration of ideas and riffs that we'd come up with together while trying to write as many songs as we could. There were probably four or five song ideas that didn't make the cut once we decided to produce a full album rather than an EP."

Betrayer of Kings not only has a fantastic fantasy cover, but some of the most barbaric heavy metal ever is included in this LP! Heavy and menacing, epic and catchy, it kind of reminds me of Omen's *Warning of Danger* mixed with Medieval Steel and Sinister Angel. "Never Ending Battle" is an eternal epic metal hymn, and so is "Run from the Devil," whereas "Fight to the End" is simply menacing! Even though *Betrayer of Kings* has its mediocre moments, this shouldn't turn you off, because when Salem's Wych nail it, they do it really hard.

When asked about other private hard rock/metal releases, Keith says, "John Zilke, whose studio we used, put together a project called Atlantis and the record *Straight Through the Heart*, and he released a pressing a little while after we had ours out." Salem's Wych did play a good number of shows throughout their existence, and Keith tells me, "Our first big gig that Randy got us where we opened up for Yngwie Malmsteen in La Porte, Indiana, is simply my all-time favorite. We played in front of about 5,000 people and I was scared shitless but had an awesome time. In 2015, the Ragnarokkr metal fest reunion gig at Reggies Rock Club in Chicago was great! We didn't have a lot of time to get ready for that gig, but the crowd that night loved us anyways! They knew the lyrics and sang along; it was an experience I won't forget!"

Salem's Wych called it a day initially in 1988, and Keith says, "Eventually, back then, it resulted in Mark leaving this area for Los Angeles and the breakup of the album lineup. His leaving for California was very disappointing for me, but he was being told by major labels that in order for Salem's Wych to be successful, he had to either move to the East or West Coast. So, he moved to the West Coast."

In L.A., Mark Gast played in Raging Storm with no luck, and Salem's Wych got back together in 2000, recording an album that was sadly never released. Keith adds that, after appearing and disappearing in the 2010s, "We did that reunion gig at Ragnarokkr in Chicago at Reggies. In talking to Mark at that time, he told me that he wished like hell that he would have done it different. He didn't regret the move, but he did wish that he would have at least kept Bill and me in the band. Ron and Tom, after the album's release, kind of wanted to head in a different direction, while Mark, Bill and I were metal to the core. So, there was several reasons for the album lineup's demise." Salem's Wych state remains unknown even today, but I suspect they are on hold.

"Nowadays, there is great support for original bands in our area, and with the internet, the sky is the limit depending on how hard you want to work at it," Keith concludes. "As an old-school guy, I love my old collection of vinyl! Can I have bitter moments about the internet? Sure I can. Can I have positive internet moments? Hell yeah! You and I would be having a much more difficult time trying to communicate! I love the fact that the internet has created a worldwide community of vinyl enthusiasts and enables them to shop across the world for their favorite classic albums! The fact that an album that I helped put together and we worked our asses off for back in 1986 has become a worldwide vinyl metal collector's classic just boggles my mind! I'm proud and honored to have been a part of it all! So, thanks to the internet and social media and YouTube and Facebook, local bands have a huge open path to get their music out into the world. Unlike back when you had to hope you could get signed by a label to have a chance at success. If a band can get a video to go viral on the internet? You never know! So, while I'm old-school and love my vinyl, I can never say that artists having more avenues to get their own material out is a bad thing."

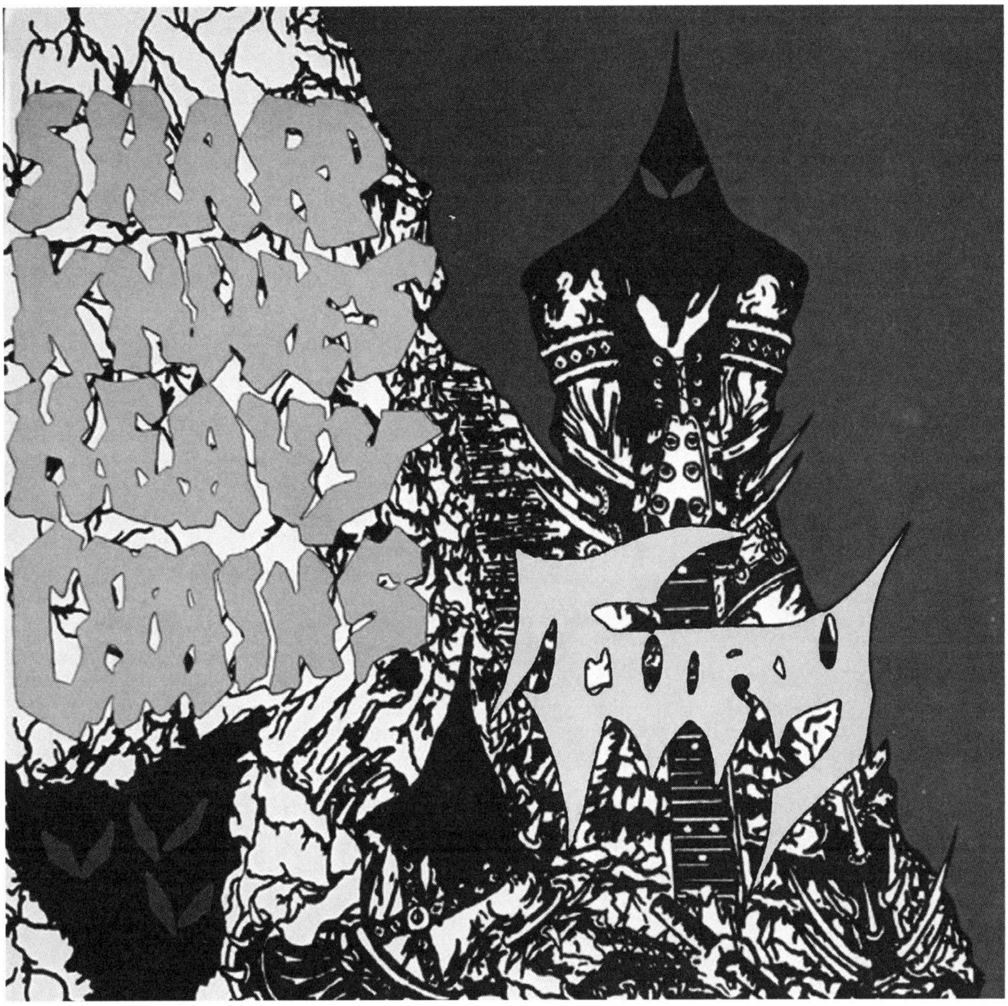

FURY

FROM HAMILTON, OHIO, FURY WAS ANOTHER CLASSY CROSSOVER HARD rock-to-heavy metal band that had roots in the 1970s. Initially describing their sound as "energetic hard rock," later in the eighties Fury went on to become a fully metal band in terms of sound. "Fury was formed by me, Nick Rotundo, on guitar, and Jimi Dee Gadd on drums in around 1981," Nick narrates. "I had been in a band called Midnight Lightning. Jimi Dee Gadd had been in several local bands prior to Fury. Me and Jimi Dee had heard of Pat Bishop (bass guitar), who was playing in another local band. We approached Pat and asked him to come and jam with us. We then asked Pat to join the band. He did. We then heard of Don Delph (vocals), who was playing in a local band, asked him to come and jam. Don was then asked to join the band. Fury was born!

"Our musical influences were pretty much everything hard rock and metal during the late 1970s and early to mid-1980s," Nick says when asked about the band's influences. "Some of our favorites during that time period were Y&T, Thin Lizzy, Saxon, Motörhead, Van Halen, Krokus, AC/DC, and Aerosmith. Jimi Dee was a big Steven Tyler fan. Two records were instrumental (pardon the pun) in my development as a lead guitarist: *Smash Hits* by Jimi Hendrix and Van Halen's first album."

In 1978, Fury released their first demo, containing three songs of proto-metal hard rock, a very promising cassette. "We were one of the earliest hard rock/metal bands in the Hamilton/Fairfield/Middletown/Cincinnati area," Nick offers. "So, to most of the older locals, we were too hard, loud, and raw (which was a nice compliment, haha)! Bogart's and Annie's in Cincinnati were our favorite places to play."

Nick also recalls Prizoner and Centaur from their area, citing them as "some metal bands that have had an impact on us," adding, "Fury did a show with Foghat in 1983 at Bogart's in Cincinnati, which stands up until today as my favorite show with Fury. But my personal favorite and most memorable show was playing some songs with Lonnie Mack at a couple of his gigs in the early 1980s."

Five years after their formation, and with the American metal wave ready to explode for good, Fury decided to record and release their first twelve-inch mini-LP, *Fury*. It came out in 1983 on their own label, Furyous Records, and Nick describes what led to its release:

"We were turned down by most major labels of the time in 1983—the exception being Geffen Records ... but that did not work out. Bill Halverson saw Fury live at Bogart's, contacted us, came to a band practice (in my parents' basement), and then asked us if we would like to make an album that he would produce/engineer. We said YES! We then recorded the *Fury* twelve-inch at QCA Studios in Cincinnati with Bill producing and engineering the album. We then had the completed album distributed globally. The album inserts were put into the albums by us, by hand—we had control of everything."

The *Fury* twelve-inch will shock even the most hardcore metalheads with its ultra-heavy sound. The drums and guitars literally sound like they are going to explode, even though Fury are still a hard 'n' heavy band and not power/thrash metal. However, in terms of quality and style, I find *Fury* uneven. There are great heavy metal tracks (such as the excellent "Bonified Freak" and "Time Waister"), but on the other hand, the Southern rock-influenced "Potted Delite" and "Closet Case" are pretty mediocre. *Fury*'s best track is the opus "Flash Four," a hard rocker's wet dream, but overall, I find *Fury* to be a mixed bag.

"This resurgence of interest in private records/bands is partly fueled by the lack of quality material being produced/released by the major labels, I believe. The major labels have always been 'false' and 'posers,'" Nick adds. "Also, in the early 1980s, major-market commercial radio stations were also just like the major labels, 'F & P,' to the extent that local Cincinnati's WEBN-FM radio station would only play bands like Fury, AC/DC, Accept, and UFO after midnight on a Saturday night! It is very gratifying to have the Fury releases still being enjoyed by people all over the world! For me, it has been and still is all about being able to create and perform music that people dig and enjoy."

A rehearsal tape was released in late 1983 and contained covers of Jefferson Airplane ("White Rabbit"), Alice Cooper ("School's Out"), and Montrose ("Rock the Nation"). Fury was one of the few exceptions to the American private metal rule in that they went on

CUT TO THE CHASE:

Fury's *Sharp Knives, Heavy Chains* EP will appeal to all those who are into the raw metal sound of NWOBHM—with a special American metal touch, of course—and it is recommended. The *Fury* twelve-inch, on the other hand, is good, though not essential.

to release another record on their own in 1984! The twelve-inch EP *Sharp Knives, Heavy Chains* was released through their own Furyous Records, and this time Fury headed for an all-out-metal approach. Reminiscent of Judas Priest (*Killing Machine* and *British Steel* era), with a NWOBHM flavor of Savage and Saxon, *Sharp Knives, Heavy Chains* contained four songs, with the title track and "Brutus" being the absolute highlights. Overall, this is their best moment and is the record that will appeal most to fans of true metal. This raw style is something I dig so much.

Fury never got the attention of record labels, and they went on to disband later in the mid-1980s. Nick Rotundo still plays and performs music, while Jim Kekic also played in Valiant.

"I do believe there is an underground scene. In today's world, the indie/underground scene is more of a home-recording kind of thing," Nick says. "Downloading has been going on since the invention of recording devices. However, it is much easier today. To me, downloading is a double-edged sword. Bad for making any mônev from artist creations. Great for exposure and gaining more fans. 'Sometimes you have to spend money to make money,' or, as I called it back in 1985 on the *Sharp Knives, Heavy Chains* EP, 'live for the money today.'"

DEAD SILENCE

ANOTHER BAND THAT CROSSED OVER FROM HARD ROCK TO HEAVY METAL, Dead Silence from Denver, Colorado, is a band that left its footprint on American metal history with only a single seven-inch—but what a seven-inch it was!

Formed in 1980, guitarist Brooke Besser says, "In the late 1970s, I was playing in a band that played stuff that wasn't really my cup of tea. We had a progressive jazz drummer, a black funky guy on bass, and a second guitar player who was into jazzy stuff. When we did rock songs, we didn't do them well. We had a young singer/guitarist who was always looking for a better gig. When he did find something else and the bassist went into the Army (without ever mentioning that little fact to us), the band broke up and I was ready to move on. I eventually answered an ad in the paper and found Ed, who was with a drummer. I went over and jammed with them, and we ended up playing UFO's 'Rock Bottom.' We kind of hit it off because UFO was one of my favorite bands and Golden Earring was Ed's favorite band. We eventually started looking for a bass player and all moved into a rental house together. We went through a couple bass players, and eventually the drummer left. We went through auditions of dozens of terrible drummers and we finally found Perry, who was 18 years old and just came over from Hawaii. We parted ways with the bass player and went to the newspaper again, where we eventually found Ken on bass, and we were set. This was sometime in 1980."

Brooke goes on: "We were interested in doing originals and hard rock music that was not played on the radio every day. As well as playing a lot of Scorpions, UFO, lesser-known Aerosmith, Alice Cooper, Golden Earring, et cetera, which was one of the reasons that we didn't really make it into the big A-level clubs. Me and Ed made a pretty good songwriting team, so we had visions beyond just playing other bands' music. Not a lot of bands in the big clubs played original music. I am not sure if they didn't write original songs or if the big booking agencies just wouldn't let them play them. The band was pretty much relegated to the B-level clubs around town and finding other gigs.

"Our biggest musical influences were anything that had to do with Michael Schenker; so UFO, Scorpions, and the Michael Schenker Group," Brooke adds. "We played a lot of Scorpions, some UFO, and a couple Michael Schenker songs ('Rock Bottom' was always our big closer). Ed was a huge Golden Earring fan, and so was I, so we did several of their songs ... but the most influential album was probably Scorpions' *Animal Magnetism*. This was primarily because it came out at the time we were putting songs together. We did four songs off of this album. For me, this was not Scorpions' best album, as I thought *Lovedrive* was their best album at the time, but the songs were new and more straightforward to play."

Dead Silence didn't follow the glam metal trend that was just starting to emerge and focussed mostly on the music, with a sheer passion for the 1970s hard rock sounds. "The music scene in Denver was primarily bands playing cover songs with the goal of being on the road with the big talent agencies. Playing original music was not really the thing. I think we were kind of unique, in that most of the other bands around were probably more concerned about their hair and the size of their PA system. We were not in any way a big hair band. I would consider us more like UFO back in the late seventies. We were pretty normal guys who were not all glammed up. That just wasn't really us; we didn't have that look."

However, Dead Silence were also impressed by the new metal sounds arriving from the UK too; NWOBHM had already been producing tons of privately released stuff, and by 1984 Dead Silence had been together for four years, having not yet released anything. "We eventually decided that we needed to try to see if we could actually land any type of recording contract with our original music, so we took what we thought were our two best original songs and decided that we would record them," Brooke adds regarding their seven-inch. "We had a little foray into recording on a four-track recorder that our sound man borrowed from a friend. I actually bought the recording equipment and we just did it in the basement of the house. We recorded 'Can't Stop' and 'Dead Serious,' found a company to press the 45 RPM vinyl record. We had maybe 150 records pressed, which we signed and sold many at a record signing party, and sold them at gigs. It is unclear whether these signed copies are more valuable than the unsigned version. Unfortunately, our Dead Silence T-shirts were bigger sellers than the records...

"We sent them out to record companies," Brooke continues, "only to receive back rejection letters about the material was not strong enough, and many that simply said that they don't accept unsolicited recordings. While the record companies gave us the cold shoulder, the rock critic for the *Denver Post* actually reviewed the record. His name was G. Brown, and he said the songs were as strong as anything he heard being played on the radio. Unfortunately, we didn't even know of this review until somebody later brought it to our attention. I had to go dig through a friend of my parents' recycle newspaper stack to find it. It didn't do us any good in the end, but at least it was some reinforcement that the songs were decent.

CUT TO THE CHASE:

Dead Silence's only seven-inch is a real treat, not just for people into the "retro" [sic] metal sound of the early 1980s, but for all fans of American metal too. Check out the band's Facebook page by searching for 'Dead Silence 8085.' Back to the seven-inch: Any fan of early Riot will love it. Its quality is undeniable, so record labels, take notice and re-release all their stuff on a compilation LP!

"This was pretty much the end of the purpose for Dead Silence," Brooke says, "and shortly after, Perry informed us that he was going back to Hawaii. We tried but never could really find another drummer, and eventually the interest in the whole thing, at least on my part, began to wane until eventually the band fell apart. Before Perry left, I had him lay down all of the drum tracks to 17 songs. I had gone in and done a click track that Perry could play along with. After Perry left, me and Ed spent the next few weeks laying down the rest of the instruments and vocals to the songs. A lot of these songs were in pretty raw form, so I went and wrote additional guitar parts for the songs. There is one song, 'Run Again,' which was a song written and sung by me that the band never did at all. In the process, we remixed 'Can't Stop' and 'Dead Serious,' so they sound much better than on the record. Unfortunately, we didn't have all the songs perfected while we were actually playing."

The (ironically named) *The Long Silence Is Over...* seven-inch was released in 1984, and I'm not exaggerating when I say it's an absolute classic of eighties American privately released metal records! Everything here is totally professional, from start to finish: the production is not muddy at all—on the contrary, it's super powerful. In terms of songwriting, the two songs ("Can't Stop" and "Dead Serious") are full of unbridled, unparalleled enthusiasm! "Can't Stop" is a galloping—and phenomenal—rocker, like a mix of early Iron Maiden with UFO, featuring killer lead guitar work and a great chorus, whereas "Dead Serious" kicks off with a total 1970s melody (akin to Wishbone Ash), and progresses into a melodic powerhouse, sitting comfortably in between hard rock and heavy metal, while in the end it explodes. Absolutely top-rate material! Tremendous stuff here, people!

Dead Silence kept it up until 1985, performing live locally in Denver. "As far as the club scene went, our best venue was a bar named Sam's. It was up on Lookout Mountain, just west of Golden, and overlooked Denver to the east. This was a big club back in the days of 3.2% beer for 18-year-olds that used to have a 'drown night' every Wednesday with all-you-could-drink beer. So, drunk 18-year-olds driving down a mountain late at night, what could go wrong there? However, that preceded Dead Silence, and the bar was still popular, but not as much so at the time. The memorable thing for all bands was the fact that the bar was close to a lot of radio and TV towers, so everything that we plugged into electrical outlets buzzed horribly. The only partial solution was to wrap everything in aluminum foil, including amps and cords, then play loud enough to cover up the buzzing. We played there regularly and always had a good time with good receptive crowds. The best single gig we played was an event put on by a friend of Ken's that he called 'The Major Rager.' This was outdoors with a big scaffold stage, kegs of beer, and LOTS of people. This was definitely the closest we came to a big concert feel. This is where our live promo shots came from."

In 2011, Dead Silence released a compilation CD, also named *The Long Silence Is Over...*, that contains all their recorded material, plus previously unreleased stuff, and as you can imagine, it is totally mandatory. Too bad that a record label didn't offer them a contract for a record release. This means that this (self-released) compilation is a total rarity. "We weren't really plugged into what other bands were doing, but I have my doubts about them releasing any records," Brooke responds when asked about other bands in Denver that released records on their own.

"The resurgence of heavy metal surprises me," Brooke adds. "It has been going on for a while, though. Years back I was contacted out of the blue by a guy from Georgia. He sent me a letter, finding my address through our copyright claims to our songs. Not knowing anything about this whole vinyl collector's thing, I sold him several of our records for five bucks. I later stumbled upon the fact that he had sold them on eBay for around 45 bucks each, so I figured out that scam and don't do that anymore. However, there are others who are trying to do the same thing. I actually listed one record on eBay to see what would happen, and it sold for around 17 dollars. However, instead of the guy actually paying me, he wanted to buy a whole bunch more for cheap. I just recently had a couple people from Facebook trying to scam me out of the records. I haven't quite figured out if these record collectors look for any record by any obscure band, no matter what the quality of the music or the recordings, or whether the music has to be good. If it is the latter, then I am flattered that our music is sought-after. However, if they are interested in the music, we have better recordings of the two original songs on the 45 plus another 13 songs on MP3 download sites."

Brooke concludes, "There is probably an underground scene since modern-day music has become so lame. We have unfortunately reached a point where I believe that rock music is almost dead, at least in the United States. All of the interest in the Dead Silence material is from Europe. I think that being able to distribute music so easily online is great; however, it is fraught with the ability to obtain the music for free. I would like to see our songs sold and receive a few checks, but at this point, I am more interested in keeping our music alive online, whether people download it for free or not. Otherwise, they are just files sitting on my computer that will not see the light of day."

TYRANT'S REIGN

FORMED IN INDIANA IN 1984 AND THEN RELOCATING TO CHICAGO, TYRANT'S Reign are one of the most raging and ferocious bands included in this book; their power/speed/thrash amalgam is simply menacing, and bands of this style like Agent Steel or Realm pale in comparison. Drummer Gabriel Anthony tells their story:

"We formed in the early 1980s in Indiana, and then moved into the suburbs of Chicago, with Karl (Miller, guitar) and Randy (Baron, vocals), with other previous members Jeff Bagherpour (guitar) and Carlos Reices (drums). Tyrant's Reign recorded an unreleased three-song demo (*Without Warning*) and the style of the band then was more rock than metal. I was recruited to replace the drummer, we practiced, wrote, and did gigs, and then a year later, Chris Nelken (guitar) came into the band. With this current lineup, everything really started to get more serious.

TYRANT'S REIGN PROMO PHOTO COURTESY GABRIEL ANTHONY

"For everyone in Tyrant's Reign, our goal was to collaborate and just express common interests in music and to put a band together to perform and join our growing and vibrant local music scene. Personally, when I joined Tyrant's Reign shortly after that early demo, I had introduced thrash metal and my heavier background, and we all gravitated as a band into that style more. I remember way back at one rehearsal, I brought three albums to show the guys; it was Motörhead's *Ace of Spades*, early Mercyful Fate, and Metallica *Kill 'Em All.*"

In 1986, Tyrant's Reign released their second demo, *Untamed*, and the change of direction was already evident. Bombastic, catchy, and super-powerful power/speed/thrash metal that sounded like no other band—actually, Tyrant's Reign predated bands like Powermad or Realm. They are just in between the aforementioned styles, like a harsher early Overkill, a more manic Anthrax, or a more melodic Metallica. Check out "Kill or Be Killed" and your head will explode! But this was just the beginning...

"Nowadays the scene is very different, but years ago, when metal and rock were commercially popular, there were many rock, metal, and other genre bands around Chicago," Gabriel explains. "The city and suburban music venues were all around and offered killer sound stages and lighting for bands. Local music fanzines were in every record store to advertise as well. it's very sad for up-and-coming bands, I think, now. Then, most music fans in our town were metalheads or rockers."

Tyrant's Reign decided that it was time to release a record as soon as possible, and this was the 1987 EP *Year of the Tyrants* on their own label, Cynical Records. Gabriel narrates:

"After trying to achieve a beneficial record label for support that we needed, we decided to release our music ourselves under our own label. I started Cynical Records. We had followed the example of many metal bands and the worldwide metal fan base with pen pals through many metal magazines. Word of mouth and performing and touring with other out-of-state thrash and metal bands and selling our music and merch. Although we still pursued that distribution deal with a recognized record company and had signed with outside management The band had played many local shows and sold merch to put ourselves in the studio and record *Year of the Tyrants*. I worked in a local printing company, I had artist friends, created the EP artwork, perfected the trademarked logo, and had our first 500 EPs on vinyl pressed. I distributed and networked for consignment deals with local, national, and international record stores to sell our records."

CUT TO THE CHASE:

You really need Tyrant's Reign's *Year of the Tyrants* EP, especially if you are a fan of the raw, über-powerful, strikingly amazing American power/speed/thrash that very few bands played to such perfection! I love the fact that they have also filtered hardcore/punk influences into their sound, but for you true metalheads: Don't think this is a crossover record. It is manic metal, played at unbelievable levels of belligerence. Now, the bad news: You'll get very few chances to find the original on Cynical Records, but you can get the reissue on the German label Heavy Forces Records. Could we hope for another reissue soon?

Year of the Tyrants is just unbelievable! Some of the craziest, over-the-edge metal to be recorded on vinyl is what blasts through your speakers when the needle hits the record. Yes, Slayer or Dark Angel or Sodom might have been way more brutal, but this is like comparing apples and oranges, since Tyrant's Reign retain their classic metal approach—even though this is played to the maximum ferocity. What I also actually love on this record are the touches of hardcore/punk that come out of nowhere (like on "Jack the Ripper" or "Reign of Terror"), all filtered through their passion for pure metal. Each and every song smokes, and this is a record that would appeal equally to those who are into bands like Helstar and Holy Terror, as well as those into early Slayer or even crossover hardcore!

Tyrant's Reign imparted their sheer sonic power to many shows during that time, and as Gabriel recalls, "We had played a local high school auditorium when our popularity and metal music was at its peak and Tyrant's Reign was a local force to be reckoned with. We had a pyro tech who had brought real concert flame towers (during sound check, we watched the high flames on each side of the stage touch the auditorium ceiling, in fear of catching it on fire). The show was a packed house of friends, families, metalheads and rockers. I even remember stage diving into the frenzied dense crowd after that show. We sold a lot of our merch and we had become a household name to the metal community. This is by far our favorite show!"

Gabriel also remembers the thriving metal scene of Chicago: "There were so many underground bands, and this is including some bands you may have heard of who actually got that deal like Wrath and Realm. Or others like The Gruesomes (punk metal), Quick Change (thrash metal), Mortor, Neurotoxin, and so many other bands started independently releasing..."

In 1989, Tyrant's Reign released another excellent demo (*Judge & Jury*), with three songs ("Passage to Eternity" being one of the best they ever wrote) of wild power/thrash. Sadly, they split up in 1990, with members appearing over the next decades in bands like David Shankle Group, Revelation, Spirit Web, Winterkill—as well as original guitarist Karl Miller, later guitarist Michael Giordano, and bassist Phil Fouch playing with their old band, War Cry.

A live album was released during their hiatus (1998's *No Your Not Dreaming...Tyrant's Reign Live*) that included the show at the Jabberwocky in Milwaukee, Wisconsin, in December of 1987, and the band were back together in 2003, releasing the compilation CD *Tyrant's Reign* (later to be re-released as a double LP named *Fragments in Time*) the following year. As of 2021, the band is still together, playing local shows and exclusive appearances in festivals.

"I think it's amazing that the young metalheads are checking out Tyrant's Reign," Gabriel smiles. "Bands today still make great music, and the production of it has gotten so much better, but the music is a sign of times, it's not like it was then. I believe the younger generation of metalheads are hearing this and finding this out now. Tyrant's Reign and I personally are grateful to know that our music has inspired and reached so many worldwide. I really want the band to record new material and actually had started the process; it's harder now only because, as I say, for all of us, life gets in the way. But never say never! We have two tracks in the works. After all, we have to make it in the underground that is still existing and still growing! I see it every day. Also, look at South America now. There's a new generation of metalheads. New metal today is kicking ass.

"I think when the world and humanity face trouble, metal music becomes more popular—it's a vent, a release," Gabriel concludes. "The power of metal is strong and forever, and its fan base is loyal like no other. As of today, with internet and downloading music: Yes, bands get around much faster, and there is so much out there. Everyone is a record producer and a label with a computer and a recording program at home. Yes, it's different. Not as personal, like when you're looking through an album, seeing the pics, and reading the lyrics and credits while listening to its contents. Bands lose when their music is simply copied, shared, and posted. Yes, it's great for popularity, but it's like baking boxes of free pastries: soon, you run out of dough..."

XCEL

XCEL FORMED IN 1985 IN PORT NECHES, TEXAS, AND WHILE THEY WERE VERY short-lived, their musical output was tremendous. Kevin Cox, founder and lead guitarist, says that "Xcel was basically made up of the remaining members of the band Wizzard. Peter Voight (bass) and Barry Duncan (guitar) were in Wizzard when I went to watch them play, and I knew Peter from playing high school football together. I joined Wizzard shortly before their original drummer quit due to other obligations. Peter, Barry, and I auditioned drummers and singers immediately. Dag Gabourel (drums) and Kevin Luke (vocals) were the last remaining pieces. From there, we started writing original material."

"I remember meeting Kevin Cox at football practice," Peter Voight agrees. "We hit it off right away. We had a lot of the same taste in music. From that day on, we have been close friends. It was the love of metal that formed Xcel."

"For me, it was the love of music," Kevin corroborates. "Specifically rock. I grew up as a child listening to my older brother's Led Zeppelin, Deep Purple, and Black Sabbath albums. So, I was exposed to that genre of music sooner than most kids my age. Then, when I was a little bit older, I discovered Kiss, and I was forever hooked. I wanted to learn guitar, and I wanted to be Paul Stanley. My brother snuck me into a Blackfoot concert when I was probably nine years old. A couple of years later, I finally convinced my parents to let me see Kiss. My brother took me to see them when I was about 11 years old. My parents finally bought me a cheap electric guitar when I was 15 or 16, and I would sit and learn anything I could pick up by ear. I would go and watch other local bands and knew that I wanted to do that too.

"I eventually auditioned for a band called Wizzard that Peter and Barry were in," Kevin continues. "Barry was leaving for another band, and they had suggested that I audition to replace him. I ended up playing with Wizzard and writing original material for them. Barry eventually wanted to come back, and Peter, Barry, and I decided to form Xcel to do original material with a fresh start."

"Yes, it was the love of music for me as well," Peter says. "Just like Kevin, I had older siblings, so I grew up listening to Led Zeppelin, Black Sabbath, Deep Purple, Bachman-Turner Overdrive, and Grand Funk Railroad. I would have to say that Kiss played a huge impact on me."

As for their influences? Xcel were just great fans of the hottest metal around. "Our biggest influences would have been Queensrÿche, Iron Maiden, and Judas Priest," Kevin mentions, and Peter agrees. "I think you can hear their influence in our music. For me personally, the biggest and original influence for me was the album *Alive II* by Kiss. I studied everything about that album. I was also inspired by Ozzy's *Blizzard of Ozz* and *Diary of a Madman*, Queensrÿche's debut EP and *The Warning*, and Iron Maiden's *Number of the Beast* and *Live After Death*. In recent years, I have really been into bands like Primal Fear and Dream Evil. Both of those bands were the direction I saw Xcel heading toward if we were still going. That was the sound I was striving for in the music I was writing."

However, things for Xcel weren't a bed of roses in their small Texas town. Peter says, "Country and western music was the music of choice for live bands in our little area of Texas. It was hard being a heavy band that played 95 percent original material. After a short while, people started to take notice, and we started to build a reputation as a great live band." Kevin is way more denouncing, adding that their hometown scene was "In short, horrible. Where we were from, it was mostly country and western and cover bands. I don't think people knew what to make of us with original material. I would say we had a decent following locally, but we always knew we needed to branch out beyond our local scene. Unfortunately, the music scene nationally was starting to change toward a more grunge sound, like Nirvana and Pearl Jam."

Xcel were committed not to give up so easily, and they were determined to release a record—and what better way than to do it themselves? "Our intent was to do exactly what Queensrÿche had done with their EP," Kevin says. "We all loved them. So, we thought we should do an eight-song album. We felt that it would show anyone interested that we are willing to do the work and that we definitely had the drive. The owner of the recording studio added us to their label for the pressing of the album. These guys were really nice and flexible with us, but unfortunately, they didn't know how to mix a hard rock album, and we didn't know enough either to step in and change things. This studio mainly did only country and western music. So, I don't think they were they were sure what to do with wide-open Marshall amplifiers and one of the hardest-hitting drummers around.

"For me," Kevin continues, "the *Deliver This Dream* album is both a source of pride and embarrassment. Our music was far better than the way the recording sounded. I think if you had seen us play live, you would see the difference, and people would tell us how much heavier we sounded than the album showed. We picked eight songs that we thought would give interested parties a variety of the things we were writing. In my opinion, the newer material we were writing was better than what is on the album. I loved the new songs and was eager to press them with an engineer who knew what they were doing. Unfortunately, that never came to fruition. So, there is at least one more Xcel album that no one will ever get to hear. The fact that *Deliver This Dream* is still hanging around after all these years stuns me. I've always felt that if you liked that stuff, then you would have really liked the newer stuff."

"We knew it would be the best way to get our music out. Apparently, it worked, because 33 years later, we are still talking about it," Peter says. "We could have done a lot of things differently while recording it, but we just had no idea at the time what we were doing and put all our trust into the hands of someone who had not recorded a heavy band before. I agree with Kevin that *Deliver This Dream* is both a source of pride and embarrassment. Now, that said, I think the reason it has lasted so long is that the quality of the material was really good, even though the recording of that material was not. I so wish we could have recorded another couple of albums so the newer material could have been released. I think it would still be relevant today."

Deliver This Dream was released through Xcel's label Tri Records in 1986, and what a beautiful piece of classic American metal it is! Everything here is over the top—except for the weak production, but it still evokes tons of nostalgia and offers so much authenticity. From the amazing "Vision" to the powerhouse "Hold Your Faith," and the sparkling "Beware the Night" to the Maiden-like "Deliver This Dream," this is one of the best records that the eighties-era American underground metal scene ever released! All the quality and youth passion of early Queensrÿche, mixed with early Dickinson-era Maiden, but filtered through an epic and melodic style, this LP is not to be missed.

Xcel played a good number of shows during its existence, and both Kevin and Peter mention the same show when asked to choose a fave. "Without question, our January 3rd, 1986 debut show at the Port Arthur Civic Center is my favorite," Peter says. "We took a page from the Kiss playbook and wanted to come out big. We put that whole thing on by ourselves, bought airtime with a local radio station, had ticket giveaways, and promoted it entirely on our own. The radio station would not help us at all and completely ignored us. So, we bought time and forced it down their throats. We sold it out, and there was still a line outside the door. They started stamping hands. There has been no other band since to pull that off the way we did. I think that is something we can claim as being true to this day, and I am really proud of that. It caught attention from bigger cities and ultimately landed us with a manager based out of Houston."

Contrary to what most people believe, the 1987 *Last Ride of Ichabod Crane* seven-inch wasn't released independently, but on the small California-based label Accent Records. This seven-

CUT TO THE CHASE:

Ah, *Deliver This Dream* is simply a must-have for everyone who's into early Queensrÿche, early Heir Apparent, or Bruce-era Iron Maiden (up until *Powerslave*). This is one of the best LPs to ever come out of the independent American metal scene, but be warned: It is really hard to find nowadays!

inch included different versions of the two songs ("Teaser" and the title track) that were previously released on *Deliver This Dream*—again, though, fantastic stuff. Sadly, this was Xcel's swan song, and the band never reformed nor released anything else.

"The only other band that I know that released anything from our area was Akela," Peter recalls when asked about the indie scene on the Gulf Coast of Texas at the time. "I think they released an album. I know they were on a show called *Star Search* here in the States..."

Deliver This Dream gained massive cult status among metalheads the next decades, and Kevin says, "I had no idea that *Deliver This Dream* is a highly paid collector's item. But I am honored, fascinated, and amused by it. I truly am. We put our hearts and souls into that band, and I enjoyed every second of it. It killed me when we broke up, and I still miss it dearly. However, I don't quite understand what the interest is all about. It excites me to a degree because I am confident the unreleased material was far better. I would hope the interest is because people genuinely liked Xcel as opposed to it just being something pressed privately and hard to find."

Peter adds, "All I can say is I had no idea that I would still be talking about *Deliver This Dream* 33-plus years later. I am honored by it all."

As Kevin concludes, with Peter agreeing: "I think the underground scene may be alive and well in Europe. If there is a scene in the U.S., that is news to me! The music in the U.S. is complete garbage. It is autotuned, overproduced nonsense. That is what sells here. Therefore, we don't get a lot of good bands coming through here unless it is a major act. I had much rather see a real musician get up there and make mistakes and everything. I can do without the dance moves, backup singers, and lip synching. As far as music being accessible via downloading, I am okay with that. However, I do think the artists should be compensated for their work and efforts."

IRON CROSS

THIS BAND RELEASED ONE OF THE MOST SOUGHT-AFTER PRIVATE METAL LPS, which heavy metal record collectors worldwide consider a holy grail—even in times when vinyl records were ridiculously cheap, this LP was very expensive to get! Iron Cross was formed in the Pensacola, Florida, area in 1979. Friends Tony Blair (drums, vocals), Mike Skelton (guitar, vocals—R.I.P. 2014), and Max Chuites (bass) were the original three members, and they played their first show as Iron Cross on New Year's Eve of 1979. Tony and Mike had a love for seventies hard rock, especially the theatrical bands and the macabre, and this influenced the band's sound and image.

After a few changes, Iron Cross' lineup became Mike Skelton (vocals, guitar), Rex Alan (guitar, vocals), Dan Bippes (bass, vocals), and Tony Blair (drums, vocals). "We mainly just wanted to emulate the bands who influenced us the most," Rex admits. "Black Sabbath,

CUT TO THE CHASE:

Are you into bands like early Omen, Satan's Host, or early Jag Panzer? You really need the 1986 *Iron Cross* LP. It's by no means an exaggeration to say that this is a crowning moment not just for private metal, but for American metal in general! Rough as hell, this is blue-collar power metal that will demolish your house.

Kiss, Alice Cooper, Uriah Heep, and Deep Purple. For me, the most significant record was Kiss' *Alive*. I was a true Kiss fanatic in the 1970s.

"Back in the day, the scene in Pensacola and nearby was very active," Rex tells me. "There were many heavy metal bands, like Azrael and Naphobia, to name a few. And the locals treated us very well. We filled most of the local venues, and we put on shows ourselves and had as many as 2,500 to 3,000 people show up." The music style of Iron Cross didn't follow the slick (or so-called "white-collar") American heavy/power metal. With influences ranging from some of the heaviest NWOBHM (like Witchfinder General and Angelwitch) and Judas Priest at their heaviest, Iron Cross were a truly monstrous act—something that's evident in their first, privately released 1986 LP, *Iron Cross*.

Rex describes the release of their first LP:

"We put the record out on a private label as the few record deals we were getting offered were very one-sided. Most of the labels wanted you to sign away the rights to your songs, which we refused to do. So, we just decided to do it ourselves. What was the procedure behind its production and release? It was recorded at Main Street Recording Studios in Winter Garden, Florida, over about three months' time. My big brother, Michael, financed the album for us, so we weren't pressured to move very quickly. We just booked the studio for 12 hours at a time, usually overnight, just got in and recorded and worked on the material."

Absolutely crushing, demonic, raging, American power metal of the highest class was the result! *Iron Cross*' initial pressing was just 100 copies, and to this day, it remains one of the most beloved records to the fans of American power metal. As mentioned, they sound like a pumped-up, testosterone-boosted NWOBHM band blended with the perfection of American metal (in terms of technical proficiency and production), and you simply can't go wrong with songs like the menacing "Demons," the heavyweight pounder "Dark Dreams of Evil" (which boasts exceptional vocals), the opening rager "Demon's Disciple," or the crushing cover of Angelwitch's "Angel of Death." This is just perfect American power metal played with absolute ferocity. It really can't go much harder in this style!

Sadly, in their heyday, Iron Cross never received a proper contract from a metal label, and that's a damn shame because their recorded output that followed the *Iron Cross* LP was still phenomenal. The *Die Like That* 1987 cassette EP and 1988 *You Could Die Like That* demo were even rawer—just power metal to the max. Songs like "Die Like That" and the Motörhead/Iron Maiden-ish "Queen of Deception," and "Arch Angel" are wild and crazy. Something that should be mentioned, though, is that Iron Cross never gave it up, and although the band hasn't got many releases under its belt, it's been continuously active since 1979!

"The most dedicated Iron Cross fans are in Europe, hands down," Rex says. "The best Iron Cross shows, then, should be the one in Athens, Greece, and then at the Keep It True Festival in Germany."

Two compilation albums of Iron Cross songs were released in 2000 and 2001—the 2000 one being a splendid double LP released on O.P.M. Records—and the band self-released their *2004 American Tour* CD in 2004. Luckily, the Greek label Eat Metal Records reissued the *Iron Cross* LP in 2017, so new generations of metalheads could enjoy this masterpiece.

"Definitely there is a huge underground scene today," Rex says. "You can be successful and very popular without any label support whatsoever due to the internet. It's helped bands like Iron Cross stay alive. I think that downloading is a great thing too. I was a big fan of Napster and hated to see it go. I would check out a song or two then go buy the CD or album after I made sure it was something I wanted to purchase. It really helps the fans also. If they just have a favorite song, they can just download that and pay for it, and the bands are still making something from it. We'll see where it goes in the future though."

The record collectors' market has caused the price of the *Iron Cross* LP to skyrocket, especially in the last ten years, and Rex concludes, "I think that the interest in small, private bands of the 1980s is really great. For us, it couldn't have come at a better time, and it helped cement our place in metal history. However, the fact that the *Iron Cross* LP has fetched such insane prices truly blows my mind. I hope that they're buying it for the music and not just for the collectible value!"

WINTERKAT

IN SAN ANTONIO, TEXAS, WINTERKAT ROSE FROM THE ASHES OF LIQUID SKY, a band that had appeared on the 99.5 *KISS Homegrown* radio station compilation LP in 1981. Guitarist Jonathan Grell had appeared in that group and formed Winterkat with vocalist Ric Swanson, drummer Gerardo Ramirez, and bassist Dean Vallecillo (the latter pair both being ex-Heyoka members).

"Yes, Winterkat was formed from members of Liquid Sky," Jonathan confirms. "Perhaps you heard the song 'Cry for the King,' written by myself and Steve Cooper. It was a passion that started in junior high school and ignited when Liquid Sky made it onto the radio.

"The South Texas rock scene was thriving when I grew up," Jonathan recalls. "We were treated well locally and regionally, enjoying airplay on the major rock stations and nurtured by one of the all-time great DJs, Joe Anthony, 'The Godfather.' The inspiration for Winterkat was progressive rock bands like Yes, Rush, Saga, et cetera, and also classical music, especially J.S. Bach. As a guitarist, I was influenced by Schenker, Uli Roth, Al Di Meola, Christopher Parkening, Segovia, et cetera. Later on, I got into the blues greats."

CUT TO THE CHASE:

Fans of Dokken, Ratt, and fairly more obscure bands like Letchen Grey will enjoy the two Winterkat records, as well as those into Praying Mantis or even Ten!

In 1983, the band released a self-titled five-song mini-LP on their own Winterkat Records label. Although Gerardo Ramirez played keyboards on the album, Ruben Castaneda from San Antonio AOR band Myth was used for live shows, and Jonathan adds, "We were young and didn't know any better. That's why we decided to put out our records on our own, haha! However, it worked and got us on the air and playing with national acts..."

The band's 1983 *Winterkat* mini-LP has five songs of catchy ultra-melodic hard rock/metal, with great tracks such as the opening "Dreamer," "What Do You Want (Out of Your Life)" and "Let the Music Take You." Mid-tempo or ballad, the songs on *Winterkat* sound surprisingly mature, and it is definitely recommended for metalheads who want a little pause from the harsher sounds. I dare say that, in some cases, Winterkat remind me of Praying Mantis!

Changes in Winterkat's lineup later took place, with Ric Swanson leaving to form AOR band Nightwork in 1985, releasing a self-titled album in 1986. He was replaced at the Winterkat mic by Michael Steele Grothues, another former Heyoka member. "I can recall one other band that was putting out records on its own," Jonathan adds. "It was Ultra, my old guitar teacher's band."

Another mini-LP, *The Struggle*, was issued (again on their own) on Momentum International Records in 1985, featuring a cover of Jimi Hendrix's "Little Wing" and a rendition of "Minuet III" by Bach, alongside three originals. Heavier than before, with more metallic tendencies, *The Struggle* has great songs like "The Light of Day" and "Life of Changes," and is a step forward in all aspects.

Winterkat struggled on until the early nineties, but by this time, many of the band's key players had moved on to other projects. Bassist Dean Vallecillo went on to join Minneapolis band Dare Force, performing on their 1989 *Firepower* album. Jonathan Grell founded Dirty Water with singer Rhett Forrester, formerly of Riot. This band demoed material, but the project came to a screeching halt in 1994 when Rhett was tragically murdered. After Winterkat, Jonathan founded Suite 16, an alliance with ex-S.A. Slayer and Riot members Bobby Jarzombek and Don Van Stavern. Jonathan later went on to join the Southern rock group Mudpie, which included former members of MSG, Salty Dog, and Steelhouse Lane, releasing a self-titled CD in 2002.

"I have been into music for four decades, so I played more shows than I can remember," Jonathan concludes. "I enjoyed the shows with my bands Liquid Sky, Winterkat, and Mudpie. I also enjoyed playing shows with MSG!"

Winterkat are no longer active, having called it a day in the mid-1990s.

MANIA

THE INDISPUTABLE IMPACT OF THE EARLY EIGHTIES JUDAS PRIEST RECORDS on the American metal scene can be found in large proportions in totally diverse styles, from hair/glam metal to speed/thrash. Judas Priest were bigger than either Iron Maiden and Black Sabbath in the first half of the eighties in the U.S., as evidenced by their appearance at San Bernardino's 1983 US Festival with Quiet Riot, Mötley Crüe, Ozzy Osbourne, Triumph, Scorpions, and Van Halen, which drew upwards of 670,000 attendants! In general, Judas Priest's style has been more American-friendly since the *Sin After Sin* LP, compared to the gloomy style of Black Sabbath and the totally British—and absolutely European—approach of Iron Maiden.

Mania is one of the countless bands that took the *Screaming for Vengeance* and *Defenders of the Faith* formula and blended it with the lite style of Dokken and Ratt. Formed in Houston,

Texas, in 1984, guitarist Steve Wilbanks tells me, "Mania basically evolved from a few prior bands that the other guitarist, Joe Reyes, and I had been involved with for a couple of years, before finally landing on the lineup that eventually recorded the first album, *No Lullabies !!* The drummer, Jesse York, joined sometime shortly after Joe and I had ceased doing cover tunes live and began focusing on original material. I also owned a sound company at the time that engineered shows for live bands, a couple of which were bands that the singer, Stacey Richards, was fronting. Stacey just happened to stop by our rehearsal hall one day, sat in with the band for a few tunes, and everything just clicked. It seemed like a perfect fit for all, and he joined the band right away. The bassist, John Smith, joined right around the time we recorded that first album. We were all a bit burned out on doing gigs while playing cover material and everyone seemed to have a similar desire to showcase our original material and to perform a 'show,' rather than the nightly routine of playing three to four sets of other people's material. We were naturally much more inspired and driven by the original material, which gave us the ability to showcase who we were artistically."

CUT TO THE CHASE:

Mania's *No Lullabies!!* is wholeheartedly recommended for any fans of melodic American metal; it's a good LP, nothing to flip out about, but you can find at least some great songs in there. Not a classic, not an epic/ true metal holy grail, *No Lullabies!!* is coming from a time and place that seems so far away today. If I could use two words to describe it, it would be *youth* and *carefree*.

In terms of influences, Steve replies, "So many come to mind from that era—mostly guitar-oriented artists. All the usual suspects ... like Michael Schenker, Iron Maiden, Dio, Van Halen, Dokken, and Judas Priest. I believe Mania's sound was inevitably influenced and unavoidably a bit derivative of all of them, as well as others. I think it would be really hard to put a finger on any single record. That was just a great period in the evolution of the hard rock scene.

"Being from Texas had its advantages and disadvantages," Steve adds. "We were not in the middle of the L.A. scene, so were not exposed to certain elements and people that might have helped advance where we were at the time as a band, but hailing from Texas allowed us to perhaps stand out from the crowd a bit. That said, Texas rock fans treated us like royalty!"

Creating a buzz around their name, Mania decided to chase their dreams, thus releasing their first twelve-inch, *No Lullabies !!*, via the help of Stratagem Records—which was a studio, not an official label. Steve sheds a little light:

"We were approached by Stratagem Records and, to put it simply, they 'offered us a deal we couldn't refuse.' Additionally, by working with an independent label, we were allowed to retain much more control of our product and image than we might have with another larger label. The whole recording process was pretty quick. We had been rehearsing pretty frequently for live shows, so we were pretty tight as a unit at the time. We just chose a handful of tunes, went into the studio, and knocked them out. Most of the raw basic tracks actually made it to the final mix."

No Lullabies !! was under the production of Fred Remmert (vocalist and guitarist of the new wave band The Zone), and it contained some classic, melodic American metal. Initially, I was unimpressed, but after subsequent listens, I have to admit that Mania can write good songs, and when they actually do it, they strike hard! "Treat Me This Way" is a total Accept-meets-Priest anthem, whereas the frantic and melodic "Cut Ya Down to Size" is worth the price of this LP alone! "Licensed to Kill" is another fine tune, this time more in the Iron Maiden vein, with a slight Rush edge—even though the party metal element is very strong. The rest of the LP is mostly hard 'n' heavy metal in the American way, not bad but not great either. But yes, *No Lullabies !!* has at least three songs that any fan of melodic American metal will love.

"We did have a really nice response to a show we did with Yngwie Malmsteen, but there were many quite memorable shows," Steve says. About other bands who also went indie, he replies, "One of my favorite bands that took the same route as we did was a band from San Antonio, Texas, called Winterkat. I later worked with their vocalist Mike Grothues in a few later projects. Fantastic guy and phenomenal voice!"

Mania were laid to rest by 1988, with no reunions whatsoever. The resurgence of interest toward private metal records has helped *No Lullabies !!* see the light of day lately, and Steve comments, "I think it's fantastic! In this day and age, it is actually possible for smaller labels to be able to garner way more exposure for their bands by utilizing the internet than was possible back then. It was really tough for a band to be significantly noticed if they didn't have a video in MTV's rotation. It seems that YouTube has recently emerged as a wonderful marketing tool for labels that might've previously had difficulty reaching their target market. It's certainly flattering that our record is a collector's item; unfortunately, the high street price for the album as a collector's item is likely more indicative of the less-than-desired numbers of units that actually were sold, scooped up at the time, and are still floating around.

"I do see a resurgence of the old-school bands," Steve concludes. "It seems more apparent to us, judging from many recent solicitations to release (and re-release) some old and previously unreleased material. I'm all for it, as I'm personally not a fan of rap and other genres that are so prevalent nowadays. Unfortunately, it is evident that musical ability is no longer necessary to sell records. I really appreciate the current ability to audition and obtain material that is sometimes obscure, hard to get, and/or out of print. I recently read that Peter Frampton had stated he only received 1,700 dollars in royalties for 55 million streams of his tunes! I just hope the laws get sorted out soon so that the artists are finally compensated justly for their work."

NIGHTCHILD

THERE WAS A SPECIFIC TIME IN THE MID-EIGHTIES WHEN INDIANAPOLIS ROCK bands, whether they were punk, metal, hard rock, or garage, were connected by one name: Paul Mahern, vocalist for the Zero Boys. The reason for that is that Mahern was responsible for producing most of the great names from Indianapolis, from Sloppy Seconds to Transgression, from Killing Children to Nightchild.

The story of Nightchild begins when guitarist Randy Joe Duke met bassist Bill Bruton in 1978. "We didn't become friends fast, but we became aware of each other," Randy admits. "We didn't jam together for another year or so. We began using the name Nightchild for the first time in May of 1981. We took it from the title of one of the songs I'd written in 1980. I was always a fan of horror films and fiction, especially the vampire genre, and I was often inspired to write about them. Bill didn't care about vampires, but he thought it sounded cool. The band went through many personnel changes over the years. It was early in 1983 before we added Ron

Brewer on vocals. Brandon Johnson (drums) had been with us for at least a year by then. That was the lineup on the record and all the way up to the end.

"I think we all have that primal drive to seek out others who share our desires and values, to bond and join forces with. So, we can create a shared identity to rise above whatever circumstance we have been born into and belong to something bigger than ourselves. Seems like that usually begins with a 'core two,' like when John met Paul or when Gene met Paul, and then the recruiting begins. Bill and I were that 'core two' for Nightchild. Even though he joined last, Ron was our third," Randy narrates. "As far as musical influences, we were all about the same age, from the same city, and we had all come of age in the golden years of rock 'n' roll. We all listened to the same artists, saw the same concerts, hung the same posters on our walls, wore the same T-shirts, and liked the same videos on MTV. There was definitely some divergence here and there, but we had far more in common than we differed on. To be honest, I can't really speak for Brandon or his tastes, but the rest of us liked our rock 'n' roll lean, raw, and true. One vocal, one guitar, bass and drums, and sparse back-up vocals, and only if and when the song absolutely called for it.

"We liked our stages that way too," Randy continues. "No big-ass pointless wall of amps. No fog machines, no fireworks. We didn't like anything to be fake, or there merely for show. We believed in less is more, and that carried over into how we presented ourselves onstage as well. What we wore onstage was what we wore every day. As we progressed and grew as a band, we stripped it down to the bare bones. In fact, my biggest disappointment is that right before we broke up, we were the best version of the band we ever were, and none of it got recorded, and no one saw it."

Describing the Indianapolis scene back then, Randy mentions, "There was no original hard rock/metal scene here in Indy when we started. No one was doing what we were doing. There were lots of hard rock/metal cover bands, and there were also local bands doing originals, but they were more of the melodic rock, pop rock. Indianapolis was home to some great punk bands in the early 1980s like Zero Boys, and there was still a punk scene, but it was cliquish. When we began, the metalheads and punks didn't mix in Indy, but that changed over time. There had also been some all-original hard rock bands in the 1970s here in Indy, but they had already come and gone. I couldn't tell you what the scene was like then. All I know is we had to create our own scene, and it was a lot of hard work. In fact, I think one of the best things we did for Indianapolis was open up some hard rock/metal venues and lay a path for the original hard rock/metal bands that followed. There were some I really liked, young bands inspired by Metallica and Slayer, and far too many glammy, big-hair, Spandex-wearing ones for my taste."

In 1985, Nightchild went on to release their own piece of vinyl, the *Remember the Faithful* seven-inch, and Randy explains, "Bill and I had both been avid vinyl collectors for years, and it had always been our plan to release a single on colored vinyl and follow it up with an LP release. We knew it would set us apart from the crowd. We loved vinyl, and recording records was one of the main reasons we formed a band. People today probably have no idea how expensive and complicated each phase of production was back then. Each step required tremendous resolve. I won't bore you with all the BS and minutiae of the ordeal, but long story short: After many months of focused toil, we finally had 1,000 copies of our own seven-inch, 45 RPM record on 'transparent porcelain and blood-red' vinyl."

Remember the Faithful contains two songs (the title track and "Hero"), with a pretty raw approach that reminds me of early Accept, with mid-tempo heavyweights that will please fans of this kind of metal. Plus, Nightchild offered a good number of shows through their existence. As Randy says, "One was in September of 1984 when we were part of a concert for the U.S. Nationals crowd at Indianapolis Raceway Park in Clermont, Indiana. That show was dynamic and magic in many ways, and for many reasons, and it kept us inspired for quite a while. It was also the largest crowd we ever played for. Another was in Marion, Indiana, when we headlined a metal show at a local VFW. As we were in the closing jam of our final song, the crowd pressed up against the stage, with the front row laying on top of it and banging their fists on the stage in rhythm with the song. It was sending a vibration through the stage that we could all feel through our feet. The harder they banged, the harder we rocked, and we were completely in sync as with each other in a metal mindmeld ... when, either by the weight of their bodies against the front or some other reason, the entire front of the stage collapsed just as we finished. It was one helluva climax! Luckily, no one got hurt."

Randy continues, "I also can't let this question go without a shout-out and salute to Oliver's in Speedway, Indiana. It was a huge all-ages venue full of high school students who we knew listened to a local metal show that was broadcast through their school. The club had a huge backroom and stage that was a perfect place for metal shows. We knew the owner, but he didn't want anything to do with a metal crowd—but he loved money, so we appealed to that side of him. We told him about the radio show and how we had been booked as guests for an upcoming episode and hoped to have a concert to promote. The free advertisement on the radio seemed to pique his interest, so we asked him to give us a shot on his deadest night, which was Sunday. He finally gave in. The deal was we could charge at the door but we had to split it with him. He really didn't expect anyone to show up, but we had over 400 kids in there on our first night. That was July 27, 1986. After that, he wanted us to play there every Sunday, but I told him that wasn't a good idea and that there should be a different band every Sunday. That gave Bill and myself another unpaying job, finding bands to fill in the other Sundays with. We agreed to play the following Sunday, but we eventually got 'Heavy Metal Sundays' at Oliver's going strong, and it had a long, healthy run. I know we played and recorded a show there in September of '86, but I think that may have been our last show there. After Nightchild broke up a few months later, the owner contacted me and hired me to manage the club and book the bands. I did it for a year or so, for the cause and to save some money, but I had no real interest in crossing over into promotion. It was a very important venue here in Indiana for the indie metal/punk scene and for touring independent bands from all across the country, as well several signed national acts."

Two demos followed—the 1986 demo and the 1987 *No Pain, No Gain* demo, still with the same Accept-influenced metal, only this time with a slight American metal approach—but it's still definitely Accept-oriented again. Nightchild called it quits in 1987, with Randy Joe Duke playing in the psychedelic rock band Direwolf later in the nineties. "There was a very good punk band called Sloppy Seconds that had several seven-inch releases on their own," Randy recalls, when asked about private metal releases from Indianapolis in that era. "I didn't

CUT TO THE CHASE:

If you are a hardcore early Accept fan, you will definitely fall for Nightchild's seven-inch. It is good (yet not crucial) traditional mid-tempo heavy metal in the tradition of the German metal bands—albeit more American, of course.

see their first one until after we broke up in 1987. I'd say there were far more punk releases on vinyl than rock or metal here in Indianapolis. It seemed like most metal and rock bands only released on cassette, which was understandable at the time."

On the subject of the resurgence of interest in obscure metal bands, Randy comments, "I'm also honored to know that there are people still interested in collecting our 45. Bill and I are still good friends, and we always contact each other when we see one pop up. It's crazy to see some of the prices they bring on eBay and elsewhere. It's hard to believe we once hustled to sell them for three dollars each."

About the current metal underground scene, Randy says, "Even though I'm no longer involved, I see posts on social media and see flyers in stores and venues. I have no doubt it is alive and well here in Indy, in fact, I'd think it's safe to say there are far more many independent all-original bands today than there were in the 1980s. As far as downloading goes, it's not going away, and there is no way to fight it. So, I accept it and think it's great, as long as the source material they're using is good. I find and get sent links all the time to Nightchild material popping up here and there from Germany, Romania, and elsewhere, and you wonder how they discovered you, but I feel honored by it. I often wonder how they found some of the tracks they use. Some are really obscure. I've heard some links that had horrible compressing and audio quality, but there are some that sound pretty good, considering what sources they're using. I'm humbled when someone has obviously taken a lot of time and trouble to represent us. The songs are copyrighted, though, so I appreciate it when they mention that as well.

"By the way," Randy adds, "that brings up a new development in the Nightchild story. I recently discovered an old master tape of one of our last shows at 'Oliver's Under 21 Club' from September of 1986. It doesn't have the entire show, but it sounds pretty damn good and is the most honest representation of who we were. Bill and I have talked about releasing it on twelve-inch colored vinyl, but we aren't sure. It's a lot to think about, but maybe. I'll let you know."

PROWLER (SANTA FE, NM)

PROWLER FROM SANTA FE ARE ONE OF THE FEW EXCEPTIONS INCLUDED IN this book, seeing as their self-financed release wasn't a vinyl record like the others. Their inclusion here is based on the fact that their recorded output was simply tremendous! Formed in 1981, Prowler's story has many ups and downs—a relocation to Los Angeles in search of fame, a disbandment in 1995—but today, the band is back together again, re-recording their old songs.

"All of us have grown up around music and played instruments in high school. Some of the guys have played in other groups but it wasn't until we got together that we knew that we might have something," Cedric Griego, Prowler's guitarist, says. Prowler suffered from constant changes in lineups; however, the classic lineup that released the first cassette was Cedric Griego (guitar), Steve Montoya (vocals), Ed Brondo (guitar), Dave Smith (drums), and Louie Medina (bass).

CUT TO THE CHASE:

Both of Prowler's indie releases rule. I just wish that somebody would notice them and re-release everything they recorded into a CD/LP collection, since we're talking about top-notch heavy/power metal that you rarely see today! Haven't found copies for sale, but I guess those two go for big bucks.

"Our most basic influences were Black Sabbath, Judas Priest, and of course Iron Maiden. There were many great bands back in the day and some very cool albums, but one imported album that changed everything was *Killers* by Iron Maiden," Cedric tells me.

While the metal heatwave was already hitting all over the U.S., Santa Fe wasn't the coolest place for a metal band back then. "Not much of a music scene, at least for our style of music, sadly, in Santa Fe. Most of the music at the time was rock 'n' roll, but here in New Mexico it was more of a Spanish-influenced style. But even though we were in that little scene, we did have great local crowds. New Mexico has a deep love for all kinds of music."

Prowler sadly missed the train on getting signed to a major or indie metal label, but after eight years, they managed to put out one of the greatest independent releases that American metal ever offered. Cedric tells the story:

"Each of the band members pooled our money for the recordings. Not easy because we were totally broke, because we had to buy our own equipment. After moving to L.A., the original members reunited and recorded two new songs. We hoped that this release would get us heard by some record label. So, our cassette, *Prowler*, was released in 1989. A five-song EP, with three songs ('Fortune Hunter,' 'Dressed to Kill,' and 'Dreams') being recorded at Creative Music in Albuquerque, New Mexico, in 1983. 'Washed Out Rebel' and 'The Hunting' were recorded at Woodcliff Studios in Sherman Oaks, California, in 1988. By the time we released our music, we had lost the drummer and guitar player. With a new lineup, the band came back to New Mexico for a show and released it there. Most of the cassette tapes were sold to our friends and family."

Prowler's 1989 cassette is an unbelievable treasure of American metal! It doesn't get any better when talking about indie metal releases of the 1980s—this cassette oozes with energy and passion for raw, heavy, powerful metal of the highest class. Their approach reminds me of another excellent American band, Steel Assassin, and songs like the epic "Dressed to Kill" and the perfect "Washed Out Rebel," reminiscent of a beefed-up Ruffians, are simply metal hymns. However, my favorite is "Fortune Hunter," which starts with a Judas Priest-like riff and then evolves into a menacing metal tune. Raging, with tons of power!

Prowler were lucky enough to perform with some great metal acts of their day. Cedric adds, "The two most memorable shows were our first show at the Whisky a Go Go—you can find a video of that on YouTube. Another show was at the Dancing Waters Club in San Pedro, when we opened for Vicious Rumors." Prowler, though, was still able to release their own EP, unlike other bands in the area. When asked about other local indie releases, Cedric answers, "There were not too many bands in Santa Fe in those days. Albuquerque had the most bands, but I never really heard if anyone released their music..."

Prowler kept it up until 1995, and their self-released 1994 CD-EP is excellent too, again in the same style—tuneful, catchy, very powerful heavy/power metal. But what a pity that no one offered them a chance to release something on a label.

"I believe that there were a lot of bands that never had an opportunity to release their music. You can never have too much heavy metal, so your hunger for great metal gets bigger, and this is when you dig the underground," Cedric replies when asked about the current state of the metal underground. "I do believe there is a great underground scene today for sure. But I believe it's in Europe, not so much here in the United States. Downloading for us is a good thing—we have always wanted to share music with the world, and finally, there's no record label to take control of our music. Prowler never really had the money to record ... and that only got better."

As of 2020, Prowler are back together again, and Cedric adds, "We are in the process of recording some of that old music. It's a very slow process—it's hard to get everybody together at once, so everything is being done via the internet," since members now live in different states.

After the first disbandment of Prowler, various members played in many bands. Steve Montoya, the singer, has also released an album called *A New Beginning* with his band called Savage Wizdom; Steve Cordova played in Fear of God; Duayne Howard played in Project Steiger and Anger Mgt.; Dean Scavone in Heavy the World; Chris Young in Overture; and James Jones in Severmind, Gutwrench, and Wasted Tracy.

MILITIA

A BAND WITH ONE OF THE HIGHEST CULT STATUSES IN THE HISTORY OF American metal, Militia from Austin, Texas, is a band that holds a very special place in the hearts of all fans of true metal—makes sense, since their sonic, lyrical, and visual stance is metal to the max!

"Militia was already formed before I had joined in late 1983 or maybe early 1984," vocalist Mike Soliz narrates. "It was formed by Phil Achee, Robert Willingham, and Tony Smith, later to be joined by guitarist Jesse Villegas. Funny thing is that I was not a singer at all. I was a drummer. It just happened when Jason McMaster of Watchtower came over to my house, as we were high school friends, and were in a cover band called Fallen Angel before moving on to other groups. Anyway, me and my friends were playing 'Metal Thrashing Mad' by Anthrax and I was singing and drumming. And after that, Jason suggested I try out for this band called Militia. So, there I was, wanting to drum like Charlie Benante, and I ended up wanting to sing like Neil Turbin!"

Militia's sonic attack took its cues from many classic metal acts, but again, their metal was played in an absolute ferocious rage, on the edge of the subgenre of power/speed/thrash.

"Our biggest influences were the usual suspects: Maiden, Priest, Mercyful Fate, Accept, and then came the early thrash," Mike admits. "Metallica, Slayer, Megadeth, but for me, it was *Fistful of Metal* by Anthrax that left the greatest impression on me. It had everything I needed to hear in metal, such as speed, great guitar work, and high-pitched vocal madness—and of course, the drumming was top-shelf."

In 1985, Militia went on to record their first demo, *Regiments of Death*, which was only a slight hint of what was coming around the corner: raging, crazy, maximum metal with super catchy songwriting! Songs like "Metal Axe" are absolute bangers, sounding like Slayer's *Show No Mercy* gone power metal—crazy stuff! "At first, there was no scene here in Austin, Texas, though, so it was very hard for us," Mike recalls. "This was a rock 'n' roll town. Most of the metal concerts were 80 miles south in San Antonio, Texas. Now, looking back, it seems bands like Militia and Watchtower were very instrumental in creating a metal scene in the early eighties. It was Chris Gates (of the hardcore punk band Big Boys) who really got this thing rolling. He started putting on shows at the infamous Ritz Theater downtown. The scene grew quickly; the potential for metal shows was increasing, as was the size of the crowds. We started bringing in bands from San Antonio, like S.A. Slayer, Karion, Wyzard, and Syrus, to name a few. And a brotherhood was formed between us and San Antonio, Militia's home away from home."

Militia weren't about to lose time, and in 1986 they recorded and released their first piece of vinyl, the twelve-inch *The Sybling*, on their own label, Scythe Records. Mike explains, "The decision to release independently was really not much of a choice. As a matter of fact, *The Sybling* EP was actually made more for label shopping, and of course, you may know by now that only 100 were printed. There are only 94 in existence now. As for the procedure to record it, that was pretty straightforward: four guys excited to be in a studio and just pressed record! Looking back, I always wish I could have done better, but then it wouldn't be this raw moment in time."

More technical and way crazier than their first demo, Militia, in just three songs, managed to put out something totally unique: a real diamond of not just privately released metal but of American metal in general! All three songs are absolutely top-class, but allow me to offer a special mention of "Salem Square." This song just sounds out of this world! Kicking off with a mental progressive/jazz style and then evolving into total power/thrash dynamite, where everything's on fire. Overall, if you're getting only a handful of American private metal releases, be sure to get *The Sybling*.

Militia played shows locally and recorded one more demo (*No Submission*) before disbanding later in 1986. "The most memorable show was the L.A. Slayer vs. S.A. Slayer show in San Antonio. Militia and Syrus were also on the bill. After our sound check, there was a gigantic roar from the crowd outside the venue. We knew then that this was going to be a historic night!" Mike laughs. And as for other significant private metal releases from Austin, Mike refers to an LP that wasn't privately released, but it fell under the umbrella of a small indie label: "The only release I can think of was Watchtower's *Energetic Dissasembly* on Zombo Records. One of the most radical, outside-the-box-thinking masterpieces."

CUT TO THE CHASE:

If you are not yet familiar with Militia, try to think of a mix of Watchtower, early Slayer, and Helstar (at their most technical). Although even then, you are not even halfway there, since Militia definitely has its own very characteristic sound! As for *The Sybling* EP, the original pressing goes for a lot of money in online auctions, and it's one of the hardest ones to get. It's the music that matters, though, so pick up the compilation LP *The Second Coming* and/or the Cult Metal Classics re-release of *The Sybling*, and enjoy one of the greatest bands included in this book!

Militia members later appeared in (great) bands such as Assalant, Karion, Awake, and Oblivion Knight. However, European metalheads never lost their interest in Militia, which is the reason the band got together again in 2008, appearing live at the Keep It True XII festival. They're still active today (as of 2021). They also released a record in 2012, *Strength and Honor*, along with compilations and re-releases of *The Sybling*!

"I think record collecting has always been there, but now it's our turn," Mike adds. "Our metal generation that is reaching back and collecting, now that we're not as young as we used to be, and in a sort of nostalgic way, we're buying back our youth. Trying to remember what it was like holding that vinyl record we used to listen to and stare at for hours. An expensive habit for sure! As for Militia's *The Sybling* EP going for so much money, that is something we never would have conceived of. But someone, somewhere, somehow decided that's the rarest of the rare, and it has been snowballing ever since. I'm sure it's because we only had 100 printed—that's all we could afford to have printed."

Finally, Mike describes the underground metal scene in his own words: "I think the underground scene is small, at least here in Austin, the way it started out. Belonging only to the few. There are younger kids getting into the old-school metal, probably passed on to them by their parents. I can honestly say I don't get out as much anymore. As for easy access to downloading, we live in a different age, obviously. I remember being very excited about being able to have our music reach virtually millions of people all over the globe with the touch of a button in the very early stages of the internet, but now, we and many others are just a drop of water in an endless ocean. But you do discover new bands that way as well. I guess we call this progress!"

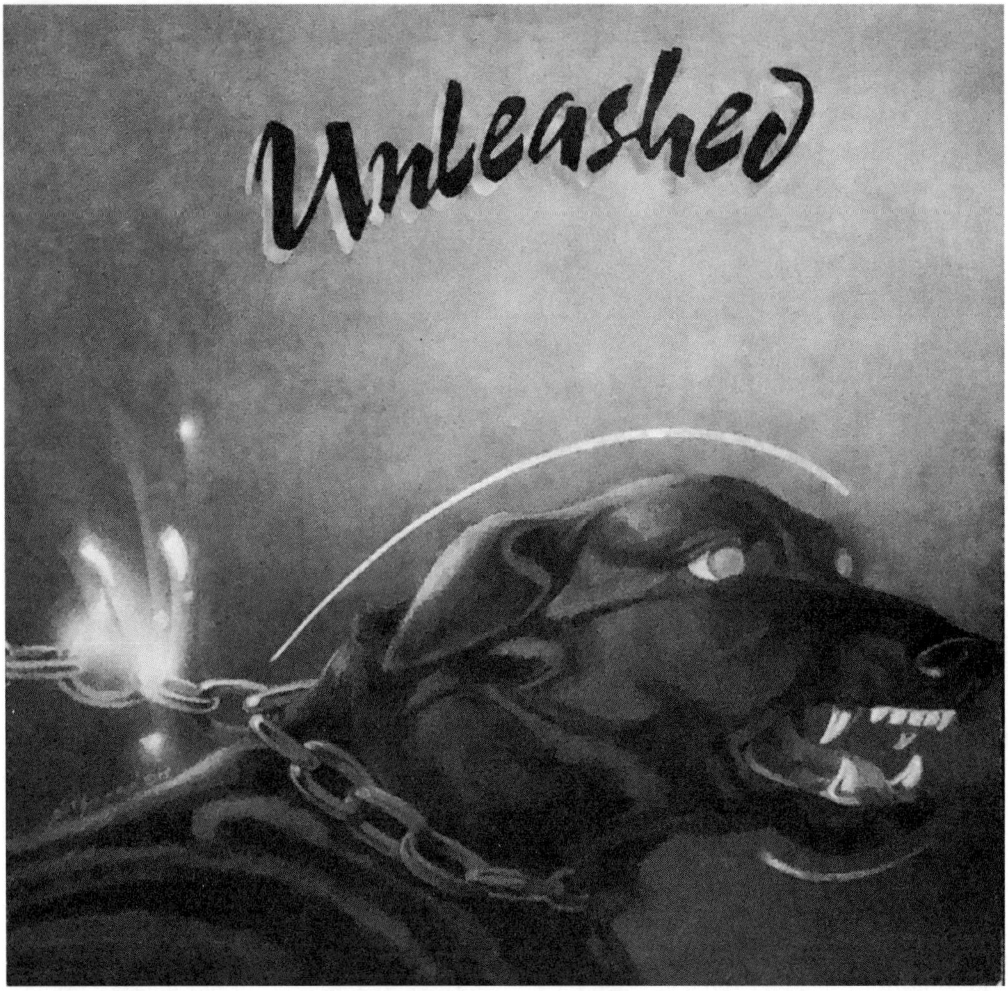

UNLEASHED

NOT TO BE CONFUSED WITH THE SWEDISH DEATH METAL BAND, UNLEASHED from St. Charles, Illinois, was a very powerful heavy/power band that left its mark by releasing one twelve-inch EP and one cassette. Formed by brothers Gary and Gerald Guzman, who had already been playing in bands together for about five years prior to Unleashed—Gerald played guitar and Gary played bass guitar—they started out just like any other young musicians, playing covers of their favorite songs. Gerald met a few musicians in high school and he would have them over to jam, and among those musicians were Eric Anderson, who played guitar and sang, and Daniel Thomas, who played drums. Eventually, the four of them came together to form the band that became Unleashed in 1985.

"The motivation was pretty simple: We were four kids who lived in the same town in the Chicago suburbs. We all listened to the same music and wanted to play all of the music we loved!" Gary says. "Everyone in Unleashed pretty much listened to the same bands—mostly hard rock and heavy metal. Some of our favorite bands and albums at the time were Metallica's *Ride the Lightning*, Iron Maiden's *Number of the Beast*, S.O.D.'s *Speak English or Die*, Anthrax's *Spreading the Disease*, Dio's *The Last in Line*, Loudness' *Thunder in the East*, and Yngwie J. Malmsteen's Rising Force's *Marching Out*. All of these albums were a big inspiration to us!"

Being from the suburbs of Chicago, Unleashed got the chance to be a part of a scene where heavy metal was happening in full force. "The local hard rock/heavy metal scene in Chicago was great at the time," Gary says. "There were many excellent bands who were playing some amazing original music. We were very inspired by them to start writing our own original music. Since we were all under 21 at the time (I was only 15, and the rest of the guys were 19), we were still lucky to see a lot of these bands because they would play all-ages shows all the time. We eventually signed with a local management team who began to book us shows in the same venues as the local bands we admired. Many of these bands were very friendly to us and supported us, allowing us to open shows for them and giving us great advice! We gradually built a local following and their support was amazing! There were many other Chicago bands at the time who had independent releases. For example, the bands Paradoxx and Hammeron both had albums out on the independent Chicago label Silver Fin Records and they were some of the most popular bands on the local scene at the time. Also, Damien Thorne was an excellent local metal band who had a great album called *Sign of the Jackal*."

The release of Unleashed's 1985 twelve-inch EP came via the help of their management, as Gary tells it: "Our original plan was just to record a four-song demo to send to press and venues, for promotion and to book local gigs. Fortunately, our management company had the funds to not only finance the recording but also finance the pressing of an EP on vinyl and cassette. They looked at us as a 'viable property' that could be marketed successfully, since we were all so young in age. So, thanks to our management company, we had a proper budget to book a professional recording studio and sound engineer for a high-quality recording. We also had the ability to hire a superior record manufacturer, a talented art director for the album cover and promotional materials, and an excellent marketing staff. So, we were fortunate to be able to do that and experience it, since many other bands didn't get that opportunity like we did."

Unleashed's 1985 EP, which was released on their own label, D.K.P. Productions, is a real metal powerhouse. The production is exceptional, offering Unleashed so much sonic power through its heavy, loud, clear guitars. And as for the songs, the four tracks range from good ("Cry for Revenge") to very good ("Obsession") to excellent ("Growing Fear" and "Search for the Truth"). Unleashed is definitely heavy metal; however, its sound is unbelievably heavy, reminiscent of some of the thrash bands of that era! Still melodic and traditional, though, this EP is a real treat.

Unleashed created a buzz around their name and scored slots on various gigs after the release of their EP. "We were able to share the stage with many great national bands, such as L.A. Guns and Killer Dwarfs," Gary mentions. "The most memorable show for me personally was when we got an offer to open for the band Helix in Minneapolis in the spring of 1988. It was a weeknight show, but we definitely wanted to play it, since it would have been great exposure for our band, and it would open up a new market for us. Unfortunately, I was the

CUT TO THE CHASE:

If you love your metal mean yet still classically based, pick up Unleashed's twelve-inch EP. In terms of sound, it reminds me of Ion Britton and Ray Gunn, heavy and very powerful, but overall, this is a very unique recording.

only one who was still in high school, and the gig was the night before I was to have my final exams! The only solution was for us to drive up to Minneapolis from Chicago (which is about a six-and-a-half-hour drive), perform the show, and then drive back to Chicago overnight so I could complete my exams. The plan was for me to study on the whole drive up to Minneapolis, and then sleep on the drive back. Luckily, everything worked out! We played a good show and got a great response, drove there and back with no problems, and I still did very well on my final exams!"

No luck getting signed, though, and Unleashed released their own 1988 promo cassette, which I sadly can't review since it hasn't been available anywhere for ages—not even Gary owns a copy. And this was the end of the band's short-lived career. Right afterward, Gary went on to play with Defcon, a hard rock/AOR band from Akron, Ohio, alongside Mark Matthews (who later sang for Jani Lane's solo band) and Shawn Zavodney (later in Slammin' Gladys and Warrant), and release three cassettes, eventually disbanding in 1990.

"Those privately released records are a sign of the times, and they capture a certain sound and vibe that can't be replicated today," Gary says. "Everything back then was recorded analog—with the warm sound of vocals and instruments recorded to tape. Also, the musicianship and performances are REAL. There was no Pro Tools studio trickery and no autotune! Musicians had to really play their instruments and play them well—there was no quick editing to make an average musician sound amazing! So, I understand why rock fans are seeking out recordings from this era.

"I'm sure an underground scene exists—even though I don't keep up with what bands are out there nowadays. My opinion is torn on music today. On one hand, I think it's great that bands are able to record themselves on their own computers and equipment and release their music online for fans to hear it immediately. They don't have to save hundreds of dollars to go into a studio to record, or spend a lot of money to put their music on physical product, such as CDs or vinyl, like we did back in the day. But on the other hand, I really hate the fact that people can now download an entire CD online within a minute illegally, and the artist doesn't receive ANY money from it. As a music fan in the eighties, there was an excitement about discovering a band's music through the radio or on MTV, going out to the record store to buy the album, and then listening to the album while checking out the album artwork and reading the lyrics or credits. Unfortunately, music fans nowadays just don't get that."

HAMMER WITCH

In the American metal history of the 1980s, Hammer Witch's case is pretty unique. I don't recall another band like them or Hexx, which started as a power metal band and then transformed into death metal after a few years! The band was founded in New Orleans, Louisiana, back in 1985 by bassist Wayne Abney, guitarist/vocalist Frankie Dee, drummer Terry Sims, and guitarist George David.

"We were originally a five-piece band (although our first vocalist's name is unavailable), and the band's core eighties lineup was forged after Frankie, Wayne, George, and Terry decided to go four-piece," Wayne says. "With all new material and enough songs for a complete set of their own music, the band toured the New Orleans area circuit doing the club scene and opening for national acts when possible. After recording our first demo, the realization set in that we needed to explore new territories and expand our horizons because the material proved to be too brutal for the slower-paced scene and commercialized market of our surroundings. Frankie

Dee's former bandmate from Trashed, Bo Topousis, had since moved to Fort Worth, Texas, and formed the band Irun, consisting of displaced Louisiana musicians who were seeking a more liberal metal environment. Upon seeing the scene, Bo urged the members of Hammer Witch to 'come to the promised land' of Dallas, Texas, which we did in late 1985 or early 1986. When Irun, after going back to Louisiana briefly, broke up in late 1986, guitarist/sound engineer Bo Topousis went back to Texas to be Hammer Witch's sound engineer while looking for a new band. When George unexpectedly left Hammer Witch, Bo stepped in as guitarist and brought Irun's drummer Sal Torneo in to replace Terry.

"My motivation was to play some music and have the ability to perform the music in front of an audience," Wayne continues. "Playing heavy music was the fix for me, and getting to jam was always and is still now the most important thing in my life. Sure, there are other things that take priority, like making money and eating, but on my deathbed, if you asked me what the thing I enjoyed most, it would be my fucking music!

"As far as influences go, sure, music influenced me, but not like you assume," Wayne says. "My influences mostly come from growing up in the streets of New Orleans East where you learned to become a man. You learned how to fight, you learned how to win, you learned how to lose. You watched the toughest become the weakest, the biggest become the smallest and the other way around, all in the drop of a hat. You learned about honor, you learned about pride and how to survive. You learned how quickly your life could change at the drop of a hat. So, as you can see my real influences don't have a lot to do with music but to do with life, and it reflects in all of my songs. But here is what you are looking for: Black Sabbath, Iron Maiden, Judas Priest ... fuck, the list goes on. The records that left the greatest impression on me were the ones I did with my band or bands. I mean, there are just too many bands that did great albums to list. From Black Sabbath's first album to Deep Purple, Van Halen, to Slayer in the old days, and all the old-school thrash bands."

"The first thing I can remember is a few guys jamming in a little room in the city," Frank adds. "I lived on the Northshore of Lake Pontchartrain, about 45 minutes away. It was more country back then. I went into the city to gig a little. I got the invite to come and jam in the little room. So, I did, and it was fun, but we needed a bass player. I said, 'When you get a bass player, call me.' Anyway, they called me the next week and said 'We got a guy, come on down.' I walked in and there was Wayne standing there, shredding on bass. It was raw, man! We all started jamming and the energy was awesome. We were not too great, but there was a lot of excitement. The band was called Tyrant. We played gigs for a couple of years. I moved back into New Orleans. Eventually, we hit some brick walls, people thought our singer was awful. So, we fired him, recorded a demo with me singing, changed our name to Hammer Witch, and moved to Dallas.

"I did not want to work regular jobs," Frank continues, "even though we all did when we had to. I still do. I was in love with music. Creating and jamming with my brothers was the best thing to me. And the band's biggest influences were Iron Maiden, Black Sabbath, Judas Priest, Ozzy, and Dio, with a little Van Halen sprinkle. My all-time favorite album is *Sabotage* by Black Sabbath!"

"The scene where I lived (New Orleans, Louisiana) was poser central," Wayne says, "and by that, I mean most bands were playing covers and trying to blend in a couple of originals if they could get away with it. They played the regular circuit, you know the type, the hair metal bands. Sure, I did that shit too when I was younger, but then realized how much more important and gratifying it was to play strictly original music. Hammer Witch took a hit when we decided to be a total original band and put a record out as far as bookings and getting gigs went. But everything comes with a price, and we decided to take the chance, and now you can see the results of that risk. Shit, a collector's item, right? Fuck 'em. Most of the local bands treated us good, but there were ones that just treated us like shit and tried to stop us at every turn. These bands were some of the biggest ones in town at the time and kind of had some pull with promoters and clubs. They did everything from using booking agents to blackball us to getting the regular clubs not to book us. They used tactics like accusing us of playing devil's music and not fitting into their acceptable musical genres. So, Hammer Witch was dead in the water but still had our music and our pride and found other options, like taking our music to the world and not getting stuck in the hometown nonsense. We packed up their cars and vans and moved the whole band to Texas and lived in a one-room apartment with four guys living on the floor. We took to the Dallas scene with a four-track demo, which later became the *Return to Salem* album."

In 1986, Hammer Witch released the (good) *Demo '86*, but it was nowhere near what was about to explode the next year, with their 1987 self-release of the *Return to Salem* twelve-inch EP. "We went with a private press because we couldn't get any label interest at the time, and we wanted our music out in the world," Wayne admits. "I was friends with Rex Brown from Pantera and he turned me on to Independent Distribution, which could get our record distributed worldwide. I contacted them, and they said they would distribute the release into all Sound Warehouse locations around the world. After a price was negotiated, we boxed up records and shipped them out. Before you know it, you could walk into a Sound Warehouse throughout the world and pick up Hammer Witch's *Return to Salem* record. It was great, and soon after, Z Rock was playing our song 'Brainchild' on regular rotation.

"*Return to Salem* was recorded in Denton, Texas, with a guy named Terry Stemmons as engineer," Wayne continues. "The key to any good recording is having the right people involved with the production. With Terry on board, all that was left was the performance from the band. We were hungry to put this release out and hit the studio with a purpose, and it showed in the release. We nailed it with each instrument, and the recording began to grow bigger and better. Starting with the sound of the drum tracks and moving to the bass and guitar, we listened to the songs grow into something bigger than we imagined. When the record was finished, we worked on the artwork and the typesetting for the record cover. If you notice, we released it on DTA Records. That stands for Dee, Torneo, Abney—our last names. Then when we went to get the record pressed, we found out we had to get it mastered first. Man, after the mastering process, it really turned the recording into a monster. A recording that could hold its own with any record put out on the labels at that time. Then we released the best we could, like selling at gigs and wherever we could get fans to buy. After we got on with Independent Distribution is when we got the worldwide recognition."

Return to Salem is a marvel of American power metal, simple as that. With songs like "Live for Metal" (with its Overkill-meets-Armored Saint style) or the heavyweight steamroller "Judgement Day," and of course the opening "Burned at the Stake," Hammer Witch sound like they're on fire. It's a totally professional recording and a technically proficient approach—all band members are amazing musicians—and they managed to reach the peak from their early start. The future looked bright. "We had received quite a bit of airplay on the short-lived metal station Z Rock, and the EP later became a collector's item," Wayne adds. "We also had already built a decent following, when personal differences resulted in the exit of Frankie in late 1989—something that stopped us for a few years, sadly."

Wayne took over on vocals, and by word of mouth, Darrin Kobetich was brought on board as guitar player. Darrin had jammed with Hammer Witch onstage two years earlier but ended up joining the ill-fated reincarnation of one of DFW's pioneer metal bands, Boss Tweed. Needless to say, he wasn't going to pass up a second chance with these dudes from the swamp. Hammer Witch immediately started working on new material and dominating Joe's Garage, a music venue in Dallas, along with other thrash bands of the day like Gammacide, Malignancy, Rotting Corpse, Rigor Mortis, Crucifix, and Morbid Scream.

So, in 1991, Hammer Witch released the *Legacy of Pain* cassette, which moved the band into a totally new direction from the first release. Crazy, aggressive, fast thrash metal was now the style of the band—frantic and ferocious stuff! "Hammer Witch did some gigs with Pantera from time to time, and since we were friends with those guys, we really had some good times with them," Wayne recalls. "Other memorable times are when we opened for Megadeth and Exciter in New Orleans and then for Wendy O. Williams in Arlington, Texas. And let's not forget the Deicide and Cancer show in Fort Worth, which broke out into a barroom brawl! As well, there were demos floating around, and you could consider them independent releases. Like Sedition, Rigor Mortis (which later signed to Capitol Records), Gammacide, Rotting Corpse, Exhorder (later signed to Roadrunner Records). Pantera also had private releases out way before they got signed."

Tired of not getting signed after all these years, in 1993 Hammer Witch released their demo *Carve Your Own Doom*, their final release, including one song of death/thrash metal. Ace stuff, like a harder Exhorder. The following year, though, saw the end of Hammer Witch. There are a few unfinished songs that never saw the light of the recording studio. The only other known recordings are a video of a 1993 gig at Dallas City Limits with poor sound quality. Two of those songs are titled "Indulge in Madness" and "Epitome of Hate."

Following the breakup of Hammer Witch, Darrin and Sal went on to form Amillion Pounds with Darrin's brother, Adam Kobetich (who also did the cover art for *Legacy*) on vox, guitar, and banjo, as well as bassist Chance Lehman. After ten years and two (and a half) recordings, that band called it quits. Since then, Darrin has been devoting his time to recording solo acoustic guitar albums and touring. Sal has played with rock band The Stink and is currently with rock band Max Cady. Wayne and Scott formed Null & Void and eventually Wayne put together another band, Mother Thumb. Both projects were short-lived.

"I think it's great, but to me, it never went away," Wayne says about the resurgence of interest in eighties American metal. "I mean, music locks in a point in time and saves it for everyone to enjoy what was going on in the band's mind, when they recorded the album. I like the resurgence because it makes me feel like we have come full circle, both as a band as well as with the fans. I just don't like the re-release thing. I have been approached many

CUT TO THE CHASE:

A required purchase for anyone who's into the classic American heavy/power metal sound, the *Return to Salem* mini-LP just rules! If Hammer Witch originated from Los Angeles or San Francisco, things might have turned out way different in their career—however, they still remain one of the greatest independent American metal bands ever. Hopefully, all of their releases will get a proper reissue someday, because their thrash/death stuff is also brilliant.

times to do a re-release from everyone from scam artists to legit companies. I can't speak for the whole band, but for me, it would take away the unique quality of the album. It just wouldn't be the same. I mean, this record was done in complete analog, from the recording to the mastering and pressing. I just don't think that putting the record out on a CD would do it justice. Sometimes, you just need to leave things as they are, and this is one of those times.

"About *Return to Salem* being a sought-after item," Wayne comments, "it's totally badass, I'm tripping, and I hope the music lives forever. Hammer Witch seems to have taken on a life of its own and grown immortal. It's like the record don't even need me or the band anymore to survive—crazy, huh? Shit, who would have ever thought this would become a collectible record. We were just some fucking kids, writing some songs, expressing our feelings, and putting them out there for people to hear. I had no idea when it happened: a friend of mine who was a record collector in New Orleans called me after the record was out for a while and told me that *Return to Salem* was on the collector's list. I remember telling him that I don't know how or why, but that it seems like a good thing. So as the years went by, I noticed that it stayed on the list and only got more desirable and expensive. Today, I think you can get one for about 360 dollars. U.S. currency. Where's my royalties?? Haha!"

Hammer Witch reunited in 2013, initially to play the tribute show for Mike Scaccia from Rigor Mortis and Ministry (R.I.P. 2012), and their status today, as of 2022, is unknown. Maybe there's something in the works? We'll see!

When prompted for his thoughts on the state of the underground metal scene today, Wayne responds, "The kids today may think they have an underground scene, but I'm not sure they realize what underground really is. This shit they call underground now is nothing compared to the old-school underground. These motherfuckers living off their daddy's nickel, talking about how they're hardcore. Let me know when they pile four fuckers in a van and leave the comfort of their hometown with nothing but a four-track tape and a dream. Because that's what Hammer Witch did; we fucking went for it and to this day have no regrets. Fuck, we used to play gigs in broke-down buildings in the middle of nowhere just to try to get our music out. Then the shit was so loud that your ears would ring like a motherfucker. Bring your own beer, liquor, whatever you needed. But it was great, and there was nothing like going to see your favorite band in a setting like this. Perfect shit that you will never forget. I'm still doing this shit, man, in my new band, Life of Scars. Yeah, man, I'm still out there looking for the underground in this bullshit. But the real underground, the dark underground that you only find on private labels, played in self-promoted gigs that the band sets up. All of these clubs with their watered-down sound systems at the new volume decibel levels are bullshit. They are worried about hurting their ears, and shit, yeah, you hardcore, you underground—whatever!!"

Regarding downloading music, Wayne concludes, "This is some more bullshit right here. It's cool in one way, but very uncool in another. Fuck, if someone can get something for free, then why buy it, right? I can't blame the fans; shit, I tell them at gigs, 'If you can't buy our music, then fuck it, steal the shit.' As long as you got people listening to your music, it is always better than them not listening to it. I got to accept the way it is, man. I can't live a fucking lie. Welcome to the new world, man. Download some Life of Scars and come to a gig. Look for us in the real underground."

DUNGEON

FORMED IN MINNEAPOLIS, MINNESOTA, IN 1983, DUNGEON IS THE KIND OF band that fans of Cirith Ungol and Omen really enjoy. After all, their approach is quite similar, and that is to say: crude, raw, and heavy epic metal.

"I joined Dungeon back in 1985. They had already formed," vocalist Buddy Hughes tells me. "Initially, it was the two Story brothers—Jon on guitar and David on drums—and a different bass player named Brian Bruzek. They had stolen me from another band. I loved their originals and joined. Their parents flipped the money for our LP release, with the bass player being John Lockner. We played some packed venues before disbanding in 1987. Jon Story wanted to go off on his own…

"It was all women, money, and fun," Buddy says. "I loved writing and recording. I was always a singer. I was in the church choir. At age nine, my mother bought me an acoustic guitar and guitar lessons, and that's when I realized how much I loved music," Buddy adds. "To me, personally, my metal gods were Led Zeppelin and Ozzy. The band back then when I joined turned me on to Riot, and they loved Schenker and did a cool rendition of 'Into the Arena.' They were also into Sabbath, especially the *Born Again* album with Ian Gillan from Deep Purple singing. But I have to admit that the record that really got me going was The Beatles' *White Album*!

CUT TO THE CHASE:

Not a milestone album, but still with many enjoyable moments, *Fortress of Rock* will definitely appeal to fans of weirder and more exotic heavy/power bands that released stuff outside of the typical style (Cirith Ungol, early Omen, and Manilla Road, for example).

"The Minneapolis original scene was hard. The cover scene, however, was rocking," Buddy recalls. "You could play three sets of covers and integrate your originals. We used to do our own gigs and rent out halls and VFWs. Then you charge at the doors and sell T-shirts and albums. The bar scene, however, was three one-hour sets of covers. I was in a lot of cover bands back then, and you could actually make a good living on the road playing the Tri-State area. The bands I was in were Mommy's Nightmare, Maniax, Pandemic, and Blitzkrieg."

In 1985, Dungeon released their first and only LP, *Fortress of Rock*, on their own label, Medieval Records. Buddy describes how things evolved:

"It was our goal, and we had the financial backing from the Story brothers' parents. I knew the studio, where I went to school with the engineer. We did preproduction in an eight-track studio called Danger Studios and then went to a 32-track analog tape machine and full studio production. Jon Story wrote all the lyrics and melodies. No one else got credit for shit. This is where Jon's ego took over and basically caused the band to break up. Dave Story got the mastering and had the album art and did most of the post-production chores. We did go out and support the album. We were in preproduction for the next album when Jon took the masters and did all the vocals, bass, and guitar. I said fuck it and joined a band called Craving Angel, with which I have two studio albums and a third one coming out pretty soon called *Mr. Hyde* on Minotauro Records. Jon had actually gotten an audition for Metal Church. Unfortunately for him, he didn't get the position. All crap aside, we still all keep in touch and respect each other.

"Back in the release of our LP," Buddy continues, "Dungeon did not have the distribution to do a worldwide release, or a U.S. release, for that matter. It was all promoted locally. Dave and I went to L.A. and New York to try to shop the album, to no avail. Locally, however, we did pack the halls and bars. We played until the demise of the band, caused by Jon's ego, his need to become a superstar in his own right."

Never mind the bad record cover. Never mind the weird production. *Fortress of Rock* is a very special record in that, even though it's not a classic LP at all, it still has many glorious moments! Tracks include the excellent instrumental "Witches Brew," the weird "Infernal Regions" that sounds like an early Cirith Ungol track, and the Accept-meets-Metal Church opening of "From Under a Rock," and these are just some of the best moments on *Fortress of*

Rock. To be fair, there are many mediocre tunes too (like "Screen Queen" or "Smash Palace"), but still, this is an above-par record for sure.

"There was Impaler, and a band from St. Paul called Regime," Buddy remembers, regarding underground metal bands from the Minneapolis area that released records on small indies. "We got our fair share of good shows with Dungeon," he adds. "But the best one would have to be the VFW in Golden Valley, Minnesota. It was a packed audience, and it just fucking rocked. There was something about that night that was magical. It was a blast, and everyone was smiling, and the place was fucking rocking..."

Dungeon released one demo in 1987 before disbanding, which included three tracks, this time in a straightforward metal style. "Teardrops in the Rain" is maybe the best song they ever recorded. But after that, they were laid to rest for once and all.

"Today's game is a shame," Buddy says. "Record companies don't develop artists like they used to. The scene here in Minnesota is being destroyed by the laws, the strict drinking licenses, and expensive taxation that makes it impossible to put up a successful club that has good rock music. There is still a thriving scene in St. Paul, though, and a resurgence in Minneapolis. I just hope we (with Craving Angel) can break these barriers and get the Twin Cities really rocking again ... but then, you have the whole downloading issue. It makes it really hard for an artist to make a living. It was hard back in the 1970s and 1980s! Now it is virtually impossible, unless you can put something on YouTube or all the other media outlets and get a million hits. You may as well play the lotto, too!"

Besides Craving Angel, which Buddy continues to play and release records with, another former Dungeon member, John Lockner, went on to play in the hard rock/metal band Gemini, releasing a CD, *The Spiritual Dimensions of Music*, in 1997.

COMMANDMENT

COMMANDMENT FROM LANSING, ILLINOIS, ARE A FAVORITE OF AMERICAN power metal fans. Formed in December of 1985, the band created a cult status around their name with their punishing and uncompromising approach toward heavy metal. "Dave Marshall, the old singer, and Kevin Clayton, the bassist, and I were in a cover band together," drummer Michael Anthony Putignano tells me. "We broke up, and Dave contacted me about six months later and played me some solos over the phone that John Remesnik (the guitarist) had recorded. Dave knew John from the area. The solos were killer, and we decided to form an original band. We wrote six songs in the first nine days and played a show at some party. It went over great, and we knew we had something. There was a second guitarist, Shawn Guiney, in the beginning, but he quit about a month in and we just continued as a four-piece."

Michael continues, "Obviously, we got tired of playing other people's songs, and thought we could write our own killer tunes. Of course, the end goal was to get a record deal, and cover bands weren't getting them. We didn't care about money or drugs or girls—that's all crap. We wanted the music to stand out and to concentrate on that. We just wanted to play. To be creative!"

When asked what Commandment's early motivations and influences were, Michael says, "I guess to emulate our idols that we grew up listening to ... the New Wave of British Heavy Metal was a big influence. Of course, Sabbath, Priest, and UFO were the other influences. Yngwie was an influence on John. Chastain, as well. The record that changed my life was Maiden's *Number of the Beast*. I played side two first because the sides weren't marked on the record, and when I heard the opening of the song 'Number of the Beast,' I was blown away and knew I wanted to play drums. Clive Burr was my biggest influence, and it's a shame he's no longer with us. And like him, I too have multiple sclerosis. Kind of a strange coincidence. Of course, we just liked most metal of our time. Thrash, speed, power, the faster the better. We really weren't too fond of the glam scene or that L.A. scene, but we listened to pretty much anything rock/ metal. That said, I would have to admit that Maiden, Priest, Overkill, and Loudness were my early influences."

Commandment went on to release their first demo in 1987, *Law of the Streets*, and exposed for the first time their very challenging and rough sound. This is American power/speed metal, reminiscent of early Attacker mixed with some early Agent Steel. Fans of this style will flip over this one, especially on tracks like "Fire When Ready" and the heavyweight "On the Attack." But the demo that showcased how serious things were came one year later: the excellent 1988 *Engraved in Stone* demo (later re-released as an LP in 1999 by O.P.M. Records) had all the qualities that Texas bands like (early) Helstar and Militia (at their most straightforward) had, with a decent dose of Iron Maiden on adrenaline. Just check out tunes like the pounding "Crystal Ball" and the killer speed metal of "Take No Prisoners." What actually makes Commandment so unique is the strange tempo changes in their songs—very atypical of most heavy metal bands!

"The scene was cool back then," Michael says about the metal scene in Illinois. "We were from the South Side/Northwest Indiana area, and getting into Chicago was kinda hard. Those bands from Chicago and the North Side thought they were better and had a bullshit attitude toward us. But we worked hard, played some shitty gigs, and eventually played Chicago a lot. Of course, the gig to get was the Saturday night slot at the Thirsty Whale. That was the goal of most bands. The Whale was the king at the time. It's no longer around, but when you drive past where it was and listen close, you can still hear the guitars in the air! The Northwest Indiana area had a few clubs that were cool. We played a lot there too. The fans were cool. I think most of them appreciated the band's efforts to try to play a killer show."

Another exception to my rule, Commandment's 1989 *Oriental Maiden/Engraved In Stone* seven-inch is in this book because the tiny indie label, Amethyst Records from West Columbia, South Carolina, released it (because they were very short of money then). The band was then offered a contract for a full LP, which was to be titled *No Mercy*—but it sadly never happened. The result was the release of the *Oriental Maiden/Engraved In Stone* seven-inch—without a picture sleeve, although there are ten copies with picture inlays that also function as a cover. Michael tells the story:

"We recorded it in two weeks, did everything on our own, and just started promoting it. We got a lot of good press from it overseas and a bit in America. We were played on a few local radio stations and one called Z Rock, which was nationwide. We never released anything on a label, unfortunately, but had some interest. Could never close the deal. Although later, a small internet label, O.P.M. Records, released the *Engraved in Stone* demo on a special-edition vinyl in 1999, which got good response and is probably instrumental in getting John and me back together—and eventually getting Commandment back together in 2008. It is bittersweet, though, since Dave Nava is no longer with us..."

CUT TO THE CHASE:

If we ever had a true-metal-o-meter, it would tilt when it heard Commandment. This is vicious, punishing ultra-metal—American power/speed metal of the highest order! Find the *Oriental Maiden/ Engraved in Stone* seven-inch in two different versions, one with silver labels and one with black labels, and also get the reissued *Engraved in Stone* LP/CD and the *No Mercy* LP!

Commandment managed to release two of their best songs on a seven-inch that's still one of American power metal's most seminal records. Kicking off with "Oriental Maiden," an epic, glorious, and fast power/speed metal track, it's evidence that Commandment should have had a full LP out in the late nineties. The B-side, "Engraved in Stone," is a menacing instrumental—terrific stuff. The *Oriental Maiden/Engraved in Stone* seven-inch is a total classic.

Sadly, by 1990, Commandment had disbanded, being disappointed by the metal/record music business and its changing climate that offered few chances to bands with a more traditional sound at the time. But from their early days, they still have some great memories. "Two shows stand out the most," Michael recalls. "A Thirsty Whale gig opening for Chicago band Tattoo. They were releasing their debut record on Metal Blade, and the place was out of control. Probably one of our best shows from a playing standpoint ever. Number two would have to be our two-night stint at the Exit Club with Slauter Xstroyes. They were a killer prog/ power metal band from the Southwest suburbs. Their singer, Jonathan Stewart, had a similar vocal style to Dave Nava, and the bands complemented each other well. Jonathan recently passed away, which was a shock. Two great singers no longer with us, but their memories will last forever. Those shows stand out the most."

In response to whether any other local bands put out indie albums, he replies, "Slauter Xstroyes and a band from our area called Tyrant's Reign had private releases. I'm sure there were others!"

Commandment got back together in 2008 and released a full LP, which was actually the record they meant to release in 1989, *No Mercy*, on Pure Steel Records. They're on the same path of greatness here, and this is highly recommended for everyone into the atypical, crazy American heavy/power metal, where everything is played to the logical limits of the genre!

"Today, there are a lot of great independent labels and a lot of great unsigned bands that deserve to be heard," Michael asserts. "The internet definitely has helped from the promotion side of it. Back in the day, promoting was sending flyers and word of mouth. Going in the back of *Metal Forces* and other magazines and finding the pen pal section to find people who listened to bands with the same musical style and sending them a flyer and bumper sticker, in the hopes they'd buy your cassette or record. Wish we had the internet back then. Of course, I'm blown away that people still remember Commandment from that long ago, and that our recordings are that sought after. It is truly humbling and makes me want to get the new Commandment CD finished..."

About the current metal underground scene, Michael says, "I think most genres of metal are still underground. The average person walking down the street has no idea who Helstar, Overkill, Death, or Sanctuary are. Most bands like this don't receive airplay on mainstream radio. Never have. Radio thinks a band like Van Halen or Nickelback are heavy metal, and that's a joke. Radio and all their management, program directors, and DJs are clueless and a bunch of clowns. Really, guys, Thin Lizzy has more than two songs. Real metal will never be mainstream, and I think most involved could give a shit. We're all right with that. We know we're the most talented musicians out there. We know we don't contrive anything. We don't care about image or award shows, which are fixed anyway. As far as downloading goes or people getting access to music via the internet, I think it's a double-edged sword. We want as many people as possible to hear our music, but we would like to be compensated somewhat for it. Back in the day, the only way anyone heard your music was at a show, or on an underground independent radio station that was on from 10 p.m. to 4 a.m. and had a range of about 50 miles. It was limited. Live shows were how it was done. Now a band can play 50 shows a year but still make a few bucks with all the online stores and downloading sites, and of course, their website. So, the downloading has helped, I think, but a band has to give a lot away to get a little back. We just want the opportunity to play and show people we still can bring it and kick ass."

Following Commandment's demise, Michael played in Throne of Serpents, Michael Anthony Putignano (his eponymous project), Wolf Messiah, Money Gunn, and Tokyo Dawn. Commandment's guitarist and bassist, John "JR3" Remesnik, later played in Exiled, Frankenshred, Throne of Serpents, St. Madness, Arsinal, and Whisper Alley (most of them power/speed bands). The late David Nava played in Nava, Money Gunn, Solitude, and Tokyo Dawn.

CROWHAVEN

A VERY UNIQUE BAND IN TERMS OF MUSIC STYLE AS WELL AS THE FACT THAT they were from rural Danville, Kentucky (not exactly a mecca of American metal), Crowhaven was formed in 1983 by Bucky Bryant and Brett Lane. They met in a local music store, and Brett and Bucky jammed together for a couple of months before bringing in local guitar sensation Rick Sargent. They later completed the lineup with bassist/keyboardist/vocalist Gary Duncil. Rick named the band Crowhaven and played with the band almost a year before leaving to help form Cain's Rage and then later POWND. Crowhaven continued with guitarist Jimmy Calhoun and played a mix of cover songs and originals. Jimmy left after a year to play more country- and blues-oriented material, and the band continued as a three-piece while honing original material for an upcoming LP.

Guitarist Bucky Bryant adds, "We had met Brad Oaks at a local Battle of the Bands competition and asked him if he would be interested in recording with us? He said, 'Sure,' and was excited about going into the studio with us! When we got together for that first rehearsal, the chemistry was just there and everybody knew this was gonna be a working unit...

"Our influences are vast!" Bucky continues. "Brett is half British and was born in London, England. His mom was born in Liverpool and had actually gone to school with Paul McCartney! Brett brought the glam influence into the band with him being a fan of bands like T. Rex, The Sweet, Slade, Maggie Bell, and The Kinks. We were all fans of The Beatles, so that influence was evident. Gary had studied music and music theory while in college and brought the technical expertise into the band with influences like Mike Oldfield, Little Feat, Dixie Dregs, Steely Dan, Talking Heads, and King Crimson. Can't forget the acoustic influence of Dan Fogelberg, Mark O'Connor, and assorted bluegrass bands. John Prine and James Taylor were also pretty standard listening in Gary's car. Gary is an accomplished finger-style acoustic guitarist."

Bucky adds, "My influences range from Buck Owens to Lamb of God! I can pretty much adapt to anything; I just love all music! My biggest influences in my playing have been Eric Clapton, Carlos Santana, Albert King, and Jimmy Page. I've studied the bluegrass work of Lester Flatt and Earl Scruggs extensively, and I'm currently learning the dobro and banjo! Brad Oaks (R.I.P.) only stated one influence that he ever got inspiration from: that was the incredible Michael Schenker. Brad had all the UFO & MSG cassettes in that old Chevy van that got us to the studio and to live gigs a few times! He idolized Michael and played so much like him! Plus, I can't deny the Southern rock influence that Gary Duncil and myself had, with bands like Lynyrd Skynyrd, Outlaws, Atlanta Rhythm Section, Allman Brothers Band, Hydra, and Molly Hatchet. It was all over the radio in the eighties in this locality. But my personal most inspirational record would have to be *Never Mind the Bollocks, Here's the Sex Pistols*. It was my coming-of-age album that completely transformed how I looked at music and the music industry! It was quite a statement to a 16-year-old kid in 1977. I kinda knew at that point that I wanted to play music professionally at some level."

Bucky also discusses how things were in the 1980s, in the Kentucky rock/metal scene: "The scene in the mid- and late 1980s in this area of Kentucky was the true epitome of a rock 'n' roll weekend! Every Thursday, Friday, or Saturday night would find you in either Richmond, Lebanon, Lexington, or Louisville, Kentucky ... enjoying or playing live music. Richmond was always a favorite with Eastern Kentucky University (my alma mater) and the row of bars and nightclubs on First Street in Richmond. You could play a different venue all three nights in one of these cities, and still not play the same venue twice in a 30-day period. Then you had the regional scene with Cincinnati, Indianapolis, and even Nashville. We truly lived in a great locality for music of all genres and styles. The local crowd has always been very receptive to us. We've even been dubbed 'Central Kentucky's best-kept metal secret.'

"We did favor the studio over live performances," Bucky says. "That was where we could create and experiment, and it always provided an outlet for our ideas and imaginations. We've recently had some local animosity with one of the younger death metal bands in our area, because we got some local attention on the reissue and the opportunity to play Ragnarokkr Metal Apocalypse in Chicago in 2014 with the newly reformed version of Crowhaven. Just some remarks about us being old men and the ever-constant 'They only recorded one album' monotonous jab. We just dismiss it as juvenile jealousy and tell them to quit singing like Cookie Monster. We've had more critics since the reissue came out than in the 25-plus years before we reformed. We still adhere to the fact that the album stands on its on merit."

In 1984, Crowhaven released a demo containing two songs (one to appear later on their LP, the excellent *The Crow*), but by 1986, they wanted to make a record. Bucky tells the story behind the recording and release of the *Emotional Adjustment* 1986 LP:

"The decision to record a vinyl LP on a private label was basically the idea of Gary Duncil, John Clark, and Jeff Carpenter. We had been practicing as a three-piece unit and really had the original compositions honed into diligently catchy and well-crafted songs. All originals as well. Gary had contacted a fellow musician from this area who's now working and living in Louisville named John Clark. They had attended college together at Campbellsville University. John had been working with Jeff Carpenter as a session musician with Jeff's newly formed label, Hit A Note Records, based out of Louisville, Kentucky. Jeff had already been working with the band Velvet Elvis, which later garnered national attention and also a couple of major label releases. Jeff was looking for bands for the label and had some major contacts within the Louisville area and independent markets. College radio stations were huge in the mid-1980s, and they were always looking for new and independent acts to play on that college circuit. Jeff and John had effectively tapped this resource and were making some huge waves within this industry. Jeff basically offered us a price and a package that we couldn't resist to make and record the album. It was pretty much a done deal after the initial meeting and procedures got finalized. With a stern budget of just 1,500 dollars and 30 hours of recording time from start to final mix, we set about recording *Emotional Adjustment* over a three-week period, starting in February of 1986.

"Jeff Carpenter was truly a master of recording and sound engineering," Bucky says. "He really brought out the very best in the band! His custom soundboard was also partially built by Tom Scholz of the great band Boston. Jeff definitely had the very best equipment as well! We basically went into the studio and played live, when we had been playing as a three-piece for the last eight months. We finished the album in about 22 hours! Trouble was? We didn't have a stellar lead guitar player. I was adequate on lead at best ... but really excelled more as a rhythm guitarist. I just rationally didn't have the style to really put the songs over the top.

"That was when we asked and auditioned Brad Oaks for the lead guitarist position in Crowhaven. It was a magical audition, and we knew from that evening that we had truly found the missing piece of the puzzle. Brad Oaks rehearsed with Crowhaven over a four-week period, learning all the songs that would later appear on *Emotional Adjustment*. The album tracks were basically complete, with only Brad's guitar parts and Gary's vocals needing to be completed and overdubbed, and the final stereo mix being satisfactory for all parties involved. We finished the album the second week of May in 1986 and the master tape was sent to Dixie Record Pressing in Nashville for our vinyl test pressings to be returned. We got those a little over a week later, and we were very satisfied with the completed project. Full-scale production was now in effect for the 300 copies of the *Emotional Adjustment* vinyl album. Our graphic artist friend, Wayne Daugherty, had been on board with the entire Crowhaven concept since the days Rick Sargent aptly named the band. His crow logo, Gandalf interpretation, custom label

CUT TO THE CHASE:

***Emotional Adjustment* isn't a 100 percent privately released record, since it was distributed via Hit A Note Records, but that really doesn't matter at all. It is one of the most unique-sounding, diverse, metal-to-the-max records you will find in this book! Get the original LP, but see if you can also score the 2013 re-release on Blood And Iron Records. This is a record that everyone who's into classic heavy metal or American power should have in their collection.**

design, and artwork are featured prominently throughout the album.

"The album was released the second week of June in 1986," Bucky continues. "But we had a problem: Dixie Record Pressing in Nashville had forgotten to put the lyric insert sheet inside the LPs ... Brett Lane and myself had to make a pilgrimage to Nashville and the manufacturing plant and have all the albums rewrapped and the lyric insert sheet placed by hand in each one of the albums. If you have one of those VERY RARE 50 albums that got released without a lyric insert sheet, you've definitely got something that will most surely increase the value of that release and your specific piece. Without a doubt! Another unknown fact surrounding the mystique of the *Emotional Adjustment* record! It was a very wild day/night in Nashville, to say the least."

Emotional Adjustment is a flawless, absolute-classic hard-rock-to-heavy-metal record that reminds me of such rare greats as Impeccable, Alkana, or Monarch. But it is even more than that; its excellent metal production brings lots of power, and every song on it introduces diverse influences! From the party metal of "Heavy Metal Darlin'" to the excellent—and almost new wave—"Don't Tell Me" and "The Crow" to the heavy Sabbathian brilliance of "Changes" and then to the NWOBHM-based "Testify," *Emotional Adjustment* just shines.

Crowhaven never split up, and they keep it up today (as of 2021), performing live from time to time since 2014, even though they haven't released anything since *Emotional Adjustment*.

When asked about his favorite Crowhaven show, Bucky responds, "The most memorable performance would most definitely be Ragnarokkr Metal Apocalypse in 2014 in Chicago, and sharing the stage with the incredible Steve Grimmett and Grim Reaper. We also got the opportunity to work with Eric Moore and the great seventies/eighties biker band, The Godz, out of Columbus, Ohio ... and played a benefit concert in Coshocton, Ohio, to help raise money for Eric's radiation treatments for throat cancer. Thrilled to say Eric is in remission and has been for a couple of years. He's just a dear friend and an incredible person, as are all the guys in Grim Reaper, as well. They've always treated us with the utmost decency and respect! The Ragnarokkr show was our first live performance in 26 years, and it just felt incredible being on stage again.

"As far as the best show from original lineup from 1986? I'd definitely say a benefit that we played in Harrodsburg, Kentucky, was the most memorable. A fellow employee at Kroger (I worked there for 19 years) had a girlfriend who was on life support following a tragic automobile accident. Her medical bills were just astronomical as the family struggled to keep her alive with their hope for her survival. Sorry to say that Anna Kephart did not survive that terrible automobile accident, but Crowhaven and another band, The Sinkhorn Family

Band, helped raise over 3,000 dollars for her care on that evening in 1987. Quite a bit of money back then."

Regarding Kentucky labels and bands from back in the day, Bucky comments, "Jeff Carpenter had many local bands on his Hit A Note record label back in 1986. Among them was a Louisville band called Velvet Elvis. They went on to be signed by Enigma Records and had a major label release in the late 1980s. Their album on Hit A Note was titled *What In The World...* and it remains a personal favorite. Almost sounding like the great band Blondie at times. Really good stuff. Another band that Jeff had on his label was Rebel Without A Cause. Plus, our great friends and local/regional band Buster Brown was releasing a couple of independent label LPs during this time. Vocalist Johnny Edwards would later go on to sing with Foreigner, Montrose, Wild Horses, and King Kobra. The drummer, James Kottak, remains a good friend, and he's played in Scorpions, Kingdom Come, and also Wild Horses."

Ending our joyful conversation, Bucky—who's a very positive person, let me tell you!—added a few words on the current underground metal scene. "Labels like High Roller, Metal Soldiers, Blood and Iron, Nightmare Records, and Skol Records have simply done some incredible and superior jobs of getting these recordings back out there and available to the metal masses. It maybe gets a little more satisfying, as I get older, especially, when a 22- or 23-year-old metalhead discovers it and contacts me, wanting info about getting a copy of Crowhaven's LP. That's pretty satisfying. I just truly want to share it with as many people as I possibly can. I'd love to know that someday, we'll record another album. But that hope may be dwindling more with each passing day. At least we have almost 40 minutes of that Crowhaven magic, captured within this recording..."

When asked about the metal underground today, he replies, "Back in the metal community, it is very much alive and well today! You have all these great and awesome metal festivals like the one Jarvis Leatherby (from Night Demon and Cirith Ungol) puts on each year, Frost and Fire in California every October. You've got Randy Kastner doing the same thing in Milwaukee each spring with RK Metal Promotions' Milwaukee Spring Bash. You've got Bob Byrne doing Legions of Metal at Reggies in Chicago every May, which replaced Ragnarokkr Metal Apocalypse! I'm talking two or three days of great metal with about 20 bands! You've also got the great European festivals like Keep It True. Always a great lineup and always a great time, no matter which festival you choose to attend."

STEEL VENGEANCE

MUSKEGON, MICHIGAN, CAN TAKE PRIDE IN ONE OF THE MOST UNDERRATED heavy metal bands ever. I know that the word *underrated* has been widely used in this book, but in the case of Steel Vengeance, there is no other word to describe them. It's a mystery (and a shame) that metalheads of today ignore the existence of this band. Formed in 1983, drummer Marshall Davis narrates their story:

"Steel Vengeance was formed in the early 1980s by guitarist/producer Michael Wickstrom in the hard rock and heavy metal tradition, similar to Judas Priest and Iron Maiden. The band has had numerous accolades throughout the 1980s such as beating out Kiss, Twisted Sister, and various other bands for the highly coveted Album of the Month title from France's *Enfer* magazine, and numerous other magazine awards and heavy metal European radio play. Their follow-up release, *Second Offense*, scored lots of acclaim as well, as did their third release, *Prisoners*. In the 1990s Steel Vengeance had a lineup change and relocated to Los Angeles and released *Never Lettin' Go* and *Live Among the Dead*. Metal Mind Productions and Psychedelic Records have remastered and re-released recently our first three albums."

"The love of heavy metal and hard rock music is the reason I formed the band," guitarist/bassist Michael Wickstrom remembers. "We loved everything ever released by Deep Purple, Led Zeppelin and Judas Priest—those were our influences. There are no particular albums per se, just the awesome music by these guys is mind-blowing. At first, nobody knew what to think of us. We are from the small town of Muskegon, Michigan. We would have to play local bars and clubs doing cover tunes and slipping in some of our originals while doing the shows. Once we released our first full-length demo, *Never Lettin' Go*, followed up by our first full-length record, *Call Off the Dogs*, we were treated like kings everywhere we went. It was a nice change, getting that respect. We opened the door for other local bands from this town by Steel Vengeance being the first ever band getting signed to a major European record label. When Marshall Davis and I left Michigan and went to Los Angeles, some of the ex-band members formed a band called Drop Hammer and got signed to a label. And now you may also know the name of another local Muskegon, Michigan, band that is pretty famous—by the name of Pop Evil. So you could say we really did open the door for these other bands."

CUT TO THE CHASE:

I always thought Steel Vengeance had a weird, nostalgic, emotional touch to their sound that reminded me of the eighties-era Angel Witch, even though their approach is way different. A funny story is that I bought *Prisoners* about 20 years ago, because its American version was on Giant Records, a label created by Uniform Choice that's released records by 7 Seconds, Verbal Assault, and Dag Nasty among others, and you know the deal: When you like some of the releases from a label, you have to get all the label's releases! It's a shame that a band as good as Steel Vengeance is still unknown by most metalheads. The *Your Time Has Come* seven-inch, though, is not a classic, just a good American metal seven-inch. However, I recommend getting *Call Off the Dogs* and *Prisoners* wholeheartedly!

In 1984, Steel Vengeance kicked off their career with the release of a self-funded, self-released seven-inch on their Kingdom Records label, *Your Time Has Come*. "That's a quick funny story," Michael responds when asked about it. "We were practicing one day, and in between songs, we stopped to talk about what we were going to do next. When we practiced, we would let some friends come over and watch us jam out. A buddy of ours brought a guy who had just started working for a company that made records. He asked us if we wanted him to print some songs on records for us. So, we jumped on it. We never did anything like this before and thought it would be a great idea. Now, back then, we had no idea how to produce, as you might have noticed by listening to that record, but it worked out for us. We had been together a year, recorded three songs on a record. We felt like rock stars, but that was short-lived once we heard how it sounded."

Mike continues, "I cannot recall how many we made of those records, but I can tell you we melted a ton of them down and made them into ashtrays, and also played Frisbee with a bunch of them too ... haha! I think Marshall Davis is the only person on Earth that still has one of those awful records! Marshall has EVERYTHING we have ever recorded, along with every single radio chart and magazine we've ever been in."

Even though Mike sounds dissatisfied with the final outcome, *Your Time Has Come* is a really good release! Very Judas Priest-influenced, its three songs have a very uplifting vibe—it's pure metal that oozes with energy, fun, and youthful recklessness! Specifically, the title song is a great tune, whereas "Black Leather" is a fist-banging beauty. *Your Time Has Come*, though, was only a small piece of what was about to come...

In 1985, Steel Vengeance released the *Never Lettin' Go* demo, which was a huge step forward. Now sounding more powerful than before, Steel Vengeance was exposing the first previews of its ultra-powerful, frenetic American metal sound, which combined Motörhead and Accept with Judas Priest. Agnès and Michel Desgranges of the French heavy metal label Black Dragon Records were intrigued by their sound and offered them a chance to release their music. Actually, all their five LPs were released on Black Dragon: *Call Off the Dogs* in 1985, *Second Offense* in 1986, *Prisoners* in 1987, *Never Lettin' Go* in 1989, and *Live Among the Dead*, 1990. Their records range from good to great, with my favorite being *Prisoners*, a sheer explosion of heavy metal mayhem in its wildest form. But then again, you can find incredible moments on all their records (e.g., "Night Turns to Day," "I Surrender," or "We Will Not be Defeated").

"Doing a concert at home, back in Muskegon, is always the best, because that's where it all started at and we have such a huge hometown fan base," Mike says, with Marshall adding, "A few years ago, there was a band called Orange October that put out a CD on their own. There were no other bands back in the day besides Steel Vengeance that put a record out on their own label. Well, maybe Pop Evil did as well, before they got famous. I think they sent one to me in the mail..."

"To be honest, I don't know why anybody would even want that very first record. Everything after that including our *Never Lettin' Go* demo was so much better," vocalist Scott Carlson adds. "There are so many underground bands out there nowadays. Just take a look at Myspace, that's all Myspace is about nowadays, along with iTunes. I think that there is so much talent out there, and it's a shame in a way, because I think the internet ruined the chances for a lot of great bands. Yet it also brought us some great bands too. So, it's up in the air regarding that question!" Mike, Scott, and Marshall agree.

Steel Vengeance split initially in the early 1990s and are back together today, after reuniting in 2007. In 2008, the band released *The Collection* on CD on their own, and at the moment (as of 2021), they are working on a new album.

PENDULUM

PENDULUM FROM SAN ANTONIO, TEXAS, FORMED IN THE HEYDAY OF THRASH metal (1986), but sadly, the band went on to release all their records on their own label, Euthanasia Music. Pendulum had the class to pursue a good career in thrash, so don't worry; the word *sadly* is only used because they never got the chance to release records on a bigger label. Vocalist/bassist Joey Yorfino tells us more:

"In 1986, I began searching for other guys to play thrash metal with. I was at a local music store, and back then, you found other musicians on bulletin boards. There was a crudely handwritten note on this board that said, 'Brutal metal band looking for bass player,' and I responded. I met Jeff and Mike Riley, the brothers who started the band, in March of 1987 and they already had a singer, a guy named Trey Hoffman. We formed that day. A few months later, we decided to add a second guitarist, and Forrest 'Bubba' Whitehead joined us, completing the original lineup. A while later, Trey left, and I took over on vocals. I was kinda forced into it because we were in the studio and someone had to sing, and the vote came down to me. We spent the next year writing, rehearsing, and recording our first eight songs, four of which ended up on the *Skull Fuck* EP. Early on, we played some great gigs opening for Armored Saint, Watchtower, and Fearless Iranians from Hell. Our motivation was being young and fearless and lucky enough to perform and create extreme metal! We formed Pendulum to thrash hard and become a band worthy of notice, but mostly to crack skulls and rebel against everything that wasn't thrash metal (haha), even though for me personally, it was Iron Maiden's *Killers* LP that stood as a game-changer. Accordingly, we were influenced by all the metal and rock of the time."

With the topic veering to the San Antonio scene of the day, Joey says, "In the late 1980s, San Antonio was predominantly punk, as in punk was the scene, with the acceptance of a few metal bands but not much attention at all. Pendulum was the city's first true thrash metal band. We played fast with blast beats and technical thrash riffing. Early on, my voice was very punkish-sounding, but we delivered thrash metal that evolved into a scene of its own. The locals were split on Pendulum; any type of extreme metal was frowned upon in the club scene. The biggest local club that featured hair metal would not let us play. They would tell us, 'You guys are too heavy,' 'We don't play that kind of music here.' So, we played at smaller underground places like Taco Land and the DMZ—both are famous places around here now. I would show up at clubs in the afternoon when the manager was there, smoke a little weed with 'em, and we had gigs. The records helped a little bit also."

While Pendulum was a few years late for the commercial outbreak of thrash metal, still they released initially the 1989 *Skull Fuck* seven-inch on their Euthanasia Music label. Joey elaborates:

"We knew we had to have a record of some kind to stand out among the crowd, so in early 1989, we released our *Skull Fuck* EP. It was a big hit with local metal guys. Only 500 were pressed, and 100 are on blood-red vinyl. We never had a second pressing. What's interesting is the story of the actual pressing. The man who was in charge of stamping out the records calls us one day and leaves a message that says, 'This is Bill, there's a problem with your record, please call me back.' The next day, we call, and he had died that night. We would tell people that this guy now haunts our record and his blood spilled into the red vinyl. The eighties and early nineties were a DIY era. We weren't going to wait for a miracle—we were determined to forge our own future!"

There is a crossover touch in Pendulum's sound, especially in the vocals; however, the result is nothing but raging, crazy, ferocious thrash metal played to its logical limits. *Skull Fuck* bears resemblance to the ultra-violent sounds of early Sacrifice (Canada), Sadus, and early Kreator with its four venomous songs, underproduced and raw as hell. *Skull Fuck* actually falls in between thrash and death metal, and it could attract fans of both, as well as metalpunks—blistering songs like "Kindred Spirit" sound like bomb blasts!

Pendulum later appeared on the 1990 *Voices of a Red God* compilation LP, alongside bands from Texas and Louisiana (with Dead Horse and Soilent Green being the most notorious ones), and also released the near-perfect *Atrocity Sin* demo, heading into a more brutal sound. Plus, they went on to perform quite regularly in the Texas area.

"The shows we did with Dead Horse were the best ones, I think," Joey recalls. "We were featured on a twelve-inch vinyl compilation record called *Voices of a Red God*, and there were a few shows in Texas and New Orleans with other bands on the record, including Dead Horse. These were great shows, but for me personally, it was the Dead Horse show where we recorded our 'Jesus Fish' video. Jeff smashed his guitar on stage in the middle of a song and fought the audience to get it back. The crowd got so violent that the management of the club ushered us off stage, put us in a room, and told us to stay put and don't come out. Tensions were high—they thought there would be a riot. Mike from Dead Horse told me, 'I love it when you guys open for us.' After us the audience of about 1,000 people were armed and ready for Dead Horse. It was one of the most raging shows I'd ever seen."

CUT TO THE CHASE:

I'm guessing that the folks who are more into traditional metal won't go mental over Pendulum's raging extreme stuff; however, *Skull Fuck* (as well as all their releases) is just a tremendous, sheer extreme metal explosion with a hardcore/ crossover edge. Of course, it is highly recommended for everyone into the brutal sounds of the late 1980s!

In 1991, Pendulum released the *Vlad the Impaler* seven-inch, again on their own label, as well as the *Vlad the Impaler* demo cassette and a split seven-inch with Spectre named *Isotopic Chaos* in 1992. The band kept it up until 1993. No reunions since then, and only drummer Mike Riley went on to later appear in another band (Doomsday).

"Well, I guess there could have been some bands from San Antonio that self-released their works, but I can't remember," Joey admits. "When we were doing Pendulum, that's all that mattered. I couldn't and wouldn't see anything past our records. We were the only thrash metal band making records in San Antonio at the time. I would have never thought in a thousand years that our little records would be a collectible item, and frankly, it blows my mind. I found out about it when I did a Google search for our label, Euthanasia Music, and the records popped up on Discogs. We did three seven-inch records, *Skull Fuck*, *Vlad the Impaler*, and a split record with another local band named Spectre called *Isotopic Chaos*. I've got a few of each left over in a box. If anyone one wants to purchase one from me, just reach out. You can also listen and watch Pendulum videos on my YouTube channel, Squidfarm Music.

"There is no underground today and never will be again," Joey adds. "Back in the day, you had to search for underground music. You heard about it through friends or at school, or someone's big brother had an album. In record stores, all metal was in the import section, even the American releases. You had to know where to look and you felt triumphant when you discovered something new—it made you feel special. Finding the underground was a mission, and underground music was something you hid from your parents; it was as far removed from mainstream as you can get. Before the internet, everyone promoted through fanzines and through the mail, you had to create a network of contacts around the world, you sent them your records and promo flyers and they would pass them on to other people through the mail. Pretty soon, you would get tons of mail from new people interested in the band—this is how I got Pendulum's music all over the planet. It took lots of time and footwork and thought and money, and that underground will never exist again."

RUDE AWAKENING

BURLINGTON, IOWA, THE SEAT OF DES MOINES COUNTY, ISN'T EXACTLY FAMOUS for its heavy metal bands. But you might be surprised. For one, it's the hometown of Rude Awakening, a young group of kids who released their own spectacular album, which is one of the rarest in American metal.

"Come on, we were barely 14, and this was a way to meet girls, of course," says vocalist Jerry Darnold when asked about the motivation to start the band. "We were just friends from school who wanted to play rock 'n' roll, so we thought, hey, let's put a band together. We were into the music of the day. If it had loud distorted guitars, we liked it. Van Halen and Kiss for sure. At that time, Van Halen's debut record and Kiss' *Alive* were the top records for me...

"Believe it or not, there were many bands in the Burlington area at the time. We just wanted to be part of the music scene. We were just kids, so we thought we had something to prove.

CUT TO THE CHASE:

Now considered a holy grail of American underground metal, *Bound for Glory* is a great record for what it is: mid-tempo, classic, stomping, and powerful American metal of its day and time. If you are a fan of this style, you simply need to get it! This is a very rare item, though, and as Jerry mentioned, nowadays it can scarcely be found, and at ridiculous prices. A reissue soon, maybe?

When people heard us, we were well received. When we first started playing together, we learned covers from the day. Ozzy, Kiss, Scorpions, and so on. But at first, we did not have a singer, so we just did instrumentals. Once we had a singer, we decided to write our own songs to separate us from the other cover bands."

Rude Awakening released their first and only LP just two years after their formation. It was 1986 when the band—with the lineup being Daryl Downer on bass, Matt Waugh on drums, Scott Jaeger on guitar, Dave Schwarm on rhythm guitar, and Jerry Darnold on vocals—put out their record through their own label, Rudiment Records. "When we went to the studio to record, we were ready. We stuck to a practice schedule prior to recording, so we knew what we wanted. In 1984 and 1985, there weren't many studios in our area, so we found a studio in Decatur, Illinois, that had eight-track reel-to-reel recording capabilities. A big deal at that time. As I recall, we only spent a few weekends there doing tracks, and the process was pretty quick for our first experience."

Bound for Glory is a real hidden jewel of American metal. Balancing between the American sounds of early Dokken and the British tradition of NWOBHM (as well as a strong flavor of Iron Maiden), this is a release that will shock anybody into digging this sound. Songs like the title track and the closing "Deranged" could drive you crazy, whereas overall the style of *Bound for Glory* is American mid-tempo classic heavy metal.

Rude Awakening also played some good shows during their short-lived existence: "At that age, every show was a great new experience. Probably playing in our local auditorium at our local music festival right before Joan Jett played on the outdoor stage. That was the first time any of us got to play on a big stage before," Jerry adds.

"Did you know that in Burlington, there were many bands that released some demos/cassettes?" Jerry recalls. "One that comes to mind is Krystal Vizhun. They were our high school band competition, and I think they put out one or two cassettes."

Rude Awakening came to an end in 1987 or early 1988. However, their echo can still be heard today through die-hard collectors of the rarest indie metal stuff. "I think it's quite amazing. I mean here it is, almost 35 years after the release of this album, when I barely knew how to play anymore, and it has all this interest. It blows my mind," Jerry says. "When I heard that our album was selling as a sort of collectible, I thought, 'What? To whom?' Then I saw it had sold on eBay for 500 dollars and another one had sold for 1,200 dollars. I did a Google search and discovered our album on these vintage independent metal vinyl records sites—I could not believe it. All I can say is I wish I had more records to sell, but I only have my one copy and always will. If I remember right, we only pressed 200 of these.

"There is definitely still an underground scene," Jerry concludes. "There probably always will be in any genre. Music has always been about discovery for me. I could care less about what's on the radio. I prefer to dig deeper and not take the spoon-fed stuff. That's where you find the real music and musicians ... however, downloading, to me? That's just a sign of the time we are living in. Everything happens in an instant, and most people crave that. Downloading songs is cool and all, but I'm an album guy and always will be. I enjoy the physical aspect of recordings, whether it's vinyl, cassette, or CD—it's all about reading the credits and appreciating the artwork. When I like an artist or band, chances are I will like the whole album."

heroes of the METAL underground

NEVER FORGET THE WARRIORS

IN THIS FINAL CHAPTER, MORE THAN 700 BANDS/RECORDS OF AMERICAN privately released metal are included, along with a small review and price market research. Many great bands here for which I either couldn't track down any of their members for an interview or they would just always forget to schedule one. But please just regard it as a useful guide! That is this chapter's purpose.

Kicking off with **CENTAUR**'s *There's a Storm Coming* seven-inch, by a Cortland, New York-area hard 'n' heavy band: The two songs were written/produced by Dave Feinstein and Carl Canedy of the Rods and sung by Peter Gerber. Two very AC/DC-fueled anthems, definitely above par—however, there's no info out there about the price of this one. **ARSYNAL** from Las Vegas, Nevada, was Mark Stewart's (Thrust/Axehammer) band, and in 1987, they released the seven-inch *Mean Line/You Think It's Luv* on their own label, Razor's Edge Records); it's good melodic metal, especially on "Mean Line." Arsynal also released a demo in 1988, *The Genesis,* and a compilation named *Millennium* was released in 2020. On the more melodic side of things, **EARGAZM** from Illinois released two private records, the *Eargazm* LP and the *Try a Little Longer/Nuthin' Lasts Forever* seven-inch, both in 1981, on their Earresistible Records label; melodic and slick American hard rock (not AOR, though), good for fans of this style. **BLIND BEGGAR**, from Lakeland, Florida, released just one twelve-inch in 1985, *Winds of War*, that contained four songs of hard/heavy metal; raw and powerful but not too inspired, even though "Virgin's Child" is a decent song. So many people are getting crazy over the 1986 *Metal Merchant* EP by Houston's **METAL MERCHANT**, and I can understand why: classic, shining American steel, with a definite Judas Priest edge, and good songs like "What Does It Feel Like" and "Sacrifice." One of the rarest and priciest items to get, *Metal Merchant* is nearly impossible to find today.

From Redwood City, California, **REDVETTE** released a very enjoyable hard 'n' heavy LP (*Redvette*) in 1982; not a classic for sure, but still nice stuff. "Coast to Coast" is a good song, and this one's worth getting. In the same style, if heading slightly more into AOR, **RECEIVER** from Hollywood, California, released their *Receiver* EP in 1981; not bad, but not crucial. **HAVEN** from Cleveland, Ohio, released two independent records, 1984's *Turn It Up/Get Ready* seven-inch and the 1985 *Haven* twelve-inch. "Turn It Up" was also released as a video clip, and overall, Haven's output is pretty basic hard 'n' heavy stuff; nothing too spectacular, even though "Rebel of the World" is a good one. **G.T. WATIES'** 1988 LP, *Steal the Thunder*, is a very special record; G.T. Waties himself, who's responsible for guitars, bass, keyboard and vocals on "I Love 'Em All," has written everything here, accompanied by two drummers and two female singers. Highly melodic and classy metal, guitar-driven—a great one for sure. **QUASIMODO** was a fairly obscure quartet from Corpus Christi, Texas, and their 1984 *Down and Out/You Want It* seven-inch on their own Opus Magnum Records label was melodic and well-written American metal, not far away from what Riot were doing in the late 1970s and early 1980s. Obvious NWOBHM influence here, and both songs are real classy acts, with "Down and Out" being the winner. **RAMMPAGE** from Florida has one of the most dramatic stories in the history of American metal: all three members of the band died of drug overdoses. However, the musical legacy that they left us on their only record, the 1987 *Rammpage Debut EP* twelve-inch, is pretty good. Guitarist Mark McClain might be a little too rambling on his endless solos, but songs like "Die Tryin'" and "Locked Down" are fine examples of classic heavy metal. *Rammpage Debut EP* was released with two covers, one red and one black. I couldn't find **STRIKER**'s 1985 *Ready and Willing* seven-inch anywhere in order to review it, so I will just note the info about them: hailing from Converse, Texas, the music's hard 'n' heavy, and *Ready and Willing* is a fairly rare item.

MONARCH from Newnan, Georgia, released one of the priciest and sought-after items, the excellent 1983 *As Your Kingdom Falls* LP; bordering between hard rock and heavy metal, with a definite epic feel, *As Your Kingdom Falls* is a total classic—reminiscent of Ashbury and the like. Just check out "You Won't Be Denied." **EMPYRE** from Long Island sound pretty mixed to me, since sometimes they remind me of a more watered-down Manilla Road or Wishbone Ash, and the next minute they have a definite hard rock/AOR style, and all this through an R.E.M. sound! Virgin Steele's Jack Starr is a guest guitarist on their 1986 twelve-inch *The Foundation*, and some songs, like "The Never-Ending Battle," are really good. They self-released another record (well, CD) in 1989, *No More Running Away*, which was good too. I have found no info whatsoever about **D.F.X.** other than that they hailed from Netcong, New Jersey; that their 1985 twelve-inch EP, *No Frills*, was issued in a plain white twelve-inch sleeve; and that it's a cross between heavy metal and hard rock. In 1984, **ECLIPSE** from California released the *True-Luv* LP on their own East Ways Productions label, and it's a pretty hard rock record with a progressive edge. "Fall of the Curtain" is an okay song, but I can't say that I was too excited about this LP. **FUTURE SOUTH** from New Mexico released the *Another World/Lady in White* seven-inch on an unknown 1980s date, and their musical style has a definite Kiss touch, mixed with some Scorpions. I didn't flip out over this one, even though "Lady in White" has an incredible guitar solo. Another very mysterious seven-inch, **NEW MUSIC** released *The River/The Jester*, a so-called hard/heavy record, in 1985.

HOTT ROXX from Cincinnati released just one seven-inch, the 1987 *Point Blank* (on their Broad Horizons Records): four songs of NWOBHM-influenced metal, with the excellent "Stargazer" being worth the price of admission. **PANDA** from Atlanta only released one LP, which mixed heavy metal with AOR, in 1988, and what makes an impression here is the total professionalism both in the recording and in the execution of their songs. Not a fan of AOR, but their *All the Pink* LP will definitely satisfy the fans of this sound—it's a minor classic in this vein. Very pricey to obtain, so get ready to break the piggy bank for this one. **RARE BREED** from Concord, California, released the 1987 twelve-inch *Rare Breed* on their own Fowl Mouth Records label, which was a very heavy, underproduced classic American metal with female vocals. "Twisted Words" is a good song. **RARE BREED** (a.k.a. Rarebreed) from New Jersey, on the other hand, released the 1987 *Rare Breed* album, again with female vocals (from Myra Ciardi), but they were better than the Concord band of the same name. Absolutely terrific American metal, and songs like "Blast Off" are real keepers. **PRISONER** from Dallas/Fort Worth, Texas, released their *Heavy Metal in My Soul* seven-inch in 1985, and of the 500 copies that were pressed, only 350 were made available to the public. Eric Knudson nowadays is the guitarist of Phantom-X; while the title song is a metal party anthem, the flip side ("It's Your Time") is a rager, reminiscent mostly of NWOBHM, even though it lacks technical proficiency both on the bad solos and vocals. **INFRA RED** from Chicago and its 1985 *Red Alert* twelve-inch

EP has a very early 1980s Judas Priest vibe, with a slight Van Halen touch, and songs like "Keep On Running" will definitely please the fans of the aforementioned. Decent EP, although it's still pricey to obtain. **HOT SHOT** from Mill Hill, Connecticut, went for a mix of American and British metal styles on their traditional heavy metal *Deep of the Night* seven-inch, with the title song being a real metal hymn!

New York City's **FRIGID BICH** is active today (as of 2021), and their first release, 1981's *Call Us Robinhoods* seven-inch, is a minor classic of early American metal! Raw and vicious, like NWOBHM on adrenaline, the title song and the B-side, "You're No Loser," are hymns of raw metal. Get this one for sure. Again from New York City, **CINEMA** released the 1986 LP *Break the Silence* and the *So Lost In Love* twelve-inch on their own Esquire Records label. AOR hard rock, very melodic with a slight metal edge, and the fans of this style will appreciate it. **AXMINSTER** from Boston followed a total American melodic metal route on the 1984 *Rock and Roll Infection* seven-inch. Party metal, but still rougher than glam metal, with the title song being a steamroller (for this style). The flip side of "Teenage Livin'" reminds me of a mix of Def Leppard and Kiss. **ROXX** from Miami, Florida, was formed by members of the power-pop band Z-Cars, and their 1983 *Miami* seven-inch is reportedly hard 'n' heavy; I couldn't find it, though, in order to review it. Some members later played in Diving for Pearls. On the other hand, another **ROXX**, this one from Nashville, Tennessee, was a heavy metal combo, and their 1987 twelve-inch EP *Roxx* (on their label, Rude Records) is good; get it just for "Nuclear War," a real true heavy metal hymn. The rest of this twelve-inch is in between Judas Priest and Dokken. **BLACK DIAMOND** from Detroit was an independent glam metal act, and the 1988 twelve-inch EP *Bending the Rules* isn't something crucial—this band kind of reminds me of a poor man's Poison, especially on songs like "Thinking Of."

AKILLA from New York City was a power/thrash band, with the thrash element deriving from their music and the power element from the vocals of Mike Villamena. The band released two records independently, 1988's *As for Me, As for You* LP and 1989's *The Cursed* LP. *As for Me, As for You* suffers from very bad production, but it is definitely still enjoyable, while *The Cursed* is the better of the two, with good songs such as "No Emotion" and "Abstract Illusion" that fans of, say, Flotsam and Jetsam will appreciate. **WIZARD** from Pittsburgh, Pennsylvania, had a contribution on the 1980 compilation LP *WDVE: Pittsburgh Rocks Album* with their song "Blind Man," and the *Down From Under* seven-inch is very NWOBHM-influenced. This actually sounds like a lost British metal seven-inch from that era! Rough and gruff-sounding metal, overall good stuff, with "Apostle of Greed" being a great song. **TEMPERED STEEL** from Glenwood, Illinois, released the *Precious Metal* LP on their Heart 65 Records in 1988; it's melodic metal, but nothing too spectacular, even though "Legend" is a very nice song. A pretty weird story behind **HYDE**, from Glendale, California: The band formed in the early 1980s, and in 1986 released the *Hyde* LP, a good party-metal LP, on their own label, Apollo Records. They later changed their name to **JEKYLL** and released the *Play Doctor* mini-LP in 1988, still in the same musical vein. **DEZIRE** was from Jamestown, Tennessee, and their hard rock-to-metal crossover is just okay. The 1985 *The Awakening* LP is oddly pricey considering the quality of the material. In the case of **AIREBORNE** from Trenton, New Jersey, we're talking about very obscure stuff; only a twelve-inch with no picture sleeve that has two songs ("Cold Eyes" and "Rock and Rollers"), reportedly heavy metal. Couldn't find it to review it. **NARATA**, from Las Vegas, is another major obscurity! One seven-inch released in 1984 contained the songs "The Quest" and "Life Before Your Time." In the case of Narata, the asking price is totally understandable, since what we have here is top-class hard 'n' heavy metal with a good Thin Lizzy influence, as well as shades of Black Sabbath. Yes, it is rough-sounding and amateurish, but you can see a band shining behind all this. Both songs rule.

FIGHTER from Nashville, Tennessee, was a power trio, and their traditional heavy metal on the 1986 *No Pain, No Gain* LP on their Rowdy Records label bears resemblance to Judas Priest (*Killing Machine* and *British Steel*), and it's simply perfect for fans of this style. Songs like the title track or "Fire in the Sky" are real metal tunes. **LUCKY 13** from Los Angeles also performed under the name Nasty Angel and released their *Lookin' for Trouble* seven-inch in 1987, which is tuneful melodic glam metal. **MADD HATTER** from Houston went for a more barbaric metal approach on their 1985 *Madd Hatter* LP, released on their Cosmos Records label; tracks like "You're in the Real World" or "Fight the Dragon" sound like Judas Priest on steroids, and it's not your usual Texan metal, with the high-pitched vocals and the crazy, abnormal rhythms. It's good, but I think that it gained much popularity among collectors due to its fantastic cover art. The crazy-obscure hunt continuing, **CAB** from California played something in between heavy and doom metal on their 1986 *Just Another Day* seven-inch; the title song is in this style, while the flip side of "Given Dreams" is the real treat here: melodic, dreamy classic metal. **TANGRAM** from Hartford, Connecticut, was a short-lived hard rock/metal band that included Rob Rock and David Pine, among others; their *Take It from the Top* seven-inch, though, is a rarity. I couldn't find it anywhere to review it. Some of the craziest in terms of rarity are the two releases of **LIQUID EARTH**; formed in 1974 in Orange County, California, their two 1984 releases, the *Lion's Den* seven-inch and the *Molten Rock* twelve-inch, are prototypes of top-class heavy metal, with "Lion's Den" being an unbelievably great track. The band resurfaced in the late 2000s and released two (also rare) CDs.

MAINLINE, from Mesa, Arizona, on their amateurish 1983 *Mainline* LP (via Deal With It! Records) played a hard 'n' heavy crossover style, but it's very uninspired. Only for completists. **EMMY STRUT** from Davenport, Iowa, released a decent but underproduced American metal twelve-inch (*Emmy Strut*) in 1985, which you should at least check out for "No Escape." Drummer Sean Schipper played later in Zoetrope and Loknut. **PANZER** from San Jose, California, is another highly obscure band/release: their 1980 *Thunder and Lightning* seven-inch is a hard rock/heavy metal crossover, good for fans of UFO, with "Shotgun" being a dynamite heavy rocker. **TIGRON** from New York City and their 1984 *Breakaway* seven-inch remains a huge mystery; it's reportedly heavy metal, but I couldn't find it anywhere in order to review it. **RACE** from West Palm Beach, Florida, was reportedly a heavy/hard rock band whose 1989 *Onehandonthewheel* twelve-inch is more on the AOR side of things, with slightly harder-rockin' songs (such as "One Hand on the Wheel"). **FORCES** from El Paso, Texas, are a different story, though, with technical melodic heavy/power metal that reaches levels of greatness on songs like "Give Me a Chance" or "Action." Sadly, the low production values kill the material on their 1986 *Talk Is Cheap* twelve-inch, but this is still definitely good. **MADRID** from Ohio was a duo, and even though in terms of appearance they looked like a glam metal act, they sounded like a weird, slightly progressive hard rock band on their 1986 LP *Dreams*. Songs like the instrumental "Tales of Talbot" will blow your mind, whereas the title track is a total anthem!

THE LIVING END (formed initially as The End, playing hardcore punk) from San Jose, California, was the glam metal band that Adam Segal formed with Chris Lentz (both of the hardcore band The Faction), alongside John Haugh (of the punk band Mistaken Identity). The band's 1989 *I Am the City/Insanity* seven-inch isn't anything too memorable, but it's well played and above par for this style. **SAVINO** from New York City sound like an American heavy metal band playing glam metal; if you can bear with their absolutely moronic lyrics (e.g., "Fat Chicks" ... duh), you can enjoy power/speed tracks such as "Take A Bath" or "Blitzed Again." But overall, their 1988 LP *Sex Mentally Assaulted* is not recommended. They even released two more CDs in the nineties—sheesh! **LACE** from Queens, New York, formed in 1980 and released one demo in 1984 and a 1985 seven-inch, *Nervous Breakdown*, which reminds of a mix between Riot and Twisted Sister. It's heavy but at the same time melodic, with the title song all by itself being a great reason to get it. **SONIC RAGE** from Illinois released the seven-inch *Will You Always Be Mine* in 1985, an obscurity that wasn't available anywhere. Reportedly heavy metal/hard rock crossover, this one fetches serious money. **WHITE NOISE** from Phoenix, on their 1981 *Different* LP, expressed their own version of hard rock/heavy metal with a heavy boogie rock influence on songs like "Dancing Bear" and "Gonna Skate." Not bad, but not spectacular either. Guitarist Darryl Ogawa later formed **SLAYER** (Phoenix) and released the *Dangerous Appetite* twelve-inch in 1982.

RAZAR from Anchorage, Alaska, and their 1984 *Decadence & Discipline* LP, are a big surprise for those into melodic metal/hard rock; songs like "Quest for Strange" or "Long Shadows" have a great metal quality, and overall, fans of these styles should check it out. Another hard-to-heavy crossover LP is 1983's *Petroffied* by **PEEPING TOM** from New Brighton, Pennsylvania; good, melodic, and sometimes very catchy stuff, like "I Won't Feel the Pain Anymore" or "Without You." In 1982, **CZAR** from Schenectady, New York, released one hands-down great American metal seven-inch, *Iron Curtain*. While the title song is a NWOBHM/Witchfinder General-flavored heavy doomster, the flip side of "Black Sunday" is a real epic, in line with early Manilla Road—tremendous stuff! **HOLY DANGER** was a short-lived Christian metal band from Eugene, Oregon, that featured Dee Harrington of Saint and Guy Ritter and Gary Lenaire when they were pre-Tourniquet. They released two cassettes in 1986, but prior to that they put out 1985's *I Wanna Rock* seven-inch, which was mostly hard rock/metal. Good, but not something too special. **DRAGONNE** from Los Angeles enjoy a good cult status to this day, which is pretty justifiable. First of all, Jeff Scott Soto was the producer of their 1988 self-released twelve-inch mini-LP, *On Dragons Wings*; additionally, the fantasy cover art on this LP is the one that's driving all the fans of epic/power metal nuts. On a strictly musical level, Dragonne are enjoyable, but by no means are they a classic American heavy/power band. Still, though, the quality is here, especially on songs like "On Dragonne's Wings" and the heavyweight "Long Way"—very strong stuff. Dragonne also released a demo in 1991, and their drummer Chris Amesquita played in the hardcore/crossover The Mofo Homeboys (alongside members of Agent Steel), and currently performs with the progressive thrashers Typhon and Power Syndicate. A very beloved band by fans of American metal is **ION BRITTON** (from

Lincolnton, North Carolina) and this is because they balance between the white-collar American power metal and the blue-collar one! Their 1987 twelve-inch *Eat Metal* is a classic of American underground metal, including inspired tracks like "Eat Metal," "Mind Grind" and "Illusionation." Ion Britton sounds like a weird mix of Iron Maiden with the vocals from King Diamond (but more on the power metal side), and some Fifth Angel (the first LP). The band is still active too! Back to crazy rarities, the only release by the New Orleans band **ROYAL ORLEANS**, the 1981 seven-inch *Husslin' in Hollywood*, remains a mystery, since I couldn't find it anywhere in order to review. But it is reportedly heavy metal.

WHITE KNIGHT from Knoxville, Pennsylvania, released their first seven-inch *When the Night Comes Around* on the small local indie label JTM Records. In the same year, they self-released the *Are You Ready to Rock* seven-inch. The band's style is reportedly hard rock/metal crossover, although I couldn't find their stuff to review. **PARAGON** from Lafayette, Louisiana, only released one seven-inch, but what greatness it held! The 1982 *Image Chamber* seven-inch includes two songs of well-played, metallic hard rock with a touch of raw Led Zeppelin, and "Dancing Meriadoc" is a real hymn! Be sure not to miss this one if you're into this sound. Very little info is available on **MANIAK** from Utah; one LP in 1981, *Here It Comes!*, is described as heavy metal/hard rock. **LABYRINTH** from Minneapolis existed from 1979 to 1986, and their only release, the independent *So Wild* LP from 1985, is a classy metallic hard rock record. Very professional, technical, and inspired, Labyrinth is another example of how high the bar was for many bands of that era—check out songs like "So Wild" and "We Don't Care." Fans of high-pitched vocals in American power metal, e.g., a cross between early Queensrÿche and Steel Assassin, will wet their pants when they hear **RELLIK** from San Jose, California, and their 1986 *Remember the Future* twelve-inch EP. This one shreds. You get four songs of top-class American heavy/power metal, with "Dream Killer" and "Beg, Borrow, or Steal" being the absolute hits of this record. Get this one for sure, but also get the *Killer* 2001 compilation LP from Doomed Planet Records that includes many of their demo recordings. **COVEN** (a.k.a. Coven 13) from Detroit are still active to this day, and their 1987 *Worship New Gods* LP is a minor classic of the doom metal genre. Even though I'm not a fan of this style, this is a top-notch LP, with influences ranging from Black Sabbath (both Ozzy and Dio eras), Saint Vitus (with the same punk edge), and Pentagram. Coven enjoys a cult status from doom metal fans and later released two more records. The *Worship New Gods* LP in its original form is surely not a cheap buy. **CONTAGIOUS** from Downey, California, is another Christian metal band of the era, and their Judas Priest-meets-Dokken melodic metal is heavy and catchy—if you can bear with the Christian lyrics on their 1987 *Be Ready* twelve-inch. Great guitar work here, and pretty inspired anthems, with the best ones being "Jesus Is the Way" and "Nowhere to Run." They released one more LP (*Free Indeed*, in 1988) on the small Christian independent label Regency Records.

STORM from Tomahawk, Wisconsin, started in 1979 and kept it up until 2005, then paused, and they got back together again in 2011—their current status is unknown. They only released one seven-inch in 1988, *Darkness/Storm*, and while "Darkness" is a blues-based, NWOBHM-inspired metallic hard rocker, "Storm" is a real metal rager, rough and powerful. Drummer Eddie Buerger later played in Chainsnap and Nightchild. A real mystery, **SYBARIS** from Philadelphia released their own seven-inch, *Summers Gone*, in 1986, but it's nowhere to be found in order to review. They changed their name to Tyrants Temple and released a CD in 2011 (another private release). **JONAS GRUMBY** from Cincinnati, Ohio, released one of the most bombastic American power metal seven-inches—yes, we're talking about the *Cry of the Ripper* seven-inch from 1985. The title song is a real ripper, somehow reminding me of the Danish heavy metal band Randy. Top stuff, and the B-side, "Short Engagements," is a good, demonic mid-tempo tune. They also released one demo in 1986 and then faded away, with drummer Jim Brink later appearing in Naked Truth and Thruster. **ELESSAR** from Cleveland, Ohio, released the 1984 twelve-inch EP *Defy the King* on their own label, and later that year Iron Works re-released it. Despite the great fantasy cover, this is not epic metal, but it's still decent melodic metal, with the best tracks being "Getting to Me" and "This Is My Life." Elessar split up in 1986, and soon members Frank Nerone and Andy Mrazek would join guitarist Mike Brody and co-found Equinox, taking a more heavy/power approach. **FIRSTRYKE** from Tulsa, Oklahoma, formed initially as Slayer, and they are active today. Their first LP, 1986's *Just a Nightmare*, is a good example of the American metal sound, balancing between the party metal atmosphere of Mötley Crüe (at their hardest) and the heavier early W.A.S.P. Plus there are memorable songs such as "Grab a Piece" and "Black Prince" (this is their masterpiece). They released another LP too: *Welcome to the Revolution*, in 2014. **PSYCHIC WARRIORS** from Bethlehem, Pennsylvania, wasn't a pure metal band by any means, but the kind of blended heavy metal, hard rock, and progressive rock on their 1980 seven-inch *Among the Ruins* is weird, heavy, and melodic, with the B-side "Clinical Approach Nightmare" being massive. This is mandatory listening for anyone into the harder-to-get-into stuff of that era.

Very obscure stuff in the case of **PREMONITION** from Santa Clarita, California; they released one privately pressed hard rock seven-inch (*Glitter Girl*) in 1980, but this isn't available anywhere. **PREMONITION** from Orland Park, Illinois (a suburb of Chicago) are harder to define; on their *When Four Become One* twelve-inch EP, they have three AOR songs and one dynamite metal song ("The Answer")—wish there were more like that, even though their EP is definitely of high quality! **UPPER ECHELON** from Seattle, Washington, released one of the most underrated classics of that era, with their 1984 *Surface Tension* twelve-inch EP which contains four absolutely amazing American metal songs! This one will please fans of true and epic metal at the same time, since two songs are all-out metal attacks and two have a more epic feel. Just listen to "Drivin' Mean" and "Evil Songs." Terrific stuff! **MAGNUM FORCE** from Torrance, California, on their sole release, the 1985 *Straight Ahead* LP, was mostly a hard rock outfit, but with a very heavy sound; "Woman of the Past" and "My Future" are two very good songs in this style, while the LP includes some live stuff too. Fans of very rough hard rock will appreciate this one, and it's not a super rarity, nor it is expensive. On the polar opposite of the hard rock spectrum from Magnum Force is **TOUR DE FORCE** from Illinois; their 1980 *Dreams of Rock and Roll* LP is a mix of hard rock with AOR, but it's not as mellow as you'd imagine, and this is due to the powerful heavy metal soloing and rhythms. Yes, there's a definite Boston and Styx approach here, but there is Deep Purple and (some) Judas Priest too, especially on songs like "Revenge" and "Cosmic Sleuth" (even though the latter has a power-pop feeling too). Don't let the pretty idiotic name of **RAVEN BITCH**, from Janesville, Wisconsin, turn you off, 'cause their first twelve-inch, 1987's *Tear Down the Walls*, contains some of the most ferocious American power metal ever, which sometimes bordered on thrash. Sounding like a more structured Destructor or a more controlled Powerlord, *Tear Down the Walls* includes such greats as "East III Gates" and "Tear Down the Walls." Raven Bitch released one live CD in 1994 and another CD, 2002's *Mental Disruption*, in the same style.

MARINER from Dearborn Heights, Michigan, has a pretty extensive history that dates back to the late 1960s! It took them quite a while to release their own vinyl (*Sweet Horizon* LP, 1981), which is enjoyable melodic hard rock, as is their 1983 *Mariner* twelve-inch—both released on their Tidal Wave Records and Tapes label. They later provided their songs for movies (such as *Stranger by Night* and *Animal Instincts III*); now that's quite a piece of info! **STATE OF SHOCK** from Lincoln, Nebraska released only one twelve-inch EP (*S.O.S.*, on their label, S.O.T.A. Records), a minor shining diamond in the history of American metal. Melodic heavy/power with a rough edge, and yet so inspired, with great songs like as "Nothing I Can Do" and "Turn Around." It can be a bit pricey, though. Bet you already know **ABATTOIR** from Los Angeles—if you don't, visit your nearest record store right now and start with their classic power/speed metal LPs *Vicious Attack* and *The Only Safe Place*. Classic stuff! However, prior to the release of *Vicious Attack*, Abattoir self-released one seven-inch that exists only as an acetate, *The Game of Death/Stronger Than Evil* (1984). Two absolutely smashing songs, it's power metal that sounds like Iron Maiden crossed with Motörhead—fantastic! This is an item of huge rarity, but no worries, because both versions are on *Vicious Attack*. **PRECISION** from Midland, Texas, on their 1983 *Precision* LP offered their own brand of hard rock with a very slight metal edge, and definitely some good songs are there, like "Walk Away" and "Texas." John Hibbitts' (vocals) father financed this release!

AIRSTRIKE from Lincoln, Nebraska, formed in 1986 and split up in 1988, and they released the 1986 LP *Initial Attack* on their label, Direct Hit Records, which is a mixed bag. When they play pure heavy metal (like on the title song or "Right Before Your Eyes") they're ripping, but when they're heading for more hard rock/AOR territory, they sound pretty mediocre. Still, though, the heavy metal songs are enough to seal the deal here. In 1986, **RUST** from Friendswood, Texas, released their *The Last Laugh* LP—it's very average and totally unmemorable heavy metal, only for completists. **THREAT** from Detroit released just one seven-inch (*Runaway/Insane*) in 1985, and it's raging and galloping classic heavy metal, with "Runaway" being an exciting track, reminding me of early Riot! **PHERNALIA** from New Jersey and their *Right to Life* LP remain sinfully unknown—a pity, since this record is a real banger of heavy metal/hard rock crossover. Just check out "Right to Life" or "Wake Up." Plus, it's not that expensive. **BURNING DESIRE**, also from Detroit, and their melodic classic heavy metal on the *Break Free* twelve-inch (1987) is enjoyable at least, with the best tracks being the awesome "Turn Away" and "Never Enough." **MESSENDGER** from South Georgia was mostly a Southern/hard rock band with some metal songs (like the excellent "Strangers" and "Tomorrow's Dreams") on their 1982 *Messendger* LP (initially released on their JAB Records); another private release by Messendger, the 1982 *Strangers/Be-Bob-A-Lula* seven-inch, featured songs off the LP. Those items are some of the lowest-priced that you can find in this book, but they're by no means of lesser quality.

Obscurities continued: **CAUTION** from Auburn, New Hampshire, presented a very enjoyable, NWOBHM-inspired seven-inch (*I Don't Know/Want Me Bad*). The date of the release is unknown, but I bet it's somewhere between 1980 and 1983. Plus, there's not even any sales history available on this one! Continuing with Auburn, New Hampshire, **BLACK BRAND** and their 1979 *Runaway/Head on to Hell* record was a mix of heavy metal with a slight punk touch—raw and good stuff. Finally, **SHADOW BOXER** (also from Auburn, New Hampshire) released their own piece of plastic in 1979, the *Love Letters* seven-inch, which is raw hard rock that you should get if you like that kind of stuff. **BLIND OWL** (Gardena, California) started out in the 1970s and released the excellent melodic metal *Lady of America* seven-inch, which included two songs, both reminiscent of a harsher-sounding Q5. Awesome and inspired stuff. Guitarist Mike Ricketts is the one behind the Clinton, Iowa, band **HYPER**; their 1985 *Active* LP will please fans of hard rock/AOR, and "Power to Do" is a fine song. **RAY GUNN** from Seattle released one of the most underrated classic American power metal LPs, the 1987 *Ray Gunn* LP (on My Records). Comparisons with early Vicious Rumors and Metal Church come to mind in this (overall great) record, with strong songs like "Don't You Dare" and the exciting "Watching You." You need this LP like air and water. Members of Ray Gunn later appeared in Reverend and Mindshaker. Of course, you all know **MANILLA ROAD** from Wichita, Kansas—although the band's sadly no longer with us, due to the passing of Mark Shelton in 2018. Manilla Road released their first three records (*Invasion, Metal*, and *Crystal Logic*) on their own Roadster Records. If you are about to pick one, choose *Crystal Logic*, one of the most brilliant metal records ever, regardless of genre. Manilla Road's quality is undeniable, and they kept up releasing top-notch stuff for four decades!

REAL STEEL from Flint, Michigan, is a very special kind of band who released just one seven-inch, the 1988 *Viking Queen* LP, and their sound is tremendously raw—totally menacing epic metal of the highest order. "Viking Queen" and "Excalibur" have to be heard to be believed! As you can imagine, this one is fetching serious bucks. **VAUGHN** released a Christian metal twelve-inch named *Holy Metal* that's pretty hard to find today. People flip over *Holy Metal*, but to my ears, this is just uninspired and amateur hard rock/metal so I'll pass. **BOLTS** from Detroit had a more progressive hard-rock orientation, sounding like a cross between early Styx and early eighties American metal on the pretty good 1982 seven-inch *Long Journey/The Reason*. Mysteriously, this remains a cheap item. **FLEURY** from Denver released an album (*Fleury*, in 1988) that received high praise from both fans of glam and fans of classic heavy metal; it must be the weird combination of ultra-heavy guitars with party metal. It is good, though, especially when it heads for a total metal approach (e.g., "Pacific Dream"). **BLIND TAXI** from Charlotte, North Carolina, and their melodic metal on the 1987 *Blind Taxi* twelve-inch is pretty fun (and definitely professional), especially on songs like "Stranger" and "The Jokes On You." I would prefer it to be a bit more rough, though. I have no clue or info on **EVERYONE'S DAUGHTER**'s only release, the 1986 *Take Me Home* seven-inch, other than that it has a female vocalist, and it's either from Kansas or Missouri.

SNOW WHITE from Anchorage, Alaska, formed in 1980 and released their 1985 twelve-inch, *New Messiah*, including three songs (and the same ones, played backwards, on side B); while this is not a major classic, still it's a damn fine record, and "New Messiah" especially is a real killer! **AXIS** (Cleveland, Ohio) on their 1985 *Slightly Tilted* LP went for a melodic metal approach (not AOR), presenting a good mix of classic with commercial metal—they even had saxophones! There are some nice ideas in songs like "Burnin Up" and "Get Nervous." Not something to flip out about. A band that I wanted so much to include with their own chapter, L.A.'s **GRAVEN IMAGE**, still stands as one of the most notorious in the world among metal collectors. Unfortunately, founding member and guitarist Rob Griffin didn't grant me an interview, telling me that the Graven Image days are over for good, and that he feels that he has put so much effort into this band without recognition. Anyway, their 1984 twelve-inch *People in Hell Want Ice Water* and 1987 *Warn the Children* 1987 twelve-inch were released on their own label (Rockhaus Records), even though *Warn the Children* can be also considered an Azra release too. Both ultra-classics of American power metal, you should definitely get them if you're into this prime sound of early Savatage and Jag Panzer. **KING COBRA** (Omaha, Nebraska) was a good hard rock/heavy metal crossover band, and their 1983 *Think Fast* seven-inch is reminiscent of NWOBHM bands like Gaskin or Ethel the Frog.

VON DYMON (Columbus, Ohio) formed in 1985 and are still active today! However, their style of melodic metal on the 1986 *Von Dymon* seven-inch leaves me cold, and so does their 2008 stuff (the *The Best I Can* single). No info on **TRYAX** (Albuquerque, New Mexico), other than that they released the *Le Commencer* EP in 1987. Not something memorable, just plain decent hard rock/metal, with a good vocalist. Bet the name **QUICK CHANGE** (Chicago) is familiar to many of you; they became mostly known for their thrash metal records (especially the 1988 *Circus of Death* LP), but did you know that they started in 1981 as a pure heavy metal band? This is evident in their self-released 1984 *Someone Is Watching Me* seven-inch. Even though it sounds rough in terms of production, this is a very good release—quirky, melodic, and totally cool heavy metal—especially "Someone Is Watching Me" is way above good! Quick Change remain active until today too. **PHENOMENON** from San Diego formed in 1978 and included three later-to-become-famous members: bassist Gregory Boaz of Tex and the Horseheads, Robbin Crosby of Ratt, and Paramore McCarty of Warrior. Their only release, the 1980 seven-inch *The Final Word*, is a stellar release that sounds like Judas Priest crossed with NWOBHM, Kiss, and Thin Lizzy—the title song is shredding! **DEZARK** from Houston have gained insane cult status among metal collectors in the world, and this is why their 1986 *Dezark* twelve-inch EP goes for crazy money. It contains one AOR song ("Broken Silence") and three heavy metal ones, all good stuff. **CHINA WHITE** (Albany, New York) formed in 1982 and were active for many years (the last year being 2019), releasing demos and one full-length. They also released, on their own, the 1986 *Heavy Metal Thunder* seven-inch, that contained one decent song ("Death from Above") and is mostly based on the tradition of NWOBHM. Nothing too exciting, but completists might want it. **MONARCH** (Newnan, Georgia) will drive you crazy in a good way if you're a fan of Ashbury and early Manilla Road; it's epic and melodic hard rock (with a slight metal influence), on their only *As Your Kingdom Falls* 1983 LP, which is a classic of this style. You should get it by any means, if just for the massive "Vorspeil/Mystery of Life."

OBLIVEION from Ohio on their 1988 *Rockin' on the Good/Side* seven-inch were nothing but a melodic Christian metal combo, no classic for sure. No review or further info on **PANTARA**, a band that released the *Rise Above/Rock Spirit* seven-inch in 1989. Reportedly heavy metal. **ROK BERGADE** from Houston didn't follow their fellow Texans' stylistic metal approach, and their 1983 *The Attack Is On* LP sounds like it was released on a rainy day in the

British countryside in early 1980s—yes, it's totally NWOBHM-influenced! And it is a really emotional, good release, with catchy songs like "Too Far from Yesterday" and "Just a Dream," plus a great Supremes cover, "You Keep Me Hanging On." *The Attack Is On* is wholeheartedly recommended. **THRUSTER** (Cincinnati, Ohio) have been active since 1983, and their 1985 seven-inch *Back in Time/Excellorate* will drive all fans of true metal crazy, 'cause it contains two songs of pure American metal with that characteristic mix of Judas Priest with Iron Maiden. (In their case, the Priest influence is slightly more evident than Maiden's.) Both songs shred! They also released the 1986 *M.I.A.* cassette, still in the same (awesome) style—be sure not to miss the vinyl reissue on this one. **VALHALLA** was a progressive metal band from Pittsburgh, Pennsylvania, that formed in 1979 as Snowblind, and released their self-titled LP in 1984, which still remains a huge classic for fans of Warlord or any melodic/epic metal act. Songs like "Looking for the Light" and "Ship of Dreams" have that definite magical American metal touch. On the other hand, **VALHALLA** from San Jose formed in 1984 and released in 1985 the *Valhalla* twelve-inch EP (on their own label, Valkyrie Records), which was nowhere near any epic metal approach. Good, melodic metal with a slight glam touch, okay but not a classic. **DARK AGE** (Stow, Ohio) on their 1986 *Star Trippin'* seven-inch presented some good ideas, in terms of music; however, the vocals (of a very young metalhead) killed it. Just for mega-collectors, and you can get this one for 30 to 40 bucks. **NIGHTCRAWLER** formed in Cleveland in 1984 as Intruder and released the *Soldier in Time* LP in 1987; balancing among Queensrÿche, Fates Warning, and early Mystic Force, songs like "Hangman" and "Past Life" are real treats, with *Soldier in Time* being a very exciting release for all fans of this technical American power metal style. They kept releasing material up to 1998 and were together until 2016. **BLACKKOUT** (St. Petersburg, Florida) released in 1985 the excellent American power metal *Black & Blue/ Fallout* seven-inch, a sheer rager of hot pumping metal of the highest order! They released one cassette in 1989 (*Ignorance of Man*, which is again brilliant) and have been back together again since 2017. **LIGHTNING STRIKES** from Los Angeles included Rob Math of Leatherwolf, and their 1985 *Lottery Tickets / Lightning Strikes* seven-inch is unbelievable, totally classic American metal, containing two real anthems. I bet every fan of this style will go apeshit! "Lightning Strikes" is a tune that should be on the playlist of every real metal fan. They also reformed in 2011, releasing the *Lightning Strikes* LP in 2016, and it's a great comeback. However, the *Lottery Tickets/Lightning Strikes* seven-inch is on the wish lists of many metal collectors worldwide and remains a huge rarity.

BLACK ONYX (Detroit) included members of David Neil Cline, Wizzard and Halloween, and were a short-lived band. Surprise!—these guys sounded like a meatier, more powerful Ozzy Osbourne (or his band, anyway) on their *Armageddon Skies* 1987 seven-inch. Pounding and raw, this one will please all of Ozzy's solo career fans. Cleveland's **SABRE** formed in 1983 and released the 1984 *Sabre* demo cassette and the 1985 *City of Flames* seven-inch. Heroic, top-quality American heavy/power metal, with two inspired and powerful songs—the title track is a classy and delicate hymn. However, a crazy story is behind the band's bass player, Paul Constantinescu, who kidnapped the 24-year-old actress Satara Stratton in Hollywood in 2010 and held her captive for ten months, until he was arrested! **RITUAL** (Livingston, New Jersey) formed in 1984 and kept it up until 2019 under various names/forms, but the band has an absolute disgrace in their history: Bill Farley renamed the band New Minority in 1994 and released one LP of nationalist white-power metal. Therefore, I am not gonna review their 1987 LP *Let the Metal Play*. It's a sad fact that this kind of neo-Nazi trash sometimes finds its way to spread propaganda to young (mostly) innocent kids. **LANDSLIDE** (Denver) formed in 1981, and the band's first LP in 1987, *Is Hard Rock*, was released on their own Glamour Boy Records. Melodic with lots of keyboards, this one's okay for the fans of this style, as is Landslide's 1989 *Bad Reputation* EP. *Is Hard Rock* isn't pricey at all, ranging from 20 to 30 dollars. **BATTLE AXE** (Waupun, Wisconsin) formed in 1979 and released 1986's *We're on the Attack* LP, which is mediocre heavy/glam metal. Another very mysterious band/release, **RAZOR** from St. Louis and its only *Saloonatic/I've Seen Better Daze* seven-inch (1985) is rough and hot American heavy/power metal, with "Saloonatic" being the best of the two songs. A major rarity, though.

More into hard rock rather than heavy metal was the sole release of **DESERT ESKIMO** (Yucca Valley, California); their 1982 LP is melodic hard rock. I would guess that fans of this style will love it, but I don't. **LOOSELY TIGHT** (Phoenix) were Pat Dixon's (later in Icon) first band, and their 1981 *Fightin' Society* is a bright and shining diamond of American hard rock. It's not metal, but there are echoes of Thin Lizzy, early Riot, and UFO in this excellent LP, with beautiful songs like "These Walls Between" and "From Another Place." This is one of the few times that a hard rock LP will be in the final "must-have American metal" list, but believe me, *Fightin' Society* totally deserves it. **LIQUID MIRROR** (Honolulu/Los Angeles) formed in 1985 by ex-members of the American heavy/power metal band Rat Attack; however, their musical approach was much different from their previous band's. The heavy/glam metal on their *Kicked Out of Fantasy* 1987 LP isn't anything spectacular—and you already know that I'm not a huge fan of this kind of stuff. **KRAYZ** from Rochester, New York, offered their own version of melodic hard rock on their 1986 *Dreamer* LP, and this one will please the fans of this sound. There's definitely quality stuff here, like "Follow the Sun." **FILTHY RICH** (Houston) included later members of the 1990s power metal band Mr. Sinister; they released two records on their own, the 1986 *Rock It Around* LP and the 1987 *Taking Time/Searching* seven-inch, both of which are enjoyable metal at least, reminiscent of Ruffians and early Armored Saint. "Louder Harder" is maybe their best song. No clue about the band **DIAMOND** and their promo twelve-inch, *Luxury*, which is reportedly melodic metal. **CHANCE** (Lansing, Michigan) released their *Take It!* LP in 1984—it's forgettable melodic hard rock/AOR.

HAZARDOUS WASTE (Pelham, New Hampshire) lives up to their name, with their venomous raw metal sounding super exciting on the 1986 *Half Life/Danger Zone* seven-inch—this is motor-metal that will make fans of Frigid Bich go nuts. They are still active today and released one compilation in 2007 and one CD-EP (*Life's a Hazard*) in 2009, both in the same style. Punk label Welfare Records found 300 copies of the original 1986 pressing and added a limited-edition picture sleeve! Keeping up with bombastic metal, **KRIMSON KROSS** (Houston) formed in 1982 and released the ultra-rare *Dogs of War/God Bless the Damned* seven-inch in 1984, and you should definitely get this if you want your metal mean. Members later formed the thrash metal band Crucial Surge. **BUCKINGHAM** (Manomet, Massachusetts) sounded like a cross between Legend and early Manilla Road on their 1981 *She Waits* seven-inch, hard rockin' and epic. They also released one cassette in 1982. **SAVIOR** from Wisconsin was a project created by singer Jay Vockroth consisting of him and three other local musicians; hard rock/AOR is their style on the privately pressed *Echo's of Love* LP from 1985, which has religious lyrics ... duh! Couldn't find either the audio files or the actual LP by **ANGELFIRE** out of Aurora, Colorado; reportedly, their 1983 LP *Look in my Mind* is hard rock/prog. **FORTRESS** (Kansas City, Missouri) formed in 1980 and featured the three Vogel brothers. Drummer Gary Vogel passed away before the release of their 1985 self-titled album; Fortress has a huge Judas Priest influence (with some American hard rock in), but it surely is a great example of this style—songs like "Metal Meltdown" and "Breakin' the Skin" will please fans of *Point of Entry* and *Screaming for Vengeance* (with some Quiet Riot in there to boot).

DESTROYER from Telford, Pennsylvania, formed in 1985, and is still active today as Slik Helvetika, pursuing a good underground career in classic heavy metal. However, their beginning was more glam/metal, evident in their 1988 self-released *Optimum D.S.I.* mini-LP. Ratt (or maybe Mötley Crüe?) wannabes, this one is pretty stale and uninspired, but completists may want it. Try Slik Helvetika—it's by far a better band. Haven't found any info on where **THE BOYZ** were from, nor any audio of their 1982 seven-inch *Don't Cry/Fortune Teller*, only that Ronnie Montrose produced it. It's reportedly a hard rock/metal band. You all know **HAWAII** (from Honolulu) because of Marty Friedman, Gary St. Pierre (later of Vicious Rumors), and longtime Journey drummer Deen Castronovo. In the beginning, Hawaii was one of the most raging and inspired power/speed metal bands of their time, and they went for a more American metal sound on their 1984 *Loud Wild and Heavy* twelve-inch EP and 1985 *The Natives Are Restless* LP. The latter was initially released on the band's own label, Shockwaves, and both are absolutely crucial releases if you have even a slight interest in classic metal in general. Pick those two up, as well as their 1983 *One Nation Underground* LP on Shrapnel, which is their most extreme. A crazy weird release is the 1983 split seven-inch between **DANA ANDERSON AND TOMMY BRODERICK**; whereas Dana Anderson's song ("Ragtime") is country rock, Tommy Broderick's song "Nowhere to Run" is a typical early eighties American metal song, with all the NWOBHM influences! **KILLEN** from New York City had one of the most atrocious covers in the history of heavy metal on their 1988 *Killen* LP (Victora Records). Plus, its production was rather mediocre—says someone who loves underproduced stuff! However, in musical terms, *Killen* is ace! Bordering between heavy and power metal, with epic songs like "Challenge of Eternity" and the pounding "Stricken by Darkness," *Killen* is not to be missed. The band's 1989 EP *Restless is The Witch* is in exactly the same style, and they also recorded a second album between 1989 and 1990, produced by Carl Canedy, but it was never released. They're currently active, having reunited in 2015.

DED ENGINE (East Lansing, Michigan) formed in 1980, and their first release was the 1983 *Limited Edition* EP cassette. Their self-released 1983 *Two Bad* seven-inch is just a fantastic piece of Judas Priest-tinged street metal. "Renegade" is a real tune that all fans of raw metal will love! Get their two LPs, *Ded Engine* (1985) and *Hold a Grudge* (1988), as well. I always thought that **METALWOLF** (Richboro, Pennsylvania) was a barbaric and furious American metal combo, but I was wrong; the band is mostly into the delicate metal sounds of Keel and Ratt, albeit more heavy—or, dare I say, with a harsher Judas Priest tone. Still, *Down to the Wire* is a good LP for all fans of this sound. The band renamed itself in 1989 as

WOLVZ, when they released the even more melodic/AOR-oriented *Down & Dirty* LP. As Metalwolf, it released another record (the *Metalwolf* CD in 1993) and are currently active (as of 2021). From Lansing, Michigan, **27 NORTH** is another band in the tradition of late seventies/early eighties Judas Priest, and the 1986 *Strike While the Iron's Hot* twelve-inch is definitely worth getting, especially for songs like "The Outlaw" and "Reach into the Dark." Approximately 150 copies were pressed. I have no further info on the Christian metal band **ALMIGHTY**, only that it released one seven-inch single in 1985 (*Be There/Ride to Heaven*). There's another Christian metal band named **ALMIGHTY**, though, and this time with a strange story behind it! The group was originally founded in the Philippines and emigrated to Hillside, New Jersey, in the late eighties, where they published their only *Cries of Prey* twelve-inch. And what a great heavy/power release this is! Underproduced and raw, the title song is an eternal hymn, while "Justice for All" is simply haunting.

HAWK (Los Angeles) was a band that included later superstars of hard rock and heavy metal Scott Travis (Judas Priest), Matt Sorum, David Fefolt, and Lonnie Miller, among many others. Formed in 1984, the band's *Hawk* 1986 LP was released on guitarist Doug Marks' Metal Method Productions label, and it's unbelievably exceptional. The LP sounds like a cross between Dio and Judas Priest, and everything is on the highest level: musicianship, production and inspiration. Just check out songs like "Tell the Truth" and "Witches Burning." They later released some CDs with demos/unreleased songs, all of equally high quality. **WHITE LION** (NYC), on their 1984 *One Of A Kind* LP, presented their own version of good, melodic metal—actually, this is way more than good! Songs like "Crank It Up" and "Sign of the Night" are high-class melodic metal with NWOBHM production. **WYNCH** (Rancho Cordova, California) included Dan McNay (later in Jack Russell's Great White), and the band's 1984 *Bad Manners* twelve-inch is a strange mix of barbaric, raw heavy metal and glam. At least two songs are above par ("Bad Manners" and "Had Enough"). **LEGION** (Cleveland) was formed by Dave Belanger and Doug King, previously of Cleveland metal band Defiance, and their sole release, the 1986 twelve-inch *Legion* (on the band's own Reeltime Records), includes one good song ("You Have to Pay") and three pretty uninspired ones. **VICE** (Corona, California) will make you go nuts if you love your metal speedy and mean! The 1984 twelve-inch *Vice* (on the band's label, Reil Records) is a minor classic of this sound—four songs, all brilliant, with my faves being "Two Wheel Thunder" and "Battle Cat." They released another cassette in 1988 (*Under Cover Lover*), which is also good. **BACKLASH** (Indianapolis) released a pretty average LP in 1986 (*Backlash*, on their label, AGF Records)—well, at least there's one good song on it, "Down the Hatch." They also released a CD in 1992 (*Go Ahead*).

On the hard rock side, **ZISH** from Laureldale, Pennsylvania, released the very nice *Original Sin* LP in 1987, which will please fans of American hard rock. **BAD AXE** (Flint, Michigan) included Tommy Scott (Halloween, Godsmack, Lillian Axe) and formed in 1975. In 1986, the band released *Contradiction to the Rule*, a real jewel of American metal (albeit with a slight hard rock edge), with fantastic songs like "All the Dead Magicians" and "The Last Knight." Not a cheap release, sadly. On their 1981 *Check Your Package* LP, **RALLOCK** (Dallas) balanced between hard rock, AOR, and power pop (you already know my love for power pop!). It's a nice, definitive, melodic LP with charming songs like "DDT" and "Venomous Lady," but I'm guessing that fans of real metal won't like this one. No clue where **RED RUIN** were from; however, their only seven-inch, 1985's *Better Red than Dead*, includes two hot heavyweights of American metal, with "Commando" being the better one, thanks to its pounding rhythm. **SMITHWORKS** (Tulsa, Oklahoma) were a hard rock band, and their 1986 self-released *Covered In Blood* (Roar Records) is a decent LP, but nothing more than that. Its fantasy cover spreads frenzy among collectors, though, which is why its price keeps going up. **SLAVEN** (Los Angeles) will surely lift some spirits with the 1985 *Slave to the Heart* twelve-inch EP and its good, melodic, mid-tempo heavy metal. Michael J. Hollander was also a member of Dark Angel and Viking, while Jerry Frazier was an ex-member of Sentinel Beast.

WHITE ASH (Detroit) are another classy-sounding American heavy/power combo, in the Detroit style, and their 1983 *Live with Rock 'N' Roll/The Spell* seven-inch balances between American proto-power metal and NWOBHM. A real charmer. **SNAKE ROCK** (Lakewood, Ohio) was one of the earliest hard rock/metal bands that released a record on their own label, with the excellent *Animal in Captivity* seven-inch in 1979. They also released the 1982 *Down and Dirty/I Don't Care* seven-inch (again on their own label), this time with more of a party metal style, and kept releasing cassettes until the late eighties. **X-CALIBER** from Ohio released only one perfect hard-rockin' metal seven-inch, 1981's *Fire!*, with the fantastic "Dark Stranger." Get this one now! That said, X-Caliber didn't come out of nowhere, since guitarist Marty Soski has been releasing great music since the sixties (!), initially with the garage rockers Inside Experience (see the *Be on My Way* seven-inch from 1969), and then with the hard rockers Lance (the *Marilyn* seven-inch from 1976). After X-Caliber, he formed the pure heavy metal **BLACK ROSE** and released the (again excellent) 1983 *Sidewinder / Slow Down* seven-inch. "Sidewinder" is a huge anthem! **STRYCHNINE** from Kent, Washington, released one of the hottest unknown gems of American private metal, the bombastic 1984 *No Escape* seven-inch, which will drive all fans of early American power metal crazy—in the best way possible! Both songs rule, and Strychnine released some more demos before disbanding in 1987, with two members heading for the speed/thrashers Panic. Detroit's **STREET ELITE** were one of the first bands for drummer Chuck Behler (later of Megadeth), and their 1985 *One Class Act* seven-inch is classic American power metal, with high-pitched vocals. It's technical and passionate, not far from bands like Ion Britton or Liege Lord. "The Battle" is a superb song, and the technical skills of Street Elite are breathtaking!

ARMADA from Lansing, Michigan, pursued quite a career in Christian metal/hard rock, with their first LP, *All Four One*, being privately released in 1986. Nothing too exceptional, it's a very Van Halen-influenced record with good musicianship and recording, but way too mellow for me. Still, this will be nice for fans of the style. The band released many more records up until to 2002, but *All Four One* has no past sales history! **NEMESIS** (Union, New Jersey) included J.J. Moore on drums (Doom Oath, DTA, Instigation, Necrophile, Blood Feast, Reverend) and their top-quality 1988 American power metal seven-inch *Pain (The Equalizer)*, which followed the 1987 cassette *Metal Christmas*, sadly remains mostly unknown. Fans of tuneful, melodic American power metal will love the pounding rhythm of "Pain (The Equalizer)," as well as the excellent vocals of Bartley Collins. However, the high point is "Nemesis," a dramatic epic metal song. Irresistible stuff! Formed in Albany, New York, in 1983 as Blitzkrieg, then changing its name to Blade, Legion, Blind Legion, and **LOST BREED**, this doom metal outfit is still active, although it's relocated to North Hollywood. The 1989 privately released seven-inch *The Desert Fox/No Hope* is an outstanding piece of vinyl, and I really like that it's mostly based on the American heavy/power sound, rather than doom metal. "The Desert Fox" is a fist-banging anthem, melodic and pounding, whereas "No Hope" is another excellent classic American metal tune. Scott "Wino" Weinrich (The Obsessed, Saint Vitus, et cetera) joined the band right afterward, and Lost Breed took a turn toward doom metal—still classy, but not my type of thing. **LUCKY 13** (Los Angeles) also went by the name Nasty Angel, and as you can imagine, they are a glam metal combo, with one release, 1987's *Lookin' for Trouble/Ride the Wind* seven-inch. Not my favorite style of music—I'll pass. **DARK AGE** (Los Angeles) were such a weird band! Formed by ex-members of Christian Death and Mournblade (punk rock), their only release, the 1984 *Dark Age* twelve-inch on the band's Gnarly Records (later re-released by RoadRunner), is a phenomenal pure heavy metal rager! The only drawback for me is the high-pitched vocals of Robert Stevens (well, in some cases), but overall, this is a masterpiece of American metal. Yes, there is a strong Iron Maiden influence here, but how can you go wrong with tracks like "Warrior" and "Metal Axe"? Brilliant stuff.

AMBUSH (Vineland, New Jersey) had a pretty good career, releasing three CDs and one compilation between 1984 and 2006, but their first vinyl offering was the 1987 twelve-inch EP *Ambush*, released on the band's own label, EMR Records. This is mediocre heavy/hard rock with a strong Mötley Crüe influence. **ROXX** from Miami, on their Puerto Rico-recorded 1983 seven-inch *Shout/Imitations of You*, initially gave me the impression (from the record cover) that they're another early glam metal band. What a fool was I! Perfect traditional heavy metal (like The Rods and Riot) is to be found in their two songs—they're gutsy and so inspired. Just check out "Shout." Couldn't get my hands on **RAMPAGE**'s (St. Louis) 1983 *Cosmic Warrior* seven-inch; I only know that it is reportedly a mix of heavy metal and hard rock. Glam/sleaze metal is the style of Dallas-based **VALANTINO** on their 1989 self-released *Wretched Böyz* LP; I'm not impressed at all, but fans of this style will want it. **THE BLITZ** (Appleton, Wisconsin), on the other hand, released only one very good American hard rock LP, 1988's *Get It On*, which is melodic and cute. No review on **LYAR** (Meriden, Connecticut) and their 1989 *This One's For Me* twelve-inch EP; reviews mention it being hard rock/AOR, and I found only one instance that it was sold in the past. Couldn't find the sole twelve-inch EP by **SPRINGBREAK** (Long Island) anywhere; hard rock/AOR is their bag on *Images Ala Matrix* (1986), which goes for insane prices. **NITRO** from Tennessee released a fairly obscure LP, the 1984 *Not Just Another Pretty Face*, on their own Lawson Brothers. It's mid-tempo hard/heavy metal—good stuff. Again, I sadly couldn't get hold of yet another record to review it, the New Jersey AOR/hard rock combo **THE CLUB** and their 1988 twelve-inch EP, *First Impressions*. **PARAGON** from Illinois put out a 1984 ultra-scarce twelve-inch EP that remains a massive rarity to this day. Its four tracks have a late-seventies Judas Priest influence that's mostly evident on the songs "America" and "Iron Tiger." Great production, too, on a twelve-inch that's surely a winner of classic heavy metal but sells for crazy money.

AMETHYST (Chicago) released only one twelve-inch EP, 1984's *Outside of Nowhere*, that makes metal collectors across the globe go wild! With a price ranging between 1,500 and

2,000 dollars, *Outside of Nowhere* remains one of the most sought-after records included in this book, with only 100 copies ever made. As for its musical value, well, this is classic early eighties American metal, melodic and rough, and "Outside of Nowhere" and "With You" are its brightest moments! **C.I.A.** from Baltimore brought the hard rock/heavy metal edge with their 1981 *Top Secret (Central Intelligence Agency)* seven-inch, a beefy stunner of this style. Just check out "Devil Cashes In"! **CROSSROADS** (Katonah, New York) and their only seven-inch, the 1984 *Lost/Heritage* record, sounds like a cross between early eighties heavy metal (Riot) and late seventies hard rock (White Wing). Enjoyable but nothing too classic. **DARK AGES** (Seattle), on the other hand, presented a very strange mix of heavy metal with goth rock on the 1987 *Medieval Sorcery* twelve-inch EP. I tend to like it, especially when things get down to a more punk aesthetic, but I wouldn't recommend it to metalheads. **LABONTE** (Massachusetts) released one LP, *The Beginning*, and one promo seven-inch, *Life Has Only Begun* b/w *Turning Up Roses*, both in 1983 on their own Vision Records. LaBonte was a Christian metal/hard rock project by the vocalist Kathy LaBonte, and in musical terms, *The Beginning* sounds surprisingly fresh after all these years. **LESTER MADDOX** (Columbus, Ohio) was more than a controversial heavy/power combo. Taking its name from the American Democratic party politician in the fifties through the seventies who was also a staunch segregationist during the civil rights movement in the USA, sadly, Lester Maddox is maybe the first white power metal band. I'll neither review nor recommend their records—this kind of stuff is just pathetic. **LEGEND** (Lilburn, Georgia) is a fairly obscure band, and the 1988 LP *Realms of Reality* is the usual mix of hard rock with heavy metal. The magic behind this one is based on its flaws, and it's more than cool for any fan of this style. **REX VECTOR** (New York City) on the 1985 *Breathe Fire* seven-inch played crude, raw, classic American metal with a very punkish production; nothing to flip out over, though, even if the title track is their strongest effort. **ILLUSION** (Tyler, Texas) and their 1985 *Without You/He Needs Her* seven-inch will drive all the Rainbow (between 1980 and 1984) fans crazy with their melodic, gutsy, hard 'n' heavy metal. "He Needs Her" will stick in your mind for days!

No info on where **MEL GILBO & ANVIL** were from; however, the *Crazy/Kick* seven-inch (1981) is a real shining diamond of pumping heavy metal/rock. "Crazy" is a fantastic tune, straight out of NWOBHM. **CATALYST** (St. Louis) were reportedly a hard rock/metal crossover act, but I couldn't find their 1981 *Wrath Of The Lamb/One Of A Kind* seven-inch anywhere—a true rarity. **LEONARD THE DOG** (Seattle) will definitely appeal to fans of party/glam metal, although it's mixed with AOR here. They are definitely too slick for my taste; however, songs like "Dead End Street" are fun. Get their *Day by Day* 1989 LP. **FAR EAST** (Goldsboro, North Carolina) released one of the most sought-after private metal records in 1984, the menacing *Ripper Slasher/Screaming in the Night* seven-inch. "Ripper Slasher" is simply ace, whereas the flip side is a mid-tempo heavyweight. Only three or four copies of this seven-inch exist, because the band destroyed all copies in the nineties, and it's sold a few times for crazy prices! **FIRSTBORN** (Golden, Colorado) released their only LP, *FirstBorn*, in 1984. It's AOR/hard rock and is okay for this kind of stuff, I suppose, but a bit pricey. **SKYWALKER** (Schaumburg, Illinois) is bringing classic hard rock, and fans of Uriah Heep, Scorpions, and Deep Purple will definitely like the *High Flyer* LP from 1982. Check out songs like "High Flyer."

CRITICAL MASS (Covina, California) is another hard rock/metal combo. Their sole 1985 LP, *Critical Mass*, was never released with a picture sleeve, and all copies came with a signed letter. It's enjoyable but still pretty basic. **KEVIN WET** (a.k.a. Kevin Mullay, from Portland, Oregon) was a hard rock artist who recorded two self-released twelve-inches, *Wet* and *Hard Attack* respectively, with his band between 1980 and 1981. Mediocre to say the least, and boring and tedious at its worst. **PROPHACY** (Spokane, Washington) caught me by surprise when I heard the first track of the 1985 *Rock & Roll Nightmare* LP, "Thank You Ladies." Awful hard rock, generic as fuck. However, the rest of the LP is pure gold—classic American metal that will drive you nuts. Just check out "Jekyll and Hide" and "Nightmare." Not a 100 percent private-metal release, but has to be mentioned: **AGGRESSION** from Concord, California, released their only seven-inch, 1986's *Aggression/Secretary Strut,* on Relentless Records, started by Tambre Bryant. This is the same label on which Villain released *Only Time Will Tell*. A heavy metal/hard rock crossover, sadly, not something special.

No review, unfortunately, on **PANZER** (San Jose, California) and their 1980 seven-inch, *Thunder and Lightning*, but it's reportedly hard rock. The same (no review!) applies to **THEE AFTERMATH** (Delray Beach, Florida) and their 1988 LP *At The Threshold*; again, this is reported as being hard rock/metal. **SQUADRON** (Woburn, Massachusetts) and their party-hard rock on the 1982 *First Mission* LP is highly enjoyable. Good, melodic, American hard rock here—just check out "Always on the Make" and "Let Me Out of This Place." In 1986, **FREEMASONS** (unknown location) released two LPs of melodic hard rock, *Forty-Eight Hours* and *Does Anybody Know*, pressing 200 copies of each, on the band's own label, Eagle's Flight Records. Some of the weirdest and most unique American private metal releases were by **JOE STEP** from Michigan; 1981's *Good Luck* seven-inch and 1982's *Sacrifice* LP are heavy metal mixed with psychedelia. Songs like "Love" or "Stepin On" are odd but charming, and both records are recommended for any metalhead who likes their metal to be outside the box. When I first saw the record cover of **THE UNAFRAID**'s (Massachusetts) 1985 *You Know What I Mean/ Streetlight Angels* seven-inch, it reminded me of a garage rock band, but I was wrong. This is a decent hard rock/metal crossover, not party/glam stuff, with "Streetlight Angels" being the better track—straight out of the NWOBHM class. **STEFFAN RODD** (Newark, New Jersey) was the first band of drummer Glen Evans (Nuclear Assault, TT Quick, C.I.A., Harter Attack). Their 1984 *Steffan Rodd* seven-inch release is NWOBHM-influenced American metal, raw and genuine, while the very Motörhead-esque "Blow Your Face Off" is a really venomous track, worth the admission price all by itself.

Let's refer to some bands that later went on to gain much exposure, though, some even making it in the music industry on a commercial level. Starting off, it's **METROPOLIS USA** (Tampa, Florida) and their 1978 *Let's Get Rowdy* seven-inch on the Atlantis label, which was attached to the studio Atlantis Recording Studio. Raw hard rock here, but passionate, plus "Let's Get Rowdy" is a fine tune. They later changed their name to **AVATAR**, and while their 1983 *City Beneath the Surface* seven-inch isn't a private metal release (it was on the tiny indie Par Records), it is regarded as one of the most fundamental for the indie metal scene. You already know this one, as well as the fact that Avatar went on to change their name yet again, to **SAVATAGE**, and a massive career followed. **TWISTED SISTER** (Long Island) released their own private metal records before signing to the UK indie punk label Secret Records; their 1979 *I'll Never Grow Up, Now!/Under the Blade* seven-inch is a huge classic, and so is the 1980 *Bad Boys (Of Rock 'n' Roll)* seven-inch (both released on Twisted Sister Records). Out of L.A., **QUIET RIOT**'s first release was the 1975 *Suicidal Show* seven-inch (which goes for big money—500 to 600 bucks). However, in 1980, they released another record on their own, the 1980 *Slick Black Cadillac* seven-inch, pressing only 100 copies of this one. Also from Los Angeles, **DOKKEN**'s first release was the 1979 *Hard Rock Woman* seven-inch, on their own Hard Records of L.A., that sounded much rougher than their later stuff. Very good hard rock/metal. **RATT** from San Diego released 100 copies of their first seven-inch, 1980's *Drivin' on E*, on their Pearcy Records. The raw, unpolished hard rock/metal is mixed with a party element here, and even if I still prefer it over the band's later bubblegum glam stuff, this style leaves me cold. And now it's time for a band that I really can't bear, **MÖTLEY CRÜE** (Los Angeles); their first two releases, the *Stick To Your Guns/Toast Of The Town* seven-inch and *Too Fast For Love* LP, were released on their own label, Leathur Records, in 1981. I know that most of you are fans of this band, and I could say that there are a few songs on their debut (like the title track or "Live Wire"—both songs that have a strong punk element) that I like, but I was never a fan of them, nor will I be in the future. Biased or not, Mötley Crüe and their ilk gave heavy metal a terrible name in the eighties, and even though (as you know already) I am not a metalhead, it's a damn shame that heavy metal was associated with the hair bands that cared more about looks rather than lyrics or music. It took ages for metal bands that were serious, genuine, and authentic, like Cirith Ungol, Brocas Helm, or Manilla Road, to gain some recognition because everything was looted by glam metal and its all-consuming media exposure. Anyway, it's your choice. **TT QUICK** (Osbornville, New Jersey) went the other way around: after releasing some LPs on semi-major labels, they went on to release two records on their own label, Halycon Records. The 1989 *Sloppy Seconds* LP is a mixed release. When TT Quick focus on classic American metal, they are simply amazing, with anthems like "Eye of the Storm" and "Method of Madness," but when they head for a more hard-rock style of songwriting, they sound stale. Get *Sloppy Seconds*, and if you like TT Quick, the other private release is the 1992 *Thrown Together – Live* CD. Okay, you all know **THE GREAT KAT**; you either love her or hate her. Truth is that I can't stand either her music or her style. Her first release (as Kat) was the 1986 twelve-inch *Satan Says* EP on her own label, Death Records, Inc. **MYSTIC-FORCE** (Baltimore) are an exception to the rule of this book, since they released *Shipwrecked with the Wicked* twelve-inch EP in 1990; however, they had been active since 1983, plus the aforementioned twelve-inch EP is a magical work of art. If you like your progressive metal with lots of power, hooks, and catchy melodies, this should be the number-one record on your list. Mystic-Force kept on releasing excellent records through the 1990s and 2000s, but sadly, they never caught much attention from metalheads, only gaining a cult following. Get the *Shipwrecked with the Wicked* twelve-inch (its original first press on Killer Pro-Duction Records), and be sure to check out the rest of the band's discography. Continuing on with the heavyweights of American private metal, **SLAUTER XSTROYES** (Chicago) are another case of a highly unique and original power/progressive metal combo; the band's still active to this day, and its first LP, the 1985 self-released *Winter Kill* album, is a real rager of American underground metal. Awkward, quirky, hard to digest, but highly enjoyable and absolutely ahead of its time, *Winter Kill* is total class, with fantastic songs like "The Stage" and "Black Rose and Thorns." Also get their 1998 *Free The Beast* LP (even weirder and more challenging!). The original version of *Winter Kill* can be very pricey, though.

LEGEND (New Haven, Connecticut) had reached legendary status in the pre-internet days, with their 1979 *Fröm the Fjörds* LP being at the top of metal collectors' wish lists all around the world. Formed in 1978 as Judge, Legend released *Fröm the Fjörds* on Empire Records, which mixes hard rock with early heavy metal and psychedelic rock, creating a very original style, akin to early Manilla Road records. As you can imagine, this is fantastic. The band's 1978 demo, *Before the Fjords*, was also released on vinyl in 2020 by the Greek label Cult Rock Classics. Legend is actually back together today (!), having reunited in 2018. If you can imagine a blend of Rush, Wishbone Ash and Rainbow, get *Fröm the Fjörds*, because songs like "The Wizard's Vengeance" will blow your mind. The original version, though, is pretty expensive. **MYTH** (New Haven, Connecticut), on their 1984 *Metal to the Pedal* seven-inch, offered high-octane, raging, and raw American heavy/power metal that, even if it lacked in terms of production, certainly had the power and ferocity. The title song is damn near perfection. Also, an unreleased full-album cassette under the same name (*Metal to the Pedal*) has been recorded, and again, it's just excellent barbaric metal. **RELLIK** (Norfolk, Virginia) played the Tidewater Virginia hard rock/metal scene (also known as the Little Creek Road circuit!) from the mid-1980s to the early 1990s, including clubs like On Stage, Skippers, Antwon's, and King Street Pub. The band released its only seven-inch in 1985, the very good *Looking for Something/Fighting Back*. Heavy and melodic at the same time, it had a definite late-seventies Judas Priest influence as well as an ethereal/magical touch, taken from Rainbow and Scorpions. Just listen to "Looking for Something." **THE HEAT** (Seattle) were a hard rock/glam combo that released the *In The Flesh* twelve-inch mini-LP (Crystal Disc Records) in 1989, but I couldn't find it anywhere to review it. **THYNN ICE** (Concord, California) is another exception to the "between 1980 and 1989" rule, and this is due to the fact that a) they formed in 1985, and b) their 1992 test-pressing *Thynn Ice* LP is one of the most glorious moments in the history of American metal! Top-notch power metal with a progressive edge, this album, with tunes like "Victim of the Fall," will please any fan of this sound. The original is nearly impossible to find—only 20 copies ever existed—so you'd better get the reissue on No Remorse Records. If you still want the first (test) pressing, get ready to spend big bucks.

VIRGIN STEEL (Pittston, Pennsylvania) released their 1984 *Walkin with My Radio* seven-inch, and to this day, it remains one of the least-known American private metal recordings; only a few copies of it were pressed, and most of them were given as gifts to friends! Virgin Steel recorded 20 more songs between 1986 and 1988 at WVIA Public Broadcasting in Pennsylvania, and vocalist/bassist Tony Garuba also played in Totally Lost Cause, The Jeffrey James Band, and Bare Knuckle. Currently, he plays in Canedy (of Carl Canedy fame). No review on *Walkin with My Radio*, since I couldn't find it, and I found it offered by a seller only once. **VXN** (Toledo, Ohio) formed in 1986, released the *VXN* twelve-inch EP in 1987 and the *The Question* cassette in 1988, before changing its name to Edwin Dare—this band is still active today, with three CD releases. As for the VXN twelve-inch, it's a beautiful example of smooth heavy/power metal, with a slight AOR/melodic hard rock element. Overall, VXN can appeal to fans of both camps with ease, something that only a few bands could achieve with success. Great songs like "The Backburner" and "Start from the Start" are examples of their awesomeness. **TORA ORPHAN** from Raleigh, North Carolina, was a short-lived heavy metal band that included Kevin Stiles (Rok Ledded, Sanity Station, Resonance) on drums and it released the superb 1984 *Don't Stand in My Way/I Need Your Love* seven-inch. With a definite hard rock edge to their Iron Maiden approach, Tora Orphan offered two pumping, exciting tracks, on a record where everything sounds unbelievably professional! Check out both tracks—this is a killer private American metal release that's sadly a bit pricey. Again from Raleigh, North Carolina, **THEATRICS** was guitarist John Custer's (Cry of Love, Dag, Corrosion of Conformity) first band; its 1983 *Deceived Children* seven-inch is a massive American metal release, containing two tracks of classic heavy metal with a strong Judas Priest influence. It's inspired and classy—just check out the title song and find out for yourselves. **ROCK ANGEL** (Lansing, Michigan) is reported as a classic metal band on the *Kick'in in the Black* seven-inch (1986); sadly, couldn't find it in order to review it. **RIP** (New York City) released one twelve-inch EP that will appeal to all fans of Ozzy, Judas Priest, and Accept, the 1987 *Give Me the Night*; not something to flip out over, but it's still good, meat-and-potatoes heavy metal, with "I Don't Know Why" being the best track here. **MARK LOWREY** (Los Angeles) will make the hearts of metalheads (who want their metal raw and filthy) pump faster with his total barbaric approach on the 1985 *Rusty Mark in the Metal Palace* LP; "Metal Madness" makes Venom sound like virtuosos in comparison, but this roughness adds to the beauty of songs like "Iron Metal Steel" and "Metal Legends." You know the deal: get it if you are into this sound.

Don't be fooled by **STEEL MOON**'s (Cortez, Colorado) fantasy epic cover on their 1983 *Fast Forward* LP; this is by no means heavy/power metal, but it's still a very enjoyable record of hard rock/heavy psych. Steel Moon also released two more CDs in the 2000s, which were more classic heavy metal. The thriving Detroit metal scene of the eighties also offered us **WAGES OF SIN**, whose *Wages of Sin* 1986 LP (on their own label, Sant Records) is a very special release. There are unusual song structures ("Pleasures of the Flesh" and "Back from the Dead"), but it's not bad at all; this will mostly appeal to fans of weird metal. I like it. **SINNER** (Milwaukee) released only a single seven-inch in 1984 (on their label, Flat Black Records), and it's hard rock/heavy metal, like a cross between American hard rock and Diamond Head. "Street Walker" and "Hard Drivin'" are very good tunes, so fans of this style should check it out. Back in Detroit, **LIMOUSINE** was reportedly a hard rock/metal act on their two releases, the *With Me Tonite/Runnin'* and *You've Got the Power/Natural Fact* seven-inches. No info on the date either of them were released, and I couldn't find them anywhere in order to review them. However, did you know that their founder, guitarist Rick Craig, played in Halloween, Humble Pie, Ichabod Krane, Noon, Sleepy Hollow, and the mighty MC5? **PROTOTYPE** (Northridge, California) included Dwight Cliff and Michael John Smith (both ex-Savage Grace) and their 1985 *One of a Kind* seven-inch was something in between heavy metal and AOR, with a huge Van Halen influence. It's just okay for fans of this style. **WICKED STEP** (San Antonio, Texas) formed as early as 1975, and their 1980 seven-inch *Enticing Woman/Jimi Hendrix* (on their Music Lovers Records label) is—as expected—a hard rock/metal combo. Real good stuff here, even though only 100 copies were released (almost all of which were given to friends and family). **HARLOW** (Kansas City, Missouri) was a hard rock/glam metal that was formed in 1985; their 1986 *Rock The Box* seven-inch (Leathar Records) is in the tradition of Mötley Crüe and Ratt, not something I really fancy. **HYKSOS** (Los Angeles) formed in 1981 and appeared on the *Metal Massacre II* LP compilation, before releasing their 1982 eponymous *Hyksos* LP. This is crushing American proto-power metal, and even though Mark Bradley's vocals are annoying when they get high-pitched (his low/medium range is good), this is a phenomenal LP! Their sound and style were two or three years ahead of their time, with excellent songs such as "In the Past" and "Strut" or the menacing "I Wanted You." Don't let the image of **WHITE HOTT** (Des Moines, Iowa) misguide you; we're talking about top-class heavy metal, with all the best qualities that American bands brought to the table in that period. The band's 1987 *Angel In Leather* twelve-inch EP is a real masterpiece, and White Hott sounds like a cross between Dio, Grim Reaper, and Queensrÿche. Check out songs like "Running for My Life" and "Angel in Leather"—unbelievable stuff! **WANTED** (Troy, Alabama) released its *Take Control/It's Over Now* seven-inch in 1984; it's gutsy, powerful classic heavy metal with a raw edge, and both songs are really good. The band also released the *Pray For Dawn* demo (1985) in the same style—very cool stuff indeed. **THE HERITAGE** (Fresno, California) included Chuck and Jerry Leal from Electric Eels and Sharon Jordan-Leal of Groundstar, and released the *Doomsday Heritage* seven-inch that included two re-recorded/re-released songs that were originally done by Electric Eels. Good hard rock/metal. **ROCK CLEF** (Los Angeles) included drummer Achim Britfeld of The Landsharks and was highly melodic on their 1983 *Trippin/No More* seven-inch, with "No More" being a thrilling, hard-and-heavy track. Basically, Rock Clef sounded more NWOBHM than American. **WEAPONS** (Detroit) was formed by ex-members of Cub Koda & The Points and released two LPs on medium-sized labels (*Captive Audience* in 1985 and *Second Thoughts* in 1990) as well as the 1986 *Summer in the City/Easy to Please* seven-inch on their own label, Military Records. More on the hard rock side of things rather than heavy metal, but still enjoyable.

THE UNINVITED (Louisville, Kentucky), on their sole LP, 1986's *Systemwreck* on their Metalcore label, present a great amalgam of crossover thrash that I missed in my book *Crossover The Edge*, and I really enjoy songs like "Pushin the Grave" and "At the Top"—they have a very Venice/Suicidal feel. No wonder, since Albert Durig was in the classic KBD punk band The Endtables in the seventies! **RAW ENERGY** (Columbus, Ohio) followed a different way of thrash on their 1988 *White Stallion* twelve-inch EP, as it was more on the classic metal side of thrash. A good EP, with "Black Rider" being a great song. **INFRARED** (Los Angeles) on their *Metal to Metal* seven-inch (1985) presents its own version of raging metal with a huge dose of Judas Priest; the endless guitar licks are a bit annoying, though. Anyway, the title song is nice. **SATIN STEEL** (Erie, Pennsylvania, and then Hollywood) lasted from 1980 to 1987, but the band only managed to release one record, the very good 1985 *Kick Me Where It Hurts* seven-inch. Nostalgic, raw, good heavy metal with great guitar solos—the title song is awesome! Members of Satin Steel later appeared in Damien Steele, Mythologic, and Andeavor. **WANTED BREED** (Los Angeles) released one record on their own label, B Records, in 1986: the *Knights in Armor* LP, which you should get just for three songs. "Walk Away," "Fighting Soldiers," and "Knights in Armor," are all good, solid American metal. Other than that, this is by no means a mandatory purchase; it's pretty good though. An interesting fact is that in 2012, the band re-emerged with a new lineup (which is partially unknown) and ended up releasing an album titled *Galactic Warriors*.

A crazy story behind **R.A.F.** out of Indianapolis: the group accepted an offer to tour in Peru in 1987 and it was a highly successful event. They released their only LP, *Hammered to the Wall*, in 1988 via a Peruvian indie label (Delta Discos), and this is a good but neither memorable nor exceptional hard rock/metal LP of great rarity. **SWEET POISON** from Atwater, California, followed the party/glam metal route on their *Until Death Do Us Part* seven-inch in 1984, on their T.W.A.T. label. It's nothing spectacular, but "Pedal to the Metal" is a fine tune. No info of past sales on that one, though. **IMAGE** (Memphis, Tennessee) formed in 1976 and released one of the most monstrous American metal records, 1986's *Image* twelve-inch EP, a perfect blend of NWOBHM with early American metal. This album is a real treat, with the best song being "The Raven." My guess is that fans of Manilla Road will love this band. "Scarlet Demons" even reaches Riot levels of greatness! Image are still active today and have released three more records since this one; however, getting hold of their *Image* twelve-inch EP is a pain, 'cause it's super rare and not cheap at all. **MAINIAX** from Spartanburg, South Carolina, formed in 1981, and their 1986 *Boys Night Out* LP (on their Sharps And Flats Unlimited label) is a mixed bag. When Mainiax head for an all-out metal approach, they are simply terrific, classic heavy metal ("Life of Crime," "Love Machine," "Yellow Star," and "Halloween"), with a huge dose of doomy Black Sabbath and Deep Purple. However, there are moments of weakness—that is, more commercial AOR rock—but when Mainiax are good, they really shred. Members later played in 4 A.M. and Shovelhead. **SNAKEBYTE** from San Diego bordered between heavy metal and hard rock, with a definite party attitude on their *Snakebyte* 1986 LP; I'd guess that fans of Dokken, W.A.S.P., and Ratt will like them—they are catchy for sure (but not for me).

CRYSYS (Portland, Oregon) included Mark Laskowski of Iscariot and The Hell Candidates, and the 1981 *Hard As Rock* LP was initially released on their own Long St. Records label (later re-released by Metalworks Records). It's a prototype of hard rock/metal crossover, one of the greatest records to ever be released in this style. Songs like "Running" and "Fire Light" are real gems, while "Satan's World" is a real rager. Get it at any cost! The band split in 1991 just after releasing a tape called *Crysys Strykes*. On their 1985 *Explosive Rock* seven-inch, **WARHEAD** (Columbia, South Carolina) expressed their own brand of classic American metal in the vein of Riot/Judas Priest. Two great and super-catchy songs that could have been a NWOBHM release too—ace! They also released the 1986 *Tonight We Rock* cassette (in the same style), and all their stuff has been re-released by Heaven and Hell Records on the 2014 *Explosive Rock* CD compilation. Pick up the *Explosive Rock* seven-inch—it's great! Couldn't find **SILVER TYLER**'s *Girls Can't Play?* 1988 LP anywhere, but it's reportedly a New York City hard-rock band. **MATINEE** (San Francisco) were a hard rock/AOR band, and my guess is that fans of Boston, REO Speedwagon, and Bricklin will enjoy their 1986 *Matinee* twelve-inch EP, which goes for 80 to 100 bucks. **OBSESSION** (Sarasota, Florida) released one good hard rock seven-inch on 1982, titled *Running*. It's okay for fans of this style.

DRUID from Groton, Massachusetts, has gained great cult status through the heavy metal underground circuit, partly because their sound and approach was highly unique on their two self-released records on Crossbone Records: the *Four Curses* seven-inch (1986) and the

1988 *Vampire Cult* LP, the latter of which was later re-released by Black Dragon Records with a different sleeve. Weird, mystical, and dark power/doom metal, with influences ranging from Black Sabbath to Venom and Judas Priest. Get them both—this is very original and 100 percent metal. **SACRED SWORD** (Egg Harbor Township, New Jersey) kicked off as a hard rock band with slight metal tendencies on their 1985 *Give Em Hell* LP. It's good, but nothing too special. Their later 1988 demo was definitely metal, though. **RENEGADE** (Otho, Iowa) has a long history: formed in the sixties as West Minist'r, the band released some hidden gems of garage rock before heading to a harder-rock sound with Renegade. Their 1981 *Rescue Me/Don't Stop—Let's Rock* seven-inch is highly recommended for those who love the heavy hard rock of the seventies mixed with blues. **IRON CROSS** (Pittsburgh) released only one LP of classic American metal (1985's *Warhead*), which had slight speed tendencies ("Waiting for the Axe") as well as power metal ones (the excellent "Chain Gang" or "Send for the Cross"). They later changed both their name (to Holocross) and musical direction (to thrash metal), releasing two nearly flawless records! *Warhead*, though, is recommended. **HERESY** (New York City) released two records that were a mix of hard rock and progressive rock, the 1985 *At the Door* LP and the 1990 *A Far Cry* CD. A fun fact: On *At The Door*, there's a guest appearance by Steve Vai, who was a great friend of bassist John Sergio!

Not much info out there on **HIGH RISK**, and their 1982 *The See'er/Pot of Gold* seven-inch is reportedly a heavy metal single, but I couldn't find it anywhere to review it. **BEOWULF** (Dayton, Ohio) released only one highly obscure seven-inch, 1981's *Sailing*; the title track is good hard-rock-meets-NWOBHM, whereas the B-side, "Waiting for You," is more on the bluesy rock side. There's only one recorded instance of a past sale of *Sailing* that I could find. On their 1982 *Why/The Sack* seven-inch, **RUBY TOPAZ** from Massachusetts had a definite Led Zeppelin touch, blended with early American hard/heavy metal, and "Why" is a good song. **WICKED SIN** (Rahway, New Jersey) formed in 1984 and are active again today after a big pause—the band's 1986 *Rockin' Roll Party Queens* seven-inch is more than decent party metal. **AMARANTH** (San Jose, California) was guitarist Simon Bibby's (later of My Silent Wake and Seventh Angel) first band, and the 1986 *You Set Me on Fire/Next to Me* seven-inch (on their own label, Excursion Records) is a great American metal release in the vein of early W.A.S.P. **ARGUS** (Tampa) formed in 1980 (and are now active again), with future members of bands like Nocturnus and Brutality. However, Argus are by no means a death metal band, and their semi-classic 1983 twelve-inch *Argus* is nothing but melodic, classy American metal, based on the tradition of NWOBHM (like Diamond Head). Check out the awesome "Another Gloomy Day."

SQUADRAN from New York City formed in 1979 and have a very interesting story; they auditioned to be Ozzy Osbourne's backing band after he had left Black Sabbath but were told that he was looking for better-known artists! There's enjoyable yet not mandatory classic American proto-metal on their 1980 *Fly Away/The Wall* seven-inch. **VIOLATION** (Livermore, California) formed in 1977 and their only recorded effort, the 1982 *Meet Me At Midnight* seven-inch, is total NWOBHM worship, with "Balls Out" being an amazing tune! **LODESTONE** (Camarillo, California) on their 1981 *Lodestone* LP head for an all-out hard rock sound, but I'm not impressed. It's okay for the fans of this style, I think. However, it is something of a rarity in the collector's market. **ARSENAL** from Terre Haute, Indiana, formed in 1979 and released only one LP of lo-fi, rough hard rock (*Arsenal*, which was released in either 1981 or 1983). It's nothing to flip out over. Still, "Come Out to Play" is a nice tune. **ABRAXAS** (Cleveland) was Carl Baldassarre's first band, before he formed the prog-rock projects Witsend and Syzygy. The 1980 *Pretty Poison/Paradise Rising* seven-inch is a fantastic melodic metal gem, with two catchy, fresh, fun songs. Actually, they remind me of a band from the same era but a different continent, Praying Mantis.

SHIRE (Los Angeles) formed in 1983 (and are now again active, since 2014) by musicians who also appeared in bands such as the excellent Attakk and Drills, while Izzy Stradlin of Guns N' Roses was a member of this band for a while too! The 1984 *Shire* twelve-inch EP is a great melodic metal record with a good dose of Scorpions and Judas Priest, and tunes like "Do You Know What It's Like" are real keepers! **DEATHCORP** (Detroit) are one of the musical exceptions of this book—raging thrash metal that sounds more European (e.g., Kreator/Sodom) than American. The 1989 *Rest in Pieces* twelve-inch will please all the fans of this barbaric kind of aural assault. Great, indeed. **BRAT** (Largo, Florida) formed in 1981 and members later appeared in bands like Vengeance Incorporated, Urban Vault, and Silent Scream; this hard/heavy blend is more than good on their 1982 *Steal Your Heart Away* seven-inch. This is a Par Records release, and it's beyond the limits of this book but ... anyway, this is an item of major rarity. **DUBIEL** (Raleigh, North Carolina) was an entertaining party metal band that released two records before changing their name to DuBeel. Fans of the more lightweight stuff will enjoy their 1986 *Dubiel* twelve-inch, while things went a bit harder and more metallic on their 1988 *Dubiel* LP. **IRONHAWK** (Chicago) formed in 1981 and released the *To the Point!* twelve-inch on their own label, Chrome Records. Absolutely crushing, top-notch American metal that blends Riot and Y&T with NWOBHM, such as on exciting tracks like "Dreams of Fortune" and the perfect "Crie Out."

You might not be familiar with **MANSFIELD** (Los Angeles), but it's the first band of Jerry Best (Dio, Lion) and Doug Aldritch (Dio, Lion, Whitesnake, Foreigner, and House of Lords, among many others). The *Gonna Rock You/Overdrive* seven-inch is a hard 'n' heavy rarity, that contains two fine anthems (with "Overdrive" being way above fine—it actually borrows a little bit from Judas Priest's "Electric Eye"!). **POWERLORD** (Oklahoma City) formed in early 1984 by Tony Gourley, with his brother Bob (formerly of Dark Angel and appearing in one show with Slayer!), and Brian Massey joining the band in mid-1984, and singer Dane Cook (not the comedian of the same name) later that year. After a frenetic 1985 demo (*Evil Dead*), Powerlord dropped a bomb with the power/thrash rager, *The Awakening*, in 1986. *The Awakening* reminds one of other amphetamine-fueled American acts like Savage Grace or Abattoir, but even more vicious and vile! Songs like "The Invasion of the Lords" or "Masters of Death" are simply ferocious. **DOUBLE CROSS** (New Jersey) released one seven-inch in 1987, *I Like It Hot/Are You Ready to Rock*, which is a major obscurity; there's seemingly no info on the band out there, I couldn't find it anywhere to review it, and there's no recorded past sales history on this one! Reportedly, it's classic American metal. **THE END** (Philadelphia) formed in 1980 and released the twelve-inch *The End* EP in 1981; the band renamed itself Brat in 1988, and overall, their melodic American metal is absolutely fantastic! No info on *The End* EP regarding past sales, but you should get Brat's re-released *The End* CD (Heaven and Hell Records) from 2019, 'cause it includes everything they released.

Speaking of grandiose hard-rock-to-heavy metal crossover, **DESIRE** (Cincinnati) formed in 1981 and released one excellent LP in this style in 1983—it's Riot meets NWOBHM and Moxy! One 500 copies were pressed of the *Cry at the Sky* LP, and songs like "Crank It Up" and "Reality Is a Crutch" will make your heart stomp, if you fancy this style! Be sure to also get the 2019 *Screamer on the Rocks* CD (Heaven and Hell Records), which includes the lost recordings of *Cry at the Sky*. **METAL AXXE** (Tyler, Texas) was another band with a seven-inch, 1986's *We're Gonna Rock You (Tonight)*, that includes two anthems, with "Heavy Metal Thunder" being the best. Metal Axxe actually balances between American party metal and NWOBHM, and these tracks are both enjoyable. The band recorded several more songs that were mostly left unfinished but have been made available for streaming on YouTube. **TYRANNY** (Los Angeles) included later members of Graven Image, Malisha, and Sinister Scream, and they released the *Rock It/She Ain't Comin' Back* seven-inch in 1979 on their label, Riff Records. According to Rob Griffin, 500 copies were released, and the result was great American metal: "Rock It" is a bombastic anthem! The original seven-inch is rare and pricey, but you can get the cheaper re-release on O.P.M. Records. You already read the piece on Hendrickson, but did you know that Gary Hendrickson's first band was **GENOCIDE** out of Salt Lake City? With clear influences from Uriah Heep, Whitesnake, and Deep Purple, Genocide delivers the goods on the 1982 LP *Too Long*. Songs like the title track or "Living Dead Co." are pure hard 'n' heavy anthems, and "Too Long" is highly recommended.

Exceptions continued: **MACBETH** from New York City was the first band of bassist Ned Meloni (later of Burning Starr, Devil Childe, Guardians of the Flame, Monarch, Pentagram, Phantom Lord, Reverence, and Thrasher); their 1978 *Didn't Mean (To Come This Far)/Freight Train* seven-inch is an amazing American hard rock/proto-metal record! With a huge dose of Black Sabbath, both songs rule—even if I have a slight preference for "Freight Train." **SHYZGIFTER** (Canton, Ohio) was a band that included a young Dan Heller (you can read all about it in his argv01.medium.com story). Active from 1979 to 1983, the band released the 1981 seven-inch *Edit It Out/To End to Begin*, a beautiful piece of vinyl! Shyzgifter sounds so exotic, super nostalgic, and very sentimental ... "To End to Begin" is an amazing song for sure. The band recorded many more songs in the same style of early-eighties American metal, so be sure to check them out. Bet you all know Omen and Savage Grace, right? What you might not know is that before those bands, Kenny Powell, Steve Wittig, and Roger Sisson played with **RAPID FIRE** (Broken Arrow, Oklahoma), which released the *School Days* seven-inch in 1980. It's basic—but good—early American metal that goes for crazy money. Also, did you know that the notorious glam metal band **CINDERELLA** (Clifton Heights, Pennsylvania) released their first record in 1984 on their own? Their *Shake Me!/Nobody's Fool* seven-inch goes for big bucks, of course.

TYLER CAPONE (Merrimack, New Hampshire) offered just one release to the world of American hard/heavy metal, the *Tyler Capone* 1982 LP (Saphire Records), which is a fascinating record. Songs like "Escape" and "Love Gone Bad" are top-class, and this is a mandatory LP for sure. Another obscure crossover hard 'n' heavy combo, **AERA** from Connecticut were formed by the three Lupinsky brothers and lead singer Kevin Musfeldt. In 1984, the band released the *Aera* LP on their own label, LPC Records; again, just like Tyler Capone, this stuff is wild! Highly recommended for all the fans of this blend. Couldn't find any other info regarding **BLACK MAGIC** (Detroit) except that they released the *Discover the Magic* ten-inch in 1982, which is reportedly a heavy metal record. No audio files available, no info on past sales. **PARAGON** (Tucson, Arizona) released a pretty unknown (even for the most die-hard collectors) LP named *Gonna Getcha* in 1983; it's more than tuneful hard rock/AOR with female vocals and catchy numbers, such as "Love's Gonna Getcha." In the same style, **GANGSTER** (Michigan) was female-fronted as well, and their 1988 *Gangster* LP (on their label, Balistidae Records) is another fine hard-rock/AOR record of the era—just a little bit rougher, though. There's another metal band named **GANGSTER** (unknown location), and its 1981 *So Long Our Love* seven-inch is an absolutely amazing piece of early American metal that actually sounds more British than American! Both songs ("Gangster" and "So Long Our Love") sound like they came from directly out of NWOBHM, à la Dragster, Tredegar, or Paralex. Good luck finding that seven-inch, 'cause I haven't found it anywhere.

TRIXX (San Francisco) are fairly unknown, but their story is wild. The band members were friends with The Residents and The Tubes, and they played with early SF punk bands such as Dead Kennedys! Their 1979 *Trixx* LP is a blend of hard rock and heavy metal with a punk touch, and a great record too! Only 100 copies were released, and songs like "House Calls" and "Cheap Thrills" are pure rockers. **REVOLVER** (New Braunfels, Texas) were another hard 'n' heavy band (with more Southern rock influences), and their 1979 *A Piece of the Action!* LP contains some great proto-American metal tracks such as "In and Out of Heaven" and "Magic in Your Soul." **SIDE KIXX** (New Jersey) released one of the funniest-looking record covers ever on the 1989 *Talk of the Town* LP, but in music terms, this is melodic glam metal, just like their fellow New Jerseyans Trixter. *Talk of the Town* is highly recommended for fans of this style (although not for me).

Back to the major obscurities: **ONCE UPON A TIME** from Baton Rouge, Louisiana, was a difficult band to describe; the sound is very NWOBHM, like the whole of the eighties didn't happen and they're still stuck in the seventies, and I'm telling you this because their *I'll Take My Time/The Fall of Englantine* seven-inch was released in 1989! Plus, there's a punk edge to it. It's really good, but the price of this one reaches crazy levels. Couldn't get my hands on the audio files or the seven-inch that **VOYAGER** (Michigan) released in 1988, titled *Tied Up/Mess with the Best*—it's reportedly hard rock/metal, and the band released it in two versions: red and white.

LLAMA (Coram, New York) was the baby of Diane Shaljian (vocals) and Frank Losardo (guitar, keyboards); they were active from the early eighties up until 1992, and the band's track "Landslide" was included on the 1981 *Homegrown Album* compilation LP, alongside Twisted Sister, Good Rats, and Zebra! Llama's self-released twelve-inch EP *The Time Has Come* is a very enjoyable American hard-rock record, and Llama also released one cassette album in 1992, *Llama*. Another unsung Chicago band of heroes, **THIRTEEN THIRTEEN** (a.k.a. **1313**), was included on the Silver Fin Records *Chicago Metal Works Battalion #2* compilation LP from 1986, and the 1985 *Silent Hero/Nation Of Strangers* seven-inch is nothing but hot, top-quality Chicago metal à la Hammeron on the excellent track "Silent Hero," while "Nation of Strangers" is more AOR-directed. Get it for "Silent Hero." **SCROOGE** (Rhode Island) released their only seven-inch, *A Waste of My Time/Cheap Love,* on their own label, Cheap Records. There's a mystery surrounding this record, since some sources mention it being released in 1979 and others in 1980. This is the usual (good) crossover between hard rock and early metal of the time. **TROOPER** (Lewiston, Maine) was a high school heavy metal band that was included on the 1989 *Rock Off '88: The Winners* compilation LP. Trooper released its *In The Dark* seven-inch in 1987, and it's their take on Judas Priest mixed with some early Iron Maiden. Two (good) songs here, with "In the Dark" being the better of the pair. Still, though, nothing to flip over. **XCALIBUR** (San Diego) included Warren DeMartini (of Ratt fame) for a while, and their approach is similar on their 1986 *Strangers/Locked in Love* seven-inch. It's glam/party metal, nothing too spectacular.

Crazy obscure would have been the best way to describe **SLAYTER**; their *Up, Up, and Away/City Limits* seven-inch was released in the eighties (don't know where the band were from), and it is evidently heavy metal. Of course, I couldn't find it anywhere to review it. **IT BAND** (location unknown) released the *Pen in Hand/You Can Do It* seven-inch in 1983, and it's nothing too memorable, just plain American hard/glam metal. I'll pass. **WALLY PASSET & BENNY PETRELLA** were two San Diego musicians (a vocalist and guitarist and a bassist/guitarist/keyboardist, respectively) who released the *Slip Away/Truth About You* seven-inch in 1980. It's good, hard 'n' heavy in the style of Yesterday and Today. Later, both musicians appeared in **KING NEPTUNE** (a post-Snakebyte band out of San Diego), releasing the nice *The Mystic Sea* seven-inch in 1988. This record is rough, hard, and heavy, with "The Mystic Sea" being a damn catchy song! **ZEUS** (East Norristown, Pennsylvania) on their 1986 *She's Gonna Rock It* seven-inch are nothing but a fun-to-listen-to glam/metal band. There are some excellent solos on the title song. Another band called **ZEUS**, this time from an unknown location, released a highly obscure *Nursery Rhyme Crimes* seven-inch in 1982 on their own Olympian Records—I couldn't find it to review it, but it's reviewed as a good hard/heavy crossover. And finally, a third band named **ZEUS**, again of unknown origin, released the *Treat 'Em Right* seven-inch in 1983; no review, no info, no past sales!

ZAR (Indiana) offer their great, melodic hard rock/metal that follows the 1970s formula, rather than the glam/party style, on the *No One Like Her* seven-inch (released in either 1983 or 1984). **SACRED REIGN** (Portland, Oregon) are an exception to the "privately released" rule, but they had to be mentioned, since their 1988 *Torn/Your Eyes* seven-inch was released on the exclusively garage/punk Tombstone Records label of Fred and Toody Cole (Dead Moon, The Rats, Pierced Arrows, et cetera). This is a very unique record because it was recorded in mono, as were all the bands on this label. The *Torn/Your Eyes* seven-inch has a definite Queensrÿche flavor in its melodic heavy/power metal (which is great). Members later played in the hard rock/metal Mirror Mirror. **MESSAGE** (Albuquerque) released the *Factory Wired/Puppet Fun* seven-inch in 1982, which contains good ideas in terms of music but sounds very inconsistent ... another hard rock/metal crossover here. **DARKSTONE** (Buffalo, New York) had kept up the hard rock tradition of the seventies in their *Back on Top/Lonely in Love* seven-inch, mixed with the then-emerging sounds of L.A. glam metal. Okay for the fans. **ROK SALLY** (Madison, Wisconsin) was a glam/metal band that loved Van Halen and Def Leppard, which is evident on the 1988 *Blind Attitude/Head On Strong* seven-inch: good, melodic, very well executed stuff that fans of this style will definitely appreciate (check out "Sleepless Nights"). The band also put out a 1990 cassette record (*Rok Sally*). Only 400 copies of *Blind Attitude/Head On Strong* were released. **BUSTER CHERRIE** (Detroit) released the *Sweet Evil/Surrender* seven-inch in 1979, which sounded like a very rough hard-rock/metal crossover, with an added Stooges-esque rage—this is highly recommended, of course.

Another very mysterious band and release, **DAMAGE** from Houston's *I Was There/High Roller* seven-inch has been reported as classic American metal, but there's no info out there on the release date, nor on past sales history. **AXESS** were originally from Monson, Massachusetts, but the band's only release, the 1986 *Don't Need You/You're in Trouble* seven-inch, was recorded by the band in the UK while they were in the military! Fantastic American metal in the vein of early eighties Judas Priest with some Queensrÿche guitars mixed in. Both songs are spectacular, especially "You're in Trouble." I have no clue about **MAXXIS** and its *Vengeful Lover* seven-inch; there's no info anywhere, only that this record was reviewed as "decent glam/metal" in one fanzine. **HOLIDAY SHARK** (New York City) went for a hard-rock/metal sound on their only record, *Stars at Twenty-Five* 1984 seven-inch, which is simply amazing! Holiday Shark definitely had the qualities to pursue a much bigger career, but sadly, they didn't. You can't imagine how professional this band sounds, even today—"Stars at Twenty-Five" holds up as a great song! **REDDI KILLOWATT** (New Orleans) was having an identity crisis on their 1979 *Liquid Lady* seven-inch, wherein they presented their own brand of hard 'n' heavy; it's good, but not something to flip out over. What actually is more significant is the fact that guitarist Terry Kilgore later appeared in the David Lee Roth Band! **PREZENCE** (Louisiana) released their 1982 *The Journey* seven-inch on their label, Master-Trak Records, and it's an unbelievable hidden gem of hard rock/progressive metal. If life was fair, they would have continued on, achieving much higher status and fame. "The Journey" is a magnificent track. **SABOTAGE** (Ohio) released the *Hell Raiser/Would You* seven-inch in 1980 on the small indie label ARV International, while their second record was totally independent, 1982's *Gentle Minds* seven-inch (on their Espionage Records). This is charming hard rock/metal crossover—definitely nostalgic but still good.

HUNTER BRUCKS BAND (Detroit) released the *Motorcity Crank* seven-inch in 1983, which included one bombastic hard 'n' heavy anthem ("Motorcity Crank") with a huge dose of MC5 thrown in, and one metal ballad ("It's Over"). Recommended for fans of this style. **WHEELZ OF STEEL** from Mequon, Wisconsin, gained massive cult status in the eighties and nineties with their crude hard rock; their 1983 *Volume One* LP is nothing to get excited about in musical terms—uninspired hard rock with a drum machine. But what's actually impressive about this record is that the band comprised two brothers, Rich and Ray Markowski, who were disabled, performing the entire album from their wheelchairs. **WIZARD** (San Francisco) released the 1983 *Dying by the Telephone* seven-inch and the 1985 *Marlin, Grog, Madman & The Bomb* LP on their own label, Wizard Records. Great party/hard rock/metal stuff, and fun to listen to (especially "Open Season"). Sadly, vocalist Perry Marlin left this world in 2021. **TRIPLE FORTÉ** (Appleton, Wisconsin) could be mistaken for a NWOBHM band! Their approach on the (highly obscure) *Triple Forté* twelve-inch from 1983 is rough yet melodic, and while this record is nothing to freak out about, it contains good songs like "Black Mirror" and "Brainwave Overload."

STRANGLERS OF BÖMBAY (Hialeah, Florida) is another crazy mysterious band with a rare release, the 1984 *Lonely Women/The Rap* seven-inch. "Lonely Woman" is a nice American metal anthem, while the party rock of "The Rap" leaves me cold. More AOR and hard rock than metal, **INTENTS** (Miami) released the *....Rock That Stands Alone* LP in 1987 (on the band's label, Rising Trax Records), and it should appeal to fans of the aforementioned subgenres, but I'd imagine that true metalheads won't go mental over this. Still, Intents could pull off a fine tune or two, like "Run Run." Similarly, **RADIEUX** from Santa Ana, California, was a band of AOR/hard rock aficionados; the 1986 *Radieux* twelve-inch is a good example of this style, yet it's gone largely unnoticed, even by hardcore fans. **INFLITE** (Irving, Texas) took a slightly more progressive route in their hard rock/AOR on the 1985 *First in Flite* LP and the *Games* seven-inch; sounding like a cross between Van Halen, Foreigner, and Styx, these are definitely good releases, with catchy anthems like "Games" and "Red Hot Tonite." **LIC TRIKS** (Montrose, Michigan), on the other hand, were a very melodic hard 'n' heavy band, with a definite NWOBHM sound, akin to acts like Saracen or Jameson Raid. Their 1982 *Lights of Broadway/Sweet Venom* seven-inch is just total sweetness, with "Lights of Broadway" being absolute class! Get this one now.

More crazy stories from the deep underground of American private metal: **CHUCK "CT" THOMPSON** (New York City) was a guitarist/multi-instrumentalist who owned the Spike Bar, a gay bar in Chelsea, Manhattan, and was also its main DJ. Chuck both DJed and performed hard rock and metal at the Spike, and in 1988, he released the *Balls to the Wall* twelve-inch, on which he played all instruments and also sang (accompanied by a drum machine). Weird but good hard rock/metal. I have no idea where **MEAT THE RABBIT** were from, and the same applies to the music on their sole release, the 1986 *Meat The Rabbit* LP (on Vertical Bag Records). It's reportedly a hard 'n' heavy combo, but I have no further info. Another crazy obscurity, this time by the band named **OPEN** from Newport Beach, California: their *Looking for Zero* 1987 LP blends progressive rock and psychedelia with hard rock/metal in an absolutely frenetic way! Fantastic tracks like "Mars" or "Silence" are just examples from this highly original record—go get it if you fancy stuff that's hard to digest. **MAINLINE** (Nebraska) was a super-exciting, hard-rock-to-metal combo (with the emphasis on metal), although with none of the later glam/metal approaches of the American metal scene. It's rough and ready crossover metal/hard rock, with great tracks such as "Too Late" on their only release, the 1983 *Mainline* LP (on Deal With It! Records). **MONARCH** (from Baltimore/Washington, D.C.) appeared on two compilations (the *WAVA FM 105 Washington Rocks* LP in 1982 and the *WAVA FM 105 Washington Rocks Too!* LP in 1983) and were lucky enough to release their own piece of vinyl, the 1982 *All I Wanted Was You/Love of Yesterday* seven-inch. This is beautiful hard rock/metal, and both songs rule with their melodic style reminiscent of UFO and seventies-era Scorpions, especially "Love of Yesterday."

MOXY ROXX (Waukesha, Wisconsin) released two records on their own: the 1985 *Time/Dreams* seven-inch (Emotion Records) and the 1986 *Victims of the Night* twelve-inch—melodic, well-played, and nostalgic hard rock/metal with a definite AOR touch. While overall I'm not a fan of this style, I can't say that songs like "Summer Nights" or "Armed and Dangerous" aren't nice! Fans of the aforementioned subgenres will definitely love them. **LIX** (originally from Texas, and later Los Angeles) included Paul "Turk" Henry (of the rock 'n' rollers Hobbit), and the band's only release, 1988's *Lix* LP on Lixicle Records, is just an example of brilliant melodic metal (not hard rock or AOR). Just check out songs like "Guardians." Get this one. **DECEPTION** (Philadelphia) was a hard rock/metal combo that released the (largely unknown) *First Cuts* 1983 LP; sadly, it's nowhere to be found to review it. No info on **SOUTHPAW** (Booneville, Mississippi), other than that they were playing hard rock/metal on their 1982 *Spring/Cold Heart* seven-inch. **FRISKY ARCHER** (unknown origin) on their 1980 *Patterns of the Nighttime* seven-inch present their own brand of hard rock/metal with a punk edge; although I can't stand the vocals, "Mystery Inside Tears" is an interesting song. **INVASION** was possibly from Maryland, and their very mysterious *R.I.P./School's Out* seven-inch (that never came with a cover) is another one that I couldn't review because their stuff couldn't be found anywhere! **EUPHORIA** (Las Vegas) had a total NWOBHM sound on their 1980 *Lazarus* seven-inch—very Thin Lizzy-influenced! Two great, melodic, rough 'n' ready songs. Absolutely excellent, especially "Sword by My Side"!

SATYRE (Turnersville, New Jersey) had their only seven-inch, the 1986 *Freedom*, produced by Bo Blaze, who was a member of Deadly Blessing for a while. This is punchy hard rock/metal with female vocals, and both songs rule, especially "Freedom." No idea where **LISA BAKER** was from, and no info on her rare 1986 *Every Girls Got a Fantasy* seven-inch, other than that it is reviewed in zines of the day as a "mellow hard rock to metal blend." With a name like **LIVE WIRE** (Aransa Pass, Texas), you can imagine that the band's basic influence was Mötley Crüe on its 1985 *Feel The Fire/Time For Action* seven-inch. I guess this is okay for this style, but I really can't stand the vocalist. **FINAL DAWN** (Los Angeles) included Brett Michael Phillips, who was a member of Megadeth for a while, and released two seven-inches on their own label, G.P. Records: *Need Some Action/Running Hard* and *The Quake Has Come*. Both were released in 1987 and included the same two songs. Great, powerful heavy metal that sounds like a blend between Saxon and Judas Priest! "Running Hard" is a hymn! **RIVAL** (Weston, Connecticut) released two seven-inches too, *Rival* and *Estate of the Art* (in 1981 and 1982 respectively), on their Original Record Company label. It's somewhere in between AOR and hard rock, and nothing spectacular. Like Rival, **HARDKNOX** (West Haven, Connecticut) balanced between AOR and hard rock; however, they were far better on their (self-released) 1980 *Magical Man* seven-inch, 1980 *Hardknox* LP, and 1982 *I'm in Love Again* seven-inch. Sweet and mellow stuff here, and definitely power-pop-influenced too, but very inspired and great fun to listen to—just check out "Anyway Love" and "Second Place."

You can read a whole chapter on **ZOETROPE** (Chicago) in my book *Crossover The Edge*, with a great interview from Louis Svitek; however, before heading for a total metal/punk approach, Zoetrope's first, self-released seven-inch, the 1980 *The Right Way* EP, was released on Zoetrope Music and sold only directly from the band between 1980 and 1983. As for its musical style, it was somewhere in between heavy metal and hard rock, with clear NWOBHM, Motörhead and Thin Lizzy influences. Two of these are classic tracks, and especially "Call 33"—such a catchy tune! Totally recommended. Another band I covered in *Crossover The Edge*, **MIND OVER FOUR** (Orange County, California) kicked off as a weird garage/psych/hard rock combo on their first release, the 1984 *Desperate Expression* twelve-inch EP. What's crazy about this record is that the band's logo and information were silkscreened over the top of other artists' album covers (which were found at, and sometimes even purchased in bulk from, thrift stores), and each record was pressed by hand by members of the band at a small pressing plant in Orange County! You already know the deal regarding Mind Over Four; this is one of the most unique-sounding bands ever to come out of the heavy metal subculture, and *Desperate Expression* is weird, crazy, and definitely not for the fainthearted! **THE ALMIGHTY STRUT** (Detroit) began life as Strut in 1976, changing their name to The Almighty Strut sometime in the early eighties to distinguish themselves from the many other bands using the name. An early lineup featured Charlie Huhn, former vocalist/rhythm guitarist for Ted Nugent's band. In 1984, The Almighty Strut released the *Undercover* seven-inch on USA Records Inc. and later self-released the 1986 *Summertime With You* seven-inch. *Undercover* is a good hard rock seven-inch, while I'll pass on *Summertime With You*—very mediocre AOR/hard rock. From Albany, New York, **BLIND LEGION** formed in 1983 as Blitzkrieg, then Blade (for a few weeks), before changing their name to Legion and releasing the superb *Nice Guys Finish Last* seven-inch in 1984. Containing two ultra-heavy, powerful and brutal American metal tracks, it's a great record by a great band. Between the two songs on this seven-inch, allow me to prefer "Used to Be Blind" with its obvious European/NWOBHM style (like Judas Priest meets Diamond Head). After this record, Legion continued as Blind Legion, releasing several good demos, only to split up in 1987—members later appeared in the doom metal band Lost Breed and the classic American metal band Cardiac Noose.

CONTENDER formed in Gurnee, Illinois, in 1981 as **MORNING STAR**; under their original name, the band released one LP, 1983's *Morning Star*, which was a mellow hard rock/AOR record and pretty good for this style. As Contender, they went slightly harder (even though they were still full-on Christian), releasing the *Contender* LP and the *Missing Link/Contender Demo* seven-inch, both in 1985, on their own Purified Rock label. Okay for fans of the aforementioned style, I suppose. Even though **KNIGHTMARE II** (Los Angeles) have a pretty extensive discography of quality American metal, they rarely get mention nowadays. However, their 1985 *Death Do Us Part* twelve-inch and 1984 *Warlord* seven-inch are both magnificent examples of raw, mid-tempo, classic American metal, with awesome songs like "Promised Land," "Goin' Insane," or "Warlord"—it's Judas Priest meets Accept! More releases followed; however, those first two were on vocalist Rotten Rod Carlock's label (Raucous Records); the same applies to Rotten Rod's next band, **THE ROD SQUAD**, and their only release, the very exciting, pounding American metal of 1990's *Body Heater/Die Hard* seven-inch. "Die Hard" is such a beauty! **TRILOGY** (Queens, New York City) on their 1984 *Songs for a Rock and Roll Night* LP (Costar Records) offered their own brand of melodic hard rock/metal, with the emphasis on the metal side—kinda like a harder Twisted Sister or a mid-tempo W.A.S.P. Not groundbreaking, but still highly enjoyable stuff here. "Let's Rock" is such a tune! **SILENT LISTENER** (New York City) included Greg Livesay (later of Livesay fame), and the band's 1986 *Veterans Of The Fight* twelve-inch (Rival Records USA) is a hidden diamond of American metal! Powerful and catchy, again in the Judas Priest/Accept vein, with superb songs like "Veterans of the Fight" and "Seasons of the Witch." Unfortunately, guitarist Stevie Dee passed away in Florida in the mid-nineties.

Bassist Scott Novello is performing cover tunes in the Bahamas today, but if you love pure, classic American metal, you should get the *Veterans Of The Fight* twelve-inch!

THE OATH (Greenville, South Carolina) released two seven-inches in 1988, *Cemetery Road* and *Out of the Blue,* on their own label, Gopher Broke Records, but neither were available for me to review them. Various sources mention that their musical style balanced between hard rock and blues rock. **JIM GILLETTE** was a vocalist for bands like Nitro, Organ Donor, Slut, and TUFF while he was married to Lita Ford from 1994 to 2011; however, his career started with a self-released LP, 1987's *Proud to Be Loud* (on his own Loud Crowd label). This hair/glam metal drives fans of this style crazy, but it leaves me totally cold. Back in the mellow camp, **PASSENGER** from St. Louis went on to release the 1983 *Passenger* LP (on Broken Prairie Records) and the *Steal My Heart* seven-inch/twelve-inch, somewhere between hard rock and AOR. What differentiates them from their ilk are the harsh production values that offer an edge to their songs (which are good, like "Now I Know"), but I guess this was unintentional. It's okay stuff for the fans of the aforementioned styles. From Concord, California, **AL SMITH GROUP** released the *Young Girls on Ice* seven-inch in 1981, and it's a sweet little piece of guitar hard rock/AOR—actually, Al Smith's guitar-playing virtuosity is phenomenal! The band is still active, performing local shows from time to time. Another band that pursued quite an extensive career (even winning the grand prize in MTV's *Basement Tapes* competition in 1983) is **RAIL** from Bellevue, Washington; formed in 1970, the band released a good number of their records on their own label, Dynasty Records, such as the 1980 *Arrival* LP, the 1985 *Rail Three* LP, and the 2001 *Adio* compilation CD. Imagine a cross between Van Halen, Boston, and Kiss, and you get the idea. If you are a fan of any of those bands, you will love Rail, especially the *Rail Three* LP with songs like "Her Majesty"—excellent stuff! Rail is still active to this day (as of 2021). **MESSAGE** (New Jersey) was Richie Sambora's and Alec John Such's first band before joining Bon Jovi, and it also included the late Dean Fasano of Prophet fame. In 1982, Message released the *Lessons* LP on their own label, Dream Disc, and as you can imagine, this is already very commercial but highly proficient hard rock/AOR. Message reunited in the nineties and released two more records.

TOYZ (Miami) formed in 1979 and released the *Rock N Roll Love Affair* seven-inch in 1980, which included two powerful hard rock anthems. Then the band broke up and returned in 1982 as **Z TOYZ**, releasing the great *American Dream* seven-inch—which included "The Lonely Ones," later to be covered by Dee Snider on his *Widowmaker* album! Z Toyz gained some attention when the video for their song "Miami Breakdown" made it to the finals of the MTV *Basement Tapes* contest in 1985, but the band sadly never released an LP, due to the company they signed to going bankrupt! **BOIS D'ARK** (Edna, Texas) was the band of Jesse De La O (of DeLaO Records), who released two very mysterious seven-inches: 1980's *Exposition Hall* and 1986's *Dressed to Kill*. Both of them are reportedly a hard rock/heavy metal crossover, like a harsher Y&T, but I couldn't find either of them in order to find out. **INTRUDERS** (Fresno) featured the vocalist Wayne Garabedian (later of the progsters Mantra Sunrise and punk band The Subtractions), and the 1986 *Intruders* twelve-inch (on Big Rock Productions) is a glam/metal amalgam with a very punk edge, reminiscent of The Joneses. I really like The Joneses, but Intruders aren't nearly as good at songwriting. Another case of an ultra-weird band,

SCREAMER from Flushing, Queens (New York City), included Punky Lazar of Frenchee—the band's only release, 1986's *Therapy For The Silent Mind* seven-inch, crossed post-punk with Misfits and NWOBHM. Just imagine Randy (Denmark) with a keyboardy post-punk edge. Ace! "Run Jacky Run" is a great tune, and the flip side "Bitch's Hell" is more rockish. Even though heavy metal purists won't like it, this is just a magnificent record. **INSIDEOUT** (Wallingford, Connecticut) could have been a much better band, as they had both the qualities and the technical proficiency, which is evident in their 1985 *Sinners Psyche* seven-inch. Actually, they should've dropped the glam/metal orientation in favor of a more power-metal sound, and the vocalist should have stopped sounding like Brian Tatler gone hair metal. Still, though, in musical terms, *Sinners Psyche* (especially the title song) is enjoyable. **BACKWARD GLANCE** (of unknown origin) are another band whose release I couldn't find anywhere—the 1984 *You'll Be Sorry* seven-inch is reviewed as a hard rock band with female vocals.

ONKOR (unknown origin) released the ridiculously rare and unknown seven-inch, 1985's *I Need Love/No Money No Honey*, on their own; it's glam/metal with lots of power but no hooks. Again in glam metal territory, **SNATCH** (New York City) released the 1985 twelve-inch EP *If the Party's in Your Mouth...We're Comin'* on their own label, Snatch Records. Fans of that style will love it (especially songs like "Hear It"), but I can't stand that kind of stuff, sorry. **ORGANIZED CONFUSION** (Wilmington, Massachusetts) and their spooky, weird, angular hard rock/metal on 1982's *Runnin' All Over/Wife Beater* seven-inch is a good example of crossover hard rock/metal. This record is rough and hard, with "Runnin' All Over" being the better of the two tracks. Sadly, I couldn't find the only record by **ESSIE X AND THE BANNED** (Livonia, Michigan), the *2 Bad 2 Be 4 Given* seven-inch (1985). It's described as hard rock/metal with female vocals, but no review on this little piece of plastic was available. **BLOOD** (Hauppauge, New York) released two crude attempts at raw heavy metal on their 1985 *Fly All Night* seven-inch and *Teaser* seven-inch, both having a definite punk edge, and "Teaser" is a nice tune. The band later changed its name to **SHORES OF EVENING** and kept up recording on their own label, Blood Records. The original purpose of their creative gathering was to record a soundtrack to a storyline that was crafted by Billy Schmitt, a local writer who wanted to create a musical production shaped by Viking mythology, native legends, and traditional folklore. The sound of the recording is influenced by jazz, rock, and heavy metal, as evidenced by the diverse playing styles found here. The 1985 *Shore of Evening* LP was recorded over one weekend, prior to the members finishing their studies at the Art Institute, and to this day, it remains a very challenging LP that blends psychedelia, classic rock, heavy metal, and progressive with punk. You have to hear it to believe it! Just listen to songs like "Go Home" or the instrumental "Does It Ever Change."

ROX SEDAN was another melodic heavy metal combo from Indianapolis, in line with Dokken and early Ratt aesthetically. Their 1984 *Tools for Toys/No Stragglers* seven-inch is a little diamond of this style, and even better were their two demos released in 1985! **INTRUDER** (Long Island) was a hard rock band that released only one seven-inch single and one compilation track (1986's *Arctic Records Presents* LP). The *69/Rock On* 1987 seven-inch is a good, quality release of hard rock/party metal, overproduced and fun to listen to. No review on **DANNY PRAZ AND THE ROCK PATROL**'s (Cincinnati) only twelve-inch, 1987's *Games/*

Crazy. As reported, this is a blend of hard rock with arena rock—Danny Praz was a member of the Cincinnati band Excalibur that released one psych/hard rock seven-inch in 1980 (*Draft Card Blues*). **MALTEZE** (Los Angeles) was a party/hard rock band in the beginning, fronted by Barbara Malteze (later of Cosmic Dust Devils, Shiver, The Dust Devils, The Tipsy Gypsies, and Time Square) on ther first release, the 1987 *We Came 2 Rock* twelve-inch. Good but not spectacular. However, the band's turn into a total heavy metal outfit was brilliant on the 1989 *Raise Your Voices/Rain* seven-inch and especially on the *Count Your Blessings* CD in 1990. Songs like "Rain" and "Blessed Are the Strong" are totally crushing, breathtaking heavy metal! Bet you all know the classic death metal band **OBITUARY** from Brandon, Florida; they kicked off as **XECUTIONER** in 1984, and among the raging demos they released (before changing their name to Obituary in 1988), the band also self-released a seven-inch, the classic 1985 *Metal Up Your Ass*. Of course, this is raw, vicious, and venomous thrash metal, bordering on the then-emerging death metal of Possessed. Obviously, this is a killer! **DIAMOND** (North Woodmere, New York) released just one LP, but what a great melodic piece of metal brilliance it was! Featuring vocalist Matt L'Amour of Pantera and Rob Dexter of Battle Brat, Diamond's only offering was the 1987 *Diamond* LP on their own label, Mijems Records, which included quality stuff such as "Lonely in Love" and "Fight Fire with Fire." Get this one now!

EARL VALENTINE (Stamford, Connecticut) was the musical project of vocalist Earl Valentine, who released the 1987 *Night Blindness* LP, sounding like a harsher Foreigner. This is melodic hard rock/AOR, totally recommended for fans of this style. Valentine went on to make two more self-released records (in the form of CDs in the late eighties), although his first musical attempt was the 1982 **MANTIS** LP on his own label, Impact Records. Mantis is great pomp/arena rock, like a cross between Foreigner, Boston, and Styx. From Minneapolis, Minnesota, **DUAL EDGE** was a Christian metal band that put out a good LP on this style, 1987's *Knock 'Em Alive* (initially released on the band's own label, Edge Records). With lots of Judas Priest and Stryper influences, Dual Edge could pull out a good tune such as "Fight for the Light" and "New Life," even though their lyrical output is just boring. **FAITH OF STEEL** (Dallas) was also a Christian metal band, and their only release, the 1986 *Metal with Meaning* seven-inch, and while I'll pass on their lyrical style, their music is nothing but nostalgic, classic American metal. Two songs might well give you goosebumps here, "Metal with Meaning" and the excellent "Our Savior." Get it. As mentioned in the Decoy Paris section, the band that Decoy Paris derived from was **HEAD FIRST** (Chicago), which formed in 1984; more hard-rock-oriented than Decoy Paris, they released one seven-inch in 1984, *She's Hot/The Same Way*, and you should pick this up for "The Same Way," which is a steamroller hard rock/metal anthem! Absolutely fantastic stuff, though the B-side, "She's Hot," is not that wild. **JAGGED EDGE** (initially from Cleveland and then relocating to Los Angeles) was a traditional metal band that released a good number of demos, as well as two seven-inches, *Jagged Edge* in 1982 and *Hand of the Master* in 1983. It's weird—and pretty rough—American metal, lacking hooks but with great power. Jagged Edge changed both musical direction and name in 1989, going forward as L.A. Law, with a more melodic hard rock/metal sound. Some interesting trivia here is that the band released its stuff as Jagged Edge via its own label, Hot Records, and this label name and logo were both later taken without permission by an unrelated Greek label that releases unauthorized bootleg material by rare and underground heavy metal bands!

JOKER (Chicago) formed in 1985 and are still active to this day (as of 2022), with a number of professional, melodic heavy metal releases under their belt; the self-released *Party for Your Life/Remember* seven-inch from 1988 will definitely appeal to fans of Lillian Axe, for example. However, there's real potential here to attract more hardcore metalheads too. Try this one. **KERY DOLL** (Maywood, California) formed in 1981 and definitely could have made it big if the circumstances were right, 'cause the *'Til Death Do Us Part* twelve-inch picture disc (on the band's own label, Krypt Kicker Records is enjoyable, hard rock/glam/metal that sounds so mature. In 2011, vocalist Kery Doll released an album called *Rock 'N Roll Freakshow* under the band name Doll (featuring ex-members of Salty Dog and Pretty Boy Floyd). Ah, **KRATOS** from Cleveland! Kratos is a band that those into obscure metal either love or hate—I tend to be one of the ones who like them. Formed in 1983, the band went on to self-release the 1986 *Speed Demon* cassette, the 1986 *Iron Beast* twelve-inch, and the 1997 *Kratos* CD. Kratos plays their own brand of heavy/speed metal that's pretty rough. There is a definite punk influence on *Iron Beast*, especially in songs like "Chainsaw" and "Save Their Souls," while "Armageddon" is a heavy metal heavyweight. Fans of Destructor, early Exciter, and Stormtrooper (*Armies of the Night*) will flip over this one, as will the current crop of metalpunks worldwide. As for me? Recommended, of course, but true metalheads will definitely have objections. **LORD** (San Francisco) was a totally different case; formed in 1986, this heavy metal was based on the seventies sound: the 1988 *The Second Coming* LP is melodic, delicate, and, well, perfect. With influences ranging from Judas Priest, Scorpions, MSG, and Thin Lizzy combined with Mercyful Fate (especially in cases of vocal delivery), Lord managed to create a spectacular heavy metal monument in just one release. Anthems like "Burnin'" and "Snow" are unbelievable, and "Back to the Asylum" is an epic that tears down the walls. Get it at any cost. **MALISHA** (Los Angeles) formed in 1982, including Kim LaChance of Vixen, and released the *Bound for L.A.* demo in 1983, to be followed by the exceptional melodic metal *Serve Your Savage Beast* LP in 1986 (on the band's label, Shardan Kane Record Co.). This record contains highly unique, inspired, and magical American metal with killer songs like "Love for the Day," "Step Through Eternity," and "Power Flight." Great stuff from a band/record that's sadly been lost in time, and wholeheartedly recommended, especially to those who like their metal exotic, mythical, and weird.

MERCENARY (New Haven, Connecticut) was a progressive metal band with ex-Legend (*Fröm the Fjörds*) members Kevin Nugent and Fred Melillo on guitars and keyboards respectively. They managed to put out two near-perfect releases, the 1982 *She's Evil/Plastic Eyes* seven-inch and the 1989 *Tribute* cassette, both mandatory for everyone into progressive metal. Even though I'm not a fan of such complex stuff, songs like "She's Evil" and "Plastic Eyes" are tremendous—especially since they were released back in 1982! Get 'em both! **MYSSTRESS** (Eugene, Oregon) formed as Fallout in 1984, changed their name in 1985, and released the *Mysstress* twelve-inch in 1986 and the *Mysstress* demo cassette in 1988. This is raging ultra-powerful American metal, with four songs that ooze with power. "Keep the Drive" and "Take on the World" are perfect examples of their metallic dynamic, so *Mysstress* is a record that will satisfy anybody who's into bands like Wild Dogs or Anvil. Sadly, Mysstress changed their name to Zoo Gang in 1989 and started playing mainstream hard rock, releasing a self-titled full-length in 1992. **PENTAGRAM** from Washington, D.C. needs a whole book of their own. Formed in 1971, the band is (along with Black Sabbath, of course) a pioneer of the doom metal sound, and self-released three seven-inches in the 1970s. Pentagram's first full-length LP, 1985's *Pentagram* (on the band's own label, Pentagram Records), is a monument of this sound, a perfect, chaotic, ultra-heavy doom metal record that's raw and rockin' (unlike the Euro style of epic doom metal). Lots of great records in this style followed, so there's quite a big discography to choose from, but be sure to get *Pentagram* in your collection because songs like "Sinister" or "Death Row" are simply menacing. **OVERLORD** (Seattle) sounded like a cross between Judas Priest and Accept (if less inspired or talented) on the 1982 *Broken Toys* twelve-inch, released on the band's own label, Sad City Records. Still, though, this is pretty enjoyable, and songs like "Had Enough" or "Blame It on the Kids" are definitely winners. **RAGING SAINT** (Austin, Texas) was another glam/metal combo, and the band self-released the *I Want Your Love/Sad but True* seven-inch in 1988. It's overproduced glam metal, in the tradition of Warrant, Mötley Crüe, et cetera. I have zero interest in this subgenre, but fans will be satisfied.

SPECTRE (San Francisco) released just one record, the 1985 *Lady of the Night* album, which bordered between hard rock and melodic metal and was really nice in terms of inspiration and execution. Yes, there are (many) ballads, but still ... listen to "Walk Tight," the excellent "Searchin,'" and "On the Run," and you'll get the idea. Plus, a great vocalist too! **STRIKER** from New Jersey, though, is a totally different story—you like your metal rough, raw, powerful, and metal to the max? Look no further, 'cause the 1982 *Striker/Finish You Off* seven-inch (on the band's label, Striker Records) is one of the most glowing moments in American metal—unbelievably powerful and inspired! Too bad Striker didn't get the chance to record more stuff. Another hard/heavy crossover band is **TAILGUNNER** (of unknown origin), and their 1983 *Tailgunner* LP (released on the band's own label, Rapid Records); I consider this one a minor classic of this sound due to its roaring guitars and excellent power. Tailgunner sounds like a cross between early Iron Maiden, Mountain, and The Stooges! "Reach 'n' Out," "Why," and "Spice Is Nice" are among the highlights of an excellent record! Highly recommended. **MYTH** (Maryland) was a highly obscure band that released the *True Myth/Satan's Lair* seven-inch in 1980; of course, I couldn't get my hands on it, since it is super-rare, so no review on that one. The same applies for **DEUCE** (of unknown origin) and its *I Live For Rock And Roll/ Small Town Blues* seven-inch; reportedly, this was a hard rock/metal hybrid, but the record's nowhere to be found. **WARMINISTER** (Dayton, Ohio) was the first band of Benny Bodine (later of Four Star Revival), and their only release, the 1986 *Out of the Ashes* twelve-inch, is a mixed bag. WarMinister balances between the classic American metal sound of Armored Saint and the glam metal of Mötley Crüe, and even though the record has good songs (like the title track or "Get Started"), I wish it had headed for a more hardcore, strict American metal sound. Still good, though.

In 1986, **GOLD DUST** (Massachusetts) released a hard rock/metal monster that drives collectors across the world crazy with its ultra-thick power chords and its crude, raw style! The *Gold Dust* LP shares similarities with bands like Crowhaven or Legend, and you should check out songs like "Hard Road" or "The Maze"—terrific stuff! Sadly, only 300 copies of

Gold Dust were pressed, although the band also released the (even more rare) *Before It's Too Late/Kodachrome* seven-inch in 1988! **THE DAVE WAGNER BAND** (San Antonio, Texas) was the brainchild of guitar virtuoso Dave Wagner, and in 1986 the band released the *Tell Me/Night Fighter* seven-inch, which is good shred metal. **ARYON** (Newark, California) formed in 1982 and included Bruce Sedlacek (later of Robyn Danger), and in 1983 released the *Rebels of the Night* LP and the *Alcatraz* seven-inch—that included two songs off the LP—on their own label, South Bay Records. This is the kind of American metal that was played prior to 1983, with no glam, thrash, or power metal approach. *Rebels of the Night* is more than a decent LP with huge Judas Priest and Accept influences, and "Love and Pain" is a really good song. **VICE** (first Connecticut and then Los Angeles) formed in 1983 and included the guitar hero Chris Impellitteri and the notorious vocalist Rob Rock. I know that fans of hair metal are going nuts over the 1987 *Hot...Just Lookin' At You* LP, 'cause it contains everything that the fans of this style want: fun, overproduced, technically proficient party metal/hard rock. Yep, this one is mandatory for fans, but I can't stand this stuff, sorry. Another band called **VICE**, this time from Albuquerque, New Mexico, took a hard rock/glam metal approach too, although pretty uninspired (with the exception of "War Child") on their only release, the 1984 *Vice* twelve-inch on Positive Records. **THE ROCK CORPS** (from the suburbs of Chicago) was another short-lived band; however, the 1984 *Rock Corps/The Lords of Light* seven-inch is nothing but nostalgic, melodic, and highly authentic American metal (pre-power days), with "The Lords of Light" being a galloping—almost epic—anthem! Get this one if you like your American metal with a huge NWOBHM influence. **WARZWOLF** (Phoenix) is a band that will be beloved by every fan of NWOBHM mixed with American metal, as well as metalheads who want their metal played mean! The 1987 *Valley of the Shadow* LP on the band's label, Raindancer Records, remains at the top of many wish lists all over the world—songs like "Black Hawk" and "Sonoran Run" are unbelievable epic metal anthems, plus there's the thunderous cover of Blondie's "Call Me." This is a mandatory purchase, of course!

REVENGE (first Florida, then Hinckley, Ohio) sounded absolutely rough and had a charming amateurish approach on their 1987 *Freedom of Choice* LP (on R.E.I. Records), sounding almost like if Venom had gone American metal. I could compare them to acts like Black Virgin, partially due to the female vocalist, Kim Solak. "Rock-n-Roll Star" is a good song too. Revenge kept it up until the late 2000s, releasing one demo (the *1992 Demo Tape*) and the 2006 *Titties-N-Beer* CD. **DANGERFACE** was a short-lived American hard rock/AOR trio formed in Los Angeles in 1982 when singer/guitarist Gary Robertson hooked up with bassist Tony Cavazo and drummer Stephen Quadros—both formerly of the American hard 'n' heavy band Snow, mentioned earlier in this book. More like hard power-pop with a slight touch of hard rock, the band's only release, the *Dangerface* 1983 twelve-inch, is worth checking out for yourselves. However, this is way too mellow for me. **ZOOT** (from either Maxville, Oregon, or Maxville, Wisconsin) are one of the bands that I have to dig really deep in order to find their 1980 *Rocking The Galaxy/I Need Someone* seven-inch. It's top-class hard 'n' heavy metal, with influences ranging from Led Zeppelin to Mountain, so fans of this style, you should track it down. "I Need Someone" is a sweet song. Another crazy obscurity is **JUZT NUTZ** from Evanston, Illinois, and their 1980 or 1981 *Rats/Electrified Lady* seven-inch. Hard rock is the starting point here too, but it kind of mixes with (my beloved) seventies punk—there's a huge Stooges influence here (especially on "Rats"). And obviously, I like it very much! **ROCKNEE** from Los Angeles had quite an extensive career in the 1980s, releasing demos, CD EPs, and compilations as well as the 1986 *Rocknee* LP on their own label. This is hard rock/glam that's very well played, and fans will definitely like it. **SHADOWFOX** from Philadelphia got their first ten-inch, the *Stealer* EP, on an indie label (Mark Records), but its next two releases, the 1985 *First Blood* LP and the 1985 *She's Got It* seven-inch, were released through the band's own label, Ariel Records. Very tame (but still professional) hard rock/AOR, it's recommended to anyone who's into this stuff.

PROWLER (New York City) initially released their *Prowling Death Squad* twelve-inch EP in 1986 on the band's label, Tursha Records, containing three songs of excellent power/thrash metal with a good punk edge. "Thrash and Bang" as well as "Sudden Death" are headbanging ragers! New Renaissance Records re-released it with two extra songs—all tracks are great here too! **RATED X** (Kearny, New Jersey) on their only LP, 1987's *Matter of Taste*, balanced between heavy and power metal with super-exciting results! They kind of use the Iron Maiden formula in their songs, blending it with the classic American metal sound, creating great songs like the title track and "Captain Crunch." Dismiss the bad record cover and focus on the music, 'cause this is serious, nearly classic American metal! On the other hand, **RATED X** from Miami was a glam/hair metal band (albeit with a strong heavy metal sound) that released their only seven-inch, *Stranger/Make You Mine*, in 1985. I have to admit that they're really good, and this is because their classic metal influences give them a pretty inspiring approach ("Stranger" is a near-perfect song!). Yep, you are all familiar with **PANTERA** from Arlington, Texas, as well as their story, so this will just be a reminder: Pantera formed in 1981 as a glam metal band, releasing three decent records on their own label, Metal Magic Records (the *Metal Magic* LP in 1983, the *Projects in the Jungle* LP in 1984, and the *I Am the Night* LP in 1985). However, the great record of Pantera's so-called independent era was the 1988 *Power Metal* LP—the first one with Phil Anselmo on vocals. In some cases, such as the title song, they sound like Riot's *Thundersteel* (only not as wild), which means fast, electric, total American power metal! Later, Pantera changed musical direction to groove metal, which leaves me totally cold. Plus, people need to stop calling their nineties music "hardcore"—it has nothing to do with hardcore! **NEW YORK** (Rock Hill, South Carolina) released the 1984 *Carry the Torch* twelve-inch (on the band's label, Tinker's Damm Productions), and even if it's overall a hard/heavy glam record, it contains one tremendous American metal song, "Nite Flyer." This song alone is a good reason for you to get this twelve-inch!

Another crazy obscurity, **LIVE WIRE** from Georgia and its 1984 *Live Wire/Mood to Rock* seven-inch, is nowhere to be found, so I can't give it a proper review. **THE PLADS** (from Ketchikan, Alaska) were a pretty weird—but really good—case of a band that kind of mixed punk with new wave and classic heavy metal on their two releases, the 1982 *Calling Girls* seven-inch and the 1983 *Domine Deus* LP. I'm a sucker for this stuff, but I wouldn't recommend them to hardcore metalheads. Ah, come on, "Domine Deus" is a great song! **STRYKEN** (Austin/Cedar Park, Texas) followed the then-emerging Christian heavy metal path, and even though I'm totally opposed to its message, the 1986 *Rock On/Surprise* seven-inch and 1987 *First Strike* LP are very well-played melodic heavy metal. Obvious Stryper influences here, along with great tunes like "One Way" or "State of Emergency." Both records may appeal to either metalheads of fans of glam/metal. **BROS GRIMM** (Columbus, Ohio) was a straight hard rock act that released two records on their own label, the 1983 *Numbers* LP and the 1988 *Good Times* LP. Nothing to flip over, but overall it's decent stuff for fans of American hard rock (especially Van Halen). **SEDUCE** (Detroit) formed in 1980, and the band's most famous moment was its appearance in the documentary *The Decline of Western Civilization Part II: The Metal Years* with a performance of "Crash Landing" and an interview. However, it still remains very sad that Seduce could never establish a career in the world of heavy metal, because their first 1985 LP, *Seduce*, released on their Psycho-Mania Records label, is one of the best records featured in this book! High-energy, ultra-power heavy metal to the maximum, *Seduce* is simply an eternal monument of heavy metal; songs like "Viper's Bite," the raging "Streets," and the heavyweight "Face to Face" are definite highlights of a nearly flawless LP that reminds me of Armored Saint or early Lizzy Borden. Seduce kept it up, releasing one more LP, the 1988 *Too Much Ain't Enough* album, but the band took a turn toward glam/metal here, and even though they did it with style, this second LP pales in comparison to the first. And now, it's time for a completely different release: the 1986 self-released split seven-inch by **KIL D' KOR** and **MAX PLÄNCK**, named *The Northwest Connection*. **KIL D' KOR** was from Seattle and had already released three demos, whereas **MAX PLÄNCK** was from Port Townsend, Washington, having previously released the 1985 *Kill the Pain* demo. While the Kil D' Kor side included one fist-banging, roaring heavy/speed anthem ("Chained Angel"), Max Plänck are the definite winner here, with the weird heavy metal rock 'n' roller "Fucked Up."

INTRINSIC (San Luis Obispo, California) formed in 1984 and are still active to this day (as of 2022), with a total of five releases. The first, self-released 1987 *Intrinsic* LP, released on the band's No Wimp Records label, remains a phenomenal record of technical heavy/power/speed metal that all fans of later Liege Lord, or those who can imagine Iron Maiden played at 45 RPM, should get! Weird but unique, powerful, and inspired, *Intrinsic* includes great songs such as "Ahead of the Game," the astonishing instrumental "Compo," and the ferocious "Possessor"—heavy metal played with maximum passion! Be sure to get their later records too if you like *Intrinsic*. **HOBBIT** (Tyler, Texas) are considered the originators of "fantasy rock" (whatever this means), but to my ears, they sound like a weird mix of progressive rock with AOR on all the band's records that were released independently. They formed in the late 1970s and kept it up until the early '10s. You can try the self-released *Take Me Tonight* 1980 seven-inch, the *Midyear's Eve* twelve-inch, and the *Need Your Love/Love Is Forever* seven-inch as well as their CDs. Obviously, not my favorite style of music. **ROLAND QUEST** (unknown origin) released just one mysterious seven-inch in 1985, the *Vixen/I Really Wanna Show* on their Ultra Records. "Vixen" is a good heavy metal stomper, while "I Really Wanna Show" has a more rockish sound. **HARD KNOX** (Oak Ridge, Tennessee) followed the glam/metal path too, although with an extra-powerful sound, on their 1985 *Mark of the Rocker* LP. Yes, there is a total Mötley Crüe influence, but the band has a much dirtier and more powerful sound, as well as some nice songs like "Get Up" or "Combat Alley." Recommended for fans. Another band that pursued quite an extensive career in the 1980s, achieving some success, is **ST. ELMO'S FIRE**

from Sacramento/Citrus Heights, California. Having formed in 1979 and still active today, St. Elmo's Fire created their own brand of melodic metal across many releases (with maybe their peak being the 1988 *Warning from the Sky* LP). However, their first, self-financed release, the 1982 *Really in Love/Too Bad* seven-inch, sounds like a cross of hard rock and power-pop punk, reminiscent of Cheap Trick. I'm definitely a sucker for this kind of stuff (and "Really in Love" is an amazing, super-catchy song), but would not recommend this one to metalheads. (Maybe the B-side, "Too Bad," which has a more straightforward metal edge, will do the job for them though!) The band released 2,000 copies of the *Really in Love/Too Bad* seven-inch, but all fans of melodic metal should at least have one St. Elmo's Fire record in their collection! **BENT SIRKIS** from Middletown, New York, released a good number of demos throughout their existence (from 1985 to 1994), but the first release was the 1985 *Stop Your Bitchin' (And Put Your Fist In The Air)/Pay It In Blood* seven-inch (on the band's own label, Evil Records). Fans of Atomkraft, Venom, Bulldozer, or even Mayhem (Portland, Oregon), look no further, because this is the kind of stuff you love: raw, underproduced speed/thrash metal with a definite punk influence. "Pay It In Blood" is a raw rager!

BASHFUL (Mt. Union, Pennsylvania) on their 1985 *Bashful* twelve-inch EP kind of reminded me of the NWOBHM band Grim Reaper—that is, heavy metal with a hard rock background, mid-tempo, with catchy songs and brilliant production. "Axshun," "Into the Battle," and "White Line Fever" are examples of prototypical, straightforward American metal, and *Bashful* is certainly a very good record. Bashful released a few more demos, and the 1990 *Down For The Count* CD was on the hard rock side of things. **BISHOP STEEL** (Kansas City) was a fantastic heavy/power metal band with two near-perfect releases, the 1987 *Hold On* seven-inch and the 1991 *Killing Asylum* twelve-inch (the latter only had 300 copies released). Some people are turned off by the bad recordings, but this shouldn't discourage you; what we have in the case of Bishop Steel is true, eclectic, inspired American heavy/power that borders on darker-sounding bands of the time (like Exxplorer). "Hold On," "Killing Asylum," and "On and On" are masterpieces, and if you have even a slight connection with American metal, you should check them out! Bishop Steel released some demos too, and if I had to pick from the two vinyl record releases, I would get *Killing Asylum* for sure! Another heavy/power outfit, **DAMIEN** from Toledo, Ohio, formed in 1981 and are still active to this day, with an impressive catalog of releases including four LPs, two compilations, and one demo. However, the band's second LP, 1989's *Stop This War*, was released via its own label, Mondo Records, and of course, this is just a top-shelf release of unbelievably crushing heavy/power metal! Actually, *Stop This War* is a world-class metal release, drawing inspiration from Judas Priest, Metal Church, Accept, as well as Ozzy, with anthems like "Stormwind," the instrumental "30 St. Clair," or the title crusher! Get it, but be sure to get Damien's other records too! **DAVID NEIL CLINE** (Detroit) was a super-talented guitarist who sadly committed suicide in 2015. His band, David Neil Cline, released the *A Fit Of Rage* twelve-inch EP in 1987 and the *Malefic Influence* LP in 1989 (on the band's own label, Gazochtahagen Records), and both releases were blistering shred metal à la Malmsteen, with influences mostly in the heavy/power metal scene with a good dose of Iron Maiden. Although *A Fit Of Rage* is more metallic, it is *Malefic Influence* that's absolutely flawless, with a more hard rock approach. The title song is a true masterwork, while "We Just

Don't Care" is a Maiden-ish steamroller—overall, we're talking about killer stuff. Get all of David Neil Cline's records (there are some more CDs) if you fancy a mix of shred metal with American heavy/hard metal.

DIETRICH (Santa Barbara, California) gained some fame in the eighties due to their inclusion on the 1982 *Metal Massacre II* compilation. Formed as Avalanche in 1979, the band released the 1982 ten-inch, *Red Alert*, on their own label, DieRich Productions. Nothing thrilling, *Red Alert* includes some good hard 'n' heavy moments, such as the title track. Other than that, you won't flip for this one. **DIRECT TOUCH** (Dover, New Jersey) was a very unique band, combining AOR/melodic metal with American power metal on all their releases, which were on the band's own label, variously styled as Andromedia Unlimited Records or Andromedia Records. They released the 1986 *Meaning To Life* twelve-inch, and in 1987 the *Girls Want Money* twelve-inch, *You've Got Something* seven-inch and *Rock You ('Til It Hurts)* twelve-inch (as well as one demo). Direct Touch's sound blends NWOBHM, American metal, and AOR, and you should listen to songs like "Rock You ('Til It Hurts)," "Dreamer," and "Meaning to Life." We are talking about marvelous stuff here! Post-breakup, Tim Rybar (FKA Rip Rybarski) and Bob Ernst performed with Tim Rybar's eponymous band (releasing two good cassettes in 1989 and 1992). The crazy story of **DWARR** (Columbia, South Carolina) is that the band was formed in 1981 by Duane Dwarr, who played all instruments and vocals, and are active still today (as of 2022). This remains one of the most enigmatic, crazy, eclectic bands that American metal ever saw! Dwarr blends heavy metal with doom and psychedelic rock, and all their stuff (four LPs/CDs) was released on the band's own label. The first release, the 1985 *Starting Over* LP, is a dark and cryptic masterpiece, massively dreamy and nostalgic, and I'd guess that fans of very early Manilla Road would love it. Their next LP, 1986's *Animals*, is more straightforward, less weird, but equally great, drawing a little more influence from Sabbath's Ozzy era. Recommended, of course, but beware, 'cause it's gonna be a trippy ride! **AUGUST REDMOON** (Anaheim, California) formed in 1980, changed their name to Terracuda in 1983, released one demo, and changed their name again to Eden in 1984, releasing some demos and one LP. The band seems to be inactive since 2013. August Redmoon released one of the most notorious American independent metal records in 1982, the *Fools Are Never Alone* twelve-inch EP (initially on the band's own Fools Are Never Alone label): it's melodic, commercially driven heavy metal (but not glam/poser stuff) and an overall pretty intriguing record. Actually, all songs are good, with "Jeckyll 'N' Hyde" being excellent. Get it.

Time to go full-on extreme, with a band that most people in the metal camp like. **SADUS** (Antioch, California) were, of course, one of the earliest purveyors of death/thrash metal, having formed in 1985 and releasing three demos before dropping the bomb with their first LP, 1988's *Illusions*, on the band's own label, Sadus Records. Technically crazy, absolutely frenetic, adrenaline-fueled death/thrash of the highest degree, *Illusions* was later re-released as *Chemical Exposure*, and every song on it will melt your face. Tracks like "Sadus Attack," "Certain Death," and "Torture" (with a crazy bass solo from Steve DiGiorgio), have to be heard to be believed. Even if you are not a fan of extreme metal, you must have *Illusions* in your collection; just imagine Kreator slamming with Slayer in an early Slaughter show, and you'll get the idea! Sadus, of course, are still active today, and you should pick up all their stuff, 'cause they rule. **EMERALD** (New Brunswick, New Jersey) formed in 1982, and up until 1987, they recorded many demos, although without releasing them. What they released was the 1985 *High Roller/Ladies Of The Night* seven-inch and the 1987 *Queen of My Dreams/Bad* demo; the seven-inch sounds like it was recorded on a cold winter day in the Midlands of England, during the heyday of NWOBHM! Judas Priest, Saxon, UFO, Tygers of Pan Tang ... all those bands come to mind when listening to "High Roller," while "Ladies Of The Night" has a slight punk touch (Misfits?). A great seven-inch nevertheless. Just like Direct Touch, **FLYNN** (California) followed the same route of blending heavy/power and AOR on the twelve-inch *Say You'll Stay* (released on the band's label, Shontod Records). You know the drill here: this is very talented and original stuff (like Queensrÿche meets Lillian Axe), and songs like "Say You'll Stay" and "Don't Walk Away" are just masterpieces. Highly recommended. **FLYNN THOMAS** (Montana) released the *Dangerous Friends* cassette in 1982 and the *Dangerous Friends/The Desert Prelude* seven-inch in 1984 on the band's own label, Bleeding Heart Records. It's hard rock with a metal touch, professionally executed, with good songwriting skills ("Dangerous Friends" is a fine tune). Flynn Thomas went on to release a picture-disc LP in 1987, the enjoyable *Dangerous Friends*, on David Thomas Richards' Masque Records. **EXCALIBUR** (Cincinnati) on the 1985 *Gotta Have Your Love Tonight/City of Light* seven-inch has that gutsy early-eighties Judas Priest sound, and both songs are way above par. Check out the YouTube videos of Excalibur's Battle of the Bands appearance for Cincinnati's 102.7 WEBN in 1984!

VIKING (Boston) was the musical project of Luís Gil Bettencourt and his brothers, Roberto Bettencourt (bass guitar) and Nuno Bettencourt (who would later become the guitarist of Extreme). Formed in the late 1970s as Alien, Viking released just one seven-inch, 1982's *Short Tale*, which included two songs of progressive/hard rock. It's ridiculously rare, and I couldn't find it anywhere. Speaking of Extreme members, Gary Cherone also played in a band that independently released a record: **THE DREAM** (Malden, Massachusetts) put out one really good melodic metal LP in 1983, which is titled *E.P.*, that included cute and mellow (but still pretty inspired) songs like "Mutha (Don't Wanna Go To School Today)," which was also released as a video clip, and "See The Light." Good for fans of melodic metal. **FORGOTTEN CHILD** (Los Angeles) sounds like a cross between AC/DC and Accept, playing American metal! The 1986 *Forgotten Child* LP is nearly perfect: pure heavy metal that was fed a steady diet of seventies hard rock and metal. Fans of the aforementioned bands, you need to hear songs like "Forgotten Child" or "Witness"—this LP is for you. They also released one demo in 1989 (*Rock & Roll Salvation*) that went in more of a hard rock direction. Plus, it has to be mentioned that prior to Forgotten Child, guitarist Robert Cromwell McKinney started a project called Fallen Angels with Dave Mustaine, where he cowrote material that was later reworked into tracks on the first Megadeth album! I got familiar with **HEATHER LEATHER** (San Antonio, Texas) through their inclusion on the hardcore/punk *Metal Moo Cow* compilation LP; they formed in 1980 and are still active today (as of 2022). The band comprises three sisters (Ruth Garza, Sandie Garza, and Sylvia Garza). Their self-released 1985 *We Came to Destroy/Child Molester* seven-inch has gotten pretty bad reviews, but I have to be totally honest: I like it! It's sloppy, chaotic, and messy (the sound on "We Came to Destroy" reminds me somehow of the Flyboys), whereas the B-side, "Child Molester," is a totally nasty (at least lyrically) metal/rocker. Then there's **VIRGIN STEELE** (Long Island), of course ... you already read the foreword by David DeFeis, but it has to be mentioned here too. Virgin Steele formed in 1981 and are still (as of 2022) active, releasing a great number of records, with at least five of them considered huge classics in the metal community. The band's first release, the 1982 *Virgin Steele* LP, was released through their own label, V.S. Records, having pressed 10,000 copies! If I were to pick just one Virgin Steele record for a newbie, it would be *Noble Savage* (1985)—it's a brilliant starting point.

Back in the American hard rock camp, **STREET THEATRE** (Lubbock, Texas) on their 1982 *Rock N' Roll Forever* LP (released with two different pressings/covers by the band's label, Excalibur Records) went for a crude, raw, and powerful approach, combining Kiss with UFO (among many others). Things get pretty dirty and wild in songs like the title track or "Sweet Little Sugar" and "Rave On." Street Theatre also released two seven-inches in the 1970s. Be sure to get *Rock N' Roll Forever* if you are a fan of pure, pre-glam, American hard rock. **DAMMAJ** (San Francisco) formed in 1981 and are still active to this day (as of 2022), and their first release was the 1982 *Beats the Hell Outta Me* seven-inch (on the band's own label, Dammaj Records). It's good crossover hard rock/metal, but things get really serious with the addition of the Gilbert brothers (Mick, Rich, and Steve), who originated from my beloved Luton, England—overall a pretty rough place. *Dammaj* went on to sign to Roadrunner Records and release their metallic masterpiece, the *Mutiny* LP, in 1986. "Devils & Angels" is a huge hymn on a spectacular American metal record! **SEDUCER** (from Plainville, Massachusetts) kicked off in 1983 with the *Malibu Sands/Shot In The Dark* seven-inch that was mostly power pop; their next release (also self-released on the band's own North Ridge Corp. label), the 1988 *Seducer* LP, went toward a hard rock/AOR sound. It's a fun listen, mellow and innocent, and it sounds so nostalgic today. Check out "Without You" and "Caught On You"—really nice tunes! Utah isn't notorious for its heavy metal scene; however, **CRISIS** from Salt Lake City formed in 1979 and remain active to this day (as of 2022) under the name Hard Bargain. After one demo, the band went on to release the total classic twelve-inch *Armed To The Teeth* (1984) on Bullet Records, which was actually a British label that released mostly NWOBHM stuff! Crisis was mostly connected with the NWOBHM sound rather than the American metal sound, rough and raw with no commercial tendencies. The band then self-released the *Kick It Out* cassette (1986) and the *Keep Fighting* seven-inch (also in 1986), containing the same style of songwriting, reminiscent of Raven and Jaguar! *Keep Fighting* is a classic. **SWORD** (Cincinnati) formed in 1978 and kept it up (with some pauses) until the mid-aughts; the hard rock/metal crossover is mostly based on the British sound (Deep Purple meets NWOBHM). Both songs on the 1982 *Call Out His Name/Run Away* seven-inch are melodic and totally classy, especially "Run Away." In 2001, Sword later released the *MT. 10:34* CD that I unfortunately couldn't get hold of in order to review.

HEAD ON (San Francisco) was a hard rock outfit that formed in 1980 and disbanded in 1984, including members of future bands such as Sea Hags, Arcade, Castle Blak, Guns N' Roses, and Mad Reign. The 1982 *Throw The Book/Ready Go* (released on an eight-inch flexi disc!) is nothing but a mix of seventies glam with hard rock, kinda like Slade, New York Dolls, or T. Rex, if more 1980s. There's also a compilation in existence, the 2011 *Washington & Battery* CD. **UNCLE SAM** (Kent, Washington) released all their records via their own Emerald Records label: the *Welcome* *to America* twelve-inch (1984), the *Rise Up Proud Eagle* seven-inch (1985), and the *America America* LP (1985). Oh, those (damn) patriots! Music-wise, though, this was a good melodic hard rock band with influences from Boston, Styx, and Van Halen, and it could definitely pull off a fine tune (such as "Redcoat" or "Forever Free"). The *America America* LP is totally recommended for fans of the style. Time to go way different, with **TOXIMIA** from New York City, which formed in 1985. Toximia was the first official band of drummer Sal Abruscato (later of A Pale Horse Named Death, Life of Agony, Type O Negative, My Mortality, and Supermassiv). The band released the 1986 *Another Beautiful Day* demo cassette, while their first LP, the 1987 *War* (on the band's own label, Kiva Records), was a real rager! Thrash metal with slight crossover tendencies, this is reminiscent of Carnivore, Slayer, and Venom, and has that definite NYHC edge with a Dirty Rotten Imbeciles fuse. Crazy stuff, and songs like "Radiation Sickness" and "Ultra-Violence" will make you bounce off the walls, but it probably won't appeal to hardcore true metalheads. Got no idea where **TRIPLE-X** was from—the only thing I know about them is that they were (reportedly) a melodic American metal band on the 1988 *Bad Reputation/Cheap Thrills* seven-inch (released on the band's label, She-Fox Records). **THE KINGDOM** (Los Angeles) reminded me of a California version of Sacred Blade on their only LP, the 1988 *The Kingdom* (Cherry Love Productions): dreamy, weird, but very melodic heavy/power metal. Songs like "An Early Frost of Blue" and "The Beautiful Dream" could be described as "ethereal metal" or something like that! Definitely unique. Although this one is only recommended to those who fancy really strange things, *The Kingdom* is a spectacular record.

THE MEZMERIST (Los Angeles) has THE definitive backstory in the world of privately released American metal. Formed in 1982, the band recruited Black Sabbath's Bill Ward as their drummer for the release of their 1983 *The Innocent, The Forsaken, The Guilty* twelve-inch, of which 500 copies were issued. Crazily weird, haunting, and eerie metal that spawned from Black Sabbath, Mercyful Fate, and Coven, filtered through an atmosphere that reminds me of an LSD nightmare. Psychedelic heavy/hard metal, maybe? I really don't know how to describe it, but this is one of the best records that eighties American metal ever put out. **STEEL WARRIORS** (New York City) was formed in 1982 by vocalist, bassist, and guitarist Steve Scott; the crude metal/hard rock on the 1984 *Steel Warriors* twelve-inch isn't that good or memorable, although it has its charm. The second twelve-inch, 1985's *On The Road To Hell*, was slightly better in terms of songwriting (the title song is actually great). Okay for completists, I suppose. **SACRED FEW** (Cleveland) formed in 1977 and reunited in 2016 after a long hiatus, until vocalist Sandy Kruger's death in early 2022. Over the last few years, the band's gained some exposure due to Sandy's guest appearance on Savage Master's *Lady of Steel* LP. The music is simple, very enjoyable female-fronted heavy metal, and the guitar melodies of Sandy's then-partner, Wolfgang Kruger, are totally cool and catchy. The band's first offering, the 1983 *Sacred Few/Lowrider* seven-inch, is a pretty fun listen, but things got pretty serious on the semi-classic *Beyond The Iron Walls* 1985 LP! "Wildlife," "Are You Out There?" and the excellent "Sea of Thought" are just pure, heavy metal rockers, and if you can imagine a NWOBHM conversion to American standards with female vocals, this is it. A must-have release. **SABOTAGE** (Detroit) formed in 1982 and had connections with Messiah—drummer Glenn Gugel was the brother of Messiah vocalist Chuck Gugel, while both bands released records on Messiah's IHM Records label. Sabotage's first self-released 1984 twelve-inch, *Cloudborne*, is their finest moment: it's classy, melodic heavy metal with amazing songs like "Purgatory" and "Prophecies." That said, the 1985 *Sabotage* twelve-inch EP contains their best anthem, "Deadly Game." *Sabotage* is mostly a hard rock/AOR sound, rather than melodic heavy metal, but I recommend both records.

Just like the case of Sacred Few, **LUCRECIA** (Los Angeles) was a female-fronted metal band with an eerie, haunting style that could be described as atypical or extraordinary. Formed in 1980, Lucrecia released the mediocre *The Hunter* b/w *No One Gets Out Alive* seven-inch in 1986 on the band's own label, Zylon Records. However, their next effort, the *Lucrecia* 1988 LP, is intriguing: check it out for yourselves, but be forewarned that this is some of the most unconventional eighties American metal you'll ever hear, with truly crazy song structures. Check out the songs "We Ain't Kids No More," "Prelude to Hell/No One Gets Out Alive," and the perfect "Shadow." Christian heavy metal, oh, that plague! Still though, **MALACHIA** (Los Angeles) was a pretty cool band that followed the path of Iron Maiden and early Queensrÿche on their (self-released on Wayde Records) *Under The Blade* 1986 LP. Songs like "Red Sunrise" and "Master's Call" are good stuff and definitely hold a romantic and nostalgic feeling that only those melodic eighties American metal bands could pull off. Malachia later also released the *Red Sunrise* 1987 LP (on the indie L.A.-area Christian label, Victoria Ltd.), while Steve Ayola played with the aforementioned (excellent) Hawk. No words, though, can describe the genius, the talent, and the finesse of **MESSIAH**, from Detroit. Formed in 1979, Messiah followed a different route from their Detroit peers, and instead of performing raging, noisy metal, the band set out to create their own melodic, mesmerizing epic metal on two perfect releases, the 1984 *Final Warning* LP and the 1985 *Going Insane* twelve-inch (both released on the band's label, IHM Records). While *Final Warning* has more in common with Omen (or even early Heir Apparent), *Going Insane* reminds me of Warlord, and of course, both are highly recommended. I would express a preference for *Final Warning*, though, because of "Who's to Blame" or the title track. **MISTREATER** (Cleveland) formed in 1978, and upholds the tradition of mixing American hard rock (like Buffalo) with heavy metal (like Black Sabbath), releasing stuff that nowadays is considered classic. The small Indiana label 700 West released the 1980 *Hell's Fire/Baby Blue* seven-inch, and Mistreater went on to self-release the superb *Hell's*Fire* 1981 LP. Each and every song here is a hit—allow me to express my preference for the steamroller "Big A" or the mystic epic "Lies/Graverobber." Mistreater released another record, 1987's *Swami*, on their own label, Mistreater Records, that was slightly more metallic and equally great. Just check out songs like "Rellik" or "Black Angel."

Mistreater's story is also connected with another band, **SCARUM** (also from Cleveland). In the early eighties, Larry Nottingham left Mistreater and was replaced by Dave Hall on guitar. A few years later, Dave Hall passed away, and Larry Nottingham rejoined Mistreater for their second LP, *Swami*, and brought the rest of Scarum with him. The lineup on that LP is identical to Scarum's, only with Curt Leudy on vocals. On the first seven-inch, *Feeling Grave/Misery* (1980), the band's name is spelled "Scarem," and on the second and last seven-inch, *Scarum* (1981), the name changes, as the band had officially changed the spelling in late 1980. Of the two self-released seven-inches, I prefer *Feeling Grave/Misery*, which includes two terrific heavy metal/hard rock tunes that share the same spirit with the then-ongoing NWOBHM. "Misery" is a real powerhouse! **ODIN** (Los Angeles) is another very weird case of a band: they formed in 1980 as Tempest and are still active today (as of 2022). The band's first release, the 1983 *Caution!* seven-inch, includes some really hot American metal, but sadly, the vocalist's glam metal style kills it for me. A shame, since "Midnight Flight" and "The Blade" are great songs. Exactly the same applies to the 1985 *Don't Take No For An Answer* twelve-inch—man, what a bummer. Later in the eighties, Odin went for a more melodic metal sound on the 1987 *The Gods Must Be Crazy* twelve-inch and the 1988 *Fight For Your Life* LP, with the former being self-released and the latter released by Japan's Victor Records! The band's last release was the 2008 *Human Animal* CD (again, self-released). Members of Odin appeared also in bands such as Drive, Armored Saint, Madam X, BulletBoys, Malice, and countless others. **OVERLORDE** (Ironia, New Jersey) is one of those East Coast metal bands that wrote history in the underground metal circuit. Formed in 1985, Overlorde released the 1987 *Overlorde* twelve-inch, a bright moment not just for the underground but for American metal as a whole! Released on the band's own label, Strike Zone Records, in a 500-copy run, *Overlorde* remains a rarity and a very sought-after item on the wish lists of metal collectors worldwide—which is totally understandable, 'cause this is just frenetic American heavy/power metal all the way. As true and genuine as it gets! All five songs rule, but my fave is the mental "Snow Giant," which somehow reminds me of Upper Echelon's "Drivin' Mean." Overlorde also released two demos, followed by the near-perfect *Return of the Snow Giant* LP in 2004 on the Greek label Sonic Age/ Cult Metal Classics. The band's still going strong as of 2022, planning to release a new album!

THATCHER (Orlando) included some later-to-be-famous musicians, such as Rick Rozz (Death, Massacre) and Bob Rossi (Rob Rock). The band's only recording, the 1985 *Destined To Conquer* twelve-inch on their own label, Fahrenheit Records, is nothing but a good American metal record in the tradition of Judas Priest, (mostly) blended with early Dickinson-era Iron Maiden. What it lacks in performance or production, Thatcher gains from passion, with songs like "Speed Demon" and "Esmeralda." Nice stuff. **TED GEORGE** (Versailles, Ohio) played all instruments on his 1984 *Chained Heat/Rock-n-Roll Dreams* seven-inch. It's decent and basic hard rock/metal, and Ted also played with **WITCH** (Dayton, Ohio), self-releasing the now-ultra-rare *Salem's Rise* 1985 LP. That one's weird—but good—hard rock to metal crossover, with no glam elements and a dark psych edge! Songs like "Loki," "Poison," or the excellent title track make *Salem's Rise* a record that you should track down as well.

Now let's talk about some records that I couldn't find in order to review them, all of them being small, private pressings. The first one is **DIVA JETTA** (unknown origin) and their 1986 *Diva Jetta* seven-inch (classic heavy metal). **ZARDOZ** (Schaumburg, IL) and the hard rock 1981 *Elaine* seven-inch. **THE DRIFT** (Boston) and the 1983 *Gimme The Night* seven-inch, which is reported as hard rock (and Billy Sheehan was the bass player!). **SCARLET FURY** (unknown origin) released the hard rock *Just a Fool* seven-inch in 1983. **PASSION** (Waynesboro, Virginia) went for the glam metal sound on the *Kerri/Think We Found Love* seven-inch. **PATI ADAM** (New Haven, Connecticut) is reported as a glam/metal act on the *Let's Love* seven-inch. **PUPPETEER** (Lakewood, Colorado) released two seven-inches of hard rock/AOR, 1984's *Borderline* and 1987's *Puppeteer*. **INVISIBLE ENEMY** (Parma, Ohio) went for pure heavy metal on the 1983 *Ritual Beast* seven-inch. **AVALANCHE** (unknown origin), which released the *Avalanche* twelve-inch on the band's label, The Reference Point Records, is mentioned as a hard rock/psych combo. **THE STAX** (unknown origin) headed for hard rock on the *Turn Out The Lights/There'll Be Times* seven-inch in 1981. **RODAN** (Beverly Hills), another hard rock/AOR combo, put out the *Tears Of Happiness/You're Gonna Lose* seven-inch in 1982. **BANTHER** (Minneapolis) was a hard rock band that released the 1988 *Banther* LP. **THE ENEMY** was a hard rock band from Massachusetts that released two seven-inches, 1982's *America Rocks* and 1983's *Random Factor*. **DEFIANT** (Portland, Oregon) pursued the hard 'n' heavy crossover sound on the 1987 *Girl Next Door* seven-inch. **POWER SQUADRON** (unknown origin) and its 1985 heavy metal *Nightwind* LP. **RENEGADE** (Haverhill, Massachusetts) released two hard rock seven-inches in 1982, *Missing You* and *You Keep Me Hanging On*. **LOST ANGELES** (L.A.) is mentioned as a hard rock/AOR band on the 1984 twelve-inch *Lost Angeles*. **TUFF LUCK** (Springfield, Illinois) was another hard rock act, releasing the *I Wanna See You/Don't You Know* seven-inch in 1987. **NIGHTFALL** (unknown origin) aimed for a blend of hard rock and Southern rock on the 1981 *Phase One* seven-inch. **MOBIUS STRIP** (Indianapolis) was a pure hard rock band on the 1981 *Mobius Strip* LP.

LITTLE BIG BAND (Eugene, Oregon) also followed the hard rock style on the 1982 *Little Big Band* seven-inch. **LABANSKY** (Woodburn, Oregon) is another hard rock/AOR act on the 1987 *Talk To Me* seven-inch. **INVADER** (unknown origin) released the *Wear Me Out/Stay A Little Longer* seven-inch, which is reported to be hard rock/heavy metal, on the band's own label, Emanon Records. **AURA** (unknown origin) is also mentioned as a hard rock/heavy outfit on the 1982 *Aura* seven-inch. **LYNX** (Huntington, Indiana) was a pure hard rock act on the 1982 *Lynx* seven-inch, released on the band's label, Projection Unlimited Records. **LETHAL INJECTION** (New Jersey) was reviewed as a "primitive clunky U.S. metal act" in regard to the 1985 *Out For Blood* seven-inch. **C.O.A.** from Spring Hill, Florida, released the heavy metal *C.O.A.* seven-inch in 1983 on the band's own M & M Productions label. **WRATH** (California) and the 1984 *Love Cage/Power On Power* seven-inch is considered an impossible-to-find hard 'n' heavy record. **GUNRUNNER** (Herrin, Illinois) on the 1985 *Make It Quick* seven-inch was reviewed as a "mediocre hard rock act." **DOGFACE** (Spokane, Washington) went for a full-on hard rock sound on the 1983 *No Strings Attached* seven-inch. The same hard rock approach is given as a description for **THE BRUCE TELLER NETWORK** (Philadelphia) on the 1983 *Phila. Radio* seven-inch. **AQUILLA** (unknown origin) was reportedly a heavy metal act on the *Rock The Night* 1985 seven-inch. Not a damn idea where **THE KNIGHTS** are from, only that the *The Way I Feel/Going Out* 1982 seven-inch is presumably heavy metal. **CELLAR JAM** (New Jersey) was reportedly a hard rock band on the 1988 *Cellar Jam I* LP. No info on where **THE JACK** originated, but the 1985 *Cheat To Win* LP is mentioned as a hard rock record. **U.N.I.** (unknown origin) went for a classic hard rock sound on the *Out Of Control/Firestorm* 1981 release. **NOISE BOYS** (Blacksburg, Virginia) followed the hard rock route on the 1987 *Noise Boys* LP. The same musical direction applies to **ZINK** (St. Paul) and the 1982 *Zink* LP. **GLASS HAMMER** (Redondo Beach, California) went for the party/glam metal direction on the *976-Eazy* LP in 1989. **AXIS** (Lewiston, Maine) is described as a heavy/hard/progressive combo on the 1982 *That Girl/Wild Child* seven-inch. **2 PLUS 2** (Sellersville, Pennsylvania) was another hard rock band, releasing its own *Two Girls* seven-inch in 1985.

WYZARD (San Antonio, Texas) released in 1984 one of the records that true metalheads literally go crazy over, the *Future Knights* twelve-inch, which got a re-release treatment later that year and was renamed *Knights Of Metal* (with a slightly different cover). It's American heavy/power metal to the max—heavy, heroic, and classy, this is one of the finest independent metal releases of the 1980s. Wyzard wrote straightforward, catchy, bloody great tunes like "Future Knights" or my favorite, "Crystal City." A must-have! Members of Wyzard also played in the excellent King's Ransom. **RIVELL** (New Jersey) released two records on their own label, the 1982 *R* seven-inch and the 1983 *Touch* seven-inch; balancing between melodic metal and hard rock, Rivell could surely pull off some fine songs, like "The Dancer" or "Danger." Now that I think about it, the band has a Diamond Head/NWOBHM aesthetic. **CLOSING SPEED** (Orange County, California) formed in 1982 and had a very interesting story: vocalist/guitarist Nick Karafotis and drummer Jim Mulligan went to school with Metallica's James Hetfield (Brea Olinda High School, class of 1981), and Mulligan later played in a band named Leather Charm with James! Closing Speed released only one record, the 1987 *The Life* twelve-inch, which contained passionate, melodic hard rock/metal (pre-glam style) and is highly recommended! Another hard rock act, **PREZENCE** from San Antonio, Texas, started off as a high school band out of Clark High School. Their first release was on the small local label Teardrop Records (as Shawn Sahm and Prezence, and the release was the twelve-inch *Life In The City*), while the band's sophomore release was the 1985 *Rock Louder/Over You* seven-inch, which can be described as shining hard rock/metal! Both songs rule, with "Over You" being my favorite. Get this one now! **WINTERHAWK** (San Diego) has one of the most interesting stories in the history of independently released hard rock/metal; formed in 1978 on the Rincon Indian Reservation in San Diego County, Winterhawk may have been the first Native American hard rock/metal band. The band released the 1979 *Electric Warriors* LP and the *Dog Soldier* LP (1980) on their own label, Mother Earth Records, and later the 1984 *Good Golly Miss Molly/Rock And Roll Soldier* seven-inch on the small indie label Starman Records. Winterhawk fused heavy metal with native instruments and wrote lyrics about oppression at the hands of the white man, and all the albums are total classics, with *Dog Soldier* being highly recommended.

JASON GO (Orlando) released the privately pressed *Bitter Love* LP in 1989, in a 100-copy run. All songs and instruments were written/performed by Jason Go, and the result is excellent melodic metal with a fuzzy production that only adds to its character, while the basic lyrical theme is about love. Jason Go was super talented and could write very catchy, melancholic stuff, e.g., "Give Me a Chance" or "Captured by Love." **MAXWELL BUGGSY BAND** (Cleveland) was a short-lived hard rock combo, and their sole release, the 1983 *Cloak and Dagger* LP, held some secret diamonds in that style, such as "Video Eyes" and "Cloak and Dagger." As expected, this is rough classic American hard rock, with none of the later melodic/glam influences. Taking a totally different approach in their hard rock, **PUMPHOUSE** from Towanda, Pennsylvania, released the 1981 *Pumphouse* LP on their own Chisel Records label—a weird blend of hard rock, AOR and psychedelic rock that's quite charming and melodic. Haunting female vocals add a great flavor to a record with anthems like "S-Pan-Yol" and "You Gotta Hold On Me." **SYN** (of unknown origin) might have had an amateurish approach in their (very early) heavy/power metal, but the power is undeniable on the 1983 *Tears Of Rain/Future*

Rock Star seven-inch, which was self-released on the Blue Records label. Surely for completists of this style, both songs share an innocent and beautiful style—especially "Future Rock Star." **ALBION** (of unknown origin) was a fairly obscure hard 'n' heavy act with a female vocalist, and the 1980 *Wings of Fortune/Albion* seven-inch contains two good, mesmerizing songs ("Wings of Fortune" is the best one). **ZARLA** (Detroit) released two seven-inches, *You Lose Again/I Hate To Work* and *What You Are/Uncle Ray* on the band's Zarla Bros. label, with no known release date. Both records are a mysterious blend of hard rock with progressive rock, but they sound pretty weak, sorry. Back to the classic American metal sound, the guys in **KRIMSON KROSS** (Houston) were clearly huge Iron Maiden fans, as evidenced by their 1984 *Dogs of War/God Bless the Damned* seven-inch. Good stuff here. Check out "Dogs of War"—if you can handle the whole "2 Minutes to Midnight" appropriation, you will love it.

BLACK RYDER (Huntington, New York) self-released two seven-inches in 1982, *Black Ryder* and *All Night Long*. However, I find both records weak in terms of execution and songwriting. This music is hard 'n' heavy, but it's not catchy or memorable. **BLESSED CARRION** from Whitney, Texas, had that underproduced, nostalgic, melodic American metal sound on the 1989 *Concrete Queen/Go For The Money* seven-inch (released on Pristine Records). It's a nice release for completists or fans of Q5 and Queensrÿche. **GAVALDON** (Los Angeles) included Phil Woodward (later of Sahara), and their 1986 *Free Me* seven-inch contains two songs; while "Induced Current" isn't something spectacular, the title song is a real anthem of heavy/power metal, and you should pick it up just for that track! **CHRONIC PHONICS** from Mukilteo, Washington, included Corey Rivers (of Babylon and Nemesis fame) and Mark Welling (of Babylon, Bloodgood, and Tempest). The band's 1982 *Life of Illusion/Beyond the Screen* seven-inch is just good, enjoyable American hard rock/metal. Mark Welling later played with **PERENNIAL** (Seattle), releasing the *You're the Ones* twelve-inch in 1984, which sounded like a blend between early Ratt and Judas Priest (with a tendency toward a more metallic approach) and contained killer songs like "Devil's Preacher." Yep, this is great. **FALLOUT** (Brooklyn) comprised future Type O Negative members Peter Steele (he'd later join Carnivore and Repulsion too, billed under his birth name, Peter Ratajczyk) on bass and vocals and Josh Silver on keyboards, as well as John Campos (Original Sin) on guitars, and Louie Beateaux (then billed as Lou Beato, later of Agnostic Front) on drums. The band lasted from 1979 to 1983, and their sole release, the 1981 *Rock Hard* seven-inch (self-released on Silver Records) is one of the most sought-after items by collectors worldwide. The title song is a strange metal/hard rocker with weird synths, but it's totally unique and so inspired. Kinda reminds me of a cross between UFO and Devo! "Batteries Not Included" on the B-side is a real heavyweight monster (with a Deep Purple influence), and of course, *Rock Hard* is totally recommended. **ORIGINAL SIN** (also from Brooklyn) was a different case; the 1982 *Original Sin* seven-inch (again released on Silver Records) was way calmer than Fallout: more melodic hard rock, with wailing soprano vocals by Cheryl Alter. "Already Gone" is a marvelous song!

Another exception to the rule, **PARADOXX** (Chicago) is included in this book because their labelmates (on Silver Fin Records) Hammeron are also included, and because the 1985 *Plan of Attak* twelve-inch remains to this day one of the rarest collector's items that American metal ever produced, with a fascinating story behind it. *Plan of Attak* has never been available for retail sales. Only 50 copies were picked up by the band to be distributed to press and friends at a release party. Due to the band's displeasure with the mix and the graphic layout they never retrieved the rest of the copies from the pressing plant, where they were eventually recycled, so the first 50 were the only existing copies! In musical terms, *Plan of Attak* is good, melodic metal in the Chicago tradition, with a style reminiscent of Decoy Paris, Malice, and Hammeron and a healthy dose of Judas Priest. It got an overrated status due to its rarity, but songs like "Black Siren" and "Don't Let Go" are definite winners! Paradoxx are active again today (as of 2022), and in the eighties and nineties, members appeared in bands like Radakka, Bird of Prey, and of course, in Manowar (Dave Shankle). **RHOADS** (Los Angeles) was a short-lived hard/heavy metal band, but included in their ranks some pretty famous people, like Nick Menza (Megadeth), John Goodwin (Rude Awakening), Kelly Garni (Quiet Riot), and of course Kelle Rhoads, the brother of the late Randy Rhoads! The 1986 *Into the Future* LP is a very enjoyable hard 'n' heavy record, with some great songs like the awesome "Expedition (to the Red Planet)" and "Into the Future." Rhoads actually reminds me of a more hard-rockin' version of bands like Fifth Angel, TKO, and Q5. **SIN** (California) put out two records on its own Caligula Records, the 1985 *Damn the Preacher* seven-inch and the 1988 *Praised For Their Music, Damned For Their Lyrics* LP. It's mediocre hard rock that's okay for the fans, I suppose. **STEELER** (first from Nashville and later relocating to Los Angeles) featured future superstars of the metal scene. First of all, it was the band that Swedish guitar virtuoso Yngwie Malmsteen joined upon his arrival to the United States. The band was founded by vocalist Ron Keel and later morphed into (the much more commercially successful) Keel. Rik Fox of W.A.S.P. and Sin was also a member, alongside Mitch Perry (Asia/David Lee Roth), Bobby Marks (Dokken, London) and Greg Chaisson (Badlands, Legs Diamond). Steeler released a very strong, hard rock/heavy metal on Shrapnel Records (*Steeler*, 1983), but prior to this, the band put out their own *Cold Day In Hell/Take Her Down* seven-inch in 1982. It's top-notch American hard rock/heavy metal with strong Deep Purple and early-eighties Rainbow influences, albeit with a heavier approach. Get it.

SKY DANCER (Iowa) formed in the mid-seventies and released the *Alive* LP as a private pressing in 1977, followed by the 1981 *Old Wires/Can't Take It* seven-inch on the band's own label, Platinum Records. Fans of Uriah Heep, Deep Purple, and barbaric hard rock, look no further: get them both and enjoy tunes like "Rock And Roll Sweeetheart." Okay, time to present a band that was (alongside Pentagram) the first to take the Black Sabbath direction and set it off in full effect: **FORCE**, from Gaithersburg, Maryland, formed in 1976 and was one of the first bands to carry the "doom metal" tag, releasing the 1981 *Force* twelve-inch on their own label, Alaca Records. Songs like "The Beast" or "Do It Again" show their total Black Sabbath worship, with the alto vocals of frontwoman Simona Queen. *Force* suffers from bad production, but its historical value is undeniable. Yeah, it might not be THE crucial privately pressed record, but still! Later in the eighties, Force changed their name to Rat Salad and released one split LP in 1994 with Obstination and Asylum. Some members of Force also formed the seminal doom metal act Iron Man, with quite a long and extensive career (from 1988 to 2018) that included many classic releases of the genre. **BARREN CROSS** (Los Angeles) is maybe the longest-standing American Christian metal band, having formed in 1983 and still keeping it up today. Lots of records of classic, pure American metal in their discography, but everything started from their 1985 *Believe* EP. While the whole Christian metal thing makes me wanna puke (lyrically), in musical terms, Barren Cross was amazing, like a cross between Dio and Armored Saint! So, musically, songs like "Give Your Life" or "Believe" are fantastic. It's up to you to get it or not. You a fan of the (early) melodic metal of Dokken and Ratt? **DESPERATE ANGEL** (Denver) is for you. The 1985 *Desperate Angel/Kid Rocker* seven-inch was released in a 300-copy run, and both songs are of high quality for this style. **JUMBO** (San Antonio) released the ultra-weird *Jumbo* seven-inch in 1986, which contains an instrumental cover of the theme to *The Godfather*, and a B-side, the bombastic American metal of "Let it Rock." Obscure but overall incredible stuff here. **DRY RUN** (Hellertown, Pennsylvania) had an amateurish—but cool—sound and approach to hard rock/glam on the 1985 *The Way She Walks/Close My Eyes* seven-inch and the *Dry Run* twelve-inch (also 1985). The band later changed its name to Dirty Blonde, veering more toward the glam side of things.

ARMED FORCES from New York City formed in 1980, and the 1984 *Let There Be Metal* twelve-inch is certainly heavy and furious, but I can't stand the singing style of Kevin Burns. King Diamond sounds like a baritone compared to this guy! Still enjoyable stuff, though. The band changed its name to Armed Force in 1985 and released the much better semi-classic of heavy/speed metal, the *Heavy Artillery* LP, on Iron Works in 1986. Get that one, 'cause it's a rager! **TWO TIMER** (Springfield, Virginia) released only one seven-inch, the 1982 *Words On The Telephone/Shake It Right* record. It's highly enjoyable classic American metal with a hard rock edge, and its influences are directly from the NWOBHM. **DOC ROCKIT** (Spokane, Washington) formed in 1974, and the band's first two releases were on small indie labels: the 1978 *There She Goes/Drive Like Hell* seven-inch and the 1979 *Doc Rockit* LP were on Primo Sound and P.S. Records, respectively. However, the 1989 *Azugi* LP was released on the band's own label, Azugi Records, and is simply one of the most glowing moments of American hard/heavy metal (emphasis on hard). Melodic and simple with no glam overtones, *Azugi* is highly recommended for all fans of, say, early 1980s Judas Priest. Actually, you should just get all the Doc Rockit records. **JIM DOFKA** is a phenomenal guitarist, active starting in the mid-1980s and still today, and while he hasn't released an LP/seven-inch privately, he should be mentioned here because with **DOFKA**, **BRICK MISTRESS**, and **SCREAMER**, he privately released cassette albums between 1989 and 1990. Dofka's *Toxic Wasteland* (1989) is a massive record of power/speed metal that combines the ferocity of thrash with neoclassical elements, all through inspired songs. Ace! Keep an eye out for Jim Dofka's work, as he regrettably remains under the radar of even the most dedicated metalheads. Not only is **WITCH** (Los Angeles) still active today (as of 2022), the band counts alumni from Bitch, Leatherwolf, Armored Saint, and Jagged Edge in their ranks! Forming in 1983, Witch released two records via their own label, O.T.T. Records: the 1984 *The Hex Is On* twelve-inch and the 1987 *Nobody Sleeps* twelve-inch. Later on, Witch headed in a glam metal direction, and even though the stuff from that period was cool, it's not crucial. However, when they focus on heavier directions (like in "Nervous Wreck"), they're really good! Witch reunited in 2008 and are now more into classic heavy metal than glam. Good call!

Still in the hard rock genre (although with a more metallic edge), **ELECTRIC EELS** from Fresno, California, released the very eclectic 1984 *Electric Eels* LP on their own label,

Gaffenburg Records. Songs like "Speed Kills" sound like Iron Maiden gone hard rock, while "She's a Lady" has that strong Judas Priest/Accept style. Worth getting the LP for sure. **24 K** (New Orleans) on the 1980 *I Gotta Know* seven-inch had a strange—yet nice—mix of pure hard rock with power pop (a huge Cheap Trick influence here!), and "I Gotta Know" is a fine tune. Get it. **APPRENTESS** from Virginia Beach, Virginia, suffered from an identity crisis: on the 1985 *I Need a Woman/Headless Horseman* seven-inch, they couldn't decide if they wanted to be Mötley Crüe or Iron Maiden, which is most evident on the song "Headless Horseman." It's actually quite good if you're aiming for the Iron Maiden approach. **BAD CONNECTION** (Duquesne, Pennsylvania) were self-proclaimed "commercial heavy metal rock n' roll," and this is the case on both releases, the *Wasted Time/(You Can) Still Rock In The U.S.A.* seven-inch and the *Bad Connection* LP—both of which were self-released in 1985. Yep, it's party metal, as you can imagine, but nothing special. **THE BURN** (of unknown origin) released in 1986 the *Let Yourself Go/Dangerline* seven-inch; it's poppy hard rock/AOR but not something to flip out about. **COUNT HEARTBREAK** (Seattle) on the 1981 *Weredog/Love Is Sepulchral* seven-inch balanced between blues rock and hard rock, like a harder version of early Bad Company. Not a fan of this style, but I figure that those who are will appreciate this record.

EXIDUS (Texas) self-released the 1983 *Reaper/Solution* seven-inch on their own label, Rising Sun Records; there's a definite Sabbath-meets-NWOBHM influence here, with the epic overtones of Legend and (early) Manilla Road, and this seven-inch is an absolute classic. A scheduled-to-be-released LP (*Opening Doors*) never came out, but you can still grab *Reaper/Solution*. **THE FLYING SIXTY NINE** (Manchester, New Hampshire) was actually a backing band for GG Allin for a while, but on the 1986 *Scream Queen/On With The Show* seven-inch, this brand of glam/metal is actually reminiscent of Mötley Crüe (and it is mediocre). **FLYTE** (Michigan) self-released three seven-inches, 1983's *Movin' Faster*, 1984's *I See You* and 1985's *It Doesn't Matter*. Party/glam metal all the way, it's overproduced and has obvious Van Halen and Ratt influences—fans of this style will definitely like it. **FUTURE REFERENCE** (of unknown origin) followed the same hard rock/party metal path on their only recorded effort, the 1987 *Won't Let Go/Life That You Lose* seven-inch. "Life That You Lose" is the better of the two, a nice anthem. I have no idea what **GATOR** (Nashville) sounds like—reports mention that the 1984 *Rockin' Man/Free-Wheelin'* seven-inch is like a cross between Southern rock and NWOBHM. **HABITS** (unknown origin) on the 1980 *Blondie* seven-inch aimed for a crossover between hard rock and power pop, with flavors of Cheap Trick. It's okay but not crucial. **HELLION** (New York City) included members who later went on to form the hard rock/AOR Melidian. Hellion released two self-financed records, the 1983 *One Way Or Another* seven-inch and the 1984 *Dangerous Maneuvers* LP, both of which contain some very nice melodic hard rock—"Ain't No Hesitating" and "One Way Or Another" are beautiful songs. **HIGH VOLTAGE** (Cranston, Rhode Island), despite their name, didn't have any obvious AC/DC influences on the 1981 *Blazing Rock* seven-inch, but the record does sound like it was made in the tradition of NWOBHM. The title song is almost great! Fans of bands like Trespass: get this one.

IMPACT (unknown origin) released the *Impossible Love/Lost Art* seven-inch in 1981 on the band's label, Future Rock; with a good dose of punk, this is a hard rock seven-inch, rough and ready for action. Both songs are above average—in fact, they are actually very good! On the 1988 *Stonecold/First Time* seven-inch, **ISAIAH** (unknown origin) aimed for a glam/hard rock style, but it's nothing too memorable or significant. **KARIZMA** (unknown origin) was a hard rock act (with lots of pop leanings) on the 1981 *Soups On/Love Bites* seven-inch; it's very mellow and not-so-inspired stuff here, sadly. **KILLER MANTEE** (New Jersey or New York City) was the first band of the glam/punk rocker Sammy Serious (The Zeros, Serious Suicide). The 1983 *Red Lipstick* seven-inch is a good hard 'n' heavy rocker record, with the title song being the best track. **LYRE** (New York City) was a group of Ross The Boss (Manowar, Dictators) protégés, as he was the producer on all of their seven-inches. Lyre released three seven-inches in the eighties—*Hungarian Rocksody/A Long Road Home*, *Mirror Mirror/Mirage*, and *It Could Be You/A Time And A Song*) in the Rainbow/Dio vein. It's definitely high-quality stuff—check out songs like "A Long Road" or "It Could Be You." **MANTIS** (Norristown, Pennsylvania) was a hard rock combo, but the 1983 *Forever with You* seven-inch is pretty mediocre. **METRO HOTEL** (Southern California) went for a hard rock/AOR style on the 1981 *Somebody's Kid/Back To The Grindstone* seven-inch, and "Somebody's Kid" is a good song that balances between both styles (with a slight prog edge). Okay, time for a massive classic release and band: **THE OBSESSED** from Maryland formed in 1976 under the name Warhorse, and by 1980, the band had changed its name to The Obsessed. Their first record, the 1983 *The Obsessed* seven-inch (self-released on Invictus Records), contains three songs, and the doom-meets-American-hardcore is reminiscent of a more venomous Saint Vitus. "Indestroy" is a bomb-blast on its own! This one's mandatory, of course, as are most later records (such as the *Lunar Womb* LP) from a band that was crucial to the American underground.

No idea where **ONE EIGHTY** was from, nor do I have any clue about the musical style on the 1984 *U.S.A.* seven-inch; reportedly, it's amateurish, party-hard rock. The exact same words apply to **ONE TO CREATE** and the 1988 *When You Dance/Love Wasn't In Your Eyes* seven-inch; again, it's called a mediocre and forgettable hard rock record. **ROCK ANGEL** (Boston) and the 1985 *Kick'in In The Black/I Won't Cry No More* seven-inch contains at least the excellent "Kick'in In The Black," an almost heavy/power anthem—great stuff! The B-side of "I Won't Cry No More" is sadly generic. **ROCKHOUSS** (Terre Haute, Indiana) and the 1981 *I Can't Wait/Prime Time* seven-inch is just an unmemorable, mediocre, and very amateurish hard rock record. **ROZE** (Ottumwa, Iowa) was actually a more-than-decent hard rock/metal band that self-released the 1981 *All The Day/Whippin' Junior Into Shape* seven-inch, the 1982 *Shine A Light* LP, and the 1988 *Born To Rock* LP (as well as the *Happy Nightcrawler* seven-inch on the small indie label Angry Young Records). If you're choosing one of their records, get the *Shine A Light* LP 'cause it contains some really good songs in the seventies Riot tradition, such as "She's Outside Waitin.'" **VISION** (Jacksonville, Florida) included Billy Powell and Leon Wilkeson (both from Lynyrd Skynyrd), and the first LP, 1984's *Vision*, was self-released via Dynamis Records and was a blend of hard rock, AOR, and Southern rock. Fans of these styles will definitely appreciate it, but it leaves me cold. **SITTIN' PRETTY** from New Jersey had a tragic story that ended the band right after the release of their 1988 self-titled LP: singer Tommy Lee died in an automobile accident. Sittin' Pretty's only release (on their Denim Records) was a good blend of heavy/glam—commercially driven but still done with gusto and style.

SILVERHOUSE (unknown origin) went for a weird blend of country rock with hard rock on the 1980 *Weariness/Lady Marian* seven-inch. Well, I can't say that I'm a fan in this case. **UFORIA** (Cleveland) self-released all their output: two seven-inches (*Out of Control* from 1980 and *Harley Rider's Worm Song*, release date unknown) and one LP (*Uforia*, 1990). It's good classic American hard rock that's rooted in the 1970s style (rather than having any glam influence). Back to the extreme stuff, **VACANT GRAVE** from Manchester, Missouri, formed in 1985 and released a good number of demos/cassettes, as well as the raging 1987 *Eternal Nightmare/ Crystal White Funeral* seven-inch, a cross between Sadus and Slayer that's fast, heavy, out-of-control thrash metal. A good one! **VALIANT** (Cleveland) self-released two seven-inches, the 1980 *Never Ending Scheme Of Love* seven-inch and the 1982 *Can't Escape From Me* seven-inch, which contain some pretty wild hard/heavy metal—epic with a seventies aesthetic. "Never Ending Scheme of Love" is a magnificent tune! **WHITE HAWK** (of unknown origin) self-released two records in the 1980s, the 1984 *Mercede Lady* twelve-inch and the *Mercede Lady/No Place To Hide* seven-inch (also in 1984), as well as a CD in 2001, *Songs From Watzlanco*. It's okay hard-to-heavy crossover, but nothing to write home about. **YOUR BROTHER** (Spartanburg, South Carolina) is another majorly obscure band, which self-released the 1986 *Say Goodbye* seven-inch with the title song on both sides. In between hard rock and progressive rock, this is a decent but still forgettable record.

And of course, **DARK KNIGHT** from New York City and their almost-perfect 1984 *Dark Knight* twelve-inch—raging heavy/power metal! No idea where **WHITEHORSE** was from, but the 1986 *Choice Of Paths/Talk To Your Man* seven-inch is a very enjoyable guitar-based hard rock record in the 1970s tradition. **GYPSY SAVAGE** from New Orleans released, via the band's own World Records label, the *Gypsy Savage* LP and the *Never Drop Out* seven-inch (both in 1984). More AOR rather than hard rock, I'd imagine that fans of this style will enjoy them both. **SCARLET** (Columbus, Ohio) released a good number of records via their own label, Bazer Records, such as the 1982 *No Intimidation* seven-inch, the 1983 *Scarlet* LP, and the 1985 *Phantasm* LP (with more releases following in the 2000s). Fans of melodic (but powerful) classic American metal will fall in love with them all, especially the *Scarlet* LP—this was the band's hardest moment, before going for a more Ratt/Dokken style. Just listen to "She Tastes Like Metal." **AIRKRAFT** (Eau Claire, Wisconsin) had more than seven releases on their own label, Ark and Premier Records, playing a singular brand of hard rock/AOR. Fans of this style should at least check out the 1983 *Let's Take Off* LP. **AMERICADE** from Brooklyn had members who went on to play with White Lion, Black Sabbath, The Scream, and Ted Nugent; the band released the 1981 *Americade* twelve-inch and the 1982 *American Metal* LP on their own label, Adem Records. Both are rough-and-ready hard rock highly recommended for fans of, say, early Quiet Riot.

ANVIL CHORUS (San Francisco) is a very historic band of its era, as members went on to play with bands like Blind Illusion, Vicious Rumors, Heathen, Leviathan, and Metal Church. The 1982 *Blondes In Black* seven-inch holds up even today as a great example of NWOBHM-influenced classic American metal, with two melodic but highly inspired songs ("Once Again" is almost perfect). Get this one! **CONSPIRACY** formed in 1976 in Ventura, California, and was the first band of drummer Ronny Appoldt, later of Hallows Eve! No speed/thrash here, though, just heavy crossover metal/hard rock on the 1982 *Conspiracy* LP, so get this LP if you are a fan of this style. I find it to be a little boring. **HAWKEY** (Detroit) was a project of guitarist Michael Hawkey (R.I.P., 2022), and former Ted Nugent vocalist Charlie Huhn. The 1986 *Hawkey* LP is a blend of American hard rock and an AC/DC aesthetic—very high-quality songs here, such as the excellent "City Sidewalks" and "Shake a Leg." Fans of those styles: don't sleep on this one! **HENDRICKSON** (Salt Lake City), on the other hand, released one very good LP of classic American metal, 1987's *Maestro*. Guitarists Gary Hendrickson's past with Genocide has been mentioned earlier (and I tend to prefer the Genocide side of his catalog), but still, *Maestro* includes some great moments such as "Human on the Run" and "Counting on a Fantasy." **MALIBU BARBI** (San Francisco) formed in 1982 as Rude Girl and changed their name in 1986; this heavy/power metal band comprised all women, was fronted by Chastain vocalist Leather Leone, and sounded powerful as hell on the 1987 *Rude Girls* twelve-inch. Crazy, frantic heavy/power metal with a slight punk edge, these two songs are ready to rip you apart! A real highlight of eighties American metal, this record is totally recommended for everyone (even for guys who are into punk, like, ahem, yours truly). Fun fact: the song "When Lightning Strikes" was written in memory of Cliff Burton. Malibu Barbi later released another record, the 1992 *Ain't Life Swell* seven-inch, that was more punk than metal—still excellent though.

SAINT (Chicago) formed in 1980, and their only offering for that decade was the 1982 *Original Sin* LP on the band's own label, Heaven Records. The production genius of Ian Burgess (who was affiliated with the hardcore and punk scene in Chicago) imparted a very unique style to the album, and songs like "Time After Time" remind me of what The Cult did a few years later! Melodic hard rock with great hooks, *Original Sin* is a real unknown gem. Saint reunited later in the aughts, releasing some compilations and CD singles.

Finally, I would like to add three more records that I couldn't find anywhere to review: **PARADOX** and the *Shock Wave* seven-inch, **RICK KAISER** and the *Falling Angel/Escape* seven-inch, and **PANZER** and the 1980 *Thunder and Lightning* seven-inch.

AFTERWORD

"WE ALL STARTED OUT LISTENING TO CLASSIC ROCK, ZEPPELIN, CREAM, Hendrix, and Sabbath. We were obsessed with heavy metal and hard rock; it was almost like our club after school to play music." Those words by Liege Lord's Anthony Truglio pretty much say everything about how the American metal bands of the eighties were treating their music: first and foremost, they were fans too.

In between the megastars of American metal (Queensrÿche, Megadeth, Metallica, et cetera) and the countless indie or demo-only metal bands in every town and city, there were bands that made some of the best metal ever to be released on record. Heir Apparent with its *Graceful Inheritance*, Liege Lord and the monstrous *Master Control*, Lady Killer, Jag Panzer and their definition of American steel of *Ample Destruction*, Omen and *Battle Cry*, Vicious Rumors, Armored Saint, as well as bands like Fates Warning and Savatage that gained much more exposure in the nineties—there are literally thousands of records released in the eighties American metal era that even today remain stone-cold classics.

"We never made money from records. Most record deals back then were far less favorable toward the artists," Truglio continues. And this is the sad truth. This was the main reason that a great majority of all those bands split up by the early 1990s. It must have been a real pain to work on your material for years, with money out of your own pocket, only to receive hardly anything in return.

"Seventies rock music was new and groundbreaking and was still being invented, creating a great desire to be a part of it," Beowulf's Chuck Gauld says. "We used to ditch the last couple of classes in high school, pile in my car, and drive to Long Beach to watch the filming of a TV show called *Don Kirshner's Rock Concert*. The tickets were free, and you never knew who was playing, I saw T-Rex, UFO, Kiss, Blue Öyster Cult and, many others, adding to the fire and excitement of playing music."

The prevalence of American private metal recordings exploded in the 1980s, but they initially began in the 1970s. Just to namedrop a few bands and records, there were **ARROW** and their 1977 *Coming Attractions* LP, **MAD DOG** and their *617* LP, **MANHOLE** and the 1978 *Sassy Woman* seven-inch, **TRIAD** and the 1976 *Feel Good Song* seven-inch, **LIMOUSINE**'s *We've Got the Power* seven-inch, **ARMAGEDDON** and the 1979 *Armageddon/Johnny* seven-inch, **KRACKER** and the 1978 *Kracker* LP, **TAHANAKO** and the 1976 *Nite Thunder* seven-inch, **QUARTZ** and the 1977 *Travellin' Man/Soothe Me* seven-inch, **TALAS'** 1979 self-titled LP, **ECLIPSE** and the 1977 *Back Street Queen/Slave Driver* record, **BAD AXE** and the 1977 *Cry for Me/All You Can Stand* seven-inch, **SUGARCREEK**'s 1981 *Speed Limit/Dragon Attack* seven-inch, **WIZARD**'s 1979 *So Much I Wanna See/Sweet Thing* record, **DOUGLAS IDAHO**'s 1974 *Prince of Darkness* seven-inch, **NITE FIRE**—and its first release, the 1979 *Maggie* seven-inch (and a good number of releases in the eighties too), **SWEET CRYSTAL** and the 1977 *Warlords* seven-inch, **ELECTRIC LEAL** and the 1976 *Loaded with Love/All Night Long* seven-inch, **BUSTER CHERRIE** and the 1979 *Sweet Evil/Surrender* seven-inch, **THE MAXX BAND** and their 1977 *Whiplash* seven-inch, **WHIRLWIND** and 1979's *King of Kings/Down the Road* seven-inch, **MAX LAZER** and the 1977

Saints of Rock N' Roll seven-inch, **BASSTAR AMBER** and the 1979 *Black Clouds* seven-inch, **DAMASCUS BAND** and the 1979 *Super Star/Oh Mama* seven-inch, **DARTANYUN** and 1978's *Shootin for the Big One/Hot to Trot* seven-inch, the notorious L.A.-based Christian heavy metal band **BARNABAS** and their first release, the 1979 *Directory Assistance/Nicodemus* seven-inch, **TY BARC** and the 1978 *Whisper/Borderline* seven-inch, **BLACKOUT** and the *Hell Bent Metal* and *Not Enough Love* seven-inches (both released in 1979), **EZRA** and the 1977 *Livin'/Teasers* seven-inch, **DAVE FEINSTEIN**'s 1978 *Midnight Lady/Ship on a Stormy Sea* seven-inch, **JUDGE** and the 1979 *RARZ/Aramis (The Lover)* seven-inch, **LAZER** and the 1979 *Sweet Roll/Demon's Daughter* seven-inch, **GENOCIDE** and the 1978 *I'll Be Around/Let's Go, Tonight's The Night* seven-inch, **LAZER** and the 1979 *Lady Luck/Miles Away* seven-inch, **AXXE** from Lubbock, Texas, which released the 1978 *Rock Away the City/Through the Night* seven-inch, and which was later renamed as **IMPECCABLE** and released the 1979 *Live on the Rox* LP ... the list is endless.

"Good music will always be sought after," guitarist Mick Sweda of Stormtrooper says, "and I'm honored that we are considered such. I think metal fans have a particular affinity for searching out and promoting bands that rocked them. It has been the prime motivator for many bands' surging careers. I don't know about our Stormtrooper EP being a collector's item, but I am pleased that anyone was entertained by it. That was the point of doing it at all."

"In fact, as I understand it, the whole Christian rock genre was still sort of in its infancy stage (in the mid/late 1980s)," says guitarist Doug Middleton of Straightaway, "and it was just starting to evolve and ramp as a result of rising bands such as Stryper."

"We recorded the first Rottweiller cassette, played several shows around Seattle—including the Paramount Theater with Heir Apparent—but the demo was never released," drummer Doug Marrapodi from Rottweiller says. "We had financing from backers fall through a couple times, and it was tough to release anything ourselves. At the time, the Seattle grunge scene was growing rapidly, and metal was slowly being pushed aside. The band eventually broke up in about 1986."

Many metal bands of that era released their albums on cassettes, since they couldn't afford to put out a vinyl record. We're not talking about demos, but full-length records here, and bands like **IO KINGDOMS**, **ADRIAN DODZ**, **ATTAXE** and its 1990 *Are You Ready* album, **AXIS** and the 1988 *No Man's Land* album, **CYANIDE** and *Sleaze Queen* in 1989, **HERO**'s 1988 album *Risen*, **L.O.U.D.** and the 1989 *Stand on the Rock* cassette, **ROUGH HONOR** and their 1987 *The Right to Rock* album, **STRAIGHTWAY**'s 1988 *One Way to Heaven* cassette, **THE REGIME** and the 1987 *Dead Serious* album, **WITHOUT WARNING** and their excellent 1989 *The Dawn of a New Day*, **ZION** and the 1989 *Thunder from the Mountain*, **APOSTLE** and their 1985 *White Metal* album, **CRITICAL MASS** and the 1985 *Death Dealer* album, **MISSDEMEANOR**, **SAVAGE SILENCE**, **MATRIXX**, and **FORTRESS OF SOLITUDE**, **POWERSURGE** and the 1986 *Elements of Metal* album, **SHEER GREED** and the 1986 *Roadkill* album, **VIKTEM** and *The Queen Lives On*, **VIOLET WIND** and *Now That We're Alone*, **BANSHEE** and their first pressing of *Cry in the Night*, **LEGGESY**, **ALYZE**, **ARCHANGEL**, **FULL ARMOR**, **MISTREATED** and *One More for the Road*, **MÄDEL FANG** and the 1987 *She's Alright* demo, **OBLIVIAX** and the excellent power metal of *I Know What You're After*, **ROXALT** and *Get Ready*, **SABER** and *Call to Glory*, **LAZARUS SIN** and the American metal greatness of *Intracranial Mass*, **MAJESTIC RYTE**'s 1988 cassette (a real gem), **NINJA**'s *S.W.A.K.*, **JIM DOFKA**'s *Concerto*, **TRUCE IN BLOOD** and *Nictophobic*, **WAXWING** and the *Appetizer*, **WICKED TEAZE**'s self-titled cassette, **ANDROMEDA** and *Calm Before the Storm*, **BLACK MASTER** and *Caught Red Handed*, **HEAVYNESS** and *Lock Me Out*, **METAL X** and *X Marks the Spot*, **PERFECT ISOLATION** and *No Fear*, **RAYZE** and *Kickin' Your Hyde*, **SINISTER FORCE**'s and **WIDOW MAKER**'s self-titled cassettes, **TAKER**'s *Blood*, **KING'S RANSOM** and the perfection of *Curators of the Realm*, **CRUCIFIX** and their 1989 self-titled cassette, **D.T. SEIZURE** and *Name Your Poison*, **DAGGAHOGGETT** and *Land Of The Dead*, **FINAL AXE** and the 1989 Christian power metal classic *Beyond Hell's Gate*, **WHITE WITCH**'s mystical and weird but great American metal on *Hell Is Doomed* (which reminds me of a cruder version of early Queensrÿche), **LOFTON** and the excellent 1988 demo *Straight Between the Eyes*, **CRUELLA D'VILLE** and the near-perfect dark heavy metal of their self-titled 1988 cassette (as well as many of the band's demo releases), **ENVIRONMENTAL HAZZARD** from Cleveland and their 1989 self-titled cassette of heavy/thrash, **REBELLION** from Fall River/Westport, Massachusetts, with their own brand of progressive Christian metal on the 1989 *Does Anybody Care?* cassette, and many, many more.

"I believe in history repeating itself," says Without Warning's vocalist Gary Capriotti, "and with the technology of easy access and information, it can be again very popular, and the large trade market will help that..."

"We put out our own records because we didn't have record company backing," says Rob Swanson, bass player of Lixx Array. "We became friends with a good sound engineer who worked at the L.A. clubs and did producing as well—John Graves, an awesome guy! We went and did our recording with him, and he mixed down the records. We looked into cassettes and CDs, got our artwork done, and forwarded all the stuff to the company to make them, and then we went after the record stores to get our stuff on the shelf. That was the most difficult task."

Moreover, with the exception of Metal Blade and Megaforce Records, there was a huge amount of lesser-known, tiny, or mid-sized indie metal labels, such as **AZRA RECORDS** from Maywood, California (and its subsidiaries Condor Classix, Iron Works, Masque Records, Metal Storm Records, N.S.F.D. Records, Rockhaus Records, and Trans-Euro Records). This label's catalog included some bands that were to become much more famous (Jag Panzer, Overkill, Dark Angel, Liege Lord), alongside more obscure bands like Graven Image, Stiletto, Rychus Syn, Stormtrooper, Commander, Hans Naughty, or Lethyl. There's **PRISTINE RECORDS** from Whitney, Texas, which released seven-inches almost exclusively, for bands like Blessed Carrion, Naked Driver, Dark Prophets, and Thin Ice. **THIRD AVENUE MUSIC** from Pittsfield, Massachusetts, with Powerage and Eclipse. **STARMAN RECORDS** from Sacramento that released stuff by Winterhawk, Sunlight, and V.C. & The Saucers. **ALBATROSS RECORDS** from Seattle that offered Q5's masterpiece *Steel The Light* LP and Widow's *Gone Too Far*. **ROCK CITY RECORDS** from Ohio and the Ginger Roxx, Spoyld, and Raven Slaughter releases. **DETROIT DUNKLEY RECORDS** and All Systems Go and The Naked Truth. **AMKEN RECORDS** and releases by Red Machete, Kid Salas, and T-Minus. **REINDEER RECORDS** from Portland, Maine, and Trooper or Fatal Sacrifice. **MUSIC CITY RECORDS** from Nashville and its releases by Teaser. **KIDERIAN RECORDS PRODUCTIONS** from Chicago and Torn Orphan and Puppetteer. **BOSSTOWN RECORDS** from Boston and releases by Trapper. **KOALATOWN RECORDS** (Dayton, Ohio) and Wizard. **TROPICAL RECORDS** with Leatherwolf, Strut, and Blacksmith.

COOK'S MUSIC and Mike Criswell Band and Night Force. **DOUBLE EAGLE RECORDS** from Cambridge, Massachusetts, and Rage. **ACE RECORDS** and Big Boys. **LARK RECORDS** from Waynesboro, Virginia, and Trigger Happy. **BMC RECORDS** from Cary, North Carolina, and Protégé, Alias Mangler, Sleeping Giant and Token. **BMF RECORDS AND TAPES** and Tora Orphan, Far East, Lemaj, Zebroid, The Works, and Theatrics. **USA RECORDS**, which among others released *First Licks*, the 1985 LP from L.A. heavy metal band Foreplay. **MIRROR RECORDS INC.** from Rochester, New York, a garage punk label that also released records by Immaculate Mary and Dirty Looks. **INSAN RECORDS** from Long Beach, New York, that released a record by Inner Sanctum, Mike Portnoy's first band. **OUR GANG ENTERTAINMENT** from Cleveland and the LP by Link. **GRUDGE RECORDS** and American Angel, Lords of the Crimson Alliance, and Damien Thorne. **HEARTLAND RECORDS** from Pasadena, California, and Marshall Law with Holy Smoke. **WORLD RECORDS** that released among many others the only LP by the great Matakopas. **EXECUTIVE RECORDS** from Raleigh and releases by Maxx Warrior, Nantucket, and Sidewinder. **R.S.V.P. RECORDS** and the bands Split The Dark and Northstar. Christian rock labels such as **PATMOS RECORDS**, which released some great ones like Philadelphia (the *Tell the Truth* LP is so sweet) and Terms of Peace. **SOUNDPLEX CREATIONS** from Arkansas that released records by Quest and Voyager. **EVER RAT RECORDS** with releases by Coven, Lethal Dose, Sashay, and Show & Tell, among many others. **WEB RECORDS** from Denver that released the (now considered a classic) first Satan's Host LP, as well as a Hammers Rule record. Even foreign labels such as Dream Records or Shades Records released stuff by American bands like Orphan Allies, Sinful, Agentz, and ESP. **C.O.M.A. RECORDS** from Seattle with releases from Mace, Strike, and Mistrust.

Continuing on, there was **EARTH RECORDS** from Houston and Xcitor. **BLUSTARR**, with releases by 33 1/3 and Teeth. **MARK RECORDS** with hundreds of releases, plus a very few heavy metal-related ones, such as the Madd Hatter LP. **RELENTLESS RECORDS**, of course, from Concord, California, which released Villain and Aggression records. **GOLDEN EAGLE RECORDS** with many releases in the 1970s, which also released *Troupe*'s only seven-inch in 1980. **BLACK HAWK RECORDS** from Gibsonburg, Ohio, that released among others the 1980 seven-inch by Rizzo. **GOLDUST RECORDS** from Las Cruces, New Mexico, and Voltz. **DME RECORDS** that released records by Paradox and Dare Force. **HOT BOX RECORDS** with two releases, one of them being Entity's *Heartplay* twelve-inch. **SMALL WORLD RECORDS** from Huntsville, Alabama, that released (among others) Hatterfox's LP. **MONTAGNE RECORDS** and **BALDWIN SOUND PRODUCTIONS** from Pennsylvania that released records by the perfect crossover hard rock/metal Full Moon. **TEARDROP RECORDS** that released the Shawn Sahm And Prezence twelve-inch. **ROCKDUSTER RECORDS** that released stuff by Broken Ice, Lynx, 50/50, and the heavyweights Cerebus (whose 1986 *Too Late to Pray* LP is a minor classic).

"I always liked studio production, so in 1983, we started our own studio," says Mitch Viegut, guitarist of Airkraft. "First a 16-track and then a 24-track MCI with two-inch tape. So, I started engineering records for many local and regional groups. We started Première Records and

Studios. The studio was mainly for Airkraft, but we released many records ... We ended up with international distribution with Relativity Records."

"The metal scene in New York in the late seventies and early eighties was incredible," Gerard de Marigny, guitarist of Americade, says. "It was the heyday of metal, and there were so many great local bands, musicians, and venues to play. We were treated like celebrities wherever we went and packed every show we ever played with thousands. We decided to put out on our own label for a few reasons—first, new wave was what most of the major labels wanted in New York in 1981, and then, we also wanted full control over our music and the recording."

A few bands also self-released their albums on CD; of course, this happened at the tail end of the eighties, with bands like **ACHERON** and the 1989 *Prophecies Unholy* CD, **MACH I** and the 1989 self-titled CD, **REDRUM** and the *Power Corrupts* CD (1989 again), **FULL ARMOR** and the 1988 *Limited Edition 1988* 4-song EP. **SQUADRON** and the perfect power metal of the 1989 *Fatal Strike* CD (as well as the 1991 *Storming the Desert* cassette), **LADY SABRE** (who also released a cassette album, the 1988 *Under a Strange Spell*) with the beautiful melodic hard rock of *Enchanted* (1989), and **HARLET** with 1988's *25 Gets a Ride*, another crowning moment in American metal.

"Seattle had a booming scene back in the eighties," says Ronny Munroe, vocalist of Paladin, "and the fans were great. As long as you were halfway good, you got respect and people would come back to see you. In turn, that made the bands want to practice more and get better for the fans—and for themselves, of course ... Plus, most every band had those kind of [private] releases. Like Perennial, Sato, Coven, and Queensrÿche."

Compilations also had a major role in the privately released American metal scene; regional or national, metalheads of the 1980s could find unknown bands that released just one LP or seven-inch or a single track on a compilation! They're too numerous to mention; however, I will namedrop a few, such as *Chicago Class Of '85*, *U.S. Metal Vol. I*, the *Metal Massacre* series of course, *L.A. Steel*, and *Metal That Matters*, as well as the more obscure ones (or compilations that include a mix of styles, like pop/rock and punk and heavy metal) such as *Santa Barbara 1988 - Collection 1 Vol. 1*, *KZEL Oregon's Best Rock*, *American Underground* 3LP, *KZOM 104 Shootin' For the Stars*, *Q-102 Plays Favorites Stroh's Superstar Talent Search*, *ComPILEation 1986*, *Righteous Metal*, *KMEL's New Oasis*, *Strictly Taboo*, *In Between The Lines 1988*, *Metal Madness Volume One*, *Cleveland Metal*, *Cleveland's Heavy Metal: Etched In Steel*, *Northwest Metalfest*, *Raising Hell In Texas: Rare Tracks, Vol. 4*, *The Metaluna Syndrome*, *Q-FM-96 Hometown Album Project Volume 3*, *Home Grown '84*, *WLLZ Motor City Rocks III*, *Heavy Artillery* ... so many compilations, and I just wish somebody in the future would write a book on the American metal compilation LPs of the 1980s.

"We wanted people to have our music in their possession to listen to whenever they wanted," says Jim Dofka, guitarist of Dofka, Screamer, and Brick Mistress. "Self-releasing seemed like the next logical step. The corporate music industry was in the bigger cities like Los Angeles and New York. We didn't think we fit the style that the industry was pushing anyhow, and we wanted to be true to ourselves. We were making money playing shows and had the finances to pay for everything ourselves, so we did."

"When we were gathering the material that was recorded, a local company called Disc Makers had an offer out for a package of 500 CDs and 1,000 cassettes with the use of an artist for the cover, so we went with that," says drummer Jim McKenna of Squadron. "CDs were just coming out then, I believe. The guy who recorded the songs was forming a production company, and we signed a contract with them to help book shows and distribute the album to local record stores. The scene back then seemed to be limited to a few really good places to play. Maybe we weren't aware then. We were always mismatched with other bands on the bill back then. People seemed to like us, but it was hard to build a following."

"We decided to press and release on our own label and distribute through Important Records," Punky Peru, drummer of Witch, says. "We were hoping to get a bigger record label deal, since we wouldn't be tied down. It might have been a better decision to release on Combat, which was owned by Important Records. That is what Metallica did, which gave them distribution. We actually paid for the recording, which was low-budget."

"It's interesting that people seek out unknown groups like they do," says Bill Menchen, guitarist for Final Axe. "Maybe they want to enjoy something special that a non-mainstream group can deliver. You know, it took me so long to get to this point. As I look back, I feel fairly satisfied. My dreams didn't come true, but I tracked Robert Sweet on 13 of my studio albums. And I put out a lot of straightforward gospel lyrics. Without telling people the most important thing they need to hear, any accomplishment would be tainted. So, I'm fairly satisfied."

"We couldn't afford to go to Quadradial, which was our number-one choice," says Chris Warren, guitarist of Lady Sabre. "Criteria, which is now Power Station, was sterile and way expensive. Essentially, the cost made the decision for us. I taught myself how to record, from the Fostex eight-track to the twelve-track AKAI. These recording were always demos. I had spoken to Michael Wagner through Atlantic and our attorney, and I was hoping to proceed toward working with him and a killer drummer, all of that. Meanwhile, I learned MIDI and multitrack recording, spent a full year holed up, finishing the album. But sadly, there was very little real support. Mostly the lip service and the backstabbing/climb-over-you kind of stuff. There was a following for us, but we were past high-school age, and we relied on our ads and the gigs we could land due to regular lineup failures, in reference to the aforesaid local ambitions. No real display of intelligence or foresight on the part of the other bands and musicians, more the 'screw them and help myself' mode. Of course, there were the usual few nice people along the way."

"We turned down a national record deal with Combat Records," says Jeff Pittinger, vocalist of White Witch. "We won a contest on MTV's *Heavy Metal Mania* on Wednesday nights! We were chosen as the number-one new upcoming metal band, and we turned that deal down for various reasons ... We told everyone that it might take us 30 years, but we will be back!"

"Back in the eighties, record labels ruled the day, and everyone wanted to get on a record label," Todd Michael Hall, vocalist of Harlet, says. "The goal was to be signed, which everyone associated with making it. We mailed our demo tapes and CDs all over the place. We paid to be on the sampler CD at the Foundations Forum convention and also played as many club shows as we could. There were a lot of bands trying to get signed, and we were not as polished and mature in our songwriting as others. Being from a small town did not help either. We had heard about bands getting signed after selling a lot of albums on their own, so we thought we would give it a shot. It was, and still is, much harder than you would think to get people to notice you and shell out money for your CD. It was pretty easy to put out your own CD if you had the money, and it was not really that expensive either. We used Disc Makers, and they are still around to this day. We got a package of 1,000 cassettes and 500 CDs for around 3,300 dollars. For the people who really love original eighties metal, the music is essentially their 'gold,' in my analogy. There is only so much original eighties metal. It is by definition a finite quantity. Once you finish sifting through all of the signed artists released by major record labels, if you want to find more, you have no choice but to look for the independent releases. I have seen people selling original Harlet CDs on eBay for quite a bit of money, and in some ways, it makes me cringe, because it isn't a great album, like *Piece of Mind* by Iron Maiden. But if I consider the value based on the fact that it is rare, then I guess it makes sense."

"We pressed 1,000 copies of it," says Darren Welch, guitarist for Axxe and Impeccable, referring to Impeccable's 1979 *Live on the Rox* album. "I believe we pressed 200 of the Axxe single. The recording of the live album was fun, but I believe we had all had too much Jack Daniel's and other things distracting us during its production. At least I know I did. But it is what it is, and we always had too much fun at our performances. The original band was only together for two or two and a half years—it was over by 1979. We still performed as Impeccable in various forms until about '80 or '81. The fact that people pay what they do for original copies of the single and the live album is surprising, and also flattering. We just wanted to make our own music like our influences had done. It's too bad we couldn't keep it together any longer than we did, but I'm fortunate to have been a part of it. I think it's really great, all the renewed interest in metal bands and other types groups that put out music on their own, privately. It's really so much work, and it was much more challenging back then, as compared to the DIY musicians of today. Almost anyone can make and record music today with all the digital platforms and technology available now. But it still costs money."

"The scene around North Carolina at the time we decided to start recording our own songs was one of many big cover acts," says Scott Board, vocalist of Cerebus. "Many of the bands were 'locked in,' so to speak, to only play covers, with no interest in ever attempting original music. We always felt that we believed in ourselves and each other as strong enough players and writers to really go for it and be proud of what we put on tape, even if it never reached anyone's ears."

"Our gigs were few and far between due to the monopoly of showcase places controlled by certain booking agents," Laith Alani, guitarist of Orphan Allies, says. "I had been working at my father's convenience store and had many customers, one of whom was an agent for a porno star (the famous Seka). He was interested in seeing if he could get his friend (Doc McGee of Bon Jovi and Mötley Crüe fame) to get us a record contract and some representation. He went to meet him in Florida, but he returned with the news that his friend was too busy to help us but said we certainly had the talent."

"We had one self-produced EP done with Keith Collins," says Rick Bales, vocalist and guitarist of Cruella D'Ville. "It was a demo, but it was a very professionally produced demo. We sold a few thousand of them at shows. The other two releases we had were with Statue Records and with Sun City Records. Both were independent record companies, but the records were not produced by the band themselves. For the EP, we hired Keith Collins as a producer. We had a very limited budget, obviously, since we were paying out of our pockets, but he and the engineer Doug Johnstone were amazing and produced a very professional product. We then had cassettes mass-produced and sold them at shows."

"In the late eighties, much of the scene was cover bands," says Wade Laszlo, guitarist of Acheron. "To get any bookings, you had play covers. We refused and booked our own shows at clubs like Fernando's and Williams Underground. I like to think we, as Acheron and then as The Unholy, were instrumental in playing all original songs in local venues. The locals treated us well. Metal fans in Minneapolis were great."

"My family moved to a city called Revere, Massachusetts, when I was about ten years old," says Louis D'Augusta, vocalist of Mass. "I remember pulling down the street to our new home and my drum set was in the back of the pickup truck, and my new next-door neighbor came over and said, 'Wow, you have a drum set! I want to play drums too!' I told him, 'No way, you're going to play guitar!' So, a few months later, we took the money he made at his confirmation and bought his first electric guitar. He didn't know anything about guitar, and we both learned a few riffs, like 'Smoke on the Water,' 'Wild Thing,' '25 or 6 to 4,' and kept playing those tunes over and over. That neighbor was Gene, and we have been playing now together for over 25 years. Kevin was a local kid who Gene knew from high school, and Gene asked him to join us because he played bass. So, after playing as a three-piece for a few years, I came up front to sing lead, and we finally decided on a new drummer, and we officially became known as Mass in 1982 ... We released our four-song EP called *Mass* in 1984, and it sold over 10,000 copies. We then signed with RCA Records and released our first full-length album, *New Birth*, in 1985."

"There were so many bands we loved," says Guy Walkden, the guitarist of Rebellion. "The image of Kiss—Ace was so cool. We loved Maiden, but I remember all of us agreeing on Queensrÿche as one of the biggest influences. Every album was epic. Me, my cousin, and Ed Snow, the singer of Rebellion, went to see Metallica on the Justice Tour, and our whole reason for even going was only 'cause Queensrÿche was opening, and they were spectacular! Then the following year, they blew up with the *Empire* album. I can honestly say that's the one band all of Rebellion can agree on as a huge influence! But as for some of other favorite bands, they were Thin Lizzy, Gary Moore, TNT, The Clash, The Cure, Joy Division, The Smiths, New Model Army, Killing Joke, Warrior Soul, The Police, Gary Numan, Eric Johnson, Prince, Bowie, Zep, Floyd, Purple. There were lots of other local acts that made demos back then, like Sirath, Legend, Emissary, Excalibur, and Hammersmyth, just to name a few. Everyone wanted to get their music out there."

"I started renting out this old abandoned church," says Jim Springer, guitarist of Torment, "and we'd try to bring in vendors to sell stuff when we played, and we had a bunch of punk bands open up for us. We created quite the scene over there at this old church place. We would give the guys who owned it a portion of what we earned. Then people started interviewing us on the radio locally. And all kinds of other metal bands started coming out of the blue, and I think it really started something over there."

"Our record was self-produced, and tapes and LPs were submitted to many companies," says Gary Hendrickson, guitarist of Genocide and Hendrickson, "but it never got any real interest. I always knew the songs were special and were very intricate and complicated for the time, but until I really started working on the 35th Anniversary release mixes, I was shocked to hear how intricate much of this music is, and I can really appreciate it now! For a 20-year-old kid from Utah to pull this off was crazy. In the nineties, I heard Dream Theater for the first time and I went, 'Shit! This is what Genocide would sound like if we would have stayed together!' Lyrically, however, the songs are not exactly art; sex was all that kids from Salt Lake thought about, and I was no exception ... It is very exciting and humbling to have this record appreciated so much, and it truly seems to have achieved cult status. I had put this record behind me and moved on when I was contacted by Manos at Sonic Age Records, and then John at OPM Records in the mid-nineties. It is because of their efforts that the record as been reborn, and that it's now sought after on vinyl. I'm satisfied with knowing that the music is finally being heard and appreciated. Both Manos and John agreed to contribute in the liner notes of the anniversary release, and I'm very honored that they accepted, and happy that Cult Metal Classics is licensed to release the record in Europe!"

"We loved Motörhead, Demon, Black Sabbath," says Ronny Appoldt of Conspiracy and later of Hallows Eve. "When Ozzy came to town with Randy Rhoads, it was just amazing. Me and Jeff Huning [guitarist] were writing all the music/lyrics on the *Conspiracy* LP. We really didn't have any other means. We were just some young kids—I'd just dropped out of high school—and what we really wanted to do was to release our music on a vinyl record. The only other band that I recall releasing their own music from our area was the great Cirith Ungol. Mesmerizing stuff, from music to image!"

List of the Best Privately Released Records in the United States, 1980–1989

THIS IS A LIST THAT CAN BE USED AS A GUIDE TO THE AMERICAN UNDERGROUND metal of the 1980s. Of course, this is not a list ranked by preference or who did it best, but an introduction for those who want to get more familiar with this stuff. And of course, there are some (minor) exceptions to the 1980–1989 privately released vinyl rule!

Hammer Witch – *Return to Salem* 1987 LP
Prophecy – *Prophecy* 1984 LP
Malisha – *Serve Your Savage Beast* 1986 LP
X-Caliber – *Warriors of the Night* 1986 LP
Upper Echelon – Surface Tension 1984 12"
Raven Bitch – Tear Down The Walls 1987 12"
Abattoir – "The Game of Death"/"Stronger Than Evil" 7"
Hawaii – Loud Wild And Heavy 1984 12" EP
Seduce – *Seduce* 1985 LP
Powerlord – *The Awakening* 1986 LP
Fallout – Rock Hard 1981 7"
Xcel – Deliver This Dream 1986 LP
Valhalla – Valhalla 1984 12"
Twisted Sister – "I'll Never Grow Up, Now!"/"Under The Blade" 1979 7"
Zoetrope – The Right Way 1980 7"
Carnage – *Carnage* 1986 LP
Spectral Incursion – Spectral Incursion 1989 12"
Manilla Road – *Crystal Logic* 1983 LP
Brocas Helm – *Black Death* 1988 LP
Hammeron – *Nothin' To Do But Rock* 1986 LP
Abraxas – "Pretty Poison"/"Paradise Rising" 1980 7"
Malibu Barbi – Rude Girls 1987 12"
Rellik – Remember The Future 1986 12"
Tyler Capone – *Tyler Capone* 1982 LP
Roxx – "Shout"/"Imitations Of You" 1983 7"
Siren – Metro-Mercenary 1984 7"
Knightmare II – Warlord 1984 7"
Tyrant's Reign – Year Of The Tyrants 1987 12"
Head First – "She's Hot"/"The Same Way" 1984 7"
Silent Listener – *Veterans Of The Fight* 1986 LP
Paragon – "Image Chamber"/"Dancing Meriadoc" 1982 7"
Flynn – Say You'll Stay 1985 12"
Euphoria – Lazarus 1980 7"
White Lion – *One Of A Kind* 1984 LP

The Obsessed – The Obsessed 1983 7"
Gold Dust – *Gold Dust* 1986 LP
Narata – "The Quest"/"Life Before Your Time" 1984 7"
Ray Gunn – Ray Gunn 1987 12"
Lix – *Lix* 1988 LP
Exidus – "Reaper"/"Solution" 1983 7"
Xcursion – *Ready To Roll* 1984 LP
Krimson Kross – Dogs Of War 1984 7"
Closing Speed – *The Life* 1987 LP
Hawk – *Hawk* 1986 LP
Legion – Nice Guys Finish Last 1984 7"
Shyzgifter – "Edit It Out"/"To End To Begin" 1981 7"
Blacksmith – Blacksmith 1986 12"
Madrid – *Dreams* 1986 LP
Medieval Steel – Medieval Steel 1984 12"
Tora Orphan – "Don't Stand In My Way"/"I Need Your Love" 1984 7"
Final Dawn – "Need Some Action"/"Running Hard" 1987 7"
Strychnine – No Escape 1984 7"
Cirith Ungol – *Frost And Fire* 1981 LP
Winterhawk – *Dog Soldier* 1980 LP
Blackkout – "Black & Blue"/"Fallout" 1985 7"
Shawn Sahm And Prezence – Life In The City 1983 12"
Real Steel – Viking Queen 1988 7"
Prowler – Prowling Death Squad 1986 12"
Thruster – "Back In Time"/"Excellorater" 1985 7"
Mark Lowrey – *Rusty Mark In The Metal Palace* 1985 LP
Hazardous Waste – "Half Life"/"Danger Zone" 1986 7"
C.I.A. – Top Secret (Central Intelligence Agency) 1981 7"
Emerald – "High Roller"/"Ladies Of The Night" 1985 7"
August Redmoon – Fools Are Never Alone 1982 12"
Purgatory – Purgatory 1985 12"
Crisis – Keep Fighting 1986 7"
Theatrics – Deceived Children 1983 7"
Street Elite – One Class Act 1985 7"
Faith Of Steel – "Metal With Meaning"/"Our Saviour" 1986 7"
Psychic Warriors – "Among The Ruins"/"Clinical Approach Nightmare" 1980 7"
Scarem – "Feeling Grave"/"Misery" 1981 7"
Lord – *The Second Coming* 1988 LP
The Kingdom – *The Kingdom* 1988 LP
Ivory Tiger – Metal Mountain 1986 12"
The Rock Corps – "Rock Corps"/"The Lords Of Light" 1984 7"
Axess – "Don't Need You"/"You're In Trouble" 1986 7"

Image – Image 1986 12"
Rellik – "Looking For Something"/"Fighting Back" 1985 7"
Mercenary – "She's Evil"/"Plastic Eyes" 1982 7"
Illusion – "Without You"/"He Needs Her" 1985 7"
Taist Of Iron – *Resurrection* 1984 LP
Lightning Strikes – "Lottery Tickets"/"Lightning Strikes" 1985 7"
Jonas Grumby – "Cry Of The Ripper"/"Short Engagements" 1986 7"
CAB – "Just Another Day"/"Given Dreams" 1986 7"
Murder Suite – Laugh Now, Cry Later 1985 7"
Sadus – *Illusions* 1988 LP
Lofton – *Straight Between The Eyes* 1988 cassette
Exxplorer (as Explorer) – *Symphonies Of Steel* 1984 LP
Ion Britton – Eat Metal 1987 12"
Resless – Restless Metal 1984 7"
Stryken – *First Strike* 1987 LP
Holiday Shark – "Stars At Twenty-Five"/"Shake Up The World" 1984 7"
Dokken – Hard Rock Woman 1979 7"
Tailgunner – *Tailgunner* 1983 LP
Messiah – *Final Warning* 1984 LP
Rated X – Matter Of Taste 1987 12"
Quick Change – "Someone Is Watching Me"/"One Night Love" 1984 7"
Commandment – "Oriental Maiden"/"Engraved In Stone" 1989 7"
Liquid Earth – Molten Rock 1984 12"
Lost Breed – "The Desert Fox"/"No Hope" 1989 7"
Kratos – Iron Beast 1986 12"
Dofka – *Toxic Wasteland* 1990 cassette
Bad Axe – *Contradiction To The Rule* 1986 LP
Voyeur – First Glance 1986 7"
Tempered Steel – *Precious Metal* 1988 LP
Striker – "Striker"/"Finish You Off" 1982 7"
Dark Age – Dark Age 1984 12"
Nemesis – Pain (The Equalizer) 1988 7"
Warzwolf – *Valley Of The Shadow* 1987 LP
Prezence – The Journey 1982 7"
Direct Touch – Meaning To Life 1986 12"
Virgin Steele – *Virgin Steele* 1982 LP
Kryst The Conqueror – *Deliver Us From Evil* 1989 CD
White Boy And The Average Rat Band – *White Boy And The Average Rat Band* 1980 LP
Breaker – "Blood Money"/"Afraid Of The Dark" 1983 7"
Ironhawk – *To The Point!* 1983 LP
VXN – VXN 1987 12"
Stryker – *Stryker* 1985 LP

Violation – Meet Me At Midnight 1982 7"
Intrinsic – *Intrinsic* 1988 LP
Forgotten Child – *Forgotten Child* 1986 LP
Bashful – Bashful 1985 12"
Steeler – "Cold Day In Hell"/"Take Her Down" 1982 7"
White Hott – Angel In Leather 1987 12"
Doc Rockit – *Azugi* 1989 LP
Militia – The Sybling 1985 12"
Ruffians – Ruffians 1985 12"
Labyrinth – *So Wild* 1985 LP
Ashbury – *Endless Skies* 1983 LP
Electric Eels – *Electric Eels* 1984 LP
Villain – *Only Time Will Tell* 1986 LP
Nightcrawler – *Soldier In Time* 1989 LP
Far East – "Ripper Slasher"/"Screaming In The Night" 1984 7"
David Neil Cline – *Malefic Influence* 1989 LP
Steffan Rodd – Steffan Rodd 1984 7"
Open – *Looking For Zero* 1987 LP
Desire – *Cry At The Sky* 1983 LP
Barren Cross – Believe 1985 12" EP
White Witch – *Hell Is Doomed* 1988 cassette
Rok Bergade – *The Attack Is On* 1983 LP
Aera – *Aera* 1984 LP
Loosely Tight – *Fightin' Society* 1981 LP
Sorcery – *Till Death Do We Part* 1980 LP
Gotham – (12 O'Clock And) All Is Well 1989 7"
Dark Knight – Dark Knight 1984 12"
Mistreater – *Hell's*Fire* 1981 LP
S.A. Slayer – *Go For The Throat* 1988 LP
Almighty – Cries of Prey 1989 12"
Valor – *Fight For Your Life* 1988 LP
Iron Cross – *Iron Cross* LP
Bishop Steel – Killing Asylum 1991 12"
Czar – Iron Curtain 1982 7"
Frigid Bich – "Call Us Robinhoods"/"You're No Loser" 1981 7"
Diamond – *Diamond* 1987 LP
Mysstress – Mysstress 1986 12"
Executioner – Metal Up Your Ass 1985 7"
Vice – Vice 1984 12"
Knightmare – *Evil Dreams* 1989 LP
Soldier – *Babylon* 1988 cassette
Damien – *Stop This War* 1989 LP

Black Rose – "Sidewinder"/"Slow Down" 1980 7"
Crowhaven – *Emotional Adjustment* 1987 LP
Phenomenon – "The Final Word"/"Ain't No Doubt About It" 1980 7"
Anvil Chorus – Blondes In Black 1982 7"
Winterhawk – *Revival* 1982 LP
Shadow – *Iron Umbrella* 1989 LP
X-Caliber – Fire! 1981 7"
Mystic-Force – Shipwrecked With The Wicked 1990 12"
Bent Sirkis – Stop Your Bitchin' (And Put Your Fist In The Air) 1985 7"
Killen – *Killen* 1988 LP
Wyzard – Knights Of Metal 1984 12"
Salem's Wych – *Betrayer Of Kings* 1986 LP
Decoy Paris – Love On The Run 1987 12"
Crysys – *Hard As Rock* 1981 LP
Sabotage – Cloudborne 1984 12"
Monarch – *As Your Kingdom Falls* 1983 LP
Black Onyx – "Armageddon Skies"/"Miss Fire" 1987 7"
Amethyst – Outside Of Nowhere 1984 12"
Ded Engine – Two Bad 1983 7"
Overlorde – Overlorde 1987 12'
Fighter – *No Pain No Gain* 1986 LP
Graven Image – People In Hell Want Ice Water 1984 12"
Metal Merchant – Metal Merchant 1986 12"
Sacred Rite – *Sacred Rite* 1984 LP
Paradoxx – Plan Of Attak 1985 12"
Sacred Few – *Beyond The Iron Walls* 1985 LP
Alias – *Metal To Infinity* 1989 LP
Sabre – City Of Flames 1985 7"
Myth – "Metal To The Pedal"/"Rock Or Die" 1984 7"
Pentagram – *Pentagram* 1985 LP
Saint – *Original Sin* 1982 LP

THANKS LIST

IT WAS A MAGNIFICENT TRIP GOING THROUGH THE DAYS OF INDIE AMERICAN metal; as a non-metalhead, I find this movement to be (alongside NWOBHM) the most original, genuine, authentic that metal ever had to offer. The DIY aspect will always be a game-changer in terms of authenticity, plus I even found myself loving some bands (such as Spectral Incursion and Street Child) for both their music and lyrics.

I would like to thank all the people who were part of this book, one way or another. First of all, Ian Glasper, for he's the one who offered me the opportunity to start writing books. Jessica Parfrey and Christina Ward of Feral House for believing in me right from the start, and for their help and patience. Professor Yannis Skarpelos for his help and kindness. David Gamage of Earth Island. Tim Cundle, a real brother and an awesome human being. Our families, who always supported us. David DeFeis, a real gentleman. All the musicians who were included with interviews, but especially Michael Hawkey, who passed away a few days before this book was completed. Rex Coward (R.I.P.), Kenny Burck and his spouse Aria, Heidi Black, Dino Alden, Greg Lindstrom for being super nice, John Nomikos (who was always like "Come on, kid, go get some sleep!"), Tom Gattis, Brian Thoryk, David Lynn Chaney, Don Cooper, Nick Karafotis, Arthur Melonas, Dead Serios Lee, Duane Weider, Lenny Spickle, Bucky Bryant, Mike Normandin and Joe Bredow for their gifts, David Calabrese, Michael Soliz, Craig Behrhorst, Marshall Davis, Graham Batting (always love your hardcore and punk affinity), Rob Origlio, Tommy Sisco, Daniel Nottage ... basically, everyone!

Friends, worldwide. From the ones you met and have great times with, such as Stevil Minta and James Sherry and Christopher Owens, to the ones who you can't wait to meet, such as Michele Giorgi, Patrick Grindstaff, and Todd Norin. Friends in Greece, all of you, especially the ones who supported me through very hard times: Makis and Irene, Christine and Spyro, Gregory Tsol, Polis and Natasa, Chris Chai, Leon, Oi Tolloi, George Vita, Kyriaki Karag, Periklis/Lena/Jordan, Stelios P., Niki and Santos, Foivos T., Foivos K., Gregory K., Misail, Beloved Dimi Periergos, Kostis Giov, Peter Bakidis, the Papadopoulos Brothers, Yanni Zikidis, Oliver Doh, Moof Porotic, Elen Sui, Marselos, Vlospa, Bob, Minmin, Tzouvalekis, Iskender and Ntelos, George Pirou, Achil Bok, and Vasilis Skoulas. Great people like Haris Tsak, Giannis Koul, Apostolis Themelis, Vagelis Kamaretsos, George Liverpool, Chris Gkoutzi, Jim Vassis of The Antinormals. Professor Pantelis Vatikiotis, and everyone in Panteion University. The antifascists of P.A.O.K, Isovitis, Stergios—everybody. Billy Alexa the whirlwind ultra-core speed merchant commando. Professor Waksman for inspiration.

To the loving memory of Chris "Papi" and Nikos Lambadas, who sadly passed away way too soon, leaving us with great memories; both had huge hearts and offered their love without any compromise, and we really miss them. Scarecrow Records, Lotus Records, Eat Metal Records, Andreas at No Remorse Records for his help. To my parents, who always dealt with my huge mess, as well as my sister. To my spouse's parents, who are always supporting us. To the Karakostas family, a family that includes us too. But most of all, to my spouse, Nikoletta, and my daughter, Amaryllis: the two human beings who shine on me every day, show me their love, and support me as much as they can. It's a huge blessing to have them. Now it's time for her to sing along with MC5's "American Ruse"!

If you didn't find your name on the list, please forgive me. It wasn't on purpose.

Till the next book: Stay positive, and listen to Wipers!